RECIPIENT OF THE 2020 INDEPENDENT PUBLISHER (IPPY) BOOK AWARD'S GOLD MEDAL FOR BEST REGIONAL NON-FICTION BOOK, U.S. NORTHEAST REGION.

"Seider looks behind the artistic side of the Berkshires and uncovers a rich and nuanced history of the region's workers and their struggles for justice and dignity. From the building of the Hoosac Tunnel through the rise and fall of the textile and later the electronics industry, Seider combines a rigorous history with the prose style of an essayist, creating a highly readable and engaging volume. I dare you to open up this book to any page and try to put it down. Without a doubt this is the definitive book on work and labor in the Berkshires and should be in every school, every B&B, and in the hands of anyone who wants to know the real story of the Berkshires."

– Tom Juravich, Professor of Labor Studies and Sociology,
University of Massachusetts, Amherst

"Out of the mills and into our consciousness come the cordwainers, the Knights of St. Crispin, the textile operatives—and their descendants. Maynard Seider has painstakingly restored these 'gritty' working class stories. Those of us who love the beauty of the industrial towns of the Berkshires are in his debt for filling in the history of these ethnic communities and those who walked these streets—who worked, organized their unions, strikes, cooperatives—and survived with a minimum of worldly goods but an abundance of forbearance, courage and dignity."

– Jane LaTour, author of *Sisters in the Brotherhoods: Working Women Organizing for Equality in New York City*

"Seider opens up issues that transcend northern Berkshire County and shines a clarifying light on the ugly transformations that have occurred all across the United States over the past half-century as working class people have suffered at the hands of politicians, cultural elitists, and corporations that have abandoned workers in pursuit . . . of greater and greate he reader in

detailed local history that simultaneously opens one's mind to the tragedy that has resulted in the concentration of wealth in the hands of the super–wealthy at the expense of regular people. His analysis of the fraudulence of the cultural economy as 'savior' is of great importance in understanding the 'upscaling' of the few at the expense of the many."

– Ed Curtin, sociologist, Massachusetts College of Liberal Arts (http://edwardcurtin.com/)

"Reading *The Gritty Berkshires* was like seeing the words fly off the pages. I found myself reading out loud even though I was alone. Guess I thought those words must be shared. It's a fantastic read. Research must have taken forever."

– Jack Boulger (1935–2019), former president of American Federation of Technical Engineers/International Federation of Professional and Technical Engineers, Local 101, Sprague Electric

"Of all the books I have read about the history of North Adams and the northern Berkshires, *The Gritty Berkshires* is the most comprehensive and wide ranging. Written in an accessible and plainspoken style, it covers more than two centuries, all the way up to the present . . . . In his final chapters, Seider addresses the swift economic decline of the region, and the ongoing experiment to revive the economy with cultural tourism, most notably the state funding of . . . MASS MoCA. *The Gritty Berkshires* is invaluable to local colleges and secondary schools, especially because the author's critical writing raises so many issues in need of serious discussion."

– Joe Manning, author of *Steeples: Sketches of North Adams* and *Disappearing Into North Adams*

"*The Gritty Berkshires* exposes aspects of North Adams and its environs rarely seen or willfully overlooked by the tourists who descend upon the Berkshires for rest and cultural enrichment. Written with passion and conviction, Seider charts the history of North Berkshire from the perspective of the working people who staffed its vaunted mills and factories through the industrial revolution to the rusty current day. The voice of the workers left stranded by plant closings and disappointed by schemes to substitute art galleries for the factories comes through with growing force . . . . The text is enriched by pages upon pages of photographs as well as sketches of entrepreneurs, both industrial and cultural, of labor leaders, everyday working men and women, and community activists who fought back, not only with protests but also with reconstruction schemes of their own. The result is an exemplary people's history of great importance."

– Bruce Laurie, Professor of History Emeritus, University of Massachusetts, Amherst, and author of *Rebels: Sketches of Northampton Abolotionists* and "Chaotic Freedom in Civil War Louisiana: The Origins of an Iconic Image," *Massachusetts Review*, Working Title Series (November, 2016)

"Finally a current book to tell such an important story. . . This book offers a detailed, comprehensive, and compelling look at the struggles and accomplishments of immigrants to the North Berkshires from the nineteenth century to the present. These stories until now have remained largely untold, hidden away in research papers and library vaults. Through his years of research and the writing of the book, Seider has given an invaluable gift to this community and its future generations."

– Deborah Sala, Northern Berkshire public school educator and author of *Brick by Brick*, a history of North Adams for students

"Seider illuminates what has too long remained in the dark—the lives of the working men and women who built North Berkshire. He does this with respect and affection. This book is a historical game changer."

– Ben Jacques, Professor Emeritus of English, Massachusetts College of Liberal Arts, and author of *In Graves Unmarked: Slavery and Abolition in Stoneham, Massachusetts*

"*The Gritty Berkshires* is a must read for anyone interested in learning (or teaching) about the history of working people in North Berkshire County or in U.S. labor history generally. I have lived in the area for almost 40 years and, for example, never knew that the most militant workers at Sprague Electric in the 1970s were the almost exclusively female clerical workers. The biographical portraits that Seider paints of contemporary local labor leaders make me want to seek out those I don't already know."

– Susan Birns, Professor Emerita of Anthropology, Massachusetts College of Liberal Arts and community activist

"Maynard Seider's mission is to counter the narratives of today's depressed communities 'without any history to be proud of' and to understand how working people built 'their communities, at home and at work.' This people's history identifies their resentment of injustice as a driver of their community's development. While North

Berkshire's story of economic and labor struggles is ever so similar to other old industrial communities in the Northeast and Midwest, Seider makes clear how important place is, especially to the labor movement's understanding of what it is up against, the power of local businessmen, their corporations, and their larger geographical connections . . . . Reading this book was a pleasure; it anticipated what I wanted to learn and told me in a style that speaks to folks who need to understand our story from our own point of view."

– Jon Weissman, President Emeritus, National Association of Letter Carriers Western Mass. Branch 46; former Western Massachusetts Jobs With Justice Secretary and Coordinator; currently Massachusetts Jobs With Justice Western Regional Council leader

"A delightful window into two centuries of working–class history in one small geographical area: its rise, flourishing factories, active unions, militant actions, and subsequent decline. The focus on a single region reveals the connections among the various factories and employers, assorted ethnic groups, the different parts of people's lives, and the ways one era's struggles shape the next's realities. Impressively researched, profoundly political, and a stimulating read."

– Dan Clawson, Professor of Sociology, University of Massachusetts, Amherst, and author of *The Next Upsurge: Labor and the New Social Movements*

"*The Gritty Berkshires* brings to light underreported and sometimes grisly details such as the injuries and deaths of often unnamed laborers who worked in the mills and dug the Hoosac Tunnel, the local dependence on slavery to provide cotton to the mills, political leaders and business owners who obstructed anti–slavery legislation, and recruitment and cross–burning by the Ku Klux Klan. This history is brought to life with personal accounts, interviews, photographs, and other historical documentation of working people . . . . Although focused on the northern Berkshire region, the experiences and lessons are universal to people and communities navigating away from industrialization."

– Anne Thidemann French, Retired School Adjustment Counselor and Service Learning Coordinator with the North Adams public schools

"Through vignettes and illustrative stories of wins and losses, Seider has humanized union leaders, rank and file workers, their families and communities who found strength and courage to become often reluctant activists. While the northern Berkshires may seem isolated from national and global developments, this readable account of over two centuries of local labor history conclusively illustrates how citizens played a role in the human drama of world economic and political battles. Although workers and their families lacked resources, the author demonstrates how ordinary folks became "local heroes" . . . who collectively responded to the challenges of duplicitous factory owners and non–responsive political elites. This is an important story about real people, who, in the face of corporate and government power, sought survival and justice for their workplaces and their towns.

– Dr. Robert Bence, Professor of History and Political Science,
Massachusetts College of Liberal Arts

"*The Gritty Berkshires* is a truly gritty history—highlighting the community's life and struggles from the ground up, and refusing to romanticize either the past or the present. From North Berkshire's roots in the 19th century to contemporary struggles around disinvestment, this book paints a complex portrait of those who really built the area, and what neglect and ignorance of that history means to all of us. We come to appreciate both the militancy and resilience of the workers, and the all-too-frequent denial of reality on the part of the powerful. *The Gritty Berkshires* offers the best of local history, rich with photos and personal stories, yet located within a larger national context."

– Martha Ackelsberg, William R. Kenan Jr., Professor of Government
and the Study of Women and Gender, emerita, Smith College

"Draw a line a few degrees east of north from New York City and then another a few degrees north of west from Boston. The lines intersect in the northern Berkshires, where high culture and big money go out to play. And now, the rest of the story: the tales of the miners who dug a nearly five-mile-long tunnel through the Hoosac Mountain that made North Adams a transit hub for its 19th-century textile mills and shoe factories. As well, Maynard Seider tells the stories of the electronics workers who made the area a hotbed of mid 20th-century industrial technology. This is social history from the bottom up and a cautionary tale about economic development schemes . . . . MASS MoCA . . . may be a nice amenity, but the costs of deindustrialization are not so easy to wish away. Maynard Seider has written clearly, and documented fully, the story of the Berkshires that lies behind the white tablecloths of the lovely inns so prized by metropolitan sophisticates."

– Robert J.S. Ross, PhD, Research Professor of Sociology, Clark University;
President, Sweatfree Purchasing Consortium; and author, *Slaves to Fashion:
Poverty and Abuse in the New Sweatshops*

"From the building of the Hoosac Tunnel, the importation of Chinese immigrants to break a shoemaker's strike, the rise and fall of Sprague Electric, and the closing of North Adams Regional Hospital, Seider documents the victories won and the losses suffered by workers over one hundred and fifty years of struggles to shape their own lives and to provide a better future for themselves and their families. Deeply researched, clearly written, nuanced, and engaging, *The Gritty Berkshires* is an important contribution to our understanding of the people and communities of the Berkshires and the labor history of New England."

– Ely M. Janis, Associate Professor of History, Massachusetts College of Liberal Arts, and author of *A Greater Ireland: The Land League and Transatlantic Nationalism in Gilded Age America*

THE GRITTY BERKSHIRES

Men working inside the Hoosac Tunnel.
(No date, North Adams Public Library).

MASS MoCA, from Marshall Street in North Adams, Massachusetts.
(Beyond My Ken - CC BY-SA 4.0)

THE GRITTY BERKSHIRES

A PEOPLE'S HISTORY FROM THE HOOSAC TUNNEL TO MASS MoCA

Maynard Seider

White River Press
Amherst, Massachusetts

First published 2019 by White River Press
PO Box 3561, Amherst, MA 01004
www.whiteriverpress.com

Paperback ISBN: 978-1887043-39-7
Ebook ISBN: 978-1-887043-50-2

Book and Cover Design:
Douglas Lufkin, Lufkin Graphic Designs, Norwich, VT 05055
www.lufkingraphics.com

Photo Credits:
Front cover, moving clock-wise and starting on the upper left: North Adams Historical Society collection; "Soldiers of Production" *Transcript*; "AFTE Strike" Randy Trabold, *Transcript*; "I Pay More Taxes" photo by Gillian Jones, *The North Adams Transcript*, New England Newspapers Inc.; "We Are Family" Seider photo; "We Are One" photo by Gillian Jones, *The North Adams Transcript*, New England Newspapers Inc.; and the middle photo of Addie Card, photo by Lewis Hine, 1910.

Back cover, photo of author by Sheila Peltz Weinberg.

Library of Congress Cataloging-in-Publication Data
Names: Seider, Maynard, 1943- author.
Title: The gritty Berkshires : a people's history from the Hoosac Tunnel to Mass MoCA / Maynard Seider.
Other titles: People's history from the Hoosac Tunnel to Mass MoCA
Description: Amherst, Massachusetts : White River Press, [2018]
Identifiers: LCCN 2018030737 | ISBN 9781887043397 (pbk. : alk. paper)
Subjects: LCSH: Berkshire County (Mass.)--History. | Working class--Massachusetts--Berkshire County--History, | Manufacturing industries--Massachusetts--Berkshire County--History. | Berkshire County (Mass.)--Economic conditions.
Classification: LCC F72.B5 S45 2018 | DDC 974.4/1--dc23
LC record available athttps://lccn.loc.gov/2018030737

DEDICATION

To the people of North Berkshire,
past, present, and future.

Parts of several chapters are based on previously published articles by the author in the *Historical Journal of Massachusetts*:

- Chapters Nine, Ten, Eleven, and the beginning of Chapter Fourteen—"The Great Depression in the Northern Berkshires: The New Deal, Textile Union Organizing, and a Pro-Labor Mayor," 45, 2 (Summer 2017).
- Chapter Twelve—"The CIO in Rural Massachusetts: Sprague Electric and North Adams 1937–1944," 23, 1 (Winter 1994).
- Chapter Eighteen—"Mr. Sprague Did Not Believe the People Would Do It": The Sprague Electric Strike in North Adams, 1970," 42, 1 (Winter 2014).
- Thanks to L. Mara Dodge, Editorial Director, and the journal for permission.
- Sections of Chapters Twenty-Four, and Twenty-Nine are based on materials in the author's documentary, *Farewell to Factory Towns?* (2012).

DEFINITION

grit-ty (grit e) adj. **1.** consisting of, containing, or resembling grit; sandy. **2.** resolute and courageous; plucky. *

*Mary Proctor & Bill Matuszeski, *Gritty Cites: A Second Look at Allentown, Bethlehem, Bridgeport, Hoboken, Lancaster, Norwich, Paterson, Reading, Trenton, Troy, Waterbury and Wilmington* (Philadelphia: Temple University Press, 1978), inside cover.

MAPS

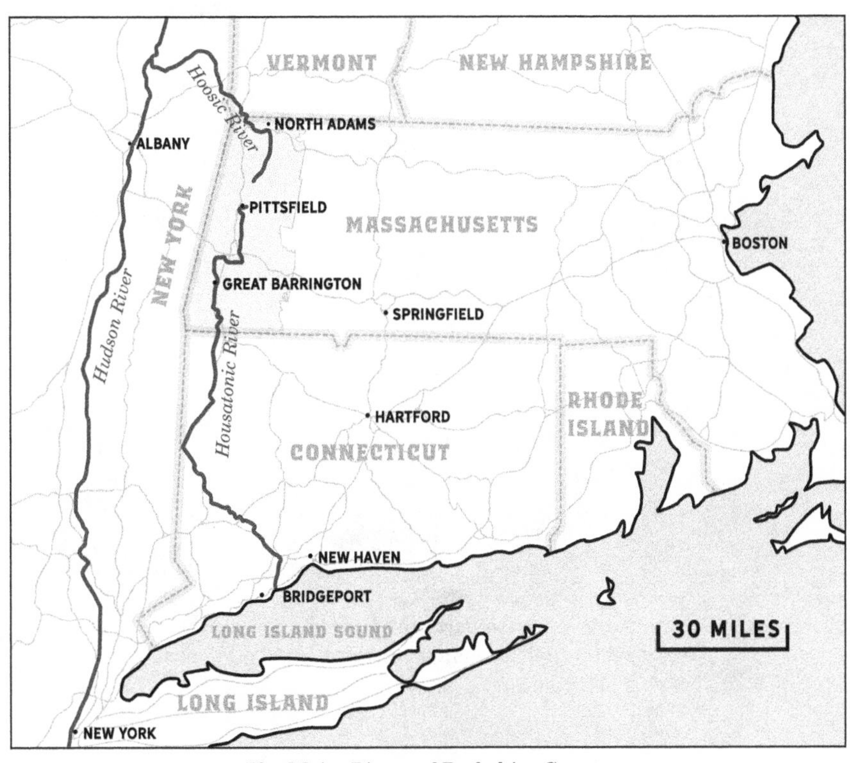

The Major Rivers of Berkshire County

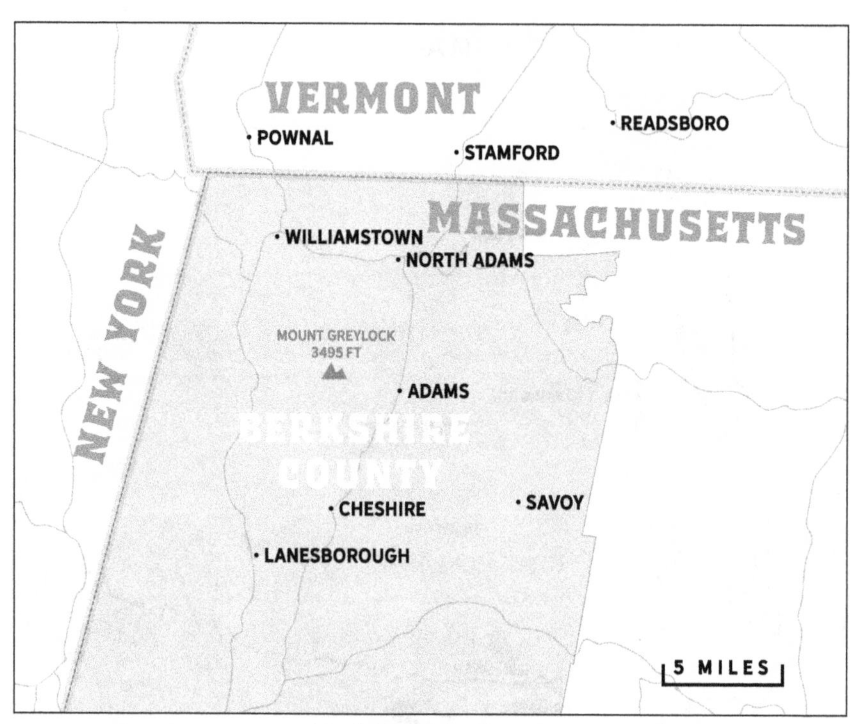

North Berkshire County
including the area extending into southwestern Vermont

CONTENTS

INTRODUCTION

"Poverty, discontent, and conflict were there [in 1870 North Adams], but one would hardly know it from reading the Transcript.*"*

—Richard Bennett,
"The Crispins, Calvin, and the Chinese"

"Why am I so without hope? . . . [T]he answer was rooted in a downbeat philosophy I had inherited from the city I am from: North Adams, Massachusetts."

—Nancy Kelly, director/writer/
narrator of the documentary
Downside Up (2002)

"WELCOME TO THE BERKSHIRES: America's Premier Cultural Resort." For most outsiders, including those who first view this sign on the Massachusetts Turnpike, Berkshire County calls to mind the natural beauty of its hills and rivers, summer theater and music, varied winter sports, and year-round attendance at numerous museums. But in this westernmost county in Massachusetts, gritty industrial cities and towns also dot the landscape, and although smaller than the state's better-known mill towns such as Lawrence, Lowell, and Holyoke, they nonetheless share some of the same physical and historical characteristics. One of these cities is North Adams. Situated in the northwestern corner of Massachusetts on the Hoosic River in the shadow of Mount Greylock, the state's tallest mountain, North Adams is just a few miles from Vermont to the north and New York State to the west.

Before visiting North Adams in 1977, I had never been to the Berkshires: I had the outsider's view of it as a lovely tourist destination. Starting off from Amherst, and after more than an hour of scenic driving on two-lane country roads, I passed through Adams on Route 8, south of my final destination. And there, in the middle of an intersection, stood a statue of William McKinley. President McKinley? Up to this point Washington and Lincoln had been the only presidents I had ever seen memorialized by statues. And now, McKinley? Here? I knew him only as the president who had led the country into the Spanish-American War. Had this monument been erected to honor him for taking control of Cuba, for adding the Philippines, Hawaii, Puerto Rico, and Guam to the country's possessions?

If I had stopped the car and walked over to the statue, one of the engravings near the base would have informed me about McKinley's leadership in protecting American industry, which was, in fact, the reason for the statue. I knew nothing of the 1890 McKinley Tariff, passed when the future president served in the House of Representatives. Just beyond McKinley I saw red brick mill buildings on the right, several still in operation, and a long line of single-story brick housing on the left. I later learned that the Plunkett family, the most famous residents of Adams (with the possible exception of the Anthonys, whose daughter, Susan B., was born there in 1820, but who left in 1826) had been the big cotton mill owners in town and good friends of McKinley and his wife. The president had made three trips to Adams and stayed in the Plunkett mansion; on his last trip he laid the cornerstone for the beautiful yellow brick library that stands just south of his statue's raised right arm. In September 1901, when an assassin's bullet took McKinley's life, Adams became the first community in the country to install such a memorial. Apparently the mill owners had wanted to show their gratitude for his tariff, a piece of legislation that raised the price of British textiles, and allowed domestic producers like the Plunketts to escape foreign competition, grow their markets, and expand their operations.

I had a lot to learn. In North Adams, where, in 1978, I would start teaching at what is now Massachusetts College of Liberal Arts (MCLA), I would discover a rich industrial history. It had previously been a textile town, but since the 1940s, Sprague Electric Company had become its leading manufacturer, producing capacitors—components that store electrical energy—for the domestic, aerospace, and military markets. I had grown up in a union household, had worked in a transformer factory in California, and, as a sociologist, had a strong interest in blue-collar work and activism.[1] North Adams, then, seemed a good fit for my interests.

I went on to teach at the college for thirty-two years, during which time I also supervised students who interned at local unions; I developed the course "Social History of North Adams," and I joined other academics, industrial and healthcare workers in establishing the Northern Berkshire Labor Coalition. The coalition began right when deindustrialization hit North Adams in the mid-1980s. Sprague's closure, along with cuts in needed social programs, brought a wave of despair into the area. The coalition served as a vehicle to bring people together from a variety of workplaces so they could get to know each other, brainstorm, and support one another. Those meetings led to the publication of a newspaper, educational classes, picketing and strike support, and assistance with worker-ownership projects.

With the disappearance of factory jobs, our work shifted, and so did the focus of the social history classes I taught, as we observed and speculated about what would come next. About a year later, we learned that efforts were underway to create a new, huge museum of contemporary art that would occupy the buildings where a print works and a capacitor manufacturing plant had stood. Soon after, a group of us got together to write a local history play.

Called *The Sprague Years* and performed in 1995 for audiences that ranged from area schoolchildren to Sprague retirees, the play dramatized the history of contested labor relations at Sprague and concluded by raising questions about the role of the prospective museum. When the museum—the Massachusetts Museum of Contemporary Art (MASS MoCA)—opened in 1999 with a mission to advance the economic development of the hard-hit region, my students and I tried to evaluate that promise. Later, I worked with others on a documentary film project, and in 2012, we completed *Farewell to Factory Towns?* The film chronicles the industrialization and deindustrialization of North Adams, the coming of MASS MoCA, and the subsequent social and economic consequences. It premiered at MCLA and played at community forums and cable access television stations throughout western Massachusetts and at numerous film festivals outside of the region.

With the completion of the film, I decided to edit some of the written material I had already completed on local labor history and to work further on its integration, a project that would encompass material starting at the beginning of the nineteenth century and continuing to the present. Hence this book.

THE NORTH BERKSHIRE REGION

During most of the nineteenth century, the area we now call North Adams was the north village of the town of Adams. As the north village industrialized in the mid-1800s, however, it developed a separate identity from the more agricultural south village. Ultimately, in 1878, North Adams separated from Adams and became its own town. In 1896, as it continued to grow, North Adams incorporated a mayor-council form of government, as it transitioned from town to city.[2] It has always been the largest community in the region, the center for markets and work, but is also integrally tied in to its neighboring towns.

Most similar to North Adams, Adams also has a rich industrial history, though with some continuation of its agricultural heritage. Clarksburg and Williamstown—smaller towns along the north and main branches of the Hoosic River—share an industrial past, though Clarksburg now displays a more rural look while Williamstown seems energized by its prestigious landmark, Williams College.[3] Cheshire, Savoy, and Lanesborough are smaller area communities without much commerce today, but they help make up what's called North Berkshire, along with the town of Florida, whose altitude of 1,895 feet makes it the highest community in the state. Even more intriguing, within Florida can be found the area of the central shaft of the Hoosac Tunnel. There, one can easily imagine the scenes of workers with pickaxes leaving their crowded shanties that filled this area more than a century and a half ago.

The region extends beyond the state line and includes the communities of Stamford, Readsboro, Pownal, and North Pownal, Vermont. The latter, in particular, has an important mill history, notably from the 1934 textile strike. While the focus of this book will be the city of North Adams, the coverage includes the entire North Berkshire[4] area.

Two mountain ranges—Hoosac to the east and Taconic to the west—that are part of the lengthy Appalachians, serve as boundaries to the region. The Hoosic River traverses the area and provided the waterpower for the early mills that facilitated the growth of manufacturing in this scenic valley.[5] In North Adams, the north branch of the river heads toward Clarksburg, while the main branch travels west to Williamstown, north through southwestern Vermont, and then on to New York State, eventually emptying into the Hudson River. A different river system, the Housatonic, runs through the central and southern parts of Berkshire County and provides power to Pittsfield and Dalton, and then on to Lee and Great Barrington. It continues to cut through the valley into Connecticut and ultimately drains into Long Island Sound. Geologically, the two rivers and their watersheds divide the county north and south: beginning as springs that emanate in a field at the base of Mount Greylock, part of the Taconic Range, the water that flows north becomes the Hoosic, and the one to the south becomes the Housatonic.[6]

The area's natural features helped spur the growth of industry in North Berkshire. Entrepreneurs chose to build mills by the Hoosic River in order to take advantage of its abundant power. In the 1850s, the state, along with several private investors, chose the Hoosac Range as a site to drill a 4.75-mile railway tunnel that would offer a western gateway for local and regional trade. It would take twenty years and the deaths of nearly 200 workers for the Hoosac Tunnel to be completed.

Already well-known as the home of the tunnel, North Adams achieved national publicity in 1870 when its largest shoe manufacturer, Calvin Sampson, imported seventy-five young Chinese men to replace striking workers who were members of a secret union of shoemakers called the Knights of St. Crispin. That event marked the first time that industrialists brought Chinese workers east of the Mississippi to break a strike.[7]

By 1900, with a population of 24,200, North Adams surpassed Pittsfield to become the largest community in Berkshire County. Immigrants and the children of immigrants from Ireland, Italy, French Canada, and Poland predominated, although smaller numbers of Russian Jews, Welsh, and African-Americans also settled in the area. North Adams not only served as the trading center and railroad hub for the communities of North Berkshire, but also for some rural towns in nearby Vermont and New York. Because of the mountains to the east and west, North Berkshire residents have tended to live and work within their region. Historically, while some have headed south to find work in Pittsfield, they generally have not ventured west to Troy, east to Greenfield, or southeast to Northampton. Residents long had access to one or two newspapers that covered their region and, with a single state representative representing them, North Berkshire's political integration was assured.[8]

In the 1920s, as sixteen passenger trains a day moved into and out of North Adams, one writer described the area as:

> nervous with the energy of twentieth century America. No city of twenty-five thousand people in New England has a greater variety of retail establishments: merchants must stock goods for workers of different nationalities and

> notions, and for a large farming population, whose lean pocketbooks force their owners to "close buying."[9]

With the ups and downs of the textile industry, however, hard times often meant that wages stayed low and, in many households, both adults labored in local factories.

Textiles and shoe production remained dominant as late as 1940. In a city whose total population (including children) numbered nearly 23,000, some 6,600 workers worked in nine large mills.[10] As textiles declined, capacitor production at the expanding Sprague Electric Company increased. Employing the bulk of the region's workforce, Sprague—with over 4,000 employees at its height in the mid-1960s—became the leading producer of capacitors in the world. Yet, just two decades later, Sprague closed its doors, and the region's residents—along with millions of others in similar communities in the Northeast and Midwest—had to face the difficult consequences of deindustrialization. Questions about the future, the state's subsidy of a massive new art museum, the closing of the region's 132-year-old hospital, and the viability of a service economy continue to face the region's population to this day.

WORKING CLASS ACTIVISM & HISTORY FROM BELOW

This book, which tells the story of the working class in North Adams and North Berkshire from the start of the nineteenth century to the present, will situate the area within a broader context. In doing so, the major economic and social forces that have dominated the nation and changed over time will be assessed as they have impacted North Adams and the surrounding area. In many ways, the history of the region has a great deal in common with other small and medium-sized mill towns in New England, New York State, and the Midwest.[11] While a good deal has been written about the birth and development of manufacturing in sizeable cities, much remains to be learned about the process of industrialization in these smaller communities. In fact, the smaller-scale production in those towns and villages is more typical of the industrialization that developed during the first part of the nineteenth century. According to one historian of that era, "most American factories during the Industrial Revolution were relatively small concerns, owned by proprietorships and partnerships, located in small towns or rural areas, and operated by relatively modest work forces and locally resident entrepreneurs."[12]

Nineteenth–century historians of North Adams and Berkshire County, subscribing to the "great man" theory of history, focused their attention on the lives and careers of the leading industrialists and politicians—men of wealth. From the writings of historians like J. E. Smith and William Spear, one can learn about the entrepreneurial skills of Sanford Blackinton, woolen mill owner and the richest man in the county; the innovative labor relations of Calvin Sampson, pioneer of importing those young Chinese men to break the labor strike at his shoe factory; and the Shanley brothers, managers who supervised the construction of the massive undertaking of the Hoosac Tunnel.[13]

But these sources do not inform us about the lives and work of the thousands of unnamed laborers who actually dug the tunnel, including the scores who didn't survive. Even into the twentieth and twenty-first centuries, the histories that have been written about the tunnel have centered on the financial, political, and technological aspects of the huge project. Ironically, a sizeable volume on the tunnel, published in 2015 and titled *Builders of the Hoosac Tunnel,*[14] does not examine the lives of those who dirtied their hands and lost their lives actually *building* the tunnel, but, instead, only recounts the story of civil engineering, of the host of engineers who played a part in planning and replanning the way in which the tunnel would make its way through the Hoosac range. Simply put, to use the language of the new labor history, most of the historical sources and writing on local labor history practiced "history from above," rather than "history from below."[15]

Similarly, while celebrating the textile captains of industry, the nineteenth-century historians omitted the crucial fact that they constructed their wealth on slave-produced cotton. No mention is made of the fact that William C. Plunkett, the founder of the Plunkett textile fortune with mills in Adams, North Adams, Williamstown, and North Pownal, Vermont, strongly supported the Fugitive Slave Act of 1850, a piece of legislation that fomented protest in Boston and "No" votes in his hometown of Adams. Plunkett was serving as lieutenant governor in 1854 when, in a landmark trial, the state of Massachusetts sent Anthony Burns back into slavery in Virginia after he had escaped to Boston.[16]

Discussions of slavery in nineteenth-century and early twentieth-century histories, while few, put a positive spin on North Berkshire. For example, in his chapter on "Prominent Citizens," W.F. Spear highlights the role that Captain Jeremiah Colgrove, a Revolutionary War veteran and North Adams mill owner, played in hiding and protecting a woman who had escaped from slavery in New York State.[17] We also learn that the northern link of the three underground railroad lines that cut into the Berkshires passed through Williamstown and North Adams on the way to Greenfield; that no escaped slaves were ever captured in the county; and that the North Adams home of Henry L. Dawes—a member of the U.S. House of Representatives—was "[a] frequent stopping place."[18] By highlighting the positive and omitting the negative, and by not examining the source of the cotton that North Berkshire textile manufacturers used, these historians kept their readers from seeing the financial and social relationship between the "lords of the lash and the lords of the loom," in the memorable phrase of Charles Sumner.[19]

Ephraim Williams Jr., the founder of Williams College and commander of Fort Massachusetts, the state's westernmost line of defense against attack in the French and Indian War, stands out as the preeminent eighteenth-century figure in

North Berkshire. The writers of the standard histories of that era generally portray Williams as a military man, protector of Fort Massachusetts, and say not a word about his slave holdings nor his land grabs from the Native population.

Williams's father, Ephraim Williams Sr., moved to Stockbridge in southern Berkshire County in 1739 after the General Court in Boston granted him a favorable land deal. Previously, Williams Sr. had lived in Newton, Massachusetts, where his family had played an important role for several generations. The court had set up Stockbridge as a "Mission" community, one where Europeans and Indians would live together, with the objective of Christianizing the native people. The chief missionary at Stockbridge, John Sergeant, had a reputation for friendship and respect among the Indians, despite his goal of cultural appropriation. The senior Williams, however, had the opposite reputation. Called "conniving and unscrupulous. . . , his ceaseless plotting to take over Indian lands was destined at last to be instrumental in undermining all that Sergeant was trying to do."[20]

Ephraim Williams Sr. also looked north to the area now called Williamstown, where he appropriated additional land. According to local historian Robert R.R. Brooks, Ephraim Jr. received his command of numerous forts east to the Connecticut River and north to Charlestown, New Hampshire, including Fort Massachusetts, because of his father's connections.[21]

Born in 1715, little is known of Ephraim Jr.'s early biography except that, after the death of his mother in 1718, his grandfather raised him and his younger brother. Then, when he was an adult, the record shows him traveling to England, Spain, and Holland.[22] He later spent time in Stockbridge, where his father lived, and he registered as a surveyor in 1742, becoming known in town as "The Surveyor." He represented Stockbridge at the General Court in Boston for nearly a year, from the end of May 1744 to the end of April 1745. That same year, with the onset of King George's War, his military career commenced as he received a captain's commission. Initially assigned to Fort Shirley in Franklin County, he moved on to command Fort Massachusetts, in the western border area in what is now North Adams and Williamstown.

French soldiers attacked and destroyed Fort Massachusetts in August of 1746 while Captain Williams was in Albany, but he helped repel another attack in 1748 at the rebuilt fort. The General Court rewarded the soldiers and their commander with land grants: Williams received a 200-acre farm next to the fort while the state gave the seventeen men under his command individual lots of lesser amounts in West Hoosac (later Williamstown).[23] With a peace treaty in place later that year, Williams stayed in command, remaining at the fort until 1752.

Not everyone agreed with the state's generous land grants to Williams and his men. In August 1751, eight Schaghticoke chiefs traveled to Fort Massachusetts with a different message, claiming that "the land was theirs, and the English had no business to Settle it Until such time as they had purchased [it] of them . . . ." When they named a price, Captain Williams is said to have replied that the "price was too high and . . . [that] the English '*now* held the land by Right of Conquest.'"[24]

On June 7, 1753, Williams resigned his command of the fort in return for his commission as major of the southern regiment of the Hampshire militia. Less than two years later, with the outbreak of the French and Indian War, colonists prepared to march against the French-fortified outposts all the way north to Canada. Major Williams received the rank of colonel, and was tasked with helping to capture Crown Point on Lake Champlain. The campaign did not go well, and Williams's commander ordered him to undergo a reconnaissance mission. On September 8, 1755, Williams led his men into an ambush and was killed almost immediately. Williams College historian Leverett Wilson Spring describes the action as follows: "Though an experienced frontiersman and familiar with the tactics of border warfare, he failed to protect his front and flanks with scouts and consequently fell into a disastrous ambuscade."[25]

Fearful of such a quick end, the 40-year old Williams had written his will less than two months earlier, before the battle had begun.

Ephraim Williams Jr. left part of his fortune to found the college that bears his surname. The standard North Berkshire histories do not tell us how Ephraim Jr. amassed his land or that he owned slaves. In 1750, however, he sold "a certain negro boy named Prince aged about nine years, a servant for life" to Israel Williams of Hatfield for 225 pounds.[26] In 1755, not long before Williams died in battle, he bought a 16-year-old slave, Romano, from John Charles Jr., for fifty-three pounds and change. The bill of sale stated that Williams had the "good and Lawful Right to sell and Dispose of him . . . . During his Natural Life," and that the slave was Williams's "sole property."[27]

Childless and unmarried, in his final will, he left his home, his land, and his three slaves, Moni, London, and Cloe, to his brothers, stipulating that his mother and sisters be cared for.[28] The last request in his will stated that whatever remained of his lands, wealth, and interest "be appropriated towards the support and maintenance of a free school" if the town of its location would be named after him (it was, Williamstown), and if it were determined to be within the boundary of Massachusetts (it was).[29] And so, in 1793, with money from the sale of the founder's slaves, Williams College became a reality.

Most current popular writing on Berkshire County does not deal with industrial history at all, but details its natural beauty and the role the county played in the post-Civil War period, the Gilded Age. Such books as Carole Owens's *The Berkshire Cottages: A Vanishing Era* (Stockbridge: Cottage Press, 1984) and *Houses of the Berkshires* (New York: Acanthus Press, 2011) by Richards S. Jackson Jr. and Cornelia Brooks Gilder, exemplify the genre that focuses on the mansions that the railroad and industrial titans built for country living. To the extent that industrial history and the history of working people tend to be ignored, this book hopes to fill that gap.[30]

THE NINETEENTH CENTURY

Michael Seif, in a review of nineteenth-century local history, notes with surprise "that there is not more evidence of labor unrest" in North Adams. He quickly adds, though, that the lack of a written record of numerous strikes may not reflect a quiescent labor force, but that the problem might lie in the manner in which traditional history tends to be written, from the point of view of the economic and political elites of the day. In the case at hand, for example, "The *Transcript*, the city's principal newspaper, tended to be sympathetic to and supportive of the manufacturing community. If there were a strike or a serious labor incident in one of the mills, it did not rate headline treatment in a newspaper whose owners believed in the aspirations of the business community as an article of faith."[31]

Richard Bennett echoes that view in his analysis of the unprecedented use of Chinese labor to break the 1870 North Adams shoe strike: "Poverty, discontent, and conflict were there, but one would hardly know it from reading the *Transcript*."[32] As noted earlier, the standard nineteenth-century histories of Berkshire County, such as those produced by Beers and Spear, display similar biases. Further, many of the working people in the area were illiterate, and even those who could read and write were not likely to keep diaries or written records relating to work.

Some sources do exist, however, that help rectify this imbalance. The annual reports from the Massachusetts Bureau of Statistics of Labor (MBSL), begun in 1869 under labor and reformist pressure, provide periodic reviews of strike and lockout activity in the state and, through other investigations carried out by bureau personnel, offer additional assessments of workplace activism. For example, the 1880 report chronicles strikes in the state from 1825 through 1879: the bureau identified 159 strikes and lockouts during that period. Of that total, twelve occurred in North Berkshire (nine in the North village and two in the South village of Adams, and one in rural Lanesborough).[33]

That number of North Berkshire incidents appears very significant when compared with similar activity that the 1880 report summarizes for larger, more well-known industrial cities in the state: Lynn, 14; Lowell, 10; Fall River, 8; and New Bedford, 6.[34] This comparison, based simply on the number of strikes and lockouts, would suggest that the North Berkshire region produced a high level of militancy in contrast to the larger industrial cities in the eastern part of the state.[35]

The narrative description for each of the strikes, while brief in many instances, adds flavor to the quantitative findings and offers insight into the factory conditions of the era and into worker culture. The first notation to a local strike occurs in 1853 when "[t]he operatives at Arnold & Company's factory in Adams . . . secured an increase of pay after a strike of two days in the latter part of April."[36] The writers of the report spend less than a full sentence on this strike, reserving more space for longer strikes that involved more employees. Yet one should note in this case that the Adams strikers achieved success, a result reached by workers only 11 percent of the time during this review period. Five years later, when operatives at Blackinton, a village between Adams and Williamstown, won a short strike, the context of the textile strikes of 1858 merits consideration:

> The manufacturers of textiles throughout New England had found it necessary to reduce rates during the dull season. As business now began to mend, the operatives, in various mills, impatient to reap part of the benefit which they felt this revival was bringing to employers, struck for a return to prices previously paid. . . . Of this class were brief strikes at Salem, Newburyport, and West Springfield. The operatives at the Blackinton Mills. . . were more fortunate; there, the desired increase was almost immediately granted.[37]

Instances of worker solidarity beyond their own workplace can be found in MBSL accounts. For example, in 1870, weavers struck two woolen mills in South Adams, at B.F. Phillips & Company and at P. Blackinton, demanding that wages be restored to previous rates. The weavers stayed out for eight days, but ultimately returned to work without a wage hike.[38] Nonetheless, while the account doesn't specify it, one might assume that *both* groups of workers coordinated their activities.

The next local strike cited by the bureau leaves no ambiguity about worker cooperation, this time by different occupational groups within the same factory. In 1872, weavers producing cloth from fine cotton struck the Renfrew Manufacturing Company of South Adams over a reduction in wages. The company then proceeded to redistribute the looms, adding the work of the strikers to the work already performed by the remaining weavers, who specialized in working with the coarser cotton. "To this the coarse weavers objected and also left." The issue had nothing to do with which group produced cloth for a different market, based on a "finer," more desirable finish or not. Rather the remaining weavers objected to the increase in their workload. The total number of striking workers, which had then grown to 175, stayed out another two weeks. However, unable to win the strike, they accepted the company's terms and all returned at the same time.[39]

In September 1873, the abrupt closing of a major banking house, Jay Cooke & Company, led to a banking crisis and subsequent stock market crash. While historians disagree on the proximate cause, rapid overbuilding of railroads after the end of the Civil War had brought many risky companies into the national mix. The Northern Pacific Railroad ran into financial difficulties that its main banker, Jay Cooke, couldn't fix. Its closing precipitated a domino effect within the banking community and the stock market, hastening a national depression that was called a "panic" in those days. The economic downturn lasted at least until 1877,[40] and led to wage cuts throughout Massachusetts.[41] The bureau records what happened next:

> The decline was accepted in the hope that it would be temporary only; but, after the opening of the year 1874, no prospect appearing of a voluntary increase on the part of the employers, strikes occurred in several factories to force a return to prices previously paid. As might have been predicted, these were generally failures. Trade was constantly decreasing in volume, and the outlook was not encouraging. In spite of this, however, the operatives at various woolen mills in North Adams, after contesting the matter three days, early in January, succeeded in obtaining a slight advance in wages. We have no other such instance to record.[42]

The bureau provides no further details, though it should be noted not only that wage increases were won during a very difficult time, but that the operatives from several mills had coordinated their efforts to make it happen.

Community support added another key dimension to a reported strike in the spring of 1878 at the Beaver Cotton Mill on the north branch of the Hoosic River.[43] When management proposed a 10 percent wage reduction for two months as an "experiment" during a business slump, the workforce split on acceptance. About one-half refused to work under those conditions. The owners responded by closing the mill, but "[a]s long as the strike continued, the help was sustained by contributions from the employe[e]s at other mills in the vicinity."[44]

The bureau's 1880 review of past strikes certainly aids in locating and quantifying strike activity. Further, its narrative, while concise, offers inferences into the culture of working people, their sense of fairness, of cooperation, and of solidarity.[45] By the late nineteenth century, the evidence from sources other than the mainstream press suggests that, while the struggles of North Berkshire industrial workers did not always result in immediate gain, at times they exhibited a strong sense of unity and class solidarity.[46] They unionized and struck as the situation demanded, in events often unreported by the local press. Yet they still continued to labor long hours often under insecure working conditions.

THE TWENTIETH CENTURY AND BEYOND

On through the twentieth century and into the new millennium, the conditions of working people generally improved, though they suffered during cycles of economic decline. The press bias of the nineteenth century continued on into the new century, resulting in the downplaying or ignoring of workers' struggles and successes, while lionizing the achievements of the "captains of industry."[47] However, by examining a wider variety of sources and trying to describe and evaluate the lives of the working people of North Berkshire, a greater understanding might be reached about their roles in building their communities, at home and at work.

Besides the print media that characterized nineteenth-century sources, the twentieth century brought with it the medium of film, a source that, like print, could be subject to a variety of bias and obfuscation. One documentary film, *Downside Up: How Art Can Change the Spirit of a Place*, which includes a focus on North Adams industrial history, exemplifies these problems. In 2002, *Downside Up* premiered in front of a large crowd in North Adams, at the Hunter Center at MASS MoCA. The documentary, written, narrated, and directed by local native Nancy Kelly, received funding from the Corporation for Public Broadcasting, Independent Television Service, the Massachusetts Foundation for the Humanities, and numerous local organizations. In addition, the Ford Foundation funded a six-community "Listening Tour," with screenings and discussions on the importance of the arts in community development.[48]

The film "tells the story of how a contemporary art museum saved [Nancy Kelly's] small Massachusetts hometown," which "decided its only hope for survival was within the world of contemporary art."[49] The North Adams newspaper, the

Transcript, awarded Kelly a place on its list of the Top 33 Very Influential People of 2002, "the folks in Northern Berkshire County and Southwestern Vermont who've had a significant and positive influence on our community," as she "cast North Adams as the star in her film . . . ."[50]

Bolstered by an initial $35 million grant from the state of Massachusetts, MASS MoCA had opened in 1999 in the same buildings where many thousands of local residents had labored producing printed textiles for Arnold Print Works and electronic components for Sprague Electric during most of the twentieth century. In the film, Kelly spends a significant amount of time visiting MoCA and discussing its art with her family. But what does that teach about the North Adams working class and its history?

In the opening scene of ocean waves, Kelly's voice remembers a dream she had of nearly drowning and contemplating the question, "Do you want to live?" After thinking it over, she decided that she did, but wondered, "Why am I so without hope?" Then she says, "[T]he answer was rooted in a downbeat philosophy I had inherited from the city I am from: North Adams, Massachusetts."

With this bleak introduction to the city and its history, Kelly goes on to point out national newspaper headlines that support her negative perception. Growing up in North Adams, with many family members employed at Sprague Electric, she confesses, "I was in training to be a factory worker." In a discussion with her uncle, he tells her of an earlier time when his wife quit work at Sprague after just one morning, exclaiming that "they want robots" there. In a later scene, her uncle recounts a "really terrible experience," when he returned to North Adams after being away for five or six years. A friend suggested he go to a local bar for a drink; in the bar he saw "all these kids I'd gone to grammar school with, now grown up. They had no teeth. They were just rotting away, just drinking their lives away. It was shocking to me . . . . They couldn't get out of that environment. There was no place to go."

In a particularly moving scene at the museum, Kelly's father disparages the repetitive work Kelly's grandmother had performed while working at Sprague. In response, Kelly says, "Glad I didn't work there." To which her father replies, "You wouldn't like it."

The only other reference to North Adams working class people comes later in the film when Kelly visits Nancy Fitzpatrick, who manages the upscale "Porches Inn" near MoCA. At the time of the filming, the inn, which had been refashioned from five old two-story wooden structures, former worker apartments, had not yet been completely renovated. The interview with Fitzpatrick, whose family owns the iconic Red Lion Inn in Stockbridge, took place in an apartment with debris and junk scattered all about. In the scene, Fitzpatrick comments: "I think this does show something about this community and the difficulty that some people in it are having with change. You know there's a certain amount of hostility in the way this was left by the people who lived here . . . ."

Toward the end of the film, children are shown creating art out of "beach" sand that had been donated by a local artist and filled a downtown street. With the addition of the museum and the increased interest in art, Kelly concludes that "the kids growing up in North Adams [will] have a much more positive philosophy of life," presumably than she did when the factories dominated the town. Ironically, Kelly, the child who came of age in that industrial era did grow up to become a very well respected documentarian. On the whole, *Downside Up* presents a narrative of a depressed community, without any history to be proud of. Previous industrial workers are described as robots, as drunks, and with no agency to make things better on their own. The message to the residents of North Adams seems to be to sit back, don't do anything, and wait for the arts and the museum to improve life for everyone.

Given its power and popularity, the film serves as an even more powerful equivalent of the nineteenth-century local newspaper, recapitulating its "history from above" perspective and anti-working class bias. To discover working class activism in the second half of the twentieth century, whether from union organizing, forming coalitions, striking, or trying to build worker-owned enterprises, one must turn to other sources, and be mindful of the biases of the mainstream media.[51]

In writing about the work and life of industrial workers, I have been aided by interviews, diaries, college theses, historical articles and books, union and corporate archives, and by my own experiences teaching and living in North Adams and participating in community-labor coalitions. Notwithstanding my own pro-labor point of view, I hope this helps broaden the historical and sociological picture of the evolution of a New England region, and highlights the role that working people played as the area and the country moved through industrialization and deindustrialization to a post-industrial society.

The statue stands in McKinley Square in the center of Adams, near the Plunkett mills. William B. Plunkett, a close friend of the assassinated president, provided a good deal of the money for the statue, sculpted by Augustus Lukeman. When it was dedicated on October 10, 1903, it made Adams the first U.S. community to erect a statue of William McKinley. (William Carney, *A Berkshire Sourcebook*; Adams Historical Society; photo courtesy of Paul W. Marino)

NOTES

1 Maynard Seider, *A Year in the Life of a Factory* (Chicago: Charles H. Kerr, 1993), originally published by Singlejack Books, San Pedro, California, 1984). This book is an ethnography of my factory experience.

2 The mother town of Adams, incorporated in 1778, was named in honor of Samuel Adams, a Revolutionary War leader, signatory to the Declaration of Independence, and governor of Massachusetts. When North Adams became independent, the south village simply decided to remain Adams. W.F. Spear, *History of North Adams, Mass., 1749–1885* (North Adams: Hoosac Valley News Printing House, 1885).

3 By the time the Hoosic River flowed through Williamstown, its power had declined and the volume of the smaller Green River's flow was too low for significant industry to develop. "The town had its factories . . . [b]ut in comparison to the industries of Adams, North Adams and Pittsfield they were modest in size and were never able to destroy the rural character of the landscape." Robert R.R. Brooks, editor, *Williamstown: The First Two Hundred Years, 1753–1953 and Twenty Years Later, 1953–1973* (Williamstown Historical Commission, 1974, second edition), 103.

Today, in the summer, the Williamstown Theater Festival brings many tourists to the town who also enjoy the shops and restaurants on Spring Street. At the top of the street stands a sign with the town's motto: "The Village Beautiful." Within a few blocks are the structures of two former mills, one, on the site of a wildcat strike in 1985, now renovated into luxury condominiums (http://harschrealestate.com/by-location/williamstown/).

4 The focus on the Northern Berkshires, which I call the Gritty Berkshires, is not to suggest that the remainder of the county doesn't share some of the same mill history, labor struggles, and contemporary economic problems. Refer to, for example: Katie Johnston, "Tourism booms but locals struggle: Behind the two worlds of the Berkshires," *Boston Globe,* September 15, 2017. Johnston writes of the increase in poverty in the county, of low-paying tourist-centered jobs, and of transportation difficulties that face residents throughout the county.

Food insecurity, particularly for children, is a serious problem throughout the Berkshires. About one third of children in the county "lack consistent access to nutritious food," compared to 20 percent of western Massachusetts children. Jenn Smith, "Groups redouble efforts to reduce food insecurity in Berkshires," *Berkshire Eagle,* April 11, 2016.

5 Sometimes the mountain range is spelled Hoosic and the river Hoosac, but Hoosac and Hoosic are most commonly used for the mountain, respectively, and the river. Historian John H. Lockwood writes that the southern part of Adams possessed richer soil, but the northern part had "the greater water power [which] gave factory sites a wonderful opportunity to carry forward their numerous enterprises." John H. Lockwood, *Western Massachusetts: a history, 1636–1925,* Vol. 2 (New York: Lewis Historical Publishing Company, 1926), 491.)

6 Richard D. Birdsall, *Berkshire County: A Cultural History* (New Haven: Yale University Press, 1959). Birdsall divides the county geographically into two parts: "the northern area, drained by the impetuous, north-flowing Hoosic River, could boast the most rugged terrain in the county" with its towns "tucked into narrow valleys under the protecting shadow of Mount Greylock" (3–4). Also see, Judith A. McGaw, *Most Wonderful Machine: Mechanization and Social Change in Berkshire Paper Making, 1801–1885* (Princeton, N.J.: Princeton University Press, 1887), 23. Of course, mill owners also used the rivers as sewers for the dyes and other industrial waste products that spewed out of their buildings. In Chapter VI, "My Birth and Family," of his autobiography, W.E.B. Du Bois writes that he "was born by a golden river." He later explains that the Housatonic "was 'golden'" in part because of the waste from the paper and woolen mills in Great Barrington. W.E.B. Du Bois, *The Autobiography of W.E.B. Du Bois: A Soliloquy on Viewing My Life from the Last Decade of Its First Century* (New York: International Publishers, 1968), 61.

7 Terrence E. Coyne, "The Hoosac Tunnel: Massachusetts' Western Gateway," *Historical Journal of Massachusetts*, 23: 1 (Winter 1995), on the building of the tunnel. For an early article on the Chinese in North Adams, see Frederick Rudolph, "Chinamen in Yankeedom: Anti-Unionism in Massachusetts in 1870," *American Historical Review* 53 (October 1947). For a more recent analysis of the Chinese experience, see Anthony W. Lee, *A Shoemaker's Story: Being Chiefly about French Canadian Immigrants, Enterprising Photographers, Rascal Yankees, and Chinese Cobblers in a Nineteenth-Century Town* (Princeton: Princeton University Press, 2008).

8 That North Berkshire sense of regional identity exists to this day with the largest human services organization, the North Berkshire Community Coalition, still going strong after more than twenty-five years. In the 1980s, two regional coalitions used "North Berkshire" as part of their identification: the Northern Berkshire Welfare Coalition and Northern Berkshire Labor Coalition, both of which played roles in combating the consequences of welfare cutbacks and deindustrialization.

9 Federal Writers' Project of the Works Progress Administration for Massachusetts, *The Berkshire Hills* (New York: Funk & Wagnalls Company, 1939), 10.

10 Jay Louis Nierenberg, *North Adams: a New England Mill Town: A Political, Economic, and Psychological Study* (Williamstown, MA: Williams College, 1942), 122.

11 Yet, like all communities, North Adams possesses some unique qualities, including a number of "biggest" and "firsts." The Arnold Print Works, situated on a twenty-six-acre building site off the downtown, was at one time the largest print works in the world. Sprague Electric, which next used those buildings, became the biggest producer of capacitors in the world, and the current tenant, Massachusetts Museum of Contemporary Art (MASS MoCA) is now the largest contemporary art museum in the country. Also, the Hoosac Tunnel, completed in 1876 and stretching from Florida (Mass.) Mountain in the eastern edge of the region to North Adams,

ranked as the second longest rail tunnel in the world. And in Adams, the Berkshire Cotton Mill complex was one of the country's largest textile mills. In 1870, the first group of Chinese men to break a strike east of the Mississippi arrived in North Adams at C.T. Sampson's shoe factory.

12 McGaw, 8.

13 J.E.A. Smith, editor, *History of Berkshire County, Massachusetts, with Biographical Sketches of its Prominent Men, 1885,* two volumes (New York: J.B. Beers Co., 1885); and see Spear.

14 Cliff Schexnayder, *Builders of the Hoosac Tunnel: Baldwin, Crocker, Haupt, Doane, Shanley* (Portsmouth, NH: Peter E. Randall, 2015).

15 Bruce Levine et al., *Who Built America: Working People and the Nation's Economy, Politics, Culture and Society,* two volumes (New York: Pantheon Books, 1989, 1992); and Howard Zinn, *A People's History of the United States* (New York: Harper Collins, 1995, revised and updated) for examples of "history from below."

16 Mark W.Carter, *Adams, Massachusetts, And The American Civil War* (Williamstown: Williams College, 1976), 15.

17 Spear, 89–90.

18 Carter, 15.

19 Sumner, a strong anti-slavery advocate, was among 5,000 "conscience" Whig delegates who gathered in Worcester on June 10, 1848, to protest the national Whig Party choice of slaveholder General Zachary Taylor as its presidential nominee. In his speech, Sumner called Taylor's nomination "the result of a vast conspiracy 'between the cotton-planters and flesh-mongers of Louisiana and Mississippi and the cotton-spinners and traffickers of New England—between the lords of the lash and the lords of the loom.'" Soon Sumner joined the Free Soil Party and in 1851, as a Democrat, was elected to the U.S. Senate, where he continued to distinguish himself with his powerful anti-slavery speeches. Robert F. Dalzell Jr., *Enterprising Elite: The Boston Associates and the World They Made* (New York: W.W. Norton, 1987), 202, Ch. 6.

20 Birdsall, 37. Birdsall, a cultural historian, writes that Sergeant asked Colonel John Stoddard to "choose four model families who might come to live in Stockbridge as a general civilizing influence." Birdsall finds it ironic that the choice of Ephraim Williams Sr. proved the opposite.

21 Brooks, 2, 3, 14.

22 Leverett Wilson Spring, *A History of Williams College* (Boston: Houghton Mifflin Company, 1917), 1; and Grace Niles, *The Hoosac Valley: Its legends and its history* (New York: Putnam's Sons, 1912), 145.

23 Niles, 150.

24 Niles, 150, and notes ix and x. In his history of Williams College, Spring refers to what must be the same interaction, occurring during the peaceful period, 1748–1752: "On one occasion the usual routine was interrupted by the appearance of a deputation of Indians, who claimed to own the land

upon which the fort stood and wanted to be paid for it. These enterprising aborigines did not succeed in collecting their bill" (7). Not surprisingly, while talk emerged about negotiations between the state and the Native Americans over land ownership, nothing came of it. Soon virtually all members of all the native communities had left the area. "By the end of 1759, more than one thousand English families had migrated into the northern part of Berkshire County without making payment to the tribe for the lands on which they settled." (Miles, 283.) Thanks to a Williams College student paper, "The mountains! The mountains!: Slavery in Williamstown, MA," by Selena Castro, I learned of the Schaghticoke land demand in Niles. Selena Castro's paper was written for the class "Theories and Methods of American Studies" (AMST 301), Spring, 2016, taught by Dorothy Wang.

25 Spring, 13.

26 The phrase, "a servant for life," was a euphemism for "slave." Robert H. Romer, "Higher Education and Slavery in Western Massachusetts," *The Journal of Blacks in Higher Education*, No. 46 (Winter, 2004–5): 98–101, 99.

27 Romer, *Slavery in the Connecticut Valley. . .* , 163. In a chapter subtitled "Deliberate Amnesia," Romer discusses the omission of slaveholding citizens from the local histories of Connecticut Valley communities. "We prefer to remember the 'good things'—the efforts to help slaves escape from the South. . . . This process of forgetting, a process I often call 'deliberate amnesia,' gives a distorted view of history, it tends to render invisible the many, many blacks and Indians whom New Englanders had enslaved. Slavery has sometimes been referred to as the 'Peculiar Institution'—New England slavery might be termed the 'Forgotten Institution'" (241–2).

28 Craig Steven Wilder, *Ebony & Ivy: Race, Slavery, and the Troubled History of America's Universities* (New York: Bloomsbury Press, 2013), 154.

29 See, e.g., Wilder. The specific section of Williams's will that bequeaths his slaves to his heirs lists the "properties" as such: "my homestead at Stockbridge, with all the buildings and appurtenances thereunto belonging, with all the stock of cattle and Negro servants now upon the place . . . ." Frederick Rudolph, editor, *Perspectives: A Williams Anthology* (Williamstown: Williams College, 1983), 2. On property documents slaves might be listed as "servants," "servants for life," or just "Negroes," but they were in fact slaves (Romer, "Higher Education. . . ," 99). Wilder lists three slaves included in the will of Ephraim Williams: "Moni, an adult woman, a boy named London, and a girl called Cloe" (154). It may be that Romano, the teenage slave that Williams purchased prior to his death, was also known as London.

30 Certainly exceptions exist, such as two labor-oriented studies of General Electric in Pittsfield by June Nash, *From Tank Town to High Tech* (Albany: State University of New York Press, 1989); and Max H. Kirsh, *In the Wake of the Giant: Multinational Restructuring and Uneven Development in a New England Community* (Albany: State University of New York Press, 1998), but nothing comparable has been published covering North or South Berkshire County. Two social histories do examine rural industrialization in western Massachusetts, but do not include the Berkshires: Jonathan

Prude, *The Coming of Industrial Order: Town and Factory Life in Rural Massachusetts, 1810–1860* (Cambridge, MA: Cambridge University Press, 1983); and Christopher Clark, *The Roots of Rural Capitalism: Western Massachusetts: 1780–1860* (Ithaca: Cornell University Press, 1990). Prude focuses on three small towns in Worcester County and Prude on communities in Hampshire, Hampden, and Franklin County. For a contemporary description and analysis of a Rust Belt region some 70 miles south of North Berkshire, see historian/activist Jeremy Brecher, *Banded Together: Economic Democratization in the Brass Valley* (Urbana: University of Illinois Press, 2011). Here Brecher not only takes the reader through the deindustrialization that devastated the Naugatuck Valley area of western Connecticut, but offers examples of how the community revitalized itself.

Today, most tourists to Berkshire County come to enjoy the scenery, the still bucolic nature that pervades the region, as well as the arts, the museums, the dance, the theater, and the music. If they were to read the county's daily newspaper, the *Berkshire Eagle*, they would more likely learn of the Berkshire's current "cultural" amenities, its natural beauty, and its Gilded Age gentry than of the history and problems of its blue collar people. Illustrative of the paper's focus are two regular contributors, the afore-mentioned Carole Owens and Lauren R. Stevens. For examples of their columns, see Carole Owens, "The Good Millionaire," *Berkshire Eagle*, October 4, 2016, and Lauren R. Stevens, "Many Joys of Hiking in a Berkshire Autumn," *Berkshire Eagle*, October 2, 2016. As if to underline its fascination with the Gilded Age and the opulent industrialists, financiers, and railroad tycoons who built mansions in Lenox and Stockbridge, the *Eagle* editors argue that the Lenox middle and high schools should proudly hold onto their nickname, "The Millionaires." The editors wrote that "the nickname should be embraced because it keeps a part of Berkshire history alive." *Berkshire Eagle,* June 28, 2017. This, despite the fact that students found it "offensive" and voted by a 2–1 margin to drop the name.

31 Michael Seif (Storch Associates and Michael Seif), *Historic Documentation Report for Western Gateway Heritage Park* (Commonwealth of Massachusetts: Department of Environmental Management, 1981), 36. For ease of use and continuity, I will refer to the newspaper throughout its existence as the *Transcript.* During my teaching career in North Adams from 1978 to 2010, everyone referred to it as the *Transcript.* The paper began in 1843, published in the North Village, as the *Weekly Transcript.* It changed ownership and names several times, becoming the *Adams Transcript* in 1858 and the *North Adams Transcript* in 1882. The latter name change reflected North Adams's separation from Adams four years earlier. The paper became a daily in 1895 and remained so until its demise in 2014 (from a history of the newspaper by Philip A. Lee, long-time editor, first published in 1975 and reprinted in the *Transcript,* Sesquicentennial Edition, November 19, 1993).

32 Richard V. Bennett, *The Crispis, Calvin, and the Chinese*, (Middletown, CT: Wesleyan University, 1986), 11 and Ch. VIII.

33 Massachusetts Bureau of Statistics of Labor, 1880.

34 Ibid., 64.

35 As part of a single strike, the Bureau includes workforces from more than one mill, and even from different towns, that may have joined a local or regional strike. Thus, for example, an 1878 woolen strike in North Berkshire involved operatives from three mills. However, North Adams is "credited" with the strike as it started at Blackinton village, although workers at a Williamstown mill also joined in.

36 Ibid. 14. That same year, Millard shoeworkers in North Adams also struck. *Transcript*, June 30, 1853.

37 Ibid., 16, emphasis added. Years later, the village of Blackinton became part of North Adams.

38 Ibid., 29.

39 Ibid., 32.

40 Scott Mixon, "The Crisis of 1873: Perspectives from Multiple Asset Classes," *Journal of Economic History*, 78, 3 (September, 2008): 727–757.

41 The depression also hit local shoe factories, including Sampson's with his Chinese workers, as well as the worker-owned shoe cooperative staffed by Crispin workers who had earlier struck Sampson's firm.

42 Ibid., 32, emphasis added.

43 Over half a century later, with textile production at an end, that mill would become the first home of Sprague Specialties, later to be renamed Sprague Electric Company. At the start of World War II, Sprague outgrew the Beaver mill on its way to become the world's leading producer of capacitors.

44 Ibid.

45 Yet, from other research and annual reports produced by the Bureau, we know that its 1880 listing is incomplete. In fact, Carroll Wright, the director of the Massachusetts Bureau of Labor (and later U.S. labor commissioner), while sensitive to the conditions and needs of labor, "subordinated unions to the point of near invisibility," basically ignoring the growth of the Knights of Labor and the early years of the American Federation of Labor. Henry F. Bedford, editor, *Their Lives & Numbers: The Condition of Working People in Massachusetts, 1870–1910* (Ithaca, NY: Cornell University Press, 1995), 10.

46 Writing in 1995, sociologist Sharon Zukin refers to the North Adams workforce during the late nineteenth century as "quiescent," specifically referencing Knights of St. Crispin shoemakers who lost their jobs to the Chinese men who were imported by Calvin Sampson to break a strike. Left unsaid is not only the effort that the Crispins engaged in to organize the Chinese, but also their own successful effort to start their own worker-owned cooperative shoe factory. (See Chapter 3 for details.) Sharon Zukin, *The Culture of Cities* (Cambridge, MA: Blackwell Publishers, 1995), 85.

47 See James W. Loewen, *Lies My Teacher Told Me: Everything Your American History Textbook Got Wrong,* revised and updated (New York: Simon & Schuster, 2007) for similar biases in American history texts; and Howard Zinn, for a classic example of examining history through the lives and struggles of working people.

48 Also, PBS *Independent Lens* selected *Downside Up: How Art Can Change the Spirit of a Place* to be shown as part of its series.

49 Saratoga Springs, NY, press release, May 30, 2002. Also, see www.downsideupthemovie.org

50 *Transcript,* October 18, 2002.

51 For alternative sources on local industrial history, see, for example, Stewart Burns, "Capacitors and Community: Women Workers at Sprague Electric, 1930–1980," *The Public Historian,* Vol. 11, No. 4 (Fall 1989): 61–81; and Robert Paul Gabrielsky, "The Evolution of the Marshall Street Complex in North Adams," *Historical Journal of Massachusetts* (Winter, 1991): 24–42.

CHAPTER ONE

NORTH BERKSHIRE INDUSTRIALIZES

"When Adams' artisans first engaged in textile manufacturing there was no Waltham, Lowell, Lawrence . . . or Paterson in the Northeast. Rather, in dozens of small rural communities throughout the region, people witnessed the spread of little . . . textile mills."

—Timothy Coogan

On August 19, 1858, the women strikers "ended up at Harmony Hall where they heard speeches call[ing] for united resistance against the millowners of North Adams."

—Timothy Coogan

"Cotton thread holds the union together; unites John C. Calhoun and Abbott Lawrence."

—Ralph Waldo Emerson

INTRODUCTION

EUROPEANS came relatively late to the Berkshires, not until the first part of the eighteenth century. A century earlier, to the east, English settlers had established communities along the Connecticut River in Springfield, Northampton, and Hatfield. To the west, the Dutch had founded Albany by the Hudson in 1623. But Berkshire County remained mostly forested and inhabited by Indians at the site of the town of Housatonic. Authors of one history of Berkshire County write that prospective settlers worried about the Dutch, who "were not desired as neighbors"; feared that the local Indians could not "be kept in quietness"; and were alarmed about French and Indian invasions from Canada, "that their habitations would be exposed to conflagration, and their persons to the tomahawk and scalping knife."[1]

A Westfield Indian peace treaty in 1724 opened up southern Berkshire County for English settlement. Seven years later, with boundaries clarified between New York, Connecticut, and Massachusetts, the parties signed additional treaties. In the north, in the late 1730s, the state permitted a survey of East Hoosick (later named Adams), West Hoosick (later named Williamstown), and Clarksburg, not for immediate settlement but to serve as a defense against French and Indian invaders. To that end, the locals built Fort Massachusetts in 1741, but the British did not establish total control of the area until 1746,[2] after Colonel Ephraim Williams Jr. had perished in the ambush near Lake George, New York, during the French and Indian War.[3]

In the 1750s and 1760s the North Berkshires became populated by English men and women who had previously lived in central and eastern Massachusetts as well as Rhode Island. Besides engaging in lumbering and farming, they also fought in the Revolutionary War. Some were landless, some day laborers, some skilled workers: "blacksmiths. . . , carpenters, joiners, masons, tanners, coopers, brickmakers, and cobblers." In general, farming was predominant in the more fertile land in the southern part of East Hoosac, while the stronger currents of the Hoosic River to the north favored industry. Both north and south became incorporated as the town of Adams in 1778, named in honor of Samuel Adams, a Revolutionary War leader, signatory to the Declaration of Independence, and governor of Massachusetts, 1794–1798. In 1811, the settlers established the first cotton mill in the north village.[4]

North Adams, as the north village became known when it separated in 1878, served as the trading center and railroad hub for rural communities in the northern Berkshires and in neighboring Vermont and New York State. Its relative isolation did not, however, insulate it and its neighboring towns from the vagaries of business cycles and nineteenth-century wars. Its mill owners and industrialists followed the main chance, and the workers of the region tried to protect themselves, forming unions and fraternal organizations, striking the factories owned by the emerging capitalist class, and cooperating with each other to enhance their standard of living.

The North Berkshire geography limited the region but also offered it opportunities. Mill owners took advantage of the Hoosic River's power to build by its banks. Later, in the 1850s, the state, as well as several private investors, chose the Hoosac range to its east as a site to drill a railway tunnel offering a Western "gateway" for local and regional trade.

Located at the foot of Mount Greylock and between the Hoosac and Taconic ranges, North Adams had enjoyed a southerly rail connection with Pittsfield since 1846. As the new railroad also connected to the Boston-Albany line, local residents could then take the train to the state capital.[5] Prior to that, weekly stagecoach rides from Albany and Greenfield provided primary inter-regional travel.[6]

Reverend Washington Gladden, minister of the North Adams First Congregational Church and a leader of the Social Gospel movement, describes such a stagecoach ride over the Hoosac Mountain:

> When the heats of noon are past, and the sun begins to sink behind the Hoosac mountain we will prepare for our stage ride of eight miles to North Adams. Persons who have been [on] this overland trip have discovered that the true luxury and glory of travel are only to be found in the stage coaches . . . . The grand scenery and the bracing air of the mountains are full of delicious intoxication . . . . Jim [our driver] learned his trade in a long apprenticeship among the White Hills, and he is fond of talking

about that region; and yet he maintains that the scenery over the Hoosac is hardly surpassed in that famous resort of travelers.[7]

FARMING, DEBT, AND RADICALISM

Before the development of the mill economy, residents of Adams worked the land, farming, raising sheep, and lumbering, and they engaged in artisan labor and milling. A significant minority owned no land. Even for those who owned farms, a shortage of capital led to debt and many lost their farms. Distrustful of the well-to-do folks in Boston and the power of state control, the voters of Adams rejected the state's first constitution in 1780.

According to historian Timothy Coogan, the creditors wanted the small farmers and workers to pay off their debts in currency like silver. Not only were the residents of towns like Adams strapped for cash, but the town itself could hardly find the funds to pay its employees and maintain a militia. And so the demand arose, from communities like Adams to the state legislature, to print and legitimize a paper currency.[8]

The legislature refused, and in towns across the Berkshires and in neighboring counties, preparations began in 1786 for what would soon be called Shays' Rebellion. As the courts enforced the debts, which many saw as illegitimate, the rebels, including more than twenty from Adams, focused their anger on them. They marched on the courts in Northampton and Springfield and had some immediate successes in stopping proceedings. In response, the governor sent in the state militia to quash the uprising.

Though the rebels lost, most of them received amnesty, and the legislature waived state and local taxes for one year. However, the total debt remained the same, and the government refused to issue paper currency. Without capital and with indebted land, farming became less and less an option for the people of North Berkshire. As the century came to an end, the future for Adams residents appeared to favor industry.[9]

THE BEGINNINGS OF INDUSTRIALIZATION

By the turn of the nineteenth century, records exist of prototypes of textile-type mills along the north branch of the Hoosic River. In 1801, David Estes is credited with the first construction of buildings to clean (card) wool and clean (dress) cloth.[10] Textile mills, both cotton and woolen, and iron forges processing local ore burgeoned after the War of 1812, aided by the embargo of English goods. "[W]ithin a few years 'the whole of the north branch of the Hoosac from the Beaver down to Blackinton was taken up by water claims and a series of mills built along its stream.'"[11] These local developments mirrored the statewide textile manufacturing increase during the same period, influenced by the restrictions on English imports. By 1860, Massachusetts' cloth output had expanded to over 400 million yards from the 1826 figure of 23 million yards.[12]

Geographer R.C. Estall traces the concentration of New England cotton mills to the rivers of the area in southern Maine, Rhode Island, Connecticut, New Hampshire, and eastern Massachusetts. Although North Berkshire lay outside that area, Estall wrote: "Adams and North Adams provide two of the very few examples of significant cotton textile development in areas that may truly be considered 'inland.'"[13]

The 1850 census marked the official shift of the town from agriculture to industry, since more factory workers than farmers now resided in Adams.[14] In a period of only two decades, the town's population doubled, and the percentage of employment in manufacturing rose from about 25 percent in Adams (1820) to almost 66 percent (1840), reflecting the source of the county's earliest textile development. Now the site of the biggest manufacturing center in the western part of the state, Adams ranked second to Lowell statewide in number of factories.[15]

Adams possessed nineteen of the county's thirty-one cotton mills in 1837, and cotton and woolen textile production increased even faster after 1842 when the Adams-Pittsfield railroad link opened.[16] In 1859, one reporter "described North Adams as a 'bright and thriving' village with about three thousand people, and 'a line of manufacturing establishments running along the Hoosac River for three quarters of a mile.'"[17] The mills tended to be small, in the Rhode Island style, unlike the heavily invested, sizeable operations in Lowell. In Lowell, also known as the Waltham model, wealthy capitalists financed the building of large mills and boarding houses where they encouraged young women from rural New England to live and work.[18] In Adams, the owners and managers of the smaller mills lived nearby and hired their employees locally. In fact, at that time, the Adams industrial setting proved more representative of New England mill work than did the Waltham model.

POLITICS AND THE SLAVERY ISSUE

Without a ready supply of cheap cotton picked by enslaved people in the South, Northern textile mills would never have been able to become financially successful, to grow and enhance the development of a wealthy industrial region. As historian Edward E. Baptiste expresses it, "the same work of hands that built a wealthy south enabled the free states to create the world's second industrial revolution. . . , one [that] began in the cotton mills of Massachusetts and Rhode Island."[19] One could say that without slavery, there would be no Lowell, no Lawrence. While pro-slavery sentiment tended to be muted in the North, Whig politicians and northern industrialists knew the role that slavery played in their region and supported it, sometimes quietly, sometimes not.

William C. Plunkett would become one such Whig politician. Born in 1799 in Lenox to Irish immigrants, Plunkett and his descendants dominated North Berkshire textile production into the middle of the twentieth century. He graduated from Lenox Academy and taught school for awhile in Lee and Lanesboro.

Historians differ on the specifics, but in Lanesboro he favorably impressed a local merchant, Thomas Durant. Under very good terms, Durant made him a partner, and a few years later Plunkett moved to Adams, where he changed careers.[20]

In 1829, he took over management of the Adams South Village Cotton and Woolen Manufacturing Company. The mill had begun operation in 1814 with thirty-one stockholders and stayed open even during the depression that followed the end of the War of 1812.[21] By 1831, Plunkett had enough capital to buy out all of the stockholders and become the sole owner. He improved the machinery and increased production, doubling the number of spindles and looms on the main floor.

About five years later, when a brother-in-law of Plunkett's obtained a quarter interest in the operation, the mill became known as Plunkett & Wheeler. In 1844, they enlarged the building, and by the time of the Civil War, the business had become very profitable. Wheeler became a full partner, and the mill expanded with a new rear building and a dye-house.[22]

While William C. Plunkett maintained his role in building the textile business in Adams, he complemented that status in the political arena as well. He served in numerous local political capacities including town meeting moderator, selectman, highway surveyor, bridge commissioner, and fire warden. Statewide, he won election as the Whig candidate to the State Senate in 1840. As the Democratic Party fell into decline, with losses after the 1837 "panic," the Whig Party moved into ascendance. According to Kenneth Goode, "William C. Plunkett, the foremost politician among Adams' economic elite, rode the crest of the Whig wave when he was elected state senator on that ticket in 1840."[23] Plunkett served several times in the state House of Representatives; on the Governor's Council in 1852; as a delegate to the constitutional convention in 1853; and in 1854, his highest office, lieutenant governor to Governor Emory Washburn.[24]

The Whig Party in Massachusetts, controlled by the textile industrialists, predominantly the Boston Associates—men like Nathan Appleton, Amos and Abbott Lawrence in Lowell—

favored the tariff, which protected their manufactured goods from the British. Despite a growing abolitionist sentiment in Boston and the North, they also refused to take an anti-slavery position, which would have inflamed their Southern allies, who provided them the slave-picked cotton that allowed them to make huge profits.[25] As Ralph Waldo Emerson summed it up, "Cotton thread holds the union together; unites John C. Calhoun [the South's leading spokesman for slavery] and Abbott Lawrence [one of the North's wealthiest textile industrialists]."[26]

This was the political party that William C. Plunkett represented when he won election to the Massachusetts State Senate in 1840, the same year that Whig candidate William Henry Harrison won the presidential election. With his cotton interests back in Adams, Plunkett would have supported the strong Whig position on the tariff. While the residents of Adams favored the protective tariff, they remained outspoken against slavery, unlike the Whigs, who tried to ignore the issue.

In Massachusetts, the struggle over slavery grew fiercer with the annexation of Texas in 1845 and the western territories that were gained in 1848 at the end of the Mexican-American War. Two years later, federal legislation known as the "Compromise of 1850" passed with the following provisions: California was to be admitted to the union as a free state; New Mexico and Utah would become territories with no prohibition of slavery; the slave trade, but not slavery, was banned in Washington D.C.; and a more restrictive and punishing Fugitive-Slave Law came into force.

The so-called compromise did not diminish the battle over slavery, and in Boston, the Fugitive Slave Law, which mandated the return of escaped slaves, was particularly hated. Adams residents felt the same, and supported Underground Railroad lines that ran through to Berkshire County, including one that went over the mountains to Williamstown.[27]

Anti-slavery sentiment grew even stronger after the passage of the Kansas-Nebraska Act of 1854, leaving the question of slavery up to the individual state or territory.[28] The textile industrialists, known as the "Cotton Whigs," opposed the Kansas-Nebraska Act, having publicly objected to any territorial expansion of slavery. Nonetheless, they and their party had committed themselves to upholding the law of the land, and that included the Fugitive Slave Act. "As realistic men of business and capital, the Yankee manufacturers felt obligated to retain the faith and goodwill of a Southern plantation economy whose production of cotton created personal fortunes already being reckoned in millions of dollars."[29]

At a March 13, 1854, town meeting, Adams voters sent the following resolution to the House of Representatives and the Senate: "We solemnly protest against the passage of what is known as the 'Nebraska Bill,' and the repeal or any modification of existing prohibitions of slavery over freedom in a government founded to secure to all men the inalienable rights of life, liberty, and the pursuit of happiness."[30] Already angered by the Fugitive Slave Act of 1850, Berkshire County residents as a whole had been switching their political allegiance from the Whigs to the Republicans. Nonetheless, Adams's best known citizen and politician, William C. Plunkett, had ascended to the office of lieutenant governor, joining his fellow Whig Governor Emory Washburn. Disunity characterized the state Whigs with the rift between the conservative Cotton Whigs and the outspoken anti-slavery "Conscience Whigs" widening.

> **ANTHONY BURNS IS CAPTURED IN BOSTON. A MAN KIDNAPPED.**—A Public Meeting will be held at Faneuil Hall this (Friday) evening, May 26, at 7 o'clock, to secure justice for a man claimed as a slave by a Virginia kidnapper, and imprisoned in Boston Court House, in defiance of the laws of Massachusetts. Shall he be plunged into the hell of Virginia slavery by a Massachusetts Judge of Probate?

Through this handbill and word of mouth, residents of Boston and its environs learned that Anthony Burns, a man who had escaped his enslavement in Virginia, had been captured in 1854, and was scheduled to be returned to captivity based on the Fugitive Slave Law. Thousands and thousands of anti-slavery citizens turned out for meetings, court appearances, and demonstrations to free Burns: his capture had created much publicity, and a leading historian on the case called Burns "[t]he most famous slave in America."[31] Burns was the third slave captured in Boston under the Fugitive Slave Law. Three years earlier, another former Virginia slave, Shadrach Minkins, had been arrested under the new law, but "had the good fortune to be rescued and spirited off to freedom by irate Bostonians"—an act which Whig Senator Daniel Webster called "a case of treason." Two months after that, however, guarded by more than a hundred Boston police, the state sent Thomas Sims, a waiter who had escaped to Boston from Georgia, back into slavery.[32]

When Anthony Burns later faced a return to slavery, despite the efforts of his lawyers, he lost in court. He might well have been freed by citizens' force: an already existing Vigilance Committee seemed up for the task, and would likely have been successful if only the local city marshals had been guarding Burns. But a hasty attempt at rescue, which resulted in the killing of one guard, had failed, and the mayor and governor had called for U.S. troops to intervene. President Franklin Pierce gave the order, and a sizeable militia subsequently guarded the prisoner. One local newspaper called it "evidence of the illegal and immoral deployment of the state's military power, a sign of guilt and perfidious weakness in Mayor Smith and Governor Washburn." Earlier, when members of the Vigilance Committee had presented a legal writ to the governor to free Burns, Washburn turned it down acting as "cold as an icicle."[33]

In his journal, well-known anti-slavery activist Henry Ingersoll Bowditch described the taking of Anthony Burns to the port to transport him back to slavery:

> In full broad daylight, in the middle of the day, in front of the assembled merchant princes of

> State Street, with a right royal cortege of two companies of United States troops, and cannon loaded with grape, and all the military of Suffolk County, the poor slave was escorted, as with regal splendor to the end of Long Wharf. There he was received on board the revenue cutter Morris, and is now probably far away towards the hell that is prepared for him in Virginia.[34]

Months later, speaking at an anti-slavery meeting in Worcester, Wendell Phillips, Boston's leading abolitionist orator, proclaimed that Governor Washburn "has committed a higher crime than murder . . . . [H]e has deserted his post and skulked from his duty, from cold cowardice, while a citizen of the State was kidnapped and carried into slavery, in violation of the laws he had sworn to support." The reporter, covering the meeting, noted that "[t]he strong and indignant rebukes administered by Mr. Phillips to Gov. Washburn repeatedly brought down the applause of the house."[35]

The behavior of the state's leading elected officials and their wealthy supporters, members of the Whig Party, so infuriated the bulk of the population that in the next election the Whigs went down to defeat, never to return to power. That included Governor Washburn, who in a bid for reelection, garnered only 21 percent of the vote, losing to the "Know Nothing" candidate, Henry J. Gardner. William C. Plunkett, in attempting reelection to lieutenant governor, suffered a similar devastating defeat.[36] In a famous sermon, "The New Crime Against Humanity," Boston's leading minister and friend of Emerson, Theodore Parker, blamed the rendition of Anthony Burns on Boston's "men of wealth and fashion" who exhibited a "hard-hearted indifference to freedom and justice." "[T]he weak pliancy of Governor Washburn and Mayor Smith" incurred some of the wrath of Parker. The minister did not criticize the ordinary citizens of Boston and pointed out that "[n]ot a single pro-slavery measure has ever been popular with the mass of men in New England or Massachusetts."[37]

During the entire Burns affair, Governor Emory Washburn's lieutenant, William C. Plunkett, made not one public statement. His apparent support for Washburn's actions placed him in opposition to his anti-slavery constituents back in Adams.[38] Plunkett clearly backed the Fugitive Slave Law, as one newspaper account prior to Burns's capture made plain. A lengthy report in the *Liberator* excoriated the speakers and attendees at a birthday party for former Secretary of State Daniel Webster on January 18, 1854—an event that was held despite the fact that Webster had been dead for two years. Webster had voted in favor of the Fugitive Slave Act in the U.S. Senate and had spoken out for its enforcement numerous times, earning him the enmity of the growing anti-slavery population in Massachusetts. In examining the names of the birthday party invitees, the *Liberator* reporter concluded "[T]he sum total of independent manhood among them all, amounted exactly to a cipher." They posthumously awarded Webster "adulation bestowed upon his memory. Every one of the speakers called good evil, and evil good." When it came time for Lieutenant Governor Plunkett to speak, he "responded in a felicitous manner, making the alarming announcement that 'Massachusetts and Daniel Webster are one and indivisible.'" This led the reporter to add, "We trust this is a mere hallucination of the brain; though, if it be a true representation of the exact position of the old Bay State, there is a daily need of the annual ejaculation, 'God save the Commonwealth of Massachusetts.'"[39]

If Plunkett's paean to Webster reached the voters back home in Adams, one assumes they would have been outraged. The voters in Adams were so opposed to the Whig policies of Washburn and Plunkett that less than 1 percent of them voted Whig in the 1855 vote for governor, a percentage lower than the Berkshire County total (1.5 percent) and the state total (9.7 percent).[40]

Perhaps, surprisingly, nowhere in the historical record, with the exception of the *Liberator* article, can any bill, policy, or political program that Plunkett favored or opposed be located. In the obituaries to Plunkett when he died in 1884, there is no mention of his Whig politics or his support of the Fugitive Slave Act: newspaper accounts only list the offices he held and his local contributions.[41] In a long memorial sermon, Reverend Edward Hungerford stated that on "moral questions," Plunkett "was always on the side of purity and right . . . . He was a man of convictions. He was a manufacturer, and believed that he knew what was for the interest of manufacturers and laborers alike . . . . He worked for his party because his party represented principles . . . . Gen. Plunkett was first and dearest a Christian gentleman." Hungerford does say that Plunkett "made enemies," but doesn't say why, or because of what issues. At Plunkett's funeral, the very popular Reverend Mark Hopkins, former president of Williams College, called Plunkett a man of "[i]ntegrity" and a man "identified with the interests and honor of the county and of the State."[42]

Historian Hamilton Child lists the numerous state and local political offices that Plunkett held, but nowhere mentions a specific bill or policy that he favored in any of those offices. He does call him "a progressive man in every respect, and good schools and school-houses were always advocated by him." Child goes on to write of Plunkett's "most prominent" role in the local Congregational church, including that of deacon, and the fact that "[h]e had also been superintendent of the Sunday school for forty-two consecutive years." Historian John Lockwood also lists Plunkett's many political offices, local and state, but omits any word of his specific political contributions. Instead, all Lockwood tells us is that "Mr. Plunkett was a man of strong convictions, slow to make up his mind, weighing well the pros and cons of a question, but when once his opinion was formed, it became unalterable under the facts." Joseph Addison Wilk, author of a dissertation on the town of Adams, writes of Plunkett's industrial role in the town's development, but entirely omits his political career. And a corporate brochure, celebrating the centennial of the Plunkett mills, similarly says not a word of William C. Plunkett's political life.[43]

Based on the historical record, the thrust of Plunkett's life, beyond his business accomplishments, show him to be a hard-working, church-going man of principle, though the content of those principles remain vague.[44]

THE DEVELOPMENT OF A CAPITALIST CLASS AND A WORKING CLASS

By the middle of the nineteenth century, a developing capitalist class had become visible in Berkshire County along with an industrial working class. In 1860, 60 percent of the workforce in the North village found employment in manufacturing, a total of 1,350 employees. Most produced cotton and woolen products, and a distant third made boots and shoes. Mill workers labored thirteen hours a day under dangerous conditions but barely made a living. Factory wages for shoemakers averaged just $1.70 a day, and Hoosac Tunnel laborers made just $1.40 a day, "a meager sum even then."[45]

The lot of the employers could hardly have been different. In a study of wealth in Berkshire County, Christopher D. Hardy ranked Adams as second only to Pittsfield in the number of economic elites within its boundaries in 1860.[46] Hardy used $25,000 in real and personal estate holdings as an elite cutoff point, and found that only three-tenths of 1 percent of the county's population exceeded that figure. Nearly 15 percent of that group lived in Adams in 1860, a significant rise from the 2 percent of a comparable group that resided in Adams in 1800. Fifteen of the twenty-two members of the Adams elite engaged in manufacturing.

For the most part, "the county's manufacturing elite in 1860 . . . was made up of men who came from modest backgrounds, started small mills, and ultimately acquired sizable fortunes." Sanford Blackinton, for example, was born on a farm but at the age of 16 began an apprenticeship to the original mill owner in the village that later took Blackinton's name. In 1821, Blackinton started his own mill with two others, and by 1860, the value of the property he owned totaled almost a quarter of a million dollars.[47]

Hardy found that in 1800, the top Berkshire County wealth holders did not possess significantly more wealth than the class just below them. That changed by 1860: not only had sizeable differences in the value of personal and real property grown to exist within the wealthiest group, but a significant gap had developed between it and the class below. Stratification had increased in Adams and in the county, and one could now speak of the "truly wealthy."[48] Racial stratification and the oppression and exploitation of slaves also contributed to the fortunes of the industrial elite as the raw material for the textile production, cotton, made its way to the Berkshires, shipped in bales from the slave South.

The increased industrialization, mechanization, and stratification meant that mill workers saw little hope of escaping their laboring status individually, and that concerted, cooperative action amongst themselves became their best opportunity to improve their living standards. Thus the strike grew to become a weapon used more and more. In fact, as noted in the Introduction, from 1830 to 1880, workers in the area of Adams (both North and South) engaged in more strikes than in the more well-known industrial cities like Lowell and Fall River.[49]

Timothy Coogan carefully delineated the changes in Adams as industry shifted from its more familial earlier stages to a colder, more distant and corporate style:

> The paternalistic world of the 1830s and early 1840s was unlike any other that came before or after . . . . [T]he relationship between owners and workers consequently had not yet been shattered by the strain of class or ethnicity. . . . [I]n that pre-railroad and pre-immigrant era of antebellum Adams, the chances for class harmony and sentimental bonding seemed high indeed. Yet, such harmonious relations did not endure for long, especially after the 1850s. Thereafter, strikes would continue to plague this new mill town and the age of paternalism would seem all but gone.[50]

The Civil War and its immediate aftermath brought rapid growth to the region. North Adams's population nearly doubled (from 6,924 to 12,090) from 1860 to 1870, and the number of its cotton looms climbed from twenty-two in 1840 to over 200 by 1870. Diverse but continuous waves of immigrants helped to form the growing industrial labor force, making Adams the most industrialized community in the Berkshires by 1860. First came the Irish in the 1830s, followed by the Welsh and the French Canadians in the 1860s, and the Italians towards century's end.[51]

By 1850, more than 20 percent of the Adams population had been born outside of the United States. In 1855, close to 1,500 foreign-born residents lived in Adams out of a total population of almost 7,000; in 1855, the Irish made up the largest number of immigrants, followed by the English, Scots, and Germans.[52] While the mill owners remained predominantly Protestant, the mostly working-class immigrant population practiced Catholicism.

Prior to the rapid industrialization, the early mill workers of the 1830s and 1840s in Adams had tended to be native born; often they were young women who came to town from their farms and rural communities. From Timothy Coogan we learn of one, Sarah Sanders, who, in 1830, left her family's log cabin in Savoy at the age of 12 to work in a small mill in Adams. Work began each morning at six and concluded at 8:30 p.m. every day except Sunday. When Sarah began work, she earned fifty cents a week plus board, and after five or six years of work, had a wage of $1.50 a week, but without board.[53] Mill workers of that time labored in close proximity with their supervisors and even the mill owners, and that closeness and paternalism tended to bring about generally peaceful labor relations.

The pace of work intensified in the 1850s and 1860s and led to an increase in industrial accidents and labor strife. Stories of these accidents, many of which resulted from the new machines, filled the local papers. In 1864, one such article described the case of a new worker who "seriously broke his arm in two places because he did not properly know how to run the crank on a machine; whereas another worker at the Union cotton factory seriously injured himself when his finger got ripped off while he was working with the gearing."[54] While workers with little or no training got maimed or worse, mill managers and owners escaped any such harm, a new reality which served to heighten the class differences in the growing factory system.

Although one strike occurred as early as 1853 at Oliver Arnold & Company, labor relations really heated up in the late 1850s, again at the Arnold mill, an action that led to a near general strike throughout the town.[55] Arnold's female weavers struck for both higher wages and payment in cash on August 19, 1858. The weavers rebelled against the custom of receiving pay in credit, or "scrip," a practice which forced them to purchase goods, often overpriced, at the company's store.

The women took to the street and marched in line to the A.P. Butler & Company mill, shouting slogans and "waving their bonnets." Reinforced by Butler workers, the procession moved to Sylvander Johnson's warp mill, singing along the way. Then they walked on to Braytonville and the A.W. Richardson & Company where more mill workers joined their ranks. Meanwhile, another march of 140 female operatives, reminiscent of the militant young women workers who had struck the mills of Lowell,[56] headed down Main Street carrying their colorful banners along the way.

Everyone ended up at the Harmony Hall meetinghouse, where they heard speeches advocating solidarity against the mill owners. The following day, another procession of striking workers took to the streets, preceded by a band. Over a hundred people joined with banners that exclaimed: "The Laborer is Worthy of His Hire" and "Give Us Our Old Wages." The marchers once again met at Harmony Hall with resolutions calling for higher wages and payment in cash. Despite general ridicule from the press, the women workers would not be dissuaded and the demonstrations continued for two additional days.[57]

In 1864, Arnold's female operatives struck again. According to one newspaper account, those who refused to honor the strike were "threatened by their gentle feminine former co-laborers with a coat of tar and feathers." Weavers and tunnel miners also struck that year. The Adams mill workers demanded fewer hours—from as many as thirteen hours a day to eleven, a demand similar to those made by mill workers in the eastern part of the state.[58] Of course, the workers wanted their weekly pay to remain the same, but with fewer hours. The fight over the length of the working day would continue well into the twentieth century, and would be the spark that ignited the famous Lawrence "Bread and Roses" strike of 1912 (see Chapter Eight).

A year later, mill workers from throughout the North and South villages of Adams met in a mass meeting with the goal of shortening the oppressive work day. Described as the largest crowd to ever congregate in Adams, the group united in calling for an eleven-hour workday. Committees of workers from each mill reported to a leadership at the Universalist Church in the North Village. Despite their numbers and organization, the local workers failed to gain a shorter work day, although woolen workers in Great Barrington and in Pittsfield soon won an eleven-hour day. Adams workers remained stuck at thirteen hours. While the mill owners seemed to have won this battle, they and other well-to-do residents of Adams worried about heightened worker militancy, and also feared an increase in poverty and crime. The growing temperance movement became one response to those fears in Adams and throughout the nation.[59]

Evangelical Protestantism had emerged as a growing force in the young nation during the first half of the nineteenth century, particularly in the cities. Although it led to varied manifestations, one major strand focused on the behavior of the developing industrial workforce. Within a context of moral reform, its adherents lectured on the evils of liquor, calling for temperance, even abstinence from drink and the saloon. For some the concern may have been strictly moral, for others worry that beer and liquor would inhibit workplace productivity and engender absenteeism. Temperance societies sprang up across the country and in New York, and "one temperance leader personally secured some 180,000 total-abstinence pledges, including several fire companies who signed up en masse, in the years from 1833 to 1842."[60] The movement, aided by the formation of the Woman's Christian Temperance Union in 1873, continued throughout the rest of the nineteenth century and into the twentieth, climaxing with the legalization of Prohibition in 1920.

Through their church activism, the leading businessmen of North Berkshire approved of a moralistic campaign against the use of alcohol. Historian Matthew Bryson writes that "[m]ost churches strongly supported total abstinence, one of [shoe entrepreneur George W.] Chase's favorite projects and a goal of many industrialists, who deemed liquor a corrupting influence that reduced both the morality and the productivity of their workforce." Chase founded the Baptist Sunday school and served as a deacon at the Congregational church. From Bryson's point of view, the time that Chase spent supporting his religious activities "not only benefited his soul, it also helped his business."[61]

Other shoe manufacturers with significant involvement in their churches included George Millard, who contributed to the rebuilding of the First Baptist Church after an 1849 fire; Calvin Sampson, the treasurer and deacon of the First Baptist Church; and J.M. Canedy, a superintendent, and W.J. Wilkinson, a deacon, of the same Baptist church. On the textile side, William C. Plunkett supported a variety of churches, Baptist, Episcopal, and Congregational. He started the very first Sunday school in Adams, and served as its superintendent for forty-two years. Plunkett's eulogist declared that on "moral questions he was always on the side of purity and right" and "[h]e was strictly temperate."[62]

As industrialization increased, farm work declined, and less than 5 percent of the workforce in Adams was engaged in agriculture by the time of the Civil War.[63] Immigrants continued to settle in the region, and by 1870 one-third of the population had been born outside of the United States, chiefly from Ireland

and French Canada. During the 1870s, Adams, composed of both the North and South Villages, ranked as the "fastest growing town in Massachusetts."[64] With its emphasis on textile and shoe production, it typified New England's industrializing towns. *Harper's* called it "one of the busiest little towns, humming and smoking with various industry."[65] Yet, at the same time, the construction of the Hoosac Tunnel brought North Berkshire national publicity and a somewhat unique identity starting at the middle of the nineteenth century.

Rebuilding of Arnold Print Works (1872–1874) after a fire (North Adams Public Library collection).

Bust of Anthony Burns, surrounded by episodes of his life (John Andrews, engraver, Library of Congress).

NOTES

1 David Dudley Field and Chester Dewey, *A History of the County of Berkshire, Massachusetts, in Two Parts: The First Being a General View of the County; the Second, an Account of the Several Towns* (Berkshire County: S.W. Bush, 1829), 10; and Clinton Q. Richmond, "Adams and North Adams," *New England Magazine*, 21 (1899–1900): 61–81, 161.

2 John Lockwood et al., editors, *Western Massachusetts: A History, 1636–1925*, Vol. I (New York: Lewis Historical Publishing Company, 1926), 417; and Timothy Coogan, *The Forging of a New Mill Town: North and South Adams, Massachusetts, 1780–1860* (New York: Ph.D. thesis, New York University, 1992), 49.

3 W.F. Spear, *History of North Adams, Massachusetts, 1749–1885* (North Adams: Hoosac Valley News Printing House, 1885), pp. 9–10; Clinton Q. Richmond III, *An Annotated Bibliography of North Adams, Berkshire County, Massachusetts* (Brookline, MA: Muddy River Press, 1999), in which Richmond writes that Spear "chose to essentially rewrite most of the Morris history (A.H. Morris, "Interesting Facts in the Early History of North Adams," the *Adams Transcript*, 1859–1860) and Vol. I of Hamilton Child's Gazetteer of Berkshire County, Massachusetts, 1725–1885 (Syracuse: Journal Office), 18.

4 Field and Dewey, 11; quote from Coogan, 58; and Richmond, 170. W. F. Spear, writing in 1885, noted that the Hoosac River proved to be more powerful at the time of European settlement ("the Hoosac river then being much deeper than now"), 13. A similar point is made in J.E.A. Smith, editor, *History of Berkshire County, Massachusetts with Biographical Sketches of its Prominent Men*, 2 volumes (New York: J.B. Beers Company, 1885): "Although the land was poor, the great water power—the Hoosac River being then much deeper than now—and the probability of the early erection of mills here attracted the attention of settlers" (464).

5 Eugene F. Michalenko, *In This Valley: A Concise History of Adams, Massachusetts* (Adams, MA: Adams Specialty and Printing Company, 2002), 4.

6 Frederick Rudolph, "Chinamen in Yankeedom: Anti-Unionism in Massachusetts in 1870," *The American Historical Review* (October, 1947): 1–29, 3.

7 Spear, 497–8.

8 See Coogan, 82–85. A century later, indebted farmers in the South made the same demand on the Congress as part of the Populist movement. See, e.g., Lawrence Goodwyn, *Democratic Promise: The Populist Moment in America* (New York: Oxford University Press, 1976).

9 See Coogan, 98–102; and Bruce Levine, Stephen Brier et al., editors, *Who Built America? Working People and the Nation's Economy, Politics, Culture, and Society*, Vol. 1 (New York: Pantheon Books, 1989), Chapter Four.

10 Spear, 29.

11 Arnold Bossi, "The Traditions and Spirit of the Arnold Print Works," *The Arnold Print,* Vol. II, no. 6 (North Adams, MA: 1919), 1; and Houghton thesis, 18.

12 Alexander Keyssar, *Out of Work: The first century of unemployment in Massachusetts* (Cambridge, MA: Cambridge University Press, 1986), 22.

13 R. C. Estall, *New England: A Study in Industrial Adjustment* (New York: Praeger, 1966), 72. Estall, however, offers no explanation for the North Berkshire "inland" concentration.

14 Sesquicentennial edition of the *Transcript*, North Adams, MA, Nov. 19, 1993.

15 Coogan, 273–4.

16 Arnold, 75 and 82.

17 Janet Ellen Roberts, *A History of the French Canadians in North Adams* (Williamstown, MA: Williams College, 1975), 22, from Anthony F. Parise, North Adams and the Hoosac Tunnel (Williamstown, MA: Williams College, 1971), 8.

18 Robert F. Dalzell Jr., *Enterprising Elite: The Boston Associates and the World They Made* (New York: W.W. Norton & Co., 1987).

19 Edward E. Baptist, *The Half Has Never Been Told: Slavery and the Making of American Capitalism* (New York: Basic Books, 2014), 312.

20 Lockwood (139) offers the most detail of Plunkett's relationship with Durant. See also John Addison Wilk, *A History of Adams, Massachusetts* (Ph.D. thesis, University of Ottawa, 1945), 152; and Orra L. Stone, *History of Massachusetts Industries: Their Inception, Growth and Success,* Vol. 1 (Boston: S.J. Clarke Publishing Co., 1930), 88. At some point early in his career, Plunkett served in the militia, which brought him the nickname General Plunkett. Wilk confuses Durant with his same-named son, who became vice president of the Union Pacific Railroad and an activist in national finance and politics (email from William Kolis, 1/27/2018).

21 William H. Pierson, *Industrial Architecture in the Berkshires* (New Haven: Yale University dissertation, 1949, photocopy, 1972), 120. With the 1815 peace treaty of Ghent, British cotton once again overwhelmed the market leading to the closing of most Adams cotton mills, with the exception of the Adams South Village operation and one or two others (Stone, 88).

22 Wilk.

23 Kenneth Goode, *Economic Change and Political Behavior: Berkshire County, Massachusetts, 1831–1860* (Williamstown, MA: Williams College, 1976).

24 Lockwood, 139; *Transcript*, January 24, 1884, 2; Hamilton Child, *Gazetteer of Berkshire County, Massachusetts, 1725–1885* (Syracuse: Journal Office, 1885), 100.

25 Robert F. Dalzell Jr., *Enterprising Elite: The Boston Associates and the World They Made* (New York: W.W. Norton, 1987).

26 Thomas H. O'Connor, *Lords of the Loom: Cotton Whigs and the Coming of the Civil War* (New York: Scribner's, 1968).

27 Mark W. Carter, *Adams, Massachusetts and the American Civil War* (Williamstown, MA: Williams College, 1976), 14–15.

28 Bruce Levine, Stephen Brier, et al., 393–398.

29 O'Connor, 101.

30 Carter, 15.

31 Albert J. Von Frank, *The Trials of Anthony Burns: Freedom and Slavery in Emerson's Boston* (Cambridge, MA: Harvard University Press, 1998), 233.

32 O'Connor, 97 and 96.

33 Von Frank, 216 and 354.

34 Vincent Y. Bowditch, *Life and Correspondence of Henry Ingersoll Bowditch* (Boston: Houghton Mifflin Co., 1902, Vol. I), 263–4.

35 *The Liberator*, September 29, 1854, 3.

36 Ibid., January 12, 1855, 3.

37 Parker, 262.

38 The *Adams Transcript* began as a Whig newspaper in 1843 and did not support the Republican Party until after 1854 (Carter, 18). "The decade before the Civil War was a period of ferment and change in politics but *The Transcript* continued its traditional vigorous support of the Whig party as long as it could despite the growing feelings against slavery of which the Whigs were tolerant. It continued too, its admiration for Daniel Webster, long its hero until his great Compromise Speech in the Senate in March of 1850" (Philip A. Lee, 1975, long-time editor of the *Transcript* reprinted in the paper's Sesquicentennial Edition, Nov. 19, 1993). The Whig affiliation may very well have kept the paper from criticizing Plunkett, though Plunkett remained an admirer of Webster at least through the beginning of 1854.

39 The *Liberator*, January 27, 1854, 2.

40 Goode, 20.

41 For example, "An Old-Time Democrat Dead," *Boston Sunday Globe,* January 20, 1884, p. 2.

42 "A Memorial discourse delivered at the funeral of Gen. Wm.C. Plunkett in the First Congregational Church, Adams, Massachusetts, Tuesday, January 22, 1884 by Rev. Edward Hungerford with remarks by Rev. Mark Hopkins, D.D., ex-president of Williams College" (Boston: Franklin Press: Rand, Avery & Co., 1884).

43 Child, 100; John Lockwood; Wilk; "W.C. Plunkett & Sons: 1814–1914, One Hundred Years of Business" (Berkshire Cotton Manufacturing Company, incorporated 1899).

44 Margaret Plunkett Lord, the great-great-granddaughter of William C. Plunkett, had a great-grandmother on her mother's side who harbored "runaway slaves" at her home on the underground railroad in Johnstown, New York (phone conversation with author, February 8, 2017).

45 Michael Seif (Storch Associates and Michael Seif), *Historic Documentation for Western Gateway Heritage Park.* Commonwealth of Massachusetts: Department of Environmental Management, 1981, 26; and Carter, 74.

46 Christopher D. Hardy, *The Reaction of Local Elites to Modernization: Berkshire County, Mass., 1800–1860* (Williamstown, MA: Williams College, 1976).

47 Ibid., 38, 49, 97.

48 Ibid., 38–41, 90.

49 Coogan, 43.

50 Ibid., 350–351.

51 Ibid. 448; Robert Paul Gabrielsky, "The Evolution of the Marshall Street Complex in North Adams," *Histortical Journal of Massachusetts*, Winter, 1991: 24–42, 25.

52 Data from Coogan, 427.

53 Coogan, 361.

54 Coogan, 432–433, from the *Transcript*, August 4, 1864. In a visit to North Adams, Nathaniel Hawthorne wrote about the "factories [with] the machinery whizzing" and the dangers they posed: "A steam engine in a factory . . . posses[es] a malignant spirit; it catches one man's arm, and pulls it off; seizes another by the coattails, and almost grapples him bodily; catches a girl by the hair, and scalps her; and finally draws a man, and crushes him to death" (Coogan, 341, 431, from Nathaniel Hawthorne, *The American Notebooks* (Boston: Ticknor and Fields, 1868).

55 Coogan, 433, 424.

56 Mary H. Blewett, editor, "Introduction" in *Surviving Hard Times: The Working People of Lowell* (Lowell, MA: Lowell Museum, 1982).

57 Coogan, 437–440.

58 Ibid., 452–3.

59 Ibid., 454–5.

60 Paul Boyer, *Urban Masses and Moral Order in America, 1820–1920* (Cambridge, MA: Harvard University Press, 1978), 77. Boyer points out that the movement failed to enact prohibition in the cities it focused on. However in Lowell, where the young women employees lived in company housing, a strict code enforced by the older female boarding house minders appeared to maintain a liquor-free environment (78–79).

61 Mathew S. Bryson, *The North Adams Shoe Manufacturers: How They Created a Successful Industry Only to Abandon It* (Williamstown, MA: Williams College, 1999), 85.

62 Bryson, 85–86; Reverend Edward Hungerford, "Memorial Discourse."

63 Coogan, 447.

64 Bryson, 8.

65 Ibid., 8.

CHAPTER TWO

"TELL ME WHAT WERE THEIR NAMES . . . ?"[1]

It all started with a list of thirty-five names, men who had died in accidents building the Hoosac Tunnel. In 1981, Charles (Chuck) Cahoon, a native of North Adams, studied that list and wanted to know more about the men who bore through that mountain. He wanted to know their names: he had always been interested in history. Previously, he had served in the Army and had worked in engineering at GE in Pittsfield.

A railroad buff, in 1971 he had accepted the invitation of Tony Talarico to serve on the committee planning the centennial celebration of the completion of the tunnel. Thanks to the city of North Adams, the committee acquired a railroad car near the old station that served as a temporary museum on the building of the tunnel. Later, when the Heritage State Park opened, the committee became the North Adams Historical Society and got space for a real museum.

Chuck wondered about all the other men who had died whose names didn't appear on that list of thirty-five. *The New York Times* had once written that the construction of the Hoosac Tunnel had claimed 199 "casualties."[2] From his own Army experience, Chuck knew that didn't mean they were all fatalities, but how many had actually died? A common figure that many had accepted—and that was engraved on a plaque at the corner of Main Street and Ashland Avenue—read 195.

Chuck got to work. Most of all, he wanted to honor those who had died by naming them. He was familiar with memorial honor rolls in cities and towns throughout the country; he knew of the names memorialized from the sinking of the Arizona at Pearl Harbor and the names of those killed in Vietnam on the most famous wall of all, in Washington D.C. But he also knew of a tradition of honoring men who died not in battle, but in the workplace, in pursuing their occupation. In particular, he had seen the film, *The Perfect Storm,* and was moved by the memorial to the men who had perished while fishing off of the coast of Massachusetts.

Beginning with the original list, which noted the dates of the accidents, Chuck then went to the records of the two newspapers that had covered the area in the nineteenth century. He learned that injuries and fatalities occurred from 1855 to 1880. From those accounts, he found more information and, in some cases, the names of other workers. But often those injured or killed were simply listed as "an Irishman" or a "tool boy" or were given no identity at all. Chuck continued checking newspaper records, discovered other dates and accidents, but often encountered other nameless fatalities. One such example comes from the *Adams Transcript,* July 1, 1869:

> Two men were killed at the Central Shaft and one severely injured on Tuesday afternoon [29 June 1869]. Five of the miners on the lower platform, 60 feet from the bottom of the shaft, entered the bucket to ascend to the next platform when the bucket was lowered so suddenly and violently as to throw out three who were precipitated to the bottom, instantly killing two and seriously injuring the other. We do not learn their names.

Years after his mission had begun, Chuck combed the North Adams Vital Records for the tunnel period, and found actual names that he could match with the dates of the accidents. He did the same in the town of Florida, where many of the men would have been buried. In both cases, he followed cases of men injured to see if they eventually died of their injuries.

The result: he has verified and named 112 men who died in the building of the Hoosac Tunnel. Still, he knows his task has not been completed.[3]

The plaque, which stands on stone from the tunnel, is located at the corner of Main and Ashland St., North Adams. Dedicated October 13, 1975. (*Transcript*, January 20, 1976; photo courtesy of Gene Carlson)

This granite memorial sits on Old Shaft Road in Florida, Mass. It is a 2016 replacement stone for the original (2013), which lacked the name of a thirteenth victim. Now, the name of Joseph Messier can be found at the bottom, center, where previously "Unknown" was carved. (*Berkshire Eagle*, November 11, 2013)

NOTES

1 "Tell me what were their names . . . ?" So goes the chorus written by Woodie Guthrie in his 1941 song "The Sinking of the Reuben James," the first U.S. naval ship hit by German U-boats in World War II. For Guthrie, it reflected the importance of naming the dead, in a sense giving them life. (See http://www.woodyguthrie.org/Lyrics/Sinking_Of_The_Reuben_James.htm.)

In 1948, a plane with 28 Mexican farm laborers crashed in Los Gatos, California. U.S. Immigration officials had sent the workers back to Mexico, and a newspaper account of the dead referred to them only as "deportees." This inspired Guthrie to write "Plane Wreck of Los Gatos," and, while he did not know their names, he gave them names in his song: "Juan, Rosalita, Jesus y Maria." In 2017, after years of investigation, Tim Z. Hernandez, a renowned poet and son of a farmworker, came up with the names of the "deportees" and wrote about it in his book *All They Will Call You*. Now, at the site of the mass grave in Los Gatos, there is a memorial with the names of most of the workers. (See https://ww2.kqed.org/news/2017/07/14/immortalized-by-woody-guthrie-deportees-who-died-in-plane-crash-are-nameless-no-longer.) The work that Charles Cahoon has done and continues to do reminded me of the messages of both songs, the importance of naming.

2 *New York Times*, March 16, 1880.

3 The newspaper articles about the accidents and a chronological and alphabetical listing of the victims can be found on the website of the Boston & Maine Railroad Historical Society (bmrrhs.org). Click on: online-archives and then online-reference materials, and then find three citations for Charles Cahoon. He begins with the following: "The building of the Hoosac Tunnel required very hard labor under difficult and dangerous conditions. Many workmen lost their lives and others [were] seriously injured in this arduous task. Their stories are revealed in various news accounts and vital records of the time. These stories are presented as a memorial to those who lost their lives and were injured during the construction of the Hoosac Tunnel, which has been justly called one of the World's greatest achievements."

CHAPTER THREE

THREE DISTINCTIVE NINETEENTH-CENTURY WORKPLACES

THE CONSTRUCTION of a nearly five-mile-long tunnel through the Hoosac Mountain, a huge undertaking which attracted some 1,000 laborers, added a frontier environment to the area, and a dangerous setting in which to work. With its high cost, bruising political battles, and unexpectedly lengthy times of completion, the Hoosac Tunnel was the state's "Big Dig," foreshadowing Boston's own struggle to remake its highway system over a century later.[1] For two previous decades, beginning in 1854, North Berkshire received an inordinate amount of attention from the statehouse and legislature in Boston, industrialists eager for a rail route to the Midwest, and members of the press who covered the controversial and costly project with zeal.

THE HOOSAC TUNNEL

> *"The West Shaft [Tunnel] workers conducted a successful strike after the bucket crushed the skull of one of their number. They refused to go back to work until the bucket's hemp rope was replaced with an iron cable."*
>
> —Terrence Coyne[2]

Although the southern rail connection already in place had opened up the region's trade with Pittsfield, and indirectly with

Boston, the local business class had a grander scheme in mind: a tunnel through the Hoosac range, which would not only make the region's link with Boston more direct, but when combined with a rail line to Albany, 40 miles to the west, would place North Adams at the hub of a transportation center to the western United States. Further, goods from the west would more easily be transported to Boston where they could be shipped to England and other European destinations. (The Legislature had scrapped an earlier plan to build a canal from western Massachusetts to the Erie Canal when the expense of erecting more than 200 locks over the Berkshires had been deemed too extravagant.[3]) The rail connection would, its local boosters hoped, "represent an open door to the riches of the Golden West," earning North Adams its motto, "We hold the Western Gateway."[4]

Despite the local boosters, construction of the tunnel, which was started in 1854 and completed in 1875, proved both frustrating and perilous, costing the lives of close to 200 workmen—many of whose names Chuck Cahoon still searches for. The tunnel's construction force numbered more than 1,000—Irish, English, French-Canadian, and Italian—adding what many perceived as a dangerous element to an already diversified workforce engaged in the manufacture of a range of products which now included woolen and cotton goods, shoes, and textile machinery.[5]

Scenes around the shafts while work was going on seemed reminiscent of mining camps in the far West, with rows of small cabins and cheap boardinghouses where the tunnel workers slept and ate. They were a mixture of races and creeds . . . children poured in and out of the squalid houses where women, speaking foreign tongues, were busy with cooking and babies. Roughly dressed men, black with grime, went in and out of the diggings.[6]

While the names of many of the tunnelers have been, to date, lost to history, we do know that Constante Rosasco, thought to be the first Italian to migrate to North Adams, came to town originally in 1864 to work on the tunnel. Four years later, he went back to Italy to bring his family over, but did not return until 1872, when he resumed laboring on the tunnel.[7] In the interim, in 1867, the name of another worker, Thomas Mallory, became known, and he has remained to this day the most famous tunneler, or miner as they were called, due to a tragic accident and his personal heroism.

On October 19, 1867, a gas explosion at the tunnel's central shaft led to the collapse of a building at the shaft's opening, causing fiery wood, a thousand pounds of drills, a mining car, machinery, and a bucket of rocks to fall down upon a work group of thirteen men who were at the bottom.[8] In describing the scene, historian Terrence E. Coyne writes: "[O]nly one man had the courage to descend and survey the disaster . . . Thomas Mallory." Mallory apparently tied a rope around himself, gave instructions to those holding the rope at the shaft opening, and began his descent. The flame on his lamp went out as he neared the bottom, but he continued. He saw no one and no bodies; he signaled to be lifted, but as he neared the top, he fainted from the noxious gas. He regained consciousness and in the next days went down twice more, but with no luck. The *Transcript* called him "a genuine hero . . . a brave, modest man."[9]

The loss of the thirteen men in that incident made the explosion the deadliest accident in the tunnel's history, and hereafter it came to be called "the bloody pit."[10] (See the end of Chapter Two for a photo of the memorial to the thirteen men.)

Dozens more men met their death, and even more were injured, in numerous accidents after 1867, before the tunnel's completion. Despite the sacrifices of its workforce and the accomplishments of its engineers, the nearly five-mile-long tunnel did not become the great economic boon its proponents had promised, partly because, ironically, the tunnel allowed cheaper goods from the sizeable eastern Massachusetts cotton mills to be sold in North Berkshire, negatively impacting several mills in Williamstown.[11]

Nonetheless, North Adams had become "a Western gateway," and its residents enjoyed the sight and revenue of numerous passenger and freight trains coming through on a regular basis. The tunnel did lead to some industrial growth in what was then called the North Village, and helped precipitate the decision for the North to separate and become North Adams in 1878.[12]

By 1880, 125 freight trains a day lumbered through North Adams.[13] In what may well be an exaggeration, in 1885, one historian claimed that "[e]ven the much boasted Springfield, with its years of development and prestige, is not today a more important railroad center than North Adams . . . ."[14] At the time the tunnel proved to be the longest in the United States, and the second longest in the world. A collision in the tunnel in 1882 resulted in the deaths of eight workers and injuries to thirty others and led to increasing calls to build a local hospital. In March of 1884, the North Adams Hospital opened.[15] While the names of leading industrialists of that era like C.T. Sampson and Albert C. Houghton have become associated with the financing of the hospital, in 1890 the *Transcript* wrote: "[T]he funds that support the hospital come almost entirely from contributions from the citizens and churches of North Adams . . . ."[16]

No full-scale social or labor history has yet been carried out on the tunnel workers. In the numerous economic, political, and technological studies that have been completed, few references have been made to worker militancy or strike activity. The 1880 Massachusetts Bureau of Statistics of Labor (MBSL) *Report* does not officially credit Hoosac workers with a strike but, almost parenthetically, and intriguingly, recognizes such activity there. As mentioned in the introductory chapter, a strike had occurred in North Adams by workers in a small railway tunnel in 1875. The laborers were fired after demanding more money; the following paragraph from the bureau report merits quoting in full:

> A new force of men was engaged. The strikers assailed the newcomers with stones, and sought to drive them away, but without success. While the Hoosac Tunnel was in process of construction, numerous similar strikes occurred; but of these no record remains. They were usually accompanied with rioting and considerable destruction of

> property, but generally resulted in the defeat of the workmen.[17]

Terrence Coyne has more to tell us about Tunnel worker strikes:

> Under [unsafe] conditions strikes were inevitable and apparently they met with a fair amount of success. The West Shaft workers conducted a successful strike after the bucket crushed the skull of one of their number. They refused to go back to work until the bucket's hemp rope was replaced with an iron cable . . . . They also struck for higher wages . . . .[18]

Coyne then quotes a reporter for the *Troy Times* who wrote: "[S]ome papers have been severe about the strikes of the men but no reasonable man could see the men at their work and denounce them for asking $1.25 for '[such] labors.'"

On the whole the local papers, enthusiastic backers of the tunnel project, tended to ignore the difficult conditions of the workers, and even the names of some of the men killed building the massive enterprise. One report went like this: "Another Irishman [was] killed at the tunnel. The fuse had been lit but the blast was late. [The victim checked] . . . but just at the moment the blast went off and a small piece of rock struck the poor fellow's head and broke it."[19]

Even worse, a lengthy article from *Scribner's Magazine* blames the tunnelers for their own injuries and deaths:

> Several serious accidents have occurred at the tunnel through [the] use [of nitroglycerine], but these, so far as the circumstances are known, have been occasioned by inexcusable carelessness . . . .

Later in the article, the writer continues:

> Most of those at the central shaft are Cornish miners, and their life-long experience in such

> holes in the ground has made them reckless of danger. The fatal accidents that frequently occur among them have no effect to make them more cautious.[20]

The state legislature, chief funders of the massive undertaking, ignored the health and safety issues that the tunnelers faced: "No committee busied itself with investigations into the circumstances attending the loss of . . . lives in its construction; that was an accepted hazard . . . ."[21]

Many of the unmarried Irish tunnel workers lived in the shanties described in 1871 by the tunnel paymaster:

> There are about 25 double shanties and 8 single shanties, at the East end of the Tunnel. There are 7 double shanties and 8 single shanties, at the central shaft; at the West end, 18 double shanties and 20 single shanties . . . . At a great many of the shanties, they keep boarders . . . . The miners, rockmen, &c., who have no families board at the shanties. They are filthy, dirty places."[22]

The paymaster quickly added, however, that the tenants "are all healthy. There is no more healthy class of men, that I know of, than the miners." While the miners may have been able to survive their housing conditions, the work itself proved not as hospitable. The same man reported on the occurrence of

> *90 and 100 fatal accidents since the tunnel was first started.* He went on to say that there were many accidents that were not fatal; men got their eyes put out and limbs broken; but *got over it.* In some cases of accident, the State made compensation: the man noted that if a man was badly hurt, his case was considered and they frequently gave him $100 or $300, and that $500 was the most ever paid.[23]

In 1868, the state contracted with Walter and Francis Shanley from Canada to take charge of finishing the tunnel. Their supervision extended to the shanties, which the state rented to the Shanleys for company housing. The miners apparently paid no additional rent to them, at least while work continued. If work stopped, due to a mechanical problem, for example, the men wouldn't be paid. In addition, as the state contract specified, "The contractors shall use their best efforts to keep intoxicating liquors from their employe[e]s, and to promote orderly conduct among them; and shall, when required by the engineer, discharge any men who shall be careless, negligent, or incompetent, or guilty of conduct prejudicial to good order."[24]

The same volume of the MBSL also described the working conditions of the tunnel laborers. By that time, three shifts of men worked round the clock six days a week for two dollars a day. When not working or sleeping, the men cut wood for fuel and drew water for the family at "a considerable distance, being obtained from a brook at the mouth of the tunnel." If they had cash, they shopped at the stores in town, but could only get credit at the company store where, according to the state investigator, "charges for goods . . . are *much higher than at the village stores*." One investigator reported:

> One of the workmen informed us, that, having been sick and unable to work, he received no wages for six months, during which he subsisted on his credit at the store. He had resumed work, but had received no wages, and did not expect to receive any, until the debt which accrued during his sickness, was discharged . . . . [He] also stated, that a good many workmen came there without money, and were obliged to trade at the store, under the order system, in order to subsist until they received their first month's wages; and it sometimes happened that such person's wages, at the end of the month, would be insufficient

> to discharge his indebtedness, *and he would be kept from month to month in this way, without having any ready money.*[25]

The report briefly noted the throat diseases caused by the temperature differences between the tunnel and the surface. At times, a priest from St. Francis Church in North Adams, one-and-a-half miles away, held Mass at the central location and "in that residential area of Florida known as Hoosac Tunnel . . . . They are not, as a general rule, regular church-goers, but their children mostly go to Sunday school."[26] As for the school for workers' children, the report offered more detail here. One hundred and forty students reported to *one* teacher who stated "it was impossible to do them any justice, or to teach them much, there were so many." Along with the teacher, they were crammed into the school house, 50 feet by 30 feet and 9 feet high. The report deemed it "wholly unfit," like the shanties where the children lived with their families. Perhaps surprisingly, most of the pupils did in fact learn how to read.[27]

THE BLACKINTON WOOLEN MILL

> *After the Civil War, agitation by textile workers throughout Berkshire County prodded most local mill owners, including Blackinton, to reduce the work day to eleven hours. This change was supported by the local paper writing that "free labor slavery in the North is going the same road as slave labor in the south, as an inevitable consequence of the abolishment of the latter."*
>
> —Elizabeth Baker

By 1864, fed by government orders for Union Army uniforms, the Blackinton Woolen Company had become the largest in Berkshire County.[28] The mill's management actively recruited skilled workers including a significant number from Wales. In fact, the 1870 census revealed that of the 848 people of Welsh ancestry in Massachusetts, 543 lived in Adams (which would include the North prior to the split in 1878). Of those 543, the census listed 514 as laboring in the woolen industry. Many had come from Newton, Wales, and lived in Blackinton village, a separate community between the North Village and Williamstown, with its own school, church, post office, firehouse, retail stores, and cemetery.[29]

Elizabeth Baker, in her social history of Blackinton, illustrates the importance of examining a variety of historical sources to document worker activity. She homes in on three Blackinton village strikes, one more than the MBSL 1880 report lists. Further, her exhaustive reading of the local press along with an informative diary kept by Oscar Archer, Sanford Blackinton's right hand man, yields the important social and cultural contexts around the strikes.

Baker discusses a strike in 1858—one that had been organized to regain the wage level the workers lost during a previous downturn—and notes that the *Transcript* "vigorously denied the existence of a strike at Blackinton, calling it a 'rumor.'" Baker concludes in this instance that, while one could not be sure, a finding in the MBSL had "more credibility than the *Transcript*'s."[30]

In 1865, a show of solidarity (without recourse to a strike) by Blackinton workers brought them a shorter working day. It happened at the end of the Civil War, when textile operatives in Berkshire County were still putting in twelve- to thirteen-hour days, despite decades of agitation for a state law mandating a ten-hour day. That September, textile workers throughout the county held meetings and wrote petitions to their employers asking for an eleven-hour day. This time, within a week, Blackinton and most of the other local mill owners acquiesced. No doubt the workers and the *Transcript* saw the end of chattel slavery as one more reason to reduce *wage slavery*. The local paper took the side of the workers in this case, stating: "[F]ree labor slavery in the North is going the same road as slave labor in the south, as an inevitable consequence of the abolishment of the latter."[31]

A strike, however, nearly occurred at Blackinton in November 1873, an event ignored by both the bureau and the

Transcript, but recorded in Oscar Archer's diary. The workers had met and taken a vote to strike after seeing their wages cut by 12.5 percent. They had been forced to accept a half-time workweek following the financial crash of October, and now Blackinton wanted them to return to a full week but with a significant cut in wages. Archer claims to have talked the operatives out of a strike by stressing the financial difficulties of the firm along with the threat of job loss if they did strike.[32]

The economic effects of the Panic of 1873 lingered over the next several years, and on January 1, 1876, Sanford Blackinton followed other local mill owners in reducing wages by 10 percent. An eight-day strike, *not* reported by the bureau, followed. Baker's research offers insight into the reasons for the strike: a new superintendent had been installed at the Braytonville mill, and many workers held him responsible for the wage cut. Perhaps more importantly, the reduction came "at a time when the workers, according to Archer, thought the mill to be profitable."[33]

Another, more extensive, strike, this one covered by the bureau, followed in the fall of the year. Hard times had returned, and Blackinton enacted wage cuts of 10 and 15 percent in June. In July, the mill switched to three-quarters time plus forty-five minutes, but the workers, as the bureau indicates, received no wages for the "extra" forty-five minutes. They protested, but to no avail.

Finally, on October 20, they revolted. After working eight and three-quarters hours—the number of hours for which they were getting paid—they walked out, demanding exactly three-quarters time for three-quarters wages. They were immediately discharged and the mill was closed. Within a week, the operatives at Braytonville and the Glen were also on strike. At issue in this strike, as it had been in January, was the belief of the workers that times had improved enough to warrant normal wages.

Sanford Blackinton responded by announcing that strikers living in company houses would be evicted, and that they would receive no credit from the company stores. Workers who could leave town did, while others organized a committee to solicit help from residents of surrounding towns. They managed to stay out for three-and-one-half weeks, but ultimately lost the strike, returning to work to receive the same rate of pay which had precipitated the strike.[34]

THE C.T. SAMPSON SHOE FACTORY

> *The self-restraint of the working-people of North Adams, in the presence of this irritating spectacle [watching 75 Chinese men exiting the train to break a strike] was a source of gratitude . . . . In truth, the experience of North Adams with the Chinamen was an encouraging instance of the absorbent power of good sense and good will. . . .*
>
> —Washington Gladden

> *When Sampson had Ah Coon [the leader of the Chinese strikers] arrested, about forty Chinese workers "stormed the jail," leading the constable to call for help from the watching crowd . . . . [T]hey attacked the Chinese with "an uncalled for display of spite and brutality."*
>
> —Richard V. Bennett

> *"The workers and passersby who visited violence on the striking Chinese let loose a fury born out of unemployment, the frustrations of hunger and poverty, the unfair labor practices adopted by northeast manufacturers all these magnified by the Panic."*
>
> —Anthony Lee

As with many of the other rising industrial centers in the state, North Berkshire's growth emanated from the production of shoes and boots as well as textiles. Earliest production centered on the craft model where a skilled shoemaker would make his product in a shop behind his house, and then sell the shoes to traveling merchants. Prior to the emergence of the factory system, a similar process prevailed in centers of shoe production such as Lynn, where the craft of shoemaking focused on the individual who would make the entire product in his own shop.[35]

By the middle of the nineteenth century, this practice had begun to change. Merchants had gained more power and individual craftsmen lost leverage and prestige. Soon, the individual shoemaker's control of his craft and his shop collapsed. In 1850, Ingraham, Millard, & Co., led by shoe merchant George Millard, had moved to a central shop on Eagle Street with about fifty employees, where specialization and piecework predominated. The cutters and fitters worked there, making parts of the uppers for the shoes.

Others took the cut leather back to their homes to stitch the upper and bottom of the shoe together on their own benches with their own tools. Eventually, the labor was subdivided even more as teams of "four or five of these . . . shoemakers would get together and forward the shoe by each one performing his specified process."[36]

Millard thus became the first manufacturer of boots and shoes in North Adams. The shift from individual craft production to a quasi-manufacturing model did not always go smoothly. Millard's hiring of a pieceworker at a lower wage in 1853 led to a short strike by the rest of his employees. As reported by the *Transcript,* Millard's action:

> aroused the pride of the "craft," and most of the journeymen in their employ protested against the reduction on the ground that they might soon be served in the same way . . . . [They] showed their displeasure to the new employee in a manner peculiar to themselves, and he saw fit to leave his seat, whether through fears of personal safety or the mode of warfare carried on against him we cannot tell.[37]

In 1858, most of Millard's employees struck again, this time to stop him from paying their wages in scrip. "While the manufacturer's checks were accepted freely by local shopkeepers and merchants, if the shoemakers wanted cash, they had to redeem the notes with Millard at a two percent discount."[38]

The North Adams shoe industry took off from 1845 to 1855,

as measured by number of workers, production per worker, and total output. From a high of 6,000 pairs of shoes made in 1845, output reached almost 33,000 pairs ten years later.[39] But for the workers, making a family wage proved difficult. In 1860, most of the fifty-nine French-Canadian men who lived in North Adams worked in the shoe factories, and they had one thing in common—a lack of money. According to historian Janet Roberts: "At a time when most of the people in town had at least $100 as the value of their personal estate, half of the twenty French-Canadian families had less than fifty dollars, and for another six families, the valuation was nothing."[40]

Although George Millard played an important role in the region's shoe making growth, his cousin, Calvin T. Sampson, soon surpassed him, becoming a leading manufacturer in the 1860s and later a national figure for his role in breaking an 1870 strike. Sampson's ancestry harkened back to the European "founding" of the new nation, seven generations removed from the Plymouth Colony's Abraham Sampson. In 1850, Calvin briefly worked as a salesman for Millard, but soon became an employer, opening his own shop. The Civil War, however, played havoc with Sampson and other northern shoemakers, as retailers in the South didn't pay their debts. Sampson would have found a market in orders for the Union Army, but stubbornly refused to switch his operation from women's shoes.[41]

Determined to expand, Sampson rented a tannery on Eagle Street and had an 18-foot addition built. He took advantage of the abundant water power from the Hoosic River and bought new machinery, including a pegging machine that could produce the bottoms for 600 shoes a day. Now, Sampson's entire labor force could work in the same building, performing the cutting and bottoming, thus making it North Adams's first factory.[42]

By 1867, steam powered his machines and his business continued to grow, leading Sampson to buy a new building on Marshall Street. In 1870, his firm's production of 400 cases a month outpaced the four other local shoe manufacturers, Millard/Whitman, Cady Brothers, N.L. & E.R. Millard, and

Parker Brothers. Sampson, as was the case with many of his fellow industrialists, expanded his influence in political, financial, civic, religious, and philanthropic realms. He backed the Republican Party with his money and served as president of the North Adams Savings Bank and director of the Adams National Bank. He was a deacon and treasurer at the First Baptist Church, and helped to found North Adams Hospital and its public library. Sampson contributed $15,000 as an endowment to the hospital.[43] Outside of his connections with other shoe and boot industrialists, Sampson had a good working relationship with leading textile manufacturer Albert C. Houghton. They both belonged to a manufacturer's club, "a group that consisted of several of the town's most prominent industrialists who met at the Wilson House to discuss the affairs of the town."

Sampson's uncle and predecessor in shoe manufacturing, George Millard, belonged to Sampson's First Baptist Church,[44] and was a major contributor to its rebuilding after a fire in 1849. Millard also involved himself in promoting rail links to North Berkshire, as a subscriber to the Pittsfield and North Adams Railroad and fund-raising committee member for the Troy & Greenfield Railroad. The Cady brothers both served as trustees at the North Adams Savings Bank, while W.G. added a directorship at the North Adams National Bank, and H.T. gained a directorship at the Berkshire National Bank and at the Adams Gas & Light Company. Both involved themselves in politics: W.G. on the Board of Public Works and Chairman of the Board of Selectmen; H.T. in the Massachusetts State Senate and later as the second mayor of the city of North Adams (1898–1899), succeeding Albert C. Houghton.[45]

By 1870, while Calvin Sampson prospered, he now faced greater worker opposition in the form of a new labor union. As artisanship faded and more and more shoe workers became deskilled, their individual power declined, and the need for organization and solidarity for what they had become—factory workers—increased. In 1870, the census used the term "laborers" for the factory workers, instead of "shoemakers," the first time that had occurred.[46]

The Knights of St. Crispin, a secret union of workers in the footwear industry, found a sympathetic workforce in North Adams, as they did in much of the rest of the country. First organized in 1867, the Knights rapidly grew, becoming the nation's largest labor union. By 1870, they had enrolled anywhere from one-third to one-half of all men working in shoe factories. Statewide, the Crispins formed one of the most formidable labor organizations in New England, with some 40,000 members.[47]

In North Adams, French-Canadian men formed the bulk of its membership. Relatively new to the area, the men had migrated from Quebec, part of a huge exodus of more than 250,000 farmers who left Canada between 1850 and 1870, seeking a better living than hardscrabble farming provided them and their families. Industrialists in New England actively recruited the French Canadians (whom they called the "Chinese of the Eastern States"), and the men, often without families, initially found work in western Massachusetts, notably in Holyoke and North Adams.[48]

From a total of some 100 French Canadians in North Berkshire in 1860, increased immigration by 1871 brought that number up to 1,100 in North Adams and 550 in Adams. The higher French-Canadian population necessitated a French-speaking pastor to serve the 200 families who now lived in the region. The 1870 census demonstrated that the shoe and boot industry continued to be the occupation where more French-Canadian men worked than any other, with eighty-three so employed. Reflective of the common use of child labor, that figure includes four boys, ages 10–14, and eleven boys, ages 15–19. In addition, eleven women toiled there, a figure that included five girls between the ages of 10 and 19.[49]

United by culture, history, and class, the shoe-making men supported each other and brought that solidarity into the Crispins. As a union, the Knights of St. Crispin advocated for shorter workdays, higher wages, and the right to see the company's books to base their wages on the firm's profits. In fact, they proved so successful in agitating for better working conditions and wages, that they led the area's leading shoe manufacturer, Calvin Sampson, to fire them. When Sampson recruited replacement workers to North Adams, his fired Crispins persuaded them not to take the jobs. Finally, in 1870, Sampson wrote his name into the history books by importing the seventy-five Chinese men from California to break the union's power in 1870.[50]

Sampson's assistant, George Chase, had journeyed to San Francisco and signed a contract with a Chinese agency—Kwong, Chong, Wing, & Company—to provide the workers. They "came from China to California as emigrants seeking their fortunes, just as emigrants from Ireland, Germany, France and England come every day."[51] The *Transcript* tried to normalize the immigrants, but neglected to tell its readers that the Chinese men were in fact contract workers, who had agreed to work three years for Sampson for as long as eleven hours a day. Not at all like the Irish or Germans, French, or English—who migrated to the United States voluntarily, without employee restrictions—the Chinese could more aptly be characterized as indentured servants, with stipulations to hours, pay and years of service. (In the national political struggle that would later erupt and lead to the Chinese Exclusion Act of 1882, American workers generally supported Chinese immigration but not contract labor, by Chinese or any other ethnic group.[52])

On June 13, 1870, when the Chinese recruits arrived at the North Adams railroad station, a large crowd watched, probably more in wonderment than in anger, since most, if not all, of the locals would have never seen any Chinese person, let alone seventy-five at one time. The national press, including reporters from New York, Boston, and Springfield, journeyed to North Adams to record the spectacle, and they witnessed a curious, hostile, but generally non-violent crowd. Though protected by the police, newspaper accounts reported the arrests of two men for throwing stones, one of whom served a night in jail.[53]

However, the Crispins, who had lost their jobs, remained disciplined, and maintained their focus on their employer and his (mis)deeds. They did not blame or scapegoat the Chinese strikebreakers.

Washington Gladden, who served the North Adams Congregational Church from 1866 to 1871, summarized this very unusual chapter in North Adams history as follows:

> The self-restraint of the working-people of North Adams, in the presence of this irritating spectacle, was a cause for gratitude. Although these Chinamen continued to live in the community for several years, there was very little disposition to interfere with them; they were permitted to go and come without insult or annoyance. The philanthropists of the community soon made these Orientals the object of their care, and various well-meant endeavors to teach them the English language and fit them for self-support and citizenship were promptly set in operation. In truth, the experience of North Adams with the Chinamen was an encouraging instance of the absorbent power of good sense and good will in an American community, in dealing with an acute case of social inflammation.[54]

Exceptions to the "good will" that Gladden referred to, however, did occur, exemplified by beatings of Chinese workers as they walked through town and of dirty water being poured on them. (Later, during a strike by the Chinese workers and an attempt to free a colleague from the local jail, a crowd of townspeople viciously attacked the Chinese, nearly killing two of them.) For the most part, though, most threats were directed at Sampson, who was blamed for the Crispin walkout and Chinese hiring.[55]

Word spread, and workers throughout the East and Midwest organized meetings to protest Sampson's use of contract labor. Just two days after the Chinese men had arrived, an assemblage in Troy, just over the Taconic Mountain range from North Adams, heard an iron molder speak. With anger intensified by the end of the Civil War five years earlier,

Donald Campbell spoke out against "[t]his new system of slavery." Up to 4,000 people gathered in North Adams a week later to hear Samuel P. Cummings, a Crispin leader, denounce the system of contract labor. Cummings did not attack the Chinese workers, but rather told the crowd "they should extend a hearty welcome . . . to all men of whatever race and color . . . ." In fact, Cummings called on his fellow Crispins to organize Sampson's new workforce into the Knights of St. Crispin. In addition, "Cummings recoiled at having 'to mention Sampson's name, but he did not wish to pollute his lips with it any oftener than possible, for it was such men as him who were their enemies, and whom they must protect themselves against.'" Similar meetings attacking the system of contract labor followed in New York City, Albany, Boston, Cincinnati, and Chicago.[56]

Besides helping to put North Adams on the national map as the tunnel had previously done, Sampson's union-busting experiment brought him low-wage labor and high profits for the next three years. Still, in solidarity with the Crispins who lost their jobs, workers at the other shoe factories in North Adams went on strike. The owners of Parker Bros., Cady Bros., and Millard & Whitman then "offered their old hands work at a reduction of ten per cent, but this was not accepted." However, enough of the former employees as well as new workers accepted the new terms, and production began anew.[57]

The Crispins tried, unsuccessfully, to organize the Chinese workers into a Crispin lodge, but they found success of their own in starting a new factory, acquiring a building on Brooklyn Street. Less than a month after the Chinese arrived in town, thirty-one Crispins bought and began operating a worker-owned cooperative that directly competed with Sampson. The North Adams Cooperative Shoe Factory began operations with $6,000 in capital from sixty shares of stock. Most of the workers owned shares, but not all, as state law prohibited women from becoming shareholders. The co-op employed forty-four: thirty-five men and nine women. Ethnically diverse, the workforce included Irish and French-Canadian Catholics as well as "native" Protestants, reflected in the names of co-op officers such as "Oliver Wood, Timothy Riordan, Napoleon Poquette, and Sherman Bateman."[58] Unlike Sampson's top-down, capitalistic enterprise, the North Adams Cooperative Shoe Factory operated "as a 'little democracy, where the men [sic] do as they like, and enjoy the privilege,' with 'no one to command and none to obey.'"[59]

In September, following the lead of the Crispins' venture, a former Sampson employee (William Vial) founded a second cooperative. Along with the Knights of Labor, who also successfully organized in the region, the Crispins favored the cooperative as a positive way for workers to step outside of the wage exploitation system. French-Canadian shoemakers first formed a cooperative in St. John's, New Brunswick, in February 1869, and within a few years dozens of shoe co-ops had been established throughout the Northeast from Maine to Baltimore.[60]

Smaller than Sampson's shop, the Crispins' co-op in North Adams utilized only six sewing machines and one pegging machine, in contrast to the thirty-five sewing and three pegging machines at Sampson's. The co-op's capital stock increased by $4,000 and tallied a profit of $1,000 at the end of four months. When a business decline forced a closure of the other shoe factories in town in November, only the co-op, along with Sampson's factory, remained in operation.[61]

Working around the clock, the Crispins produced 100 cases of shoes a month, managing one quarter the output that Sampson's workers manufactured. Mimicking the famous photograph that Sampson had taken of the Chinese workers in front of his factory, the Crispins had a photo taken of themselves as co-op workers. An examination of the Crispin photo by Anthony Lee indicates that the Crispins, along with other workers they hired, actually posed themselves by one side of Sampson's factory! Rather than pose by their own wooden shop, they preferred to be, almost literally, in Sampson's face. "It was a deliberate, pugnacious, provocative gesture, not to say an indication of stealth and wiliness."[62] Not hesitant to show their former boss that they could produce on their own, one Crispin, Isaac Tyler, met Sampson in town just prior to starting the cooperative. When Sampson remarked, "I understand you are going to manufacture goods," Tyler let it be known that the Crispin factory would be "as close to [Sampson] as possible."[63]

In its 1880 history, the MBSL reported two strikes at Sampson's, one in 1868 and the other the nationally famous 1870 turnout. From the bureau's narrative and from other sources, the pivotal role of the Crispins has been noted in both events. An examination of the 1871 annual report from the bureau, which includes nineteen pages of testimony from Sampson and six shoemakers about the events of 1870, adds further insights into both strikes and to the role of the union. It also mentions a third strike, in 1861.[64]

That strike report has the added credibility that Sampson testified to it. The importance of the event is heightened by its origins—a protest against the introduction of new machinery—and its implications about worker culture and the desire for independence and self-control, reminiscent of earlier Luddite actions in England.[65] Sampson began manufacturing shoes in 1858; two years later he claimed that his factory produced sixty pairs a day. He said:

> Introduced the Wells pegging machine, the first made, in 1861. This was about as early as the use of improved machinery became common. The effect of this machine was to increase the number of persons employed. At first, however, all my men left the shop. They said the use of machinery would throw them out of employment; but the foreman told them not to be alarmed, as it would increase the number of hands required. Two-thirds of the men who left were French Canadians. They were out two or three weeks, and then came back to work. They had no organization; but it was the old English

experience of strikes against the introduction of machinery.[66]

Later on, Sampson discussed additional experiences with machinery in his shop. Here, one gets the sense that the workers had learned to deal with the new technology not by striking, but by engaging in sabotage: "I undertook to run lasting machines; but the men managed to make it cost me more than to do lasting by hand. The same has been true of other laborsaving machinery. There has been no strike against machinery since the introduction of the pegging machine alluded to."[67]

The testimony of Daniel Luther, who previously worked as a foreman for Sampson, provided more detail on the strike of 1868. At that time, 1871, Luther was working elsewhere: "The . . . strike [of 1868] was general through the town, and included the shop where I am now working. It was a strike against a reduction of wages to the extent of one dollar per case. We had been waiting for work for three weeks, but were unwilling to work at the reduction. Very few went back. In the course of a month new help was hired, apprentices—most of them in town."[68]

The 1880 report provides no mention of the general shoe strike to which Luther testified. The report credits Crispin dissatisfaction with a non-Crispin worker at Sampson's with the strike's origin, but from reading all of the testimony in the 1871 report, it seems likely that wage cuts helped to precipitate the 1868 strike.

The report does not mention that the Chinese strike-breaking in 1870 led to a short solidarity strike at the other shoe factories in North Adams and a 10 percent wage cut, as the owners "now had access to two new pools of workers, the former employees of Sampson and the Chinese." Nor is there any mention of rebellion by the Chinese workers in either the MBSL or Frederick Rudolph's classic account of the Chinese in North Adams. According to the *Providence Journal,* the Chinese workers themselves struck Sampson twice that year. The shoemakers wanted to negotiate a new contract with Sampson, and they had little trust in their foreman, Charlie Sing.[69]

Ah Coon led the first strike in August when a dozen or so men stopped working. Because the Chinese men lived in the same building where they worked, the strike led to a bizarre daily scenario. The striking men refused to climb the stairs from their living quarters on the ground floor to the bottoming room on the second floor, preferring instead to hunker in their bunks and take up space in the dormitory while the workdays passed. They still ate and drank and communed with the men who continued to work, and still took advantage of the stipulation that Sampson had to supply them with room and partial board.[70]

Despite Sing's efforts to increase production among the non-striking Chinese workers, orders could not be fulfilled and Sampson had to contract out for more Chinese men from California to take up the slack. The spirit of resistance reached the non-strikers, and, even before the additional workers arrived, they demanded that a new foreman be appointed to replace Sing.

When the men struck a second time just two months later, Sampson retaliated by discharging them. The strikers blamed Sing and, according to the local paper, "threatened to kill Sing, and Ah Coon got hold of a pistol for the purpose."[71] When Sampson had Ah Coon arrested, about forty Chinese workers "stormed the jail," leading the constable to call for help from the watching crowd. According to the *Transcript*,[72] they attacked the Chinese with "an uncalled for display of spite and brutality."

The crowd used "clubs, stones, brass knuckles . . . and began cracking skulls," leaving two Chinese men "close to dying." At that point, Charlie Sing needed an armed guard, and Sampson moved the strikers to a separate part of the factory.[73] Ah Coon was given a night in jail and a fine of about twenty-five dollars.[74] Without money and a job, Ah Coon had no choice but to leave the area.

Sampson brought in fifteen new Chinese recruits, first quarantining them from the veterans, as if to keep an infection of militancy at bay. He continued to employ his Chinese workforce until 1880 when the last of the contracts ended.

Whether Sampson kept his word to pay for the men's rail trip back to California is not known, but we do know that only two of the Chinese men remained in North Adams.[75]

Anthony Lee helps to put the 1873 events into context, pointing out "how much the men became entangled in historical developments completely characteristic of Reconstruction New England: The workers and passersby who visited violence on the striking Chinese let loose a fury born out of unemployment, the frustrations of hunger and poverty, the unfair labor practices adopted by northeast manufacturers—all these magnified by the Panic." As for the Chinese themselves, they could only be unhappy with their indentured status, a position of "near-servitude," forced to live "among westerners whose language they only roughly understood, whose laws and provisions they . . . had no ability to change . . . and whose behavior patronized and belittled them . . . ."[76]

The times had changed, "the labor question having arrived in North Adams" in a somewhat virulent form."[77] Or, as one historian of that era saw it, "The aristocracy of North Adams may well have been in embryo; but so was the challenge."[78] To protect themselves from this growing power imbalance within the industrial economy, North Berkshire workers continued to use the weapon of the strike. This was the option utilized at Blackinton, which had no union, and at Sampson's shoe factory, which had a militant local of the largest national union of its time, the Knights of St. Crispin. The Crispins, like the soon to be dominant Knights of Labor, favored worker cooperatives, where workers could escape wage exploitation entirely and democratically control their work environment.

The press in the Northeast, including the *Transcript*, backed the cooperative model, certainly as a substitute for strikes.[79] During that first season, the MBSL reported: "The men at work speak with pride of their new feelings of self-reliance and freedom, as well as of the quality of their work and the tendencies developed toward a more economical production than before." A reporter for the *New York Tribune* "described the cooperative factory as a 'little democracy,' where 'the men do as they like, and enjoy the privilege.' There is . . . 'no one to command and none to obey.'"[80] As Steve Leikin, an historian of nineteenth-century cooperatives, sees it, the "shoe workers in North Adams attempted to exert control over their work life and community under new conditions of increasing industrial inequality and instability. They set out with a bravado fueled by republican and democratic sentiments . . . ."[81]

Cooperatives appeared to be a popular model for Massachusetts workers at that time, and not just for Crispins, as the reports from the same MBSL volume offer accounts of a co-op grocery in Randolph, a co-op and ten supply stores in Fall River, a machine shop co-op in Greenfield, a co-op that manufactured stoves in Somerset, and a cigar makers' co-op in Westfield. Along with eighteen other shoe co-ops throughout the state, the North Adams operation continued to survive. The Panic of 1873, however, proved its downfall as it did for many capitalist firms, and the Crispin co-op closed down by March of that year, after about two-and-a-half years in existence.[82] However, spurred on by the Knights of Labor's cooperative ideology, hundreds of cooperatives, stores, and factories in the Northeast and Midwest got off the ground in the 1880s and 1890s.[83]

By the 1870s, industrialization and the growth of the factory system meant that the working class had become more and more dependent on capitalist employers for their jobs, jobs that industrialists discarded during downturns in the economy. The Massachusetts Bureau of Statistics of Labor made that point clearly in its 1871 annual report, declaring that worker earnings were dependent "upon continuous health and continuous work. But with the exception of some few indoor employments, continuous work is the exception and not the rule."[84]

Historian Alexander Keyssar writes that in each decade from 1870 to 1920, downturns occurred at least once, so much so that these shifts came to be seen as "normal." Keyssar added that a 70-year-old man in 1921 would have lived through "six major cyclical downturns" and roughly the same number of lesser declines.[85]

Hoosac Tunnel Family (this photo, and following two photos, from the North Adams Historical Society collection, 1865–1875 period).

Hoosac Tunnel Housing

Hoosac Tunnel Workers

West Portal, Hoosac Tunnel, during construction (no date, North Adams Public Library).

Men working inside tunnel (no date, North Adams Public Library).

Blackinton Mill workers (no date, North Adams Public Library).

View of Blackinton Mill, from the west, 1890 (photo courtesy of Paul W. Marino).

Drawing of Chinese workers at Sampson's shoe factory (*Harper's* Magazine, no date).

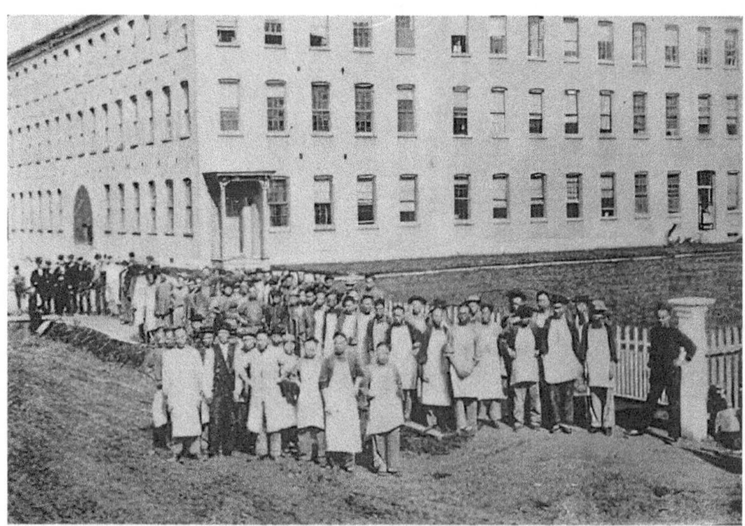

Chinese workers in front of factory, around 1875 (Henry Ward).

Knights of St. Crispin and supporters, who started shoe manufacturing cooperative, 1870 (photographer unknown).

NOTES

1 Popularly known as the Big Dig, the Central Artery/Tunnel Project disrupted traffic in Boston for fifteen years and came in way over budget. For a retrospective on the Big Dig, its plusses and minuses, see Anthony Flint, "10 Years later, did the Big Dig deliver?" *Boston Sunday Globe Magazine,* December 29, 2015.

2 Terrence Edward Coyne, *The Hoosac Tunnel* (Ph.D. dissertation, Clark University, Worcester, MA, 1992), 151.

3 *Boston Sunday Globe*, July 27, 2003, M12.

4 Terrence E. Coyne, "The Hoosac Tunnel: Massachusetts' Western Gateway," *Historical Journal of Massachusetts* (Winter 1995), 1–20, 6–7. In 1860, a local newspaper waxed indignant when England's Prince of Wales visited Lenox, in the southern part of the county, but ignored the tunnel: "[I]t seems curious that the Prince should have gone right by the Hoosac Tunnel, the greatest in the world, without expressing the desire to take a royal peep." (18)

5 Frederick Rudolph, "Chinamen in Yankeedom: Anti-Unionism in Massachusetts in 1870," *American Historical Review* 53 (October 1947).

6 Federal Writers Project, *The Berkshire Hills* (New York: Funk & Wagnalls, 1939), 3.

7 Mark Rondeau, *A People of Faith, Hope and Love: The First 100 Years of St. Anthony of Padua Parish, 1903–2003* (The St. Anthony 100th Anniversary Committee, 2003) 4.

8 Details from Coyne, *The Hoosac Tunnel*, 283, and Gene Carlson & Tina Peters, 2.

9 Coyne, 284, dissertation, note to *Transcript,* October 24, 1867. Before Mallory descended, he handed an onlooker a note that was apparently his will in an envelope: "If I don't come out of this alive you can open this. If I do give it back" (Lydia Ballou, *Hoosac Trails,* November 2011) .

10 Carlson & Peters, 2. For a compilation by Charles (Chuck) Cahoon of the names of those killed and injured during the construction of the tunnel, see https://mail.google.com/mail/u/0/#inbox/1607c429de0d0841?projector=1. Prior to beginning work on the tunnel, Mallory served with the Union forces in the Civil War. He went on to live in North Adams and had the life that one could write a dramatic play or opera about. Carlson & Peters summarize his life as follows: Mallory "sailed the oceans of the world, served in one of the bloodiest wars in history, witnessed and took part in the rescue efforts of one of the most horrific catastrophes at the Hoosac tunnel, traveled across the continental United States, made shoes, earned a reputation of honesty and sobriety, protected the people of North Adams, assailed villains, and survived villainous accusations" (8). For a memoir of one who knew Mallory, see Lydia Ballou, *Hoosac Trails,* November 2011.

11 After the tunnel opened, three cotton mills in Williamstown suffered sizeable losses and soon closed down. See Theodore W. Ruger, *Changing*

Times: A Study of Industrial Transformation and Working-Class Culture in Nineteenth-Century Williamstown (Williamstown, MA: Williams College, 1990), 23–24. Also see Daniel Edmund Powell, *Another Williamstown: The Cotton Textile Industry in a New England Community 1826–1929* (Williamstown, MA: Williams College, 1979): As Williamstown's cotton mill owners "had anticipated, the Tunnel made efficient, inexpensive rail transportation available—particularly to areas in Eastern Massachusetts. But rather than increasing the salability of Williamstown products by widening the radius in which potential markets could be found, the improvement of transportation connections led to the near extinction of the cotton industry in the community" (48). See also Carin Lynn Cole, *Between Two Worlds: The Business Career of Albert C. Houghton* (Williamstown, MA: Williams College, 1991): The tunnel "did not provide the increase in trade that was expected" (40–41).

12 Writing at the turn of the twentieth century, Clinton Q. Richmond hails the progressive spirit of the North Adams populace: "It was during these struggles to secure railroad outlets and push forward the interests of the Hoosac Tunnel that the citizens of the town acquired the faculty of standing as a unit for any broad public improvement benefiting the whole community. This spirit was again exemplified in recent years, when the citizens of North Adams united as one man to secure the location of a State Normal School in the city." "Adams and North Adams," *New England Magazine,* 21 (1899–1900), 161–1, 175. Richmond could have also added the wide community support for the region's first hospital (see endnote 16).

13 Elizabeth Baker, "Blackinton: A Case Study of Industrialism, 1856–1876," *Historical Journal of Massachusetts* (January, 1981),15–26, 17.

14 W.F. Spear, *History of North Adams, Mass., 1749–1885* (North Adams: Hoosac Valley News Printing House, 1885), 513.

15 Paul Donovan, *North Adams Regional Hospital: A Historical Perspective, Part 1: 1882–1910,* Ch. Two (n.d., author's email address: emsportmed2015 @gmail.com).

16 "North Adams and Vicinity Illustrated," *Transcript* (1897), 32. Referring to the people and churches of North Adams, the quotation continues "and as they have never failed in the past to enable it to proceed on its course of mercy, it is not probable that in the future they will fail to carry on the policy that has already proven so successful." Seven years earlier, Mary Hunter Williams, Chair of the Board of Control of the hospital, made the following comment after discussing gifts to the hospital, noting that she and the board "beg[a]n to feel the embarrassment of riches" from the contributions of "'the people of Northern Berkshire" (Donovan, 29). While significant contributions came from wealthy residents like A.C. Houghton and C.T. Sampson, the non-rich gave also. That included help from people in Adams and Williamstown, as well as North Adams. Besides individual gifts, local churches took up collections for hospital expenses (*Transcript,* November 6, 1890, 8).

17 Massachusetts Bureau of Statistics of Labor, 1880, emphasis added (MBSL).

18 Coyne, The Hoosac Tunnel, 151.

19 "What were their names . . . ?" for the research done by Charles Cahoon on the fatalities and injuries suffered by the Hoosac Tunnel workers.

20 *Scribner's Magazine*, Vol. I, 10, 151, 156.

21 Edward Kirkland, *Men, Cities and Transportation,* Vol. II (Cambridge, MA: Harvard University Press, 1969), 414.

22 MBSL, 1872, 440–1.

23 Ibid., 441, emphasis in original.

24 Ibid., 441–2.

25 Ibid., 346, emphasis in original.

26 Joseph Day, *Dew Upon the Mountains: A History of St. Francis of Assisi Parish, North Adams Massachusetts in the Berkshires* (North Adams, MA: St. Francis of Assisi Parish, 1989), 35.

27 MBSL, 1872, 346.

28 Baker, 16.

29 Andy Etman, *Sanford Blackinton, His Mill, and a Wool Sorter Named John W. Jones* (North Adams, MA: Massachusetts College of Liberal Arts, SOCI 500, paper, 2006).

30 Baker, 12.

31 Baker, 13–14.

32 Baker, 14.

33 Baker, 19.

34 Baker, 16–17.

35 Alan Dawley, *Class and Community: The Industrial Revolution in Lynn* (Cambridge, MA: Harvard University Press, 1976).

36 Matthew S. Bryson, *The North Adams shoe manufacturers: how they created a successful industry only to abandon it* (Williamstown, MA: Williams College, 1999), 27.

37 *Transcript,* June 30, 1853, 4.; "A Great Berkshire Industry," *The Berkshire Hills,* Vol. 3, No. 6, February 1, 1903.

38 Bryson, 46.

39 Bryson, 29, 33.

40 Janet E. Roberts, *A History of the French Canadians in North Adams* (Williamstown, MA: Williams College, 1975), 34, reported in Michael Seif (Storch Associates and Michael Seif), *Historic Documentation Report for Western Gateway Heritage Park* (Commonwealth of Massachusetts: Department of Environmental Management, 1981), 39.

41 Bryson, 29.

42 Bryson, 40–41.

43 *Transcript,* "North Adams and Vicinity Illustrated" (1897), 32.

44 Bryson, 88.

45 Bryson, 83–87.

46 Bryson, 49, 111.

47 Dawley, 175; Henry F. Bedford, editor, *Their Lives & Numbers: The Condition of Working People in Massachusetts, 1870–1900* (Ithaca, NY: Cornell University Press, 1995), 3.

48 Anthony W. Lee, *A Shoemaker's Story: Being Chiefly about French Canadian Immigrants, Enterprising Photographers, Rascal Yankees, and Chinese Cobblers in a Nineteenth-Century Factory Town* (Princeton: Princeton University Press, 2008), 149.

49 Roberts, 23, 69. The second biggest occupational group of the French Canadians worked in the cotton and woolen mills, with more women (forty-six) than men (thiry-three). Included were girls and boys as young as 10–12. An all-male workforce served as the third largest occupational group, with a total of fifty-one men laboring in the Hoosac Tunnel, including nine teenagers, aged 13–19.

50 Bryson, 111; Daniel Pidgeon, *Old World Questions and New World Answers* (London, 1884), 146–150; MBSL, 1880.

51 *Transcript,* June 23, 1870, 2.

52 Andrew Gyory, *Closing the Gate: Race, Politics and the Chinese Exclusion Act* (Chapel Hill: University of North Carolina Press, 1998), 40. Gyory argues that American workers made a distinction between contract labor and normal immigration, opposing the former, but not the latter for the Chinese. Gyory concludes that the passage of the 1882 Chinese Exclusion Act, which prohibited the immigration of Chinese laborers, resulted from both national political parties, the Republicans and Democrats, scapegoating the Chinese, trying to divert attention of the electorate from a shortage of good jobs and a weak economy. Anthony Lee argues that most scholars disagree with Gyory, and find anti-Chinese attitudes among Eastern workers, not differing on the issue of contract labor. As for Lee, "[M]y own claim is not an either-or proposition. There is plenty of evidence to support both labor's demand for exclusion and its plea for accommodation, suggesting that workers were quite split on their attitudes toward the Chinese and exclusion" (292). Both authors, Gyory and Lee, steadfastly argue against the racist exclusion act and its ongoing consequences. Gyory writes, "The law's legacy, in the form of future restrictions and anti-Asian racism, lingers to this day. Like the Fugitive Slave Act of 1850, the Chinese exclusion act of 1882 remains one of the most infamous and tragic statutes in American history . . . . More than a century after its passage, the [a]ct still haunts the nation's treatment of immigrants and immigration" (258–9). For Lee, as with the end of Reconstruction, "[t]he act was the second such policy to renege on the promise to invite the country's most abject laborers to obtain the privileges of freedom, equality, and participatory and communal democracy . . . ." Further, by "making a more explicit equation

between race and class . . .," it "made whiteness a marker"—a fundamental societal value that the Chinese could not meet, but the French Canadians could" (271–2).

53 Richard V. Bennett, *The Crispins, Calvin, and the Chinese.* (Middletown, CT: Wesleyan University), 57.

54 Washington Gladden, *From the Hub to the Hudson: with sketches of nature, history and industry in north-western Massachusetts* (Greenfield, MA: E.D. Merriam, 1870), 173.

55 Lee, 172.

56 Interestingly, at a North Adams Central Labor union meeting a quarter of a century later, similar ethnic sentiments were voiced regarding Italian labor. In a discussion about hiring "cheap Italian labor" for work at the reservoir and the possible use of the "Padrone' system," the union argued that ethnic discrimination was not being contemplated: "[T]he Central Labor union makes no distinction as regards nationality, but do most earnestly protest as citizens and voters against the importation of cheap alien labor for it is a detriment to . . . the welfare of the community" (*Transcript,* July 17, 1895).

57 *Transcript*, June 23, 1870, 2.

58 Steve Leikin, *The Practical Utopians: American Workers and the Cooperative Movement in the Gilded Age* (Detroit: Wayne State University Press, 2005), xvi.

59 Rudolph, 23 and quote in Leikin, xvi, from *New York Tribune.*

60 Lee, 181.

61 Bennett, 66–67.

62 Lee, 182.

63 Leikin, xvi.

64 Rudolph; MBSL, 1871.

65 The Luddites of early nineteenth-century England did smash machines to save workers' jobs. "Luddite direct action can be seen as taking from the relatively rich in order to give back (or keep) what was due to the workers (many of whom were poor)," from Steven E. Jones, *Against Technology: From the Luddites to Neo-Luddism* (New York: Rutledge, 2006), 47.

66 MBSL, 1871, 98.

67 Ibid., 99.

68 Ibid., 109, 110.

69 Rudolph, 2; Bennett, 65; Bryson, 5; and Lee, 254.

70 Lee, 255.

71 Lee, 256.

72 Bennett, 100.

73 Lee, 257.

74 Bennett, 100–101.

75 Lee, 257, 269.

76 Lee, 257–258. For a fascinating and provocative historical novel based on the Chinese sojourn in North Adams, see Karen Shepard, *The Celestials* (Portland, OR: Tin House Books, 2013).

77 Gladden, 171.

78 Rudolph, 7. Writing about a time some three decades earlier, Social Gospel minister Washington Gladden described a different era: "North Adams was . . . a good sample of a New England democracy . . . . Indeed, there was nothing resembling a social stratification in . . . North Adams at that day . . . . That class consciousness which some of our industrial leaders are so eager to cultivate would have been wholly inconceivable to the people of this New England town" (Gladden, 160–161).

79 Ibid.

80 Leikin, xvi.

81 MBSL, 1872, 456; Leikin, xvi.

82 MBSL, 1872, 454-457; Bennett, 95–96.

83 See Leikin for examples of coal mining, shoe and barrel making cooperatives, with a focus on Stoneham, Massachusetts, and Minneapolis.

84 Quoted in Alexander Keyssar, *Out of Work: The first century of unemployment in Massachusetts* (Cambridge, MA: Cambridge University Press, 1986), 36.

85 Ibid., 47.

CHAPTER FOUR

THE KNIGHTS OF LABOR, WORKER CULTURE, AND THE CELEBRATION OF LABOR DAY

W.G. Cady & Co., N.L. Millard and the C.T. Sampson Company have opened their shoe factories as "free shops," and announce that they have got through being directed by labor organizations of any kind.

—*Transcript,* March 25, 1886

I have seen little children at the tender ages of eight, nine and ten years, some right here in North Adams, working right in the Union [mill] . . . . Is it not an everlasting shame and disgrace?

—James Woodacre, Knights of Labor, at first Labor Day celebration in North Adams, 1886

Our capital and capitalists have been developed here from humble beginnings and through assiduous labor. As a result we have had little class distinction and no idle wealth."

—Mayor Albert C. Houghton, 1897

DESPITE THE HARD TIMES OF THE PANIC and its aftermath, labor activism continued in the region. In 1876, for example, 600 Blackinton workers, mostly Welsh and English, responded to wage cuts and shortened hours by striking for three-and-a-half weeks.[1] The Knights of Labor, the nation's largest union, continued to advance the cause of working people, both in and out of the workplace, during the 1880s. Generally speaking, the Knights favored worker-run cooperatives, and. while they advocated for labor in capitalist operations, particularly pushing for an eight-hour day, they tended not to favor strikes.

Local industrialists worried about the growing membership of the Knights in North Berkshire. Reflecting that worry, in the spring of 1886, the *Transcript* published an editorial counseling "Patience" in labor troubles. While the editorial didn't mention any specific local disagreement, it referenced "the particular trouble in this village . . . ." The newspaper's summary of past labor relations in North Berkshire presented an inaccurate and idyllic view:

> For almost the first time in its history, the business interests of this village are threatened with injury from a disagreement between labor and capital. During all the trying years of the past, the relations between the manufacturers and their employees have been pleasant and mutually profitable, and the concord has resulted in the rapid growth and prosperity of this community . . . . There has been peace here, justice and fair wages in most cases, prompt payments, friendship and courtesy, on both sides . . . . We were in hopes that this history would not be marred by the disturbances that have rent other places, and we hope still that the good feelings of the past will be able to lead all parties to an amicable and wise settlement and adjustment.[2]

A page later in the same issue of the paper, a very lengthy article ("CAPITAL AND LABOR"), subtitled "THE WAGE QUESTION," covered a sermon delivered by Rev. Mr. Rowley on Sunday at the First Baptist Church, quoting the minister at length. Rowley spoke to a capacity crowd and, in a more moralistic voice, counseled the same patience that the paper's editor had offered. Rowley spoke of his concern for workers and for the poor, noting that, at another place where he spent seven years, he "saw the mansions of the managers of this monopoly and the hovels of the poor people they employed" and reminded his listeners that he was "always ready to help the weakest in the fight." He vaguely referred to a great strike out West, but told his audience: "Because some workingmen have wrongs, it doesn't follow that all workingmen have wrongs." Then to emphasize that point, and to bring it home, he added, "Because employers are unjust in Illinois, that is no reason that they are unjust in North Adams."

Regarding North Adams, Rowley worried about a possible strike in the shoe industry, a strike that Rowley thought unnecessary, since "I am told by shoe manufacturers, in whose word I have as much confidence as in my own, that unless a better and higher market shall be found for their shoes, a larger advance in wages will be simply impossible." Then, turning to turmoil in the area's two print mills, the minister relied on the words of the mill managers, who "say that they are paying all that they can afford to pay while competing with other similar industries." Rowley made reference to a strike in a neighboring area that cost the workers dearly "because capital could better afford to be idle than to raise the wages of labor." Finally, he beseeched his audience not to strike: "In the interests of order and good government, of your homes and families, in the name of all that that is sacred and dear to the highest well-being of our common life as dwellers in the same community, I plead with you to save North Adams from a calamity, from which it could not soon recover."

In that same issue of the newspaper, two brief items pointed to other labor strife, one a "rumor" that "local house girls" (cleaners) would strike for higher pay, and news that the *Transcript*'s paperboys actually struck for increased wages. As far as the "house girls" were concerned, "It is not yet ascertained whether they belong to the Knights of Labor."

But, as readers would learn if they read further, the editor's and minister's concerns most likely centered not on "house girls" or newspaper boys, but on the shoe and print work industries.

A much larger news story covered the situation at the shoe factories and the print works. A committee of the Knights of Labor had "request[ed] more pay to all unskilled workmen in both the Arnold and Freeman print works," but the mill owners, Houghton and Bracewell, turned them down, arguing that they paid comparable market rates, and in some cases even more. The Knights stated that they would not strike for higher wages, but "will try to bring it about in some other way." Cognizant of Mr. Bracewell's sympathy for the condition of his employees, the Knights still felt "his sympathy did not go far enough."

As for the shoe industry, the Knights claimed that they had helped bring about an increase in wages for the stitchers at Whitman, Canedy & Company. Regardless of any current disputes, the news report concluded that "[w]hatever comes, the leaders of the Knights of Labor can probably be depended on to do nothing rash or precipitate." While the editor and news writer of the *Transcript* seemed to argue that patience and worker calm will prevail, a small item in the same edition of the paper suggested that positions, at least in the case of the shoe manufacturers, have significantly hardened: "W.G. Cady & Company, N.L. Millard and the C.T. Sampson company have opened their shoe factories as 'free shops,' and announce that they have got through being directed by labor organizations of any kind." That notice may have been meant not only for the Knights of Labor, but also for the American Federation of Labor, newly born, whose affiliated membership included a union of shoe workers.

TEXTILES REIGN SUPREME: THE ARNOLD BROTHERS AND WILLIAM B. PLUNKETT

During the last quarter of the nineteenth century, shoe and boot manufacturing in North Adams surged, spawning the introduction of tanneries. At the same time, the production of cotton textiles increased. Improvements in the national economy clearly aided both industries. Integrated operations leading to the dyeing and printing of cloth bolstered the local textile sector and, by the end of the century, textile manufacturing held the number-one spot in the North Adams economy.[3]

Emigrants from Rhode Island, Oliver, Harvey, and John Arnold, had started several textile enterprises beginning in 1829 in North Adams, though not as a threesome until 1843. In 1861, they built their own print works on Marshall Street, and production began in 1863. Spurred by increased prices for cotton goods during the Civil War and demand for Union army uniforms, the firm did very well, its holdings increasing sevenfold from 1860 to 1870, amid continued expansion.

A fire in 1871 destroyed the company's eight buildings, but the Arnolds rebuilt on a different site a year later, though still on Marshall Street. At that time, F.H. Arnold, Harvey's son, came on board, while Oliver and John sold their shares to Albert C. Houghton, a future president of the print works and later the first mayor of North Adams.[4]

While the Panic of 1873 hurt their business, as it did the other companies in town, a year later the print works showed a profit of $100,000. The Dunn Credit Bureau characterized the print works owners as "shrewd, calculating, persevering businessmen" whose operation was now "the most successful in the country." An integrated operation, the company owned four textile plants in North Berkshire to manufacture the cloth, and built a series of mill buildings on its sprawling Marshall Street site for the printing operation. By 1883, with some 2,000 employees, Arnold Print Works (APW) had become the largest print dyeing plant in the world, and the buildings on its site had increased to twenty-six. The print works also maintained an office in Paris to keep in contact with the latest developments in fashion and an office in New York to design the new patterns. APW continued to do well despite growing Southern textile competition, in part by utilizing "new machinery . . . , follow[ing] fashion trends closely . . . , and diversifying its products."[5]

Houghton, often referred to as A.C. Houghton, a successful land speculator and now the treasurer of the company, had been purchasing more and more of the equity from the Arnold brothers, and by 1876 had become the main force at the print works. In 1882, he gained complete control and soon added eight new buildings, including a packing, engineering, dye, and dry house. The new brick building for dyeing print cloth indigo blue was "probably the largest building in the world for that purpose." In 1888 APW's profits of $143,000 proved larger than any other manufacturer in North Adams.[6]

The continued success of APW helped push textiles past the boot and shoe industry and by the mid-1890s it had become the most profitable industry in North Adams. Each day, 1,000 employees at the mill turned out 200,000 yards of fabric. With the Eclipse and Beaver mills, two other Arnold assets in North Adams, another 1,000 workers produced the cotton cloth for the print works. Additional cotton cloth came from mills the firm owned in Williamstown and North Pownal, Vermont. At its height, 3,200 employees worked for the huge print works. Besides the printed cloth, the company produced stuffed animals. Historian Alexander Keyssar notes that the high sales of that product meant that APW employees had steadier work in 1895 than did textile workers in other state textile communities.[7]

APW's size and the vertical integration of its cotton mills allowed it to compete with the immense mills of eastern Massachusetts. One historian of the Williamstown mill owned by APW credits its survival amidst the downfall of neighboring Williamstown cotton mills to the "cooperative network" of the four feeder mills and the parent APW.[8] Low labor costs undoubtedly helped APW's bottom line and, as with other local industries, the print works employed youngsters "between 10 and 15 years of age, and some under" for eleven hours a day.[9] Nationwide, corporations, including those that dominated an industry, had replaced small businesses and family firms. One biographer of Albert C. Houghton compares his innovations and successes with vertical integration to the careers of John D. Rockefeller and Andrew Carnegie in the oil and steel industries, and writes, "The success of the Arnold Print Works as a vertically integrated corporation paralleled changes occurring in the economy as a whole."[10]

As with other local industrialists, Houghton expanded his influence beyond the world of business. He served as a trustee of Williams College for nearly twenty years and was appointed a commissioner to the Chicago World's Fair in 1893. Politically, before he switched allegiance to the Republican Party, he was a delegate to the Democratic National Convention in 1892. Locally, he helped write the North Adams charter so it could become a city in 1895, and then, running unopposed, became its first mayor. Following the model of nationally successful businessmen, Houghton turned to philanthropy, helping to found the city's first hospital and then paying off its debt of $7,500.[11]

At the start of the twentieth century, Houghton's company, the Arnold Print Works, had become the largest employer of Italian workers in North Adams. Italians, the last of the major waves of immigrants of the late nineteenth century, numbered about 250 families in 1906. They tended to live on State Street and in the Union Street area, near the print works. Tyroleans, from the former Austro-Hungarian Empire, less likely to consider themselves Italian, lived mostly on Furnace Hill.[12]

From a number of only 336 in 1893, the North Adams Italian population grew to nearly 1,500 in 1910. Reflective of the community's growth and religious conviction, they constructed St. Anthony's Church in 1906. Italians faced significant discrimination in the city, and received disproportionately low-wage manual labor work. Prior to 1900, the print works only hired Italians in what was called the "blue dip" building. There, where blue dyes were produced, the dirtiest work on the vast site took place.[13]

Given the centrality of textiles in the North Berkshire economy, it should come as no surprise that an industry manufacturing textile machinery would be born and develop in North Adams. Fourteen years after migrating from Scotland, 41-year-old James Hunter Sr. opened his long-lived family business making machine castings in a small shop alongside the

Hoosic River. The company grew, built modern brick structures on Main Street, and incorporated in 1891 as the James Hunter Machine Company. By that time, James E. Hunter, the founder's son, headed the company, which had developed a reputation for building excellent textile machinery. Also a well-respected inventor, James E. held numerous patents on his products, which could be found in mills all across the country. Well into the twentieth century, local skilled machinists continued to find work at Hunter Machine Company.[14]

The largest city in Berkshire County at the time, North Adams continued to see a rise in population, which peaked in 1900 with 24,100. Economically, textiles and shoes still served as the foundation of its industrial base, but competition from Southern mills could now be felt. While the federal tariff could not shield the region from domestic competition, it certainly protected local textile manufacturers from European producers. In Adams, an overwhelmingly textile town, its leading capitalist, William B. Plunkett, himself the grandson of Irish immigrants, had developed a strong, even "intimate" friendship with the U.S. representative from Ohio and future U.S. president, William McKinley,[15] who had crafted the federal tariff. The Plunkett family had, of course, been involved in textile manufacturing since the early nineteenth century, incorporating as the Berkshire Cotton Manufacturing Company in 1899.

Unable to find enough employees locally to work for low wages at his growing textile mills, the Plunketts encouraged immigration to Adams, mostly from Poland. While it remains unclear if any of the company's representatives actually traveled to Poland to recruit, from 1895 to 1905 a total of 1,400 Poles settled in Adams, tending to come from Galatia (once an area in central Turkey) and Russian Poland. They formed about one-seventh of the population of Adams. In 1904, they established St. Stanislaus Church there.

During the 1890s, McKinley visited Adams three times. The tariff had been a huge boost to Plunkett and other American manufacturers, since the high tax it placed on imports kept foreign competition away. (While the tariff meant more jobs for local residents, it also had the consequence of raising prices for American consumers.) When the McKinley tariff had passed in 1890, Plunkett planned a second mill. Two years later, before a crowd of over 9,000, Congressman McKinley helped dedicate the new building. On the day in 1896 that McKinley received the presidential nomination, Mill No. 3 went into production. A year later, McKinley visited Adams again, that time to lay the cornerstone for the town's new library.

In 1900, President McKinley returned to Adams to lay another cornerstone—that one for Plunkett Mill No. 4. When an assassin killed McKinley in 1901, Adams became the first town in the nation to erect a statue to his memory—the one mentioned in the Introduction. The granite and bronze likeness remains standing, facing south in McKinley Square, within sight of the former Plunkett mills. At its dedication on October 10, 1903, onlookers were entertained by an orchestra and a chorus of 125.[16] (Given the economic, political, and ideological power of the region's capitalist class, it is not surprising that, while a statue of a business-friendly president greets visitors to the center of Adams, no nineteenth-century statue exists that honors North Berkshire's textile workers or the scores of men killed building the region's "Western Gateway," the Hoosac Tunnel, in North Adams.)[17]

CLASS, CULTURE, AND SOCIAL LIFE AT THE END OF THE NINETEENTH CENTURY

Historians have referred to the "Gilded Age" as roughly the last third of the nineteenth century, a time of industrial, railroad, oil, and banking concentration. It encompasses an era when great fortunes could be made. Capitalist elites did not hide their wealth: they built great mansions in Newport, Rhode Island, in the southern Berkshires, and on Church Street in North Adams. Economist Thorstein Veblen described and explored what he called the "conspicuous consumption" of the very wealthy, who called attention to their status by their extravagant homes, parties, leisure activities, and charitable giving.[18]

In 1872, Sanford Blackinton moved from his very large house by the mill to a new, ornate mansion on lower Church Street, serving as a figurative gatekeeper to the numerous homes soon to be built by the city's elite in the coming years. At a cost of $75,000 (the equivalent of about $1.35 million in 2016), the high price reflected Blackinton's reputation as the richest man in Berkshire County. He lived there until his death at age 88 in 1885. In 1896, the city's leading industrialist, A.C. Houghton, bought the Blackinton mansion and, continuing his practice of philanthropy, donated it to the city of North Adams for its free community library, and as a memorial to his brother Andrew Jackson Houghton.[19]

Credited with the origin of the term Gilded Age, Mark Twain noted that the gold on top didn't extend very deep.[20] With industrialization accelerating and the workforce expanding, workers struggled to make a living in the booming mills. In the process, the immigrants and other industrial workers organized to form unions, and soon became part of a fast-growing and welcoming national organization, the Knights of Labor.

Statistics that describe the national labor force in 1880 show that North Berkshire's workforce was typical. First, with the rapid increase of industrialization, 80 percent of the almost three million workers employed in manufacturing worked in factories, not at home or in outbuildings producing shoes or clothing. Second, as the demand for factory workers opened the gates for immigration, immigrants comprised 42 percent of those laboring in extractive and manufacturing industries—at a time when just 13 percent of the U.S. population had been born in foreign lands.[21]

As more of the country's wealth went into the pockets of the top 1 percent and the corporations they controlled, a greater sense of class consciousness grew within the working class. A national railroad strike in the summer of 1877, often referred to as "the Great Uprising of 1877," brought violent struggle between the forces of the railroad corporations, aided by government troops, and striking rail workers. The workers had seen their wages reduced again and again since 1873, and they often worked under hazardous conditions. In Massachusetts alone, an average of forty-two railroad workers lost their lives each year from accidents.[22]

The railroad strike began on July 16th in Martinsburg, West Virginia, and led to the first-ever deployment of federal troops to put down a labor rebellion.[23] Federal and state militias joined local police forces and fired on protesting workers in a number of cities, including Baltimore, Pittsburgh, and Chicago. Battles broke out and dozens were killed and wounded, mostly protestors. While the strikers ultimately lost the war, the labor movement gained strength that continued into the 1880s. Fear of future uprisings led communities to build armories and organize local militias. Undoubtedly that was why a militia company came to be organized in North Adams on August 27, 1877.[24]

Populist parties and organizations, which focused their anger at the growing corporate power of the railroads and banks, coalesced in backing William Jennings Bryan, the Democratic Party's nominee for the presidency in 1896. That McKinley defeated him in that campaign seemed to be the downfall of the last great hope for labor, small business, and the populist spirit as the capitalist ascendancy continued. For North Berkshire, McKinley symbolized the "gilded" order.

However, the "labor question," as it had come to be called, remained a reality in the workplaces of North Berkshire, especially since only a decade had passed since the "Haymarket affair"[25]—when striking workers had gathered at Haymarket Square in Chicago in an effort to gain an eight-hour workday, and an unknown person let off a dynamite bomb, killing seven police officers and four workers, and injuring dozens of other people, which resulted in a media obsession of an anarchist threat and the ultimate downfall of the Knights of Labor and the quest for an eight-hour workday. Still, local elites in North Berkshire did their best to downplay labor strife to present a public front of unity, harmony, and opportunity for all.

In 1897, the inaugural remarks of North Adams's first mayor, former president of Arnold Print Works and one of the wealthiest men in the region, A.C. Houghton, exemplified this spirit. After highlighting "the substantial absence of labor difficulties here," Houghton went on to paint the following class picture:

> Our capital and capitalists have been developed here from humble beginnings and through assiduous labor. As a result we have had little class distinction and no idle wealth. Differences of race and religion, elsewhere hindrances to concert of action with us only increased the variety and strength of our commingled and combined ability.

A local editor went even further than the mayor: In North Adams, he argued, "there is little or no class feeling, no distinction of masses and classes . . . . No town or city in New England has less conflict of labor and capital."[26]

THE KNIGHTS OF LABOR, WORKER CULTURE, AND LABOR DAY

With the demise of the Crispins, the next major union to take root in North Berkshire, and in the nation for that matter, proved to be the Knights of Labor. The Knights opened their membership to all, with the exception of the Chinese, a group that suffered from virulent racism during that period. The Knights had grown rapidly in the 1880s, prior to the Haymarket affair, and they rode the wave of the eight-hours-a-day movement and the increased prosperity in the United States. They generally organized geographically on an industrial model, enrolling all workers regardless of skills or sex within an industry. As a national union, it reached its peak in 1886, the year of the first Labor Day celebration in the Berkshires.

The local event came just four years after the first recorded Labor Day observance in America, which had been a festive march and picnic by some 10,000 workers and their families in New York City on Sept. 5, 1882. But the practice of setting aside a special day to honor workers and specific crafts can actually be traced back to ancient times and its continuation through the Middle Ages. Then, at the end of the eighteenth century, during the French Revolution, a day in September was designated as a labor holiday. In the United States during the 1800s labor unions often used celebrations, picnics, parades, and demonstrations to rally support for the causes of working people.

In 1886 in North Berkshire, mill workers put in ten-hour days, six days a week, fifty-two weeks a year. They had Sundays off and enjoyed six unpaid annual holidays. Their only other time off came from unpaid layoffs and plant shutdowns. In the cotton mills, weekly wages averaged $6.00, with women and children making significantly less. In the woolen mills, the weekly wage averaged about $8.50, and in shoes and leather about $10.00 per week. Entire families worked in the mills, the only way in which many households could survive. Throughout the state, 10 percent of all 10–15-year-olds labored for pay, mostly in manufacturing.

The prospect of a day off at the end of the summer, even if unpaid, for rest and relaxation, must have filled local employees and their families with excitement and anticipation. And though the Knights of Labor in North Berkshire called for a seventh holiday—one to commemorate the contributions of labor—it would be eight more years before Labor Day would become a national holiday. So the local Knights stood as relative pioneers in the forefront of the celebration of labor.

They respectfully communicated to the local mill owners their desire to have production stop on the first Monday in September, which, in 1886, was the sixth. Most manufacturers and employers responded favorably to the request, and a sizeable contingent of local workers and their families—more than 3,000—attended the festivities, some of them coming by train from as far as Hoosick Falls, N.Y., and Greenfield, Massachusetts. Several railroad companies had lowered their rates for the occasion, and a local band met the travelers at the station. Many of the celebrants marched in a procession to the fairgrounds off State Road. There, led by an official of the Knights of Labor "in a blue coat and scarlet sash, manly and martial-like, on horseback," the celebration began at about ten o'clock.[27] Most of the sporting events started at 2:00 p.m., but at least one ball game, between the lasters of H.T. Cady's shoe shop and local cigar makers, began before lunch, as did the singing, provided by the Knights of Labor glee club. The regular lunchtime "dinner" cost thirty-five cents, but no record could be found of the cost of the clambake, which began at 5:00 p.m. In between the meals, the revelers had access to snacks.

In their post–Labor Day editions, both local newspapers[28] gave prominent attention to the speeches, providing excerpts and summaries. The speakers, mostly clergy, praised the contributions of working people, expressed concern about the continued low-wage immigration to the United States, lectured on the evils of alcohol, and cautioned the crowd about alleged anarchist violence and other labor radicals, such as had been witnessed at Haymarket in Chicago earlier that year.

The last speaker, James Goodacre, a leading member of the Knights of Labor, focused his speech entirely on specific problems facing labor and the need for change. A dedicated egalitarian, Goodacre demanded the right to vote for women and "equal pay for equal work." He also noted that, though this year the Knights had to ask their employers for the day off, he hoped that before too long that would no longer be necessary as workers would be their own bosses, through the cooperative movement championed by the Knights. At that time, the local shoe cooperative had already failed, but the Knights had been contemplating a retail store cooperative. Goodacre also exhorted the crowd to call for an end to the "great wrong" of child labor:

> I have seen little children at the tender ages of eight, nine and ten years, some right here in North Adams, working right in the Union [mill], and in every other mill in the land . . . . Is it not an everlasting shame and disgrace? At five minutes before six in the morning you

> can see the little ones entering the mill doors, North, South, East and West . . . . Can not we in some way stop this degrading business?[29]

Child labor proved to be a practice difficult to stop, as low wages and outright poverty in local families forced mothers and fathers to send their children into the mills to supplement the family wages. For families and individuals unable to make a living wage, the last resort proved to be the notorious "poor farm." Typically a farm run by a local family, it served as a place for destitute men, women, and children to reside and work, supported by the local town. Established in Adams in 1868, the first North Berkshire poor farm was sold to North Adams in 1884. Excerpts from the 1898 annual report of the "city almoner and overseer of the poor," William Woodhead, provides an insight into the conditions of the time as well as the attitudes of city officials:

> [T]he past year has been one of continued business depression, and . . . the expense of this department has largely increased over that of last year, increased by reason of the larger number who have been aided, and not on account of any increase in the amount given to the applicants . . . . We must bear in mind that the population of the city is increasing, and with that the work of this department must also increase. To the worthy and the needy poor, we desire to be of assistance, but with that intemperate and worthless class we have no sympathy; these are the class whose only usefulness seems to be to propagate paupers.

The North Adams poor farm, often referred to as the city infirmary, located on a section of Southview Cemetery, lasted into the 1960s, though the city's poor received a boost in the 1930s by New Deal legislation through which the federal government provided widows' benefits, Social Security for general welfare and retirees, and Aid to Dependent Children.[30]

After the speeches, a full afternoon of sporting events followed. Winners of the bicycle and foot races received cash prizes, and those with a desire to gamble wagered on the horse races with the top purse at twenty dollars. A second ball game, a five-inning affair, went to the W.L. Brown team. Not yet ready to end their holiday at sundown, North Berkshire's first Labor Day celebrants packed the Odd Fellows' Hall and danced until midnight.

For the next quarter century, the day would be celebrated, but labor and politics would not always be its focus. The sponsors of the events included temperance and nationality groups as well as unions. As political speechmaking declined, parades and sports became more central.

In 1889, militant shoe workers who had shut down four North Adams factories in a strike over wages played a central part in the Labor Day celebration. The local paper called it "by far the most successful of labor days here." A parade began on Eagle Street and included a platoon of police, the North Adams Musical Association band, two branches of the International Boot and Shoe Workers Union, representatives of the Cigar Makers' union, and the North Adams Fire Department. Marchers could be seen unfurling banners—at that time still demanding the eight-hour day.

A full slate of sporting events, including bicycle and foot races, a baseball game, and horse and dog races, drew the interest of the crowd. Another event, a "hose race" between groups of firefighters, proved to be very popular. Each team ran 200 yards with their pipe, laid out 800 feet of hose, coupled them and attached the nozzle, all vying for the fastest possible time. Before long, North Adams became a western Massachusetts center of the Firemen's Muster, with its appealing sport and pageantry.

Also that year, many in the crowd listened to a speech given by Dr. Edward McGlynn of New York, a well-known orator and supporter of the single tax. The tax, originally proposed by Henry George, would be levied on all land, whether or not it was being used. This tax would pressure speculators to utilize or sell their lands, thus lowering the cost of natural resources, raising production, and increasing the demand and wages for labor. McGlynn expressed this popular, pro-labor theory clearly and forcefully in a "strong, rich, controlling voice." He also spoke out for nationalization of the railroads, telegraphs, and telephones—all community resources needed by the entire population. As with earlier Labor Day celebrations, the night brought dancing. The local reporter pronounced all of the day's events successful and also noted: "There was no drunkenness on the streets or fair grounds, and not a single arrest was made for that offense, which can rarely be said of any holiday in North Adams."[31]

The Lasters' Protective Union sponsored the next three annual field days. In 1891, the announced speaker, who was again Dr. McGlynn, did not appear, and the following year no mention of a speaker could be found. For the first time, the press report on the 1892 celebration observed that many local folks had left town for the day on several excursions. Nonetheless, a sizeable crowd attended and enjoyed a popular tug-of-war match in which the North Adams team defeated a team from its neighbor to the south.[32]

In 1894, a non-labor-oriented sponsor, the Father Matthew Temperance Society (FMTS), organized the events of the day, which drew a crowd of 4,000–5,000.[33] As part of a powerful national trend, temperance had become a popular cause in North Berkshire in the late nineteenth century, and, without a labor sponsor, the festivities focused on sports with no mention of unions or speeches of any kind. The following year, North Adams hosted the Springfield Diocesan's FMTS; in 1896, members of the society, including local residents, traveled to Worcester for the sporting events; and in 1897, Turners Falls hosted.[34] Ethnic groups also celebrated Labor Day, with the Irish Ancient Order of Hibernians sponsoring a field day of sporting events that attracted around 1,500 to the fairgrounds in North Adams in 1896. The following year, the Italian Mutual Aid Society planned two parades, a train ride through the Hoosac Tunnel, and a banquet.[35]

The sole labor-oriented Labor Day event during this time period occurred in North Adams in 1895 when the Socialist Labor party sponsored an open-air speech at the soldier's monument on Main Street. Herbert N. Casson, the speaker, who was best known for starting a labor church in Lynn, spoke out against the monopolies, the trusts, and the need for trade unionism to improve the lot of working people. To the people of North Adams, he exclaimed, "You have here a beautiful city and with the proper laws and proper men in office you have heart enough and brains to make everything as high as your hills." He ended by specifying the creed of the socialist party: "Thou shalt not steal, nor be stolen from; thou shalt not rob nor be robbed."[36]

While the next few Labor Days seemed relatively quiet in North Berkshire, in 1899 a local contingent joined many others in Pittsfield at what might have been the largest celebration of labor ever held in the county, an event hosted by the Pittsfield Central Labor union. That same year brought with it numerous events throughout and just beyond Berkshire County, and in all cases local residents participated. By then the celebrations had become more specialized, with the workforce divided by skill, ethnicity, and politics. While local French societies met in Northampton, 800 Irish Hibernians from North Adams journeyed to Troy, the skilled United Workmen from the region headed for a field day in Dalton, and regional temperance groups convened in Westfield.[37]

The largest crowd of all, however, estimated at 8,000, congregated in Pittsfield for a field day celebration of labor unions that came from Holyoke, Easthampton, and Westfield, as well as from throughout the county. Nearly a quarter of that total arrived by rail from North Adams and Adams. In the lengthy parade, North Adams contributed two bands and a drum corps; marchers represented the building trades, cigar makers, textile workers, shoemakers, bartenders, plumbers, bakers, typographers, and iron molders. A North Adams team won the tug-of-war competition, but the local baseball team, not as fortunate, lost to Pittsfield 7–5.

Arnold Print Works transportation brigade, around turn of twentieth century (photographer unknown).

Library of Congress photo in front of Eclipse Mill by Lewis Hine, 1911, working for National Child Labor Committee. Boy with pipe in midst of child workers is Albert (Puggy) Duquette, whose father was a cotton mill spinner. Research by Joe Manning reveals that Albert went on to fight in World War I and became a professional boxer (https://morningsonmaplestreet.com/2014/11/26/albert-duquette-page-one).

Addie Card, 12 years old, stands inside of a North Pownal, Vermont, cotton mill where she worked as a spinner (Lewis Hine, 1910, Library of Congress). The mill, once owned by the Arnold Print Works, was sold to the Plunkett family's Berkshire Cotton Manufacturing Company, and later became part of the Berkshire Fine Spinning Association. Again, research by Joe Manning brought more of Addie's life to the public, and the life of her descendants as well (https://morningsoonmaplestreet.com/lewis-hine-project-index-of-stories/lewis-hine-project/).

Entitled “Young doffers in N. Pownal, Vt.,” Lewis Hine took this photo in 1910 (Library of Congress).

NOTES

1 Elizabeth Baker, Blackinton: A Case Study of Industrialism, 1856–1876," *Historical Journal of Massachusetts* (January 1981), 15.

2 *Transcript,* March 25, 1886.

3 *The Architectural Heritage of North Adams, Massachusetts* (North Adams Historical Commission, 1980), 21; See also Carin Lynn Cole, *Between Two Worlds: The Business Career of Albert C. Houghton* (Williamstown, MA: Williams College, 1991), 40.

4 From 1877 to 1910, Houghton also owned the Williamstown Manufacturing Company and "took pride in the fact that no employee under his jurisdiction ever engaged in any strikes." Houghton's boast may have been aided by the increasing post Civil War practice of hiring child labor. Daniel Edmund Powell, *Another Williamstown: The Cotton Textile Industry in a New England Community, 1826–1929* (Williamstown, MA: Williams College, 1979), 108–109.

5 "The Arnold" (North Adams Historical Society, undated),1

6 Cole, 29; W.F. Spear, *History of North Adams, Mass., 1749–1885* (North Adams: Hoosac Valley News Printing House, 1885), 34; and Cole, 67.

7 Cole, 76; Alexander Keyssar, *Out of Work: The first century of unemployment in Massachusetts* (Cambridge University Press, 1986), 119.

8 Daniel Edmund Powell, *Another Williamstown: The Cotton Textile Industry in a New England Community, 1826–1929* (Williamstown, MA: Williams College, 1979), 125. "Since the relatively small Berkshire rivers and streams could not produce enough water power to operate a factory as large as those in Lowell and Lawrence, Houghton organized a cooperative network of four textile mills which he owned in neighboring communities. . . . Acting alone, none of the enterprises would have been large enough to succeed, but together, the four factories could produce cloth at competitive prices."

9 Massachusetts Bureau of Statistics of Labor *(*MBSL*)* (1872), 351.

10 Cole, 72. See Howard Zinn, *A People's History of the United States, 1492–Present, revised and updated* (New York: Harper Perennial, 1995), 247–258, for more on Rockefeller and Carnegie and the role of the state, including the Supreme Court, in enhancing the fortunes of the industrialists who came to be called the "Robber Barons," 247–258.

11 Cole, 74. On Houghton's $7,500 contribution, see Paul Donovan, *North Adams Regional Hospital: A Historical Perspective, Part I: 1882–1910* (n.d., author's email address, emsportmed2015@gmail.com), 29.

12 *Golden Jubilee: St. Anthony's Church, North Adams, Massachusetts, 1958; The Architectural . . .*

13 Lauren R. Stevens,"Groups Have Lived in Harmony," *Berkshires Week* (September 11, 1987); Dick Tavelli and John Hauck, *The Italians in*

North Adams: A History of Their Cultural and Political Contributions (Williamstown, MA: Williams College, 1972).

14 North Adams Historical Society, with source from "North Adams and Vicinity Illustrated," *Transcript*, 1897 and Jan. 20, 1919. In 1961, with textiles in decline, a fifth generation of Hunters, James H. and Richard A., sold the company—then composed of the North Adams plant and branch operations in South Carolina and Los Angeles—to Crompton & Knowles Corporation (C & K). The Hunters continued to run the North Adams facility as a division of C & K. They built a new plant on South Church Street, which opened in 1968, and donated the land upon which the old factory stood to the city, soon the home of a new city hall. In 1973, the Hunters bought the new plant back from C & K and ran it until 1983. That year they sold it to Morrison Berkshire, thus ending 136 years of continuous Hunter family machine production and repair. According to the *Transcript,* the firm was thought to be the oldest family-owned textile machine company in the United States. (*Transcript,* October 27, 1995).

15 *Transcript*, June 27, 1919, 1.

16 William Carney, *A Berkshire Sourcebook: the history, geography, and major landmarks of Berkshire, Massachusetts* (Pittsfield, MA: Junior League of Berkshire County, 1976), 160–162.

17 A plaque memorializing the 195 men killed building the Hoosac Tunnel does stand in a mini-park on the corner of Main and Ashland Streets in North Adams.

18 Thorstein Veblen, *The Theory of the Leisure Class* (New York: Oxford, 2007), first published in 1899.

19 Sanford Blackinton's widow, Eliza, lived in the mansion until her death in 1896. "A Brief History of the Houghton Memorial Building, Now the Home of the North Adams Public Library," North Adams Public Library.

20 Mark Twain and Charles Dudley Warner, *The Gilded Age: A Novel of Today* (New York: New American Library, 1969 [1874]).

21 Leon Fink, *Workingmen's Democracy: The Knights of Labor and American Politics* (Urbana: University of Illinois Press, 1983), xii.

22 Bruce Levine, Stephen Brier, et al., *Who Built America: Working People and the Nation's Economy, Politics, Culture, and Society, Volume One: From Conquest and Colonization Through Reconstruction and the Great Uprising of 1877* (New York: Pantheon Books, 1989), 554.

23 The troops had been withdrawn from the South the previous spring by the Compromise of 1877, an agreement that permitted Rutherford Hayes's presidential election and effectively ended Reconstruction. See Levine, Brier et al., 500–513, on the end of Reconstruction.

24 Ibid., 558; Spear, 502.

25 See, for example, James Green, *Death in the Haymarket: A Story of Chicago, the First Labor Movement and the Bombing That Divided Gilded Age America* (New York: Pantheon, 2006).

26 H.G. Rowe and C.T. Fairfield, editors, *Index to North Adams and Vicinity Illustrated*, 1898 (Pittsfield, MA: Berkshire Family History Association, 1995), 12, 45.

27 *Hoosac Valley News*, September 4, 1886.

28 *Hoosac Valley News,* September 4, 1886; *Transcript,* September, 1886.

29 *Hoosac Valley News,* September 4, 1886.

30 *Transcript,* February 27, 1989. In 1962, the act was changed to Aid to Families with Dependent Children (AFDC).

31 *Transcript*, September 5, 1889.

32 Ibid., September 10, 1891; September 8, 1892.

33 Ibid., September 6, 1894.

34 Ibid., September 2, 1895; September 5, 1896; August 4, 1897.

35 Ibid., September 7, 1896; September 3, 1897. A free, non-sectarian Labor Day celebration took place at Cole's Grove in 1896 highlighted by a hypnotist, dancing, and performers of "negro specialties of song and dance . . ." (September 3, 1896). In 1898, Great Barrington hosted Labor Day sporting events which drew North Berkshire residents to that locale (September 6, 1898).

36 *Transcript,* September 2, 1895.

37 Ibid., September 5, 1899, 5; September 2, 1899, 4.

CHAPTER FIVE

"EUGENE DEBS SPEAKS TO A LARGE AUDIENCE IN ADAMS"

SO READ A HEADLINE from the *Transcript,* describing a speech that the nation's most famous and influential socialist gave on March 9, 1898, at Koehler's Turn Hall on Summer Street.[1] In the last decade of the nineteenth century, socialist parties in both Adams and North Adams regularly met, spread the message of socialism, and tried to elect their candidates to local and statewide office. On the whole, though, unionized North Berkshire workers who belonged to affiliates of the American Federation of Labor followed the lead of AFL President Samuel Gompers in rejecting socialism and fighting for reform within the established two-party system.

Nonetheless, cracks in the structure of capitalism had widened since the depression of 1893, and socialist alternatives were up for discussion. The large audience in Adams received Debs warmly: they already knew of his role in founding the American Railway Union (ARU) and his support of the Pullman Palace Car Company strikers in 1894. When Debs and the ARU had boycotted trains with Pullman cars, the strike widened, affecting rail transit in twenty-seven states. Debs and the union had refused to obey a presidential order to call off the strike, and President Grover Cleveland ordered the Army to end it. With the strike ended, a federal court convicted Debs of disobeying an injunction, and he spent six months in prison.

The story goes that Debs had become a socialist after spending his time behind bars reading books on socialist theory.

In Adams, he talked to his audience about the capitalist exploitation of labor and called on the government to take the railroad, telegraph, and telephone systems out of private monopoly control. He inspired confidence in ordinary workers; he told them that, if they studied the economic problems they faced, they would conclude that a cooperative system organized under principles of social democracy would bring them equity and fairness. Known for his oratory, Debs could "express . . . passionately . . . what people were feeling."[2] According to the *Transcript* reporter, Debs "received loud applause throughout the lecture . . ."; later, he met with members of the audience and then headed to another meeting in New Bedford.[3]

Debs went on to run for president five times from 1900 through 1920, as the candidate of the Socialist Party of America.[4] From the time that he achieved national prominence in 1895, the *Transcript* wasted no opportunities to attack him.[5] For example, in a lengthy editorial entitled "American Lawlessness," the paper compared his Chicago strike action to the Confederate troops firing at Fort Sumter. His action was said to be "an attempt, in the interest of barbarism, to overturn the conditions of civilized life."[6] Under the heading "Dangerous Debs," the paper anticipated that "[t]he intelligence of the working people of this country will save them from the unsafe leadership of men like Debs who misrepresent and malign the freest government on earth."[7] And finally, with the news that Debs's Socialist party was making inroads in Kansas, the editorialist refers to that reality as a "new affliction" to "long suffering Kansas." Specifically, the writer warns of a socialist takeover of the public schools and colleges, "of socialists and anarchists who will inspire the youth of the commonwealth with the sublime doctrines of Debsism."[8]

In Adams and North Adams, however, Daniel DeLeon's brand of socialism, not Debs's, prevailed. Here, the Socialist Labor Party, headed nationally by DeLeon, was in ascendance. Unlike Debs's, DeLeon's socialism tended to be less pragmatic, more theoretical. In addition, he possessed a contentious personality, brooking no disagreement, which led to internal disputes within the party and kept it from growing. One historian of socialist organizing at the turn of the twentieth century portrayed the two men as follows: "While DeLeon lectured the working class, Debs talked with workers. DeLeon, the cold, impersonal editor, worked with words and abstractions; Debs, the sentimental labor leader, worked with men."[9]

German immigrants made up the bulk of the Socialist Labor Party (SLP) in Adams. *Transcript* reports of meetings in Adams wrote that talks and debate took place in German.[10] In 1894, an SLP activist in Holyoke established a local edition of a national socialist paper, *Labor,* to include one or two pages of local news. Within a year, the paper seemed so popular that Adams became one of five towns in the state to produce a separate edition.[11] Yet, just a year later, disagreements within the Adams socialists led to a split, bringing about the so-called Adams section and the Cincinnati section which met in different halls.[12] Perhaps it was this split that led a statewide SLP activist to write that same year that "[t]he party in Adams, once 'one of the best,' was 'smashed to pieces.'"[13]

In North Adams, numerous assemblies and campaign rallies took place leading up to the local and state elections of 1898. Venues ranged from local meeting rooms to outdoor spaces. A leading statewide SLP speaker, Herbert N. Casson, from the Labor church of Lynn, spoke at the St. Jean Baptiste hall.[14] He castigated the legislature for spending $150,000 to exterminate the gypsy moth infestation "while people 'were crowded into tenements like sheep and actually starving in some parts of Boston.'" The local party used the Central Labor union hall for a meeting in 1897 where they discussed an increase in their numbers and preparation for future organization.[15] Monument Square proved to be a popular place for the socialists also, as lectures and even debates took place there in 1897 and 1898.[16]

In the months leading up to the 1898 elections, activity increased. In September, the party nominated Phillip Connors as its candidate for mayor of North Adams. Two open-air rallies

followed, one at Monument Square and the other at
Street. The following month, the SLP candidate for go
George R. Peare, spoke at St. Jean Baptiste hall bef
attentive audience.[17] He focused on the class structure of the nation, noting that the capitalist or upper class, composed of some 9 percent, owned 71 percent of the country's wealth. Peare stated that it was that 9 percent that made the laws, but that could be changed by votes of the working class. A crowd of 700 attended the final rally the evening before the election at the Odd Fellows Hall and was entertained by the Germania band of Adams as they listened to speakers on the meaning of socialism and the importance of voting "socialist" the following day. But most did not. SLP candidate Phillip Connors garnered only eighty-three votes, coming in fourth behind Mayor H. T. Cady.[18]

The local decline of the Socialist Labor Party mirrored what had been happening nationally and statewide. In 1898, the first year that Debs's party appeared on the state ballot, the SLP received more votes, as it also did in 1899. By 1900, the trend had reversed, and that continued through 1912, when the SLP candidate for president in Massachusetts received just 1,100 votes, less than 10 percent of the Socialist Party members.[19]

Twenty years after he spoke in Adams, Eugene Debs delivers an anti-war speech in Canton, Ohio on June 16, 1918 (Wikimedia Commons). It was a period of national repression, the "Red Scare," and Debs was sentenced to prison for ten years based on the words he used. (He was one of 900 people imprisoned under the Espionage Act.) Before his sentencing, Debs's address to the court included his most memorable short speech: "[Y]ears ago I recognized my kinship with all living beings, and I made up my mind that I was not one bit better than the meanest on earth. I said then, and I say now, that while there is a lower class, I am in it; while there is a criminal element, I am of it; while there is a soul in prison, I am not free." While in prison, Debs received over 900,000 votes as the Socialist Party candidate for president. He spent 32 months in prison until he received a pardon in 1921, at the age of 66 (Howard Zinn, *A People's History of the United States, 1492–Present,* 359).

NOTES

1 *Transcript,* March 10, 1898, 8.

2 Howard Zinn, *A People's History of the United States, 1492–Present, Revised and Updated* (New York: HarperCollins, 1995), 332..

3 *Transcript,* op. cit.

4 The party went through several name changes: initially the Social Democracy of America party, 1897; the Social Democratic Party of America, 1898; and the Socialist Party of America, 1901.

5 If Debs represented the anti-hero for the editors of the *Transcript,* then President McKinley was the hero writ large. To coincide with a visit to Adams, the newspaper published a poem in McKinley's honor by William Frederick White of Ashburnham, "Salutary to McKinley." It opens as follows:

> McKinley, McKinley is coming,
> McKinley the tried and the true,
> He is setting the spindles running;
> You'll find you've plenty to do.
>
> The cotton field loaded with harvest,
> The corn field full of the sheaves;
> The wheat fields filling the largest
> Of merchant fleets crossing the waves.
>
> "And who is McKinley?" you querry,
> A stranger I reckon you be;
> He's a comrade, citizen, soldier,
> He is bringing prosperity.

6 *Transcript,* July 19, 1895.

7 *Transcript,* September 3, 1897.

8 *Transcript,* October 18, 1897.

9 Henry F. Bedford, *Socialism and the Workers in Massachusetts, 1886–1912* (Amherst, MA: University of Massachusetts Press, 1966), 66.

10 *Transcript,* July 12, 1897 and Mar. 14, 1899.

11 Bedford, 42–43.

12 *Transcript,* August 25, 1896.

13 Bedford, 88.

14 *Transcript,* October 19, 1895.

15 *Transcript,* October 23, 1897.

16 *Transcript,* Oct. 8, 1897; Aug. 18, 1898; and Sept. 9, 1898.

17 *Transcript,* Sept. 10, 1898; Sept. 15, 1898; Sept. 16, 1898; and Oct. 27, 1898.

18 *Transcript,* Nov. 8 and Dec. 20, 1898. State-wide, Peare had 3.17 percent of the vote.

19 Bedford, 290–292.

CHAPTER SIX

THE END OF THE NINETEENTH CENTURY

School was . . . taught by nuns . . . . In the morning . . . you would have math, English, geography, and history. Then in the afternoon you had Canadian history . . . , Canadian grammar, reading and writing. They also had religion class, in French, all afternoon.

—Turn of the century curriculum in North Adams French Catholic school

Let [W.B. Plunkett] continue to build giant mills in Adams and bring presidents to lay the corner stones and dedicate them.

—*Transcript*, 1899

While this [Spanish-American War] expansion has been going on, adding new territory and population, there has also been great expansion in the commercial world; we in North Adams are realizing this in every sense of the word.

—North Adams Mayor Cady's introduction to President McKinley's speech in North Adams, 1899

SOCIAL LIFE, ETHNICITY AND LIVING CONDITIONS

The workplace and the union served as a basis of integration and solidarity, and, as earlier noted by the changing nature of the Labor Day observation, so did the ethnic group. One of the biggest groups to immigrate to North Berkshire was

French-speaking Catholics from Quebec. They had traveled there "not in quest of a higher standard of living but to avoid a lower." Part of a sizeable migration from French Canada, they left behind low-producing farms and land unable to support the growth of large families. By 1860, drawn by the lumbering and mill economy, 100 French Canadians lived in Adams. Their numbers grew to 1,650 by 1871 when a French pastor arrived to serve the region's parishioners. At the beginning of the twentieth century, French Canadians numbered 5,000, about a quarter of the local population. Most migrated from towns near Montreal, some answering the calls of recruiters who visited their villages and farms.[1] One descendant of a family that arrived in the Berkshires in 1902 could recall that "[t]he cotton and woolen mills were going full blast! There was a lot of work here . . . ."[2]

In Canada, many of the early immigrants worked as farmers or skilled craftsmen. In North Berkshire some continued to ply their trades, while others labored in the mills or on the railroad. As employees, "strike" and "layoff" became part of their new English vocabulary. They kept in touch with relatives back in Canada, often traveling back to visit. According to the 1870 census, eighty-three French-Canadian males worked in the shoe factories, including four between the ages of 10 and 14. Many of these workers may well have been members of the Knights of Saint Crispin who struck the Sampson shoe factory, leading to the importation of the young Chinese strikebreakers. "Laborer" described the occupation of sixty-four, including one not yet age 10 and four between the ages of 10 and 14. The third largest group, fifty-one, worked on the building of the Hoosac Tunnel, though Irish laborers, who migrated earlier to North Adams, easily outnumbered them there.

"Keeping House" proved to be the dominant female occupation. However in 1870, forty, including sixteen under the age of 15, worked in the cotton mills. Shoe factories employed eleven, including one girl not yet 13. Seven were listed as servants and six as woolen mill employees, including one between the age of 10 and 12.[3]

The French tended to live in the Greylock section of town, worked in the Greylock mill, worshipped at the French church across from the mill, and sent their children to the French school next to the church. Notre Dame, a second French church, larger and more ornate than the Greylock church, opened in 1888 at a cost of $70,000.[4] With its location on East Main Street, this church served a population closer to the city's downtown. Notre Dame's parishioners had settled in the Beaver section of town, and on Cliff, Minor, and Union Streets.[5]

For that first generation of French-Canadian immigrants, having space where they could live and pray in their native tongue remained a top priority. The importance of language and heritage can be seen by the following description of a local French elementary school:

> School was . . . taught by nuns . . . . You had to wear semi-uniforms, dark pants and white shirts for boys and girls had a uniform type, a jumper and blouse. In the morning, it would switch, one year you would have math, English, geography, and history. Then in the afternoon you had Canadian history, you had Canadian grammar, reading and writing. They also had religion class, in French, all afternoon.[6]

In 1848, the first known Catholic mass in town was celebrated by Irish parishioners; it was led by Father Jeremiah O'Callaghan, who had traveled to North Adams by horseback from Burlington, Vermont. By 1856, the Irish community had increased in size, enabling it to own its first church, on Center Street, a purchase from the Methodists. In 1863, Father Charles Lynch arrived in North Adams as the first Irish Catholic church pastor. Soon a new "proper church" was built thanks to "the labor of Irish workmen after their ten to twelve hour days in the mills and mines."[7]

In its 1880 report, the Labor Bureau investigated the "Social Life of Workingmen" throughout the state. By social life, they meant clubs and lodges, bands and choirs, libraries and lyceums, parks and recreational facilities, museums and theatres. It is unknown if any of the tunnel laborers participated in this social life, as the report offers no information on the background of participants. The fact that North Adams earned an "excellent" rating for its "social life"—in the top 4 percent of the more than 200 cities and towns responding—may suggest that the town had begun to develop a significant middle class, or at least elements of a solid and secure working class. The tunnelers, however, stood outside these strata.

Not all immigrant groups could be found working in the mills or tunnel. For the relatively small number of African-Americans who had emigrated from the South to North Adams, census records suggest that black men did not work in the mills until the second decade of the twentieth century. It is likely that discrimination played a role, with the first record of mill work not found until the 1920 census. In South County, however, in Lee, a photograph of Columbia Mill workers in 1885 does show two black employees among the workforce.[8]

Records exist of African-Americans settling in the White Oaks Glen section of Williamstown between 1781 and 1827.[9] According to census data, thirty-eight black residents lived in Adams as far back as 1850, a time when the North village was still part of Adams. That number increased to fifty-seven in 1870. In the 1880 census, the first one since North Adams separated from Adams, the African-American population of North Adams totaled thirty-nine. By 1900, that number had more than doubled to ninety-three. Women's occupations clustered around domestic service, and the men tended to work as laborers, teamsters, and barbers.[10]

While a few Jewish families resided in North Adams prior to 1880, migration increased from the 1880s into the first part of the twentieth century, as part of a huge wave from Russia and Eastern Europe. Many Jews who came to North Adams migrated from Vilna and surrounding areas of today's Lithuania.[11] By 1888, newspaper accounts reported that the immigrants had gathered together to celebrate High Holiday services, though not yet within a synagogue.[12] In 1890, twenty-five Jewish families lived in North Adams and, with a smaller number of Jewish families in Adams, they built their first synagogue, which opened in 1894. In Eastern Europe, facing pogroms and persecution, Jews had not been allowed to own land and many survived by peddling or operating small stores. As with all immigrant groups, a correspondence developed between the first arrivals and families and friends in the old country, bringing news of the new world and of prospects for work and survival. According to one historian, "Some of the early arrivals . . . sent back news that the area's mills and factories were booming and retail stores and markets were needed." And that early generation of Jews responded by starting small retail markets, selling shoes, groceries, furniture, and dry goods.[13]

The importance of recreation and sports has already been highlighted by the events of the Labor Day celebrations. In addition, the easy availability of hunting, fishing, swimming, and hiking in the Berkshires added to an abundance of outdoor activities. By 1886, interest in establishing a YMCA led to the organization purchasing the A.C. Houghton mansion in 1894. Needing more space and facilities, the YMCA constructed its own building in 1901 with a gym, bowling alley, and baths.[14]

Ethnic neighborhoods grew up around the mills and, for the most part, men and women walked to work, even to distant workplaces. Horse-drawn trolleys arrived in North Adams in 1886, but by the end of the decade electrical power replaced the horses. In 1904, the lines connected Adams, North Adams, and Williamstown, and extended to the mills located in the Beaver section of town and Clarksburg. The trolleys, which continued to expand throughout Berkshire County and into neighboring states, served as an important form of transportation, though they came to an end in the 1930s.[15]

EXPANSION AT HOME AND ABROAD

As mentioned earlier, with the closing of the nineteenth century, President William McKinley visited Adams to help William B. Plunkett celebrate the expansion of his textile empire, the opening of Mill No. 4 of the Berkshire Cotton Manufacturing Company. Sizeable crowds greeted the president in both Adams and North Adams, many probably also cheering America's expansion into the Caribbean (Cuba and Puerto Rico) and Asia (the Philippines). It is likely that few in that crowd had attended the huge banquet in Boston in February 1899, where President McKinley had spoken in celebration of the peace treaty with Spain after the United States had captured Cuba, Puerto Rico, and the Philippines. At the luxurious Boston event, 400 waiters served 2,000 diners in what was called "the biggest banquet in the nation's history.[16] William James, the Harvard philosopher, who helped to form the Anti-Imperialist League, wrote an angry letter to the *Boston Transcript* criticizing McKinley's speech and the massive killing of Filipinos. At another time, James had angrily proclaimed, "God damn the U.S. for its vile conduct in the Philippine Isles."[17]

By the late 1880s, shoemakers in North Berkshire had become more militant, striking at times, even though they hadn't formed official unions. Their employers, however, matched their militancy, having no hesitation in bringing in strikebreakers. A decade prior to McKinley's election in 1896, agitation by shoe workers led to a walkout by stitchers at Millard & Whitman. Two years later, Sampson Manufacturing Company lasters struck, and a year later "most of the North Adams stitchers and all of the town's cutters struck in two separate incidents." Moreover, American Federation of Labor (AFL) President Samuel Gompers sent the Federation's support to the stitchers, "an act that constituted the first union intervention in the Adams industry since the downfall of the Crispins."[18]

In 1893, George Chase brought in scabs from Boston to break a strike and, three years later, twenty-eight employees, including many "girls" in W.G. Cady's bottoming/finishing department, struck against a wage cut. John F. Tobin, general president of the Boot and Shoe Workers International Union, came to North Adams and spoke to a crowd of about 200 at the

Grand Army hall in mid-September 1898. Tobin's appearance points to the role of national organized labor and its connection with North Adams. According to the news account, in response to Tobin's talk, many workers signed up, hoping to form a local union.[19]

Within two years, the first unions of cutters and lasters did emerge, ending a twenty-year shoemaker union lull. In May of 1900, the cutters union struck Millard's in a wage protest, a strike that would continue until August. "N.L. Millard eventually appeared to secure a victory when he successfully employed scabs from Pittsfield, but the strike signified the new-found ability of the workers to unite and force a protracted dispute."[20]

The visit by President McKinley to North Adams on June 26, 1899, led to a sharp disagreement between local unions and the City Council. This controversy, however, had nothing to do with McKinley's wars or his domestic policy. In the 1880s and 1890s, local trade unions had been organizing and expanding, reflecting the national growth of the American Federation of Labor and the craft union movement. (The AFL, born in 1886, focused on organizing skilled workers, solely based on craft, such as carpenters, electricians, machinists, and masons.) Earlier, the City Council had discussed the appropriation of $400 for the presidential visit. The Council favored the allocation despite the fact that the city solicitor concluded that such an appropriation would be illegal. The Central Labor Union in North Adams, whose seventy delegates represented fourteen labor unions with a membership of 1,000, objected to the spending of public funds on the visit, also on the grounds that it would be illegal. But to emphasize the point that they supported President McKinley and wanted him to come to the city, the Central Labor Union contributed $25 of its own money to entertainment for the visit. Despite the union's position and a similar view by the *Transcript,* the Council voted a second time to use public funds.

Outside of criticism over the Council's action, a celebratory mood characterized the thousands attending the dedication ceremony in Adams and the parade in North Adams. The

Transcript, in referring to W.B. Plunkett, editorialized, "Let him continue to build giant mills in Adams and bring presidents to lay the corner stones and dedicate them." Mayor Cady, in introducing the president to the North Adams throng, praised the war McKinley so avidly pursued: "While this [Spanish-American War] expansion has been going on, adding new territory and population, there has also been great expansion in the commercial world; we in North Adams are realizing this in every sense of the word." The *Transcript* also printed lengthy excerpts from a local Congregationalist sermon the day before, which found biblical backing for the war. Support for military expansion and an accompanying jingoism increasingly characterized national public opinion. As the *Washington Post* editorialized:

> A new consciousness seems to have come upon us . . . and with it a new appetite, the yearning to show our strength . . . . Ambition, interest, land hunger, pride, the mere joy of fighting, whatever it may be, we are animated by a new sensation. We are face to face with a strange destiny. The taste of Empire is in the mouth of the people even as the taste of blood in the jungle . . . .[21]

On the whole, 1899 proved to be a very busy year for the local working class. In January, the North Adams Central Labor Union (CLU) appointed a committee to express its dissatisfaction to the Mayor for contracting work out on the new city "barn" in a manner *not* provided for by the charter. Also that month, the Barbers Union supported the idea of licensing barbers, the local Typographical Union voted to send money to help striking shoe workers in Marlborough, and the rank and file established a union at the Deerfield Valley Ice Co. The trustees of the public library received a petition from 160 North Adams Italian residents to place some books printed in their native tongue in the library.

Several examples will suffice to illustrate CLU activities through the remainder of the year, and remind us of organized labor's direct involvement in the political and social life of the city: in February, they endorsed the publication of the *Union Workman* in Springfield; in March they supported a City Council appropriation of $600 for summer open air concerts; in April they protested the introduction of a ten-hour day by contractors and supported the nine-hour day; and in May the CLU discussed the establishment of a permanent county organization for the celebration of Labor Day.

THE CENTURY ENDS

Warmer weather coincided with a rash of strikes in the region in 1899. In May, "pullers-over" at the N. L. Millard & Company shoe plant successfully struck over work and wages. In June, one group of carpenters had to strike to receive their back pay. An unsuccessful strike over wages occurred among women in the sewing room at the Blackinton mill during July. That same month, folders at the Arnold Print Works saw their strike end in compromise. In August the "boys" in the spinning and carding rooms from the Eclipse Mill struck for a wage increase for night work, and in December, they won one.

In August, carpenters successfully negotiated for the employment of union-only men in the construction of the new Richmond Hotel. A September entry in the 1900 *MBLS* annual volume carried the following interesting report on regional solidarity and labor discipline: "Central Labor Union adopted resolution of Typographical Union 316 relating to the *New York Sun*, and imposed fine of $2 on every member of CLU who purchased said paper . . . ."[22]

October saw the beginning of active work by the CLU in the political campaign. However, the next month the Lasters Union withdrew from the CLU because "that latter body brought political matters into the meeting, which is against principles of Lasters Union." Also, in November, a forty-seven-member Clerks Union organized and received a charter. On a "social note," W.C. Ellis dedicated his new shoe factory (originally built for F.J. Barber) with a dance for his employees and "about 250 of their friends."[23]

It must have been a good year for the Williamstown Manufacturing Co., as they increased wages for the second time in December. James Hunter Machine Co. bought land to build a new foundry and became a union shop, as requested by the New England delegate of the National Molders Associations. Minimum wages at Hunter also increased by twenty-five cents to $2.50 per day. Finally, local shoe cutters decided to re-affiliate with the general body of the Boot and Shoe Workers Union.

While one historian of nineteenth-century Berkshire County may have been correct about Adams in the early 1880s—"There were no capitalists in Adams"[24]—the economic and social reality of Victorian mansions and upper class lifestyles could not be ignored during the Gilded Age. As we have seen, a concentration of county elites could be found in North Berkshire, and by the end of the century they controlled significant textile holdings. They were household names—Blackinton, Arnold, Houghton, and Plunkett—and their economic and social power brought them political influence at the local and national levels. The North Berkshire press heralded their commercial accomplishments and the mayor of North Adams praised the confluence of local growth and national expansion.

Yet one needs to remember that during the same year, 1899, 41 of the city's very poor resided at what the North Adams Annual Report referred to as the "Almshouse," commonly called the "Poor Farm" or "Infirmary." A working farm inauspiciously located in Southview Cemetery, it remained a city institution until after World War II. At a time when federal relief aid remained in the distant future, those down on their luck—widows, the elderly, the disabled, and those just not able to find work—and who had no other place to turn to ended up at the "Almshouse."

If a capitalist class held sway in the region, a sizeable working class had emerged as well. Predominantly immigrant, the bulk of North Adams's 1900 population of 24,200 worshipped in the growing number of ethnically based Catholic churches. While adjusting to the industrialization of the area, local workers had demonstrated a value system that emphasized wage and hour equity for the same work, solidarity between workforces, a pride in their work and a reluctance to be deskilled, as well as a willingness to fight to maintain their employment and living standards, particularly if they felt the state of the economy warranted it.

They had their own leaders, some long since forgotten, some not, and formed their own unions, some local, some national, part of the American Federation of Labor. They had a good sense of local issues, but also responded to state and national events that affected them. They opposed child labor, and fought for wages that would allow them to keep their children in school, instead of sending them into the mills, and they agitated for a shorter work day. They used the strike and the threat of the strike to improve their status, and, when the strike option no longer existed, they tried to adapt by, for example, forming cooperatives.

By the turn of the century, two generations of unions, the Crispins and the Knights of Labor, had gone by the boards, and most of the unionization came under the auspices of the American Federation of Labor, with its craft unions of skilled workers. The local unions met as a central labor council where representatives considered matters of mutual concern and mapped out political strategy. Nationwide, the labor push for shorter hours and an eight-hour day still prevailed, a desire that would not only produce more leisure for workers, but provide more jobs for the unemployed. In 1899, the North Adams Central Labor Union proclaimed that "'lessening the hours of labor' was 'the only rational solution of this vital economic question.'"[25]

Organized labor had coalesced to meet the challenge of organized capitalism. It did so in a context, however, in which divisions within the working class could not be ignored. And so, while the Labor Day celebration of 1899 included the largest number of the region's workers ever at such an event, the day also saw local workers travel to diverse sites elsewhere that had been organized on the basis of skill, politics, and ethnicity.

Men outside the Wilson Drug Store (date unknown, North Adams Public Library).

Huge crowd to see and hear President William McKinley in Memorial Square, North Adams, on June 26, 1899 (North Adams Historical Society).

In 1897, President McKinley came to the Plunkett Park Street mansion in Adams for a one-week stay. In the photo above, left to right: W.B. Plunkett, C.T. Plunkett (standing), W.B.'s wife Lyda (sitting), President McKinley and his wife Ida Saxton McKinley. According to Eugene Michelenko, of the Adams Historical Society, the young women are nieces of Mrs. McKinley and daughters of the men above, right. "The standing men could be one of the following: Russell Alger, Secr. of War; John Long, Secr. of Navy; and Joseph McKenna, Atty. Gen. [T]hose are the men who the newspaper reported to be in Adams with the president." (Photo from Adams Historical Society)

NOTES

1 Phil Pugliese, *Transcript,* January 2, 1987.

2 Notre Dame Centennial, 6; Janet E. Roberts, *A History of the French Canadians in North Adams* (Williamstown, MA: Williams College, 1975), 23–24; Bethany Shears, *Berkshire County: Then and Now* (North Adams, MA: Massachusetts College of Liberal Arts).

3 Roberts, 69.

4 Lauren R. Stevens, "Groups Have Lived in Harmony," *Berkshires Week,* September 11, 1987.

5 Herschensohn and Reed Associates, *The Architectural Heritage of North Adams, Massachusetts,* Part I of the North Adams Historic Preservation Plan, Prepared for the North Adams Historical Commission (Ithaca, NY: Historic Preservation Planners, 1980), 20.

6 Shears, 2–3.

7 Phil Pugliese, *Transcript,* March 17, 1987.

8 David Levinson, editor, *African American Heritage in the Upper Housatonic Valley,* (Great Barrington, MA: Berkshire Publishing Group, 2006), 7. Growing up in Great Barrington, in South County in the 1870s and 1880s, W.E.B. Du Bois takes note of the following class, ethnic, and racial distinctions, stating "that most of the colored persons I saw . . . were poorer than the well-to-do whites . . . . None of the colored folk I knew were so poor, drunken and sloven as some of the lower class Americans and Irish." W.E.B. Du Bois, *The Autobiography of W.E.B. Du Bois: A Soliloquy on Viewing My Life from the Last Decade of Its First Century* (New York: International Publishers, 1968), 75. See also, David Levering Lewis, *W.E.B. Du Bois, Biography of a Race, 1868–1919* (New York: Henry Holt, 1993), Ch. 3.

9 Philip J. Pugliese Jr., *Transcript,* March 11, 1989.

10 Kailey Maloy, *Occupations of African-Americans in North Adams* (North Adams, MA: Massachusetts College of Liberal Arts, 2010).

11 Phil Pugliese, *Transcript,* August 15, 1987.

12 Carolyn Kaplan, *Congregation Beth Israel Centennial, 1995.*

13 Phil Pugliese, "Local Jews recall rich history," *Transcript,* August 15, 1987, 1,16. A second congregation, Chevra Chai Adom (known as the Ashland Street Shul) was established in 1909. The Jewish community started a Young Men's Hebrew Association (YMHA) in 1916, a center for sporting activities, and a Young Women's Hebrew Association in 1919. Other institutions that served the community included Hadassah, a Jewish Boy Scout Troop, and a chapter of the Jewish War Veterans. The two synagogues merged in 1958 and four years later dedicated a new building on Church Street. That structure served its members well for some forty years. In the 1980s and early 1990s, the Jewish community participated in the "city-wide celebration of ethnicity," La Festa (Kaplan, 23). As the

Jewish population declined, the synagogue was sold to Massachusetts College of Liberal Arts, but a new home for Congregation Beth Israel was completed in 2002 on the west side of North Adams, at the base of Mount Williams. See Carolyn Kaplan; Pink Horwitt, *Jews in Berkshire County* (Williamstown, MA: DOR Company, 1972); and Mark E. Rondeau, "North Adams Notes," *Advocate,* Oct. 24, 2001.

14 Rowe, H.G. and C.T. Fairchild, editors, *Index to North Adams and Vicinity Illustrated, 1898* (Pittsfield, MA: Berkshire Family History Association, 1995); *Old Home Week Souvenir.*

15 *Transcript,* Sesquicentennial edition, Nov. 19, 1993; Danielle Cassagio, *The Berkshire Street Railway* (North Adams, MA: Massachusetts College of Liberal Arts, 2009).

16 Howard Zinn, *A People's History of the United States 1492–Present, revised and updated edition* (New York: Harper Perennial, 1995), 307.

17 Ibid., 307.

18 *Transcript,* April 15, 1886, 4; January 1, 1885, 5; September 12, 1889, 4; and Matthew S. Bryson, *The North Adams shoe manufacturers: how they created a successful industry only to abandon it* (Williamstown, MA: Williams College, 1999), 115.

19 *Transcript,* July 12, 1891, 4 and December 8, 1896, 1; August 10, 1898, 5, and September 17, 1898, 8; Bryson, 115–116; *Transcript,* September 17, 1898, 9. There had been a press report that Gompers himself would speak in North Adams, but apparently he did not come.

20 *Transcript,* August 16, 1898 and Bryson, 116.

21 Zinn, 292.

22 MBSL 1900, 201.

23 Ibid., 227.

24 J.B. Beers, *History of Berkshire County, Massachusetts, with sketches of its prominent men, 1885* (Pittsfield, MA: Berkshire Family History Association, 1995), 469.

25 Alexander Keyssar, *Out of Work: The first century of unemployment in Massachusetts* (Cambridge, MA: Cambridge University Press, 1986), 196. Keyssar discusses several ways that unions tried to help with the reality of unemployment including the refusal of overtime, work sharing, and restricting production (185–191). Bryson, 46.

CHAPTER SEVEN

CLARENCE DARROW COMES TO TOWN

CLARENCE DARROW, probably the most well-known lawyer in the country, spoke at several venues in North Adams and Williamstown toward the end of 1925. He focused his attention on criminal law, though he had already earned a remarkable reputation as a labor lawyer and civil libertarian. Earlier in his career, Darrow had represented labor leaders like Eugene Debs and William "Big Bill" Haywood, and had recently argued the case for evolution at the Scopes "Monkey" trial in Dayton, Tennessee.

He gave his main address before a full house at Drury High School in North Adams as part of a lecture series sponsored by the Young Men's and Young Women's Hebrew Association. In a talk entitled "Heredity and Environment," Darrow focused on the latter, naming poverty as the leading cause of crime. He also made the case for improving early education as an antidote to the ignorance that also leads to crime. He castigated the penal system, stating that prisoners need treatment, not punishment. Opposed to capital punishment, he termed it "barbarous and cruel." Not without a sense of humor, the noted lawyer admitted that he had "never killed anyone but I have read a great number of obituary notices with much gratification."

Darrow also spoke at the city's Kiwanis Club and at Williams College. Expansive on his views of North Berkshire, the popular lawyer praised the *Transcript,* saying he was "greatly surprised to find a newspaper of its size and character" in such a small city. After spending some time with John Martin, clerk of the district court, Darrow called him "one of the best philosophers I have ever known." Darrow's most extensive compliments went to Rabbi Irving Miller, who was just completing his first year at Congregation House of Israel.

Miller, just 21 years of age and probably the country's youngest rabbi, had been the main proponent of the lecture series that brought Darrow to North Adams. He presided at the Drury talk, introducing Darrow as "a great legal light whose achievements will stand for a long time." In a lengthy article about a week after the lecture, the *Transcript* reported that "the young rabbi made so favorable an impression upon Mr. Darrow . . . that before his departure he discussed the question of a legal career with Rabbi Miller and made the proposal that he go to Chicago, enter law school there . . . arranging to remain with Mr. Darrow upon his matriculation." According to the newspaper, Rabbi Miller was in fact traveling to Chicago to meet with Darrow, but also stopping at Youngstown, Ohio, where he had been offered a position at "a large and important synagogue." As it turned out, though the rabbi "conferred for some time with Mr. Darrow" in Chicago, he ended up accepting the rabbinical position in Youngstown.[1]

1922 portrait of Clarence Darrow at the age of 65, three years before his visit to North Berkshire (Library of Congress).

NOTES

1 *Transcript,* December 8, 1925; December 16, 1925; December 28, 1925; and December 31, 1925. That same year, two of the country's most famous rabbis, Abba Hillel Silver and Stephen S. Wise, spoke before large crowds at Drury High School. Rabbi Silver lectured as part of the same forum series that had brought Clarence Darrow to North Adams, while Rabbi Wise—one of the leading orators in the U.S.—was invited by the Methodist Church Men's Club. Wise called for the U.S. to join the World Court and warned against the danger of Italian fascism, calling Mussolini "the most dangerous power in the world today." For Wise, the visit was his second to North Berkshire, having spoken at the Adams Congregational Church years earlier. "Little If Any Progress in Ideals In Modern Times Says Rabbi Silver," *Transcript,* December 22, 1925; "Rabbi Wise Wants U.S. in World Court; Holds Mussolini is Most Dangerous," *Transcript,* November 17, 1925.

CHAPTER EIGHT

LIFE AND WORK THROUGH THE 1920S

[C]onditions at North Adams are pretty much the same as at Lawrence . . . . Wages are low, too long hours are required, and the workers are ground by the mill owners.

—Victor I. Berger, Socialist member of Congress, Wisconsin

If conditions are as bad at North Adams as Mr. Berger says . . . I do not know anything about it.

— George P. Lawrence, member of Congress, Massachusetts

We are all 100 percent American and . . . strongly opposed to I.W.W.'s Bolsheviki and anarchists.

— Joseph R. White, United Textile Workers of America organizer, speaking in North Berkshire

THE ETHNIC MIX that typified North Adams at the turn of the century held constant during the first three decades of the 1900s. In fact, about 20 percent of its residents in 1930 had been born on foreign shores. North Berkshire's rapid population increase, largely bolstered by immigration, could be seen as a microcosm of the demographic changes in the state as a whole, with immigrants largely arriving from French Canada, Ireland, Italy, and Poland.[1] Ethnicity still helped to define neighborhood, church, club, and organizational membership. Men and women spent much of the day at their workplace, sometimes working different shifts, then one spelling the other at home taking care of the children.[2]

The Beaver mill, once a cotton mill and later the first home of Sprague Specialties, underwent a renovation by sculptor and developer Eric Rudd that was completed in 1990. The building now houses lofts, workspaces, and some retail establishments. Rudd, who lives there in a very large loft, comments on the original hard maple wood floor, a surface that shows numerous depressions:

> There's a big depression . . . where you can sink [your feet] right in. And that depression was there because somebody stood there, a number of people . . . probably six days a week, fifty two weeks a year, and they wore down the floor standing in front of a machine, working. So you have to respect the work that the people did in those mills. You also have to respect the construction to make those mills. They were all done by hand. Those gigantic mills, and all the brickwork and everything.[3]

While the local mills suffered a decline along with the rest of New England industry after World War I, factory work in textiles and other manufacturing still appeared to be plentiful in the first decade of the twentieth century. Under the leadership of A.C. Houghton, the Arnold Print Works remained the biggest and most influential textile operation in the area. Houghton had continued the integration of its operations, with corporate control over four mills supplying cotton cloth to the immense print works itself. In 1906, one historian described the print works as "one of the largest concerns in Massachusetts under single control, the leading establishment of its kind in the United States for variety and excellence of production . . . not surpassed in facilities or organization by any rival in Europe."[4]

After the popular Houghton ran unopposed for mayor, he decided to leave office after one term. Instead, he focused his attention on Arnold Print Works. In 1906, his company took in more than $9 million in sales, and Houghton himself managed the company from its New York City office.[5]

Not content with controlling the North Berkshire factories that produced the cloth and the mills that printed them, Houghton attempted to integrate his operation even further by trying to corner the market for the raw material he needed the most—cotton. He bought a huge shipment of cotton, which the *Transcript* characterized as "containing more raw cotton than could be found in all New England at the time." To do so, Houghton had to borrow a sizeable amount of money, a debt that entrapped him and Arnold Print Works the following year when the country fell into a financial panic or depression. Litigation and demands from creditors, even those who appeared to be friendly to APW, ensued over the next three years, and Houghton faced further embarrassment over failure to pay a city tax bill.

Finally, APW had to sell its local cotton mills, yet the company maintained the print works itself. Houghton's speculative attempt to increase the company's integration down the line to the control of the raw material itself ultimately led to the loss of his four feeder mills at home and the local integration that had served APW well for many years.[6]

Two of the four feeder mills were sold to a New Bedford group; the remaining two—one in North Pownal, Vermont, and the other in Williamstown—ended up in the hands of William B. Plunkett, who already owned the Greylock mill in North Adams and huge cotton mills in Adams.[7] This 1910 transaction could be seen as symbolizing the decline of the Houghton/APW empire and the expansion of the Plunkett empire, with its move further into North Berkshire and neighboring Vermont.

Despite the loss of his personal power, A.C. Houghton remained president of APW until he died in 1914. At the news of his death, the Arnold Print Works stopped work for that day; the *Transcript* referred to Houghton as "perhaps the most remarkable man that ever lived in North Adams." In his eulogy for Houghton, Franklin Carter, a past president of Williams College, worried that Houghton's contributions to the city might be forgotten as "cities are forgetful." To keep the memory alive of the man Carter called the "actual founder of North Adams," he ended his eulogy by proposing that a statue be erected in Houghton's honor.[8]

As Houghton had done previously, the Plunketts then moved to integrate their extensive operation by buying two cotton plantations in Mississippi in 1912.[9] These purchases brought better results for the Plunkett family than did Houghton's 1906 ill-fated attempt to corner the cotton market. In fact, for much of the twentieth century, the Plunketts would become the leading textile operatives in the region. They parlayed the mills they already owned into a 1929 merger, which established the Berkshire Fine Spinning Associates (BFSA), an entity that would expand their reach into eastern Massachusetts and Rhode Island. Then in 1955, BFSA merged with Hathaway Manufacturing Company, becoming Berkshire Hathaway. While some of the textile mills remained in operation, the decline of the New England textile industry continued, and soon the Plunkett family's reign would be over. (See Chapter Fourteen for a discussion of Berkshire Hathaway, the end of textile manufacturing, and the role of invester Warren Buffett.)

Although toward the end of the nineteenth-century textiles had advanced beyond the local boot and shoe industry in profitability, a new and soon-to-be growing shoe manufacturing company came on the scene in 1912. Originally called Wall, Streeter & Doyle, the firm was owned by partners who included James E. Wall, his brother Jeremiah, Edward Streeter, and Albert Doyle. By 1920, its work force of 164 employees was producing 1,000 pairs of shoes a day at the former Millard Shoe Company on Union Street. Five years later, retirements and buyouts left James Wall as the sole owner. Sales, which went directly to some 600 retail outlets, increased from just under $50,000 in 1913 to nearly $1 million in 1919.[10]

Wall, a hands-on owner, had a very anti-union reputation. (Not until more than half a century later when his son succeeded him did workers successfully vote in a union.) Low-wage Italian immigrants made up the bulk of James Wall's early employees.[11] At the Arnold Print Works, the discrimination toward Italians that had been prevalent in the late nineteenth century continued into the new century as they received few promotions and predominantly worked at manual jobs. The treatment that these workers faced at Wall and Arnold probably typified their treatment at other local workplaces, as Italians, the most recent immigrants, were likely to be supervised by Irish or French-Canadian foremen, members of immigrant groups that had arrived in North Adams earlier.[12] By 1910, Italians accounted for about one-sixth of the city's population. Many traced their roots to northern Italy or Tyrol, from the Austrian-Hungarian Empire. The latter tended to self-identify as Tyrolian, even though they had "Italian names" and spoke Italian.[13]

A much smaller immigrant group, African Americans, appeared to make small status gains as the new century enfolded. In the state as a whole, black men made up only 1.2 percent of the men in the labor force between the Civil War and the 1920s. According to the 1910 census, African American men in North Adams found work as railroad porters and as cooks, along with the more traditional employment role of general laborer. The same census listed one black merchant and one black clergyman. Black women, however, still found employment mostly as domestic servants and as laundresses.

By 1920, black men could be found working in the mills for the first time, particularly in the Arnold Print Works, likely reflecting the greater demand for cloth during World War I. In addition, individual African American men could now be found in the trades and in more prestigious occupations, including serving as a plumber, mechanic, railroad foreman, athletic trainer, horseman at a local club, head hotel bellman, and clergyman.[14] These findings seem consistent with employment data for the county as a whole with African American men working in the trades, factories, service, and hospitality industries.[15]

THE STRUGGLE TO REDUCE THE WORKWEEK

A desire to reduce the arduous workweek continued to motivate reformers nationwide. Reformist pressure in Massachusetts led the legislature to cut the maximum workweek to fifty-four hours from fifty-six, effective January 1, 1912. The new law specified the change for women and children, a population that dominated the textile industry.

Workers anticipated that the reduction in hours would not mean a proportionate decrease in pay. When, on January 11, a group of Polish women at the giant American Woolen Mill in Lawrence found out that their pay had been "shorted," they walked out. A two-month strike by tens of thousands of Lawrence workers followed, organized and mobilized by ethnicity, and led by the leaders of the Industrial Workers of the World (IWW), including Big Bill Haywood, Joseph Ettor, and Elizabeth Gurley Flynn. Unlike the dominant American Federation of Labor, which only organized skilled workers by trade, the IWW, or Wobblies, organized all workers throughout the industry, regardless of skill. Featuring banners proclaiming: "We Want Bread and Roses Too," the strike came to be called the "1912 Bread and Roses Strike," heralded as one of the most important strikes in U.S. history.

For one reporter, Ray Stannard Baker, it was the first time he heard strikers sing as they marched. Their favorite song, "The Internationale," began:

> Arise, ye prisoners of starvation! Arise, ye wretched of the earth, For justice thunders condemnation— A better world's in birth, No more tradition's chains shall bind us, Arise, ye slaves! No more in thrall! The earth shall rise on new foundations, We have been naught, we shall be all.

The strikers stayed united despite the opposition of the police and the militia, and, after two months of a cold winter, they won "significant wage increases."[16]

In North Adams, textile workers, facing the same issue as the women did in Lawrence, struck on January 12, the day after the first employees in Lawrence walked out. Sixty "girls," doffers, and winders at the Waterhouse & Howard mill located on Eagle Street, struck at noon; two hours later they "held an indignation meeting at the corner of Bank and Main streets." They were shorted for the two hours, and knew that their counterparts at the Braytonville and Briggsville mills were not. One spokesperson stated:

> We are all girls who have to work for a living. Some of us are supporting our mothers . . . but we talked it all over and decided to walk out in a body. . . . We may as well play for nothing as to work for nothing . . . . It isn't a sympathy strike. We have no union for we believed that the Waterhouse & Howard company would do what was right by us.

The strikers appeared willing to accept a compromise—"half a loaf would be better than none"—but John H. Waterhouse refused. By the next workday, all but three of the strikers had returned to work. Described by the local reporter as "affable," Waterhouse went on to say: "[T]he girls went out for a lark as much as anything else and after they had their holiday, they realized that we could not pay for work that was not done so they came back."[17]

Another strike, this one at the Hoosac Worsted Mills on January 20, proved to be short-lived. After only two days, fifty-seven of the sixty weavers who struck asked for and received their jobs back. In March, a strike of nearly 400 employees erupted at the Hoosac Cotton Company mill; another one occurred in April, that one at Arnold Print Works and Strong, Hewat & Company. Lacking local newspaper coverage, the results of these strikes are unclear.[18] However, with the Lawrence strike settled in March, mill owners throughout New England generally increased employee wages, and the wave of strikes diminished.[19]

Through the first three months of 1912, the *Transcript* gave significant coverage to the events in Lawrence, a strike of national significance. Feeling a bond with the economic struggles of the Lawrence strikers who also faced the militia's bayonets, North Berkshire workers invited representatives from Lawrence to speak at their meetings and raised money for their cause, which included benefit performances at North Adams's Empire Theater. There, fifty union musicians performed at two showings; all proceeds went to "the Destitute of Lawrence."[20]

In early March, IWW's Bill Haywood was scheduled to speak at Germania Hall in Adams, but he did not attend. A newspaper account wrote that the hall was "packed to the doors" for Haywood and that those who waited were "greatly disappointed" by his absence. "The audience waited for him patiently for two hours before dispersing and contributed a good sum of money to aid the strikers." The Adams socialists had sponsored the meeting, and a speaker "urged socialism as the only true way in which the workingmen will receive the just reward for their labor." The *Transcript* reporter wrote that "[h]is remarks were frequently applauded."[21]

Also in early March, at a Congressional committee investigating conditions in Lawrence, Representative Victor I. Berger of Wisconsin, the only socialist in Congress, spoke of the need to improve the status of textile workers in North Adams. Berger most likely mentioned North Adams because William Whitman, the president of the Arlington mills in Lawrence—the object of Berger's criticism—also owned Hoosac Cotton Mills in North Adams. Berger stated that "conditions at North Adams are pretty much the same as at Lawrence . . . . Wages are low, too long hours are required, and the workers are ground by the mill owners." Representative George P. Lawrence disagreed with Berger about the situation in North Adams and responded: "If conditions are as bad at North Adams as Mr. Berger says . . . I do not know anything about it. Of course, there is always room for improvement, and I hope the march of progress will continue, but conditions at North Adams are as good as they are anywhere on the map."[22]

At the end of World War I, the fight to reduce the workweek even further accelerated nationwide and in North Berkshire. In fact, in 1919, more than four million workers engaged in the greatest number of strikes in U.S. history. They represented 22 percent of the total workforce and a spectrum of occupations including police officers, steel workers, coal miners, telephone operators, clothing workers, shipyard workers, and textile operatives.[23] In North Berkshire, textile activism dominated.

"LOCAL WORKERS MARKING TIME" read the *Transcript* headline at the end of January 1919. The article began by noting that the eastern Massachusetts textile workers, notably in Lawrence and Lowell, were threatening to strike the following week unless their weekly hours were reduced from fifty-four to forty-eight *without* a reduction in pay. Further, textile operatives closer to the Berkshires, in Ludlow and Indian Orchard, had also joined the forty-eight-hour movement, a fact that "proved of interest to the workers in [North Adams] who are believed to be awaiting the outcome of efforts elsewhere before deciding on any definite stand."[24]

Mirroring the action seven years earlier, requesting a reduction in hours without a cut in pay, the strike began in Lawrence on February 3 when 47,000 immigrant workers walked out of their mills. They organized by ethnicity, one leader for each of twenty groups. The city and state aggressively responded to the strikers, even more so than they had in 1912. Lawrence's Mayor John Hurley brought in police from outside of the city and outlawed mass meetings. The police regularly attacked strikers, and two leaders were even kidnapped and beaten. The strike continued, but by mid-May the strikers had exhausted their funds and the mill owners desperately needed to restart production. They negotiated with the United Textile Workers, a union that had previously walked away from the strike, though not the strikers themselves, but agreed on a forty-eight hour workweek along with a 15 percent wage hike.[25]

Northern Berkshire textile workers benefitted by that

agreement as it became the new norm for state cotton and woolen employees. A sizeable front-page headline in the *Transcript* announced: "4,600 WORKERS GET BIG WAGE INCREASE," the amount agreed upon in eastern state mills. Unlike the Lawrence strikers, who had been out since the beginning of February, North Berkshire workers waited until April 30 to walk out. An organizer for the United Textile Workers of America, Joseph R. White (who would become a major figure in North Berkshire in the 1934 national textile strike), assumed leadership of the strike. Reflecting the anti-Communist rhetoric of the time, White proclaimed: "We are all 100 percent American and as such are strongly opposed to I.W.W.'s Bolsheviki and anarchists. American principles are what we intend following . . . and American principles are what will bring victory to our cause." White even added that while the strike commenced, no strikers would picket.[26]

A total of 600 workers at North Adams Manufacturing Company, Hoosac Worsted Mills Dept., and the Blackinton Company went out on strike first. About a week later on May 17, 235 Strong, Hewat & Company employees joined the walkout. That same day, the *Transcript* reported on a fund-raising dance for the strikers at the Odd Fellow's Hall; it also carried news that the North Adams Central Labor Union passed a resolution in favor of the textile strike, offering financial as well as moral support.[27] With the hours and wage resolution reached with strikers in the Eastern state mills by the end of May, a similar settlement greeted North Berkshire textile employees at the beginning of June.[28]

Not limited to the textile trade, labor activism during 1919 included a strike by Berkshire Street Railway trolley unionists; a strike by Williamstown telephone workers aided by a sympathetic walkout of linesmen; and a discussion by local police whether to join an American Federation of Labor union. Further textile activism erupted at the Berkshire and Renfrew mills in Adams where walkouts by the loomfixers and weavers calling for higher pay led to a six-week strike during the summer. Later in the year, Windsor Print Works employees struck after management fired four pro-union workers. The firings brought support for the strike by the 5,000-member Central Labor Union and by the United Textile Workers of America (UTWA). First vice-president of the UTWA, Thomas F. McMahon, came to the city to personalize his union's support. Responding to management's firing of four pro-union workers, McMahon stated that his union "will fight to see that 'real industrial democracy' prevails in this plant."[29]

REPRESSION OF LABOR AND THE RISE OF THE KU KLUX KLAN IN THE NORTH

Nationally, the government reacted to the great waves of strikes and anti-war sentiment with attacks on radicals, socialists, and the labor movement as a whole. In 1918, the Justice Department arrested the Socialist Party candidate for president, Eugene Debs, the most popular radical and labor leader of his day, for an anti-war speech that they termed "treasonous." In 1919 and 1920, President Wilson's Attorney General A. Mitchell Palmer, the enforcer of the Red Scare, ordered police raids on Communist and left-wing organizations, effectively shutting many down and even forcing some of the leadership into exile. Vigilantes fearlessly attacked IWW members while the federal government used sedition laws to harass, arrest, and repress the Wobblies. Racial hostility had also accelerated, leading to attacks on blacks in East St. Louis, Illinois (1917), and in Chicago (1919), that had resulted in the deaths of scores of African Americans and nearly two dozen whites.[30]

In 1920, the state of Massachusetts arrested Nicola Sacco and Bartolomeo Vanzetti and sentenced them to death "on the basis of flimsy circumstantial evidence."[31] One, a shoe worker and the other, a fish peddler, were, in reality, guilty only of being immigrants, anarchists, and union organizers. Despite appeals and huge, ongoing protests, both men were executed in 1927. Sacco sent a last note to his son, Dante, that read: "[R]emember always . . . in the play of happiness, don't you use all for yourself only . . . help the persecuted and victim because they are your better friends .... In this struggle of life you will find more and love and you will be loved." (Fifty years later, Massachusetts Governor Michael Dukakis received a report from his legal counsel that doubted the fairness of the trial. Dukakis then issued a proclamation detailing the prejudices and problems around the case and stated that "any disgrace should be forever removed from their names." The governor didn't offer a posthumous pardon as he had no power to grant one, but, more importantly, a pardon would have implied that the two men had been guilty.[32])

Union membership fell in the 1920s; inequality increased and working conditions declined. Anti-immigrant sentiment continued to grow, leading to a 1924 law that set quotas on immigration, severely limiting entry for Africans, Jews, and Catholics from southern and eastern Europe. Into this atmosphere, the Ku Klux Klan experienced an upsurge, particularly in the country's North and Midwest, with a particular animus toward Catholics. By 1924, the Klan's membership totaled four and a half million.[33]

The Klan actively recruited throughout New England in the 1920s, leading to violence, cross burnings, and numerous examples of anti-Catholic rhetoric. New England led the nation in foreign-born residents, and since most were Catholic—Irish, Italian, and French Canadian—they attracted the attention of the Klan. In 1926, in Massachusetts, Catholics outnumbered Jews by about eight to one and Congregationalists by about eleven to one. While instances of Klan attacks on Jews occurred, most Klan activity, again, was directed toward Catholics.[34]

Boston and Worcester became the centers of Klan activity, though smaller towns throughout the state were not immune. While the Klan could bring out large crowds of supporters and onlookers, protestors also emerged. For example, in September 1923, at a meeting of 2,500 Klan members at Mechanics and Washburn Halls in Worcester, some 25,000–30,000 protestors massed against them on Main Street. According to one newspaper report, they "confined their opposition to jeers and cat calls and the occasional dropping of stench bomb."[35]

Boston Mayor James Curley emerged as the leading political opposition figure, speaking out against the Klan and attempting to thwart their efforts to rent out space in Boston. The Legislature passed fairly weak resolutions against the Klan, like prohibiting the use of masks in public spaces. Grassroots groups, like *Les Vigilants*, most likely French-Canadian in makeup, developed to battle the Klan, who threatened to bomb and burn Catholic schools. In the summer of 1924, the KKK held meetings in Haverhill, Lancaster, and Spencer, all of which resulted in violence. Clashes with protestors involved sticks, stones, and bullets, leading to injuries and arrests. "In Lancaster alone 500 men and boys confronted 200 Klan members with sticks and stones and held them under siege for nine hours until the police were able to escort them away from their meeting place."[36]

While most of Klan activity occurred in central and eastern Massachusetts, the westernmost counties, including Berkshire County, saw burning crosses and Klan recruitment. One of the first instances of a group coming out against the Klan could be found in 1924 with a short article noting an anti-Klan resolution passed by the North Adams Kiwanis Club.[37] The following year, the *Transcript* reported a cross burning on the east side of town, off of John Street. Apparently further such cross burnings continued, and in October, several young men from Summer Street removed one burning cross and caught three men responsible for the fire. No mention of any Klan affiliation of the men appeared in the *Transcript.*[38]

Also in 1925, several contradictory articles appeared that reported allegations of a Klan organizer in North Adams. The first one, in March, headlined "KLAN ABANDONS EFFORTS IN CITY," named the organizer, C.O. Wrenn, and reported that he left the area after being exposed by the *Transcript.* The article also reported that crosses had been burned just over the city line in Clarksburg and numerous ones in Franklin County. In September, two articles appeared, alleging that an organizer, unnamed but a "well known Williamstown man," had enrolled

100 local members from Williamstown and North Adams, but without the presentation of any evidence or names.[39]

In October, North Adams residents were reported to be in attendance in a day-long meeting outside of Shelburne Falls, joining 500 Klan supporters who burned three large crosses, set off an aerial bomb, and launched a hot air balloon. Most of the Klansmen wore white robes, and the gathering appeared to be one of the largest in western Massachusetts. A similar assembly, on Whitcomb Summit, closer to North Adams, reportedly had happened a few days earlier.[40]

The following year, Klan activity in the area picked up with reports of gatherings and cross burnings in North Pownal and Pownal, Vermont; in Williamstown; on the Mohawk Trail; and in New Ashford. In all cases, the reporters noted the hometowns of the attendees, but without naming names.[41] The *Transcript* stated that an "alleged" KKK organizer had been working in North Adams for several months with two young assistants. Again, though, no names, or in this case, numbers, were mentioned. However, later that fall, three crosses were burned in separate parts of the city on the same night: in Kemp Park, in a pasture near North Eagle Street, and on a hill in Braytonville. The November 20 edition of the *Transcript* noted that the sermon to be given at the Cheshire Baptist Church the next day, Sunday, would be: "What I think of the KKK." Whether in response or not, opponents of the pastor's message burned two crosses in Cheshire the following month.[42]

The year 1925 appeared to be the peak year for the Klan in Massachusetts, with the final armed conflict between the hate group and its opponents in 1926. Activity in the North Adams area and in western Massachusetts also appeared to cease around the same time. The influence of the Klan dwindled, and the state exacted its own revenge on the rabidly anti-Catholic group by voting for the first Catholic presidential candidate, Democrat Al Smith, in 1928. While Smith barely beat Hoover statewide, carrying less than 51 percent of the vote, the Catholic Democrat won handily in Adams, with 60 percent of the vote, and in North Adams, with 57 percent.[43]

WORK AT THE END OF THE 1920S

While industrial work dominated the area, farming still remained an important occupation. Maurice Spitzer, a long-serving and well-respected doctor, grew up on a dairy farm and refers to the local dairy farmers and the vegetable farmers as "the mountain people." Both groups worked hard at tending cows and tilling the soil, then selling their goods wholesale, retail, and directly to households. Dr. Spitzer refers to the farming community as one of "three social classes" in North Adams, besides the factory workers and the "well-to-do."

At that time, the "gentry" still lived on Church Street, and had not yet made the move to Williamstown, which would later accelerate with the growth of Sprague. "Those were the days the owners set the wages, provided company housing, determined the working conditions, and in great part provided the leadership in the community," as Dr. Spitzer remembered. Of course, "[t]he factory workers and their families comprised the largest number of the population" and "[t]hese workers were known for their superior craftsmanship," whether it be, as Spitzer notes, shoes, fabrics, or biscuits.[44]

With a new decade on the horizon, North Adams boasted a diversity of industrial production from shoes, printing materials, textiles, and textile machinery, to rugs, brushes, boxes, bricks, biscuits, brass, neckties, and aluminum casting. Out of a three-story building by the railroad tracks on Ashland Street, the Clark Biscuit Company employed some 200 workers who produced cookies, crackers, and cakes. Its concentration of retail trade also served the North Berkshire region as a center for shopping. One commentator wrote of "a business boom" in North Adams toward the end of the decade, with night shifts added at Hoosac Worsted Mill and at Windsor Print Works, and increased shoe production at the Melanson plant.[45]

Workers had organized themselves into more than two dozen local unions, representing trades from barbering to yarn finishing. They included the traditional craft unions such as bricklayers, carpenters, cigar makers, electrical workers, molders, painters, plumbers, steamfitters, and tailors. At least seven distinct unions could be found in textiles and five in the shoe industry. Two different unions represented local railway workers, and a Pittsfield-based local served North Berkshire trolley employees. White-collar postal clerks had a union, as did local musicians, motion picture operators, theatrical stage employees, and newspaper typographers. Many had affiliations with the American Federation of Labor (AFL) and met regularly as part of the North Adams Central Labor Union (CLU). Working through the CLU, members of the trades fought hard for union hiring, boycotted non-union workplaces, and engaged in political action to defend their interests and those of working people in general. In 1940, when North Adams elected its first pro-labor mayor, Faxon Bowen, the CLU proved to be his biggest champion.[46]

The North Berkshire union demographics appeared to reflect that of the state as a whole, mostly with its emphasis on skilled craftsmen.[47] However, the increase in unionization among shoe workers, along with a significant number of textile employees, could also be seen in the state. Yet looking at the big picture, in the state as well as locally, the bulk of the less skilled workers, neglected by the AFL, did not belong to unions.[48]

In North Berkshire, the non-craft industrial workers who belonged to unions tended to be in relatively conservative locals that often disdained the strike weapon. To complicate matters, within any industrial plant a small number of skilled employees might belong to an AFL craft union and have little to do with the other workers. At the Arnold Print Works, for example, the printers and engravers had their own union, while the vast bulk of the less skilled employees belonged to the Calico Workers' Union #1, a weak organization. Although women made up a sizable portion of the local workforce, they comprised only about 20 percent of union members. More than 500-strong, the women unionists concentrated in seven textile locals. On the whole, given the diversity of small craft unions and the weakness of industrial unions, one would have to characterize regional labor in 1930 as relatively weak.[49]

Employees of the Boston Finishing Works (BFW), on Water Street, Williamstown, 1902 (Williamstown Historical Museum). Powered by the Green River, an earlier company began operation on the same site in 1873, manufacturing cotton twine. BFW took over the site in 1892 with a specialty in "finishing" cotton cloth which had yet to be processed. After BFW closed in 1906, the site was used to produce fabrics of corduroy and velvet. In 1930, production ceased, but began again with Cornish Wire's purchase of the buildings in 1936. From that year until 1960, Cornish produced electrical wire and cable, and became one of the biggest employers in Williamstown. In 1984, Carol Cable bought the property and continued operation until 1996. Now, the buildings have been converted to apartments for rent and sale ("History of Cable Mills," May 25, 2015; *Wikipedia).*

Sisters Maggie and Exhilda Lapan at Williamstown Manufacturing Company (Station Mill) loom, circa 1900 (Mike Miller, *Wikipedia,* Williamstown Historical Museum).

North Adams tradesmen at work (no date, North Adams Historical Society).

Improving the infrastructure in North Adams (no date, North Adams Historical Society).

Workers in the card room, the Plunketts' Berkshire Mills, Adams (Adams Historical Society).

Adams lime workers, circa 1920 (John Dickson and Will Garrison, Berkshire County Historical Society). The quarry in the town of Adams, close to the North Adams city line, is now owned by Specialty Minerals. Previous owners include Pfizer, New England Lime Quarry and Follet. The area is often simply referred to as the Adams lime quarry (https://www.mindat.org/loc-5980.html).

NOTES

1 Alexander Keyssar, *Out of Work: The first century of unemployment in Massachusetts* (Cambridge, MA: Cambridge University Press, 1986), 41.

2 "Oral History Project," Winter Study, January, 1984, North Adams State College.

3 From interview with Eric Rudd in *Farewell to Factory Towns?,* documentary written and directed by Maynard Seider, 2012.

4 Rollin Hillyer Cooke, editor, *Historic Homes and Institutions and Genealogical and Personal Memoirs of Berkshire County, Massachusetts* (New York: The Lewis Publishing Co., 1906), 206, quoted in Carol Lynn Cole, *Between Two Worlds: The Business Career of Albert C. Houghton* (Williamstown, MA: Williams College, 1991), 2–3.

5 Cole, 74, 76.

6 Cole, 76–89.

7 Ibid., 88–89.

8 Ibid., 1, 91.

9 See *Greenville (Mississippi) Weekly Democrat,* December 5, 1912, 4: "Hon. G. A. Wilson . . . has sold the well known Ashland plantation of 5000 acres . . . to a Massachusetts man named Plunkett for $190,000." Also see the *Choctaw Plaindealer,* of Ackerman, Mississippi, March 8, 1912, detailing an option to 4,528 acres of land to a Massachusetts corporation and trustee Charles T. Plunkett. This would be the Silver Creek Company (*Laurel Daily Argus,* January 8, 1912, of Mississippi). In a 1940 court case (McRae v. Ashland Plantation Co.), the court specifies that the three corporations involved—Ashland Plantation Company, Silver Creek Company, and the Berkshire Fine Spinning Associates—"had the same personnel on their boards of directors." Supreme Court of Mississippi, Division B., 187 Miss. 350 (Miss. 1940).

10 "Wall-Streeter," document (n.d.)

11 Jay Louis Nierenberg, *North Adams: New England Mill Town: A Political, Economic and Psychological Survey* (Williamstown, MA: Williams College, 1942), 132.

12 Dick Tavelli and John Hauck, *The Italians in North Adams: A History of their Cultural and Political Contributions* (Williamstown, MA: Williams College paper for Political Science and History, 1972), 19–20.

13 Phil Pugliese, *Transcript,* February 13, 1987.

14 Keyssar, 88; Kailey Maloy, *Occupations of African-Americans in North Adams* (North Adams, MA: Massachusetts College of Liberal Arts, 2010), 10.

15 David Levinson, editor, *African American Heritage in the Upper Housatonic Valley* (Great Barrington, MA: Berkshire Publishing Group, 2006), 7. As the title suggests, the Levinson book covers African American history

in the Berkshires as far north as Pittsfield. However, the Hart family of Williamstown is highlighted, including Henry Hart who started a trucking business and his daughter, Margaret Alexander Hart, "the first Black graduate of the North Adams Normal School, who went on to receive a master's degree from Teachers College, Columbia, and embarked on a distinguished teaching career" (62). The Hart family, along with the Todd, Porter, and other African American families, founded the African Methodist Episcopal Church located on Washington Avenue in North Adams. Interviewed by Philip J. Pugliese Jr., Margaret Hart affirmed that "the church gave the blacks a sense of community, as they gathered for church socials, church suppers and services. It also gave the blacks a sense of their traditions and cultures." *Transcript,* March 11, 1989.

16 James R. Green, *The World of the Worker: Labor in Twentieth Century America* (New York: Hill and Wang, 1980), 84–86.

17 *Transcript,* January 12, 1912; January 13, 1912; and January 15, 1912. An earlier article in the *Transcript* described a walkout by five employees at Braytonville's North Adams Manufacturing Co. mill. The mill's superintendent claimed that it was a dispute over money, and that the company had made no wage reduction for the shorter workweek. *Transcript,* January 9, 1912, 1.

18 *Transcript,* January 18, 19,20, 22; March 12, 13, 14, 15, 29, 1912.

19 Ibid., March 25; April 2, 1912.

20 *Transcript,* March 9 and March 11, 1912. Plans were also announced for a film benefit to be shown in the Adams Town Hall. *Transcript,* February 20, 1912, 1.

21 *Transcript,* March 2, 1912, 3. In another reference to socialism, Senator Mack of Berkshire sponsored a bill to provide food and clothing for poor children, but it received little support in the legislature. When Mack "defended his bill at length . . . Mr. Brown of Middlesex said the bill is a step toward socialism. Mr. Mack said if such legislation would make him a socialist he was proud of it." *Transcript,* March 28, 1912, 2.

22 *Transcript,* March 4, 1912, 2; Whitman was also president of four mills in New Bedford and one in Boston. *Boston Daily Globe,* Sept. 21, 1928.

23 Green, 93–99; Joshua Freeman, Nelson Lichtenstein et.al., *Who Built America?: Working People and the Nation's Economy, Politics, Culture & Society, Vol. Two* (New York: Pantheon, 1992), 258–267.

24 *Transcript,* January 29, 1919, 3.

25 "Lawrence Mill Workers strike against wage cuts, 1919," *Global Nonviolent Action Database.* nvdatabase.swarthmore.edu.

26 *Transcript,* May 21, 1919, 1; May 5, 1919, 1; May 6, 1919, 2. At the Adams Board of Trade dinner on April 8, 1919, the first speaker, Henry N. Teague, "landlord" of the Williamstown Greylock Hotel, mirrored the anti-communism of the labor leader Joseph White. Teague said, "Bolshevism and I.W.W. are the same thing. He believed that the three most effective agencies for successful reconstruction are the Catholic church, the

American federation of labor, and the attitude of the returned soldier." Then, going well beyond White into anti-Semitism, Teague noted that the leader of a labor strike in Seattle "was a Russian Jew who had been in America for only about eight months . . . [and] there should be action to prevent repetitions of such instances as this." *Transcript,* April 9, 1919, 8.

27 *Transcript,* May 5, 1919, 1; May 10, 1919, 2; May 17, 1919, 5, 10.

28 *Transcript,* May 21, 27 and 28, 1919. The future must have seemed bright for at least one local textile industrialist as Hoosac Worsted Mills planned a two-story addition to its factory, and additional employment for 600. *Transcript,* July 2, 1919.

29 *Transcript,* April 18, 1919, 14; September 20, 1919, 1; September 9, 1919, 2; August 19, 1919, 3; September 9, 1919, 6.

30 See Green, Chapters 3 and 4.

31 Green, 117.

32 Howard Zinn, *A People's History of the United States, 1492–Present,* revised and updated edition (New York: Harper, 1980, 1995), 367. https://en.wikipedia.org/wiki/Sacco_and_Vanzetti.

33 Zinn, 373.

34 Mark Paul Richard, *Not a Catholic Nation: The Ku Klux Klan Confronts New England in the 1920s* (Amherst: University of Massachusetts Press, 2015), 13.

35 Ibid., 93.

36 Ibid., 99, 111, 116.

37 *Transcript,* August 5, 1924, 5.

38 *Transcript,* July 15, October 20, 1925.

39 *Transcript,* March 27, September 17, September 23, 1925.

40 Ibid., October 13, 1925.

41 *Transcript,* May 5, May 25, July 17, July 28, August 7, August 19, December 26, 1926.

42 *Transcript,* April 28, November 26, November 20, December 20, 1926.

43 *Transcript,* November 7, 1928, 2, 6. The other five New England states voted for the Republican, Herbert Hoover.

44 Paper written by Dr. Spitzer for North Adams State College Social History class, 1984. Spitzer, who was born in 1902, describes his origins in North Berkshire as follows: "My parents came to this country from Russia, when they chose to exchange the hardships and humiliation of the Czarist Pogroms for the rocky soil of Florida Mountain in the Berkshires." They came toward the end of the nineteenth century and, without any farming experience, his father gradually cleared the land, bought some cows and, at the end of a lengthy process, "delivered milk to his customers every day." In his paper, Spitzer also wrote about the retail stores on Main and Eagle Streets, specializing in apparel, grocery, meat and fish. And "one chain

store—H.W. Woolworth, where no item was priced over 10 cents . . . ." Dr. Spitzer's wife, Mary, who worked in her husband's office and in numerous voluntary activities, became well-known for her work with the elderly. In recognition of those efforts, the Mary Spitzer Center was dedicated in 1975, and that same year she became the first recipient of the Carol Hell Memorial Award for community service. *Transcript*, March 17, 1984, 14.

45 *Boston Daily Globe*, Feb. 18, 1927.

46 Annual Report of the City of North Adams, 1933, 78, 80, 125; William Carney, *A Berkshire Sourcebook: the History, Geography and Major Landmarks of Berkshire, Massachusetts* (Pittsfield, MA: Junior League of Berkshire County, 1976), 163; and Nierenberg, Chapter 5.

47 A note on the return of striking weavers to the Norad mill in 1925 indicates, at least in this instance, the elitist view that some skilled workers displayed: the strikers said the pay schedule "for blanket weaving would not enable them to make as much as is paid a common laborer," but they also added that "the task of running two looms was an extremely difficult one." *Transcript*, Feb. 27, 1925.

48 Keyssar, 180.

49 Nierenberg, Chapters 7 and 8. Ethnic and religious differences also served to divide the workforce. Massachusetts Bureau of Statistics of Labor, 1926, 1921.

CHAPTER NINE

HARD TIMES IN NORTH BERKSHIRE

THE GREAT DEPRESSION reached its nadir in 1933 in North Berkshire and throughout the country. In their struggle to remain employed, local industrial workers changed jobs and occupations, and endured partial workweeks, temporary shut-downs, and pay cuts.[1] Younger couples moved in with their parents or in-laws, and some had to relocate elsewhere to find work. Stella Zawislak's sister moved to Albany, New York, "to do domestic work" in 1933 because "[t]here was no job in the Berkshires."[2]

For Arthur Paul Boucher, attending high school in the mid-1930s, it was a very bleak time. He lived in a condemned house and recalled:

> We had no windows, we had no heat. We had a little stove in the kitchen. My brother was stealin' electricity from the neighbors, so we could have a bulb in the kitchen. I was living with my father. He wasn't working . . . . He was a carpenter, but there was no work in those days, '29, '30, '31. One year was so bad, I went deer huntin', caught a deer, came home, and we cooked the deer with rotten tomatoes. That's what we ate all winter long. And we'd go down and steal coal behind the Windsor Print Works to keep warm.

The teenager sought work everywhere, but had no success:

> Once I went down to the city to get a snow job. The guy says to me, "Well, we can't give you a job 'cause your father owns a house." I says, "The goddam house that's condemned? What am I supposed to do, go home and eat the goddam house? Nobody's workin'. We haven't got any food, we haven't got any heat." And he says, "Sorry." That's the way it was in those times.[3]

Although Vera Uberti managed to find some work at Sprague Specialties, the times were "very rough" for her, too. Her mother had tuberculosis and lived in a sanitarium. Vera's paycheck barely covered the rent; her family was "charging" the groceries. She remembered:

> It was quite a long time before I got the grocery bill paid. Things weren't easy . . . . You ate a lot of hamburger . . . . You didn't have any frills . . . . You made do with what you had. So it was hard. . . . [F]or awhile there you didn't go to movies, or anything like that . . . . [Y]ou listened to the radio. You did a lot of reading. But it was rough for a long time . . . . [A] lot of people were out of work.

Phyllis Griswold remembered her father being unemployed before getting a WPA job. "[Y]ou made your own clothes and you grew your own food," she recalled.

Both women pointed out, though, that it seemed that everyone in the area shared the same problems.

A third woman, Ruth A. Bernardi, stated: "I don't remember them as Depression years. I mean we were all . . . sort of equal. Nobody had that much anyway. So we didn't feel as there was a depression."[4]

Bernie Auge, who grew up in the Greylock section of the city and lived in mill housing, remembers that his family ran up a bill at the company store and at a private grocer's for two and a half years during the Depression. Some eighty years later, he recalled that the bill totaled more than $115. Still, we were "fortunate to have a house and be able to eat . . . . We never missed a meal." It helped that the schools distributed free bread, and his father would go to City Hall to pick up surplus canned food. However, since the cans had no labels, you had no prior idea of what dinner would be.[5]

Despite these times of difficulty and even deprivation, the region's diverse industrial base helped many weather the 1930s. As one former teacher put it: "There were various industries here. [I]f there [had] been one industry . . . we'd have been down and out."[6]

Similarly, the local Italian community "generally worked through the depression of the 1930s without too much difficulty." According to two local researchers:

> The depression in North Adams was not so severe as it was in larger cities: the employment levels in stores and shops, in the two print works and Hunter Machine Shop, remained about the same as before, even though men who may have earned thirty-four dollars a week before were now earning eighteen a week, and sometimes had to put their whole family to work to be able to eat.[7]

A remarkable diary written in 1932 by a young Adams housewife provides day-by-day descriptions of life during that difficult year. Elsie Kleiner Koch writes of family issues, house cleaning, playing cards, and the enjoyment of movies. But money was tight, and work for her husband, Billy, in the paper mill was often infrequent. She added that Billy liked to fish and his successes helped the family, as did food from their garden.[8] The following excerpts from the diary focus on the layoffs and wage cuts from Billy's paper mill job:

> May 18: "Billy is out of work today until called for. The whole mill is down."

> June 5: "Billy is laid off until called for and then they have another 10% cut in wages."
>
> July 18: "Billy is not working yet. The mill hasn't been working very much at all lately."
>
> July 26: "They called for Billy to work from 3 to 11 today and we are so glad."
>
> September 14: "Billy just worked until noon & doesn't know when he will work again."
>
> December 1: "Billy didn't work much & they got another 10% cut starting Monday."

At the end of the diary, Elsie, by then pregnant with her first child, summarized and reflected on the year:

> I wonder what next year will bring Billy & I. This year brought us a lot of sorrow and sadness . . . . No work and no money. A 35% cut in his wages and hardly any work. I suppose we should be thankful that we still have each other. We have started a little one & perhaps after it is born things will be better for us. I hope so. If God is willing perhaps Billy, the little one & I will have some very happy years ahead of us. Billy certainly deserves happiness he is always helping me with my work. Helping his folks & my folks and also the folks downstairs.[9]

NOTES

1 Maynard Seider, "The CIO in Rural Massachusetts: Sprague Electric and North Adams, 1937–1944," *Historical Journal of Massachusetts* 22:1 (Winter 1994), 51–73.

2 On moving in with in-laws, see Florence Harris (May 16, 1988) and on leaving the Berkshires, see Stella Zawislak (May 18, 1988), both interviews from "Shifting Gears: The Changing Meaning of Work in Massachusetts, 1920–1980: North Adams, Massachusetts," Oral History Collection, University of Massachusetts, Lowell, Libraries, Lowell, MA (hereafter cited as "Shifting Gears").

3 Arthur Paul Boucher, quoted in Joe Manning, *Steeples: Sketches of North Adams* (Florence, MA: Flatiron Press, third edition, 2001), 192.

4 Vera Uberti (May 11, 1988); Phyllis Griswold (May 18, 1988); and Ruth A. Bernardi (May 19, 1988), "Shifting Gears."

5 Interview with author, October 15, 2016.

6 Interview dated January, 1984, Oral History Project, North Adams State College, Winter Study Term, 1984 (student project; notes in author's possession).

7 Dick Tavelli and John Hauck, *The Italians in North Adams: A History of their Cultural and Political Contributions* (Williamstown, MA: Williams College,1972), 21.

8 William C. Koch Jr., editor, *The Diary of Elsie Kleiner Koch: 1932* (JeanShadrack Publishing, 2008). The editor, Elsie's son, discovered the diary in 1984, after his mother died.

9 Ibid., 131.

CHAPTER TEN

THE GREAT DEPRESSION IN NORTH BERKSHIRE: CONTINUITY AND CHANGE

"Local self-sufficiency" is now merely a phrase in many places. The smaller units of government have frequently been unable to carry on, and they would have collapsed . . . if Washington and the state capitols had not come to their aid . . . . [T]he nation has been pulled out of the quicksands of despair which were pulling it down in 1931 and 1932. The remarkable surge in spirit is a cause for deep satisfaction and prayerful thanks.

—North Adams Mayor Archie Pratt,
quoting *Boston Herald* editorial

We have been living in a bosses' world, but we are building a workers' world now to plan our future destiny. Continue the fight until you win.

—Mary Hillyer, Amalgamated Clothing Workers union, at rally for striking Greylock workers in North Adams, 1934

AFTER A DROUGHT of over fifteen years without a formal North Berkshire Labor Day celebration, 1932 brought with it a colorful and well attended parade and firemen's muster. The week's entertainment centered on the muster, an early North Adams tradition, and an event that the local firemen won that year. Out-of-towners from all over New England and New York State descended on the city to partake in the muster, as well as movies, dances, concessions, a midway, and weekend ballgames.

> "True to the traditions of the old time firemen's events, several of the visiting organizations out for a good time, came early and stayed late. By Saturday night, a number of delegations were in town . . . . From then on there was no lack of hilarity, and while there were no disorders of a serious nature, it was fairly evident that stimulants were not difficult to obtain by those who wanted them."

While still referred to as Labor Day activities, there is no mention in the press of local workers or organized labor's participation, or of the rights of labor. However, there was a documented dispute between some city workers and the mayor during preparations for the week. Apparently, Mayor Johnson had originated the idea of the 1932 celebration, but he faced a setback when the project committee could not raise the necessary funds. Turning to city firemen and policemen to help out, he asked each of them to give a day's pay to help defray expenses. In what might be viewed as a gesture of labor solidarity, the city workers refused, "some taking the position that they would be willing to give a day's pay to charity but not to a fund which might be entirely absorbed by expenses, leaving nothing for charitable works."[1]

Despite the region's role as a railroad and trading center, the mountains surrounding the area limited access to other sizable communities in Massachusetts and neighboring states. This sense of isolation, and the reality of it, tended to bring with it a culture of self-sufficiency along with a skepticism—if not suspicion—of newer ideas. For the working class, this led to the formation of local, independent unions in the area's mills in which local organizers often kept outside national labor unions at bay. This perspective would be challenged by the national organizing drives of the 1930s.

Although life and work were never easy in the early decades of the twentieth century, the Great Depression became the first major crisis faced by the region and its residents. The economic collapse hit the area hard, resulting in shortened hours of work and reduced wages. Similar conditions plagued workers throughout the nation, of course, and social movements pressured the federal government to act, resulting in a variety of New Deal programs that helped to ease the pain of the Depression. That same activism led to legislation that guaranteed workers the right to form unions and collectively bargain.

A national textile strike in 1934 proved to be one harbinger of the new labor movement. The strike, which began in the South, quickly spread to New England. For three weeks, textile workers in North Adams and surrounding towns attended mass rallies, went on strike, organized in their mills, and made connections with each other in nearby workplaces. Although the national strike failed, it heightened the need for a new labor federation. In 1937, the birth of the Congress of Industrial Organizations (CIO) satisfied that need. Soon the CIO sponsored militant organizing campaigns that spread like wildfire through all branches of industry across the nation.

News of the New Deal programs, enacted during President Franklin D. Roosevelt's first two terms, reached the American people through radio, a new technological medium that broke through the relative isolation in North Berkshire and countless other rural communities in the United States. Roosevelt's famous "fireside chats" delivered a new version of an activist government to a population that had become used to a "national ideology . . . [of] laissez-faire economics and rugged individualism, and . . . [a] federal government . . . small in scope and ambition."[2]

Coincidentally, at the same time, a company built on the production of capacitors used in the commercial use of radios had set up shop in an abandoned textile mill in North Adams. Sprague Specialties (later to be renamed Sprague Electric Company) left its cramped quarters in Quincy, Massachusetts, and began to manufacture capacitors in the Beaver mill by the north branch of the Hoosic River. The company and its employees struggled during the Depression years, but World

War II orders boosted Sprague's growth in the 1940s, and postwar military, aerospace, and commercial orders combined to make the company the world's leading producer of capacitors by the 1950s. At its height, Sprague employed 4,137 workers in North Adams alone.[3]

During the 1930s, however, textile mills dominated the North Berkshire landscape. As the decade began, some 5,000 residents worked in those mills. The new economic, political, and technological forces unleashed in the 1930s first impacted the textile industry and its thousands of employees. The increased activism from the national government and a revitalized labor movement played an important role in determining how local residents would make it through the 1930s, breaking through the region's relative isolation. In their pioneering 1937 study, *Middletown in Transition: A Study in Cultural Conflicts*, sociologists Robert S. Lynd and Helen Merrell Lynd concluded that in Muncie, Indiana, "events outside the control of" the community became "[t]he major impetus" in understanding the social changes its residents underwent in the 1930s.[4] A similar finding could have been reached for North Adams.

This chapter focuses on how similar outside forces, unleashed by the Depression, affected North Berkshire, and how this previously isolated region underwent change in a deep and long-term way. The story of how North Adams and its populace dealt with and survived that decade must not only address the national forces that the Lynds highlighted, but also recognize the power of the local traditions and institutions that city residents had developed over the years. By the decade's end, North Adams adapted just in time for additional winds of change to envelop the area as a result of World War II. Since textiles served as the key area of employment in the region during the first forty years of the twentieth century, a focus on that industry helps shine light on the most important forces that impacted life in the 1930s.[5]

North Berkshire attained a population of about 43,000 by 1930. The three largest communities—North Adams (21,621), Adams (12,697), and Williamstown (3,900)—accounted for

89 percent of the total.[6] In North Adams, 20 percent of the population had been born in foreign lands, and in Adams, 24 percent. Ethnically, the Irish, French Canadians, and Italians dominated in North Adams. Next door, in Adams, Poles made up the largest ethnic group, having migrated in great numbers at the turn of the century to work in the Plunkett mills in that town.[7]

HOPE AND THE NEW DEAL

President Franklin Roosevelt's New Deal programs did make an impact in North Adams and North Berkshire, creating jobs, improving the area's infrastructure and environment, and providing relief for many in need. The legislation included aid to families in need, protection for union organizing, and Social Security. The Civilian Conservation Corps (CCC) and the Works Progress Administration (WPA) comprised two of the most important New Deal jobs programs.

The CCC employed more than three million young men who planted trees; constructed roads, campgrounds and sewerage systems; built fire towers; and brought phone service and electricity to rural America. CCC youth in North Adams excavated trails to the top of Mount Greylock, built Bascom Lodge on its summit, and constructed the Thunderbolt Ski Trail to the valley below, among other improvements. Outside of the city, another CCC contingent opened up the Savoy State Forest for recreation by building pathways, constructing log cabins, and erecting dams for water recreation.[8]

The WPA, an even larger program than the CCC, employed eight and a half million men and women across the country who built thousands of schools, airports, bridges, playgrounds, and a host of other community projects. The WPA also employed artists who painted public murals and crafted public art installations like sculptures and reliefs; actors and theater personnel who presented plays; and writers who produced guidebooks covering all of the states. WPA projects proved to be vital in North Adams during the Depression. Hundreds of unemployed men and women joined the workforce repairing and enhancing the city's infrastructure, planting trees, providing free school lunches, sewing clothes, and bringing nursing care to homebound residents. The artistic legacy of the New Deal can be viewed today in the lobby of the North Adams Post Office, where a 1942 sculpture by Louis Slobodkin stands, depicting a family man leaving his wife and child behind as he heads off to a distant mill, while a second sculpture shows men digging in what would become the Hoosac Tunnel.[9]

Beyond the material aid that the New Deal programs provided, a fresh way of looking at the national government that moved beyond self-sufficiency, seemed to be taking hold. As early as 1934, that perspective could be seen in Mayor Archie Pratt's annual address. After expressing gratitude for federal assistance which provided jobs "at fair wages" for the unemployed, he concluded his remarks with a lengthy quote from the *Boston Herald*, which he noted was "a conservative Republican newspaper." Beginning with the huge changes the country had experienced since the inauguration of FDR, the paper editorialized:

> "Local self-sufficiency" is now merely a phrase in many places. The smaller units of government have frequently been unable to carry on, and they would have collapsed . . . if Washington and the state capitols had not come to their aid. We have seen the rapid growth of a belief, strange to this country but not novel to Europe, that society owes everybody a living . . . . At least, the nation has been pulled out of the quicksands of despair which were pulling it down in 1931 and 1932. The remarkable surge in spirit is a cause for deep satisfaction and prayerful thanks.[10]

Although New Deal programs certainly helped, hardship still characterized life in Northern Berkshire. The North Adams annual reports help document the difficult times, even amidst the positive federal programs. The 1933 report put it in stark terms: "Like all other cities and towns throughout the country, North Adams had many of its inhabitants out of work [and] in a great many cases, in dire need." The city engineer described a state-funded program of street repair and the work that the previously unemployed men, many mill workers, performed. These men worked hard, with "blistered hands, aches and pains" and "stuck through the job from beginning to end." Data from the city's dental clinic for 1932 clearly indicates the nutritional problems faced by the children and the absence of preventive care for too many North Adams youngsters. Of the 404 children that the dentists examined, 89 percent had "defective teeth," and 19 percent of the total had "permanent teeth extracted." That is, one out of five second graders needed false teeth, or else they would sport one or more gaps in their mouth, with more attendant problems.[11]

In his annual address of 1935, Mayor William Johnson declared:

> "We confront a new order of things. We have to plan to carry on with less. Welfare is the great problem we have to solve. We must provide food, clothing and shelter for the unfortunate victims of the depression, people who are in need and going to be in need. No man knows the time when the call for aid will cease."[12]

At a time when Social Security and decent pensions remained a future hope, destitute individuals and families had only charity to turn to, or they would have to live in the city's "poor farm," officially called the "city infirmary." The 1937 annual report from the Commissioner of Public Welfare sounded sympathetic to the status of the 679 families (representing 2,674 persons) aided in 1936, "people, who through no fault of their own, were obliged to apply for aid because of unemployment and decreased resources." The report added that "physically able" heads of families were expected to work, presumably on a WPA project.[13]

THE BERKSHIRE FINE SPINNING ASSOCIATES AND THE GREYLOCK MILL

In North Berkshire during the Depression, local mills ran the gamut of woolen and cotton goods-related manufacturing, from the processing of raw materials to the fine printing of fabric. Woolen mills could be found in three different neighborhoods: Strong, Hewat & Company with 250 employees in Briggsville; the Blackinton Woolen Company with a work force of 175 in North Adams; and the Norad mill with 250 employees in Braytonville. (Norad had re-opened in 1934 after obtaining government loans from the Reconstruction Finance Corporation of the federal government.)

Most local employees worked in cotton mills and received lower wages than woolen workers. The Plunketts of Adams owned half a dozen local mills within the Berkshire Cotton Manufacturing Company, as well as 11,000 acres of cotton land in Mississippi.[14] While local workers might still refer to the mill they worked in by its neighborhood name (e.g., Greylock mill), more and more of these mills had fallen victim to the corporate takeover, then called a holding company operation. In 1929, the Plunketts themselves sold their sizeable holdings to one such outfit, the Berkshire Fine Spinning Associates. The BFSA now controlled thirteen factories in southern New England, including the four mills in Adams, the Greylock mill in North Adams, one mill in Williamstown, and a factory just over the Vermont border in North Pownal. While the local mills had already been integrated through Plunkett ownership, the wider consolidation of BFSA expanded the geographic connections and, in one ironic consequence, helped make it possible for thousands of mill workers in three states to participate in one of the more significant local and national strikes of the first half of the 1930s.

The BFSA, with a local labor force of between 3,000 and 4,000, manufactured light fabrics, or cotton "lawns," a first step before being printed locally at the Arnold and Windsor Print Works. The three-story brick Greylock mill stood on State Road and Protection (as in tariff protection) Avenue, where it dominated the south side of the street. Its predominantly French-Canadian mill workers rented tenements from the company on Taft Street, Dew Street, Protection Avenue, and State Road—all of which were near the plant. For the rent of two dollars a week, workers got a toilet, no bathtub, and a kitchen stove that provided the only heat for the house. Decades later, Bernie Auge remembered loading up on blankets to keep warm in the winter.[15]

The paternalistic owners allowed their employees to grow food in garden plots behind the mill and to charge their provisions at the company store during hard times. As Bernie recalled, "You bought your coal from the company. The grocery was there. They found out how much you made, and you had about twenty cents left over." Each mill had its own baseball team, and the friendly competition that ensued brought some good times to the hard-working employees.[16]

Workers worshipped at the Holy Family Church across from the mill; their children attended the school there, with English lessons in the morning and French in the afternoon, taught by the Sisters of St. Ann. It was a time when residents lived in ethnic neighborhoods near the mills where they worked. One long-time Greylock resident couldn't recall leaving his neighborhood until he enrolled in high school.[17]

Cotton manufacturing at the Greylock mill began in the cotton shed in the back, where workers cleaned the debris from bales of raw cotton with picker machines. Face masks were essential in order to avoid inhaling dust and lint from the cotton fibers. Next, carding machines untangled and aligned the fibers, making them ready for skilled speeder tenders. As future labor leader Rene Ouellette recalls:

> I was a speeder tender, making the thread. Yarn is put on a bobbin; it goes from a good size to a smaller size, to an even smaller size. It was a good job, and then if you wanted to [make] a good week's pay, you had to work overtime. I

> was making $31 a week, but after the strike I was making $17. You couldn't make it go.[18]

In the mule room, where the largest number of employees toiled, the workers spun the yarns into stronger, twisted threads on large frames (mules). The steam from the humidifiers kept the cotton damp and pliable, but produced an uncomfortable, tropical-like environment. Men went without shirts and often without shoes or socks to better endure the oppressive heat and humidity. In the slasher room, employees starched spun cotton to prepare it for the weaver. Highly skilled weavers, paid by piecework, operated the huge, noisy power looms.[19]

The production clock on each loom registered the weaver's total count. The loom fixers, all male, formed another group of highly skilled and highly paid employees. At Greylock and elsewhere, they organized their own separate union. They had joined the American Federation of Textile Operatives in 1915, and prior to 1934, they stood as the only unionized sector of the Greylock workforce. Their participation could make or break a strike, since the mill couldn't operate without them.

When the whistle blew to signal the end of the workday, each employee had to clean his or her own work area—at no extra pay. It took a subsequent strike for the workers to win paid clean-up time. Like most other mills, it sometimes remained closed for weeks when business slowed down, leaving employees with no work and no benefits. However, the relatively unskilled workers received very low wages regardless of the speed of business.

In 1936, Frank Kryston began work at Greylock as a janitor, cleaning and sweeping in the mule room. He recalls that his wages "were $10.40 a week, and we were shut down for three months through the holidays. The mill attic was full of stored cloth while they waited for a good price." Yet memories of the mill proved to be positive as well. According to Nicholas Thores, a plant supervisor who worked his way up to management from an "unskilled" status, "Greylock was a friendly mill, and we got along well with local union members."[20]

THE NATIONAL TEXTILE STRIKE OF 1934

Throughout the early 1930s the textile industry nationwide suffered from serious problems. Manufacturing had already shifted from the Northeast to the South in search of cheaper labor. By then, mill owners blamed their poor sales on foreign competition and increased wage demands. In addition, overproduction led to lower prices, mill closings, and unemployment.[21]

The textile industry was not, of course, the only Depression-era industry facing difficult circumstances. In an attempt to stabilize American industry and increase employment, President Roosevelt sent one of his key New Deal pieces of legislation, the National Industrial Recovery Act (NIRA), to Congress on May 17, 1933. The act, though very controversial, gave business leaders the right to work together and set "codes of fair competition" and avoid "destructive . . . price cutting." For labor leaders, Section 7(a) gave workers government protection to unionize and collectively bargain with their employers for the first time.[22]

Specifics of the NIRA set minimum wages ($13 a week in the North and $12 in the South) for cotton textile workers, mandated a forty-hour workweek, and ended child labor in the mills. Despite the law, textile industrialists continued to increase the notorious "stretch-out," the process of assigning individual workers more and more machines to tend, even as many as ten, and ignored many of the law's provisions, including Section 7(a). In pushing the stretch-out, employers deliberately violated the executive order "to prevent improper speeding up of work to the disadvantage of employees."[23]

By the time the national United Textile Workers of America (UTWA), an AFL affiliate, met in convention in August 1934, labor leaders and workers, whose hopes had been raised by the NIRA but dashed by employer opposition, proved ready to act. The 500 delegates of the UTWA from textile mills across the country voted to strike. Two of the delegates included

Adams local #1711 President Lucy Giroux and Secretary Delia Raymond, who represented "several hundred" employees of the Adams mills, part of the much larger Berkshire Fine Spinning Associates.[24] On the eve of Labor Day weekend, September 1, 1934, the UTWA proclaimed a national strike. The local North Adams newspaper reported the situation as follows:

> They called out 425,000 cotton workers and 100,000 wool and worsted workers from 1500 mills in 21 states, most of them in the eastern part of the country. A number of mill owners saw no support for the strike and said that the "code" had helped workers by providing more and continuous employment. Owners disliked the term "stretch-out" and would prefer to call their policy "specialization," which lightens the work load and increases wages.[25]

Support for the national strike began locally in the four big Adams mills owned by Berkshire Fine Spinning Associates (BFSA). Of the 2,900 cotton workers in Adams, only a few hundred belonged to the United Textile Workers union. However, 400 employees belonged to their own local union of Polish workers, the Textile Workers of Adams. Poles made up a significant segment of the immigrant community in Adams, and they formed a cohesive workforce in the Plunkett cotton mills. Some 1,400 Poles immigrated to Adams from 1895 to 1905, many coming directly from the Galicia region of Austrian Poland, and others from communities already in the United States, like Chicopee and New Bedford, Massachusetts. While it remains unclear whether representatives of Plunkett recruited the prospective textile workers from Europe, many—like other immigrant groups that came to the United States both before and after—heard of the availability of work in Adams from friends and relatives. For Plunkett, they represented a low-wage, hard-working workforce, one more immigrant group that hoped the reality would match their dreams in the "New World." They worked from fifty-four to sixty hours a week in the cotton mills, but received relatively low wages, laboring in the lowest paid industry in the country.[26]

Nearly thirty years earlier, in 1905, skilled Polish weavers had formed a union, "one of the largest unions ever organized in town." Some of the English-speaking Polish weavers who already belonged to a mixed weavers' union helped their compatriots with the procedures necessary to start their own organization. Composed of some 300 members, the Polish weavers joined the Adams Central Labor Union. They successfully won a wage increase and combined with representatives of the other nationalities—English, French, and German—in striking for better conditions in the mill.[27] The Polish union remained strong while some of the other unions in the plant weakened. An historian of the Polish workforce in Adams concluded that "because of its strong ties of nationality and community, [the Polish union] had succeeded in establishing a strong labor organization. . . . Despite their low wages, the Poles had built a strong financial basis for their union in a remarkably short time."[28]

The Plunkett mills had experienced increased labor-management conflict in the 1920s, a time of growing competition in the national textile industry. The Adams workers had struck twice—in 1923 and 1926. Although the union lost the first strike, the second brought a victory. In June of 1926, the company increased the pace of work, reducing the number of women on a given job from three to two. The women struck, and a week later 2,000 employees engaged in the sympathy strike. The company responded with a lockout, the union with a picket line, and the mill found itself with too few willing workers to reopen the plant. Finally, management gave in and went back to employing a full complement of three women on the job in question. The union helped support its members during that strike with more than $10,000 in strike benefits, and its membership numbers subsequently increased to 1,100.[29]

By 1934, the Polish weavers and employees in the Adams cotton mills had already built a strong foundation of solidarity and activism. Unlike the BFSA workers in neighboring North Adams and Williamstown who lacked a union, their colleagues in Adams had a small loomfixers' union, a UTWA affiliate union, and an independent Polish workers' union—the Textile Workers of Adams—that had about 400 members. Not surprisingly, then, the call to heed the national strike drew an initial answer first in Adams.[30]

While the low wages and conditions in the Adams mills clearly energized the union workers, their ethnicity proved to be the glue or power that bound them together. In examining the Polish union over time, historian Keith Melder defines it as a "Polish organization rather than a group of laborers." As members of the largest ethnic group in Adams, the Polish mill workers had a history of union struggle, but they lived, shopped, and worshipped in vibrant ethnic institutions. With a strong cultural foundation in the huge, ornate St. Stanislaus Church, the Polish community supported a parochial school, which opened in 1913, and a wide array of Polish associations and societies, including a veterans' group, a charity, and boys' and girls' clubs. Further, Polish residents could shop in numerous Polish-run retail stores and, before long, could be served by a Polish professional class. The first Polish selectman, elected in 1933, heralded the increased political power that the Adams Polish community would enjoy. If the history of the Polish union and the strong Polish communal institutions helps to explain why the walkout emanated from Adams, the absence of unionized cotton textile workers in North Adams, Clarksburg, and Williamstown suggests at least one key factor for their initial quiescence.[31]

At a mass Labor Day rally on the Valley Street grounds in Adams, UTWA long-time organizer Joseph R. White spoke before a crowd of approximately 1,000. The three local Adams unions had already met to endorse the strike. A prototype of the fiery 1930s labor leader, White directly appealed to the rank and file. Based in Cohoes, New York, he had responsibility for organizing in the Albany, New York, and North Berkshire areas. A UTWA national vice president, White represented the leadership that would break from the more conservative American Federation of Labor (AFL) in 1935 to form the militant Committee for Industrial Organizations, which became the Congress of Industrial Organizations (CIO) in 1937. Unlike the far older AFL, which organized by individual crafts, the CIO organized across an entire industry and included in a single union local the majority of workers in a factory, mill, or business. The organizing strategy of the CIO meant that their potential membership would include the vast bulk of the "so-called" unskilled workers, bringing in recent immigrants, African Americans, Catholics, and Jews.[32]

White, who had just arrived from Washington where he had participated in pre-strike meetings with other national leaders, informed his audience that the textile owners had responded to the federal code by cutting the workforce and increasing the stretch-out. He told them that workers who operated twenty looms in 1929 now cared for forty and even sixty looms. "And there have been no improvements in the looms. They are the same that were used in 1929 . . . with the result that workers are sent into tuberculosis, starvation, and death."[33]

White not only spoke of the national situation to the crowd, but also seemed well-informed on Adams's politics. He defiantly responded to a request by the town selectmen for workers to remain at work: "Well, as soon as the selectmen start to tell you what to do, it's time to stand up and tell these politicians what they need to do. . . . [W]e will know who our friends are and what to do when they come up for election in the spring." White concluded his oration by turning back to the national scene:

> I hope you people are not going to disappoint the old South. The South is out on strike now. We are trying to get this through for you because if we get a 30 hour week it will mean four weeks' work a month and four pay envelopes a month instead of only three. This is the time to get it and if you stick together you can get it.[34]

Fred Major, a leader of Local No. 1717, also addressed the crowd, as did Fred Hish of the same local. The latter spoke in Polish, making sure all of those assembled got the main points of White's talk and stayed "united."[35]

Nationally and regionally, events moved quickly. Several states in the South called out their National Guard to maintain order after an increase in violence and the deaths of several workers. By the second day, 360,000 textile workers across the South and North had joined the strike. The United Textile Workers union refused to consider arbitration until all mills nationwide had shut down. Regionally, all the Fall River mills, including the BFSA affiliates, had been idled, and, in New Bedford, 14,000 workers had closed twenty-five mills.

In Adams, the strike gained immediate success. Three hundred unionized picketers met the 1,700 morning shift employees at the BFSA plants at the six o'clock starting bell. Only two dozen or so workers crossed the lines, thus forcing the company to close down about an hour later. As for the afternoon shift, "When workers began arriving on Columbia and Hoosac streets . . . there were about 1,000 assembled and automobiles lined both sides of Hoosac street as far as Mill street and on Columbia street to Valley street from McKinley square. *Not a single employe[e] entered the mill and the power was not started.*"[36]

A well-organized workers' committee divided the pickets into groups of about twenty-five, each under the direction of a captain. A twenty-four hour a day strike headquarters operated on Spring Street at the former Hermann Hall. According to the *Transcript,* "Representatives of the employe[e]s who remained away from work today expressed themselves as much pleased with the manner in which the general strike began in Adams."[37]

In the afternoon, Joseph White spoke to 400 strikers, who enjoyed accordion music along with White's oratory. White had already met with 500 workers in Cohoes, New York, and had plans to be in Easthampton, Massachusetts later in the day.[38] As it turned out, the plants in Adams had been the only ones in the BFSA chain to be shut down on the first day of the strike; work went on not only in North Adams and Williamstown, but also in the affiliated mills in Brattleboro, eastern Massachusetts, and Rhode Island.

THE STRIKE SPREADS LOCALLY

Locally, the strike spread quickly. By the end of the week, BFSA mill workers in North Adams and in Williamstown walked off their jobs. During the supper hour on the day following the initial Adams strike, over 100 Adams unionists, men and women alike, came to Greylock to picket and talk to their fellow workers about the strike. (A *Transcript* photo, headlined: "PICKETING AT GREYLOCK MILL SUCCEEDS," pictured a line of more than a dozen women pickets with a leading placard stating: "WE ALL ARE ONE.") As was the custom, a delegation of four workers had previously informed the North Adams police chief, Michael W. Conlon, of their intentions.

The pickets moved steadily up and down before the mill carrying placards that urged fellow employees to join them, and this invitation was verbally extended to some of the Greylock help who came out of the mill during the supper hour. When the machinery started to turn again for the evening operations after the supper hour, a number of the force failed to go back in, while in the next half hour others came out by twos and threes. By 7:45 p.m., operations had been seriously crippled and the plant shut down, turning out the remainder of the night shift of approximately 250 people.[39]

The next day, picketing at Greylock began before 6:00 a.m., with only fifteen to thirty of the 250-member day shift crossing the line. Within ten minutes, even those holdouts had to leave, as the company simply shut the plant down. In an ominous note, North Adams Public Welfare Commissioner James B. Ruane stated that voluntary strikers at Greylock would be ineligible for city relief. At a BFSA plant in Warren, Rhode Island, local readers learned that fellow workers faced tear gas and police clubs as the strike there turned ugly. Nonetheless, local union officials began recruiting unaffiliated Greylock employees, and over 200 paid the one dollar membership fee to enroll in the growing union.[40]

Worker solidarity in the neighborhood emerged during this period as well, reflecting nationwide struggles of activists to protect the homes of workers and the unemployed.[41] In early September 1934, Strong, Hewat & Company attempted to auction off its mill housing in the Briggsville section of Clarksburg. In an article headlined "STRONG COMMUNITY SPIRIT IS SHOWN," a reporter described how a group of tenants, all of English background, formed their own corporation (the Co-operative Home Plan) to buy a twelve-tenement building. The local community used its power to pressure the auctioneer to reward local residents with housing at the right price.

"The assembled crowd took an active and vociferous interest in the proceedings and cries of 'sell it' were directed at the auctioneer in many cases where the occupant of the house had bid what the crowd considered a sufficient sum for the property." In one case a woman was bidding against a North Adams man for the home she occupied. The bidding started at $3,000, and as the price increased, the woman weakened in her decision to buy it. Finally, she made an offer of $4,300, and "the shouts of 'sell it' were so strong that the auctioneer stated his doubt of the advisability of any further bidding . . . and sold her the house at this price." The protests apparently continued throughout the day and, as it turned out, only four of the twenty pieces of property went to people living outside of Briggsville.[42] Community solidarity clearly overlapped with labor solidarity.

On Thursday, just three days after the Labor Day rally that had attracted 1,000, an enthusiastic crowd that now reached 2,000 filled the Valley Street grounds. Following a mini-concert by local musicians, and with the aid of an amplifying system, Joseph White reported to the gathering that the mills in Utica and Fall River had been shut down by the strikers. Then the UTWA vice president and regional organizer exhorted the crowd to "keep the Flying Brigade in action until every mill in North Adams is closed." Josephine Kaczor, from the Amalgamated Clothing Workers of America, spoke to the crowd in Polish.

Like White, she drew applause, interrupting her speech, as she commended the local strikers on their "courage," labeling the growing national strike "one of the grandest in history."[43]

That same evening, between 220 and 250 strikers from Adams and Greylock traveled to Williamstown, where they met their fellow BFSA workers at the Greylock "B" mill during their supper hour. According to the local reporter about half "shuffled up and down the sidewalk in front of the Cole avenue gate while the others walked the backyards lying between Mill and Arnold streets where many of the mill employe[e]s have homes." Replicating the pattern at the North Adams Greylock plant the night before, very few of the roughly 250-member night shift returned after the break, and the mill closed down.

The next morning, although a quarter of the 100-employee day shift crossed the picket line, management simply shut the mill down. The caption under a *Transcript* photo headlined "ADAMS PICKETS CLOSE WILLIAMSTOWN MILL" reads as follows:

> Photo shows scene at gate of Williamstown mill, varying emotions of indecision, determination, confusion and apprehension being registered by the expressions and attitudes of those leaving their work for a period, the length of which no one knows while the pickets, who do not appear in the picture, are keeping up their march.[44]

The following day, as the local strikes continued, Joseph White once again addressed an open-air mass rally of some 400 at a field near the Greylock mill. Standing on the back of a truck in the middle of the field, White spoke through an amplifying system, telling the crowd that he was "gratified to see the workers out in Greylock in view of his inability to organize them two years ago." With the cotton workers virtually all out in support of the strike, he saw the next task as one of enlisting local woolen and print workers to the cause, a unified effort that would bring stability to the industry and decent hours and wages to all textile workers. Using the popular term for groups of strikers moving from mill to mill to spread the strike, White expressed hope that "your flying squadron will go to Blackinton and Briggsville so as to have the woolen workers join in this great cause which means the stabilization of industry . . . and that can be done only by collective action." He also stated that "we want to know if the employe[e]s of local print works are with us or against us." White concluded by invoking what he called the Biblical reminder that "God helps those who help themselves."[45]

In the course of his address, White reserved his harshest words for the North Adams welfare commissioner, James Ruane, who had threatened the withholding of city aid from striking workers. White called Ruane "the first understrapper, the first small city official who has had the audacity to tell the people who employ and support him that they will not get anything if they do not agree with his policy and scab." White warned that if Ruane followed through on his threats, the mayor would be asked to fire him. If the mayor refused, White called on the voters to remove the mayor.

Mary Hillyer, a representative of the Amalgamated Clothing Workers union from Troy, New York, assailed the industry's treatment of workers over the previous few years. She called on the strikers to build good unions to "keep their employers in line and be sure of proper treatment for themselves." She concluded by exhorting the crowd to go on to greater victories: "We have been living in a bosses' world but we are building a workers' world now to plan our future destiny. Continue the fight until you win."[46]

It had been a good week for North Berkshire strike supporters. In a matter of only three days, some 4,000 local textile workers had joined the national strike. While not producing a yard of cloth, they filled their week with mass rallies, picketing, meetings, and discussions. In an atmosphere of increasing solidarity, the local workforce had discovered the power of its numbers and determination, as they forced the shutdown of one mill after another. Although beginning with a relatively small base of experienced, unionized workers, North Berkshire residents responded with enthusiasm to national events and local needs. Clearly energized by the thousands across the South and Northeast who had walked out, and spearheaded by the militant Adams textile workers who initiated the local strike, non-unionized workers in neighboring North Adams and Williamstown proved receptive to the presence and arguments of the "flying squadrons," which had become a common and very effective tactic locally and nationally. An historian of the national strike notes that "the initial success of the strikers' flying squadrons in shutting down mills, especially in the Carolinas and Georgia, gave the public ample reasons to be impressed by the UTWA's apparent formidability."[47]

A great deal had been accomplished by Friday, and with a new week not far ahead, it seemed like a good time to take stock and plan for the future. According to strike leaders, the local union membership drive had progressed nicely, with 75 percent of the Greylock mill workers already enrolled, and with plans to revive their old local. Discussion of possibly forming a new local in Williamstown continued, and a recruiting squad of two men and three women headed to that town to organize workers there. Local flying squadrons prepared to travel to the woolen mills in North Berkshire and to some of the textile mills in Brattleboro (BFSA owned) and to Pittsfield as well. With the closing of the Williamstown mill, the Hoosac mill on Union Street in North Adams remained the only local cotton mill in operation. The mill's legal receivership status kept its owners from directly running the business and also made it illegal to picket or interfere there. So while the flying squadrons stayed away, the *Transcript* reported that "personal visits had been made over the week-end to some of the mill's employees and the strike situation was discussed during the supper hour," resulting in about a quarter of the weavers walking out.[48]

The whole issue of outside help, of mobile flying squadrons, had filled the local press. It had been reported, for example, that city officials in Lawrence had barricaded their highways to keep outside strikers from entering the city. The Adams strikers had already served notice to the Pittsfield police chief of their intentions, and a *Transcript* reporter wondered in print if they would be stopped. UTWA Vice President White had an interesting perspective on the squadrons, one perhaps reflecting the geographical organizational divisions within his union. He had no problem with strikers from Adams traveling to Pittsfield, but as to reports of a Fitchburg squadron coming to North Adams, that possible event he would protest, as they would be entering "his territory." White "thought the union organization in the local territory was taking care of its own situation satisfactorily from labor's standpoint, since it had closed all the cotton mills in Northern Berkshire with one exception and plans were under way to attack the woolen mill angle and to invade Pittsfield."[49]

WOOLEN MILL WORKERS REFUSE TO STRIKE

Local woolen mills, however, remained in operation despite the call for a national strike. Joseph White encouraged the North Berkshire cotton mill strikers to bring their "flying squadron . . . to the Blackinton and Briggsville woolen mills and induce their workers to join in the general strike."[50] In response to the plans to widen the local strike, the Strong, Hewat & Company office in Briggsville, a section of Clarksburg, affirmed that they would be open on Monday and that "(w)e welcome a showdown." The company statement added that its "wages are the highest in the industry," and that "[t]here is general contentment among our workers," who "are not interested in the least in the strike movement." Indeed, this may very well have been the case. The hesitancy of the woolen workers to join the strike undoubtedly reflected their higher status and pay as compared to cotton workers. But they also feared for their jobs because at the same time that the company trumpeted their high wages, management announced a downturn in business. The decline meant, they explained, that only 80 instead of 150 workers would be needed for work on Monday.[51]

With the national strike into its second week, the number of idled textile workers had climbed to over 409,000. Violence had spread from the South into New England, and several states asked for federal troop intervention. In Honea Path, South Carolina, private guards shot and killed seven mill picketers. In Saylesville, Rhode Island, thousands of strikers trying to close down their mill battled state troopers, resulting in 132 injuries.[52] North Berkshire residents surely knew of the physical dangers of striking. The local press covered the national scene and, for example, a photo of state troopers firing tear gas appeared in the *Transcript* on September 12, 1934, under the headline: "THREE SHOT IN RHODE ISLAND TEXTILE STRIKE RIOT."

Monday arrived and fifty Adams strikers responded to Strong, Hewat's challenge by traveling to Briggsville. Unintimidated by "squads of police patrolmen appear[ing] on Church Street, taking up stations on the main approaches to the city from the south," the contingent from Adams crossed the city line. The Strong, Hewat employees spent much of the day not working, but rather meeting amongst themselves to discuss the strike and to voice their intentions. The weave shop employees began the discussions, but workers from the picker room and dye shop, the only other departments on the clock that morning, joined them. Although no union existed at Strong, Hewat, departmental committee members regularly represented the employees.[53] But, since only a reduced workforce attended the meeting, the participants decided to call in all the workers and vote again that afternoon. The full group (reported by the *Transcript* to be "the highest paid woolen workers in New England") did meet, but they voted 129–116 to oppose a strike.[54]

In contrast, after hearing an argument from an Adams striker, the company's sixty weavers decided not to return to work. They felt that the vote underrepresented "the mill's real workers" since the election had included "some people who had not worked for six months and some girls who had been working only for the summer." While refusing to work, they nonetheless "assured Mr. Hewat that they had no complaints or grievances against the mill or its management but felt that they ought to

from Adams to Cohoes, N.Y., Joseph White's hometown, to offer their help for possible picket duty. That same day, the *Transcript* printed a declaration from the eleven-member Adams strike committee, a response to the national manufacturers' refusal to accept an arbitrated settlement to the strike. Time and again in their statement, the workers compared their situation to that of the slaves in the South:

> [T]he manufacturers have invaded the rights of the workingman so deeply that they do not wish to give up their usurped ownership of the working man's right to a decent living without a bitter battle. Just as in the days of slavery the slave owners would not give up their rights to the slaves' freedom without a civil war . . . . Now will we be crushed? Will we go back 150 years and become slaves like the colored men of the South used to be? No. This strike is a strike not only to prevent future strikes but to prevent something worse than a strike. We are now fighting for a right to live as human beings are fit to live. This is not a battle of revenge but a battle for a decent living.

The strike committee had words of praise for Francis J. Gorman, the UTWA's national president, who had proclaimed that both President Roosevelt and the UTWA (unlike the textile manufacturers) did "that which was right and constitutional." Gorman criticized the manufacturers' violation of worker rights to "free speech, free picket and free public expression of our rights as given by the constitution." He also deplored the fact that workers did not have the right to work. In the words of the Adams strike committee:

> [W]hy in God's world were not we given that right during the depression? And why in God's world again do they as our bread givers, if we call them that, throw many good men and women upon pauper lists because of their so-

> called efficiency or stretch out? And where in God's world is there a law or principle which gives us the right to starve or commit slow suicide?

In contrast to the greed and selfishness of mill owners, the strike committee promoted a different ethic of the working class: "[We] working men will justly say that there is a law and principle that says 'Thou shalt not starve thyself nor permit thy neighbor to starve.' And that is why we are fighting to avoid this slow starvation in this land of plenty."[60]

At around the same time, a second candidate for the northern Berkshire district seat in the state legislature, Edmund R. St. John, spoke to members of Local 43 of the UTWA. He highlighted his strong record in support of workers and criticized two of his opponents in the upcoming primary, and argued that he had the best chance of defeating the Republican incumbent. St. John then reminded his audience of his background in organized labor as a member of the International Brotherhood of Electrical Workers. He asserted: "[S]trikes and walkouts are not new to me. I have been in both and have been chairman of a strike which cost me a job . . . . I am telling you about myself to show that my love for labor was not acquired with my desire to run for office."[61]

A few days later, in one final burst of militancy, "a crowd of cheering marchers" picketed the Berkshire Woolen and Wyandotte mills in Pittsfield where workers walked out. Albert Sprague Coolidge, a Harvard professor and Socialist candidate for U.S. Senate, addressed the crowd. He then traveled to North Adams where, that evening, at an outdoor meeting at Monument Square, Coolidge discussed the principles of socialism, and pointed out the vital differences between his party and the Democratic Party, a strong supporter of capitalism. "All that has increased under the NRA," he said, "[are] the profits of the big corporations." The candidate then "called upon the workers to unite and build up a strong, clean and independent party which should be able to win control of the government to make and carry out the laws which will be necessary to make the Socialist plan a reality."[62]

President Roosevelt had appointed Governor John G. Winant of New Hampshire to chair a three-person board to study and make recommendations for industry and labor, but the mill owners refused the board's offer to arbitrate the strike issues. It quickly became clear that the board would have no power beyond recommendations. With the national strike at a standstill and not expanding, the UTWA responded to an appeal from President Roosevelt and called off the national strike.[63]

The following day, Joseph White once again addressed the local strikers at their headquarters in Adams. He discussed the terms of the settlement, declaring it a "big victory" for the workers who are "vindicated and received everything they contended for." In reality, although the agreement made it more difficult for employers to increase employee workloads, on the critical issues of wages and benefits, the strikers achieved no gains. On the whole, the three-week strike failed to improve the material conditions of the country's textile workers.[64]

In North Berkshire, after a full month of disruption, work began again on Monday, October 1, with the local unions trying to augment the assistance that the strapped local workers needed. In Adams, the union asked merchants and others for commodities and cash contributions for a relief fund. A benefit show for the fund was held at the Atlas Theatre in Adams. In North Adams, about forty Greylock mill workers—in addition to those on welfare—received federally funded employment through the Emergency Relief Administration. Looking to the future with hope, the new union president at the Greylock mill, Henry Risch, scheduled a Sunday afternoon meeting to discuss issues about the formation of the new local.[65]

On the day the strike ended, the *Transcript* closed its coverage of it with a final attempt at healing, albeit with a "wishful thinking" paragraph:

> Particular efforts were made by the idle hands and their leaders, by mill management and by public authorities in all the Northern

> Berkshire communities to avoid irritations and conflict and consequently in this section the tie-up of production was marked by none of the incidents that occurred in other sections and it was possible for the mills to re-open and the workers to return in this vicinity today with no special local problems and no bitter local issues to be met.[66]

Using the same concept—"bitter" but employed—in a more realistic vein, a leading historian of the national strike concluded that "[t]he great strike of September 1934 left no heritage beyond bitter memories." Another historian simply called it a "full-fledged calamity for the cause of textile unionism."[67]

1935: LOCAL TEXTILE WORKERS STRIKE ON THEIR OWN

Despite the widespread activism and solidarity throughout the Northeast and South, textile industrialists held firm, and the National Recovery Administration's promises to aid workers didn't materialize. Nationally, the leadership of the United Textile Workers of America suffered a huge loss of prestige by the strike's failure. Locals expressed less confidence in the UTWA. The following year, North Berkshire workers would refuse outside union intervention during a three-month strike that began, this time, at the Greylock mill in North Adams.

Depression-era work remained slack, and in April 1935 the Greylock mill had been shut down for several weeks. The company offered to reopen the mill, but with significant wage reductions, as high as 50 percent. In a secret ballot, 450 workers voted against the reduction, while only twenty-five voted to accept it. At that time, somewhere between half and three-quarters of the 500 person workforce had been unionized. Despite the vote rejection, the company stood firm on its offer and the local newspaper headlined "GREYLOCK STRIKE LOOMS; MILL LIQUIDATION."[68]

The rank and file at the Greylock mill had elected Rene Ouellette as president of the United Textile Workers local. As Ouellette later recalled, "We went out on strike because they were going to put more work on everyone. Some workers thought unions were no good; some didn't want to pay out money for dues."[69] Dues, in fact, were very low: one dollar for joining. Faced with a weak treasury, the local tried to raise money by selling beer at dances for twenty cents a glass. This was illegal, however, and the police enforced the regulation. Nonetheless, the local union continued to hold fund-raising dances.

At the same time, in an attempt to present a united front to management, union members from throughout the Berkshire Fine Spinning chain in North Berkshire and Fall River, Massachusetts, and from the Rhode Island plants in Anthony, Albion, and Warren, had came together to form the Berkshire Textile Council. The Council held its meetings in Springfield, Massachusetts, and elected Greylock's Rene Ouellette as president. Born in Fall River where his family ran a boarding house for mill workers, Ouellette moved with his family to Utica, New York and then North Adams, where they had relatives. In 1917, at the age of 14, he went to City Hall to obtain his working papers, an act he clearly remembered almost seventy years later. He began working at Greylock, where he remained into the 1930s. By the time of his election to the local's presidency, he had eighteen years of seniority. Physically strong and outspoken, he must have been a very popular co-worker.[70]

Union organizers struggled to obtain strike support throughout the month of May. Craft unions and older skilled loom weavers opposed the strike, and division among the 2,900 employees in Adams soon became obvious. On May 17, the Textile Workers of Adams, an independent union of Polish workers, voted 400 to 40 to return to work. Even though a previous mass meeting for all Adams workers had rejected that offer, the Polish union stood as the largest—bigger than the total membership of the three local UTWA unions. More significantly, about two-thirds of all the Adams employees belonged to no union at all.[71] Additional bad news arrived from the Fall River and Rhode Island plants where, despite previous promises to strike, workers remained on the job.

The UTWA's national leadership demanded that all old wage rates must be restored or there would be a national strike. Local unions, however, refused any national intervention. Rene Ouellette recalled telling the UTWA representative, "Stay the hell away. When we need you, we will call you."[72] Locals now preferred to handle their own problems with management, since the national leadership had failed in obtaining benefits from the 1934 strike.

In one last attempt at broad-based solidarity, on June 3, the Berkshire Textile Council issued a strike call in two days if the old wages had not been restored. Unfortunately, at the same time, Loomfixers Local 43 in Adams voted to return to work. The company used both the carrot and the stick to gain that objective. They agreed to cut the loomfixers' wages by "only" a dollar a week, and they also threatened to physically remove the looms out of one of the Adams mills. With that vote, the loomfixers broke a large chunk of the regional textile solidarity.

In the meantime, the Fine Spinning workers had reached the ninth week of efforts to regain their old wage rates. Management promised to reopen the mills even if a strike became official. Everyone was feeling the economic pressure of being out of work for so long. Community pressure added to the wavering support of employees for the cause. Ouellette remembers the advice that the priest gave parishioners at the Holy Family Church, the French church, in the Greylock neighborhood: "The priest told us, 'Half a loaf is better than none.'"[73]

Still, at a mass meeting of union members, local officials continued to plan a strike if the mills dared to reopen with the wage reductions. After two more days of stalemate, the *Transcript* reported that on June 13 the BFSA had closed its Warren, Rhode Island, plant. The newspaper highlighted the economic distress faced by the unemployed Warren workers. Finally, the local union accepted defeat. As Rene Ouellette put it, "We were supposed to be one," but the company divided the workforce by offering some occupational groups better deals than others, by threatening to remove the looms out of one of the Adams mills, and finally by simply closing down the BFSA mill in Warren. "They [BFSA] told us, 'Take [the wage reductions] or we will shut the mill down here too.'"

Mill #3 in Adams reopened first with 500 employees called to work on June 17 and 300 more the following day. The returnees faced no pickets. Two days later, Greylock workers started production after a hiatus of nearly eleven weeks. The corporation applied the wage reductions unevenly, with some employees losing only a few cents and others much more. And the company demanded more productivity. As Nicholas Thores recalled, "They increased the work load. Weavers used to run eight to twelve looms; now [it has] more than doubled. Some of the people were put out of work." Weavers now had to operate ten more looms with no increase in wages. A weaver who had asked Ouellette to change his vote now apologized to him and told him, "You were right to want to strike."[74]

Ouellette's own wage went from $31 a week before the strike to $17. Immediately after the mill reopened, the company brought in the hated time and motion "systematizers" to check the worker's time rate on each job. If any job allowed a few minutes without work, the worker would incur added duties the next day. As Ouellette remembered:

> The systematizer would get on a window . . . and he'd watch us work. And if you had two minutes to yourself, he'd put that down. If I had five minutes to myself, he'd put that down, and the next day you had another pile of work to keep you busy . . . . I had to leave that job to go to the shoe shop. I put in my notice that I was done, and twenty minutes later, they knew it in Fall River [BFSA headquarters]. They were happy that I wasn't going to cause them any more trouble.[75]

Although his presidency proved to be relatively short, Ouellette "enjoyed" it, recalling that he'd been "trying to do something good for people, and it was for my own good too. I'd fight like hell." Years later, Ouellette became a heavy equipment operator for the city of North Adams and president of the public employees union. The failure of the 1934 and 1935 strikes undoubtedly weighed heavily on North Berkshire cotton mill workers. They had organized, mobilized, and sacrificed, but with little material payback. They worked without striking during the coming years, doing their best to survive the Depression. Their connection with national unions had grown, though with a skepticism of their efficacy. Even when the economy improved during the World War II years, they held back from joining the newer CIO unions, although it also appeared that the more militant CIO textile union, the Textile Workers Union of America, hesitated to organize in North Berkshire.

1937 CIO TEXTILE ORGANIZING DRIVE

By the late 1930s, with plants throughout New England, the Berkshire Fine Spinning Associates had become the "World's Largest Manufacturers of Fine Cotton Goods." Some 6,600 North Berkshire residents worked in textiles, a little more than half in BFSA plants. In March 1937, the BFSA announced a 10 percent wage increase for all its employees, thus affecting 2,750 employees in their Adams and North Adams mills. The previous October, the BFSA had increased wages by 5 percent and added a second 5 percent raise less than two months later, reflecting a national increase. With the add-on of all three raises, BFSA workers now earned over 20 percent more than that had five months earlier.

Although, at first glance, those local wage hikes seem to have been attributable to an uptick in the textile industry, they might also have been instituted as a defensive measure against militant organizing by the new labor federation, the CIO, which had just won major unionization campaigns in auto and steel. The *Transcript* noted this possibility: "The increases were announced on the eve of the campaign which the Committee for Industrial Organization has declared it would conduct to organize New England's textile workers. Sidney Hillman of New York, who will direct the unionization campaign, proclaimed yesterday [March 18, 1937] that this would be the greatest effort of the C.I.O. and the greatest effort of its kind in labor history and added 'It will succeed.'"[76] In fact, nationwide, the textile industry did try to counter the CIO drive by raising wages by 10 percent and cutting back on the typical fifty-hour workweek.[77]

Historian Clete Daniel writes about the campaign, which was led by Sidney Hillman, who also headed the Amalgamated Clothing Workers Union:

> [T]he momentum created by its triumphs in steel and autos and by the lesser but still important victories it had won in rubber, electrical manufacturing, and other mass-production industries over the preceding months, invested the CIO . . . with a mythic power and presence it would never again enjoy.[78]

These victories had been achieved through a militant and unprecedented tactic: the sit-down strike. By then an increasingly common practice employed by the CIO, the sit-down strike happened when workers refused to work, but remained in the plant until a deal, often union recognition, would be negotiated with the employer. According to Daniel, "The sit-down strike, a tactic that, by virtue of its audacity and frequency, came to symbolize the bold and unruly character of the new industrial unionism, was, by the time the TWOC appeared on the scene, an almost normal feature of the new labor organizing."[79]

Hillman's proclamation to organize textile workers came just a month before the U.S. Supreme Court affirmed the constitutionality of the Wagner Act (officially the National Labor Relations Act, but also known as the "Wagner Act" after Senator

Robert Wagner from New York), which granted workers the legal right to join unions and collectively bargain. Since the collective bargaining provision (7a) of the National Industrial Recovery Act of 1933 had been struck down by the Court in 1935—along with the entire National Recovery Administration that May—uncertainty had reigned in labor circles about legal and social support for unionization. The Supreme Court decision on April 12, 1937, that declared the Wagner Act constitutional proved to be a major victory for union campaigns.

In fact, just nine days later, the reenergized textile union, now known as the Textile Workers Organizing Committee, announced plans to organize some 10,000 textile workers in the Holyoke, Massachusetts, area under the direction of Horace A. Riviere of Manchester, New Hampshire. The CIO union expected to focus on Holyoke, with its 8,000 textile workers, but also committed to organizing in neighboring Springfield, Ludlow, Chicopee, Easthampton, Westfield, and Northampton. However, the notice excluded North Berkshire and even Berkshire County as a whole.[80]

Still in its infancy, the Textile Workers Organizing Committee (TWOC) followed the earlier organizing drives in auto and steel. Despite the omission of Berkshire County from its territory, textile workers in the southern part of the county reached out to Horace Riviere for help. From the small town of Housatonic, thirty-seven miles south of North Adams, striking workers at Monument Mills contacted Riviere for aid; he obliged, sending organizers from the Holyoke office. After a short two-week campaign, the CIO union overwhelmingly won an election at the plant by a vote of 402 to 32.[81]

Around the same time, further north in Pittsfield, 115 tannery workers at the Dichtman-Widen plant struck, demanding that the company recognize their CIO-affiliated union, the National Leather Workers Association. Further CIO organizing continued in Pittsfield with the announcement that employees of two factories, Glix Brand Underwear and Berkshire Button, would meet to discuss affiliation with the CIO's International Ladies' Garment Workers Union. In addition, the United Electrical and Radio Workers of America (UE) scheduled a union drive at the giant General Electric facility in Pittsfield. Also, in the month of April 1937, readers of the local North Berkshire newspaper learned that a CIO organizer had met with employees at Greenfield Tap and Dye Corporation, thirty-six miles to the east of North Adams, in Franklin County.[82]

The Supreme Court's decision on the Wagner Act led to an ambitious plan for organizing in North Berkshire in April. However, this ultimately unsuccessful proposal did not emanate from a CIO affiliate but from a far more conservative union. On April 15, beneath the headline "PLAN INDEPENDENT UNION OF PRINT WORKS WORKERS," *Transcript* readers learned that a national union of textile printers hoped to organize over 1,800 non-union workers in the Arnold Print Works, at plants in Adams and in North Adams, as well as at the Windsor Print Works in North Adams. The union, the Associated Workers of Printing, Finishing and Allied Industries, had a history of working with management to solve problems rather than using the strike weapon. Although the union aspired to organize all print works employees under a CIO-type industrial model, its no-strike policy sharply differentiated it from its competitor, the TWOC. As it turned out, the array of crafts within both print works led to competing interests, thus undermining any general desire for a union of all print workers. Only forty employees attended what had been billed as a "mass meeting."[83]

A local union then jumped into the print works fray, attempting to succeed where the national union had met defeat. The Calico Workers' Union, an independent union formed in 1934 at Arnold Print Works, announced its intention to organize fellow employees who had no union affiliation. They had some success with the less skilled workers, who earned significantly less than the printers and engravers who already had their own craft unions, but they could not generate large-scale worker interest.[84]

Although neither AFL nor CIO unions initiated organizing drives among North Berkshire textile workers as the 1930s neared an end, it did not mean that other workers foreswore the possibility of militant action.[85] Late in the summer of 1938, workers at the Brightwater Paper Company in the Zylonite section of Adams went out on strike. All 250 non-unionized papermaking employees walked out, protesting a five-cent-an-hour wage reduction. Frustration had built up for some time as the reduction had been put into effect two months earlier. The *Transcript* described a "sizeable group" that had assembled:

> across the road from the Brightwater plant and there seated in chairs and on steps . . . remained during the greater part of the morning discussing the strike situation in general . . . . They . . . stated that they are not organized in any union, as was the case in the past when different groups at the plant went out on short-lived strikes, but instead on "their own" . . . . It was said that today's strike is the first one at the Brightwater plant in which all of the employees, except executives and the office force, have participated.[86]

The lack of newspaper coverage suggests that the strike lasted no more than two days, and that specific work stoppage appears to be the only one in the North Berkshire region during the late 1930s. Wages of mill workers in the area increased between 1937 and 1940, a factor that might account for the absence of union activity and, as noted earlier, may have been brought about as a defensive measure by the mill owners to keep CIO organizers from their plants.[87] In Adams, the Polish unionists who initiated the local textile strike in 1934 and widened the strike with their flying squadrons, had also benefitted from wage increases, but by the late thirties, some had found other, higher wage-earning opportunities at General Electric in Pittsfield and Sprague Electric in North Adams.[88] In any case, the lack of CIO textile activity in North Berkshire, whether because of lack of interest from local workers or CIO organizers themselves, meant that the area would have to wait until 1945 for the new labor federation to take hold in the region. This gap contrasted with the nearby Pioneer Valley, where Textile Workers Union of America organizers would prove successful at organizing unions for textile workers in Holyoke, Chicopee, and Easthampton in the late 1930s and 1940s.

EXCEPTIONS: THE CIO, TRADES WORKERS, AND SPRAGUE

Although historians describe and celebrate CIO victories that sparked huge labor movements in large cities like Detroit, Akron, San Francisco, Minneapolis, and Pittsburgh, with rebellious sit-down and general strikes, the experience of smaller communities more likely matches the localism evidenced in North Berkshire. In Muncie, Indiana, for example, the representative small city that the Lynds studied in their celebrated 1937 book, *Middletown in Transition: A Study in Cultural Conflicts,* workers at General Motors also rebuffed the efforts of CIO organizers.[89]

A review of labor activism in North Berkshire during the 1930s also fails to find examples of coalitions forming between textile and other industrial workers or workers in the trades. The trades employed some 500 North Berkshire workers, many in unions that came together in the North Adams Central Labor Union (CLU). A diverse group, CLU's membership included AFL affiliates of carpenters, bricklayers, plumbers, musicians, and bartenders. More politically active, and with a longer history than any of the industrial unions, the CLU picketed non-union shops and boycotted non-union trades people.[90]

In addition to fighting for their own members, the CLU took outside political stands. For example, they advocated for an end to child labor locally and nationwide. They also opposed the North Adams City Council's proposal that mandated a police permit to picket, assemble, parade, or speak out in public, declaring those to be civil rights.[91] They might have achieved their chief citywide political influence in 1940 when they endorsed Faxon Bowen as mayor.

The case of Sprague Specialties, a new firm producing capacitors for radios, provided another significant twist to the story of unionism in the North Berkshires. While CIO organizers bypassed local textile mills, they made their way to Sprague, where they found a critical mass of support.[92] Sparked by a growing interest shown by Sprague workers, UE President James Carey traveled to North Adams in 1938, where he spoke to 400 Sprague employees. Encouraged by the UE perspective, local workers voted to form UE Local #249; not surprisingly, management refused to recognize it. Struggles continued into the 1940s as UE tried again to organize at Sprague, but lost a hotly contested election in 1944. The company supported weak independent unions for the production workers, including one that the National Labor Relations Board ruled an illegal "company union." The independent production workers union that survived remained in place until 1967, when an AFL-CIO union, the International Union of Electrical Workers (IUE) defeated it in an election.[93]

NEW DEAL SOCIAL PROGRAMS IN THE LATE 1930S

While labor organizers worked to carry out President Roosevelt's policies and support legislation to improve worker rights and the economy, many area residents continued to need help from New Deal social programs. Inconsistent reporting in the city's "Annual Reports" makes it difficult to determine the numbers and scope of the work done through the Works Progress Administration (WPA), the Civilian Conservation Corps (CCC), and other work-related New Deal programs in North Adams, but it does appear that New Deal projects came to play an even bigger role in the region by the late 1930s. For example, the 1938 report focused on the previous year's joint city-WPA work for "sewers, waterworks, sidewalks, and road construction." Emphasizing its importance to the city, and pushing back against negative stereotypes of the WPA, the report added that the work done "eliminate[d] all suggestions of 'boondoggling.'" In total, 157 men and 78 women were employed, the women most likely in WPA sewing, nursing, and household aide programs.[94]

The following year, the WPA operation continued to expand. Termed "by far the most active in WPA history," local employment rose to an average of 445. In addition to laboring outdoors on infrastructure projects, repairing five schools, and building a new city park, WPA employees updated the city's fire and cemetery records. Suggestive of the ideological change that the New Deal fostered, North Adams's conservative mayor, Francis J. O'Hara, declared: "There can be no doubt that social security, unemployment insurance, old age pensions, and aid to dependent children are all blessings and no one would want to return to the old order of caring for those out of work or infirm by disease or old age."[95]

Woman Orator Stirs Strikers

Unusual photo of Miss Josephine Kaczor of Troy, N. Y., representative of Amalgamated Clothing Workers of America, addressing open-air mass meeting of 2000 Berkshire Mills strikers in Adams, yesterday afternoon. She first greeted the crowd in English and then spoke in Polish, expressing her opinion that the strike was "one of the grandest in history."

Transcript photo (September 7, 1934) of Josephine Kaczor, who spoke to huge crowd the day before.

Rene Ouellette (far left, behind the table), age 50 in 1953, at a Greylock Sportsman's Club meeting, where Rene served as president. The 1935 textile strike leader was an avid outdoorsman and the subject of a glowing article in "Outdoor Life" (September, 1953) for his conservation efforts, which included, bringing rabbits back to the North Berkshire. (Neil Priessman photo)

Eighty-six year old Rene Ouellette playing horseshoes with North Adams Mayor John Barrett at a picnic, hosted by the Berkshire County Nutrition Program and the North Adams Council on Aging, September 7, 1989.

2000 Adams Strikers Hear Union Orators

Transcript photo (September 7, 1934) of part of the audience that heard Josephine Kaczor and other speakers at the September 6 strike rally in Adams.

Greylock mill worker housing, 40–50 Taft St. (Wendy Champney, North Adams Historical Society secretary; North Adams Historical Society photo).

As part of the "New Deal," Civilian Conservation Corps members work on the side and roof of what will become Bascom Lodge at the summit of Mount Greylock (CCC Archives).

Civilian Conservation Corps youth in front of Greylock Barracks, 1936 (CCC Archives).

As part of the "New Deal," the Works Progress Administration funded artists, including sculptors. Above is a bas-relief work by Louis Slobodkin, representing the city's industrial history, which can be found in the lobby of the North Adams Post Office. A second bas-relief by the same artist, depicting Hoosac Tunnel workers, hangs on another wall of the post office lobby (1942).

NOTES

1 *Transcript*, September 6, 1932. The lack of Labor Day celebrations reflected the weak position of organized labor. The first Labor Day in Berkshire County had been celebrated in North Adams in 1886, sponsored by the Knights of Labor. Over the next quarter century, Labor Day celebrations became more sporadic and, at times, not focused on the problems and successes of labor. After the 1932 celebration, the next known commemoration occurred in 1953, sponsored by the Textile Workers Union of America, which then played a major role in representing the cotton mill workers of North Berkshire (*Transcript,* August 29, 1953, 10).

2 Adam Cohen, *Nothing to Fear: FDR's Inner Circle and the Hundred Days That Created Modern America* (New York: Penguin Press, 2009), 11.

3. On Sprague's origins and growth, see Maynard Seider, "The Sprague Electric Strike in North Adams," 1970, *Historical Journal of Massachusetts*, 42:1 (Winter 2014) and John L. Sprague, *Sprague Electric: An Electronic Giant's Rise, Fall, and Life after Death* (North Charleston, South Carolina: CreateSpace Independent Publishing Platform, 2015).

4 Robert S. Lynd and Helen Merrell Lynd, *Middletown in Transition: A Study in Cultural Conflicts* (New York: Harcourt, Brace & World, 1937), 3.

5 L. Mara Dodge, "Anna B. Sullivan, 1903–83: The Formative Years of a Textile Mill Union Organizer (Holyoke, Massachusetts)," *Historical Journal of Massachusetts*, 36, 2, (Summer 2008) 199. Textile mills had been closing with regularity in New England since 1900. In the quarter century since 1908, twenty-five such mills had been shuttered in western Massachusetts alone. In North Berkshire, the exodus of textile manufacturing continued. The last cotton mill closed its doors in Adams in 1958, although print work, fashion and garment sewing, and military contract work would continue through the 1980s, and even, in some cases, the 1990s.

6 "Historical United States Census Total for Berkshire County Massachusetts," accessed August 15, 2016, https://en.wikipedia.org/wiki/Historical_United_States_Cenus_total_for_Berkshire_Couinty_Massachusetts.

7 North Adams population statistics from Jay Louis Nierenberg, *North Adams: New England Mill Town: A Political, Economic, and Psychological Survey* (Williamstown, MA: Williams College, 1942), 37; Adams population figures from Keith E. Melder, *The Polish Immigration in Adams, Massachusetts: A Case Study of the American Melting Pot* (Williamstown, MA: Williams College, 1954), Chapters 1 and 2.

8 Figure on CCC employment from Irving Bernstein, *A Caring Society: The New Deal, the Worker and the Great Depression* (Boston: Houghton Mifflin, 1985), 158.

9 Figure on WPA employment Bernstein, *A Caring . . .*, 313. Slobodkin visited North Adams in 1941, where he learned about the city's history and researched his subject matter. A third sculpture that the artist made for the post office, "The Mohawks," is missing. See Deborah A. Goldberg, *Louis*

Slobodkin's North Adams Reliefs (Williamstown, MA: Williams College, 1987). Photographic examples of WPA work in North Adams can be seen in *Farewell to Factory Towns?* (2012), a documentary written and directed by the author. Specifics on the projects and number of residents employed by the WPA and other government programs can be found in the North Adams annual reports throughout the 1930s and early 1940s.

10 *Annual Report of the City of North Adams*, 1935, 1213.

11 *Annual Report* . . . , 1933, 78, 80, 125.

12 *Annual Report* . . . , 1935, 9.

13 *Annual Report* . . . , 1937, 48.

14 William Carney, *A Berkshire Sourcebook: The history, geography and major landmarks of Berkshire County, Mass.* (Pittsfield: The Junior League of Berkshire County Inc., 1976), 162.

15 Interview with author, October 15, 2016.

16 "Oral History Project," Winter Study, January, 1984, North Adams State College.

17 Bernie Auge interview by author.

18 Interview with Rene Ouellette by Karen Rose and author, "Oral History Project," January 24, 1984. Ouellette went on to recount how, when he and his wife learned that the company was overcharging them for groceries, they never went back and, instead, "paid cash" at a grocery store "downstreet."

19 Bernie Auge thought the noise probably affected the workers' hearing (interview with author).

20 "Oral History Project" interviews.

21 In New England, "active spindles . . . declined to 5.4 million from 18.1; and nearly three of every eight production jobs were lost" in the period from 1919–1939. William F. Hartford, *Where is Our Responsibility? Unions and Economic Change in the New England Textile Industry, 1870–1960* (Amherst: University of Massachusetts Press, 1996), 52.

22 See Cohen, 242–247.

23 See Hartford, 59–60.

24 Hartford, 61, and *Transcript*, August 17, 1934; August 21, 1934, 8; and August 30, 1934, 12.

25 *Transcript*, September 4, 1934, 1.

26 A significant French-Canadian population also worked in the Adams mills. In 1932, UTWA organizer Horace A. Riviere from Manchester, New Hampshire, spoke to members of Local No. 1711 and also delivered a speech in French at the Notre Dame church to which all local French speakers were invited. *Transcript*, November 2, 1932. For a history of the Polish population in Adams, see Melder.

27 German families first immigrated to Adams in the 1850s and had become "a sizeable community" in the 1880s. At the height of immigration, they

numbered just under 1,000. In Adams, they found work at the Plunkett mills, the Berkshire Cotton Manufacturing Company. They joined existing churches, including the Episcopal church, and built numerous meeting places and clubs. In 1885, with Germans making up 540 of the 800 parishoners of St. Mark's Episcopal Church, the church hired a German assistant to conduct services in that language. *Transcript,* "Sesquicentennial Edition, November 19, 1993, 23, and Philip Pugliese, *Transcript,* October 10, 1987.

28 Melder, 90–91.

29 Melder, 92–3.

30 *Transcript,* August 17, 1934, 11. The Loomfixers' Union was an AFL affiliate, and the Polish union briefly joined the labor federation (AFL) through membership in the UTWA. According to an historian of the Polish community in Adams, by 1937, the union broke its affiliation "since the unskilled workers were given little service by the United Textile Workers of America" (Melder, 93). Some 1,100 textile employees worked in the three cotton mills in North Adams and Williamstown. Twenty to twenty-five loomfixers in the Hoosac Mill were unionized, though not affiliated with the UTWA. On the eve of the national strike on September 1, one local cotton mill worker said that, "as far as he could judge, most of the local employees feel that their employers are doing the best that can be done for them under existing circumstances and that there is nothing to be gained by a walk-out." *Transcript,* August 31, 1934, 3. However, within a week of the national strike, those employees in North Adams and Williamstown walked out by the hundreds.

31 As Melder puts it, "The Poles led the fight for union recognition in the town and have always been the leaders in the union organization. The union was successful because, like the other Polish societies, it was a manifestation of group unity . . . . It could be maintained through many periods of trouble because it was an organization of Poles, representing the solidarity of the Polish community" (95). Also, see Chapters 4 and 5, Melder. That generation of Polish unionists would probably not have been surprised by actions taken by their descendants some 74 years later. When the Catholic Church announced the closing of the Adams Polish Church, St. Stanislaus Kostka Parish, in 2008, its congregants began a 24/7 vigil to keep it open. The vigil continued for over three years and on day number 1,150, the Springfield Diocese announced that St. Stanislaus would reopen. The decision came down from the Vatican, no doubt impressed by the persistence and loyalty of the Adams Polish community. Lori Stabile, *Springfield Republican,* February 18, 2012.

32 White had traveled to the area the previous June, where he spoke to members of Local No. 1711 of the need to lower the workweek to increase employment opportunities for unemployed workers. White called for "30 hours work with 40 hours pay based on the present rate." *Transcript,* June 6, 1934, 10. White had visited Adams frequently in the past and had organized local branches of the UTWA. *Transcript,* September 3, 1934, 10.

33 *Transcript,* September 4, 1934, 10.

34 Ibid.

35 Ibid.

36 Ibid., emphasis added.

37 Ibid.

38 *Springfield Republican*, September 6, 1934, 1.

39 For a similar photo (*Transcript*, September 6, 1934, 3) and discussion of women's key role in the 1934 strike in another Massachusetts community, see Dodge. According to the *Springfield Republican* (September 6, 1934, 1), the work stoppage began when the bobbin boys stopped giving materials to the weavers. This newspaper put the number of Greylock strikers at 300.

40 *Transcript*, September 6, 1934, 3.

41 See Richard Cloward and Frances Fox Piven, *Poor People's Movements: How They Succeed, How They Fail* (New York: Pantheon, 1977) for examples of similar types of solidarity nationwide.

42 *Transcript*, September 4,1934,5. See also *Transcript*, August 31,1934, 2, and September 1, 1934, 5.

43 *Transcript*, September 7, 1934, 10.

44 The *Springfield Republican*, September 7, 1934, 1, is the source for the previous paragraph. For the *Transcript* photo and caption, see *Transcript*, September 7, 1934, 11. Under a headline of "PICKETERS CHARGE OFFICIAL OF MILL ENDANGERED LIVES," the *Springfield Republican*, September 7, 1934, 11, reported that strikers accused the Williamstown mill's superintendent, Silas Rooney, of driving through the picket line without warning. Also, see *Transcript*, September 8, 1934, 8.

45 *Transcript*, September 8, 1934, 5.

46 Ibid.

47 Clete Daniel, *Culture of Misfortune: An Interpretive History of Textile Unionism in the United States* (Ithaca, NY: Cornell University Press, 2001), 48.

48 *Transcript*, September 11, 1934, 2.

49 Ibid., 5.

50 Ibid., 5.

51 *Transcript*, September 11, 1934, 2.

52 Hartford, 61–62 and Howard Zinn, *A People's History of the United States, 1492-Present* (New York: Harper Perennial, 1995, revised and updated), 387–388.

53 The following year the National Labor Relations Act outlawed such arrangements as illegal company unions. In 1940, the National Labor Relations Board ruled that the first such union at Sprague Specialties was in fact a company union. See Maynard Seider, "The CIO in Rural Massachusetts: Sprague Electric and North Adams, 1937–1944." *Historical*

Journal of Massachusetts, Vol. 22, no. 1 (Winter 1994), 61..

54 *Transcript*, September 11, 1934, 3.

55 Ibid., 3.

56 Ibid., 3; "TEXTILE STRIKERS TO INVADE PITTSFIELD TUESDAY IN EFFORT TO FORCE LOCAL MILLS TO CLOSE" headlined the *Springfield Republican* (September 10, 1934, 1) with the subhead, "Flying Squadrons from Adams Will Attempt to Make 1000 Workers in Four Local Mills Join Walkout"; George P. Willison, *The History of Pittsfield, Massachusetts, 1916–1955* (Pittsfield: City of Pittsfield, Mass., 1957); *Transcript*, September 10, 1934, 3.

57 *Transcript*, September 11, 1934, 2. The hesitancy of woolen workers to strike undoubtedly reflected their higher status and pay as compared to cotton workers. Their relative conservatism may have also been influenced by other religious and ethnic factors. An interesting item in the *Transcript* immediately after Herbert Hoover's election in 1928 reported that the Blackinton woolen mill workers "[a]ll reported for work as usual . . . but their elation at the victory of Mr. Hoover was so great that they soon decided that today was no day for such every day matters as work." Management agreed to their request to close down for the day so they could celebrate. A one-hour march down Massachusetts Avenue soon followed with cheering, horn blowing, and Hoover banners. *Transcript*, November 7, 1928, 16. Perhaps the religious factor influenced these pro-Hoover woolen workers, many of Welsh Protestant background, while Catholicism predominated among the North Adams and Adams population. In the 1928 election, North Adams went for Al Smith by 57 percent to Hoover's 43 percent, and Adams did the same, defeating Hoover by a margin of 60 percent to 40 percent. In Massachusetts as a whole, Smith barely beat Hoover, carrying less than 51 percent of the vote. *Transcript*, November, 7, 1928, 2, 6.

58 *Transcript*, September 12, 1934, 10.

59 Ibid.

60 *Transcript*, September 17, 1934, 2.

61 *Transcript*, September 18, 1934, 10. Although the strike committee wanted equity, they didn't aspire to total equality. In criticizing one of the manufacturers' responses to the code, the lowering of all workers' wages towards the same minimum, they supported the recognition of all skill differences and differential rewards among textile workers—the spinner is, after all, "more skilled than the bobbin boy," and the weaver deserves "more pay than the scrubber."

62 *Transcript*, September 22, 1934, 5. Coolidge was referring to the National Recovery Administration (NRA), part of the National Industrial Recovery Act (NIRA), passed by Congress in 1933. While the collective bargaining part of it was supported by labor, management generally ignored it and the act as a whole was viewed by labor as encouraging corporate monopolistic control and pricing. In 1935, the Supreme Court ruled it unconstitutional.

63 See Daniel, Chapter 2, for a discussion of the Winant Board and reactions to it.

64 *Transcript*, September 22, 1934, 5.

65 *Transcript*, September 28, 1934, 3, 10.

66 *Transcript*, October 1, 1934, 5.

67 The "bitter" phrase from Irving Bernstein, *The Turbulent Years*, 315. The second comment from Clete Daniel who wrote: "even the most sanguine analysts ultimately agreed [that the strike] was a full-fledged calamity for the cause of textile unionism" (58). See Dodge for Anna Sullivan's "unusual bitterness" at the national union for leaving the Holyoke strikers "high and dry" (209).

68 *Transcript*, May 6, 1935, 2.

69 "Oral History Project."

70 In 1986, middle school students interviewed Rene Ouellette for a documentary project, "The Mills of North Adams" (copy housed at Visitors' Center, Western Gateway Heritage State Park, North Adams). He told the students about the difficult working conditions in the mill, the long hours of laboring, and workers' loss of fingers on the job, even in one case an entire hand. His grandson, Peter Breen, remembers hearing stories from older relatives abut Ouellette and his work life. At Greylock, he would help his fellow workers with loom problems, untangling the threads and going from machine to machine throughout the plant. "He was a very pleasant person. . . . He would talk to people. That's the way he was through life . . . . He would help people." Author interview, August 10, 2016.

71 *Transcript*, May 18, 1935, 8.

72 Rene Ouellette, "Oral History Project."

73 Ibid. Priests in Holyoke, Massachusetts made similar remarks about textile unionization and strikes. There, "vigilant pastors warned their people against the possible and probable dangers of hastily considered actions in labor relations." William F. Hartford, *The Working People of Holyoke: Class and Ethnicity in a Massachusetts Mill Town: 1850–1960* (New Brunswick, NJ: Rutgers University Press, 1990), 180.

74 *Transcript,* June 10, 1935, 8; Thores and Ouellette, "Oral History Project."

75 Nearly fifty years later, Ouellette remembered the time back in the 1930s when he picked up a man who needed a ride. When Ouellette found out that his passenger was a "systematizer," he told him to "Get the hell out." See Maynard Seider, "Remembering Work in Depression Days," *Transcript*, June 9, 1990, 6. Catherine O'Neill, who worked at Sprague during the 1930s and 1940s, also vividly recalled—about half a century later—being observed by a systematizer: "[H]e'd watch you . . . . And if he thought that you were going quite fast and you were making quite a bit of bonus, then after when he went and checked with the big shot, then . . . they would cut you down. So we all, when we saw him coming we'd kind of slow down. But you weren't fooling them . . . . I hated that . . . . He'd stand in the back and he'd watch. And he'd make you nervous. And before you know it your rates would be higher." Shifting Gears Project.

76 *Transcript*, March 19, 1937, 3.

77 Bernstein, *The Turbulent Years*, 620.

78 Daniel, 69.

79 Bernstein, *The Turbulent Years*, 500, quotes Bureau of Labor Statistics conclusion that more than half a million workers participated in nearly 600 sit-down strikes from 1936 to 1938; Daniel, 69.

80 *Transcript*, April 21, 1937, 1. As Daniel writes, "TWOC organizers were a highly visible presence in every important textile center in New England almost as soon as the [1937] campaign began . . . . [T]he legendary milltowns of New England—Fall River, New Bedford, Lawrence, Providence, Pawtucket—were again pulsating with promise as fervent TWOC organizers fanned the dying embers of textile unionism back to full candescence" (81).

81 *Transcript*, April 23, 1937, 6 and May 7, 1937, 5. Two years later, a CIO textile union successfully organized a mill even closer to North Berkshire, when the Berkshire Woolen Company of Pittsfield reached agreement with the Textile Woolen Workers' Union. *Transcript*, July 7, 1939, 5.

82 *Transcript*, April 6, 1937, 2; April 27, 1937, 5; and April 19, 1937, 7.

83 *Transcript*, April 15, 1937, 5; April 19, 1937, 14; and April 27, 1937, 5.

84 *Transcript*, May 3, 1937, 3; and Jay Louis Nierenberg, *North Adams: New England Mill Town, a Political, Economic, and Psychological Survey* (Williamstown, MA: Williams College, 1942), 136. The conservative character of this union is suggested by the following quote from an interview in 1941, when the head of the Calico Workers' Union at Windsor Print Works spoke of his opposition to both strikes and membership in national unions "on the grounds that most of the leaders are racketeers, and that his men can do better for themselves, without having to pay large dues into any large chest" (Nierenberg, 127). This type of sentiment could also be found among the leaders of the Independent Condenser Workers Union at the Sprague Electric Company. Seider, "The CIO in Rural Massachusetts."

85 Nor should it be assumed that the supposedly militant TWOC always reflected the wishes of the workers it organized. In bargaining with a textile firm that threatened to move to a lower wage area, the TWOC in Holyoke agreed to a 12.5 percent reduction at Farr Alpaca if the company officially recognized the union—this despite a 1,338–6 vote of the rank and file rejecting the wage cut (Hartford, *The Working People of Holyoke*, 192).

86 *Transcript*, August 29, 1938, 8. The strike lasted at least one more day. The vice president and general manager of the company, Henry J. Guild, just back from New York City, met with a group of about fifty strikers. No resolution followed as Guild argued that the "wage cut was in line with similar reductions in the paper industry and that none of the other paper mills have yet restored the wage cuts as business conditions at present do not warrant such action." (*Transcript*, August 30, 1938, 8).

87 See, e.g., *Transcript*, January 1, 1937, 12, "NOTABLE PROGRESS SEEN IN ADAMS DURING YEAR"; *Transcript*, March 26, 1937, 3, "LOCAL WOOLEN MILLS ANNOUNCE PAY RAISES FOR 900 WORKERS"; and Nierenberg, 182.

88 Melder, 98.

89 Similarly, the Muncie, Indiana police kept a delegation of striking United Auto Worker members from a nearby town from entering Muncie. When the Muncie Chevrolet plant had to close because it lacked parts due to the UAW strike, all 1,500 employees signed a wire to the president of General Motors that read: "We . . . wish to assure of our loyal support in the present labor crisis." Further, the workers told the governor, "We are bitterly opposed to having anyone come in and try to tell us what we need; we know what we need . . . We will go to any necessary extreme to get back to work." Lynd and Lynd, 73. For a description of the CIO upsurges in major U.S. cities, see Green, Chapter 5.

90 Nierenberg, 138.

91 *Transcript*, January 9, 1937, 3 and February 9, 1938, 5.

92 Without providing any evidence, one local analyst of CIO organizing at Sprague remarked that, if the CIO fails to organize Sprague, "defeat . . . might, psychologically, upset the C.I.O's plan to unionize the textile industry in the same city." M.S. Stedman, "The C.I.O. Comes to North Adams," *Sketch*, November, 1938, 18. See also, Ch. 12, this book.

93 See Seider, "The Sprague Electric Strike" and Chapter Eighteen, this book, for details.

94 Annual Report of the City of North Adams, 1938, 116.

95 Ibid., 1939, 112,113,10.

CHAPTER ELEVEN

THE IMPACT OF THE GREAT DEPRESSION

THE ROOSEVELT ADMINISTRATION'S NEW DEAL programs did indeed make a difference in North Adams and its surrounding communities. The union organizing drives and the solidarity networks that blossomed in the mid-1930s changed the area as well, increasing the number of workers who experienced a union consciousness. Not including the 1934 and 1935 textile strikes, the most active union members appeared to be from the trades, organized in the Central Labor Union (CLU). They followed a local tradition of activism that went back to the turn of the twentieth century; the CLU's political clout even sparked the winning campaign of Faxon Bowen in 1940, bringing the first pro-labor mayor into North Adams City Hall.[1]

Although the area had changed, that change still reflected narrow limits, a shift that resonated elsewhere. When sociologists Helen and Robert Lynd returned to "Middletown" (Muncie, Indiana) in the 1930s to explore the impact of the Great Depression on the city's institutions and social classes, they found little apparent change: the community still held to its pro-business, conservative values.[2] They noted, however, that "[a]mong the working class, tenuous and confused, new positive values are apparent in such a thing as the aroused conception of the possible role of government in bolstering the exposed position of labor by social legislation, including direct relief for the unemployed." In the 1936 presidential election,

Roosevelt received a 59 percent majority vote, despite Muncie's pro-Landon employers who were "prepared to go to great lengths to contrive to make their employees 'vote right.'"[3]

In the 1936 election in North Adams, Roosevelt received an even higher margin of victory. He defeated Alfred Landon 63 percent to 37 percent (compared to 61 percent to 37 percent nationally) despite the vehement opposition against FDR expressed by nearly all of the city's major employers.[4] Likewise, the 1940 election results in North Adams showed Roosevelt defeating Wendell Wilkie by 62 percent to 38 percent (compared to 55 percent to 45 percent nationally). North Adams and even more so Adams (where FDR defeated Wilkie by a higher margin, 71 percent to 29 percent) had become solidly Democratic and supportive of national government economic aid, including vibrant jobs programs.

Looking back over the earlier years of the century, 1924 was the last time that voters in North Adams and Adams supported a Republican presidential candidate—until 1956.[5] Both communities had bucked the national tide in 1928 and backed Al Smith, the Democratic nominee, a vote aided no doubt by Smith's Catholicism. In North Adams, for example, the French-Canadian vote had previously been overwhelmingly Republican, but in 1928, "they voted almost unanimously" for Al Smith.[6] By 1940, North Adams's working class had pushed previous ethnic political differences aside to elect the city's first pro-labor mayor, one fully associated with President Roosevelt and the New Deal.

Although a culture and lifestyle of self-sufficiency had characterized the city's working people during the pre-Depression years, the hardships of the 1930s tested their attachment to independence. In 1934, Mayor Archie Pratt told residents that "[l]ocal self-sufficiency" had outlived its usefulness. Pratt welcomed the New Deal programs that aided North Adams and the entire country. Later, in 1934 and beyond, national unions began to organize in the city and surrounding towns, breathing a greater union and national consciousness into the area, which meant that local people didn't have to do it all by themselves. Outside help had become available, amidst greater national integration.

The city had changed, as had the North Berkshires. But not completely. The CIO upsurge that spread through industrial cities such as Flint, Detroit, Akron, and Pittsburgh, for example, did not manifest itself in the northern Berkshires in the 1930s.[7] In retrospect, although the active participation of North Berkshire workers in the national strike of 1934 expanded their union consciousness, the overwhelming defeat of the strike only added to their suspicion of outside unions, thus delaying the time it took for CIO unions to receive a local welcome.[8]

Union organizing did continue in the North Berkshire textile industry into the 1940s. However, it was not until 1946 that a CIO union, the Textile Workers Union of America (TWUA), gained membership in the region. That year, the TWUA won elections at the Hoosac Cotton Mill and the BFSA's Adams and Greylock plants. The area's tradition of self-sufficiency remained but, tempered by the social changes of the previous decade, the local work force gradually became more willing to join national labor organizations, even if it took them longer than their fellow workers in large cities.

NOTES

1 See Ch. 14 for a discussion of Faxon Bowen's campaign and his mayoralty. At a December 1, 1940, Central Labor Union meeting, a proposal to form a branch of the Labor Party "was enthusiastically received" by sixteen delegates of CLU-affiliated unions, according to John F. Smith. Smith, the CLU president, announced that another meeting had been called to discuss the possibility at further length. There is, however, no record I could find of any more action on the issue. *Transcript*, December 2, 1940, 3.

2 Robert S. Lynd and Helen Merrell Lynd, *Middletown in Transition: A Study in Cultural Conflicts* (New York: Harcourt, Brace & Co., 1937). Echoing the findings of the Lynds, Jay Louis Nierenberg (*North Adams: A New England Mill Town: A Political, Economic, and Psychological Study*. Williamstown, MA: Williams College, 1942) recognizes the continued power of the business class in North Adams (227–228).

3 Lynd and Lynd, 489, 497–498.

4 See Nierenberg, Chapter 6, "How Management Thinks and Acts," for interviews with local owners and managers, most of whom vehemently opposed New Deal programs, particularly the National Labor Relations Act.

5 In 1956, both Adams and North Adams chose President Dwight Eisenhower over the Democratic candidate, Adlai Stevenson. Since that time, including the 2016 presidential election, the Democratic candidate has always been successful in both communities. Thus, Adams and North Adams stayed Democratic while the state of Massachusetts went Republican with Eisenhower in 1952 and Ronald Reagan in 1980 and 1984.

6 On Smith's religion and the Adams vote, see Keith E. Melder (*The Polish Immigration in Adams, Massachusetts: A Case Study of the American Melting Pot*. Williamstown, MA: Williams College, 1954), 105. On the French-Canadian vote in North Adams, see Nierenberg, 43.

7 Nierenberg argues that the refusal of North Adams workers to join national unions contributed to their relatively low wages and weak power position (229). See Nierenberg, Chapter 10, for comparisons of the wages of North Adams industrial and municipal employees with similar workers in other Massachusetts mill towns.

8 Of course, organizing became easier in the 1940s with the war economy and a resurgence of consumer buying power after the war. In the period from 1920 to 1940, "Massachusetts lost nearly 45 percent of its textile production jobs. But after 1940, a large infusion of military contracts, promising unprecedented profits, stabilized the regional industry and even led some manufacturers to reopen deserted plants." William F. Hartford, *The Working People of Holyoke: Class and Ethnicity in a Massachusetts Mill Town: 1850–1960*. New Brunswick, NJ: Rutgers University Press, 1990, 194. The rapid growth and development of Sprague, with its significant military contracts, during the 1940s and the 1950s exemplifies that. And the TWUA's "most important wartime growth . . . occurred in the northern branch of cotton textiles." Clete Daniel, *Culture of Misfortune: An Interpretive History of Textile Unionism in the United States*. Ithaca, NY: Cornell University Press, 2001, 194.

CHAPTER TWELVE

SPRAGUE ORGANIZING AND THE CIO 1937–1944

The first thing we did [when we formed the union] was to stop foremen from having members of their family working for them any more. Next, we got four hours of guaranteed work if we reported to work, which was no more than right. And we got rid of "gravy" jobs. Work had to be divided equally, good and bad.

—Mabel Lewitt

Sprague is in an excellent position and certainly has no basis for bellyaching . . . . [T]he company has also taken the precaution of socking away over a half million dollars. . . When things get dull . . . the people at Sprague lose their jobs and their pay envelopes, but the stock holders continue to draw dividends out of this kitty.

—UE Director of Research-Education
William Mitchell, 1938

HOME RULE—Beware of the C.I.O. Wolves in UE Clothing! . . . [Don't] sell your birthright for a filthy mess of pottage . . . . Vote I.C.W. No. 2 and Send the "Carpetbaggers" Back to Sidney Hillman.

—ICW #2 election ad, 1944

[UE] is the only real union in the electrical manufacturing industry with a record of getting things done for the members . . . VOTE UE—THE AMERICAN WAY.

—UE election ad, 1944

INTRODUCTION

ALTHOUGH THE CIO bypassed North Berkshire textile workers, organizers from the United Electrical, Radio and Machine Workers of America (UE), a founding affiliate of the CIO, traveled to North Adams during the 1930s to challenge Sprague Specialties' dominance of its work force. While textiles remained the leading employer in North Berkshire during the Great Depression, Sprague brought a different product into the market—electrical capacitors—a move that would mark the start of a significant shift in local manufacturing away from textiles (though not its end) to a focus on electrical components, both in their production and in the subsequent employment opportunities they brought to the area. This transition reflected changes in the state as a whole, as the growth of electronics replaced a diminished textile industry.[1]

This chapter looks at labor relations at Sprague during its first decade in North Adams, the strategy and tactics of the new industrial union organizing, the reactions of Sprague management, and the divided responses of the local employees. Prior to the Great Depression, national AFL unions tended to be conservative, focusing on hanging onto their specialized craft memberships. The bulk of the working population—semi-skilled workers and laborers in mass production workplaces, like steel, auto, and electrical—who had been ignored by the AFL, awaited the birth of the CIO. Corporate leaders, fearful of that future wave of unionization, established employee relation plans, or company unions. Controlled by management, these plans generally allowed worker representatives to air complaints and suggestions to management, but without any type of effective power. As Bethlehem Steel's Charles Schwab explained his company's plan, "I will not permit myself to be in a position of having labor dictate to management."[2] In some cases, the plans replaced trade unions that had been driven out, and in other cases attempted to co-opt employees from establishing rank-and-file-controlled labor organizations.

In 1935, the Wagner Act outlawed company unions. Within three years, the Depression-era militancy of the new CIO gave birth to authentic, worker-controlled unions with over four million members. In some plants, however, the company union, or a labor organization much like it, fought to stay in power and, with the help of management, keep the new CIO challenge at bay.[3] Most of the research and writing on the CIO has centered on organizing drives and successes in big cities and major factories.[4] But an examination of the hotly contested, though unsuccessful, drive in a smaller, more rural environment, helps broaden the scope of research on the social history of the CIO's first decade and, more specifically, brings our attention to a non-textile growing production field in North Berkshire.

THE DEVELOPMENT OF AN "INDEPENDENT" UNION AT SPRAGUE

"ELECTRICAL INDUSTRY EMPLOYING 1,000 TO LOCATE HERE," boldly proclaimed the banner front-page headline of the *Transcript* late in 1929.[5] It began when businessmen Robert Chapman (R.C.) Sprague, the son of a noted inventor with North Adams roots,[6] decided to move his fledgling condenser operation from Quincy to North Adams. At an old textile mill in the Beaver section of town, production of condensers (capacitors) commenced in early 1930. Young women, most without previous factory experience, made up a majority of the workforce that engaged in light manufacturing.

In 1936 the first recorded strike, a one-day walkout, occurred, and the next year employees established their first union. Participants differ as to the circumstances of the walkout's formation, and even the year of its founding, but according to "facts" presented by a National Labor Relations Board decision in 1940, the idea for the union came from Carleton Shugg, Sprague vice president and plant manager.[7]

In March 1937, a wage dispute led to a two-day strike in the can shop. Gerry Steinberg, who began his career with Sprague in Quincy and worked at the North Adams plant since its start in 1930, remembered the strike as culminating from a number of grievances "boiling over." According to Steinberg, while it started with "one small group," within a couple of hours "the entire plant was practically empty." He recalled that the strike lasted "three or four days."[8]

At that time, the U.S. Supreme Court had not yet reached a decision on the constitutionality of the Wagner Act, and that first labor organization came to be called—literally—the Sprague Company Union (SCU). The following week, Shugg ran elections for representatives and officers. The company furnished application cards, made copies of the union's constitution and bylaws, and allowed SCU meetings at the plant. As Shugg himself testified, "I think I definitely took the leadership in the formation of the Sprague Company Union."[9]

Several weeks after the formation of the SCU, a representative of an AFL union, the International Brotherhood of Electrical Workers (IBEW), spoke to a meeting of about 125 Sprague employees. When labor activist Gerry Steinberg told Shugg that his role in starting SCU would lead to a "bona fide" union entering Sprague, Shugg responded: "That is a fine way to show your appreciation of what I have done for you."[10] At the same time, Shugg also used the carrot in response to such threats by accepting an SCU request for a vacation plan and time-and-a-half wages for holiday and weekend work.

The paternalistic loyalty assumed by Shugg did permeate the employee culture, but not without a sense of workers' rights. The first generation of Sprague workers at the Beaver plant thought highly of Shugg, and while that didn't keep them from unionizing or striking, it did lead to seemingly contradictory behaviors. For example, one retiree, Emma Gould, remembered a strike when employees walked a picket line while simultaneously taking up a collection for Vice President Shugg, who lay ill at the time. Years later, Gould laughed at the incident, shaking her head, and saying, "How stupid we were! How stupid can you get—really!"

Kenny Russell, who worked in management for most of his forty-plus years at Sprague, recalled his early years on production in the can shop while Shugg still served as boss. The 200 can shop employees got together and presented a petition to Shugg requesting a raise. Despite this show of courage, they must have felt intimidated enough to protect the identity of their leaders, so they creatively fashioned a petition into a circle, leaving no single name at the top.[11]

When Gould explained the good feelings that the first generation of Sprague employees held for the plant manager (notwithstanding their low wages), she reasoned that Shugg couldn't be at fault for their pay, citing: "He didn't own the company."[12] Despite this caveat in Shugg's case, numerous workers held very strong and positive feelings for R.C. Sprague himself who, in fact, did "own the company." Throughout the interviews with former employees, the positive feelings that workers evoked for management officials like R.C. Sprague, Shugg, and long-time director of personnel Jack Washburn very much correlated with the perception that these officials treated them with respect and concern. Conversely, other top officials, including R.C. Sprague's two sons, R.C. Jr. and John, were perceived as having little use for local employees, and were viewed with scorn.

In April 1937, the Supreme Court ruled the Wagner Act constitutional, thereby upholding legislation making company unions illegal. Shugg responded to this change by suggesting to the president of the company union, Charles Dean, that the union simply change its name and its meeting place. Thus, at the beginning of May, Sprague helped create the Independent Condenser Workers Union (ICW). How independent was it? Once again, Sprague management used its stationery and duplicating facilities to print the constitution and bylaws; membership was openly sought on Sprague property and on company time; all employees became members; and, while the union was recognized as the exclusive representative by management, "it never attempted to secure a contract."[13]

Others have different memories of the union beginnings at Sprague. According to one version, in 1937 about 100 workers met with Shugg and convinced him to recognize the new local.[14] By that time, Mabel Lewitt had already worked at Sprague for two years. Along with her husband, Leonard, she recalled a key role that she played in starting the union:

> I had to walk two miles to work and I couldn't punch in until the work came down the line. Sometimes I wouldn't even work at all and they'd send me back home. Then, I would no more than get back home and they would send for me and I had to go back again . . . . And the foremen's wives were working with them, their aunts, their uncles, their brothers, you name it. So we formed ICW #1. The first thing we did was to stop foremen from having members of their family working for them any more. Next, we got four hours of guaranteed work if we reported to work, which was no more than right. And we got rid of "gravy" jobs. Work had to be divided equally, good and bad.[15]

Gerry Steinberg also remembered the ICW's origins as coming from the rank and file. Elected Chairman of the Grievance Board, the key position in the union, Steinberg felt that the workers "made reasonable attempts to keep the union dissociated from the company." Nonetheless, Steinberg recognized that, because of the paucity of information in employee hands, they were forced "to accept pretty much as gospel" Sprague's arguments in regard to wages, hours, and conditions of work.[16]

Over the next three decades, R. C. Sprague skillfully used a blend of economic and political power with a well-developed paternalism and a variety of social and recreational services to keep national unions out of the city and generally to maintain control over a relatively low-paid but dedicated labor force.[17] A small group of machine shop employees successfully organized a local of the International Association of Machinists (IAM) in 1949, but nearly two decades would pass from that point before the office, technical, and production workers would belong to national unions.

THE UNITED ELECTRICAL WORKERS UNION AND SPRAGUE, 1937–1940

The Independent Condenser Workers Union maintained its status through the latter years of the Depression, during World War II, and for twenty more years until the end of the 1960s. Yet many other electrical plants, including one just twenty miles away in Pittsfield and another only fifty miles away in Schenectady, New York, had been organized by the UE. With a reputation of Communist domination and militant action, UE had enrolled 30,000 workers in seven General Electric plants, including the two giants in Lynn, Massachusetts, and Schenectady.[18] As early as 1937, at the height of CIO organizing in the United States, the UE also expressed an interest in trying to organize at Sprague.[19] Besides General Electric, UE had already organized radio assembly shops, the prime customer for Sprague's condensers, as well as half-a-dozen condenser manufacturers in New York.

The local opportunity for the CIO union came early in 1938 when management forced Sprague employees to take a 10 percent pay cut "on the plea . . . that the company was operating in the red, and [that it was] unable to meet the competition of other manufacturers.[20] Since the ICW had no research staff by which it could present its own analysis of the financial status of Sprague and the industry, it simply accepted the company's conclusions and the 10 percent cutback. This inability to challenge the company on financial research would plague the union for the next three decades. When the ICW finally lost an election to an international union in 1967, its detractors still focused on the need to bring in a sophisticated research arm.

UE's Tom Dwyer, tasked with organizing the union at the GE plant in Pittsfield, made contacts with workers at Sprague. When he proposed to bring in a UE speaker to discuss the company's financial position, he received strong support from the rank and file. In fact, Gerry Steinberg remembered that Sprague workers initiated the meeting with the UE organizer who presented "information which contradicted" management.[21] In a June 15, 1938 letter, UE's Director of Research-Education William Mitchell claimed:

> Sprague is in an excellent position and certainly has no basis for bellyaching . . . . Not only do the assets of Sprague far overshadow the liabilities, but the company has also taken the precaution of socking away over a half million dollars—just in case things get a little dull. When things get dull of course the people at Sprague lose their jobs and their pay envelopes, but the stock holders continue to draw dividends out of this kitty.[22]

In fact, Sprague reported to its board that the company was "in a strong liquid position," and George Flood, the treasurer, announced that the company's strength justified a total dividend of $12,000.[23] During the following year, the company reported a first quarter and a second quarter profit. In August, while the "wage adjustment plan" had already been accepted by the employees, R.C. Sprague told the board about his decision to spend company funds on a new company newspaper. At a cost of no more than $300 per issue, the paper would be "a means to develop an improved relationship" with the workers, something management had been wanting to do "for some time."[24]

The next two months at Sprague brought a flurry of activity. At the beginning of March, a group of Sprague workers visited UE headquarters in New York City, where they met national union president (and CIO vice president) James Carey. They also toured several UE organized condenser factories in the metropolitan area. According to the *Transcript*, UE organizer Thomas Dwyer clarified comparable condenser industry wages and documented the relatively low wages at Sprague. The *Transcript* reporter also wrote that about twenty-five Sprague employees attended a debate at Williams College on the CIO.[25]

On March 18, Carey traveled to North Adams, where he spoke to an audience of some 400 workers. Carey argued for the benefits of a nationally organized condenser workforce with a standard minimum wage, in effect to keep individual companies from competing over wages and setting one group of employees against another. After Carey spoke, workers from three New York area condenser firms affiliated with UE discussed their own more favorable working conditions and wages. This would not be the last time that UE militants from New York and New Jersey plants journeyed to Sprague to help organize. They came from "strong, well-organized tough locals. . . . (T)hey were very militant people who really believed in spreading the word. And they understood that they had to organize these places like Sprague . . . ."[26] The North Adams workers must have been impressed, as they voted, unofficially, to affiliate with the pioneering CIO union.[27]

The momentum continued to grow. The next day, ICW's executive board announced that an affiliation vote would be taken at its meeting on March 22. By then, Sprague's management had become actively involved in heading off the possible UE affiliation. Sprague Vice President Shugg called the ICW leadership to his office and scolded them about their pro-CIO "organizational activities," warning them that they "were doing harm to the bulk of the workers."[28]

Nonetheless, the vote that evening favored UE, 51 to 46. Within three days, a charter had been issued to the new local, No. 249, with Charles Dean serving as president. Dean's willingness to take the presidency must have been a great coup to the UE faction, as he left his ICW vice presidency to do so. The new group quickly rented office space in town and enrolled twenty members.

Meanwhile, at a meeting attended by 145 employees, opponents of the UE established a new independent union, simply called Independent Condenser Workers Union #2 (ICW #2). Dean complained that the anti-CIO group did not publicize the meeting and that those who came "represented a picked group . . . and included almost all of the supervisors and assistant foremen, . . . salaried workers, and members of the laboratory staff." Dean went on to say that "while it would form a splendid basis for a mutual benefit association, it was hardly a good nucleus for a labor union."[29]

A week later, UE Local 249 filed charges with the labor board alleging that Sprague management violated the Wagner Act by helping to organize ICW #2. On another front, UE supporters initiated a series of meetings with employees, department by department, in a drive to increase their membership. Some meetings were even held outdoors, as "Sprague put pressure" on the owners of local halls to keep the CIO union from meeting in their establishments.[30]

On April 27, after repeated requests for recognition from both unions, Sprague management designated ICW #2 as the official bargaining unit for production workers, claiming that they had enrolled a majority of the employees. Despite Sprague's recognition of the independent union, UE organizers continued efforts to increase its membership. Local 49 grew in size and influence, and soon began publishing 1,000 copies of a bi-weekly newsletter with local and national labor news, editorials, sports, and a gossip column.

Meanwhile, in an interesting development, James Wall, the owner of Wall-Streeter Shoe Company, a Sprague stockholder and activist in the Democratic Party and in industrial trade associations, met with two UE local executive board members to try to convince the union to withdraw its charges to the NLRB. The union responded to Wall, whom organizer Adolph Stearns deemed "the most influential citizen in town."[31] The response was as follows:

> We wish to inform you that our body is convinced that our course of action in appealing to a Federal agency for the purpose of creating an organization for the benefit of the workers in the plant in which we work is correct. The policy of the U.E. is to increase wages, shorten hours, and better working conditions . . . . We as citizens and wage earners of this community fully appreciate your interest in maintaining the

> good name of the city of North Adams. We believe that our action in forming a local of the U.E . . . will not only aid a great number of family-heads and supporters of families to [a] higher standard of living, but will be an important factor in creating a fuller social and cultural life for our membership and all our friends.
>
> We are ready to seriously consider, at all times, all and any advice which would help us achieve our aims, which are no different than the aims of the people of North Adams as a whole. That is, to be better Americans and to make our city an example of prosperity.[32]

While Wall's original letter is not available, it seems evident from the union response that the North Adams leading industrialist made his case based on the greater good for the whole community. UE's rejoinder captured the same ideological ground, fighting for the good of "our city." Throughout these and other internal labor and labor-management battles, both sides regularly presented their individual concerns as congruent with the broad community interest. (This portrayal continued decades later into the ten-week strike in 1970, where both sides argue that they represent the community.) On a more internal basis, the company liked to argue that management and the employees were part of the same "family." During World War II, opposing unions both promoted themselves as being "American."

In late 1938, Local 249 received good news when the Labor Board's "Intermediate Report" found that Sprague had indeed violated labor law by "dominating and interfering with the formation and administration" of ICW #2. The Board recommended the withdrawal of recognition from the "Independent" union for purposes of collective bargaining and a new election. These stipulations remained provisional, however, pending approval by the national board. Over a year passed before the national board made a decision, one that reversed the regional board's pro-UE finding. On February 19, 1940, the Board concluded that ICW #1 was a company union (Sprague's "puppet"), but it held that its successor represented the production workers in an independent fashion and had not been a union "dominated" or "aided" in its start by management. Even though one Board member dissented from this conclusion, the majority ruled, and ICW #2 received further legitimacy as the representative of Sprague's blue-collar workers.[33]

UE–ICW FIGHT CONTINUES 1941–1944

The Independent Condenser Workers union may have won the battle, but UE supporters continued to fight the war. The pessimism at UE headquarters in early September 1941 over securing a beachhead at Sprague reversed itself later that month when, halfway through the contract year, a wildcat strike erupted, against the wishes of the ICW.[34] Interviews with ICW stalwarts suggest that UE activist Gerry Steinberg helped agitate for the strike. Management at first rebuffed demands from a delegation of departmental representatives; the unofficial bargaining group had asked for a 15 percent wage hike, the recovery of lunchroom privileges, additional seniority rights, and no pay penalty for the walk-out. Further, the *Transcript* reported the presence of CIO representatives in North Adams, the distribution of CIO literature to the strikers, and strike support from a UE business agent who addressed the crowd. Sprague termed the demands "unauthorized," but the company met with a four-man strike committee on the second day of the job action. Sprague satisfied the group's demands on the lunchroom and seniority, but not on the key economic issues. Three days later, the "official" bargaining committee of the ICW joined the strike committee. Five days of additional negotiation brought a settlement.[35]

The employees won about half of the wage increase they sought. They also improved their lunchroom scheduling and won a bonus payment plan. The proposals met with the approval of the workforce by a three to one margin, although less than 500 out of a total of 1,700 employees voted.

One historian of Sprague unionism interpreted the nine-day strike as not only unsuccessful, but also a setback for UE.[36] However, while UE seemed to agree with this evaluation of the strike itself, the union did not see it as a self-inflicted defeat. Instead, the relative failure of the strike heightened the optimism of UE Field Organizer Walter Mugford that the workforce might be ready to listen again to a CIO union. "There is a strong pro-C.I.O. feeling among the workers, although, there is also a very active anti-Union group. Personally, I feel that the time is now right for an active organizational campaign."[37] In addition, Mugford added that a small group from the Pittsfield General Electric local would help with the organizing.

The national union went along with Mugford's assessment and agreed to send a full-time organizer, Edith Hammer, to work in North Adams.[38] UE records leave it unclear as to whether or not Hammer ever carried out that assignment, but apparently either she or another woman organizer did spend time in town.[39]

In 1943, the UE hired veteran activist Gerry Steinberg as a full-time organizer for Sprague's 3,000 employees. By far, Steinberg was the dominant and most widely known Sprague militant.[40] Numerous Sprague employees referred to him as a Communist, labels they also attached to the CIO and the UE. The Communist charge certainly intimidated potential UE supporters. As Emma Gould remembered it, "Anybody that had dealings with Gerry they called them Communist . . . . I got out of his way, too." But while she was "scared" about his rumored affiliation, she, as was the case for most of the other respondents, "liked him as a person."[41] Opponents also recognized the skill which Steinberg went about his organizing, whether talking, listening, or buying drinks at a local tavern. One old-timer remembered him as a "pretty fair guy" and a "real good fighter," though Steinberg publicly opposed any violence.

The CIO Sprague strategy included an educational

campaign both in the shop and around the city on the advantages of the UE, and a goal of burrowing from within, of electing sympathizers to key positions, including stewards. It was a critical time for the union since, according to veteran field organizer Hugh Harley Jr., "we have the Sprague situation upside down with an excellent chance of cracking it wide open."[42]

Leo Potegal, another organizer, soon joined Steinberg, and Harley also aided the cause. The educational campaign within the union and the attempt to gain leadership seats and take over the independent union proceeded aggressively. As of late August, Steinberg reported that most of the members of the Executive Council of ICW had signed on with UE and were "now beginning to exercise their power as prescribed by their constitution and holding meetings off company time and property."[43] At the same time, supporters of UE thwarted the independent union from pushing the company's insufficient wage offer to the employees and brought in three non-Sprague condenser workers to inform the membership of the wages and conditions they received in their union shops, an action reminiscent of the 1938 campaign.[44]

As attempts escalated to bring a UE affiliation vote, the action grew even more heated. The independent union president and his executive council expelled seven UE supporters as "CIO stooges" and distributed a leaflet warning members away from a special union meeting that had been organized for an affiliation vote. Relatively few attended, but UE won the affiliation vote 124 to 1. Steinberg, perhaps somewhat optimistically, claimed that "[i]t is apparent now, that the rank-and-file Sprague worker is against the co. union leadership and will call for their removal shortly."[45]

Money remained the dominant issue, but any broad discussion of wages or union dues had to be viewed within the context of local control, a factor that aided the independent union. The pro-UE faction argued that a national union with a research staff would provide the education and information necessary to negotiate with a wealthy and powerful employer and would bring Sprague workers up to par with comparable capacitor workers elsewhere. ICW adherents countered that they had been able to negotiate raises, and a national affiliation would mean a huge increase in dues and a loss of local money to well-heeled CIO bureaucrats.

One ICW argument, as recalled by a respondent decades later, recognized the ICW's own lack of power, but nonetheless argued that UE wouldn't do any better. "So we pay 10 cents a week (in dues), we get 10 cents worth," he said. "(If we) pay 60 cents, are we going to get 60 cents worth? No!" The former employee felt that the economic issues (pay) overshadowed the political (Communist) issue. Further, he thought, some may have wanted to stay with the ICW, believing that no union, even a national one, "is gonna dictate to R.C. Sprague. This was the big thing."[46]

Who supported UE? Some felt that younger, lower-paid employees tended to back a CIO affiliation, but evidence also exists that the UE had support among machine shop workers, among the most skilled and the highest paid workers at Sprague. It does appear likely that the UE may have been less successful among the women than the men. In the late 1930s, UE's local membership was evenly split among men and women, although women made up about three quarters of Sprague's employees.[47]

On the national level, women dominated an electrical work force like Sprague's.[48] While they became union activists less frequently than men, their on-the-job friendships and gender networks formed the basis for informal work group leadership and militancy on the shop floor. Family-like, gender-based friendships also typified the Sprague work force over the years.[49]

One hypothesis held that Sprague's female employees were more difficult to unionize than men, not because of sex or gender per se, but because they were typically younger, less experienced, and less committed to maintaining their jobs at Sprague than the men. With a shorter-term outlook toward the job, the women tended to fear strikes and seemed more apt to shy away from unions. Their status also helped make them more susceptible to anti-UE arguments about outside or Communist control of the national union.[50]

Also, UE in North Adams added to these difficulties by sending in seven young male organizers for the Sprague campaign. Gossip spread about sexual liaisons between these men and women workers, increasing division within the workforce. UE organizer Hugh Harley admitted the following:

> "[W]omen liked the men and the men liked the women and sometimes two or three women would like the same man. Well, then the word would get going around that so and so on the staff is monkeying around with this particular person and then some other women would be jealous of it and they wouldn't like it and it just ended up a goddamn mess. Me included . . . . [T]here was plenty of reality so it was spread among the people and I'm sure the company didn't slow it down. And that's true in any campaign regardless of what the issue is.[51]

The added burden of major child and home care responsibilities faced by the women also made it more difficult for them to become union activists. For many women, the demands of the day simply provided no time available to even go to union meetings. However, despite this, Hugh Harley did remember two strong UE female stalwarts from the rank and file, including one "tough, hard fighting woman."[52]

During January, Harley reported that "things" were "moving" and that "[l]ocal talent" had emerged.[53] The UE petitioned the NLRB Board for an election to determine representation for the production employees. The union collected over 1,000 signatures calling for the election, out of a certified workforce of approximately 2,700. Both the independent union and the company filed briefs to forestall an election and maintain the rights of ICW #2,[54] but to no avail. UE organizers continued to build up their forces, initiating a steward's organizational system, with some sixty-six stewards in the UE corner, though time appeared to be against them. In Washington, the national union officials tried to delay the date of the vote. Nonetheless, a steward's organizational system had been initiated, and the sixty-six stewards stood in the UE corner.[55]

The membership of UE's local increased by an average of fifty-six a week throughout the month of May. The pace of activity accelerated as the August 22 voting date approached. And the results looked promising. In Hugh Harley's own words:

> [The ICW] . . . has a poor organization in the shop and in the past four weeks we have dominated the activity in most of the shop. If this trend continues we will be able to solidify our people. The ICW is not doing much for the people at the present time and there is considerable resentment against it. [But] it has very successfully raised the strike and dues issue and we have only been able to counteract it partially.
>
> We are now six organizers on the job. Each is assigned to one of the weak areas and is doing a large amount of home visiting. This is gradually getting good results. Our people are very confident that they can do a job, which is not necessarily a good sign, although in this case it helps because the [ICW] people are gradually being undermined by the confidence our people show.

Harley, however, did note, "our membership is not necessarily stable. We are not able to get big numbers of our members to wear buttons."[56]

If any adult in North Berkshire still remained unaware of the upcoming election between the two unions, by the time the second half of August rolled around that would change. With just a few days left before the voting, both sides took out huge ads in the *Transcript*, trumpeting their causes, and the UE even purchased fifteen minutes of radio time.

ICW began the campaign on August 19 with a half-page ad headlined: "HOME RULE—BEWARE OF THE C.I.O. WOLVES IN UE CLOTHING!" The ad castigated the UE supporters as outsiders, as "carpetbaggers" who "come to town like the seventeen year locusts to eat off the fat of the land and disappear after the pickings have become lean." Local readers read that a favorable UE vote would just enrich Sidney Hillman, the vice president of the CIO and at that time its most widely known and controversial leader, and bring him more Florida vacations. Rather than turning the union over to Hillman and "his henchmen," the ICW ad portrayed itself as "fearless, courageous, vigilant, and honest," and with membership dues at only $1.00 a year. The ad reminded Sprague employees not to "sell your birthright for a filthy mess of pottage." Just before the ad concluded listing three rows of a dozen ICW supporters each, a final "headline" blared out: "VOTE I.C.W. NO. 2 AND SEND THE 'CARPETBAGGERS' BACK TO SIDNEY HILLMAN."[57] At that time, Hillman, who had led the CIO's textile organizing campaign, had become one of the most recognized names within the leadership of the CIO, and a confidante of President Roosevelt.

Two days later UE responded with a half-page ad. The headline read: "SPRAGUE'S OLD TIMERS 'SPEAK UP,'" the message tried to combat the "outsider" theme and included signatures from thirteen "old-timers," each with eight to twelve years of time put in at Sprague. They stressed that the CIO union had not been thrust upon them, but had been solicited by machine shop workers "because it is the only real union in the electrical manufacturing industry with a record of getting things done for the members." The writers blamed the independent union for Sprague's low wages compared with other electrical and machine plants in the North Adams, Greenfield, and Pittsfield areas.[58]

They went on to inform their readers that "any bona-fide national organization (such as the American Legion, the Elks, the Eagles, the Moose) must have money to carry on their work."

After accusing ICW officials of "LIES, PROMISES AND A LOT OF HOT AIR," they asked their readers to "VOTE UE—THE AMERICAN WAY."[59] Just as the ideological war included the struggle over local community turf, so did the battle rage over which side better represented America and Americanism—key issues during a war, particularly for a union accused of being Communist-controlled.

In the same issue of the paper, UE ran another big ad stressing that the 1,700 members of Local 249 were North Adams people and not "The So-called 'Outsiders.'" The ad concluded with about eighty signatures listed by work areas.

Not to be outdone, ICW's ad on that same day attacked "The CIO Rabble-Rousers!!" for costing Sprague workers a raise. It pointed to UE "Empty Promises!" and "CIO Florida Vacationists." And in a bit of red-baiting, the ad also suggested some new initials referring to a CIO campaign—NAC—"sounds to us like Non-American Communists."[60]

The anti-Communist attack against UE was a common tactic nationwide and certainly at Sprague. UE's strongest antagonist, William Stackpole, "brought that issue up," claiming to know who was "communist-tinged." Stackpole complained that, while UE wrapped itself up in the American flag, its union newspaper looked almost the same as the *Daily Worker*, the Communist Party paper. While Stackpole felt that the Communist issue was enough to prevent workers from voting for UE, he had other problems with the CIO union.

Prior to working at Sprague Electric, Stackpole had been employed at General Electric in Pittsfield, where the UE represented the production workers. The stewards did "nothing" and the union wasn't "policing their [collective bargaining] contract," so Stackpole declared, "I wouldn't join it in 100 years." He even found fault with the way the union's organizers dressed, a "crummy group," standing out from all of the other labor unions. Stackpole came to Sprague in the middle of the 1944 campaign, where he jumped in immediately against UE, producing flyers for the ICW election campaign. The aggressive distribution of such propaganda leaflets was a key tactic in the union battles of the 1930s and 1940s. Just two months after coming to Sprague, Stackpole was elected chairman of the independent union's grievance committee, the main seat of power within that organization.[61]

In a prominent two-column news story on Election Day, the *Transcript* called it "the largest labor election ever held in North Adams."[62] Both unions had agreed to stop their campaigning at midnight before the day of the vote, and that truce held up. Yet, despite the best efforts of the UE organizers and supporters, the 911 UE votes fell some 400 short, and the great CIO drive came to an end, with the victory going to the ICW.[63]

The hard-fought win for the incumbent union led to an impromptu parade down Main Street. At UE headquarters, participants sang, cheered, and listened to the drum corps play. Then, after receiving a parade permit, the celebrants followed a police patrol car through the city's shopping district. According to the *Transcript*, "It was generally agreed that the election brought out more people and created more interest and enthusiasm on Main [S]treet than any municipal election in many years." The independent union scheduled a party at the Blue Room of the Richmond Hotel for Friday night, while UE activists resolved to carry out their plans for their own party at the Moose Hall. Although "CIO organizers said . . . they would keep the union office open and would 'keep up the fight,'" UE Local 249 officially disbanded before long.[64] They did, however, return to contest a 1948 election at Sprague and successfully organized a branch plant of Sprague Electric in Bennington, Vermont, in 1952.

CONCLUSION

The day after the election, the *Transcript* reported that the victory margin was "much higher than was generally anticipated. Election observers had freely predicted that only 150 to 200 votes would separate the two unions," and that as recently as a week earlier, some "observers predicted that the UE union would win easily."[65]

Why did the CIO union fail to win the Sprague membership in the late 1930s and again in the mid-1940s? A major reason, perhaps the most important one, must center on the power of the corporation along with an allied company union already in place. Sprague's electrical workers recognized the need for a partisan voice, but split over the necessity of its being an "outside," national union. The company union provided the formal bargaining and grievance structure of a union, kept dues low, and spoke to a strong "localist" ideology—one that supported an emphasis of self-sufficiency and distrust of outsiders.

R.C. Sprague played his cards well. He stayed out of the fray on the shop floor and at the bargaining table, and presented an image of the concerned father, of one who is worried about the well-being of his workforce. Very much aware of national corporate plans of paternalism, or welfare capitalism, he helped found a company union as well as a panoply of training programs, sports, music, and other leisure activities for "his" employees. He presented himself as a neutral bystander, while urging his employees to exercise their "democratic" right in the bitterly contested election of 1944. A company newspaper and a generally friendly personnel staff also aided in producing an informal, family-like atmosphere in the plant.

When the "iron fist" was called for, Sprague's plant manager enforced the 10 percent wage cut and "hung tough" on other contract and strike issues. Influential manufacturer James Wall challenged the need for the UE presence in town, and, as previously mentioned, the "independent" union resorted to red-baiting the insurgents. Opportunities for work did not abound in North Adams, and local residents had already learned that the red brick mills along the Hoosic River did not guarantee lifetime employment in shoe production or textiles. Fear of losing one's job could never be taken lightly. The new manufacturer of condensers "provided" work in a relatively hospitable environment, and the founder and his company seemed to care, as was witnessed by the sporting teams and numerous events that the company sponsored. Yet despite all of this, from time to time Sprague workers did rebel, even against R.C. Sprague and the "independent union." Perhaps the initial question should not be why did UE fail, but rather how was UE able to come so close to winning?

Years later, Stackpole expressed no surprise that over 900 Sprague employees had voted for the UE, even with the strong campaign mounted by its opponents. The UE, after all, had been "around so long" and had been "organizing . . . for a long time." Also, there were "always groups [of voters] that were dissatisfied" and UE "always had a hard core."[66]

Workers across the country were organizing by the millions in the late 1930s, and the CIO upsurge brought new unions to nearby Pittsfield, Greenfield, and Schenectady. UE projected energy, thoroughness, and honesty, qualities that resonated well with local workers. Paternalism, as an ideology, assumes an obligation by the father to care for the obedient children: when the father reneges on that social contract—as, for example, when a 10 percent wage cut by Sprague does not seem to be merited—the children may rebel. In E.P. Thompson's phrase, the "moral economy" has been violated.[67] During such periods of time, some mainstays of the status quo, such as a company union, may well be overturned.

As the national economy fluctuates and as political structures shift, opportunities for social change emerge. A group or relationship that may be stereotyped as "immutable" during one era may be quite "mutable" during another. Gary Gerstle has skillfully demonstrated the process by which Woonsocket, Rhode Island, French Canadians developed the most militant textile local in New England during the 1930s, while coming from an ethnic background that historians and union officials have traditionally stereotyped as culturally conservative.[68]

Despite its size and isolation, North Adams felt the winds of Depression-era change and New Deal ideas. Change clearly impacted traditional textile workers in North Berkshire; with the onset of electrical workers, the workplace shifted, not only in relations between employees and managers, but also through conflicts between groups of workers.[69]

Gerry Steinberg began work at Sprague Specialties in Quincy, Massachusetts, and moved to North Adams when the firm relocated there in 1930. As an employee, he became the main union organizer within the company, advocating for the United Electric Workers (UE), a founding union within the Congress of Industrial Organizations (CIO). He later left Sprague and became a full-time organizer for the UE, and played a key role in their concerted campaign at Sprague in 1944. (photo from Rhoda Steinberg)

Cartoon from the "U.E. News," a newsletter circulated at Sprague during the 1944 campaign, poking fun at the current production workers union.

NOTES

1 Robert W. Eisenmenger, *The Dynamics of Growth in New England's Economy, 1870–1964* (Middletown, CT: Wesleyan University Press, 1967), 68. Sprague would grow to be one of the largest electronics manufacturers in the state, and a harbinger of the shift in production in New England from textiles to electronics, to electronic components. "Any device that exploits the movement of electrons is . . . 'electronic' . . . . An electronic device is one in which a controlled and variable flow of electrons results in a signal containing information." Early on, such devices would use vacuum tubes and later transistors. When Sprague began, the industry it serviced, radios, "was the only large source of employment in electronic product manufacture." R. C. Estall, *New England: A Study in Industrial Adjustment* (New York: Praeger, 1966), 80.

2 David Brody, *Workers in Industrial America* (New York: Oxford University Press, 1980), 58.

3 Thomas Brooks, *Toil and Trouble* (New York: Delacorte, 1971), 192.

4 See, for example, James R. Green, *The World of the Workers: Labor in Twentieth Century America* (New York: Hill & Wang, 1980).

5 *Transcript*, October 3, 1929, 1.

6 R.C.'s grandfather, David Sprague, married Frances Julia King in 1842 and lived in Milford, Connecticut. After the tragic death of their first child, they had two sons, Frank Julian Sprague, R.C.'s father, born in 1857, and Charles May, born in 1860. In 1866, the boys' mother suffered a hemorrhage and died. David decided to head west on his own and left his two young sons with his older sister, Elvira Betsy Ann Sprague, of North Adams. Both boys went to public school and to Drury Academy. Frank, according to the *Transcript*, "the smartest boy of his age in town," graduated from the Naval Academy. He went on to have a very distinguished career as an inventor, working briefly with Thomas Edison, before forming his own company where he completed work on street railway electrification, did pioneering work on elevator technology, and became known as the "father of electric traction." His early years in North Adams apparently had no role in his son's move to the Beaver mill in North Adams in 1929. William D. Middleton & William D. Middleton III, *Frank Julian Sprague: Electrical Inventor & Engineer* (Bloomington: Indiana University Press, 2009); John L. Sprague and Joseph J. Cunningham, "A Frank Sprague Triumph: The Electrification of Grand Central Terminal," http://magazine.ieee-pes.org /januaryfebruary-2013/history-6/; and John L. Sprague, *Sprague Electric: An Electronics Giant's Rise, Fall, and Life after Death* (North Charleston, South Carolina: CreateSpace Independent Publishing Platform, 2015).

7 See Raymond C. Bliss, *A Study of Union History at the Sprague Electric Company in North Adams, Mass. 1929–1970* (Williamstown: Williams College, 1976); Stewart Burns, "Capacitors and Community: Women Workers at Sprague Electric, 1930–1980," The Public Historian (Fall 1989); and NLRB decision, 1940, Case No. c-1040.

8 George A. Piendak, *The Independent Condenser Workers Union, Local #2: A Study of Local Unionism* (Williamstown, MA: Williams College, 1965), 14; and NLRB Case No. c-1040.

9 NLRB Case No. c-1040, 4.

10 Ibid.

11 Interviews by the author with Emma Gould and Kenny Russell, 1991.

12 Interview with Gould.

13 NLRB Case No. c-1040, 5.

14 Burns, 18–19.

15 Robert Paul Gabrielsky, "The Evolution of the Marshall Street Complex in North Adams," *Historical Journal of Massachusetts*, XIX (Winter 1991), 33. One historian of Sprague unionization, Raymond Bliss (1976), makes a strong case that the ICW had always been a company union. While Gabrielsky doesn't deny this, he argues that the actions of the union over time bespoke the kind of militancy one saw early on in the CIO's development (34–35). On the whole, though, the ICW's acceptance of one-year contracts tied to Christmas bonuses and its unwillingness to bolster any research and educational capacity led to a more bureaucratic or business unionism than that practiced in the heady, CIO social movement days of the late 1930s. If Sprague's workers displayed a rank-and-file militancy, it may have been more in spite of, rather than because of, the ICW.

16 Piendak, 15–16.

17 Gabrielsky, 28–30.

18 James J. Matles and James Higgins, *Them and Us: Struggles of a Rank-and-File Union* (Englewood Cliffs, NJ: Prentice-Hall, 1974), 84.

19 James Matles to Tom Dwyer, Dcember 15, 1937, in the United Electrical Workers Union (UE) archives, Archives of Industrial Society, University of Pittsburgh.

20 Dwyer to Research Department, UE archives, February 3, 1938.

21 Piendak, 17.

22 Letter in the UE archives.

23 Sprague Board of Directors meeting, minutes, December 10, 1937.

24 Ibid., August 25, 1938.

25 *Transcript*, March 18, 1938.

26 Interview by author with Hugh Harley, retired UE organizer, 1992.

27 *Transcript*, March 19, 1938.

28 National Labor Relations Board, case c-1040, 7.

29 *Transcript*, March 24, 1938.

30 Ibid., March 26, 1938. Phone interview with Robert R.R. Brooks, 1991. Brooks, a Williams College professor, labor economist, and former New Deal

administrator, vividly recalled a pro-UE speech he gave at a street corner in North Adams more than fifty years earlier.

31 In 1942, Wall served as vice-president of the National Boot & Shoe Manufacturers Association and, regionally, was a director of the New England Shoe Association. R.C. Sprague, younger than Wall, would most resemble his friend in his trade association and political activism, though Sprague was a Republican. Wall's Democratic Party politics of the 1930s and 1940s tended to be conservative, and probably differed not much from Sprague's, and both men, of course, abhorred unions. Bernard A. Drew, "Wall and Streeter, maker of shoes," *Berkshire Eagle*, July 5, 2014.

32 Stearns to Matles, UE archives, April 20, 1938.

33 *Transcript*, February 20, 1940.

34 Matles to organizer Walter Mugford, UE archives, September 2, 1941,

35 Bliss, 21. One retiree discussed a 1941 strike in different terms, and it is unclear if his reference is to the same events. He recalls that the union hired a Williamstown lawyer, Judge Ruby, to represent them. Ruby called a meeting of the employees at a local ballpark, Noel Field, where he reported on his negotiations with the company and on what he settled for. When dissent developed over what some saw as a low figure, Ruby responded that the union had given him the power to reach an agreement without any subsequent vote from the membership. During the course of the strike, the employees carried their protest from the Beaver St. plant to downtown as they marched to the home of George Flood, Sprague's treasurer and controller, on Church St. Here again, the protest was directed at the founder's representative, and not at R.C. Sprague himself.

36 Ibid. It may be that Bliss's ICW informants exaggerated the role of the CIO union in the walkout in order to blame UE for its relative failure. While there were to be no more plant-wide strikes at Sprague until just after the end of World War II, a good deal of worker militancy nonetheless made itself felt. William Stackpole, the longtime leader of the ICW, termed the forties "'a war between Sprague and the union.'" In 1943–4 Stackpole remembered "'innumerable walkouts by plants and departments'" (Bliss, 24), and, years later, recalled the use of the quickie sit-down strike as a powerful tool (interview with author, 1990). These experiences typified workplace activism across the nation where unions officially upheld a wartime, no-strike pledge, but its members waged numerous informal, wildcat sit-in strikes to gain some immediate advantage (Green, Chapter 6).

37 Mugford to Matles, October 31, 1941.

38 Matles to Hammer, UE archives, November 5, 1941.

39 Interview by the author with Rhoda Steinberg, widow of Gerry Steinberg, 1993.

40 Piendak, 14.

41 Interview with Gould, 1991.

42 Hugh Harley to Matles, UE archives, 2.

43 Steinberg report, UE archives, August 28, 1943.

44 William Stackpole remembered that meeting, or one very similar, as a case of a UE double-cross. According to Stackpole, one of the UE outside spokesman came from Solar, a condenser company nearly in bankruptcy. Stackpole claimed that Solar paid UE to send an organizer to North Adams to foment a strike there, thus bringing more condenser business to Solar. As Stackpole recalled it, "I pinned the guy [the president of the union at Solar] down right on the Drury [High School] stage." Whether, in fact, deliberate deception had occurred, Stackpole's perception of it points to the tremendous hostility felt by both sides. (Author interview with Stackpole.)

45 Steinberg report, op cit.

46 Author interview with Sprague employee who didn't want to be identified.

47 "Sprague's Union Eyes," (local UE newsletter), December 15, 1938, 2.

48 Ronald Schatz, *The Electrical Workers: A History of Labor at General Electric and Westinghouse, 1923–1960* (Urbana, Illinois University Press, 1983), 33.

49 See, e.g., Burns. Predominantly female unions such as the Amalgamated Clothing Workers of America (ACWA) and the International Ladies' Garment Workers' Union (ILGWU) grew dramatically during the late '30s. Further, women were involved in the popular sit-in movements susceptible to anti-UE arguments about outside and Communist control of the era at, for example, Philadelphia's Pennstate Tobacco Company and two Woolworth stores in Detroit. For the most part, though, top formal leadership positions in CIO unions remained closed to women. Joshua Freeman, Nelson Lichtenstein et al., *Who Built America? Working People and the Nation's Economy, Politics, Culture, and Society* (NY: Pantheon Books, 1992), 411, 413.

50 Interview with Harley.

51 Ibid.

52 Ibid. In North Berkshire, it appears that women are more likely to become activists in their late thirties, when the bulk of their early child rearing responsibilities were over. Seider, "Labor Activists and the Life Cycle," unpublished paper. In North Berkshire, it was not uncommon for in two paycheck families, the husband would work one shift, the wife the second, and the two would share childcare responsibilities. On a national level, "women who played leading roles in labor organizing during the 1930s tended to be people living in unusual circumstances—divorcees, widows, political radicals, or members of union-conscious households." Freeman et al., 413. The female activists that Schatz studied in the electrical industry "differed crucially in their personal lives: they lived independent lives while their sister workers mostly were dutiful daughters living at home and turning over their pay to their parents." Brody, 468.

53 Harley Report, UE archives, January 22, 1944.

54 The practice of the ICW and management joining forces against UE had occurred previously and would happen again both in North Adams and in a Bennington, Vermont, branch plant.

55 Harley to Scribner, UE archives, May 10, 1944.

56 Harley to Emspak, UE archives, July 23, 1944.

57 *Transcript*, August 19, 1944. In that same edition of the newspaper, another ICW ad invited all Sprague workers to a "Victory Picnic" on Sunday, two days before the election. Food and drinks would be free and the ad concluded with a sample ballot where an "X" marked the I.C.W. No. 2 slot.

58 Ibid., August 21, 1944.

59 Ibid.

60 Ibid.

61 Author interview with Stackpole, 1990.

62 *Transcript*, August 22, 1944.

63 Ibid.

64 Ibid.

65 *Transcript*, August 23, 1944.

66 Interview by author, 1990.

67 E.P. Thompson, *The Making of the English Working Class* (London: Victor Gollancz, 1963).

68 Gary Gerstle, *Working-Class Americanism: The Politics of Labor in a Textile City, 1914–1960* (Cambridge University Press, 1989). Similar ethnic "shifts" may be detected in Sprague/North Adams history. In fact Burns (1989), seems too quick to accept a strong Catholic background as a major explanation for his respondents' "apparent conservatism."

69 As Gerstle suggests, "union development should be analyzed in terms of the struggle of competing rank-and-file groups for power and influence" (126). This kind of competition did in fact exist during Sprague's first fifteen years of operation. Robert H. Zieger adds, "We know little about the interior worlds of industrial workers of the 1930s and 1940s." "Toward the History of the CIO: A Bibliographical Report," *Labor History*, XXVIII (Fall, 1985), 509. More, as well, needs to be known about the consciousness of workplace activists, of people like Gerry Steinberg, to understand where their 'resentment of injustice' springs from and how it becomes activated. Peter Friedlander, in Brody, "The CIO after 50 Years," 468.

CHAPTER THIRTEEN

SOCIAL CLASS AND UNION MEMBERSHIP IN NORTH ADAMS

AT THE BEGINNING of World War II, the makeup of the social classes in North Adams could be described as follows: some 40 to 50 percent of the city's families made their livings from relatively "unskilled" mill work; 35 to 40 percent had white-collar or skilled blue-collar occupations; some 10 percent fell into a class of "junior executives," managers, very highly skilled workers, and some professionals; and at the economic apex, some 5 percent, stood the mill owners, big business men, well-established professionals, and the old families with significant inherited wealth.[1]

The war coincided with a shift in employment out of textiles as Sprague's share of the labor market rose significantly. Still, many North Adams residents found work in the other mills and enterprises in the city. In the early 1940s, with a population of nearly 23,000, some 6,600 North Adams workers toiled in the nine biggest mills in the cities. Next to Sprague, Arnold Print Works employed the most, at 1,450. National unions represented the skilled printers and engravers at APW, while the vast bulk of the lower paid workforce (1,350 employees) belonged to a local, independent union, the Calico Workers' Union #1.[2]

Similarly, the Calico Workers' Union #2 represented the majority of the lower paid workers at Windsor, the city's other print works, and, as with APW, the smaller group of skilled printers and engravers belonged to separate national unions. The president of the Calico Workers gave some of the same reasons for not affiliating with a national union that his counterpart at Sprague's ICW union would have stated: distrust of national leaders and an unwillingness to pay higher union dues.[3]

Even though the cotton workers at Berkshire Fine Spinning Mills belonged to a New England based national union, the American Federation of Textile Operatives, their wages remained fairly low. The woolen workers at Strong, Hewat, some 500 strong, belonged to a local, independent union but enjoyed higher wages, a typical outcome for woolen, not cotton, employees. They also participated in a group insurance plan that provided them with visiting nurse association services, disability benefits for thirteen weeks, disease and accident benefits, a small pension based on age and years of service, and death benefits to beneficiaries.[4]

The two major shoe plants in North Adams, Wall-Streeter and Gale, manufactured high-priced men's shoes and low-priced women's shoes respectively. Wall had an apparently well-deserved reputation for being vehemently anti-union, and several employees had been fired for attempting to start a union. Wall paid his workers by piece rate and, according to one worker, Wall would "fire anybody that got to know his trade too well, lest he start drawing too high a salary." The skilled workers at Gale Shoe Company belonged to a number of craft unions and, not surprisingly, made higher wages than their counterparts at Wall-Streeter. For example, the Gale cutters averaged fifty dollars a week compared to thirty dollars for the cutters that Wall employed. The less skilled workers at Gale also did better than those at Wall's, and morale seemed much higher, in large part due to the labor relations and the easier manner of Gale himself.[5] Over 1,000 employees produced shoes in North Adams during the war years, with 400 at Wall-Streeter and 675 at Gale Shoe Company.[6]

For the city's mill workers as a whole, weekly wages ran from a low of $18 for the most "unskilled" work to a high of $75 for the very skilled, unionized printers and engravers. Most of the workers fell into the less-skilled category, and wages averaged about $30 a week in 1942. While wages had generally increased by the beginning of the war, so had the cost of food, rent, and clothing, and workers in North Adams suffered a decline in their real buying power. Add that to the fact that numerous families lost the salaries of their sons and husbands as they went to war, and local residents who depended on mill employment survived on relatively tight budgets.[7]

With both parents needing to work in one of the city's mills, the workers had to find a way to share childcare, unless a relative or friend could help out. Catherine O'Neill worked nights at Sprague Electric during World War II while her husband worked days at a shoe factory, a not atypical arrangement. She went in to work at 2:30 in the afternoon; her husband came home around 4:00 p.m. Their son got home from school at 3:45, so the "girl next door" took care of him until Catherine's husband arrived. When Catherine later reflected on that time period, she said:

> Married women with children [worked at Sprague Electric] . . . . [T]heir husbands came home at night and stayed with the kids, and they went to work. That's what I did. My husband took care of my kid at night, and I went to work. And in the daytime I was home . . . . [That] wasn't unusual . . . . [The men] had to help.[8]

Pay and work conditions proved noticeably better for the city's non-mill, unionized craft workers, all part of the North Adams Central Labor Union (CLU). Some 500 workers from thirteen different craft unions, most affiliated with national unions, comprised the central union, including "55 bartenders, 20 moving picture operators, 35 carpenters, 40 bricklayers, 30 plumbers, 75 hodcarriers and building tradesmen, 50 musicians, 10 barbers, 20 typographical workers, 25 cigar-makers, 50 painters, 40 electricians, and about 30 movingmen." Each union had its own meeting, and elected representatives to the CLU monthly meetings. These unionists made up the vast bulk of the workers in each of the thirteen crafts, and demonstrated a power not seen in most of the bigger factory unions. For example, they often convinced the owners of the city's bars, hotels, and restaurants to use only union men to carry out the needed work.[9]

The CLU's president at the time, Johnny Smith, worked as a bartender at the Corner Café and also served as secretary-treasurer of the bartenders' union. The CLU membership undoubtedly expressed the highest level of labor solidarity in the area, and its actions included picketing non-union establishments and boycotting non-union craftsmen. Johnny Smith had hoped to widen the scope of the CLU power by organizing the unaffiliated workers of the city, and "to overcome the barriers thrown up by different nationalities, different plants, different crafts, and departmental organizations"—goals similar to those held by UE, the CIO union that unsuccessfully had tried to unionize Sprague's production workers.[10]

NOTES

1 Jay Louis Nierenberg, *North Adams: New England Mill Town, A Political, Economic, and Psychological Survey* (Williamstown, MA: Williams College, 1942), 192–3.

2 Nierenberg, Ch. 7.

3 Ibid., 127.

4 Ibid., 131.

5 Ibid., 132.

6 "Wall-Streeter Shoe Company," North Adams Historical Society (n.d.)

7 Nierenberg, Ch. 8.

8 Catherine O'Neill was born around 1914, worked at the Hoosac Cotton mill during summers, left high school after two years against her parents' wishes, worked at a tie factory before Sprague, and left Sprague after World War II for J.C. Penney, where she stayed for thirty years. She considers herself fortunate that her husband likes to cook, since many husbands "can't even boil water." Then the wife would have to "start something and get it ready" and "all [the man] had to do was heat it up." Interview from "Shifting Gears: The Changing Meaning of Work in Massachusetts, 1920–1980: North Adams, Massachusetts," Oral History Collection, University of Massachusetts, Lowell, Libraries, Lowell, MA.

9 Nierenberg, 137.

10 Ibid., 138, 139.

CHAPTER FOURTEEN

A PRO-LABOR MAYOR, WORLD WAR II, AND THE POSTWAR INDUSTRIAL WORKFORCE

[S]ince Bowen was just a common laborer, he was not worthy of a public office.

—Mayor Francis J. O'Hara

December 2, 1940
[A]lready [Mayor O'Hara] has started his campaign of ridicule, belittling a man who wears overalls and works with his hands . . . . HELL! I am proud of my record as laboring man!"

—Faxon Bowen's response
December 3, 1940

That generation [that lived through the Great Depression] was committed to one thing: their kids were gonna go to college. They would save ten to fifteen dollars every week out of their paychecks, whether they were making two hundred a week or fifty a week. That's why we have so many banks on Main Street."

—Mayor John Barrett III

LABOR ELECTS A MAYOR

IN 1940, FAXON BOWEN, a 64-year-old millwright who worked at the Arnold Print Works, became the first pro-labor candidate to be elected mayor of North Adams. A complex man, Bowen, the son of a county judge and the grandson of a Universalist minister, grew up in rural Vermont and New York State.[1] He had enough money to buy land in a waterpower project, but, as he put it, the New England Power Company "bought out us little fellows." He enjoyed working with his hands doing skilled work, and became known as the "poor man's Roosevelt," a spokesman for the little guy and working people. An upsurge in organized labor support led to his upset election for mayor, but he lasted only one term, as that initial labor support appeared to dissipate. In the end, Bowen proved to be more of a "good government" advocate than a supporter of unionized labor.[2]

In 1925, at age 49, Bowen moved to North Adams, where he lived at 66 Quincy Street with his mother and sister. An avid reader and civic activist, he soon became well-known to the community for his letters to the editor of the *Transcript* that criticized corruption and inefficiency in city government.[3] Adding to his mystique, he signed his letters "The Black Hound," the description of his dog. Elected to City Council in 1929 and again in 1932, Bowen resigned in 1935 to become superintendent for the Civilian Conservation Corps in Sandisfield, in southern Berkshire County, near the Connecticut border. Soon after, however, conflicts with administrators led to his firing, and he moved back to North Adams.[4]

Upon his return to politics in 1936, he ran unsuccessfully for state representative, but in 1938 the voters once more elected him to the City Council. He took office in 1939 and the following year became an outspoken advocate for a city manager form of government, known as Plan E, which would professionalize city government and lessen the power of the mayor. For Bowen and other advocates, this shift would lead to greater efficiencies in city services, lower taxes, and decrease the possibility of graft. The incumbent mayor, Dr. Francis J. O'Hara, the Democrats, and the Republicans all opposed Plan E, as did the business community, which raised the money for newspaper and radio advertising. Not surprisingly, the electorate defeated the plan on November 5, 1940.

Two days later, Bowen resigned from City Council, apparently because of Plan E's defeat. He claimed that he was "done with politics." But his exit lasted less than two weeks, and on November 18, just three weeks before the next mayoral election, Bowen announced that he would run for the city's highest office, as an independent against the incumbent Democrat, O'Hara, and the Republican challenger, Clinton E. Whitney. Bowen had always been a vocal critic of Mayor O'Hara, accusing him of graft, corruption, and waste. In his campaign, Bowen focused initially on improving city services and good government reforms such as his support for a city manager.[5]

Bowen's most prominent supporter and campaign manager, John Alberti, stood at the opposite end of the social class spectrum from him. Alberti, a graduate of Williams College and Harvard Law School and a well-known North Adams lawyer, proclaimed that Bowen was "independent in his attitude, . . . untrammeled by personal considerations, and heedless of the bridling influence of the entrenched interests. Faxon Bowen wears no man's collar."[6] Bowen focused his attacks on Mayor O'Hara's Public Works Department. He exposed kickbacks given to city employees for city business and the expenditure of high prices for real estate holdings that the city needed to buy, money that he claimed went to the Mayor's banker-friends. Alberti, meanwhile, raised questions about the source of a big contribution that Mayor O'Hara made to his church. O'Hara ignored the Bowen campaign's charges. Then, in an early December interview with a reporter, O'Hara put his foot in his mouth by stating: "[S]ince Bowen was just a common laborer, he was not worthy of a public office."[7]

That remark infuriated many in North Adams, including Bowen, who responded the next day:

> [A]lready [Mayor O'Hara] has started his campaign of ridicule, belittling a man who wears overalls and works with his hands. Sneeringly he says, "Bowen is a common laborer." Since when has this status of human

existence been a crime in America? Does the O'Hara philosophy of government create also a caste of untouchable and unapproachable aristocracy? HELL! I am proud of my record as laboring man![8]

O'Hara's disparagement of Bowen and Bowen's quick rejoinder brought energy to the challenger's campaign, particularly within a key segment of organized labor. The three biggest trades unions—those representing the carpenters, the bricklayers, and the painters—endorsed Bowen, and soon the entire North Adams Central Labor Union followed suit. Apparently the major figure in bringing that endorsement was Johnny Smith, the president of the CLU and a man whom Bowen called a "pal."[9] For Alberti, "the chief factor in Bowen's election was the glorification of the workingman's overalls. . . . This was democracy at work to the highest degree—when the working people could elect a working man to govern themselves.'"[10]

Bowen's publicity highlighted his personal laboring background and concern for working people. In fact, two planks of his electoral platform stated, "The workingman's overalls should evoke respect, and not ridicule," and "Labor should receive the recognition which it justly deserves in the civic affairs of the community." Bowen's campaign focused on accusations of graft and corruption, which he aimed at the current mayor. In addition, Bowen promised to close a city dump in the middle of a densely populated neighborhood, restore antiquated bridges, improve flood control, and distribute city business and contracts "among all citizens," showing "no partiality." Bowen also talked favorably of bringing a city-owned electrical power plant online.[11]

Revealingly, the two western Massachusetts newspapers that covered North Adams during the campaign contained virtually no discussion of labor issues, including any about Bowen's labor backing; his pro-labor platform made the *Transcript* only as a paid advertisement. Accusations of graft and influence-buying alleged by the candidates or their supporters garnered the most press attention, with Bowen and the Republican candidate attacking O'Hara, and the latter's solicitor hurling accusations against Bowen.[12]

Bowen's supporters staged two big rallies, including one reputed to be the largest in the city's history held on the evening before the election. Almost 1,000 people jammed the Sons of Italy Hall, and loudspeakers outside brought the sounds of the rally to the hundreds more who couldn't get inside. "Bowen himself spoke and the crowd went wild. There was a torchlight parade afterwards and four hundred cars, all covered with Bowen stickers, drove noisily through the excited city."[13]

On December 10, Election Day, just three weeks after Bowen first announced his candidacy, he handily won the election, receiving 4,706 votes (53.5 percent of the total), some 600 more votes than the combined totals of the Democratic incumbent (3,189) and his Republican challenger (901). It proved to be the second-largest plurality in city history for the mayor's race. Even more surprising, in a historic first, Bowen won every ward in the city, even the fifth, often called the "Silk-stocking Ward," where the city's well-to-do and professional class lived. The results showed that Bowen not only had done well among workers across lines of ethnicity and religion, but also had gained considerable support from the wealthier class tired of the corruption in city government.[14] His accomplishment seems even more notable as he entered the campaign late and defeated a two-term mayor who had the local newspaper's endorsement.[15] Bowen undoubtedly benefitted from his identification with the very popular Roosevelt New Deal programs that provided employment and economic support in the city. He also tapped into a "desire on the part of the people for at least an experiment in . . . 'Honest Government.'" The voters of the city proved ready for a change.[16]

In his inaugural address, the mayor spoke in fiscally conservative tones, highlighting the need to reduce the city's debt service, which, he explained, "now takes a ruinous proportion of our tax revenues." Identifying expenditures on relief as "the second greatest strain upon the city's finances," Bowen vowed to professionalize the welfare office, removing it from political control. He also promised to do the same with the public works department. He concluded by calling for "justice for labor . . . for the unfortunate and [for] clean government."[17]

Within one week, he tried to force the welfare commissioner to resign, asked for an outside evaluation of the welfare department, and announced that he would take on the post of Commissioner of Public Works himself (without an additional salary). He focused on ending graft and corruption in both the Welfare and Public Works Departments. He fired political appointees of the previous mayor, established civil service ratings for public works employees, and ordered inventories of equipment at the city yard. Bowen also made himself the cemeteries' superintendent, but, as with the case of the public works department, he did not take the additional salary.[18]

His first year in office saw contentious relations with the City Council, personnel controversies over Civil Service jurisdiction, and antagonistic relations with both the police and fire departments over raises. Likely reflecting the views of many others, Rene Ouellette thought Bowen was a "good mayor," but he recognized that Bowen's "rough and ready style" didn't please a lot of people.[19]

Cognizant of his support in the working class community, Bowen appointed pro-labor officials to his administration, two labor representatives to the Board of Appeals, and numerous mill workers as election officials. He also put city employees on a cost-of-living pay scale, an attempt to take politics out of the picture, and brought the issue of the city's opposition to gambling and prostitution to light.[20]

Colorful at home, Faxon Bowen gained attention regionally as well. He placed an advertisement in the newspapers for "[a] secretary smart enough to earn $50 a week and dumb enough to do the work for $18." Besides the local press, papers up in Boston and Portland, Maine, picked up the story. A woman vacationing in the Berkshires, Audrey Milner, answered the ad, got the job, and soon married the mayor. She was 37; he was 66.[21]

As he began his second year in office, Mayor Bowen claimed success in improving the operations of municipal offices as well as the conditions of North Adams streets. In his address to the City Council, Bowen also claimed victory in the fight against gambling operations in the city with the words:

> I promised the people of this City that I would close down the flagrant gambling operations. Within a month I have had a check made by the State authorities and they report "North Adams cleaner than we have ever seen it." . . . Measured by an impartial State check-up, we are freer of graft and petty rackets than we have ever been in our history as a City.[22]

Soon after that address, Bowen tried to force longtime Police Chief Michael W. Conlon to resign, charging him with not doing enough to stop gambling in the city. Conlon, in office since 1926, refused to leave, and Bowen soon found that Civil Service regulations kept him from simply firing the chief. Finally, Conlon accepted a three-month probation period "and promised to wipe out gambling, and enforce the law."[23]

Thinking back on the numerous conflicts he experienced during his first year, Bowen admitted that he "sometimes [ran] rough shod over red tape and political opposition." In 1942, he fulfilled a campaign promise to close a city dump in a poor residential neighborhood, and he tried, without success, to build a new "poor house" in a different location, outside of the city cemetery where it stood by a small farm. Still, he improved the conditions for the residents who lived there.[24]

The mayor demonstrated particular pride in starting a federally supported free lunch program for city schoolchildren that fed about 600 children a day. Since the food came from the federal government, and WPA employees cooked and served the meals, it cost the city little, less than two cents per meal. Prior to the program, many school children went home for lunch, but, often with both parents at work, "[t]his usually resulted in unbalanced diets and malnutrition, as the City's Board of Health discovered."[25]

Bowen also started and saw the completion of a major project to rip up the unused city trolley tracks for use in the war effort. Despite controversy over cost and responsibility for the project, he persevered. The mayor also gained publicity with a plan to organize a private army of men who were too old for the regular army to fight in World War II, but he dropped the plan when he learned that private armies were illegal. As his first term approached an end, his supporters called for his reelection, emphasizing his fiscal responsibility and honesty.[26]

Despite those virtues, Bowen came in second in a five-man field, losing by over 500 votes to Cornelius O'Brien. Why did the mayor lose? The *Transcript* put it simply:

> Mayor Bowen was retired from his office for the same reason that he was elected two years ago because a large number of people were tired of Dr. O'Hara. He lost this year because an even larger number of people . . . were tired of Faxon Bowen. In each instance the majority of them were not voting "for" a candidate. They were voting "against" one.

O'Brien had the strength of the Democratic Party behind him, while Bowen, an Independent, split the vote along with three other candidates. Moreover, O'Brien didn't make the mistake former Mayor O'Hara had when he'd disparaged laboring people in the 1940 campaign, which pushed the Central Labor Union to back Bowen.[27]

Bowen's City Council and mayoralty terms had been filled with controversy, including disputes over the pay of city workers. By the end of 1942, he had undoubtedly lost a good deal of the labor support he had previously held. A close reading of newspaper coverage during the campaign failed to show any indication of organized labor's support for Bowen, either from the trades or from industrial workers.

Although Bowen always highlighted the importance of labor and helping the unfortunate, he failed to articulate a strong labor *union* ideology. Perhaps he was too much of an individualist who valued the importance of hard work, regardless of the employer-employee context. This can be seen in a letter that Bowen sent to R.C. Sprague. After losing the election, Bowen, then in his late sixties, went to work as a millwright at Sprague in 1943. In 1945, he wrote to Sprague upon receiving a note from him thanking Bowen for his service on a Citizen's Committee, which had apparently been set up to help mediate a strike at Sprague. The sentiments expressed in the letter demonstrate Bowen's harsh attitude toward unions and organized labor, at least in 1945:

> While [a strike] is unthinkable to any honest man, one never knows what the herd will do, once it is stampeded . . . . The curse on all labor is its love of easy money—the philosophy of something for nothing. Wartime economy aggravated this condition and the real problem of reconversion is to get men back into the habit of working . . . . Now to tighten up the slack and to get labor to realize that it is serving its own ends by delivering a day's work for a day's pay is a problem that faces our economy all over the Nation.

Bowen went on to praise R.C. Sprague's "spirit of humanity and fair play" in contrast to the "half-brained agitators" in the community. He also praised General Electric, where he had previously worked, for its concern over the employees' "well-being," and castigated labor unions for their lack of "[k]indness and decency and fair play."[28]

The expression of these sentiments seems even more remarkable given their timing at the end of World War II, when strikes erupted over the United States, including in North Adams, as workers tried to gain the wage increases that employers had denied them during the war.[29]

ECONOMIC AND SOCIAL CONDITIONS IN THE EARLY WAR YEARS

In February 1942, the city's 6,000 industrial workers averaged a weekly wage of $26.81, significantly less than industrial workers ($38.52) in nearby Pittsfield, where many enjoyed higher pay at General Electric. In fact, of the thirty-seven cities studied that month by the state, only ten averaged weekly wages less than North Adams. Not surprisingly, most of the mill workers rented their housing, living in two- and three-family tenement buildings, often near the mills where they worked.

They made do on tight budgets, spending just on necessities. Studies of two of the major banks in the city, the North Adams National Bank and the North Adams Savings Bank, revealed over 26,000 separate personal savings accounts, a phenomenal number for a city of just 22,000 and very high even when recognizing that some of the accounts emanated from residents of other northern Berkshire and southern Vermont towns. Regarding that period of time, as noted previously, John Barrett III, North Adams's longest serving mayor (from 1984 to 2008), reflected:

> Many of those people lived through the Great Depression, and that never left them. They went without for their kids. That generation was committed to one thing: their kids were gonna go to college. They would save ten to fifteen dollars every week out of their paychecks, whether they were making two hundred a week or fifty a week. That's why we have so many banks on Main Street."[30]

The city's school system functioned to make its graduates employable, something it proved generally successful in doing. In 1940, a trade school specializing in machine shop training opened in the annex of the high school, supported mainly by the donation of machinery from Sprague Specialties, Berkshire Fine Spinning Associates, and the Hunter Machine Company. The high school also provided evening classes for many immigrant adults who wanted to learn English. The local newspaper reported that "[s]eventeen different nationalities were represented in this group, with the largest numbers being French, Italian, and Syrian."[31]

While the demand for war materials increased—e.g., many Wall-Streeter employees were producing gas masks in a cooperative effort with Sprague Electric, and others manufactured 1,000 pairs of shoes a day for the Army[32]—news of the downfall of a traditional mill in North Adams caused great alarm. At the end of March 1942, Arnold Print Works announced its liquidation due to a war-related shortage of raw materials. APW employed 1,100 at its Marshall Street plant and another 500 in their Jones Division in Adams. The news led one "man on the street" to exclaim in an interview with the *Transcript*: "'Pearl Harbor never bothered us here. We continued to live as we had lived before. But this is North Adams' Pearl Harbor.'"[33]

LABOR DURING WORLD WAR II

World War II affected textile production in North Berkshire in different ways. Because the cloth that Arnold Print Works needed for its printing operation had been diverted for military production, the long-established factory faced liquidation, and abandoned its Marshall Street headquarters. The print works survived on a smaller scale, however, and moved to neighboring Adams. On the other hand, Strong, Hewat benefitted by military orders for woolen garments in 1941 and 1942, with 60 percent of its business now in government contracts.[34]

Of course, military orders led to a huge expansion at Sprague Electric, as it replaced Arnold Print Works at Marshall Street and purchased two additional smaller former textile mills to add to its Beaver Street operation. For North Adams and the rest of the country, the huge increase in military-related production, along with the millions of workers now in the Armed Forces, brought with it a "full employment" economy and escape from the Great Depression.

Labor relations at the Strong, Hewat plant proved contentious, with a June 1942 threat by the owners to fire any workers who participated in what the employees called a lockout, but management termed a strike. Differences also emerged between the skilled weavers, numbering between 80 and 85, and the more than 300 production workers. The former negotiated separately through the Briggsville Weavers' Club and the latter as the Independent Woolen Workers' union. The larger production workers union wanted the weavers to join with them in one big union, but the more highly paid weavers refused. The weavers themselves went on strike in mid-June, leading to a cutback in the whole operation.[35]

Organizing activity continued at a rapid pace during the war years. In the spring of 1942, workers at the five plants of the Berkshire Fine Spinning Associates voted in a new union, the American Federation of Textile Operatives (AFTO), to represent them. Local unions had been part of AFTO since 1915, but now the national independent union had become entrenched in North Berkshire. Perhaps as a reward for that increase in union membership, AFTO chose North Adams to host its national convention, at its 50th anniversary year, in June.[36] It appeared to be the first (and last) time that a national union chose North Adams to hold its annual convention.

Held at two downtown hotels, some 300 delegates and friends attended the meetings. Independent for all of its half-century of existence, the union voted to explore the possibility of affiliating with the American Federation of Labor. While that appeared to be the most significant resolution passed by the delegates, they also called for a higher minimum wage and a 30-hour workweek, a schedule that would lead to greater employment. (With work plentiful during the war, the delegates were undoubtedly thinking ahead and concerned with the peaks and valleys of their particularly industries.)

Interestingly, for a union gathering, an insurance executive had been tabbed to give a major speech, a decision that reflects the conservative nature of the AFTO. Harold E. Crippen of Geddes and Crippen reminded the gathering that "[y]ou have the 40-hour week, social security and old age assistance, unemployment insurance, socialized medicine, housing, sick benefits and hospitalization, and many other of your dreams have come true." But then, presaging the corporate, right wing, anti-Communist, McCarthyite assaults that would hit labor at the end of World War II, Crippen continued:

> Most of these new ideas of social reform have been created by pressure groups and their success tends to create other pressure groups which may lead to unwise decisions, foolish legislation and, more important, may ruin individualism. Individual thoughts and actions are your heritage in this free America and only by individual thoughts and action can you preserve your heritage and control your destiny. So don't let yourselves be followers, but stand fast for your privileges that are yours so that you as individuals may continue to live in peace and harmony in this free and lovable America.[37]

Nationwide, both the AFL and the CIO supported no-strike agreements during the war. Officially, most unions went along with the agreement, but when workers saw corporate profits rise while their wages stagnated, frustration set in. In workplace after workplace, workers conducted informal, quickie strikes—without union approval—and often won their demands through direct action. Historian Howard Zinn calculates that during the course of the war, 14,000 such strikes took place, involving nearly seven million workers, "more than in any comparable period in American history."[38] According to one union official at Sprague Electric in North Adams, "innumerable walkouts by plants and departments" characterized the period of 1943–

1944.[39] Once the war ended, an unprecedented wave of strikes shook the nation, including both informal and formal strikes at Sprague Electric.

THE POSTWAR YEARS: ACTIVISM AT SPRAGUE

In late October 1945, 169 employees who worked at the paper tubular assembly department at Sprague's Beaver Street plant went on strike, one that was unauthorized by the union. Two days later, the company agreed to pay the workers on a piece-rate basis that they favored, and the walkout ended. Negotiations for a new all-plant contract had been scheduled to start on November 1, but in early October the union initiated its demand for a 30 percent wage increase. So strong was the sentiment for a significant hike that 98 percent of all Sprague employees went on strike on November 1, without waiting for negotiations to start—again without union permission. The context for the walkout and the demand for the 30 percent wage increase reflected a decline in postwar pay. When the war ended, Sprague employed 2,600 workers at its three plants in North Adams; a month later that number declined to 1,500, who then worked a shorter week. While that level increased to 2,000 and with additional hours of work, "the average take home pay was less than the higher war-time average."[40]

The strike continued, and on November 23 the company and the Independent Condenser Workers #2 (ICW) negotiating committee met in Boston with the Chairman of the state Board of Conciliation and Arbitration. Four days later, the union brought a low offer back to the membership who "jeered and booed its rejection, and resumed picketing around the Sprague plants the following day."[41] The next day, the picketers received a vote of confidence and economic support when the woolen workers at Strong, Hewat voted to each donate one dollar a week to aid the strike.[42]

Urged on by the business community, Mayor Cornelius O'Brien appointed a Citizens Committee that included a banker, a Chamber of Commerce official, and four former mayors. No union leader or labor spokesperson made the cut. The committee met with the company and the union separately and came up with a new proposal, but one that had raises tied to the company's future profits. The strikers "angrily" rejected it by a vote of 900 to 40 on December 9. However, with the strike more than five weeks long, it became difficult for the wage-less employees to keep holding out, and a week later, they settled for a one-year contract with two pre-Christmas bonuses, wage increases up to 16 percent for workers on the low end, and a 6 percent hike for those making more.[43]

About a year later, on November 4, women dry rollers engaged in a sit-down strike when management unilaterally cut the piece rate. They didn't wait for official union support, but instead acted on their own, in unison. In fact, a second group of workers—stitchers—joined them in sympathy. The protest led the company to reinstitute the previous rate and pay the strikers for the time lost, if they returned to work. They did, and both parties engaged in two lengthy give-and-take meetings to discuss the rates, who the time study person would be, and the structure of the work area.[44]

On a national level, the Cold War had started. Despite the Soviet Union's alliance with the United States during World War II, the U.S.S.R. had become the new enemy abroad. At home, corporate America mobilized against labor's resurgence, and, riding a wave of anti-Communism pushed by Congress and President Harry Truman, legislation that would severely cripple the labor movement became law in 1947. Among the provisions of the Taft-Hartley Act, states could ban the union shop; unions had less leeway to institute boycotts and solidarity strikes; and the president had the power to block a strike for ninety days if he deemed it a "national emergency." In addition, unions that refused to sign affidavits declaring their officers to be non-Communists could not compete in NLRB elections.[45] This last provision soon came home to haunt an aggressive union drive in North Adams.[46]

At the end of March 1948, the contract between the company and the production workers union at Sprague, ICW #2, was set to expire. Sensing the weakness of the ICW there, and the growing militancy of the workforce, a number of outside unions competed to win bargaining rights for the sizeable workforce. Those outside unions included the United Electrical workers (UE), which had previously tried to organize in North Adams in 1938 and 1944 when Gerry Steinberg, a production worker, led the effort internally. Now, four years after the last attempt, Steinberg had the lead again; he no longer worked at Sprague, but operated as a full-time UE organizer and had the local support of the large UE union at General Electric in Pittsfield. Division within the CIO brought two other CIO unions into the battle, the United Auto Workers (UAW) and the Textile Workers Union of America (TWUA); they were joined by the former CIO-based United Mine Workers and two AFL affiliates, the International Brotherhood of Electrical Workers and the International Association of Machinists (the IAM). Unlike the others who wished to organize all the production workers, the IAM focused only on organizing Sprague's machinists.

Frenzied activity filled the months of March and April. The competing unions held mass meetings, sent out flyers, spoke on the radio, and tried to convince the 1,900 Sprague employees to join them. At the same time, the company fought back, desperately wanting to keep the weak ICW as the certified union. R.C. Sprague spoke directly over the intercom on company time, went on the radio, and sent several letters to his employees bashing the opposition and praising the ICW. To attack the strongest union, the UE, Sprague not only painted them with the Communist brush, but added a Fascist touch: "[T]he UE-CIO has been trying the 'boring from within strategy,' just as Russia did in Czechoslovakia, Finland, and eight other countries, and as Hitler did in Norway."[47]

The vote on the new contract was scheduled for March 26. It had become clear that the UE had the biggest following, and likely was the only outside union that had a chance of unseating the ICW. Two days prior to the vote, hundreds of rank-and-file

ICW members met to consider affiliating with UE. Planning also continued for a UE-sponsored walkout from Sprague on March 25, a quickie strike that would forcefully publicize the power of the dissidents. Later that day, the *Transcript* reported the following:

> In a demonstration move, designed to show strength, 1000 employees of the Sprague Electric Company staged a "work stoppage" by walking out of the plant this morning at 10:30. There are 1900 employees on [Sprague's payroll], but the 1000 workers who ceased work this morning for a short time represented the majority of workers in the plant . . . .

The workers left at 10:30 a.m., despite a broadcast by R.C. Sprague at 8:45 a.m. "urg[ing] them to reconsider . . . ." They returned to work at 1:00 p.m. and, not surprisingly, R.C. Sprague refused to meet with representatives of their delegation.[48]

Dissident strength held as the contract failed to receive a majority vote despite the support of the ICW executive committee. The vote, 854 opposed to 579 in favor, indicated the continued influence of the UE, who had called for a "No" vote. R.C. Sprague responded on March 29 with a letter addressed "To My Fellow Workers." After voicing his disappointment, he spent a good deal of the letter warning the recipients of supporting a union (unnamed) whose "only 'tricks' are . . . unauthorized work stoppages . . . and finally, if all else fails, a full-fledged strike."[49]

With a second vote scheduled for April 7, both UE and R.C. Sprague went on the radio to seek support; the TWUA and the IAM petitioned the NLRB for recognition; and a state conciliator met to set up arrangements for the April vote. This time, the company and the ICW won, as a revised contract received 725 favorable votes to 653 against. The contract received quick signatures, but the struggle continued, as UE, the TWUA, and the IAM asked the NLRB for a third election.

On May 28, the NLRB declared that the UE could not stand for a new election as it still refused to sign the non-Communist affidavit. Most of the other unions voluntarily left, with the final withdrawal—the TWUA—coming on September 22, 1948. The ICW had a new contract, and Sprague Electric had a union it could handle. Despite the widespread dissatisfaction that production workers had with their "independent" union, and the strong campaign that UE had waged, the temper of the times—the corporate, political conservative push; the strong anti-communism; and the anti-labor provisions of the Taft-Hartley bill—meant that the status quo at Sprague would continue.[50]

POSTWAR TEXTILE ORGANIZING

Despite their failure at Sprague, the TWUA achieved success in their own industry. In 1946, the CIO union won elections at both the Adams and Greylock plants of the Berkshire Fine Spinning Associates (BFSA) and also at the Hoosac Cotton mill. The following year, the TWUA achieved bargaining rights at the Windsor Print Works, though it took an eleven-day strike in March 1948 to negotiate a contract.[51]

Continuing to gain new memberships, the TWUA moved into a local woolen mill in 1949 when the production workers at Strong, Hewat decided to leave their Independent Woolen Workers unit for the CIO.[52] With this affiliation, the production workers joined 70,000 other workers in 250 woolen mills. TWUA hoped to gain a highly desired nationwide contract. If all the locals under the contract had the same wages and benefits, it would keep any one woolen employer from claiming that its specific labor costs were too high, thus taking away one common argument that employers used to cut their workers' economic package. Now, with all labor costs the same, that contract would be the "pattern" that all new contracts would be forced to follow. Similarly, when the United Electrical Workers union tried to organize at Sprague Electric in the 1930s and 1940s, they hoped to bring wage rates for production workers up to the "pattern" developing in the capacitor industry. (See Chapter Twelve for that attempt at pattern bargaining.)

The TWUA initially prevailed at the Hoosac mill, but an independent union, the Northern Berkshire Textile Council, defeated them in 1948. A significant slump in the cotton rayon market kept the Hoosac mill closed all during the summer of 1951 and led to the layoffs of 400 employees. When it reopened, both unions, the Northern Berkshire Textile Council and the Loomfixers' Union, agreed to a "stretchout," with workers now responsible for sixty looms instead of the previously agreed upon number of fifty-four.[53] The acceptance of an increased workload had to have brought back memories to the older workers of Depression-era days.

Also in 1951, local cotton and woolen mill workers found themselves in the vortex of TWUA negotiations and the threat of a national strike. It began in February with a walkout of 70,000 woolen and worsted workers who were seeking a wage increase and pension benefits. While employees struck in Woonsocket, R.I., and in Lawrence, Massachusetts, Strong, Hewat & Company woolen workers, who were also TWUA-CIO members, voted to extend their current contract. At the same time, national union leaders warned of a cotton textile strike the middle of March if their pay and pension demands weren't met. At a meeting of union leaders and cotton mill owners in Boston, eight delegates of North Berkshire TWUA locals representing 2,400 employees attended.[54] Both sides later reached a tentative agreement, thus averting a strike. As part of the arrangement, petitions were filed with the national Wage Stabilization Board, who approved wage and cost of living adjustments to the textile employees, including those at the Adams, Greylock, and Hoosac mills.[55]

On the woolen side, the Strong, Hewat employees remained at work and received praise from company vice president Douglas Hewat "for displaying independent thinking . . . in refusing to accept the orders handed down by disinterested power hungry Union politicians." In a letter to the *Transcript*, Hewat went on to argue that woolen workers had improved their earnings over and above the cost of living and that the union demands for more went against the federal government's price policy. He ended his letter with strong words: "That these labor leaders have the audacity to defy the Government of the United States and the President that they helped elect . . . should be an eye opener to all clear thinking patriotic Americans. Let us all wake up before it's too late."

Despite Hewat's compliments to Strong, Hewat employees, they went on strike less than two weeks later. A few days after the walkout, the editors of the *Transcript,* without naming the local strikers, posted a lengthy anti-union editorial. Under the heading "The Strike Weapon," the writers insisted that "enlightened industrialists" had improved the "evils" of a previous era, but that "organized labor has not advanced as far along the road of enlightenment. It has grown in power but not in wisdom."[56]

After a four-week strike, Strong, Hewat management agreed to new terms with the local union, representing the company's 400 employees. The new contract included a raise, a cost-of-living clause, and improvements in insurance, severance, and pension benefits. Interestingly, the three company officials who represented Strong, Hewat at the settlement did not include Douglas Hewat.[57]

The TWUA increased its local membership when James Hunter Machine employees switched to the CIO union, replacing the AFL-affiliated International Association of Machinists in December 1951. The following March, the new union helped negotiate a two-year contract with higher wages along with improved vacation and insurance benefits. The TWUA then had a significant presence in North Berkshire, as the union also represented workers at the Windsor Print Works, Strong, Hewat & Company, Arnold Print Works, and the BFSA plants in North Adams and Adams, for a total of some 4,000 employees.

The BFSA plants employed 2,500 workers, but they faced a threat by the employer to cut wages or move more work to the South. With this demand, the company fell in line with similar threats from other New England cotton manufacturers, such as the Naumkeag Steam Cotton Company of Salem, Massachusetts which "constantly dangled the possibility of plant closure and flight to the South when faced with workers' demands."[58] The *Transcript* called the BFSA threat "[t]he most serious textile crisis in years" with the possibility of a local strike as workers wanted their wages brought back to their previous level.[59]

In August 1952, a lengthy dispute between local union officials at the Arnold Print Works and the national led to a rival union, the United Textile Workers (UTW), AFL, winning a representative election there. Building on that momentum, the UTW gathered enough support to merit an election to represent BFSA workers not only in Adams and North Adams but also in Brattleboro, Vermont. Gearing up for the election scheduled for February 26, 1953, the TWUA held mass meetings on the 22nd in Adams, where nearly 300 attended, and in North Adams, where 125 were present. State CIO president and state TWUA director J. William Belanger spoke along with TWUA's cotton division director, Victor Canzano, and with Henry Kullas, TWUA Berkshire director.

A day earlier, UTW's national president, George Baldanzi, addressed his supporters over the radio. Baldanzi, a former TWUA executive vice president who switched sides after he lost a bid for the TWUA presidency, "stressed the UTW's claim of providing more 'home rule' for that union's locals, [and he] attacked . . . TWUA's practice of depleting union funds to maintain costly headquarters and top-level officials in New York City." Baldanzi's critique of the CIO union echoed the ICW attack on another CIO union, UE, when it attempted to win an election at Sprague Electric in the 1940s. As it turned out, the TWUA not only won the election in Adams and North Adams, but the union also expanded its reach with a victory in Brattleboro. In mid-April, 25,000 workers in twenty-three New England mills, including the three local BFSA plants, gained a two-year contract.[60]

But an attempt by the TWUA in October 1953 to regain representation rights at the Arnold Print Works failed, as the CIO union picked up only about 40 percent of the vote. The TWUA made the effort despite an earlier "no-raiding" agreement between the CIO and the AFL, an accord that would presage the eventual merger of the two rival federations in 1955. According to Henry Kullas, the union's area director, the merger of Aspinook Corporation with the owners of APW just prior to the election played a key role in the vote. The United Textile Workers already represented two Aspinook plants as well as two other plants that gained in the merger, which in itself added further legitimacy to the UTW.[61]

Kullas maintained a strong presence in local affairs. Besides his involvement in political issues, he stayed active on the labor educational front, choosing ten union members to attend the CIO Summer Training Institute at Springfield College and conducting local classes in Brattleboro, North Adams, Adams, and Pittsfield.[62] As the key part of his union work, he supervised a dozen or so business agents and organizers at the James Hunter Machine Company in North Adams and in more than fifteen cotton and woolen mills throughout the Berkshires, from Housatonic in the south to Clarksburg in the north. His responsibility illustrated the role that textiles still played in the Berkshires even into the 1950s. In the North Adams area, the TWUA represented textile workers at all of the major plants except for the Hoosac and Arnold Print Work mills.

Befitting its role in North Berkshire labor, the TWUA sponsored a Labor Day celebration at Noel Field in 1953. While the *Transcript* mistakenly called it organized labor's first celebration of the day in North Adams history, the events recalled earlier celebrations with speeches, athletic events, and refreshments. At the end of the year, the union continued its annual Christmas party tradition for the members' children, and the Berkshire Joint Board announced its dues-paying membership at a robust 3,717.[63]

However, 1954 proved to be a worrying time for the TWUA as Windsor Print Works and Strong, Hewat & Company reduced their workloads and even demanded wage cuts. Then an interesting political situation developed in South County, at Monument Mills in Housatonic. In discussing an ongoing struggle at that plant, Henry Kullas had noted that two years earlier:

> Father Lexton supposedly advised his parishioners against TWUA-CIO. However, this year, two company representatives requested that he again interfere and he refused because they, the company, did not keep its promise to keep the mill going if the union lost in 1952. On Sunday, July 18, Father Hanrahan, in another Catholic church in Housatonic, quoted from the encyclical of Pope Leo XIII advising his parishioners of their obligation to belong to unions and the employer's obligation to provide a decent wage which will permit the breadwinners to adequately provide for the needs of their families.

Kullas went on to write, "Circumstances alter cases. In my humble opinion, we have at least a 50–50 chance of winning this election."[64] Emil Rieve, General President of the TWUA, responded: "Perhaps we can get a few other clergymen to quote from the encyclical." As it turned out, the workers at Monument Mills got the message and voted for the TWUA by a 2–1 margin on September 9.

That same year (1954), the TWUA once again hosted a Labor Day celebration, held this year in Clarksburg, for a crowd of 700. Besides Democratic Party candidates for office, speakers included Williams College Professor James M. Burns, the head of the Central Labor Union, the president of the Beverage Dispensers' Union, the local police chief, and John L. Alberti, attorney for several local unions.[65]

The TWUA, CIO, hoped to make inroads at Strong, Hewat, where the United Textile Workers union, AFL, represented the weavers. Indicative of the industrial union model of the CIO versus the AFL craft union model, Kullas wrote to President

Emil Rieve of a new program at the Adams branch of the Berkshire Fine Spinning Associates. The letter read:

> [W]e have entered into a loomfixers' training program with the company. The purpose of this training program is to secure loomfixer jobs for people who are interested in TWUA. This, I hope, will off-set some of the old time loomfixers who still think and talk craft unionism.[66]

A huge industrial merger in 1955 led to heightened anxiety within the local workforce. The region's largest textile employer, the BFSA, which also owned mills in Rhode Island and Fall River, agreed to merge with Hathaway Manufacturing Company, a firm founded in 1888 and headquartered in New Bedford. With the obvious difficulties facing New England textile mills, corporate control now moved even further away. (In 1965, the new company, Berkshire Hathaway, would be controlled by the country's most famous investor, Warren Buffett, who had begun buying stock in the firm just three years earlier. Buffett would keep the firm and its name as his main investment arm, but would gradually discard its textile mills.[67])

In 1955, however, Henry Kullas and the workers he represented had to face new contract proposals put forth by the Fall River-New Bedford Textile Manufacturers Negotiating Group, an alliance of New England textile producers that included the newly formed Berkshire Hathaway Company. Kullas soon reacted to the harsh proposals by saying: "If employers insist on their demands, they will force the people to strike."[68]

The manufacturers played the "Southern card," arguing that New England textile workers had to bring their pay level down to that of their Southern brothers and sisters in order to be competitive. But Northern textile workers had taken a pay cut in 1952 and had received no wage increases since then. A strike would affect 2,300 workers in Adams and Greylock, nearly a quarter of the 10,000 New England employees being represented in the negotiations.

The management offer focused on so-called fringe benefits, including the elimination of the automatic cost-of-living clause, the loss of five paid holidays, and the reduction of illness and hospitalization benefits. The union countered with the status quo—an acceptance of the current contract with no other changes. With neither side giving in, the strike began on April 16.

The TWUA looked for outside support and solidarity to help weather what looked like the possibility of a lengthy strike. A pro-union alliance, named the Civic Groups of Northern Berkshire, quickly formed. In addition to economic support from the TWUA's emergency strike fund, numerous local unions pitched in with checks, including the Beverage Dispensers, the Independent Condenser Workers at Sprague, the Bricklayers, and the Widen Tannery. The unions at Sprague and the one at General Electric's big plant in Pittsfield also volunteered to raise more money by soliciting from their own members at the plant gates. In addition, local merchants proved amenable to extending credit to the workers during the strike. (On an interesting political note, in responding to a request by Henry Kullas, the Williamstown selectmen called for an increase in the federal minimum wage from seventy-five cents an hour to one dollar an hour, a shift that would aid Southern workers and reduce the wage competition between workers in those two geographical areas.[69])

Both sides remained firm in their positions, and the strike continued on into July with the introduction of mediation. At the same time, at the national level, the two largest CIO unions, the United Auto Workers and the United Steelworkers, each contributed $50,000 to the textile strike fund. Referring to those generous gifts, TWUA's executive vice president, William Pollock, bluntly stated that the strikers "will not be starved into submission."[70]

A day later, the two sides reached a settlement, one that seemed palatable to the strikers. Current hourly wages stayed the same, and the workers kept their six paid holidays. The recent three-cents-an-hour increase from the cost of living escalator clause remained on the workers' paycheck, but they lost future cost-of-living clauses. The company took away some overtime provisions in the paid holidays and gained efficiencies in making work changes. Berkshire Hathaway's executive committee chairman, Seabury Stanton, noted that "the new agreement fails to completely solve the problem of our wage and fringe differentials with the Southern mills," but he hoped that a higher federal minimum wage would narrow the difference and lessen the competition.

The union's William Pollock seemed less conciliatory, stating: "[I]t is evident that this wasteful strike need never have occurred and certainly could have ended much more quickly." He added, with tongue in cheek, "I have no desire to engage in recriminations."[71] The rank and file still had to approve the proposed contract. Before the vote, the union asked Berkshire Hathaway if the workweek would include a full five days, unlike the three days before the strike. The company replied that it would, and the strikers affirmed the new contract, returning to work soon after.

Happy with the result, Lillian Dolan proclaimed: "We knew we'd win." After thirty-five years with the company, and determined not to give up earlier gains, Dolan stated: "We certainly weren't going to go backward . . . . It's wonderful to think that we'll be going back to work for what we fought so hard to get." Dolan's husband, James, worked at Sprague Electric, so they had an income during the strike. Dolan's co-worker, Elsie Brouillette, a folder-tender at the mill, expressed her happiness with the contract when she said, "With everyone so 100 per cent for us, I knew we couldn't lose." Brouillette had taken a part-time job during the strike, as did many others, though she still had to go into debt. Perhaps the striker with the largest family, fifteen children ages 2 to 21, Joseph LeFabvre, "attributed the success to stronger union organization and the cooperation of local merchants who were willing to extend credit when needed."[72]

With the thirteen-week strike settled, two months later another TWUA local plant went out on strike. Some 350 unionists at the Windsor Print Works (later a unit of the Consolidated Textile Company Inc.) walked out on September 30, 1955. At the same time, eight members of the independent guards union agreed to respect the TWUA picket lines. This proved to be a shorter strike than the Berkshire Hathaway walkout, and less than three weeks later, October 18, the two sides agreed on a settlement. Windsor employees received a pay raise, a third week of paid vacation, and improved hospitalization, surgical, and life insurance benefits.[73]

Also that year, the TWUA sponsored a Labor Day celebration, holding it this time at Williamstown's Taconic Park. The union then boasted a local membership of about 3,800, and some 1,000 celebrated on Labor Day. Besides the usual entertainment, speech making, and refreshments, the union made an interesting presentation, a plaque to James A. Hardman Jr., the *Transcript's* editor, for "integrity and fair play" during the Berkshire Hathaway strike.[74]

The year's end brought a major development in organized labor, as the two biggest labor federations merged on December 5, ushering in the AFL-CIO. Noting the change, Henry Kullas hoped that the combination would lead to more organizing in the South, higher wages, and more comparable labor costs.[75] The merger did not, however, help the Northern Berkshire textile industry, as imports and Southern competition continued to batter it. In 1956, two historic mills in North Adams, the Greylock mill, and the Windsor Print Works, closed. In addition, Kullas reported that Strong, Hewat & Company. was "in serious financial difficulty."[76]

The Windsor closing, during the first week in June, while not unexpected, came without any leadtime. Windsor's parent corporation, Consolidated, "had nothing to offer the 500 workers, many of whom had given as many as forty-five years of their lives to the Union street mill." Greylock, on the other hand, handled its closing gradually, over the summer, and most of its 550 employees had the opportunity to take jobs at the Adams Berkshire Hathaway plant. "[M]any of them took advantage of that offer, which also softened the blow somewhat." At least for a while.[77]

James Hunter Machine Company appeared to be the only local TWUA workforce that seemed to be doing well. In the fall of 1956, the company announced it had acquired a controlling interest of a Greenville, South Carolina company (W.D. Dodenhoff), which would enable Hunter Machine to have greater contact in an area where growth characterized overall textile production.

The TWUA still carried on, sending eight members to a University of Connecticut training institute, purchasing "stewards kits" for its stewards and officers, and holding its annual Labor Day celebration on September 3. By this time, fears of textile plants moving South worried union leaders less than the influx of very cheap textiles being imported from low-wage manufacturers in Asia and Latin America. Very cognizant of that competition, the union sponsored a program to pressure the president and Congress to get tougher on imports. The campaign enlisted members and others to send out about 20,000 postcards to lobby for their case. On the local level, the union informed the Pittsfield, Adams, and North Adams chambers of commerce to tell their members not to buy textiles produced outside of the United States.[78]

An end of the year column in the *Berkshire Eagle* carried a page-wide headline that read: "1956 YEAR OF CHANGE IN NORTH BERKSHIRE—PROSPECTS GOOD FOR 1957"; a sizeable subhead stated: "Area Not Defeated By Closing of Mills." Most of what consisted of good news, the main reason for the reporter's somewhat optimistic take on local manufacturing, came from a major expansion of the Cornish Wire Company's employment in Williamstown and in the Blackinton section of North Adams. But North Berkshire's gain of some 100 jobs at Cornish came at the expense of the company's closing its plant in Rutland, Vermont, a six-year-old operation. One of the biggest employers in the area, Cornish already employed 500 workers in Williamstown and 100 in Blackinton.

Cornish Wire had started its Williamstown operation in 1936 and its smaller Blackinton facility in 1953. In 1950, the

Williamstown employees had voted against affiliation with the International Union of Electrical Workers (IUE), but in 1956, both North Berkshire Cornish plants voted to join the union, which also represented employees at General Electric in Pittsfield. After six weeks of negotiations, the contract brought significantly improved benefits. Perhaps more importantly, the workers won a union shop, mandating all employees to join the union within thirty days of starting work.[79] Word of the successful negotiations at Cornish brought an upsurge in interest among some Sprague employees to leave their weak local union and affiliate with the IUE, an AFL-CIO union. However, support for that change lacked a majority, and it would be more than a decade before the Sprague production workers union would vote to join the IUE. (See Chapter Eighteen for the vote, negotiations, and a ten-week strike.)

In 1957, a significant downturn hit the local textile industry. In February, the Adams division of Berkshire Hathaway closed its Number Three mill, leading to the layoff of more than 700 employees. That crisis led Governor Foster Furcolo to call a special meeting in Adams where he proposed that some of the laid-off workers get one- to two-month temporary jobs on the state highways, a mini-WPA project. Nonetheless, the bad news continued. Even James Hunter Machine Company, a plant that had been stable in the 1940s and 1950s, reported layoffs. The closing of numerous textile plants in New England meant less of a need for new machinery; for those textile mills still in operation, they benefitted from the surplus of machines then available from liquidations and auctions.[80]

In less than two years, TWUA membership had plummeted some 40 percent down to 2,283 with the Adams division operating on a three-day schedule, while the Fort Dummer division in Brattleboro, Vermont, remained closed. Yet even with the difficult times, the union did its best, sponsoring a Labor Day celebration and continuing to provide Christmas parties for its members' children.[81]

But months later, on May 7, 1958, a bold headline spread across nearly an entire page of the *Transcript*: "BERKSHIRE

HATHAWAY DEATH SENTENCE TO BE EXECUTED IN 3 WEEKS." The company's directors had made the decision the previous day; more than 1,000 workers would lose their jobs. President Seabury Stanton didn't hedge on the decree at all. First, no more cotton would be imported; then the picker and carder room work would cease; and finally, the spinning and weaving operations, in two to three weeks.

Stanton said the company regretted the move, but had to close the operation since it had become "unprofitable." He maintained that, though they had tried to modernize the plant, the losses had continued. In addition to the costs of operation, Stanton referred to the fact that the demand for the higher quality of goods that the mill produced "has slumped substantially . . . because those goods do not lend themselves to the wash-and-wear finishes wanted by our housewives."

TWUA's Kullas criticized Stanton's announcement, especially since the mill's employees had recently agreed to increase their workloads for the same wages, a practice that Greylock mill workers had adopted just before that mill closed down. Acknowledging the reality of the closing, Kullas went on to advise his membership of the contractual benefits they should receive upon the closing, as well as the vacation pay they would be owed. The chambers of commerce in both Adams and North Adams voiced their concerns, and the president of the Northern Berkshire Development Corporation, Harry B. Smith, declared that "the organization will make intensive efforts to find tenants for the Adams mills."[82]

The closing dealt not only an economic blow to the area, but a psychological one as well. After all, it seemed as if the mills had been there forever and took up a substantial part of the town's real estate. Under a different name, the mills had opened in 1889 and "as recently as 1929 [was] the largest fine goods mill in New England." Called the Berkshire Cotton Manufacturing Company and ultimately becoming four mills, it had been started by C.T. and W. B. Plunkett, the sons of William C. Plunkett. W.C. Plunkett, as he was known, began his industrial career in the Berkshires in 1829 when he took over the management of the Adams South Village Cotton and Woolen Manufacturing Company, a mill that had begun operation as far back as 1814.

In the late nineteenth century, aided by the tariff on textile imports championed by then U.S. Representative William McKinley, the Plunketts had begun their operation. (See Chapter Four for details.) They had consolidated their own interests with the Greylock mills of North Adams, Williamstown, and North Pownal, Vermont, along with the Fort Dummer Mills of Brattleboro, Vermont, and two mills in Rhode Island, thus creating a new empire that came to be called Berkshire Fine Spinning Associates. But having "reach[ed] its peak in 1948," BFSA merged with the Hathaway Manufacturing Company in 1955 and changed its name, for a final time, to Berkshire Hathaway. But on that day on May 1956, cotton manufacturing came to an end in Berkshire County.[83]

The area had some stark facts to face: with more than 4,000 unemployed, the local unemployment rate, already high, would climb to 22 percent, and North Berkshire would rank fourth in *the country* in area unemployment. The local chambers, elected officials, and union heads including Henry Kullas and Marc H. Toureille, president of the International Union of Electrical Workers Local 229, Cornish Wire, all took action. Governor Furcolo told local legislators that he would seek more defense contracts and unemployment funds for public works projects in the area.[84]

On the federal level, Senator John F. Kennedy asked for increased unemployment compensation. The future president called the "limited House-approved unemployment bill a 'palpable fraud' and could not understand why the White House embraced the measure as its own." Kennedy also criticized the Defense Department for not providing more military contracts to area industrialists. On the federal level as well, Williams College Professor James M. Burns, an aspirant for the Democratic nomination for Congress, sent a telegram to President Eisenhower "plead[ing]" with him to call for an emergency session of Congress "to demand immediate broadening of unemployment compensation, immediate selective temporary tax cuts, expanded housing, hospital, and school construction."[85]

Local meetings continued as business people, government, union officials, and civic leaders looked for answers to the unemployment crisis. Not everyone agreed with the variety of proposals, and, at an early morning meeting on May 10, Donald LaFrance, President of the Adams Chamber of Commerce, tried to persuade those in attendance "to avoid 'hare-brain schemes' seeking state and federal assistance as the tax situation must be considered and such projects only add to the taxation burden." This didn't stop Mathew Ciempa, TWUA's business agent, from advocating for federal relief for "distressed areas," for state passage of an expanded "employment relief program," and for "an expanded public works project to give jobs to Berkshire county residents."[86]

THE DRAGON CEMENT CONTROVERSY

Just a few days later, still in May, 1958, LaFrance championed a tramway project for Mount Greylock, which he claimed would create 250 jobs, though he didn't say if federal or state funds would be needed for the project. Besides asking Berkshire Hathaway to continue temporary operations in Adams, Ciempa wanted the federal government to buy the cotton cloth that the mill would produce. And in a proposal that apparently drew no opposition at the meeting, the TWUA business agent asked Dragon Cement Company to establish a plant in Adams.[87] Dragon ultimately tried to start such a plant, a proposal that Sprague Electric Company condemned.

The Dragon proposal would, in fact, become one of the most controversial economic development proposals of the post-Berkshire Hathaway era. A front page article in the *Transcript* at the end of July carried an announcement by Dragon that it had taken out an option on 425 acres of land in the southern part of the city next to a limestone quarry, and would build a cement plant that would employ 200 people and have a yearly payroll of $800,000 (later reduced to 150 people and $750,000). The company also assured readers that the plant would "have an effective dust control and filter system."

The mayor, the city manager, and the Chamber of Commerce president all expressed pleasure at the prospect of new jobs, and a poll of local residents concurred, since jobs, especially high-paying jobs, were at a premium. Dragon began test borings, and its president called the limestone "one of the richest deposits . . . in the Northeast." A day later, perhaps the first public criticism of the project came from Fred Windover, a member of City Council and a personnel director at Sprague. Before long, on August 20, a front page *Transcript* story described Sprague Electric Company as "vigorously fighting" the plant's location. Though the plant was proposed to be be situated two miles south of the Sprague facilities, the company claimed that the dust that would be generated would harm Sprague's production. Dragon then proposed bringing in independent experts to study their plan and the dust issue, but Sprague refused the offer.

Instead, Sprague began an all-out public relations campaign to halt the plant. Management had come up with a twelve-minute color film of dirty cement plants, and showed the film to all its employees during the workday. Sprague argued that cement plant dust would blow north toward their operations a full one-third of the time, creating harm. In addition to the film, which they made available to community civic groups, the company paid for full-page opposition ads in the *Transcript* and sent letters to their employees.

Dragon responded to the dust issue by buying a three-column ad describing an old, "dirty" cement plant in New York that was located next to a GE capacitor plant and was causing no problems at all. Sprague countered with a letter from a GE official stating that the capacitors produced by GE were different from theirs. Soon, Sprague circulated petitions for their employees to sign, and 800 did. Sprague's production workers union, the ICW, drew up its own petition against the Dragon plant. But the final nail in the Dragon coffin came down when Sprague announced that they would eliminate 2,000 jobs in the city if Dragon were allowed to quarry or build the cement plant. Quickly, the city's zoning board withdrew its approval of the Dragon proposal.[88] Lest Dragon or another cement company might try again, R.C. Sprague purchased the site by the quarry and additional land next to it as well.[89]

The outlook for textiles in North Berkshire and throughout Berkshire County continued to be discouraging. News of mill closings filled Henry Kullas's Februrary 27, 1959, report to TWUA President William Pollock. Kullas plainly said: "The unemployment picture is quite serious in Adams and to a lesser degree in North Adams and Pittsfield." A "distressed area bill" had yet to be passed, but Kullas described his work for many victorious Democratic candidates (with the exception of Jim Burns) in the previous November election. The Berkshire Joint Board of TWUA hired a bus and took part in the "March of the Unemployed" in Boston and "was helpful in securing [an] extension of unemployment insurance for 13 weeks" in the state. But with union membership down to 1,200, finances obviously suffered, and the Pittsfield and North Adams union offices had to be closed. Henry Kullas delivered the saddest news towards the end of his lengthy report: "Due to our depleted finances we did not conduct the annual children's Christmas party this year."[90]

TORCHLIGHT PARADE—Faxon Bowen victory parade, above, started at 10.15 p.m. Dec. 10, 1940 and lasted at least an hour. Even the car's headlights and street lights seemed to celebrate as Faxon stands beside one of several autos carrying his supporters.

Mayor-elect Faxon Bowen (on right, with bow tie) celebrating in a victory caravan on Election Day, December, 1940, after handily defeating the incumbent mayor, Dr. Francis J. O'Hara. A solid labor vote insured Bowen's win. At far left is Attorney John N. Alberti and Angelo Scavo is driving (Trabold, *Transcript*, September 29, 1971).

FAXON BOWEN

Faxon Bowen (*Springfield Republican*, December 11, 1940).

Men working at Cornish Wire plant, Water Street, Williamstown, 1940s (Williamstown Historical Museum).

Women working at Cornish Wire plant, Water Street, Williamstown, 1940s (Williamstown Historical Museum).

Women inspecting shoes at Wall-Streeter shoe company, North Adams, circa 1940s (*Transcript*).

Sprague employees leave the plant during World War II (*Transcript*).

Women making gas masks during World War II at Sprague's Brown Street plant, 1942 (*Transcript*).

Capacitor production at Sprague's Brown Street plant, 1945 (reproduced from Sprague "Log," by Paul W. Marino).

Workers constructing Hadley Overpass, North Adams, 1946 (North Adams Public Library).

NOTES

1 Bowen's daughter believes that the source of his "honesty" and "anti-corruption" fervor can be found from both sides of the family, the religious and the judicial. Interview with Louise O'Brien by author and Chet Gallup.

2 *Transcript*, October 6, 1971,1; *Springfield Republican,* December 12, 1941, 4.

3 See Jay Louis Nierenberg, *North Adams: A New England Mill Town: A Political, Economic, and Psychological Study* (Williamstown, MA: Williams College, 1942), Chapters 5 and 9, for Bowen's biography before his election to mayor and his accomplishments as chief executive. In his obituary, the *Transcript* wrote, "He parlayed a native ability to write controversial letters to *The Transcript* into one of the most colorful political careers in the annals of North Adams history . . . ." Oct. 6, 1971.

4 *Transcript,* October 6, 1971, 1; *Springfield Republican,* December 12, 1941, 4. Earlier, he worked for the Works Progress Administration as a writer, and he directed and wrote a sociological study of Berkshire County. (Unfortunately, the author has been unable to locate a copy of the study.) At the CCC camp in Sandisfield, Bowen "claimed to have converted 600 young men from 'potential cutthroats, thieves and gangsters, into useful citizens.'" The men showed their appreciation by giving Bowen a watch and chain, "which he proudly displayed for years afterward." *Berkshire Eagle,* October 6, 1971.

5 *Springfield Republican*, November 17, 1940, 4, and December 11, 1940, 1.

6 *Transcript*, November 18, 1940.

7 Nierenberg, 85–86, 89.

8 *Transcript*, December 3, 1940.

9 Nierenberg, 138. As it turned out, however, that endorsement lacked unanimity. The president of the Bricklayers' Union, William J. Timothy, publicly stated that his union never backed candidates and that the authority to include the union in the advertisement had not been given. *Transcript*, December 10, 1940, 2; *Springfield Republican*, December 10, 1940, 4. While letters to the editor may not reflect voter sentiment, as the election neared, the *Transcript* ran three letters criticizing Bowen on December 6, 1940, and one supporting him, though that one came from Bowen himself and two others. (Of course, the possibility exists that the *Transcript* may have held back on publishing pro-Bowen letters, but that seems unlikely, since Bowen would have probably made that an issue if it were the case.) The following day, Bowen's campaign paid for three ads promoting his candidacy.

10 Nierenberg, 89.

11 Nierenberg, 86; *Transcript,* December 7, 1940, 3; Rene Ouellette interview, January 25, 1984, by the author and Karen Rose.

12 See, e.g., *Springfield Republican,* December 9, 1940, 4, and December 10, 1940, 4.

13 Nierenberg, 90.

14 *Transcript*, December 11, 1940, 2; Nierenberg, 90. Much of the Irish vote, traditionally Democratic, must have moved over to the Bowen Independent column. In addition, many French and Italian voters, who historically had tended to vote Republican, must have deserted that column to vote for Bowen. The Irish population was estimated at about 7,000, the French 4,000, and the Italian 3,000. Nierenberg, Chapter 3. According to Bowen's daughter, Louise O'Brien, his Welsh background helped him gain that ethnic group's vote, and the Italian heritage of Rose Uberti, his wife, who died in 1936, brought him success with that sizeable voting bloc. (Interview with author and Chet Gallup.)

15 *Transcript*, December 9, 1940, 2.

16 FDR defeated his Republican opponent in North Adams in 1932 by a margin of 55 percent to 45 percent; in 1936, 63 percent to 37 percent; and in 1940, 62 percent to 38 percent. As FDR's margins grew from 1932, the support for the New Deal president indicated a more class-based voting pattern in North Adams. This continued with the candidacy of Bowen, even though he ran on an Independent ticket and campaigned for only three weeks. See Nierenberg, 91, for a reporter's statement in the *Springfield Republican*, December 12, 1940, 2.

17 *Annual Report of the City of North Adams*, 1941, 9.

18 Nierenberg, 157–158.

19 Regarding Bowen's style, Ouellette remarked, "If he told you to jump, you better jump." January 24, 1984, interview with the author and Karen Rose.

20 Nierenberg, 165–166.

21 See, e.g., *Transcript*, September 25, 1941, 5, and May 25, 1942, 2. Audrey survived Bowen, lived to 91 years of age, and is buried next to him in South Readsboro, Vermont, Cemetery. Bowen's previous wife, his second, Rose Uberti, died in May, 1936, after less than two years of marriage.

22 *Annual Report of the City of North Adams*, 1942, 21; *Transcript*, January 20, 1942, 4, and December 1, 1942, 1. For a full description and analysis of Bowen's term in office, see Nierenberg, Chapter 9, "Modern Administration in Operation."

23 *Annual Report* . . . , 1942; Nierenberg, 142. In his speech to the City Council, Bowen added the following: "There will always be gambling. We could spend the total tax levy and not clean it up completely. We can, however, and it is the moral duty of every government function to, eliminate the dirty rackets which serve to strip men of their earnings and send women and children to the Welfare Department for food and shelter." Here Bowen follows his practice of pointing out the illegality of an activity, its immorality, and the hardships it places on its victims. Earlier that month, two North Adams men had pleaded guilty to running a gambling operation at a local athletic club for more than two years. Nierenberg, 167. In an interview that Nierenberg conducted with a pro-Bowen lawyer midway through the mayor's first year in office, Joe Kronick stated "that

Bowen's attacks on gambling rings and an alleged house of prostitution . . . had won him a lot of votes" in one of the city's wards. Nierenberg, 94. For more detail on the gambling issues, see Nierenberg, Chapter Five and Chapter Nine, in addition to his citations to *Transcript* reporting.

24 Nierenberg, 167–170.

25 Ibid., 164–165.

26 Nierenberg, 161.

27 *Transcript,* December 5, 1942, 3. For a full description and analysis of Bowen's term in office, see Nierenberg, Chapter 9, "Modern City Administration in Operation."

28 Sprague Company Archives, F-128, "Union Correspondence." To add to Bowen's complexity, or maybe inconsistency, in 1942, while mayor, he welcomed the American Federation of Textile Operatives to their annual convention in North Adams and claimed to have held "a union card for 40 years." *Transcript,* June 29, 1942, 3. In fact, in a long open-letter advertisement just before the election, O'Brien mentioned "Labor Unions" as one the many organizations "I have enjoyed my activities in," a statement vague enough to mean anything, but probably positive enough to keep organized labor from rebelling. *Transcript*, December 7, 1942, 2.

29 On the postwar strikes, see, for example James R. Green, *The World of the Worker: Labor in Twentieth-Century America* (New York: Hill and Wang, 1980), 193–194. In 1946, the 70-year-old Bowen was defeated again in another try for mayor. *Transcript*, December 11, 1946. In a lengthy political ad for that office, in the form of a letter signed by three supporters under a photo of Bowen, the election was portrayed as a race between the moneyed interests of the city and the interests of the "COMMON, HONEST, HARD-WORKING LABORING MAN." The ad cited the need for housing, recreation, new police and fire stations, a new court building, and flood control. And, for city workers, a "'LIVING WAGE.'" It ended: "VOTE for FAXON BOWEN—the 1946 LEADER of PROGRESS." *Transcript,* December 5, 1946. Bowen and his wife moved to Pownal, Vermont, to a house they named Arkmont, after both of their home states. He once again sought political office, as candidate for selectman of Pownal. (*Transcript,* January 17, 1952.) But it was not to be. At his death, Bowen left his wife Audrey; one son, Faxon Bowen Jr. (Springfield, Vt.); a daughter, Louise O'Brien (Shattuckville/Colrain, Mass.); twelve grandchildren; and fifteen great grandchildren.

30 Mayor John Barrett III in Joe Manning, *Disappearing into North Adams* (Florence, MA: Flatiron Press, 2001), 45.

31 Nierenberg, 202–3. The group that Nierenberg refers to as Syrian might well be the Lebanese, with roots in North Adams. (That area of the Middle East has been contested for millennia, and at one time the country we now call Lebanon existed within greater Syria.) Early on in North Adams, many of the group worked in the mills and later developed a merchant class. Phil Pugliese, *Transcript,* January 1, 1988.

32 Bernard A. Drew, "Wall and Streeter, maker of shoes," *Berkshire Eagle,* July 5, 2014.

33 Nierenberg, 187 and 220; *Transcript*, March 30, 1942.

34 *Transcript*, March 30, 1942, 3, and May 11, 1942, 2.

35 Ibid., June 22, 1942, 3.

36 Ibid., April 29, 1942, 10, and June 25, 1942, 11.

37 Ibid., June 29, 1942, 3.

38 Howard Zinn, *A People's History of the United States, 1492–Present, Revised and Updated* (New York: Harper Collins, 1995), 408.

39 Quote from William Stackpole in Raymond C. Bliss, *A Study of Union History at the Sprague Electric Company in North Adams, Massachusetts, 1929–1970* (Williamstown, MA: Williams College, 1976), 24.

40 Bliss, 26–27.

41 Bliss, 29.

42 *Transcript,* November 28, 1945.

43 Bliss, 30–33.

44 A stenographic record of the two meetings was kept (F-121, Sprague archives), so rich in detail that it became the basis for one scene of *The Sprague Years*, a 1995 play performed in the theater of North Adams State College. The dialogue illustrates the struggle for self-respect that the female workers engaged in, refusing to be called "kids," even during the "pre-feminist" 1940s. The last three pages of the record dramatically bring the dispute to a conclusion, an end to the sit-down, but point out the contentious issues involved in agreeing on a fair rate for the piecework. Two years later, another sit-down strike erupted when eyelet solderers and wire solderers (in sympathy) stopped work because of a unilateral change in the piece rate system. Only when management brought back the previous rate did they return to work (June 5 inter-office communication, Jack Washburn to R.C. Sprague Jr., June 5, 1948, Sprague archive, carton F-230).

45 "The provisions of the Taft-Hartley [Act] were many and deadly and all geared to the destruction of labor as an independent force controlled by its members and responsible to them." Richard O. Boyer and Herbert M. Morais, *Labor's Untold Story* (New York: United Electrical, Radio and Machine Workers of America, UE, 1955), 347. See also Green, Chapter Six.

46 Women had been hired in record numbers at Sprague during World War II, and, even three years after the war, they made up 58.6 percent of the work force (1,122 women, 792 men). At Sprague in 1948, 77 husbands and wives were employed, and 551 others had a spouse who worked elsewhere. For all workers employed in manufacturing in North Adams in 1948, men were predominant at 57 percent (2,867 men, 2,168 women). Sprague archives, carton F-230.

47 The quote from letter of March 24, 1948, addressed "To My Fellow Workers," from Sprague archives, carton F-121.

48 *Transcript,* March 25, 1948; typescript from R.C. Sprague, entitled "Broadcast over loud speaker system to 3 plants at 8:45 AM on 3–25–48," Sprague archive, carton F-121.

49 *Transcript,* March 27, 1948; March 29, 1948 letter from R.C. Sprague, March 29, 1948, Sprague archive, carton F-121.

50 *Transcript,* April 7, 1948; September 22, 1948; Letters from R.C. Sprague to employees, April 9, August 23, and August 30, 1948, Sprague archives, F-121. During this period, the company had been in contact with Royal Parkinson Associates for public relations and advice on fighting outside unions (see letters Sprague archives, F-121). In a very interesting letter that R.C. Sprague sent to Royal Parkinson (April 8, 1948), asking his advice on spending for public service sponsorship on the two local radio stations, he concluded as follows: "Another factor is that the radio stations certainly offer an inexpensive means of publicity to any labor union or union competing for representation at our plants. Recently both stations have been very helpful to us. Being a little hard-boiled about it they might continue to be as helpful if we were regularly supporting them financial[ly] in a modest way. Where do you think the balance lies?"

51 *Transcript,* May 3, 1948, 6.

52 *Transcript,* September 30, 1949, 8.

53 *Transcript,* August 26, 1953.

54 *Transcript,* Feb. 20 and Feb. 24, 1951.

55 *Transcript,* August 18, 1951.

56 *Transcript,* March 19, 1951.

57 *Transcript,* April 14, 1951.

58 Aviva Chomsky, *Linked Labor Histories: New England, Colombia, and the Making of a Global Working Class* (Durham, NC: Duke University Press, 2008), 97. Chomsky also points out that tax laws made it easier for companies to move South as they could deduct the losses from firms they acquired from their own future profits. In fact, banks even "encouraged large corporations to acquire New England mills only to shut them down" (97).

59 *Transcript,* January 12, 1953, 2.

60 Ibid., February 23, 1953, and April 13, 1953, 3.

61 Kullas to Rieve, October 20, 1953, TWUA archives.

62 Ibid., p. 3.

63 *Transcript,* August 29, 1953, and Kullas to Rieve, December 22, 1953, 1.

64 Kullas to Rieve, July 23, 1954, 1.

65 Rieve to Kullas, August 11, 1954, 1; Kullas to Rieve, October 7, 1954, 1; *Transcript,* September 2, 1954, 23.

66 Kullas to Rieve, October 7, 1954, 2.

67 Alice Schroeder, *The Snowball: Warren Buffett and the Business of Life* (New York: Bantam Books, 2008), 268–277 and 507–508.

68 *Transcript*, April 7, 1955, 2.

69 Ibid., June 2, 5, 6, 7, 9 and July 7 and 14, 1955.

70 Ibid., July 12, 1955.

71 Ibid., July 14, 1955, 2.

72 Ibid., July 14, 1955, 2.

73 Kullas to Rieve, October 28, 1955, 1.

74 Ibid., 1–2.

75 Ibid., December 14, 1955.

76 Kullas to Pollock, October 15, 1956, 2.

77 Maynard Leahey, *Berkshire Eagle*, December 31, 1956, 9.

78 Kullas to Pollock, October 15, 1956, 3, 4.

79 *Transcript*, May 25, 1956.

80 Kullas to Pollock, March 15, 1957, 2–3.

81 Kullas to Pollock, July 18, 1957, 4, and October 31, 1957, 3. One local even sponsored a basketball team.

82 *Transcript*, May 7, 1958, 9 and 20.

83 *Transcript*, May 7, 1958, 5. Earlier in the nineteenth century, the founding father Plunkett, William C., had purchased the North Pownal textile mill in partnership with Daniel J. Barber. Barber managed it until 1871 when the partners sold it to what became the North Pownal Manufacturing Company. Barber went on to establish tanneries in North Adams and in Blackinton. John Lockwood et al., editors, *Western Massachusetts: A History, 1636–1925,* Vol. 3 (New York: Lewis Historical Publishing Company, 1926), 38.

84 *Transcript.*, May 7, 1958, 2.

85 Ibid., May 7, 1958, 5.

86 Ibid, May 7, 1958, 3.

87 Ibid, May 10, 1958, 3.

88 Descriptions in the above paragraphs from George A. Piendak, *The Independent Condenser Workers Union, Local #2: A Study of Local Unionism* (Williamstown: Williams College, 1965).

89 Barry Werth, "The Father, the Sons, and the Town," *New England Monthly,* June, 1985, 60.

90 Kullas to Pollock, 2–3.

CHAPTER FIFTEEN:

THE WINDSOR MILL PROJECT: A PRECURSOR OF MoCA?

I really believe North Adams has something special.
—Mary Ann Beinecke
Transcript, February 12, 1975

[T]he council's vote meant that the city has missed the boat on a project that could have given it a nationwide reputation.
—Lewis C. Cuyler
Transcript, January 15, 1975

AFTER SERVING AS STORAGE SPACE for most of the years after the Windsor Print Works closed in 1956, the mill buildings became the focus of a new and innovative proposal that emerged early in 1972 by Mary Ann Beinecke. Through her Hoosuck Community Resources Corp. (HCRC), a non-profit organization, Beinecke hoped to turn the Windsor mill into an arts complex with space for skilled craftsmen to produce a variety of goods. For a city in economic decline, Beinecke's vision promised needed jobs, apprenticeship opportunities, and the attraction of a tourist economy.

For the next nearly three years, Beinecke's group wrote and received grants for refurbishing the buildings and made contacts with numerous artists and craftsmen who might work in such a center. As an engine of economic development, the project anticipated an immediate creation of 80 jobs, with another 300 over the five years that would follow, which would make the arts complex the third-largest employer in North Adams.[1]

After years of study and preparation, nearly all documents appeared to be in place for the project to go through in January 1975. But though HCRC had raised almost $2 million in proposed funding, it lacked an administrative budget for its executive director and staff to work.

On the night of January 14, Beinecke's group went before North Adams City Council and asked the city to contribute $50,000 toward its operating budget. Debate lasted an hour and the 6 to 3 vote went against HCRC. While all the councilors spoke favorably about the project, six hesitated to spend taxpayer money on something that wasn't a sure thing. Councilor Robert J. McDonough bluntly explained his negative vote: "I would rather see this $50,000 go to municipal employees—the guy who can't afford bread and butter."[2]

While additional attempts to reinvigorate the project followed, the 6 to 3 vote effectively killed it. The next day, Lewis C. Cuyler, Associate Editor of the *Transcript*, penned an essay entitled "Faith wasn't there last night." Cuyler wrote that the city's representatives had shown faith in earlier projects like flood control, the state college, a new high school, a new industrial-use facility, and in building "the finest hospital around." But spending money on the artistic reuse of the old mill buildings had given the councilors pause. Cuyler suggested the underlying reason may have been class-related. Mary Ann Beinecke came from a "wealthy family" and lived in Williamstown; Cuyler continued his editorial by suggesting: "The rich people of Williamstown had their art and lived their kinds of lives; the people in North Adams lived a different kind of life. Most of the time they got on well, but they could never be together."[3]

NOTES

1 John Edward Garstka, *A Producing and Performing Arts Complex: A Study in 19th Century Mill Recycling* (master's thesis, University of Massachusetts, Amherst, 1974). See also Courtney Taylor, *The Windsor Mill Project* (student paper, Massachusetts College of Liberal Arts, North Adams, 2010).

2 *Transcript,* January 15, 1975.

3 Ibid., January 16, 1975.

CHAPTER SIXTEEN

GOVERNMENT CONTRACTS, SAFETY ISSUES, AND WORKER ORGANIZING

"We hope to make North Adams the tent center of the world."
—Leonard Weiss, president of
Hunter Outdoor Products, 1967.

"[T]he county sometimes has to trade clean air and working conditions for steady employment."
—John J. Pignatelli, chairman,
Berkshire County Commission, 1975.

INTRODUCTION

THE LONGEST-RUNNING shoe manufacturer in the city, Wall-Streeter Shoe Company continued to operate into the 1960s, just ahead of the flood of imports in the next decade that would decimate the domestic industry. After James E. Wall's death in 1959, his son, Yale-educated Robert Wall, took over and three years later expanded the operation by renting space in the Windsor Mill. A challenge by the Boot and Shoe Workers Union, AFL-CIO, in 1964 to improve conditions for Wall-Streeter workers went down to defeat, as the union lost the NLRB election 210–141.[1] Still, with several hundred employees, Wall-Streeter remained one of the biggest employers in North Berkshire.[2]

An even bigger employer, Cornish Wire, operated plants in Williamstown and Blackinton. In the spring of 1960, negotiations for a new contract began between the International Union of Electrical Workers (IUE) and Cornish management. The union represented over 500 workers out of a total labor force of about 600. By the beginning of June, negotiations broke down as the union held firm on two issues: a cost-of-living clause and seniority rights for women employees. On June 7, 506 union members went on strike. A week later, union President Robert Curry offered to submit the differing issues to arbitration, but the company rejected the offer.[3]

In an interesting development, national IUE President James B. Carey spoke to striking Cornish workers in the company's Williamstown parking lot. Carey, who had been in Pittsfield for an IUE anniversary celebration of its representation of GE workers, promised the help of the national office to the Cornish strikers. Twenty-two years earlier, Carey, then president of the more radical United Electrical Workers union, had journeyed to North Adams to speak to about 400 Sprague workers about the benefits of UE affiliation. Carey had been one of the founders of UE, an early affiliate of the militant CIO. As the years passed, Carey had become more conservative, increasingly anti-Communist, and eventually left the UE to start a rival AFL electrical workers union, the IUE.[4]

After eighteen days, the Cornish strikers approved a new contract that included raises over a three-year period in addition to improved health benefits. The union also won some seniority changes for women's job titles. According to the *Transcript,* "[T]he job title issue was one of the most troublesome in the controversy, causing deadlocks when agreements were seen as possible on other points."[5]

In neighboring North Adams, an expanding Sprague Electric Company employed the largest labor force, some 4,000 and growing. Even so, textiles continued to play a significant role in the region. Although the production of cloth from cotton or wool had ended in the area by 1960, the sewing of cloth and fashioning it into finished products had become a key element of the industrial base. For a quarter of a century, from the early 1960s to the mid 1980s, as Sprague Electric Company reached its apex and began its decline, one could chart a parallel development in what might be called the city's sewing industry. Sparked by government Defense Department contracts for tents, duffel bags, and even gas mask hoods, hundreds of local residents found work in several companies that were housed in abandoned textile mills in North Adams and neighboring Clarksburg. While the names of the companies varied, the same owners and managers, often with questionable reputations, tended to run the operations, often out of the same mills.

Suffering from low pay and subpar health and safety conditions, workers battled for union representation, and at one company, Hunter Outdoor Products, they participated in probably the longest strike in North Adams history—23 weeks! Hunter and its associated firms dominated the sewing industry in the 1960s and 1970s and X-Tyal (pronounced X-Tile) followed in the 1980s. Just as Sprague left North Adams in 1986, these firms also abruptly closed. When Sprague departed, both it and its parent company, Penn Central, were financially viable; however, when Hunter and X-Tyal shut down, they chose bankruptcy. To make matters worse, X-Tyal left in the middle of the night, leaving its employees without their final paycheck. That action by X-Tyal, now called the "Midnight Movers," led to a variety of protests against the company, culminating in nine arrests and a federal investigation of the firm. (See Chapter Twenty for the X-Tyal era.)

HUNTER OUTDOOR WORKERS STRIKE OVER UNION REPRESENTATION

In 1961, Sports Industries (S.I.) began operating in the Greylock mill, formerly the home to a subsidiary of the Berkshire Fine Spinning Associates. By 1964, S.I. had filed for bankruptcy. Hunter Outdoor Products shared the building with S.I., but claimed to be a separate entity. However, when S.I. went out of business in 1966, its vice president and manager moved to Hunter, and its equipment and goods ended up there, too.

With sizeable government orders for duffle bags and tents in 1966, Hunter Outdoor Products hoped to expand and add hundreds of more workers. The company also produced tents for the civilian market, and its president, Leonard Weiss, boasted, "We hope to make North Adams the tent center of the world."[6] In the fall of 1967, Hunter purchased the former Hoosac Cotton Mill on Union Street to accommodate its rapid growth.

Already employing several hundred workers, but claiming a local labor shortage, the following spring Hunter brought in 50 men from New York City to bolster its workforce. Hunter's superintendent, Alfred E. Simon, claimed that the firm had "borrowed" the workers from its New York plants and had purchased an apartment house and rented big blocks of rooms in one hotel and two motels to accommodate them. The company also claimed that it provided transportation for the new employees—who were "Spanish speaking"—so that they could go home on weekends. (Roughly a century earlier, C.T. Sampson, North Adams's leading shoe manufacturer, hired 75 workers from outside the city—in that case Chinese men from San Francisco—to break a strike [see Chapter Three for details].) In the case at Hunter, however, the company claimed that the outsiders would be only temporary employees. According to Simon, when new local workers were trained to do the job, each would replace one of the "borrowed" workers, thereby hastening the outsiders' return to New York City.[7]

A year earlier, North Berkshire had been declared an Economic Development Area, achieving that designation by its "high or potentially high unemployment." With a looming labor struggle at Hunter, management's alleged reason for importing the men from New York could be questioned.[8] But first, the labor battle at Hunter involved not the new workers but rival unions.

Joseph Martin, company vice president, claimed that Hunter had a labor contract with Local 29 of the Retail, Wholesale and Department Store Union (RWDSU) out of New York City. That local represented Hunter employees in New

York, both city and state. Workers in North Adams who were opposed to Local 29 claimed they never voted for that union, but instead supported affiliation with the International Ladies' Garment Workers Union (ILGWU). Two representatives from that union had been leafleting both Hunter plants in North Adams and visiting workers' homes as well.[9]

When the case came before the National Labor Relations Board, the board determined that Hunter lacked a valid collective bargaining agreement with Local 29, and had engaged in numerous unfair labor practices. The Board compelled Hunter to withdraw its recognition of Local 29 and mandated that the company and the union return union dues to the employees.

Dissatisfaction with pay and working conditions at Hunter exacerbated tensions, and by the end of October 1968 a strike seemed likely. A strike vote was taken on October 30: the vote carried, albeit with only about one quarter of Hunter's 300 employees voting. However, more than 100 workers struck the next morning, hoping to pressure the company to recognize the ILGWU as their bargaining agent. According to the *Transcript*, "Several minor incidents occurred . . . including a striker reportedly injured when hit by a car passing through the picket line. However, except for a few shouting matches and some shoving, there was little trouble."[10] When ten of the Spanish-speaking New Yorkers refused to cross the picket line, Hunter's superintendent initially threatened them with the loss of company housing, a threat he later withdrew.[11] The national ILGWU agreed to pay the striking workers $30 a week in strike benefits along with other assistance after the first week.

By the second day, more than 50 percent of the workforce had struck. In fact, the ILGWU paid strike benefits to 168 employees at the end of that week, so one has to assume that at least that many participated in the strike by picketing. The union paid the benefits even though they had not yet gained official union recognition. In addition to daytime picketing, a six-member "Night picketing and house visiting committee" carried out those extra duties.[12]

The company filed charges with the NLRB claiming that strikers threatened those who were going to work. Hunter also used leaflets and a radio announcement to underline the alleged threats, which stated: "The FBI is now investigating." In a note given to workers along with their last pre-strike paycheck, Hunter vice president Joseph Martin said, "Rest assured that the company is not going to deal with any union just because it has hired outsiders to try and prevent you from working."[13]

On November 9, the union took out a large ad in the *Transcript* to state its case. It explained the history of the struggle against Local 29 and the NLRB decision against the company; it ended by stating that the workers "voted to strike against management's continuous harassment and denial of their dignity as human beings. They voted to strike to affirm their basic rights as human beings and American citizens."

As the strike continued, picketers successfully kept some fuel trucks from crossing their lines, the company filed a $1 million suit against the ILGWU for damages, the union countered with charges against the company of unfair labor practices, and both sides disagreed about how many employees had struck. Community support grew for the strikers, with funds coming from several local unions and from the huge Pittsfield General Electric workforce.[14] At the same time, the U.S. Immigration and Naturalization Service (INS) picked up seventeen persons from Latin American countries for violating their visa status. Some of those held by the INS were employed at Hunter, including a group that was still working in the picketed plant. Others had joined the strikers, but the situation once again raised the earlier question as to management's motivation for bringing the men from New York earlier in the year, as well as management's relationship with INS.[15]

Disturbances on the picket line led to eight arrests, including charges of assault and battery with a gun and accusations of cutting air brake hoses on a company truck. The latter charge was leveled against Joseph A. Danahy Jr. of Boston, an ILGWU organizer, who pled not guilty. In all, only two of the picket line arrests led to convictions.

On December 6, Joseph Amedeo (another ILGWU organizer) was arrested following a complaint by a non-striking worker that "she had been harassed by horn blowing as she crossed the parking lot." A patrolman on duty went to Amadeo, who was near where the horn blowing had emanated, and told him, "Picketing from a car is not allowed." Amadeo refused to give the police officer his registration and license, and after refusing to exit his car, he was arrested. At the end of December, Amadeo went to court, at which time he claimed that he might have inadvertently struck the horn with his elbow, and that he didn't get out of his car either to picket or when the officer asked him to because he had been shot in his leg in Pennsylvania several days earlier and walking out would have been difficult.[16]

In a letter to the district union headquarters, Andrew J. Dilk Sr., the local lawyer hired to represent Amedeo, described the trial testimony of Police Captain William H. Garner:

> The police officer really poured it on far beyond just the matter of just disturbance of the peace . . . . Apparently the police are bitter about the outcome; the testifying officer told Joe he would get him yet and he didn't care who knew it. There is no question that the local police are prejudiced against out-of-town organizers as against a local employer. I told Joe to watch himself from here on as they will be watching him carefully.[17]

Joe Amedeo was found "not guilty."

The strike moved into January 1969. In the beginning of the month, 125 workers received strike benefits, and a dozen continued to picket at night. At the end of February, an NLRB Trial Examiner issued a thirty-page ruling that Local 29 (the union that the company favored) and the company had been guilty of unfair labor practices in withholding Local 29 dues from employee paychecks and threatening to close the plant if employees voted for ILGWU representation.[18]

Still, Hunter refused to recognize the new union, and the strike continued. On March 19, a company representative forewarned of a factory closure and the loss of some 300 jobs because of the strike's "economic pressures." Perhaps because of these threats, on April 2 the strikers voted to end their twenty-three-week walkout, at which point Hunter Vice President Martin promised to cut the 200-employee workforce back to 150. The strike had become the longest strike in North Adams history, surpassing the twenty-two-week strike by Sprague Electric machinists in 1948.[19]

Hunter appealed the negative NLRB decision to the U.S. Court of Appeals, and it took two more years, until March 31, 1971, for the Court to reaffirm the trial examiner's ruling of unfair labor practices on the part of the company and Local 29. Finally, nearly two-and-a-half years after that, in August 1973, the company agreed to honor a decision by the workforce to be represented by the ILGWU.[20]

HEALTH, SAFETY, AND THREATS

Heated disputes over health and safety issues at Hunter reached the public in March and April of 1975. While these problems often occurred in the sewing industry, the fact that the disputes reached the press and led to North Adams officials castigating a federal anti-poverty agency proved unusual. Two employees had become sick from the gluing operation at Hunter, and, when the state denied them unemployment compensation, they sought help from the North Adams office of Western Massachusetts Legal Services (WMLS), a federally supported agency and a "War on Poverty" program.

WMLS Attorney Lee Flournoy asked the Federal Occupational Safety and Health Administration to inspect the plant to evaluate the workers' complaints. At first, Vice President Martin refused to admit the government inspectors into the plant, but they eventually entered, tested, and found seventeen health and safety violations.

The *Transcript* had interviewed workers at the plant who registered complaints that included unusual fatigue and "intense nausea," along with reports of colleagues passing out while working with the gluing operation, falling victim to the glue (toluene) and the solvent (methyl-ethyl-ketone). Rather than dealing with the complaints, Vice President Martin went after the legal services group, accusing it of "libel" and of acting with "political motivation." As an additional threat, Martin announced that the gluing operation would be transferred to a South Carolina plant and that further expansion elsewhere could cost some 500 to 750 jobs in North Adams.[21]

Remarkably, the threat to cut the workforce led North Adams Mayor Joseph Bianco to attack Western Massachusetts Legal Services, not Hunter. The mayor accused the federal agency of taking the case of former workers "who apparently would rather continue on government relief than work."[22] Bianco also filed a complaint with the state bar association that the legal services group had committed an ethical violation, but the bar association disagreed. Two county commissioners also rushed in to support Hunter's operation. Peter G. Arlos accused WMLS of being "overzealous payroll patriots," who aided in the loss of some 200 industrial jobs. Less inflammatory but frightening nonetheless, John J. Pignatelli, the commission's chairman, opined that "the county sometimes has to trade clean air and working conditions for steady employment."[23]

The county's director of WMLS, Cecil D. Driver, responded to Arlos by calling him "another politician shooting off his mouth when he doesn't know what he's talking about." Driver went on to say, "We're working with Hunter management to make it a safer and healthier place to work."

Editorially, the *Transcript* supported WMLS despite the opposition from Hunter, Mayor Bianco, and the two county commissioners:

> It's an old story for businesses to go [s]outh in search of tax benefits, cheaper labor and less stringent laws—or—as Hunter Outdoor Products . . . is saying—because of too many

> federal and state safety inspections. It is new, though, for a company to put the blame on the diligence of anti-poverty lawyers pressing health issues on behalf of employees.[24]

Finally, within a few days, Hunter and Legal Services reached a compromise in which Hunter and its sister company, Inflated Products, agreed to reduce the levels of the glue and solvent used in the gluing process. Hunter's Vice President Martin also announced that the company had decided to "reconsider . . . its moving plans."[25]

THE LAST YEARS

In fact, Hunter Outdoor Products seemed to believe in a bright North Berkshire future: in late 1974, it purchased the abandoned Strong, Hewat & Company buildings in neighboring Clarksburg. The Clarksburg buildings had been unoccupied since 1967 after sixty years of woolen manufacturing, and the new buyers expected between 200 and 250 employees to be working there in two years. Yet, around the same time, Hunter's Martin confirmed that the company had begun operating a plant in Summerville, South Carolina.[26]

At the beginning of 1976, both Hunter and Inflated announced new contracts for the production of sleeping bags from the governments of the United States, Iran, and Saudi Arabia. To fulfill the orders through 1978, the companies advertised for additional workers. Hunter also announced that, while it would maintain its government contracts, it would also produce its commercial products (sleeping bags and other outdoor equipment) under a new entity, Greylock Mountain Industries Corporation.[27]

By the fall of 1976, the early optimism of that year had dissolved as Hunter, Inflated, and Cessna Land and Leasing (a connected real estate holding company) filed for Chapter 11 bankruptcy, owing the Bank of New York about $8 million. Operations continued for a while, but less than a year later 400 workers had been laid off, leaving a workforce of only 80.[28]

Production varied over the next two years, and the company reached a high of 500 employees in the summer of 1979. Workers continued to be represented by the ILGWU, which survived a rank-and-file rebellion of employees who were dissatisfied with the help that the union provided them. The internal union protest peaked when Gail E. Bobin, a shop steward at Inflated, and Jeffrey J. Rice, an employee at Clarksburg Coating Corporation (a "sister" firm of Inflated's), filed a petition to the National Labor Relations Board asking for an election to oust the union. The two dissidents led an effort to form a new local, United Inflated Workers, as an alternative to the ILGWU, and called for an all-employee meeting. That got the attention of Paul F. Winslow, the ILGWU district manager. Winslow listened to the complaints and committed the union to the "election and training of new union officers, and tighter enforcement of contract agreements concerning seniority, grievances, and job posting."[29]

Bobin, originally from New York City, had moved to North Adams in 1974 but had worked at General Electric in Pittsfield and then migrated to Inflated when she was laid off at GE Comparing the conditions at both workplaces, Bobin remarked, "The differences just smack you in the face." Not only upset that Inflated permitted unsafe conditions, but also angry that the union hadn't intervened, Bobin remarked, "When I get angry, I don't hesitate to tell people on the top or bottom what I think." And so she went to see the vice president of Inflated, Joseph Martin, a man who had held the same postion at Hunter, and she told him, "When we settle among ourselves, we're going to come back to you for our share of the cookies."[30] Unfortunately, a short six months later, it all appeared to be over as the U.S. Bankruptcy Court in Boston declared Hunter, Inflated, and the Clarksburg subsidiary bankrupt.[31]

In March 1980, the assets of the three firms were auctioned off, attracting hundreds of business people who reportedly received good deals on various pieces of machinery. The city of North Adams, Mayor Richard Lamb, and the police department tried to stop the auction to assure that taxes owed to the city would be paid, but the bankruptcy judge restrained them. (Six years later, employees at the bankrupt X-Tyal Corporation also tried to stop an auction of the company's machinery, but were first stymied by the bankruptcy judge and later by the police.) The following month, the U.S. Attorney's office in Springfield announced the continuation of an investigation of Inflated Products and its sister firms by the Justice Department's Organized Crime and Racketeering Section—an inquiry that had begun in 1976.[32]

Also that month, William J. Nightengale, the last president of the defunct companies, announced that he intended to remove at least 1,300 barrels believed to contain flammable and toxic wastes from the Clarksburg plant. Reportedly, some of the barrels had been dumped into the Hoosic River's north branch. According to the *Transcript*, "The barrels are believed to contain varying amounts of the chemicals toluene, methyl ethyl keytone, and acetone—all solvents used in coating processes" from the Clarksburg, Hunter, and Inflated plants. While the companies no longer existed, their toxic waste remained, making a bad ending even worse to another chapter in the region's textile history.

Workers cleaning chemicals, residue at Hunter Outdoor Products, 1970s (*Transcript*).

Some of the 1,300 barrels believed to contain flammable and toxic wastes that William J. Nightengale, president of Hunter's affiliated companies, intended to remove. The barrels stand in Clarksburg, next to the north branch of the Hoosic River, by Hunter's Inflated Products, in the former Strong, Hewat buildings (*Transcript,* April 1,1980).

Auction of assets of Hunter-affiliated firms March, 1980. The city of North Adams tried to stop the auction to assure that back taxes would be paid, but the bankruptcy judge said "No" to the city (*Transcript*).

NOTES

1 "Wall-Streeter Shoe Company," North Adams Historical Society (n.d.); "Wall Says Union Lost Fair Fight, 'Now back to Job,'" *Transcript,* April 16, 1964.

2 Wall-Streeter remained in operation until the end of November, 1973 when Robert E. Wall announced, "The imports have finally killed us . . . , we can't compete with 22-cent an hour labor." The company, which had produced fine men's shoes since 1912, and had at one time employed over 400 workers, had a workforce of just 150 at the end. While those unemployed workers did receive some severance, the union-less workforce was left without pensions. (Lewis Cuyler, "Wall-Streeter to close," *Transcript,* November 28, 1973; Lewis Cuyler, "Wall-Streeter Shoes: A lot of class," *Transcript,* November 29, 1973). Just a few month later, Wall announced that Florsheim, owned by Interco., Inc., had bought out the company, and would reopen production in North Adams with Wall in charge. The plant did reopen on March 11, 1974. Before long, local interest in a union brought a United Shoe Worker (USW) organizer down from Manchester, New Hampshire. The USW represented most of Florsheim's employees in the Chicago area and Midwest. Enough local employees indicated their interest in joining the union, and in an October 2, 1974 election, the union won 77 to 40. Newly elected President Robert F. Bellard and Vice President Nancy M. LaVigne led negotiations, and three months later, January 7, 1975, they had a contract with higher wages, insurance coverage, a pension plan for future retirees, and an increase in paid holidays and vacation time. The celebration over the first union contract at that plant in sixty-two years did not last long, as six weeks later Florsheim announced that the plant would close April 1, at a time when the city's unofficial unemployment rate stood at 14 percent. Union President Ballard stated that the shutdown "has nothing to do with the union, the people, the craftsmanship, or even North Adams." To that, Wall agreed, "pointing instead to declining shoe sales across the nation" (*Transcript,* Feb. 27, 1974; Sept. 27, 1974; Oct. 2, 1974; Jan. 7, 1975; Feb. 19, 1975). In a follow-up article in the *Transcript,* "Unemployed shoe company workers face a bleak Christmas" (Dec. 20, 1975), reporter Michael W. Munley interviewed Lena Duble, who began work at Wall-Streeter in 1928 at age 14, and continued to work there except for "time off to bear two children." Now 62, Duble missed not just her regular paycheck. "It feels like part of you has been taken away," she said. "It's like losing family." Union President Bellard also commented, "It's too bad something can't be done. The government should step in and open that factory." The government didn't, but a federal program, "Trade Adjustment Assistance Program," deemed the Florsheim employees eligible for assistance since the company's closing resulted from foreign imports. The program delivered but not without some misunderstanding and anxiety due to a poorly written government letter ("Florsheim workers assured on U.S. funds," *Transcript,* Nov. 15, 1976).

3 *Transcript,* June 7, 1960 and June 13, 1960.

4 *Transcript,* June 13, 1960; Maynard Seider, "The CIO in Rural Massachusetts: Sprague Electric and North Adams, 1937–1944," *Historical Journal of Massachusetts,* XXII, 1 (Winter, 1994), 58; Richard O. Boyer and Herbert M. Morais, *Labor's Untold Story* (New York: United Electrical, Radio & Machine Workers of America, 1955).

5 *Transcript,* June 25, 1960.

6 Ibid.

7 *Transcript,* April 19, 1968.

8 On EDA designation, see Gordon Lane, *Transcript,* May 21, 1968, 3. Interestingly, earlier the same month, Lane wrote a column arguing that local firms faced a shortage of eligible workers to fill their needs (*Transcript,* May 4, 1968, 2).

9 Ibid., October 4 and November 16, 1967.

10 Gordon Lane, *Transcript,* October 31, 1968.

11 A threat reminiscent of company behavior in the nineteenth and first part of the twentieth century holding company housing as leverage in labor disputes.

12 International Ladies' Garment Workers Union (ILGWU) archives, 5780/120, Box 3, Folder 4. Kheel Center for Labor Documentation and Archives, Cornell University.

13 Gordon Lane, *Transcript,* November 1, 1968, 2.

14 *Transcript,* November 22, 1968, 2.

15 Gordon Lane, *Transcript,* November 22, 1968, 2.

16 Ibid., December 30, 1968.

17 Dilk letter of December 28, 1968, ILGWU 5780/120 Box 3, Folder 5.

18 Albano to Sol Chaikin, January 13, 1969, ILGWU 5780/120, Box 3, Folder 5.

19 Gordon Lane, *Transcript,* March 19, 1969; April 17, 1969. The machinists had earlier broken away from the production workers union and became the first Sprague employee group to join a national union, the International Association of Machinists. The IAM local, with little more than three dozen members, struck in 1948 but the production workers failed to honor their picket line.The company persevered without the machinists and "[a]fter a five-month-long strike, the IAM met total defeat" (Raymond C. Bliss, *A Study of Union History at the Sprague Electric Company in North Adams, Mass. 1929–1970.* Williamstown, MA: Williams College, 1976, 35–36). Two of its demands, an agency shop and arbitration, would not be won for itself and the other two unions until the ten-week 1970 strike (Chapter Eighteen).

20 *Transcript,* August 28, 1973.

21 Paul L. Krause, *Transcript,* April 4, 1975, 1, 24.

22 Peter Martin Nelson, *Legal Services: Emerging Institution or Crack in the Dike?* (Williamstown, MA: Williams College student paper, 1976), 23.

23 *Transcript*, April 9, 1975.

24 Nelson, 24.

25 Paul L. Krause, *Transcript*, April 8, 1975.

26 *Transcript*, January 30 and April 10, 1975.

27 Ibid., January 23, 1976.

28 Ibid., August 3, 1977.

28 James P. Therrien, "New union shop steward 'caused quite an uproar,'" *Transcript*, June 9, 1979.

30 Ibid.

31 James P. Therrien, *Transcript*, December 5, 1979.

32 Sandra E. Constantine, *Transcript*, April 23, 1980.

CHAPTER SEVENTEEN

LOCAL ACTIVISTS AND THE "FAIRNESS" DOCTRINE

FOR A NUMBER OF YEARS I had my sociology students read Lillian Rubin's *Worlds of Pain: Life in the Working Class Family.*[1] Rubin wrote clearly and with passion, and my students empathized with many in her sample of working-class men and women. However, I had become increasingly dissatisfied with one of the major themes in her book. She argued that the economic and social difficulties that members of the working class faced not only kept them down, but also made them virtually unable to escape from their painful condition. Rubin believed that, for the working class to improve their collective status, it would take a concerted effort by others to aid them. She hoped that the professional middle class might somehow fulfill that role. The working class, as Rubin saw it, had been too beaten down, too victimized and impotent to change the course of its own or the nation's history. To me, this seemed to be a one-dimensional reading of a complex group of people. My own family's work, teaching, and political experiences led me to question her fatalistic conclusion.

One way of directly testing Rubin's thesis would be to study a working-class group of known activists, a group that refused to behave as victims. I thought that by listening to the stories of this distinctive group, I might find something that they held in common—from their upbringing, their workplaces, or specific adult experiences—that helped move them onto the activist road. My initial research question went like this: *What kinds of people become labor activists?* But I soon realized that I had phrased the question in too constricting a manner. The question suggested that significant differences existed between activists and non-activists and, further, that activism and non-activism may be more or less permanent characteristics of individuals. After conducting a pilot study in which I interviewed thirteen labor leaders, I learned that the research question needed to be rephrased. So then I asked: *Under what conditions do working-class people become labor activists?*

Ironically, my decision to make this conceptual shift had followed a strong "aha" moment that I'd experienced while questioning a so-called "non-activist." I had decided I needed a control group of non-activists to help me tease out the key factors separating the two groups. One of the union officials at the local hospital gave me the names of some members of his unit who had not been involved in the union. I began to interview one of the non-activists, Nancy, an LPN in her early fifties, who had more than twenty years of experience at the hospital. About ten minutes into the interview, Nancy told me that, not long after she'd begun working there, the administration of the hospital changed, and the new regime exhibited a more controlling and bureaucratic leadership style. This shift led a group of LPNs to explore the possibility of starting a union, a process that meant a lot of phone calls, meetings with prospective unions, and numerous discussions with co-workers. Then Nancy—supposedly a "non-activist—stunned me by casually mentioning that she belonged to that pioneer group that had organized the first union.

However, her active period turned out to be relatively short-lived. One of her children suffered a critical injury, and Nancy had to cut down at her hours of work in order to spend more time at home with her daughter. Other familial obligations increased for her as well, and she literally had no time to be involved in the union or even to go to union meetings. Now, some twenty years later, with her family situation stable, Nancy thought of becoming involved with the union again. When I asked her why some people became activists, she replied:

> I think it's their way of life . . . . Most of the people I know—either their co-workers talk them into it, and they really get involved—or they have more free time and got interested and just carried on with it . . . . You get friendships in them. I always thought I would become interested in it if I hadn't gotten bogged down with other things, because I was always kind of interested in it anyway . . . . [T]he girls and fellas I know [who are active] seem to have more time . . . . They're freer to attend meetings. I think that has a lot to do with it.

In another interview, Nancy exemplified the role that gender—she, like most women of her generation, was the prime family caretaker—and life cycle played in "becoming" an activist. At that point, with all her children out of the house and no additional familial obligations, she had the extra time to pursue a union role.

I realized that becoming involved in a union was a process of "becoming," not necessarily of being born or bred an activist. I had earlier hypothesized that labor activists would have been brought up in pro-union households, and would have learned the importance of unions at the kitchen table (as I had). I soon found that not to be the case with the activists I interviewed, most of whom did not grow up in pro-union households. For the most part, the activists did not seem that different from current non-activists in terms of family background, general political ideology, or future orientation.

What I did discover, as I continued to interview activists, was that their entrée into activism began over issues of equity, or fairness, in the workplace. That was the case whether they worked in an industrial or service sector setting. One typical case involved a secretary who volunteered to fill a vacant steward's position when no one in the union helped a member who was denied a promotion that should have been hers: "She got no support . . . and it really made me angry to see a real abuse of a good employee and no one to help defend or help guide her."

In another case, John, a specifications writer at Sprague had worked there for fifteen years before he attended his first union meeting. He directly saw the weakness of the union and how the company "did whatever they wanted to do . . . not treating people fairly." Without arbitration at the end of the grievance process, the process meant little. There were simply "no answers . . . . They weren't fair with the people." Now John realized that "something needed to be changed," and he worked hard with others in a successful effort to bring in a stronger union. With that union he served on the grievance and negotiating committees, and, after a ten-week strike, helped to bring about a new contract that put arbitration into the final step of the grievance process.

Ilene, a transplant from California, began work as a sewing machine operator when she was in her early forties, after she had raised her children. She remembered growing up not liking unions, that unions to her were "Jimmy Hoffa." But she had learned about collective bargaining from the management side by having served on her town's school committee. The union recognized that expertise and asked her to serve on several negotiating committees. About ten years into her work at the textile company, when problems emerged about the viability of the company and the leadership of the union, Ilene began taking a stronger interest in the union.

As the only woman on the negotiating committee, Ilene took on the union president when she said she believed the union was "dishonest, that they were double-dipping, and that they were not giving the people a fair shake." Somewhat spontaneously, she spoke up in the cafeteria, making her accusations in public. Later, she brought in the international representatives of the union to investigate, and after a hearing, they removed the union officers from their positions. A trustee ran the union until the next scheduled election when the rank and file elected Ilene president, and subsequently reelected her twice. In thinking back over her rebellion within the union,

Ilene saw it as "something that needed to be corrected . . . . I seldom ever use the term president. I mean I'm just a person like anybody else . . . . I certainly don't have the education and background . . . except good common horse sense and fair play."

Shaun Sutliff became a union activist in his twenties. His family, of French Canadian background, goes back three generations in the region and includes two grandparents, his mother, and his wife all of whom worked for a time at Sprague Electric. After high school, Shaun worked at a limestone quarry doing quality control. He soon learned that the company encouraged employees to cheat on the tests, to certify batches of stone that did not warrant it. When asked how the workers felt about the quality control shenanigans, Shaun replied, "It took away from the dignity of the job. It's either good or it isn't."

After the quarry, Shaun enrolled at the local state college where he remembers being radicalized through some college courses. In one course, where he studied media bias, he began reading left-wing magazines like the *Nation,* the *Progressive*, and *Mother Jones*. He read an article in one of those magazines on a progressive electrical workers union, and later, tried to bring that union in when he started work at a new company in Williamstown. Only after the organizing started, did he realize that the one he had contacted was not the one he'd read about: he had mistaken the IUE for the UE. He remembered thinking: "Oh, shit, the wrong one!"

Shaun continued his political education through reading, working with other activists at the Northern Berkshire Labor Coalition, and attending labor conferences and rallies. Meanwhile at Chadbourne, the new company that processed materials for electrical capacitors, Shaun and about two dozen other relatively young workers saw their jobs as providing an opportunity to start something good. While management started off in a cooperative manner, they began to renege on "one hundred little things"—pay, quality, the speed of production, etc. The workers made a list of proposals for change. When the company said "No," the union organizing drive began. Shaun was married, but because he was not yet a father, he had the time and passion to get involved.

The company fought back with a union-busting firm, and the union lost the vote. Shaun and those who led the first drive decided not to head a second drive, not because they'd changed their minds on the need for a union, but because they needed strength and leadership from others. That in fact did develop, and a second vote went 19 to 6 in favor of the union. Shaun went on to serve on the negotiating committee and also as president. When asked how he came to be a union leader, an activist, he talked about his mother's role on the local school board. When she "got angry," she "got involved." If she bought something at the store and it didn't work, she would bring it back. In Shaun's words, she would "stand up for what's fair."

As I learned from this informal research, no one is necessarily one or the other, an activist or non-activist, nor do specific background factors necessarily push employees in a specific direction. Gender, life cycle changes, and reactions to workplace conditions all need to be factored in. To paraphrase Marx, all workers are capable of making history, but we struggle to do so under the conditions that history has dealt us.[2]

NOTES

1 New York: Basic Books, 1976.

2 "Men make their own history, but they do not make it just as they please; they do not make it under circumstances chosen by themselves, but under circumstances directly encountered, given and transmitted from the past" (Karl Marx, *The Eighteenth Brumaire of Louis Bonaparte* (New York: International Publishers, 1852).

CHAPTER EIGHTEEN:

THE 1970 STRIKE AGAINST SPRAGUE

We shouldn't be blind and deaf to the rest of the world.

—Walter Wood, president of International Union of Electrical Workers (IUE) #285

The strikers had won "a struggle for dignity, justice and security."

—Raymond C. Bliss, historian

[W]e were very happy . . . that we had framed a contract that . . . applied to almost every problem that we had . . . that we had been able to move a corporate giant like . . . Sprague into listening to us and into achieving some measure of fairness . . . .

—Jack Boulger, American Federation of Technical Employees (AFTE) activist

INTRODUCTION

WHILE THE TEXTILE INDUSTRY still played a significant role in the region in the 1960s and 1970s, its importance paled in comparison to the size and influence of Sprague Electric Company. In 1970, more than 2,000 blue- and white-collar workers in North Adams engaged in a militant ten-week strike against Sprague. The capacitor company[1] had dominated employment in the northern Berkshires for three decades and had never before faced such a significant and lengthy strike. For much of its history in North Adams, Sprague had virtually controlled its weak labor unions, leaving the workforce low-paid and ill-protected on the shop floor. So what precipitated the strike and the strong sense of camaraderie that typified the production, office, and technical workers who came together to challenge the power of the world's largest capacitor company? And what would be the consequences of the mighty upsurge of 1970, immediately after the strike and years later in the community's memory?

After orders had stagnated during the Great Depression, demand for the variety of capacitors that the company manufactured for war-related products skyrocketed during World War II, and Sprague's mostly female workforce doubled from 1,300 in 1940 to 2,600 in August 1945.[2] That workforce produced the capacitor that detonated the second atomic bomb dropped over Nagasaki, Japan. R.C. Sprague, with his naval officer background and his economic and political interests, became well known in Republican political circles as an expert in national security. In 1953, President Eisenhower offered him the post of assistant secretary of the Air Force, but Sprague turned it down, rather than sell his stock in the company.[3]

R.C. Sprague remained very active in trade association activities and kept the corporate headquarters in North Adams while the company continued to expand worldwide.[4] The company had been doing quite well since 1940, with sales and earnings steadily increasing by an average of 16.5 percent a year;[5] in 1966, local employment at Sprague reached its highest level, 4,137, an enormous number for a city of less than 20,000 people. In addition to corporate headquarters, the company maintained a large research and development center in North Adams, along with a variety of production lines at four locations throughout the city. With Vietnam War–fueled increases in defense spending and an expanding demand for electric and electronic products, Sprague's immediate future looked promising.

Nonetheless, concerns about the movement of jobs out of North Adams could not be avoided. In a well-publicized speech given by R.C. Sprague in 1957, the founder stated that it would be "very unwise" for Sprague to further expand in North Adams, as "[t]here is such a thing as being too large in any one community . . . ."[6] In fact, the company's first branch plant had already been established in Barre, Vermont, in 1945. By 1951, it had added branch plants in Wisconsin, New Hampshire, and in Bennington, Vermont. Two years later, the company headed south to North Carolina and Puerto Rico, and by 1960 had additional plants in California, Mexico, and Italy. As Japanese corporations increasingly entered the world market of capacitor and electronic component manufacturing, Sprague acted no differently than its U.S.-based competitors in scouring the globe in search of lower production costs. By 1970, some 12,000 Sprague employees worked at more than two dozen worldwide locations.

With the exception of a small workforce at the location in Barre, Vermont, North Adams employees constituted the only unionized group of Sprague workers. While the company had virtually controlled the local unions that represented the production, office, and technical workers for some three decades, a younger, more savvy, and activist workforce, which included many former G.I.s, voted in new national, AFL-CIO unions in the late 1960s. Up to that point, only the relatively small group of Sprague machinists in North Adams had national union representation. But Sprague management was about to face significant opponents.

THE COMING OF THE INTERNATIONAL UNIONS

Toward the end of 1966, production workers replaced the Independent Condenser Workers #2, a union known to be in the company's "hip pocket,"[7] with the International Union of Electrical Workers (IUE). The IUE affiliation would provide the production workers with expertise in financial analysis, contract negotiation, legal help, and strike support. Walter Wood, president of the local chapter, represented a new generation of Sprague worker, one with more formal education and greater knowledge in the area of labor relations, and more willing to challenge management. Not content to rely solely on outside help, Wood established a relationship with the Labor Relations and Research Center at the University of Massachusetts in Amherst in order to improve the local members' skills in those areas as well.[8]

Prior to the IUE, for years the ICW#2 had meekly accepted management's contract offers and, without a right to arbitration, had no leverage with which to fight grievances. A wide array of company extracurricular activities had engendered a layer of employee loyalty, and management had shrewdly offered a $100 Christmas bonus—a significant amount for employees earning only about $50 a week during the 1940s and 1950s—that was only available if the union accepted a pre-Christmas yearly contract.[9]

The decision to affiliate with a national union did not come without a struggle, but by the mid-1960s, the momentum for change and greater employee power could not be stopped. As one woman stated at a 1966 union meeting, "The people were afraid thirty years ago, but they aren't now." Her sentiments seemed to exemplify "the emergence of a more militant labor force at Sprague," as one local historian put it.[10]

Walter Wood had taken courses in labor studies at the University of Massachusetts and at Rutgers University in New Brunswick, New Jersey. He realized that Sprague employees had historically been at a disadvantage in bargaining with management since, without a research staff, they could hardly challenge the company's economic arguments. He subsequently set up an education committee and asked the Labor Center at UMass to help organize programs in labor law, grievances, and labor relations for union members. He also rented a downtown office for the union, the first permanent union office the production workers had ever had; encouraged membership to get involved in civic and political issues; and started a union practice of aiding other local unions in their organizing drives.

Wood himself had long been active playing in several drum and bugle corps, even managing one group that played in international competitions. In North Adams, he served on the local housing authority board, advocating for a labor representative, wanting to "speak for the working people . . . to [m]ake sure they got a fair shot at a vacant apartment."[11]

Throughout the 1950s and 1960s, pay increases at Sprague Electric had failed to keep pace with the cost of living, and as the company had grown, it also had become more impersonal. Many in the Sprague workforce had seemed ready for a change. In 1967, with the new union in place, the rank and file authorized—by a vote of 380 to 233—the local's negotiating committee to call a strike, if necessary, when the current contract expired in June. But Walter Wood and the committee realized that only a fraction of the membership of some 2,800 had attended that meeting, and voted, and that deep divisions existed within the membership.

Because of that, two days before the strike deadline, in an unprecedented move, the union called for an outdoor meeting at a local baseball field to hold a final vote. That time, with the membership mobilized and a crowd estimated at between 1,500 and 2,200 sitting in the bleachers, Wood stood on the diamond and, using a microphone, went over the company's contract proposal. He then expressed the negotiating committee's concern that the initial strike vote had represented only a small number of members, and, realizing that opposition to the strike existed among many workers as well as in the community, he urged acceptance of the company's meager proposal. According to the *Transcript*'s labor reporter, Gordon Lane, the rank and file "voted overwhelmingly" to accept the company's offer. While Wood later admitted that "he had 'to eat a little crow'" in reversing his position, that would not be the case three years later.[12]

Before talks began for the 1970 contract, the last segment of the workforce, composed of the technical and office workers, joined a national union, the American Federation of Technical Engineers (AFTE). Just as production workers had undergone a change that had resulted in a new affiliation, a significant shift occurred among white-collar workers as well. Future AFTE activist Jack Boulger had started working at Sprague in 1954 as a member of the weak independent office workers' union. Just two years out of high school at the time, Boulger had grown up in a working-class family. To help his family, he had worked second shift at the Strong, Hewat woolen mill all the way through high school, the same mill that employed his father.

At Sprague, Jack gradually became more and more involved with the union. Recalling that period, he later said:

> I saw some things going on that I couldn't believe. So I started doing some reading. And I started reading some of the laws. And I got ahold of some labor papers. And I said "My God," you know, you don't really know how bad something is until you find out how it should be, or how it is in other places.[13]

Boulger went on to organize a committee to decertify the independent union and bring in a national union affiliated with the AFL-CIO. In doing so, he worked very closely with Walter Wood. As Wood encouraged his union members to get involved in local civic affairs, Boulger did the same. Boulger himself became a director of the United Way and served on the Board of Trustees of the North Adams Hospital, and as president of the employee credit union at Sprague. Active in the AFTE Northeast Council, which was composed of locals from New England and New York, Jack Boulger would go on to serve as president of that union group.

Shifts in gender relations also played a role in support for the international unions and greater workplace activism at Sprague. According to one local researcher, "By the late 1960s, . . . more women remained single, or else were married and chose not to have children, thereby enabling them to complete the necessary educational requirements that had to be met in order to gain a semi-professional lab or professional job."[14] With greater independence at home and on the job, the women had more time and energy to attend union meetings and engage in strategy sessions. They were also active on the picket lines, as exemplified by Evelyn Jones, who would later be elected vice president of the production workers' union.

At that point, AFTE and the IUE joined the machinists, who already had an AFL-CIO tie, having become members of the International Association of Machinists (IAM) back in 1949. As all three unions prepared for contract talks, they knew that General Electric workers had struck the huge GE plant in Pittsfield, just 18 miles to the south, as part of a national strike. Many GE strikers lived in North Berkshire, and had friends and relatives working at Sprague. When the GE strike ended on the last day of January 1970, its employees had won significant wage increases as well as gains in vacation, pensions, sick pay, and medical benefits. R.C. Sprague had always argued that as a producer of components for the electronics industry—a "middleman," not one that could pass on costs directly to the consumer—his company couldn't be compared to General Electric and the giants of the electrical products industry. In 1970, however, that argument didn't carry much weight at home.

THE START OF NEGOTIATIONS

During the summer of 1969, Sprague management prepared to train hundreds of research and development specialists and other corporate personnel to manufacture capacitors in the event of a strike. Longtime industrial relations specialist George Bateman recalled some of the plans: "As a matter of fact, we had even prepared to live in for a period of time. So we had food, we had sleeping facilities, we had all these things, and they even built a helipad on top of one of the buildings for a helicopter to come in."[15] The company also had leased space at a new office building a block away from its main gate.

Though he had an experienced labor relations staff, R.C. Sprague liked to keep in close contact with the negotiators, asking questions, making suggestions, and enforcing final decisions. He displayed the engineer's grasp of comparable costs and wages throughout the industry, as well as the intricacies of national trade policy and international competition, skills honed by his involvement in trade association affairs and Republican politics. Sprague also possessed a sizeable ego and a secure sense of the value of his own opinions. Over the years, through company-sponsored athletic events and entertainment, through awards dinners, a company newspaper, and a radio show, and by his cultivation of an approachable, gracious yet stern "captain of the ship" persona, R.C. had benefitted from the paternalism that became synonymous with the company. He was a stubborn "father," one who did not like to be crossed, and one who believed that internal arguments should be kept within the family. Not surprisingly, he strongly opposed arbitration as the final step in the grievance process, since that would cede authority to an outsider. Approaching 70 years of age but still vigorously running the company, R.C.'s spirit and actions dominated the negotiations. He took it all personally, never really believing that *his* workers would strike. Later, when a strike appeared imminent, he proved unable to skillfully craft an acceptable contract.

Formal negotiations began in September with the unions' proposals. Besides wage and benefit demands, the company faced a call for a union shop and binding arbitration. A union shop would require new workers to join the union, and pay a union initiation fee and union dues within thirty days of being hired. Under the system of voluntary membership already in place, a significant minority of the workforce often joined just before negotiations, and then exited—along with their dues—once the new contract had been approved.

As for arbitration, it would strengthen the grievance process. Again, under the system that was in place, the outside mediator who emerged during the final step had no power to enforce a decision. Thus, step-by-step, even through the mediation, when they reached the tenth and final step, the company simply could refuse to accept the grievant's contentions, thereby weakening the whole procedure for rank-and-file workers. As one AFTE activist put it, "We were looking for something that would provide a measure of justice swiftly before we forgot what we were looking for."[16]

Winning the union shop and arbitration would not only bring real political and economic gains to the two new unions (AFTE and IUE), but would also bring a psychological triumph to them, since the local, "independent" unions had not been able to achieve either goal in their three decades of existence. In December, management presented its set of counter-proposals, which included a separate ten-cents-an-hour raise for the highest paid blue-collar workers—those in maintenance (represented by IUE) and the machine shop (the IAM local). The AFTE local considered this an affront to their members, and, as was common during that time period, the union distributed flyers that were titled: *"Living Wage. Not Insults."* Using the flyers to make their case, AFTE angrily responded to management's workforce-splitting tactic and went on to criticize the economic power that Sprague had wielded since the 1930s:

> THEY ARE RESPONSIBLE FOR THE FACT THAT MOST FAMILIES HAVE TO WORK BOTH HUSBAND AND WIFE IN ORDER TO CARVE OUT AN EXISTENCE IN OUR AREA . . . . THEY ARE RESPONSIBLE FOR THE FACT THAT WE ARE RIDICULOUSLY FAR BEHIND, IN WAGES AND BENEFITS, THAN THOSE OF OUR NEIGHBORS WHO WORK IN NEIGHBORING COMMUNITIES . . . WE ARE TIRED OF BEING EXPLOITED . . . ."[17]

The *Transcript* published a news item about the flyer, headlined: "AFTE LOCAL SAYS SPRAGUE TO BLAME FOR AREA POVERTY."[18]

Following AFTE's lead, IUE used rhetorically charged flyers to communicate with and solidify its membership, particularly on the issue of wages. Arguing that the cost of living had increased by 7.1 percent since their last raise, Local #200 proclaimed:

> LET'S MOVE FORWARD . . . NOT BACKWARDS! OUR FIGHT NOW IS FOR MORE THAN SURVIVAL ! ! !

The union went on to inform its ranks that while the average manufacturing wage, both nationwide and in Western Massachusetts, was $3.12 an hour, Sprague production and maintenance workers received an average of $2.60 an hour.[19]

As the March 1 strike deadline loomed closer, negotiations nearly collapsed. For three decades, R.C. Sprague and his industrial relations staff had used the compliant officers of the local unions to exert control over the North Adams workforce. Three times, in 1937, 1944, and in 1948, national unions waged spirited campaigns to gain a membership hold but had been defeated.[20] By 1970, Sprague's paternalism was wearing thin, as was exemplified by one of the IUE's bulletins, which stated that the company wanted its employees as partners, but "why don't we all share *as partners* in the profits from increased productivity???"[21]

On February 10, the IAM membership unanimously authorized a strike, and six days later AFTE membership gave its negotiating committee the okay to call a strike on March 1. The following day, in a special issue of its in-house newspaper, the company warned its employees, "At meetings today and tonight, IUE apparently will move ahead with its announced plan to take a strike action vote. This vote could have the most serious consequences to the Company and its employees." Despite the threat, the IUE rank and file voted to authorize its committee to call a strike if necessary, thus joining the other two unions in a concerted show of solidarity.[22]

As positions hardened, all sides used the local newspaper, the *Transcript*, to take their case to the broad community. One letter writer cautioned workers not to strike, thus raising the possibility of Sprague leaving the area, as the local textile firms had previously done. Union leaders were referred to as "Communistic," and local residents were reminded: "Thank God you have a job." On February 13 and 14, Sprague ran full-page ads in the paper, the first a letter by R.C. himself, and the second from President Bruce R. Carlson, engaging in a "good cop, bad cop" approach. While R. C. Sprague focused on reconciliation, Carlson attacked the IUE for wanting a strike.[23]

The company rejected a union suggestion for "an impartial fact-finding committee,"[24] and also turned down requests from the IUE and AFTE for data on employee productivity and corporate finances. Most notable about these requests is not that Sprague turned them down—that was probably expected—but that *now,* for the first time in more than three decades, union leaders from the production floor and the office adopted a negotiating posture with management in which both sides stood on an equal plane. In the contract negotiations, employee representatives no longer acted intimidated by complex financial and legal arguments. In the late 1930s, as we have seen, dissident workers recognized the need for such expertise, and they mobilized to affiliate with a national union, United Electrical Workers, which had a legal and research department. Unsuccessful in that and later efforts, the rank and file continued to be represented by "independent" unions that never challenged the company on its financial data and arguments.

With less than two weeks to go before the contract expired, *Transcript* editor James A. Hardman Jr. cautioned the unions about striking. He said, "The community . . . hopes the unions will be realistic in assessing what is possible, and will not embark on a fruitless battle which might cost them more, in the end, than they can gain."[25] Fifteen years earlier, Hardman and R.C. Sprague had been on opposite sides of the citywide controversy when a new company, Dragon Cement, had tried to move into North Adams. Hardman had welcomed the opportunity for the creation of 150 new jobs, while Sprague threatened to cut production at his North Adams operation—a move that would have cost the area 2,000 jobs—if the cement company's plans were allowed to proceed. Worried about Sprague's threat, the city had ruled against Dragon Cement's zoning request.[26]

THE STRIKE BEGINS

Talks between AFTE and management reached an impasse on Sunday, March 1, after 40 hours of mediator-assisted negotiations. At a final meeting, the rank and file voted to strike by a nearly 2 to 1 margin (229–123), and at midnight the first strike at Sprague since 1949 began. AFTE's membership contained the most combative members, a new generation of predominantly women clerical workers. As long-time local president Jack Boulger put it, "The young turks [provided] leadership and spoke of injustice."[27]

The strike lasted ten weeks, through the end of a Berkshire winter and the first half of spring. Sprague would never be the same, nor would the community. Years later, both participants in the strike and interested observers would recall the Sprague era as comprising the pre-strike period and the post-strike years. Many would romanticize the earlier days when Sprague was "like a family,"[28] when harmony characterized work relationships, and when the company organized a multitude of recreational and social activities off the job. Sprague constantly touched the lives of individuals, families, and generations, and many basked in the warm feelings of those memories.

Others, more hard-nosed and less sentimental, remembered the differences between the pre and post-strike periods as less clear-cut. If 1970 was a demarcation point, the line was somewhat fuzzy. The earlier years never appeared so glorious, and the beginnings of change could be traced to a time prior to 1970. These people had never really recognized R.C. as the "good father," nor the local union as the protector of their interests. They remembered the low wages, and the need for two-paycheck families to work long hours. They believed that Sprague used its considerable power to keep higher-paying industry, like Dragon Cement, out of town. They noted the postwar proliferation of domestic and overseas branch plants in low-wage, non-union settings, and they watched the numbers of the local workforce decline in the three-year period *before* the strike. While a significant minority of Sprague employees undoubtedly fell into this realist camp, and another sizeable group made up the romantic group, most production, office, and machine workers probably believed elements of both.

All the behaviors and emotions of a classic, lengthy strike manifested themselves in North Adams during those ten weeks in 1970. Many battles were fought, in and around the picket line, with some physical violence and destruction of property, but mostly with bruised and angry feelings. Only about 5 percent of the workers scabbed,[29] so Sprague received little help from experienced line and office workers. Strikers, particularly those in two-paycheck Sprague families, had a tough time of it economically, and many had their first taste of surplus government food that winter and spring. They managed to hold firm, building a common solidarity through their determined mission, singing,[30] shouting, and marching—belly to backside—on the picket line. Union leadership rose to the occasion, maintaining a disciplined rank and file, publishing numerous strike bulletins, and keeping its membership well informed of developments. In the community itself, both management and labor battled to win the hearts and minds of those outside of the Sprague (now estranged) family.

Once the final round of negotiations had broken down, AFTE spent the hours from 7:30 p.m. to midnight on March 1 preparing its membership. Still, "(i)t was very tense." The first shift came on at 7:00 a.m. One AFTE member vividly recalled the start of that first day, just after midnight:

> We made up some signs. We went out that evening. It was cold. Come morning, our people were out there and I was out there . . . and we started our picket line . . . . And the seven o'clock people come in at 6:30—[and they] *stopped* on the other side of the street. The word got out . . . . They were respecting [the picket line]. There was, Lord knows, hundreds and hundreds and hundreds of people backed up on the other side of the street . . . . "Oh, great," [I thought].[31]

En masse, as members of the dense crowd, and as individuals, IUE and IAM unionists overwhelmingly refused to cross the AFTE lines. "We were really surprised that we could stop everybody . . . . (We) did really well."[32] On March 9 the machinists' union officially went on strike, further legitimizing and broadening the picket lines. On March 19, IUE defeated an intra-union challenge and four days later officially joined AFTE and the IAM on strike.

Strikers marched in tight formation, often with two or three concentric circles winding around, making it virtually impossible for anyone to break through easily. These were not symbolic lines, but meant to keep out scabs, workers, and truckers alike. Esther Hartranft, a long-time Sprague loyalist, did cross the picket lines throughout the strike. Hartranft worked as a private secretary, a status making her ineligible for union membership. She later said:

> It was quite formidable to approach [the picketers]. And they stood shoulder to shoulder. You just had . . . to push your way through. And . . . [t]he first time I did it, I . . . got through and was a bit shook up . . . . I was advised to go to the office nurse and just get something to quiet me down, because it was, it was traumatic. I shook when I got in there . . . . I was sort of numb when I went through . . . . I'm sure there was a lot of yelling. . . . Of course the women are more vociferous than the men really.[33]

The police stayed on hand to maintain some sort of peace, and male managers made their presence known at shift changes to help female management personnel and scabs through the lines. Sprague also arranged for picket line activity to be filmed from a distance, another effort at intimidating the strikers. Evelyn Jones, a future vice president of IUE, picketed and said:

> Of course I was a big mouth as usual. I could . . . yell "Scab!" from Marshall Street to the corner of Main. They used to be at the corner of

> Main shaking their fist at me . . . . Of course the company had cameras all over the place taking our pictures. And they'd say, "Why, you're one of the ones that was picketing at such and such a place," you know? You talk about me having a file. We had a file, too.[34]

In 1970, Evelyn Jones had already been working at Sprague for twenty-four years, and she knew the meaning of the picket line. (It would be five more years before she would get involved with the union, running and being elected to the local's executive board. As she recalls, "I was fifty-two when I was elected [a]nd after that nobody could stop me." She went on to serve ten years on the board and four as vice president, the highest position that a woman had reached at IUE #200. She loved her union work and also became very involved in Democratic party politics, getting to know Governor Michael Dukakis and his secretary of labor. Outspoken at work, for the union and in politics, Evelyn would feel her power, though she still faced negativity because of her gender and later, because of her age.[35])

Not many workers crossed the picket line, but those who did heard about it, and not just from Evelyn Jones. Long-time friends yelled at scabs, "I'll never speak to you for the rest of my life!"[36] AFTE, the most confrontational of the three unions, actually published the names of scabs in their strike bulletins. Each of their early bulletins featured a verbal attack against a single scab. While IUE didn't appear to print the names of its members who scabbed, the union kept a list on a big sign in its office of the names of those who refused to picket.

By the third week of the strike, the company moved equipment from North Adams to its plant in Nashua, New Hampshire, machinery that would mean the loss of 100 jobs. But that action, and the implied threat of future job cuts, failed to weaken the strikers' resolve. AFTE responded by charging Sprague with an unfair labor practice, and IUE recommended organizing the Nashua plant. A local writer, looking at the strike in historical perspective, began her column with, "The times they are a changing" and concluded, "The father image of Sprague is gone, along with apathetic, one-sided bargaining. Unionism at Sprague is finally catching up with the times."[37]

Two weeks before the strike deadline, the company had started boarding up windows and hired a contingent of Pinkerton security police for the duration. On the second day of the strike, the police arrested an AFTE international representative for allegedly blocking a truck at the plant's main gate. Some witnesses stated that the police actually knocked him down in front of the truck. On March 4, soldered spikes were discovered in one of the plant parking lots. On the first of April, a truck owned by a service station operator who had rented trucks to Sprague to move equipment out of the plant, was torched. Two days later, fire destroyed the car of a scabbing production worker.[38]

A company action nearly led to even more violence and potential fatalities. To service its North Adams operation, Sprague hired a Troy, New York, trucking firm that specialized in delivering oil to strikebound plants. The company retrofitted its trucks as battering rams, with heavy-duty metal plates over the front bumpers and fenders. It looked and acted "like a tank, an armored vehicle," which could push blocked cars out of the way for a delivery. "They didn't care; they just rolled those cars right over." George Bateman, North Adams Director of Industrial Relations, remembers getting to one delivery and calling for police intervention just prior to the onset of possible violence. That's when he noticed that the truck drivers also carried rifles.[39]

THE PUBLIC RELATIONS BATTLE

The company presented its side of the story to the community with full-page ads in the *Transcript*. Editorially, the local radio station gave a vigorous defense of Sprague, while it tore into the union leadership for keeping the strike going. The *Transcript* editorials, while more moderate in tone, swung further and further to support the company the longer the strike lasted. R.C. Sprague spoke to local civic groups, presenting the company viewpoint, and even mailed a lengthy copy of one of his speeches to all of his employees. An ideological battle raged to see whose actions best served the interests of this somewhat ephemeral ideal called "the community." The striking unions fought that battle with all their resources, ceding no ground on the public relations front to the company. They responded in print to management attacks and what they perceived as misinformation. IUE President Walter Wood delivered point-by-point rebuttals to civic groups, specifically responding to arguments advanced by R.C. Sprague. An AFTE effort complemented the IUE through a letter-writing campaign to local businessmen, presenting the union story and inviting strike fund contributions.

Personally, R.C. Sprague made a planned and concerted effort to stay in touch with both management and hourly personnel, even those on strike. From his own notes at the conclusion of the strike: "I made a point of remaining in N.A. during [the] strike and went through [the] middle of picket lines at least four times daily. Quite a lot of friendly banter with pickets." Through it all, he made a "[p]rinciple[d] effort . . . [t]o keep emotions under control and lid from blowing off."[40]

A tougher side of R.C. Sprague would also be revealed during the strike. Early on, he publicly moved one production line out of North Adams in an obvious warning to strikers. Privately, he used his relationship with Jim Hardman, editor of the *Transcript*, to try to control the work of the paper's labor beat reporter, Gordon Lane. And with angry indignation, he fired off lengthy letters to western Massachusetts Congressional representatives Silvio Conte and Ed Boland for what he alleged was a false presentation of his company's policies.

As the strike unfolded, the *Transcript* became increasingly supportive of Sprague's negotiating position and increasingly anti-union in its editorial policy. Although daily newspapers in Springfield and Pittsfield covered North Adams news, the *Transcript* remained the most widely circulated paper in town. Four days into the strike, the paper began with a moderate "Appeal to Reason," asking the participants to keep their emotions down and reach agreement. Still not choosing sides, the next strike editorial some two weeks later portrayed both workers and management as victims of price inflation and business recession, and reminded everyone that the whole community had a stake in an early settlement.[41]

However, by March 27, the *Transcript* underwent a noticeable shift toward the company in its editorial policy. Two events had occurred in the interim that likely influenced editor James Hardman. Four days earlier, the IUE joined the other two Sprague unions on strike, dampening any hope for an early settlement, and on the 26th, R.C. Sprague delivered a lengthy speech defending the company's position before the Chamber of Commerce. The *Transcript* editorial not only referred to the substance of Sprague's speech, but accepted the founder's arguments as fact. For example, the editorialist mentioned Sprague's long-standing position that, as a manufacturer of components, not end products, it had little power over pricing and therefore had to be constrained as far as wages. Rather than critically examining the merits of the argument, the *Transcript* simply repeated it. Similarly, the newspaper uncritically accepted Sprague's argument that competition kept it from offering a higher wage.

While R.C. Sprague had always held out the possibility of closing up shop in North Adams if conditions warranted it, a few unionists now called his bluff, telling him to meet the strikers' demands or leave the city. The *Transcript* responded by criticizing the "thoughtless and irresponsible words of a small number of union officials and militant strikers," who didn't represent "the general sentiments of 3,300 workers or residents." Two weeks later, the *Transcript* reminded the strikers that their weekly losses in wages totaled $260,000, and advised them to accept the company's offer. (Grateful for the paper's support, at the strike's conclusion, R.C. Sprague sent a letter of thanks to editor James Hardman for his editorials "which were factual and informative.")[42]

THE UNION RESPONDS

As indicated earlier, the unions had displayed a well-organized and creative front during negotiations and the strike itself. They maintained that same tenor in their own public relations campaign, reacting to attacks on them by the company and media, as well as proactively reaching out to the North Berkshire community. The AFTE local wrote to local businessmen toward the beginning of the strike, making the case that the beleaguered Sprague employees shared a community of interest with them. AFTE President Ron Durant maintained that Sprague workers hadn't been able to stay even with the cost of living. Sprague "may have provided the 'economic life-blood for the entire area' as the *Transcript* editorial of March 19 suggests, but the 'decent' employment has not 'fostered prosperity.'" His message continued:

> Should we allow ourselves to be constantly threatened by Sprague Electric—that they will move out of North Adams and, therefore, sell out our self respect for a meager settlement AGAIN, which is less than the rise in Cost-of-Living, and thereby retain a lower standard of living in this area?

The union's struggle with the company for respect as well as for a fair economic package was, Durant wrote, "YOUR struggle as well. It is a struggle FOR OUR community." He argued that, with higher wages, workers would be able to spend more, and local businesses would do better. "This strike has become the chance for all of us—businesses and working men alike—to better ourselves." The union asked each business to support the strikers "both morally and financially," and also asked for a contribution to the strike fund.[43]

AFTE leadership continued to take on R.C. Sprague in their strike bulletin. A week and a half into the strike, they wrote:

> We understand Mr. Sprague toured the plants yesterday, it's like yelling down a barrel, isn't it, R.C.? Your news release sez there are 2000 people working. Betcha didn't find them, did you, R.C? If you are wondering what happened to them *LOOK* OUT YOUR WINDOW!!![44]

Adopting a mixture of sarcasm and humor, AFTE came up with a stunt that brought the strike nationwide publicity. After noting that R.C. had voluntarily taken a cut in salary from $80,000 a year to $70,000, the union passed the hat for him, collecting a total of $40. A Minneapolis newspaper picked up the wire service story and headlined it: "SORRY BOSS, $40 ALL WE CAN AFFORD."[45] The article quoted strikers as wanting to contribute more, but "we're making the lowest wages of any electrical workers in the state." R.C. and management were kept well aware of this news coverage, and corporate files held reprints of a half dozen or so similar news reports, including one from the *New York Times*.

On March 23, IUE officially joined the strike and AFTE received lots of picket line help. "I want to tell you it was a relief when somebody joined us—like getting a reprieve." It probably meant more than money. AFTE pickets, in fact, received only $4 weekly from their small local treasury, as the international union did not yet have a strike fund. However, the international office spread the word of the North Adams strike to its other local affiliates who, in turn, sent in contributions to the strikers. In particular, the AFTE local at GE in Pittsfield took up a collection every week, "like clockwork."[46]

IUE Local #200 also received help from its affiliated locals, along with resources from its more sizeable treasury and strike fund, providing each picketer $20 a week. In addition, other North Berkshire workers contributed doughnuts, coffee, cider, firewood, and moral support. As Jack Boulger recalled, "[T]here was a lot of outside help. There were people that showed up and introduced themselves. The nicest people in the world. You know, you got a problem with that lousy company, we're going to help you kind of thing."[47]

Local college students from North Adams State College and Williams College, aided the strike effort as well, helping, for example, to compile information for the strike newsletters. (The times were changing for these students as well, as they had mobilized on their respective campuses, just miles apart, to strike against the expansion of the Vietnam War into Cambodia and the killings of students at Kent State and Jackson State.)

While each of the unions had handled their negotiations separately, Boulger recalled that, once all three had officially joined the strike, "We started coordinating and it ended up . . . a completely coordinated operation."[48] In a major speech to the Lions Club about a week after IUE joined the strike, Walter Wood reiterated AFTE's outreach to the local business community: "I feel that many of you as retailers and individual business men should also be as interested as we [are], on this problem of maintaining the economic life of our community." Wood also went over the union's negotiating stance and offered a critique of R.C. Sprague's well-publicized speech to the Chamber of Commerce the week before. Wood explained the battle over the adoption of a new incentive system, and his union's insistence that the company guarantee that wages would not decline under the new bonus system. He presented economic data familiar to many in his audience: the cost of living had increased 7.4 percent since the last contract, while the company's offer of a 4.5 percent increase for each year of a two-year contract would only mean further "erosion" of the workers' "purchasing power."

Wood then turned to the issue of low-price imports leading to American job losses. He suggested several causes of the problem, none of which R. C. Sprague had touched on. First, Wood reminded his largely middle class, business audience that the U.S. electronics industry had grown to become the biggest in the world in part because of technological developments that had been "underwritten and nurtured by billions of dollars in government" funds. In fact, two-thirds of the industry's research and development money came from the federal government.

And, as Wood argued, those electronic firms that invested overseas did so with technologies developed with American tax dollars and skills developed by American workers. Though R.C. Sprague had presented the difficulty as simply a case of low wage rates winning out in a competitive, free market economy, Wood framed the problem quite differently:

> This as you can well see is not so much the problem of what might be called foreign competition, but what began as a move by some profit-hungry corporations to relocate in extremely low wage areas in an effort to exploit the use of a labor force unaware of their true value and the result: huge profits.[49]

Although Wood offered a very different perspective on the problems of the industry than did his boss, once again the local media simply accepted R.C.'s definition of the situation as reality. The local radio station and its owner, Donald Thurston, maintained a similar editorial policy toward the strike as did the *Transcript*. Thurston castigated "[t]hose irresponsible people who are saying North Adams would be better off without [Sprague] . . . . [They] should have their heads examined." Thurston also accepted R. C. Sprague's argument that the unique dilemmas of the electronics components industry kept him from paying his workers a higher wage. Also, echoing the *Transcript* editorials, Thurston focused his attack on union leadership. He argued that while a high-percentage raise might be good for union leaders, it could lead to a decline in employment. Once again, he editorialized, Northern Berkshire might revert to the social decline of the mid-1950s, when the textile industry closed down, and workers tried to survive on welfare and part-time jobs.

Thurston's radio address appeared to be the last straw for the union leaders, and the presidents of all three locals angrily responded in the "IUE Bulletin." They called Thurston "irresponsible," and in a lengthy rejoinder, they attacked his argument. They complained that neither Thurston nor the

Transcript's Hardman had asked any of the union leaders to discuss the strike issues with them. They argued that management's refusal to invest in new technology had led to the decline of the local textile industry, rather than wage demands. While Thurston had reasoned that the North Adams population decline could be traced to the demise of textiles in the mid-1950s, the union presidents pointed out that the population drop-off had, in fact, begun in the mid-1940s, and, since a good deal of the populace that left the city had simply moved to nearby communities, no substantial population change had occurred in the region.

Union leaders also criticized Thurston for failing to include the following problems in his list of local woes: the lack of housing, the need for a new school, and the preferential tax treatment some received in North Adams. They reminded Thurston that in 1970 "conditions of employment that have existed for many years, are in some areas, no longer acceptable to employees of plants represented by organized labor." They claimed to be "considerably disturbed" by Thurston's attempts "to cast suspicion on local union leadership . . . to divide the present unity that exists."[50]

As if to highlight the housing issue, while the strike continued, a huge urban renewal project brought wrecking balls to a poor neighborhood with housing and retail stores on the south side of Main Street. A prior, though smaller, program from 1958 to 1963 had focused on the Center Street area of the city where "251 of the 298 dwellings . . . were considered unsafe for human habitation." Similar descriptions fit the housing stock on the Main Street neighborhood. The following North Adams Redevelopment Authority (NARA) appraisal of a tenement building on the new renewal site can serve as an example:

> The subject property is a 2-story wood frame structure commonly called "row type housing." The interior contains four 6-room apartments made up of three rooms on the first floor, three rooms and bath on the second floor . . . . These apartments have older style one-pipe

> air heating plants, which have outlived their usefulness and are inoperable for the most part . . . . The general condition of this structure can best be described as poor and having suffered much deferred maintenance.[51]

The Main Street project had been held up because of the failure of the NARA to build new low-income housing to replace the units that would be destroyed.[52]

A SETTLEMENT IS REACHED

In late April, with negotiations going nowhere, all sides agreed to try mediation in Washington, D.C. The head of the Federal Mediation and Conciliation Service, J. Curtis Counts, led the mediators, an indication of the government's strong desire to end the strike. (Counts had previously been credited with playing an important role in halting the three-and-a-half-month national GE strike, a labor stoppage familiar to North Adams residents because of the giant GE plant in nearby Pittsfield.[53]) On May 5, after twenty-seven consecutive hours of negotiations, the parties announced a tentative agreement. It brought with it economic compromises including a 6 percent increase the first year, and 5 percent raises the second and third years of the contract. As for non-economic provisions, the unions won binding arbitration and an agency shop.[54] On May 8, all three unions approved the contract. For AFTE's Jack Boulger, the resolution brought with it a "whole spectrum of feelings, depending on how you felt to start with . . . . I think the attitude was mostly positive. We ended up with a good contract." Historian Raymond C. Bliss wrote that the strikers had won a "struggle for dignity, justice and security."[55]

The *Transcript* took a different view. On May 11, it reported that as many as 500 jobs had been lost during the strike. In an editorial entitled "No One Really Wins," the editor wrote that it "appears certain" that there "will be a severe and long term drop" in local Sprague employment. The economic gains that workers won weren't much, the paper added, given the amount of time without a paycheck. Not being able to resist a final anti-union poke, the writer modified his "no victors" thesis by claiming, "the only possible winner seems to be the national treasury" of the IUE, which gained more dues-paying members because of the agency shop provision.

How can one objectively evaluate the impact of the strike itself on the fortunes of Sprague? Even immediately before the strike, the company had been experiencing mixed bottom lines, losing money in 1968, but turning profitable in 1969.[56] After the strike, the company recorded net earnings losses in 1970 and 1971. However, at the 1971 annual meeting, the company reported that its "industry position has about recovered" and Sprague was "again enjoying its normal share of industry orders."[57] By 1972, Sprague "got back all [the] sales . . . lost [by the strike]" and claimed significant increased earnings in 1973 and 1974.

As profits continued their upward swing, outside suitors became interested. Sprague had gone public with its stock in the1950s and secured a place on the New York Stock Exchange in 1966. By 1976, Sprague Electric looked attractive enough to investors that one company that wanted to diversify, General Cable (soon to be GK Technologies), purchased it in 1976. While the Sprague family controlled a sizeable chunk of the company, some 16 percent, its holdings only represented a minority share. But according to R. C. Sprague, "If I hadn't agreed to sell at the price they were offering, I would have been vulnerable to a shareholder suit."[58]

While the company had recovered its sales and even improved its bottom line, job decline—which had begun even before the strike—continued during the 1970s, except for a small uptick under GK.[59] According to Sprague CEO Neal Welch, by 1979, Sprague, while owned by GK, had "record profits of $44 million." In 1981, Penn Central Corporation, a holding company notorious for not investing in its subsidiaries, bought GK, and by 1986 had sold off Sprague's lines, effectively closing its gates in North Adams. The fifty-six-year life of the capacitor company in North Adams had come to an end. In this regard, its ending fit the nationwide pattern of deindustrialization that ravaged manufacturing centers in the 1970s and 1980s.[60]

THE MEANING OF THE STRIKE IN COMMUNITY MEMORY

Given all of this, how would the community, and particularly former Sprague employees, remember the strike and the role of the unions as time passed? While numerous ex-Sprague workers responded to interviews in the 1980s and 1990s, no systematic, representative study of that workforce had been carried out, so no clear-cut answer to that question could be ascertained. Nearly two decades after the strike, while overseeing an oral history project in which some two dozen Sprague retirees discussed their working careers, Stewart Burns acknowledged that only one interviewee had "wholehearted praise for the strike's success."[61] Burns wrote that some who had been part of management thought the strike itself "was 'foolish.'" Others, who had originally supported the strike, came to view its consequences as harmful to the workforce.

Statements like the following characterized a number of the retirees' reactions:

> The gains "didn't impress me."
>
> [T]he strike was not a victory because "these companies will do what they want anyway."
>
> "I don't think the worker ever wins, really."

June Rock, a member of AFTE and an early striker, believed the strike "worth it" at the time even though it was ultimately "devastating" in terms of lost jobs and subsequent corporate decisions. Perhaps the most surprising sentiment coming from the interviewees belonged to Mabel Lewitt, a leader in organizing the first union at Sprague in 1937 and an active striker in 1970, while in her sixties. When questioned about the role of unions in the economy of the 1980s, she responded that unions are "no good today."

Lewitt and virtually all of Burns's interviewees had begun working at Sprague in the 1930s and 1940s and had developed strong loyalties to the earlier unions, locals that had generally cooperated with management. A sample of the new breed of worker, hired in the 1950s and 1960s, and bulwarks of the AFL-CIO-affiliated unions (a group not among the Burns sample), might well have viewed the 1970 strike and unions differently, even as hard times hit the community decades later. Jack Boulger, one of the AFTE strike leaders, for example, still had a very positive view of the strike when he was interviewed nearly two decades later in 1989:

> [W]e were very happy about . . . the fact that we had framed a contract that . . . applied to almost every problem that we had . . . . I was pretty happy with the fact that we had been able to move a corporate giant like the Sprague Electric Company into listening to us and into achieving some measure of fairness . . . . The more we dealt with them the better off things seemed to get.[62]

In 2011, when asked once again if the strike was successful, Boulger still "responded emphatically: 'Oh yeah, yes.'"[63]

Even a high-ranking secretary, one exempt from union membership, who crossed the picket line in 1970, expressed positive feelings toward the Sprague unions some eighteen years later:

> "[W]henever [the unions] made any gain, we gained also . . . which is a bit unfair . . . . They did all of the work and we did reap some of the benefit . . . . I just had a natural, or unnatural you might say, feeling that unions were not good. I take that back now. I feel that they did accomplish a great deal."[64]

Yet, even if the viewpoints of former Sprague employees are in fact more diverse than the Burns sample leads us to believe, why have some come to blame themselves for the departure of Sprague and thousands of industrial, clerical, and technical jobs from North Berkshire? How do we explain a shift in sentiment from a group of formerly pro-union workers? One tentative answer might emerge from the battle for the hearts and minds of the workers and community members that raged during the negotiations and strike. The unions and their members aggressively presented and supported a pro-worker perspective, which not only detailed the economic inequities facing Sprague employees, but also systematically critiqued the company's counter-perspective, and continually maintained the moral and logical truth of their own position.

Because of its economic and political power, the company's perspective received more support in the local print and broadcast media, but the strikers made creative and forceful use of their own resources—strike bulletins and flyers, letters to the community, speeches to community groups, social pressure to prevent strikebreaking, and a strong and aggressive picket line. Thus, from the time that negotiations started in September 1969, until the strike was settled in May 1970, one could say that a battle of counter-ideologies or viewpoints ensued. Why then had the corporate ideology emerged triumphant well after the strike, at least as indicated by Burns's research?

To try to answer this question, we need to return to the conclusion of the strike and examine developments immediately afterwards. The company couldn't claim a strike victory for itself, especially since the unions had done well on wages and had successfully gained arbitration and agency shop provisions. But Sprague could ignore those gains and focus on the wages that employees lost during the ten weeks and on the number of jobs permanently gone from the North Adams operation. Thus, while the company couldn't simply say it won, it could certainly argue that the strikers lost—and lost big, in wages and in job security.

In the battle over key political ideas since 1970, the dominant view presented by the company and the media has been one in which the local workforce made a bad decision by striking, as it led to a direct loss of much-needed jobs. As one former employee put it, the company gave the workers "the impression" that they harmed themselves by striking. "Christ, it'd been in the papers—the thing that killed Sprague's in North Adams was the 1970 strike . . . . That's all they talked about."[65] And then came the devastation of 1986, when Sprague closed up shop for good.

Add to this the dominant political and social messages of the late 1970s and 1980s that were continually being expressed by national political leaders and the media—that corporate decision makers could do no wrong, and overpaid union leaders and their selfish membership were what led to the decline of industrial America. President Reagan successfully fired unionized air traffic control workers in 1981, beginning a period of aggressive corporate attacks on unions, union contracts, and labor in general, which continued throughout that decade.[66]

For old-timers living in North Adams in the mid-1980s, the city seemed virtually deserted. The crowds that had packed Main Street restaurants during the heyday of local manufacturing had disappeared; unemployment, poverty, and homelessness were on the rise. The city's population continued its decline. As many as 5,000 jobs had vanished in the northern Berkshires in the 1980s, manufacturing jobs as well as jobs at retail outlets and other small businesses. Wages and salaries ranked the second lowest in Massachusetts. Demand for food aid and general relief increased along with a rise in abuse and school dropouts.[67] When local residents read about the "Massachusetts Miracle" in Boston newspapers, they could only wonder if their region's state boundary had shifted.

Still, in several instances, local residents tried to improve the bleak post-Sprague environment. Some industry did remain in the North Berkshires, and a new generation of industrial union activists, along with education and healthcare workers, organized the Northern Berkshire Labor Coalition. The coalition engaged in educational work connected with the Labor Center at the University of Massachusetts, Amherst; supported a wildcat strike at an electrical cable plant; aided textile workers in gaining lost paychecks from a suspicious bankruptcy; published a newspaper; and kept alive the celebration of Labor Day some 100 years after its first appearance in the Berkshires.[68] In explaining the need for the coalition, Michael O'Brien, president of the local chapter of Service Employees International Union 285 at the regional hospital, stated: "You don't need a formal education to know that when you have more than one person working at something you have strength . . . . We're militant in regards to Northern Berkshire; we're ready to fight as hard as we can, and with the cooperation of elected officials, to advance Northern Berkshire."[69]

At the same time, a group of health and human service workers coalesced to start an organization that became the Northern Berkshire Community Coalition, which engaged in community outreach, educational support, and research. The coalition, which began as a Health and Human Services organization of professionals, transitioned to one with a broader mandate and wider composition that included city residents, often organized by neighborhood.[70]

The threat of state cuts to programs for the poor led to the formation of the Northern Berkshire Welfare Coalition in 1979. With connections to Community Action and the Coalition for Basic Human Needs, the Welfare Coalition included recipients, community supporters, and legal aid paraprofessionals. The group demonstrated in Boston and in North Adams against the cuts that conservative Democratic Governor Edward J. King had proposed. They questioned the governor at an open meeting at the state college and on a local radio station. They worked with recipients, aiding with paperwork and helping to facilitate additional resources. The coalition received publicity and some success in pressuring the city to allocate money to help residents with their winter fuel bills.[71]

The state became involved as well, focusing on skills training and planning for the future, including discussions about creating a contemporary arts museum in the former Sprague buildings.[72] But the overriding reality of hard times couldn't be dismissed as former factory workers and retirees tried to survive and make sense of a changing economic landscape.

For residents of North Adams, a progressive labor voice that had been loud and clear leading up to and continuing during the 1970 strike—a countervailing force to Sprague management and the local media—had been diminished. And the national media had become more and more anti-labor as the percentage of union members shrank. At the same time, the national Democratic Party, which had found great favor in North Adams since the late 1920s, was moving further and further away from championing working-class issues and its traditional labor union base.

In 1970, the residents of North Adams broke away from Sprague corporate ideology, said "No" to workplace paternalism, and fought hard for the economic and workplace rights that had eluded them in the past. They accomplished this with a powerful counter-offensive to the company's public relations campaign and a disciplined and unified strike effort, all during a national era of strong labor movements and a supportive Democratic party. As unions weakened in the 1970s and 1980s, as deindustrialization became the new normal, and as the Democratic party moved to the right, that ten-week upsurge in 1970 in North Adams stands out more and more as a significant accomplishment, one difficult to replicate absent a major shift in the nation's economic and political landscape.

Note: The following ten photos of the 1970 strike against Sprague Electric were taken by Randy Trabold, *Transcript* photographer.

The office workers, members of the American Federation of Technical Employees, strike first on March 2, 1970. Members of the other two unions support them, respecting their picket lines, and watch behind the row of police across from the main Sprague entrance.

The tight "belly to backside" picket line kept out possible scabs.

John Shaker pickets with two children by the Sprague main gatehouse.

Women picket while police watch.

Francis A. "Frank" Forst of Jamesburg, N.J., AFTE senior international representative, arrested, charged with disorderly conduct on the second day of the strike. Forst had been called to Marshall Street when pickets refused to move, to allow company trucks to exit the plant. A North Adams police captain asked Forst to tell the pickets to move, but Forst told the pickets they had a right to block the trucks and he joined the picket line. The police got involved, pushing ensued, and when Forst fell to the ground, he was arrested. At the courthouse, strikers arrived, jamming the courthouse in support of Forst. Judge Ernest H. Rosasco stated that Forst "did stir the people up even more" and, because the trucks weren't allowed to leave, he was guilty of "disturbing the peace." Then the judge added, "I'm not greatly disturbed by this. I'm willing to continue the case for disposition if we can get along peacefully." (March 4, 1970.)

Ronald H. Durant, president of the AFTE local #101, in a lighter moment, leads AFTE strikers in strike songs. The strikers had taken popular folk tunes, like "On Top of Old Smokey" and "I've Been Working on the Railroad," and adapted Sprague strike lyrics to them.

Joseph S. Lora Jr., chief steward of the International Association of Machinists local #1794, on the left in dark coat, arguing with Sprague director of corporate facilities, John D. Washburn, while Robert Diodati, man in light coat to the right, looks on. Diodati had served as president of the office workers union in 1966, before they affiliated with AFTE, but joined management in 1969 in Sprague's industrial relations department (April 20,1970).

Walter D. Wood, president, IUE Local 200, the production workers union, strongly protests an incident involving a woman picket. IUE had joined the strike on March 23 and now, about a month later, the *Transcript* reported that "Wood's protest was one of several confrontations as picketing became rougher." Police Capt. William H. Garner is on the left, and next to Wood is Patrolman Donald F. Morin. Roger Bell, with sunglasses, AFTE communications officer, stands in the background (April 21, 1970).

Picketers attempt to block truck. Tony Tassone, with hat, is second from left, and Evelyn Robinson, with kerchief, stands in front of the police.

Donations of wood helped keep the barrel fires going and the picketers warm.

NOTES

1 A capacitor is "an electrical component, used to store a charge temporarily, consisting of two conducting surfaces separated by a nonconductor," *Encarta World English Dictionary* (New York: St. Martin's Press, 1999). Sprague had its beginning producing capacitors (also called condensers) for radios, but capacitors can be found in all electrical and electronic products. Sprague's greatest expansion occurred during World War II with weapons-related demand, and produced the capacitor that detonated the second atomic bomb dropped over Nagasaki, Japan (*Transcript*, Sesquicentennial Edition, November 19, 1993, p. 50).

2 *Berkshire Eagle*, October 8, 1984. Catherine O'Neill began working at Sprague Specialties (later it became Sprague Electric) in 1930, working forty-eight hours a week at twenty cents an hour. During the 1930s, she thought the company was "just going downhill . . . . I thought . . . this place is really going to fold up . . . but then came the war. And that's what boosted . . . Sprague's up and saved them . . . . [T]hey had . . . a lot of government work . . . . [T]hey made gas masks. And they made a lot of resistors and condensers . . . for the war . . . . Airplanes and the boats, and things like that . . . . They kept busy all during the war . . . . They were hiring people that had already had jobs someplace else. And if they wanted to work nights they hired them. . . [T]hey were even hiring married women, older women, because I know my mother worked there for awhile too." Interview from "Shifting Gears: The Changing Meaning of Work in Massachusetts, 1920–1980: North Adams, Massachusetts," University of Massachusetts, Lowell, Libraries, Lowell, MA.

3 Soon after making that decision, Sprague served as chief consultant on a Senate subcommittee that was examining continental defense, and in 1957, Eisenhower appointed him to a similar committee. On that committee, Sprague reportedly challenged General Curtis LeMay, head of the Strategic Air Command, on the command's vulnerability to a Soviet attack (Richard Rhodes, "The General and World War III," *The New Yorker*, June 19, 1995, 55). Eisenhower praised Sprague for his work on the committee (letter dated November 8, 1957, carton FF29, Sprague archives). In a letter dated September 14, 1961 (K-240, archives), Sprague wrote to President Kennedy urging him "not to give in to the Russians any longer" and to build shelters "to save the majority of our people" in the event of a nuclear war. Sprague maintained a friendship with former Vice President Nixon, and in a letter dated April 18, 1962 (N160), in which he addressed Nixon by first name, Sprague wrote, "I congratulate you on your decision to seek the Governorship of California. Particularly at this time we need men of your experience, energy and integrity in public life."

4 Sprague served as president of the Associated Industries of Massachusetts (1951–1953), president of the Radio-Electronics-TV Manufacturers Association (1956–1961) and longtime director of the Electronic Industries Association. He also held the rank of director of the First National Bank of Boston and the Federal Reserve Bank of Boston (John A. Adams, *Transcript*, September 28, 1991, 1–2).

5 Maynard Seider, "Contested Beliefs and Rebellion in a New England Mill Town: Sprague Electric Workers in North Adams," *The Mind's Eye* (Fall 1997): 39–60, for data on Sprague in the "Introduction."

6 *Berkshire Eagle*, March 29, 1957, p. 6.

7 George Bateman interview, March 15, 1993, by author; Bateman was Sprague's director of industrial relations in North Adams during the strike.

8 Walter Wood interview, "Shifting Gears Project," Center for Lowell History, University of Massachusetts, Lowell, 1988–1989; Raymond C. Bliss, *A Study of Union History at the Sprague Electric Company in North Adams, Massachusetts, 1929–1970* (Williamstown, MA: Williams College, 1976).

9 Robert Paul Gabrielsky, "The Evolution of the Marshall Street Complex," *Historical Journal of Massachusetts*, note 7 (Winter, 1991).

10 Woman's statement from ICW-IUE Archives, Box 4, 107, November 15, 1966, University of Massachusetts, Amherst; historian's quote from Raymond C. Bliss, *A Study of Union History at the Sprague Electric Company in North Adams, Massachusetts*, 1929–1970. Williamstown, MA: Williams College, 1976, 117.

11 Bliss and Walter Wood, interview, "Shifting Gears. . ."

12 Bliss, 116; *Transcript*, June 16 and June 17, 1967. The fact that the *Transcript* employed a labor reporter in 1970 speaks to the importance that the paper's owners—brothers James Jr. and Robert Hardman—placed on local coverage, and the significant role that labor and labor relations played in that era of industrial work. In 1975, the *Transcript* received the accolade of "best daily newspaper in New England." Four years later, the Hardmans sold the paper, which never returned to local control, finally ceasing publication in 2014. https://en.wikipedia.org/wiki/North-Adams-Transcript. As labor unions declined in membership and in influence, U.S. newspapers reduced their coverage of labor issues, and labor reporters became a thing of the past. When well-known labor reporter Steven Greenhouse left the *New York Times* in late 2014, the "paper of record" didn't replace him, leaving perhaps the *Wall Street Journal* as the only national newspaper with a reporter focusing on labor (David Uberti, "The labor beat is dead; long live the labor beat," *Columbia Journalism Review,* March 12, 2015).

13 Jack Boulger, interview, "Shifting Gears. . ." 13.

14 Bliss, 120.

15 Bateman interview. Research and development scientists, who worked in a facility across from the main gate and were "asked" to do production work during the strike, initially bent over and walked through a 4 ft. high tunnel under the street, thereby avoiding the pickets. However, when the strikers found out, they picketed the R and D parking lot at the end of the day, leading to a two- to three-hour hold up for the scientists to ultimately exit. After that, the scientists skipped the tunnel and took their chances going through the main gate picketers (from "Memoirs of a Salaried Scab," anonymous).

16 John Boulger interview, "Shifting Gears Project." Another area of negotiations, one of contention but of less public awareness, involved the incentive system that the company wanted to institute. It was called "Work-Factor," named after the company that designed it (Work-Factor Corporation). The production workers' union inadvertently discovered a Sprague memo in the wastebasket that detailed the new incentive goal. This chance finding allowed the union several months to prepare its responses prior to formal negotiations. Sprague had already purchased the Work Factor system and wanted to introduce it into all their plants. For management, "[t]he big problem . . . was North Adams with the union, because none of the other plants had a union. So they could put in any system they want" (Walter Wood interview by Robert Gabrielsky, "Shifting Gears. . .").

17 AFTE 101 flyer, "Unions: AFTE 1968–70" folder, F-246 carton, Sprague archives. When the company moved out of its buildings in North Adams, its records were indexed, boxed, and stored in a nearby warehouse. Those are the records that I refer to as the Sprague archives. I was given permission to examine them in the mid-1990s, but in the more recent past, the "archive" is not available to the public, and its future is uncertain. I have copies of several records that I refer to in the paper, and notes on the rest.

18 *Transcript*, January 8, 1970, 11.

19 IUE—Local 200 flyer, "Unions-IUE-1968-70" folder, F-246 carton, Sprague archives.

20 Maynard Seider, "Contested Beliefs . . ."

21 "Unions-IUE-1968-70" folder, F-246 carton, Sprague archives.

22 Bliss, 137, on the chronology, and quotation from *The Sprague Log*, North Adams, Massachusetts, Sprague Electric Company, February 17, 1970, accessed through Massachusetts College of Liberal Arts Archives, http://www.mcla.edu/library/sprague/.

23 "thank God . . ." letter to the editor by Doris M. Richards in the *Transcript*, February 14, 1970; comments on Sprague/Carlson letters from Bliss, 131–136.

24 Bliss, 137–138.

25 Bliss, 142.

26 Sprague to Hardman letter, May 12, 1970, in "Unions-general 1969–70" folder, F-246 carton, Sprague archives. Years later, with the union contract at stake, Hardman spared management from his critical pen. When the strike ended in May, R.C. Sprague personally thanked the *Transcript* editor for his support.

27 Bliss, 149–150.

28 Stewart Burns, "Capacitors and Community: Women Workers at Sprague Electric, 1930–1980," *The Public Historian*, Vol. 11, No. 4 (Fall, 1989).

29 "STRIKE 1970," from notes of R.C. Sprague, "Union Neg. Apr–Jul 1970" folder, E-379 carton.

30 Creatively changing and adding verses to such favorites as "Solidarity Forever," "I've Been Workin' on the Railroad," and "On Top of Old Smokey," the strikers sang while the picketing continued.

31 "tense" quote from Jack Boulger and second quote from Leo Cyr, interview by author, June 23, 1993.

32 Leo Cyr.

33 Esther Hartranft interview, from "Shifting Gears. . ."

34 Evelyn Jones, ibid.

35 After Marshall Street had already been shuttered, but Brown Street remained open, Evelyn worked there and wanted to run for union president. One of the most powerful men on the executive board refused to back her because "I was a woman and I was too old," and the rest of the board followed suit. As she told her interviewer, Evelyn followed the principle of "you don't get mad, you get even." She campaigned against her original antagonist when he ran for office again, and helped to defeat him. And to top it off, he lost to another woman. As the interview closed, and now in retirement, Evelyn continued her involvement in Democratic Party politics. In the spring of 1988, she was campaigning for Governor Michael Dukakis to get the nomination for president and, in one of the last remarks she made, said, "I imagine once Mike gets the nomination . . . we'll be out on (the) trail with him." "Shifting Gears. . ."

36 Burns, 21.

37 Anne L. Millet, "They're Big Boys Now," *Berkshire Eagle*, March 21, 1970, 13.

38 Bliss, 145–158.

39 Bateman interview.

40 "STRIKE 1970," Sprague archives.

41 *Transcript,* March 5 and March 19, 1970.

42 *Transcript* quotations from April 10 and April 24, 1970; letter to Hardman, May 12, 1970, in "Union Neg., April–June, 1970" folder, E-379, Sprague archives.

43 AFTE letter to businessmen, March 20, 1970, "Union Negot. Jan.–March, 1970" folder, E-379 carton, Sprague archives.

44 AFTE STRIKE BULLETIN, March 10, 1970, Sprague archives.

45 April 2, 1970, Sprague archives.

46 Boulger interview.

47 Ibid.

48 Ibid.

49 "Walter Wood talk to Lions' Club," April 1, 1970, "Union Negot. April-July 1970" folder, E-379 carton, Sprague archives.

50 "IUE #200 Bulletin," April 30, 1970, "Union Negot. April–July, 1970" folder, E-379 carton, Sprague archives.

51 The first quote comes from Ruth M. Starratt, "Urban Renewal in North Adams: A Case Study in Community Decision-Making" (Amherst: University of Massachusetts master of arts thesis, Department of Sociology and Anthropology, 1968), 24. The second quote is from Joe Manning, *Disappearing Into North Adams* (Florence, MA: Flatiron Press, 2001), 7. Manning's book contains numerous interviews and copies of documents relating to the south side of the Main Street urban renewal project, and continues on to the coming of MASS MoCA. Interviews are from tenants, landlords, government officials, and small business owners. Issues of class and poverty pervade many of the pages of Manning's book. One of the most powerful interviews illustrates the racial housing discrimination faced by an African American family (4–7). In an earlier book by Manning, *Steeples: Sketches of North Adams* (Florence, MA: Flatiron Press, 1997), his interviews with old-timers brought out their feelings about the Main Street urban renewal and led him to pursue that subject in greater depth in *Disappearring*. Both books are historical gems that give voice to the people of North Adams at a particular time, but whose memories also bring us back to an earlier period.

One aspect of the Center Street renewal, known as the Artery project, had been designed to redirect east-west traffic to more easily move in that direction rather than travel through several streets in downtown North Adams. Sprague objected to the original plan, as it would have meant the destruction of part of the company's major warehouse. In arguing for a change in the plan, Sprague raised the possibility of "curtailment of the company's operations in" North Adams (*Transcript,* July 23, 1955). R.C. Sprague again raised that possibility in a July 29 letter to Robert Hardman, the publisher of the *Transcript*, when he said: We could "move some operations out of North Adams so as to free enough space in the Marshall Street plant to continue to run a centralized warehouse. This, of course, would not be good for the community" (Sprague archive, Box K-240, "East-West Artery," copy held by author). Five days later, Sprague wrote a similar letter to the city manager of North Adams, Robert H. Harp: We could "move sufficient product lines out of the Marshall Street plant to other cities where we have already established branch plants" (ibid.). A memorandum from the Massachusetts Department of Public Works on October 6, 1955, suggests that Sprague's threats bore fruit. They would be repeated a few years later when Dragon Cement Company wanted to establish a plant in North Berkshire.

52 According to one researcher writing about the Main Street project, the NARA displayed "a disregard and/or lack of sympathy for poor, low-income residents." In May, 1971, after noting that half of those who had to relocate were low-income and paying low rents, the executive director stated: "There are some who will never be able to find another place because they are unacceptable to most landlords . . . . I think you will see us importing trailers for these 10 or 15 low income people who cannot get landlords to rent to them" (Jennifer J. Card, *From Industrial to Postindustrial: The*

Rebirth of North Adams Massachusetts [Amherst, MA: Hampshire College, 2002], 42).

53 "Sprague-Union Talks Moving to Washington," *Berkshire Eagle*, April 25, 1970.

54 An agency shop meant that all workers would either have to join the union or at least pay union dues. Not as strong as a union shop, where everyone would have to join the union, it provided a good win for the strikers.

55 Boulger interview and Bliss paper. As Bliss phrased it, "By 1970, the workers had had enough. To put a dollar sign on a struggle for dignity, justice and security is not easy" but "[t]he unions did obtain their 6% hike, cost of living adjustments, and union security and binding arbitration clauses" (165–166).

56 Bliss, 163–164.

57 "Minutes," Board of Directors, 1971, Sprague archives.

58 Quoted in Lauren R. Stevens, "Sprague Electric, and the man who started it all," *The Advocate*, March 30, 1988, 1, 6.

59 In 1966, four years prior to the strike, Sprague employment in North Adams reached its peak at 4,137. As the company shifted production elsewhere, employment dropped to 3,054 in 1969 and to 2,022 the year of the strike. By 1976, the year of the sale to General Cable, Sprague employment had declined to 1,664. Under General Cable (GK Technologies), employment increased and in 1981, with the sale to Penn Central, 1,720 employees remained in North Adams. *Berkshire Eagle*, October 8, 1984.

60 Historical evidence certainly suggests that decisions of manufacturing companies to downsize and/or move offshore would have occurred regardless of whether their workforce unionized or engaged in contentious labor relations—e.g. strikes—as the push for cheaper labor and lower regulation proved to be the dominant motivations. For an overview of the beginnings of the national wave of deindustrialization, see Barry Bluestone and Bennett Harrison, *The Deindustrialization of America: Plant Closings, Community Abandonment, and the Dismantling of Basic Industry* (New York: Basic Books, 1982). For a focus on the steel industry, see Jack Metzgar, *Striking Steel: Solidarity Remembered* (Philadelphia: Temple University Press, 2000); and for the auto industry, see Kathryn Marie Dudley, *The End of the Line: Lost Jobs, New Lives in Postindustrial America* (Chicago: Chicago University Press,1994). For a study of New England and globalization, see Aviva Chomsky, *Linked Labor Histories: New England, Colombia, and the Making of a Global Working Class* (Durham, NC: Duke University Press, 2008). For the story closer to North Adams, in western Massachusetts, see Robert Forrant, Metal Fatigue*: American Bosch and the Demise of Metalworking in the Connecticut River Valley* (Amityville, NY: Baywood Publishing Company, 2009).

61 Burns, 75. Somewhat similar sentiments are expressed in a report on conversations among fifteen women at a 1997 Sprague Retirees Club monthly meeting in Joe Manning, *Steeples: Sketches of North Adams* 3rd edition (Florence, MA: Flatiron Press), 155–169.

62 Boulger, interviewed by Robert Paul Gabrielsky, "Shifting Gears. . ." 26.

63 Alison Pincus, *The Mark of Reliability: From Sprague Electric to MASS MoCA in North Adams, MA* (Williamstown, MA: Williams College, 2012).

64 Esther Hartranft interview, "Shifting Gears . . .", 46–47.

65 Norman Chenail interview, September 23, 1992, by author. John Sprague, the founder's son and last CEO of the company, wrote: "The strike did more than cost North Adams jobs. It almost destroyed Sprague Electric." Yet, while Sprague admits that the company did eventually "recover" from the strike-related losses, he tends to blame the national unions for pushing up wages and benefits so much that the firm became uncompetitive, resulting in the loss of jobs. Thus it would seem that former Sprague employees have only themselves to blame for voting out their old "independent" unions, affiliating with IUE and AFTE, and striking for ten weeks in 1970. And, writes Sprague, "[a]s the former North Adams employees are now learning painfully, service-type jobs . . . offer neither the same level of pay or benefits as the industrial sector—if those service jobs ever materialize!" Those remarks were published in a front page story in the *Transcript* (May 27, 1993), culled from John Sprague's 1993 book, *Revitalizing U.S. Electronics: Lessons From Japan* (Boston: Butterworth-Heinemann).

66 Bennett Harrison and Barry Bluestone, *The Great U-Turn: Corporate Restructuring and the Polarizing of America* (New York: Basic Books, 1988).

67 Alan Bashevkin, "Social Costs of Economic Decline: Northern Berkshire 1980–1990," Northern Berkshire Health and Human Services Coalition, January 23, 1991. The first large indoor mall had reached the Berkshires, and for those residents with much disposable income, they now had to drive nearly twenty miles to the south to buy the clothes and accessories that had been available on Main Street during an earlier time.

68 Holly Taylor, "N. Berkshire workers form labor coalition," *Berkshire Eagle*, October 29, 1984, 18; Joseph A. Grande, "Workers, academics join to discuss saving, attracting jobs," *Transcript*, October 29, 1984, 3; John Hitchcock, "Pulitzer winner sounds warning on labor's future," *The Morning Union*, September 2, 1986, 9.

69 Holly Taylor, 18.

70 www.nbccoalition.org.

71 "Welfare group quizzes King," *Transcript*, June 15, 1979. The local newspaper editorially attacked the governor for his proposals that would hurt the poor. Entitled "More misery for poor," the lead editorial went on to state that "in this society there is no justification for empty stomachs or cold homes" (*Transcript*, March 10, 1979, 4).

72 "The Task Force Report," The Governor's Task Force on Economic Development for Northern Berkshire, assisted by Landscape Architecture and Regional Planning, University of Massachusetts, Amherst, in conjunction with LANDUSE INC., Hadley, Massachusetts, 1986; Susan C. Phillips, "Museum would generate jobs, dollars, report says," *Berkshire Eagle*, June 2, 1987, 1

CHAPTER NINETEEN

FROM COLORADO TO THE BERKSHIRES: A UNION PRESIDENT'S EDUCATION

UNLIKE MOST OF THE OTHER LOCAL ACTIVISTS who grew up in the area, Mike Wilber left North Berkshire for a significant period of time as a young adult, spending his twenties and early thirties in Colorado. Prior to that, Mike had dropped out of high school and worked at a variety of jobs for a number of companies—a small supermarket, a paper mill, a predecessor of X-Tyal, and Sprague Electric Company. Mike's father had been a production worker at a wire cable company, and, while Mike knew that his father had been involved in more than one strike, little talk of unions and labor issues took place at home. Despite his mother's admonition—"Don't make waves!"—Mike remembers that his father was outspoken.[1]

Drafted in 1969, Mike trained as a radio operator in South Carolina and as a baker in Colorado. At Fort Carson, he also earned his high school graduate equivalency degree. After his Army stint, he returned to the Berkshires and went to work at Sprague, but was laid off in less than a year. In 1973, Mike went west again and spent the next decade in Colorado. He worked in Colorado Springs, at a big plant making Jeep tops for American Motors. It was not the first union shop where Mike had worked, but it turned out to be the first one in which he took an active interest in the union itself. He became chief steward for the Amalgamated Clothing and Textile Workers Union (ACTWU) local there and, after a while, he took on the presidency of the ACTWU Rocky Mountain

District Board. Besides learning the formal skills of contract negotiation, contract maintenance, and newsletter production, Mike discovered the power of informal work groups.[2] He saw firsthand how workers could use both written and unwritten communication to slow production down and win disputes with management. Toward the end of his stay in Colorado, Mike took a management post, which afforded him a view of the shop organization he wouldn't ordinarily have had access to.

In 1983 he and his wife, Margaret, moved back to North Berkshire, to a home in North Adams. His first job back led him, coincidentally, to another ACTWU local—this time at X-Tyal. Mike worked in quality control: it didn't take long for him to learn the job and the state of labor management relationships at X-Tyal. He became involved with the union and his co-workers elected him president.

NOTES

1 Interview with author.

2 On informal work groups, see Maynard Seider, *A Year in the Life of a Factory* (Chicago: Charles H. Kerr, a Singlejack Book, 1993), 40–47, and Stan Weir, *Singlejack Solidarity* (Minneapolis: University of Minnesota Press, 2004), 235–251.

CHAPTER TWENTY:

A SWEATSHOP, A BANKRUPTCY, AND CIVIL DISOBEDIENCE

When the union's inspiration through the worker's blood shall run.
There can be no power greater anywhere beneath the sun.
Yet what force on earth is weaker than the feeble strength of one?
For the union makes us strong!
Solidarity forever! Solidarity forever! Solidarity forever!
For the union makes us strong.

—sung by X-Tyal workers and supporters trying to block the auction of the company's machinery, July 1985.

We had a feeling that we were going to be arrested . . . . I guess it didn't really matter if we got locked up. [W]e had to do something as a group to get anywhere, and we did.

—Jean Braman, union activist

If they couldn't buy the business themselves, they at least wanted everyone to know that the workers of North Berkshire are not going to be kicked around anymore.

—*Berkshire Eagle*, August 3, 1985

INTRODUCTION

BY THE MID-1980s, one textile company dominated the news. A quarter century of local textile history came to an end during an early summer weekend in 1985 when X-Tyal (xtile) International Corporation filed for bankruptcy. While X-Tyal lasted only five years in North Adams, its product, labor-management relations, and manner of leaving town matched that of four previous manufacturers—like Inflated and Hunter Outdoor Products—that had hired hundreds of local residents, mostly women, at low wages to sew tents, inflated products, and gas mask hoods for the military. Complaints of sweatshop conditions and of harassment, rumors of organized crime involvement, and the weakness of local unions pervaded the working climate of these mills that were situated in and around North Adams.

But this time, in July of 1985, the response to bankruptcy was different. This time, when X-Tyal chose to auction off its machinery, raw material, and assorted office furniture, the workers "wouldn't go gently." This time, thirteen people—including ten former X-Tyal employees—were arrested for disturbing the peace during a public auction. A local newspaper columnist described the handcuffed workers and supporters from the Northern Berkshire Labor Coalition being led out to police cruisers as singing "Solidarity Forever." The columnist added:

> Another group of demonstrators outside the mill cheered them on. As the television cameras rolled [the demonstrators] chanted "two, four, six, eight—we want the feds to investigate." If they couldn't buy the business themselves, they at least wanted everyone to know that the workers of North Berkshire are not going to be kicked around anymore.[1]

How did the words of a Wobbly, Ralph Chaplin, come to reverberate through the red brick walls of X-Tyal? Why did more than a dozen local residents resort to non-violent civil disobedience, a behavior not seen in these parts in the living memory of its natives? How did community support, including, the backing of the mayor and a recently formed labor coalition, grow so strong? The answers to these questions are well worth pursuing, and the place to begin is with the workforce at X-Tyal (pronounced X-Tile) during the first half of the 1980s.

X-TYAL: THE BEGINNING

The first public pronouncements in March 1980 about the possibility of a new company succeeding Inflated Products at the ill-fated Union Street mill elicited little cause for optimism. For two decades, local residents had labored in the textile defense contracting business, or "rags and bags as it's known in the trade," and had benefitted little from it.[2] The city of North Adams had been negotiating with X-Tyal International Corporation to begin operations with a workforce of eighty people. The company was believed to be the likely recipient of a $5 million contract that Inflated Products had not completed. According to Michael Shebanie, president of X-Tyal, the company had already purchased sewing machines and coating fabric at the Hunter and Inflated bankruptcies.

Was the cycle to be repeated again? Despite its middle name—International—X-Tyal manufactured its textile goods at two small cities (Hudson and Beacon, which were over the border in New York State) and sold most of its products to the U.S. military. The company had begun operations in 1971 and a decade later had 168 employees at its New York sites. For its North Adams operation, X-Tyal announced that William A. St. Pierre, a former Inflated executive, would be plant manager.

Early relations between the city and X-Tyal appeared amicable. The company agreed to pay North Adams the back taxes on the property, and X-Tyal general manager, William Kicara, announced that they would put their monthly property taxes into an escrow account to "avoid any problems." X-Tyal's initial contract with the government had been increased to $6 million, and Kicara hoped for a second contract that would allow the company to remain in the city even longer.[3]

While X-Tyal prepared for its April start-up, a couple of discoveries heightened local cynicism. The copper wiring inside the plant had been stripped bare, and dozens of barrels of waste stood outside. Lest anyone think the new owner could be responsible, William Kicara stated, "It's inconceivable anyone having business sense would go to the trouble of absconding with the wiring . . . ." He added, in a wonderfully prescient phrase: "It takes all kinds to make a world." By August, the workforce totaled just 34, but with more contracts (military and non-military) in the pipeline, the company anticipated significant increases. Initially, and indicative of the shortage of work in the area, 325 residents had applied for work. A bit more than a third (over 120) started work in the mill at the end of February 1981. However, with a new contract for tents in hand, the company anticipated hiring over 60 more.[4]

Over the next couple of years, the local workforce became plagued by a pattern of employment instability. A month long layoff in the summer of 1982 left most of the then 140 X-Tyal workers unemployed. Still, the company waxed optimistic over an $11 million Army contract, which they said would necessitate hiring 100 new workers.[5] The following June, with a workforce of only "about 46," Kicara announced that over 350 new workers would be hired, at a rate of 40–50 a week, to help fulfill a new $21 million contract. The X-Tyal executive expected that work to last two and a half years. He also stated that, despite the offer of space from Florida's Dade County, X-Tyal preferred to stay in North Adams.

Finally, the reality did begin to match the rhetoric, and the workforce expanded. In May 1984, 370 employees worked at X-Tyal, 300 of them members of Local 1280A of the Amalgamated Clothing and Textile Workers Union (ACTWU). With industrial work opportunities very limited in North Adams, especially with the contraction of work at Sprague, the jobs were needed, but poor working conditions became a major complaint. The sweatshop-like conditions at X-Tyal found pubic light in a May 15 article in the *Transcript*. Jean Braman, a shop steward, told a reporter that the workplace needed "better first aid provisions, and a nurse on duty" along with "higher wages." In a complaint reminiscent of the Hunter work environment, an employee referred to a chemical solvent used in the cleaning process: "The stuff gets in your skin . . . . I don't think it is good for you if it contacts your skin." A third worker faulted the condition of the bathrooms. In fact, those facilities proved to be so horrendous that workers sometimes walked two blocks down the street to use the facilities at McDonald's.

George Crosby, personnel manager, responded that the bathrooms are "being renovated" and that the chemical wash "is safe . . . according to government standards." Charles Shebanie, general manager, defended the plant against its "sweatshop" stereotype: "[I]t just isn't true, this is a normal factory situation and we do our best to deal with problems the employees might have in a rational manner." Shebanie went on to say, "We promote from within our company, the heads of departments, group leaders, and quality control personnel were all line workers at one time . . . . We do a lot of business in North Adams, using local vendors' products and increasing the cash flow in the city. We're good neighbors to the rest of the community."

According to Crosby, "We try to keep in touch on a one-to-one basis with our employees . . . . We want more people to work for the company. I'm a native in North Adams. I live in the community and I'd like to see more unemployed people find jobs here." At that time, initial base pay was $3.75 an hour, just 40¢ higher than the state minimum wage. Crosby claimed that some workers could make more than $200 a week with incentive payments. He described the wage as "better than average . . . for this area."[6]

SWEATSHOPS IN THE UNITED STATES: THEY'RE BACK

While the term "sweatshop" had been liberally used during the first part of the twentieth century to describe unsafe factories where "sweated," overworked, underpaid employees, particularly in the sewing and apparel industry, toiled, most Americans hoped and believed that the gains of the labor movement and the New Deal had left that dreary history behind. The definition of "sweatshop" has varied over time, but it usually refers to a mill or factory where safety and/or pay regulations are violated and where direct exploitation of the working and material conditions of employees—e.g. controlling the bodies of workers by restricting bathroom use—is commonplace.

By the 1980s, conditions in the U.S. apparel industry had declined to such an extent that journalists, union leaders, and sociologists argued that the sweatshop had returned. Most of the research and journalism focused on its return to major cities like New York, Los Angeles, and Philadelphia.[7] Indicative of the downturn, the typical apparel worker's pay fell from 72 percent of the average U.S. family median wage in 1947 to 42 percent in 1977. Sociologist Robert J.S. Ross, a leading student of the history of clothing sweatshops in the United States, maintains that, while clothing imports amidst "free trade" agreements that ignore labor standards stand as the leading cause of the sweatshop revival, the loss of apparel union power, the deregulation of domestic labor standards, and the increasingly concentrated power of the industry itself have aided the sweatshop's return. Researchers and journalists also focus on the workforce of the new sweatshops, "undocumented, and therefore disempowered, immigrants exploited by unscrupulous and desperate entrepreneurs."[8]

ACTIVISTS AT X-TYAL

While North Adams was obviously a much smaller community than the cities noted above, the conditions at X-Tyal, along with the causal factors listed, could be seen as contributing to overall conditions that faced the city's workforce—with one exception. North Adams workers, and North Berkshire workers for that matter, were not *recent* immigrants to the United States and, in fact, were often third- and fourth- generation descendants of white, Catholic immigrants who traveled here toward the end of the nineteenth century and the beginning of the twentieth century. North Berkshire had remained an overwhelmingly white, Catholic community, a geographic area that the great post–World War I migration of African Americans had bypassed, as had the later Hispanic migration and the post-1965 Asian migration. Yet, as a workforce that could be exploited, the white Catholic workers fit that categorization, despite their racial "privilege" and long history as U.S. citizens.[9] The reality that good paying jobs had left the area, that unemployment remained high, and that the area's isolation limited workers' commuting possibilities, all contributed to a workforce that was compelled to accept work under sweatshop conditions. While the economic, social, and even physical conditions facing the North Berkshire workforce in the mid-1980s helped allow X-Tyal to exploit its employees, the responses of these employees helped determine how far the exploitation would go.

Though many in the community had already granted X-Tyal its sweatshop status, the contents of the May 15 *Transcript* article provided the first public acknowledgement of problems at the mill. The shop steward mentioned in the article, Jean Braman, played a key role in advocating for employee rights at X-Tyal. Jean had grown up in the North Berkshire area. In her mid-thirties, she brought to the workplace the independence and spunk she had displayed earlier while working in a local welfare coalition. At X-Tyal, it didn't take her long to become involved in rank-and-file and union issues. Still a probationary employee, and not yet a member of the union, Jean quickly reacted when management fired a fellow worker. She tried to energize the other employees in her section by speaking up. She got up on a table "like Norma Rae," to inform the others about the firing.

Management responded with a warning, and Jean described the harassment that followed:

> [A supervisor] came over, and he got a little wise. [I said,] "You have no right to put your hand on me or on anybody else here. We know what we have to do. Just leave. Leave us alone." He left for a while, came back, started picking on another girl. She was really afraid, started crying. [I said,] "That's it . . . . I'm leaving. What we should do is all go down to the office." Nobody wanted to. They were afraid they were going to lose their job. I can't fight for them all, if no one's gonna be there as a group to back me up . . . . I went back downstairs, punched out and had my lunch.

Jean left the plant and found a new job, but after the X-Tyal owner looked over her favorable production record, he asked her to come back. She did, feeling that she was "a stronger person," that the "girls were behind her." The owner reprimanded the supervisor, and he soon ended up getting fired. All of this happened within Jean's first thirty days at the factory. When she became eligible to be in the union, her co-workers elected her steward.

Jean grew up in Adams, one of eight siblings. Her father worked on a farm and her mother in a local mill at the times when she wasn't a full-time "homemaker." Fluent in Polish, Jean's father spoke the language with other men in Adams. Jean graduated from high school and worked part-time in the area while raising two young children. She had her first child while still a teenager and her second at the age of 20.

Jean's first adult experience with political activism occurred not in the workplace but with the state's welfare system. She was enrolled in A.F.D.C. and joined a newly formed Welfare Coalition of recipients and advocates. She explained her activism in the following way:

> They [the welfare department] weren't doing what they should for some people . . . . I couldn't understand why some people got this and some people got that, and other people didn't get this or that [rent or food stamps]. I wanted to get involved in it, not only for myself, but [for the others]. That's about the time that the (Northern Berkshire Welfare) Coalition [got started] because we were trying to fight for more . . . . We wanted more money because of the cost of living, but we wanted more unity, I guess, in the welfare program.[10]

As an advocate, Jean helped people get food stamps, find apartments, and receive medical attention. She also served on the policy council for Head Start and on the Community Action board of directors. After her marriage ended, she took a job at X-Tyal.

Throughout the summer of 1984, the workforce at X-Tyal remained about the same (350), but with a new contract, the company announced that 150 more employees would be needed. At that time the mayor, John Barrett, had only favorable remarks to make about X-Tyal: "It's a nice thing because it's a long-range commitment of three years, it's one of the fastest growing industries in town."[11]

Within a year, Barrett's view of X-Tyal would shift 180 degrees when, at the beginning of 1985, a three-week plant shutdown idled most of the then 320 workers. Still, George Crosby "denied rumors that [the] firm is in trouble." According to Michael Wilber, the local union president, Crosby said "there is enough work for the next 18 months." The company's public stance stayed the same the next month, but Wilber complained about X-Tyal's "very secretive" style. As it turned out, William Kicara, by then president of the firm, had been discussing a declaration of bankruptcy with a New York lawyer as early as April 1985.[12]

NEGOTIATIONS

At the same time, the union found itself in very difficult negotiations with the company over a new contract. Within the plant, management adopted an even tougher disciplinary approach, at one point suspending Mike Wilber along with an outspoken co-worker. But they protested the company actions, returned to work, and union support grew stronger. A late-May meeting to discuss a possible strike drew a record turnout. As the contract expiration date drew near, X-Tyal demanded concessions including cuts in dental and medical benefits, wages, and the elimination of a "floating holiday." (The medical and dental benefits were crucial to the rank and file, many putting up with the low wages and poor working conditions in order to have the security of health insurance coverage.)

The membership rejected the givebacks and authorized its leadership to call a strike if negotiations stalled. One union steward said that the "members are prepared to strike" as "company officials want too much . . . . X-Tyal negotiators have justified the cuts because of business conditions but have not shown any desire to discuss the changes." At this point, Wilber also publicly added that he had spoken with a member of the Northern Berkshire Labor Coalition over "that group's support and . . . assistance to the X-Tyal workers."[13]

Over the weekend, the union workers voted not to strike, but also to reject the new contract. They decided to work under the old contract and continue to negotiate. The leadership of the union had concluded that management hoped to force a strike, thereby avoiding unemployment compensation costs in the event of a layoff or shutdown.

On Monday, the workers returned to their shifts, undoubtedly catching management by surprise. There was no lockout, at least not yet, but the company persisted in urging the concessionary contract on its employees. Wilber said, "Supervisors handed out copies of the contract offer to employees and a company official spoke on the intercom at 3:20 p.m., urging workers to sign it." When the workday ended ten minutes later, management had zero signatures. The workforce held its own meeting in the parking lot and once again "agreed to continue working."[14]

Work resumed the next day, despite the company threat of no signatures, no work. Wilber confirmed to a reporter that the local would "continue to work [and] fight the company through the labor board." The local met with its regional representatives and prepared unfair labor practice charges against X-Tyal including the refusal "to bargain in good faith with the union and attempting to negotiate through individual employees instead of the union." According to Wilber, the company simply presented the same proposal four times during negotiations. That week X-Tyal also instituted the new wage cuts.[15]

At the end of the week, with a lawyer from the regional union staff at the mill taking employee statements, management requested an additional negotiations meeting with the union for Monday. In that five-hour session, the rank and file voted 65 to 35 to approve a settlement. The company withdrew all of the givebacks, except for ten cents an hour in bonus pay. As Wilber put it, "It's not the greatest contract in the world, but it's the only one we could get."[16] The resulting calm prevailed for two weeks until X-Tyal announced a one-week shutdown.

THE BANKRUPTCY

The company lied to its employees. On Friday, taped to the mill's doors, nondescript but chilling signs announced the plant's closing, and padlocks underscored the message. The word spread over the weekend, and on Monday over 100 angry employees gathered there. But instead of opening that day, the company had its lawyers file for bankruptcy. Many employees had personal possessions inside that they could not retrieve. Some had come prepared with signs of protest; later that morning, a sizeable number of them (nearly 100) marched the six or seven blocks to City Hall.

Jean Braman, not surprisingly, led the way holding a cutout of a cardboard owl, identifying X-Tyal as the "MIDNIGHT MOVERS." That theme, a company that left town in the middle of the night without paying its workers, appeared on other signs held by the outraged marchers as they made their way to the plaza of the city's modern city hall. In the mayor's statement of support, he "reiterated his intention to keep the 'midnight movers' out of North Adams." As one, the community seemed to be coalescing against the manner of X-Tyal's departure, like a thief in the night, leaving a trail of deceit. Many that morning could remember a similar trail taken by X-Tyal's predecessors over the past quarter century. But with X-Tyal, the workers' and the community's reactions to the assault were stronger. And they vowed, there would be no more fly-by-night successors. (Unfortunately, nearly thirty years later, another "successor" did emerge. See Chapter Twenty-four for the precipitous closing of North Adams Regional Hospital.)

Mike Wilber argued that the company had planned the closure well in advance: "They don't care at all about the employees as long as they make their money." X-Tyal had tried to foster a strike so they wouldn't have to pay benefits to their workers: that strategy failed, but the company went into a "chapter seven" bankruptcy with debts to local retailers and their workforce. The mayor stated that he had contacted Defense Department officials who claimed that the company seemed to be doing fine financially. "They're not hurting for money," claimed Mayor John Barrett.

Other government officials came by to provide information on unemployment aid. The mayor also "called for worker solidarity and cautioned them to fight together and remember fellow employees even if they find jobs themselves. 'Everything possible will be done to find jobs for those affected by the closing,'" he said.[17]

The following day a powerful *Transcript* editorial placed the midnight movers in the same camp with Sprague Electric, North Berkshire's largest company (which had earlier lied to the community over a major layoff), and with Carol Cable, where a management contract violation led to a wildcat strike:

> The pattern is simple: Contempt for union leadership and suspicion of workers in general, when the company has the upper hand, to fawning calls for community support and public assistance, when the firm is in trouble. Refusal to provide information on major worker dislocations, and even bald-faced denials of impending events. Insistence on givebacks in wages or benefits. Threats to close down plants. Departure for low-wage areas in the South or abroad . . . . As the North Adams area struggles to recoup the economic losses of the past several months, the search for jobs must be accompanied by a search for employers who are reliable. Midnight movers can do little for the people of these hills. [18]

Over the next few weeks former X-Tyal workers and government officials held numerous meetings to deal with practical problems of personal belongings inside the mill, bounced checks, unpaid wages, and the loss of health insurance. Mike Wilber was a whirlwind, writing, calling, talking, and organizing. He continued to bring the many stories of X-Tyal to the press, including concern that a "new" X-Tyal would open again, and that the cycle of exploitation and bankruptcy would continue. At this point, with little to lose, many workers stood ready to fight the precipitous closing.

Members of the Northern Berkshire Labor Coalition and workers from other local plants came forward to support the X-Tyal workers. In an effort to save their jobs, the president of the blue-collar local at Sprague Electric brought consultants from the Industrial Cooperative Association to talk to X-Tyal workers about a possible buyout of the plant. After all, electrical workers at the Brown Street division of Sprague had nearly put together a successful worker buyout, and a similar plan had surfaced among Deerfield Paper workers in Monroe Bridge, a rural community 13 miles northeast of North Adams. And former Adams Supermarket employees soon attracted national attention by establishing the worker-owned Heritage Supermarket in North Adams.

But the luxury of time and economic resources to develop a feasible plan proved lacking. Midway through July, a fire of suspicious origin struck the Union Street mill, where X-Tyal had been its most recent tenant. Twenty-two firefighters on the scene helped confine the damage to the first floor. Investigators discovered signs of forced entry as well as the use of an accelerant. The mill was insured, but neither of the two principals who owned the mill through Toloco Industries of Poughkeepsie—coincidentally, the wife of X-Tyal's president and the widow of the previous president—could be reached for comment.

Any hope of outside help from the union's main office appeared to be dashed when headquarters informed Wilber that they viewed an inoperative plant as a defunct local. That news didn't, however, seem to faze the president of the local, who said: "We are going to try to keep the workers together and plan to have regular meetings to insure everyone is being helped. A steering committee will also be meeting this week to discuss the potential for an employee buyout of the facility and determine what is involved in such a buyout."[19]

But when the bankruptcy judge moved up the date for the auction, a buyout proposal seemed impossible. On July 23, the court announced that the auction would take place in just eight days. The focus of the union's struggle now shifted to preventing the auction. The members pooled their resources and retained a labor lawyer to help with both a possible buyout and an auction delay. As Wilber put it, "We feel it is grossly unfair to have the auction while workers still remain unpaid." At that point, twenty-five workers had still not received their last paycheck, and, of those who had, an additional twenty-five found that their checks had bounced.[20]

Wilber also announced that he had met with a representative of the Small Business Administration to discuss the possibility of a business start-up, and that meetings of former employees had been scheduled to deal with issues covering the auction, a buyout, and unemployment benefits. On Wednesday, July 30, Mike Wilber, two co-workers, and a Labor Coalition supporter drove two hours to Poughkeepsie. At the bankruptcy court there they met with their lawyer in an attempt to get an injunction to stop the auction. Meanwhile, a flurry of activity continued in North Adams.

At the close of a ninety-minute meeting at the Greylock Community Club, nearly two-dozen of the then "ex-employees" divided into committees to meet with elected officials to secure their help. Among other speakers at the meeting, Robert Patti, a representative of the International Union of Electrical Workers (IUE), "urged the unemployed workers not to let themselves 'be treated like second-class citizens.' No one's going to fight for you, fight for yourselves . . . ."[21]

Labor Coalition members had helped lobby the aides of Representative Frank Costa and Senator Peter Webber as well as Mayor Barrett. Coalition spokesman Mark White stated that the workers now had "[s]trong support . . . from elected officials, local clergy, and the general community" with hopes of preventing the auction, and of keeping companies like X-Tyal "from exploiting local workers who are seeking employment in one of the state's most job-blighted areas." Previously, Coalition members had asserted that local officials "had been less than cooperative."[22]

On the legal front in Poughkeepsie, the workers' attorney, David G. Sachs of Holyoke, cited two reasons for gaining a postponement. First, the workers simply needed more time to come up with a buyout plan; and second, they were not given the standard twenty days advance notice of the auction.

Further, the attorney held that X-Tyal's attorney had not filed all of the necessary papers. "Asked if the employees have a chance of delaying the auction, Sachs responded, 'If it were a totally lost cause, I would have said that at the outset.'"[23]

Finally, two days before the bankruptcy hearing, former X-Tyal workers met to discuss possible courses of action if the auction could not be halted. One option discussed included "a peaceful and organized protest of the sale."[24] Before that could happen, though, the legal system at Poughkeepsie had to be tested.

Unfortunately, at the end of a two-hour hearing, the judge refused to grant an injunction. X-Tyal's lawyer argued that a postponement of the auction would further economically damage his client who would have to pay additional rent at the mill. But the workers' lawyer countered that X-Tyal's rent went to a firm owned by Kicara's wife, in effect taking money from his right pocket and putting it in his left one![25] Still, the judge would not be swayed. A front-page headline—"WORKER REPS LOSE BID TO HALT X-TYAL AUCTION"—made the *Transcript* that afternoon. The article went on to note that workers would gather that night to discuss staging a protest at the auction itself.

As Jean Braman remembered that meeting:

> We had a feeling that we were going to be arrested—but we felt we were right in what we were doing and I don't think anyone was going to really stop us except for the police. We had an awful lot of people; we had an awful lot of support, not only from [our own local union], but other locals in the area—100 [percent] they were with us all the way. I guess it didn't really matter if we got locked up, if we got arrested. I felt we had to do something as a group to get anywhere, and we did.

THE PROTEST

Hours before the scheduled start of the 11:00 a.m. auction, dozens of X-Tyal workers and their supporters gathered outside of the mill. It began as a mild, overcast summer day, and the light showers held off until mid-afternoon. Tactics for the protest had been discussed the night before, signs had been made, and the crowd appeared ready. After a few short speeches, a steady picket line marched up and down the hilly sidewalk on Route 2, the Mohawk Trail, the road that greeted visitors to the city from the East.

The mood appeared to be one of optimism, even gaiety; a strong feeling of determination cut across the crowd of about 100. Their handmade signs read: "No More Midnight Movers," "Save Our Jobs," and "Federal Investigation Needed." Other signs raised questions about X-Tyal's finances and disappearing federal tax money. Verses of "Solidarity Forever" rang out loudly from the group.

The most popular chant was "Two, Four, Six, Eight, We Want the Feds to Investigate." A complementary chant, perhaps in recognition of the appearance of one member of the local clergy on the picket line, responded, "One, Three, Five, Seven, Bill Kicara Won't Go to Heaven."

Numerous members of the media arrived. The local reporters had been following the story and television stations in Springfield and Albany had also been alerted to the protest by the demonstrators. Mike Wilber told the reporters: "We'll go out with a bang . . . . We want the people in there to know that we want scavengers out of town."[26]

The mayor had driven over and huddled with the safety commissioner. For the most part, the local police stayed on the other side of the street, and did not interfere with the marchers. Unfamiliar faces driving out-of-state cars had moved into the mill parking lot and, once they had been identified as auction bidders, the protesters engaged them in conversation.

Relatively friendly discussions ensued, as the out-of-towners mostly listened to the litany of protestor complaints. The protestors also urged the prospective buyers not to bid for the equipment, as they still hoped for a worker buyout.

About an hour and a half before the auction started, tensions noticeably increased as the auctioneer arrived, along with William M. Gruner, the bankruptcy trustee. Gruner was familiar to the four protestors who had attended the court proceedings in Poughkeepsie. A tall, stocky man in his sixties, Gruner affected a folksy manner and appearance. He dressed casually and seemed to enjoy wearing white cowboy hats.

The day before, at a break in the courtroom deliberations, Gruner walked over to the visitors from North Adams and delivered a rambling monologue on the virtues of Bill Kicara. Perhaps thinking his analogy would soothe the ripped-off X-Tyal workers, Gruner laughingly told the group that Kicara was like one of those good-hearted Southern slave owners who did, in fact, take good care of his slaves. And Gruner meant it as a compliment to Kicara! So Gruner already had two strikes against him before he drove into North Adams that morning. It didn't take long before further heated arguments with the protestors added the third strike.

When the doors at last opened, both the protestors and the "legitimate" bidders poured into the building to examine the properties up for sale. Those who wanted to bid were told to sign in and get an identification number. A visibly tense auctioneer told one group of protestors that if they wanted to bid, they would have to deposit $100 in cash, just like everyone else. With that admonition, a couple of protestors went off to the bank to bring back the cash. A half hour later when they went in to sign up, they found that they had been lied to, that no such deposit requirement existed.

A line of cars deliberately drove up and down the block outside X-Tyal, and the rhythmic beeping of their horns made it difficult to hear anything that was going on inside. As eleven o'clock approached, it seemed clear that the demonstrators would try to drown out the sound of the auctioneer. With a sizeable crowd of bidders, protestors, interested observers, and several police officers, the "normal" noise might have been disconcerting enough. Gruner tried to get the police to stop the horn blowing outside, but Commissioner Arthur Kelly refused. Instead he advised Gruner to "turn around, ignore it, and go."[27] When the auctioneer tried to begin above the din, one of the protestors raised questions with him about the rules of the auction. Finally, as he attempted to start with the loud beeping and sidewalk chanting competing for the crowd's attention, two groups of protestors on the inside began to sing "Solidarity Forever."

Gruner and the auctioneer, as well as the mostly bemused and befuddled bidders and the smiling but quiet protest supporters, listened until they finished. At one point, the folksy but condescending Gruner even used his arms to lead the group in the manner of a fifth-grade music teacher. Hearing the first verse end, the auctioneer proceeded to begin once again as Gruner stopped conducting. But the singers would not be silenced. "Solidarity Forever" rang out once again. And loudly. "A call for the bidders to 'come on and join in' drew laughs from the predominantly male, middle-aged crowd. If Gruner had hoped the demonstrators would get it all out of their systems after two choruses, however, he was sadly mistaken."[28]

As a third chorus began, Gruner huddled once more with the commissioner. The latter came over to the singing group and informed them that if they persisted in singing they would be arrested for "disorderly conduct." Kelly told them that they had "made [their] point very clear." When given a choice by the commissioner, the whole group chose to be arrested.

Kelly made the arrests, and one of his officers led the group, singing still, down the stairs to the street. The crowd outside greeted them with a huge roar of approval, and that roar continued as they crossed the street to await transportation to the city jail. Before they left in a couple of patrol cars, the mayor told one of the arrestees, "You did the right thing." In a newspaper interview, the mayor said he "fully supported the workers' cause . . . . 'They have done just about everything we asked them to do,' his honor stated."[29]

A half hour later, more protestors "did the right thing," and five more were arrested for singing "Solidarity Forever" in a "disorderly" manner. The protests, while delaying the auction, even impressed some of the bidders. As one prospective buyer from Haverhill stated, "I don't blame them, doing what they're doing."[30] The police and court officers seemed to feel likewise, since they treated all thirteen arrestees respectfully. The young officer charged with processing the prisoners grinned throughout, probably never having seen so many so happy at having been arrested. All were released on their own recognizance, but told not to return to X-Tyal that afternoon. The next day, the judge ordered the case continued "without a finding" for sixty days. If those arrested stayed out of "trouble" over the next two months, any charges would be dropped.

At the end of the court session, the former X-Tyal employees thanked the local officials and police for their fair treatment. Val Rodriguez, one of the thirteen "prisoners," said:

> We want to thank Mayor (John) Barrett . . . for his support, Commissioner (Arthur J.) Kelly and the police department for treating us with respect after our arrest, and the Northern Berkshire Labor Coalition for their support and especially the three members who were arrested with us . . . . We . . . knew that the time had come to take a stand against worker exploitation . . . . We want other businesses to know that if they come into North Adams they will have us to deal with—a strong community.

Rodriguez was not a public figure. Unlike Jean and Mike, she had never been involved in any type of group activism or rebellion. In numerous ways, Val's life and work career seemed characteristic of the biographies of many working-class women in North Adams. The notoriety of her name appearing in the arrest report in the local newspaper and on radio newscasts was most unusual.

At the time of her arrest, Val was 40 years old, the fourth generation to live in the area, with parents and grandparents who had worked in the local textile and electrical equipment mills. She had dropped out of high school in her senior year in order to get married, but over twenty years later, she received her GED. In between, she helped raise three children and worked in five different factories. Val's husband had been employed at the same unionized factory for nearly two decades. The two always managed to arrange their work schedules so they could jointly care for their children. Much of Val's work experience had been in textile mills specializing in government "defense work," sewing the fabrics for gas masks, for example.

After her first child, Val worked at Sprague Electric from 1965–68. She left before the strike in 1970, and she remembers never really having "anything to do with the union—just paying the dues." As with most of her co-workers, she didn't go to union meetings. Neither did she hear much complaining. "If you worked in Sprague's, you were lucky . . . . You know because that's where the better working conditions were and the best wages were [compared to the textile mills]."[31]

Hunter Outdoor Products proved to be the first of several textile mills that she worked for. Subsequently, she went to work at a cardboard factory, which she described as "a clean sweatshop." Then she got a job at Cecile, a successor to Hunter that was "run by the same people. There was a lot of grumbling about the working conditions because they were rather bad. . . ." Employees had to work hard to make bonus, and even with that, it brought the pay to about a dollar above minimum wage.

When Cecile went out of business, Val began working at X-Tyal in 1983. After a while, management quickened the work pace, and Val agreed to become a union steward. Concerned about the chemicals used in production, she inquired about them under the "Right to Know" law. Management responded by pulling her off her job and harassing her, but Val and the union fought back by filing a grievance. Things got worse as workers found that the faulty machines and poor raw material kept them from making their bonus. Harassment continued, and workers realized that management wanted them to quit rather than wait for anticipated layoffs, as layoffs would mean higher company costs for unemployment compensation.

The work was grueling and the pay was low. Add to that the very real possibility that X-Tyal could declare bankruptcy as its predecessors had. Val, along with others, had had enough. After one complaint to the personnel manager, he responded to her: "You're upsetting everybody and you're doing this for nothing and you're just doing this to grandstand." To which Val later commented:

> And you know the guy that did this . . . , he was an area person, you know I'm saying he was born and brought up in this area. And I was twice as angry at him because I thought, "How can he do this to his people? We're his people." And he did this to us. And I think I was more angry at him than the others because the others were from New York State and we knew they were, well we always assumed that they were Mafia. [But t]his guy was local. He was not Mafia and he did this. You know, and I still haven't forgiven him for doing this. He said "Hello" to me but I won't, when I have a grudge, I keep a grudge.

The parochial and public schools in North Adams that Val attended provided no coverage of unions or labor history in the curriculum. She remembers being a dutiful, obedient child whose first major rebellion came in high school when she decided to marry a man her parents didn't approve of. Even after that, Valerie pictures herself as being "placid, a very placid type person until my late thirties, early forties." Her parents did not get involved in community, public, or workplace issues, and only mildly, in their church. The focus was "just work and come home and that was it."

But her parents did work in unionized factories, and she does remember some talk at home about the union. She explained:

> I can remember my mother talk [about the union]. She would go to union meetings and stuff . . . . She, I think, supported unions . . . . I didn't generally support unions until X-Tyal. You know because before it was more or less the unions were paid off. You paid them off but they worked for the company. That's the way it seemed when I worked for the other companies [Hunter's and Cecile's]. But when Michael became president [at X-Tyal] he really wanted something for the people. He was fighting too. He was fighting the union in Connecticut [district headquarters] and he was fighting the company. And I think, you know, that's when it all began with me and getting interested in unions and things like that.

The sewing machines and other equipment had been auctioned off for nearly $200,000, about one-fifth their value. As the mayor noted, the "chances of developing a successful buyout plan without the equipment are now slim."[32] Still, as one commentator put it, "If they couldn't buy the business themselves, they at least wanted everyone to know that the workers of North Berkshire are not going to be kicked around anymore."[33]

SEEKING HELP FROM THE FEDS

For the next six-plus months, the issues swirling around X-Tyal and the bankruptcy remained in the local news. Mike Wilber and eight former employees and supporters continued to work hard in several areas, with mixed success. One major campaign sought to recover all the money owed to workers. Secondly, the protestors tried to pressure the F.B.I. and Congress to fully investigate the millions of dollars that X-Tyal could not account for. Finally, the group hoped to ensure that a re-organized X-Tyal, using a different name, but with some of the same owners and management personnel, did not set up shop in the city. Furthermore, they hoped to keep out similar "fly-by-night," "sweatshop" operations. The nine called themselves NAGS, Nine Against Government Scams, and they met once a week at the Capitol Restaurant for coffee, sociability, and progress reports. They wrote letters to Senators John Kerry and Ted Kennedy and contacted the *Boston Globe*, *20/20*, and *60 Minutes*, hoping to garner more publicity and further investigation. They stayed in touch with the local media and also found the time to picket William Kicara (illegally, it turned out) in front of Central Berkshire District Court in Pittsfield on a wintry day more than six months after he abandoned X-Tyal.

With the signatures of more than two dozen former employees and backers, the NAGS sent a letter to the two national television networks asking them to investigate the circumstances around the bankruptcy. That letter, nearly two single-spaced pages, detailed the local history of the X-Tyal-type pattern of bankruptcies, as well as the specifics around the latest closing. The letter began:

> We would like to call your attention to what we believe is an involved scam which uses the bankruptcy laws to make a fortune for a very few people at the expense of many. The scam involves setting up a company and securing Government contracts to produce military equipment such as gas masks or tents. The company then uses millions of dollars in advances from the Government to grossly overpay for subcontracting, supplies and rent to companies owned by the principals or their relatives. In the meantime, the company builds up huge debts to legitimate companies. When the company gets far enough in debt, it declares bankruptcy and closes its doors, putting hundreds of workers out of jobs. The company's assets are then auctioned off by the Bankruptcy court where the owners buy

> their own equipment through their agents. A few months later, the company starts up again under a different name in the same geographical area to repeat the process. This is believed to be a national trend. As U.S. Representative Silvio O. Conte recently stated, "It appears more and more firms who support the Defense Department are participating in what appears to be a scam to defraud the Government out of funds by going into bankruptcy after receiving large process payments."

The group concluded their letter with the following: "We feel that the best way to ensure that an in-depth investigation of the above allegations takes place, is to get national exposure on the whole scam through a network documentary which would focus on both our local problem and the national trend."

Apparently the networks did not agree, as they showed no interest in pursuing the matter. *The Boston Globe* had one short article but without any follow-through. However, the local media did pursue the story. The Williamstown *Advocate*, for example, investigated government documents at a Defense Department office in Hartford, Connecticut, and discovered the following: X-Tyal told the government that employees received an hourly wage rate averaging $7.05 while the reality was at least $2.00 less; and the chemical/biological warfare hoods that X-Tyal produced were contracted to be sold at $7.98 per hood to the government, yet records showed the military paying at least $10.00 per hood to the company. In addition, and only months before the company closed, it received huge progress payments (advances on future production) from the government as well as a big bonus for a "cost saving change." The sizeable front page headline in the *Advocate* summed up its investigation with questions about the missing money: "DID FEDS OVERPAY X-TYAL $4M?"[34]

It took criminal charges, a default warrant, and a change of venue to bring William Kicara to court in Pittsfield, and in

February 1986, a month after the picketing, all of the former X-Tyal employees received the pay owed them. In court, Kicara "submitted to facts sufficient to warrant a guilty finding on charges of non-payment of employee wages." With the last of the money paid, the court dropped criminal charges against Kicara. Nonetheless, the overall results pleased Mike Wilber, who said, "I'm glad it at least got all the way to the courts . . . . Mr. Kicara told us that he would never move out in the middle of the night and that if there were financial problems he would let us know about it."[35]

While the protesters failed to stop the auction, their actions and the resulting publicity around it galvanized the federal government into action. Within two days of the arrests, U.S. Rep. Silvio Conte called on the attorney general's office and the House Appropriations Committee to investigate the unexpected bankruptcy and Defense Department practices of making advance payments to contractors-such as X-Tyal. A Conte spokesman claimed that while the Congressman's request for a federal investigation did come over a month after the bankruptcy, Conte had "been thinking about this option for some time." The spokesman did admit that the protest and subsequent arrests "had some bearing" on the representative's actions.[36]

Although this pleased the former X-Tyal workers and their supporters, they didn't leave the field to the feds. In fact, they accelerated their activities, meeting weekly, doing their own investigation, and continuing to publicize what they saw as a bankruptcy scam. On their own, for example, they discovered that X-Tyal had failed to pay a number of local merchants as well as the city of North Adams for various goods and services. They also learned that Toloco Industries, the owner of the mill building itself, was owned jointly by William Kicara's wife (using her maiden name) and the widow of a former X-Tyal president, and that the rent they charged X-Tyal was 75 percent higher than the going market price. With the rent factored into the Defense Department payments, the taxpayers had lost once again.

Some three weeks after Congressman Conte had publicized his calls for federal investigations, his office had little to report on. One aide had nothing to say about any response from Attorney General Meese's office except to state that a response "is not taking any longer than expected." The aide did say that the Defense Department Logistics Agency in Philadelphia had opened an office to investigate sudden closings by apparently financially sound contractors such as X-Tyal. According to the aide, the Defense Department "seems to recognize that there is a chronic problem."[37]

Two weeks later, Conte's office announced that the Attorney General's office had turned the investigation of X-Tyal over to the FBI. The Congressman's office also declared that the investigation by the House Committee on Appropriations would probably begin when Congress reconvened in the fall. Mike Wilber responded to the FBI involvement in a positive yet wary tone: "We feel good that the FBI is going to investigate." Speaking on behalf of NAGS members, Wilber added, "We want to keep this in the public eye because we want it to go all the way this time so it doesn't happen again . . . ." Later that month, Conte's office explained that, in fact, the FBI was performing an initial record check to determine whether a formal investigation of X-Tyal would be needed. But after three months had passed, neither government probe had uncovered anything on X-Tyal. On the last day of the year, Conte's office simply reaffirmed that the FBI's investigation was continuing, but "its policies prevent it from revealing the status of the probe."

The response by Conte's office failed to reassure Mike Wilber, who announced that his union planned to picket a court appearance by William Kicara, primarily "to pressure" the federal investigations. As Wilber explained, "It's not just X-Tyal that's a problem. Every time you pick up the newspaper there is a story about another company trying to rip off the government." Meanwhile, Wilber had begun to use the Freedom of Information (FOI) Act to learn the status of the FBI investigation. After a number of letters back and forth to the Department of Defense, he did receive seven pages of FOI documents. But the government had blacked out much of the content, and the information available tended to reveal nothing that was not already known (e.g. that the building X-Tyal rented went at a rate 75 percent higher than average local rates). And the FBI, despite an earlier announcement, did not issue a report.[38]

On another front, in an effort to prevent another reincarnation of X-Tyal to enter the city, the results appeared successful. Back in August, the *Transcript* reported that "Mr. Wilber said workers will not allow former X-Tyal principals to move back into North Adams under a different corporate name . . . . 'There's a few crooked people in the woodpile,' Mr. Wilber said, adding that he and others will fight to prevent such a move . . . ."[39]

Over the next few months, those sentiments appeared to be the consensus in North Adams. When new firms expressed an interest in moving to the city, they virtually had to prove they differed from X-Tyal. When A. Michael Fleming, president of a hospital uniform firm, discussed plans to move into North Adams to produce hospital-related hoods, he stated that he might also go after Defense Department contracts. However, he added: "I want to emphasize that I don't plan to operate only off of government contracts . . . . When I come [to North Adams] I also plan to be there a long time." Besides speaking with the Community Development Corporation and with Mayor John Barrett about operating in the city, Fleming met with officials of the Amalgamated local that represented X-Tyal workers.[40]

In evaluating another possible new entry into local manufacturing, the mayor "stressed that Versatile, Inc., is not another X-Tyal." The mayor also put pressure on Toloco Industries to board up and secure their property, and even threatened to raze the building. In 1986, a Community Development Corporation plan to buy the building from Toloco generated local outrage over fears that William Kicara would make a profit over the sale, while he still remained untouched by the government investigations. That plan never went through. Some wanted the boarded-up building declared a "public nuisance," while the mayor felt it should only be declared "ugly." However, he admitted that when he showed up at the fire at the plant in 1985, he said, "'Burn, baby, burn,' but it didn't."[41]

Four women assembling a tent at X-Tyal, 1981 (*Transcript*).

Jean Braman and Mike Wilber (partially obscured) hold a sign protesting X-Tyal's precipitous closing and workers without paychecks (Wilber collection).

Picket line winds its way up Rt. 2 fronting X-Tyal (Wilber collection).

Before the auction, buyers look over the machines that X-Tyal left behind (*Transcript,* July 31, 1985).

The Berkshire Eagle, Thursday, Oct. 10, 1985—15

Photos by Susan Plageman

STILL QUESTIONING X-Tyal's sudden bankruptcy filing, former employees of the firm have vowed not to let unanswered questions die. Pictured above are eight former employees and supporters who were among 13 arrested for disturbing the peace during an auction of the firm's machinery in August.

Among those arrested, Jean Braman, second from left; the author, to her left; fourth from right, Valerie Rodriguez and on the right, Mark White, Williams College student and member of the Northern Berkshire Labor Coalition.

U.S. Department of Justice

Federal Bureau of Investigation

In Reply, Please Refer to
File No.

Albany, New York
August 4, 1986

UNKNOWN SUBJECTS
DOING BUSINESS AS X-TYAL INTERNATIONAL CORPORATION
HUDSON, NEW YORK
FAG-DOD; TGP

Investigation in this matter was predicated upon the receipt of information on September 30, 1985 from the United States Department of Justice on the basis of a letter to that department from the Honorable [redacted] a Member of Congress. In his letter, representative [redacted] noted that X-TYAL INTERNATIONAL CORPORATION (X-TYAL), a Defense Contractor, had filed for bankruptcy shortly after having demonstrated that it was in sound financial shape.

Representative [redacted] stated he did not have exact evidence which would lead to a determination of wrong doing but noted that "More and more firms who support the Defense Department are participating in what appears to be a scam to defraud the government out of funds by going into bankruptcy after receiving large progress payments." He requested an investigation to determine if the government is being defrauded.

X-TYAL was in the business of manufacturing with almost 100% of its production being for the United States Department of Defense. Its headquarters were in Hudson, New York with manufacturing facilities in both Hudson, New York and North Adams, Massachusetts. The Hudson Facility manufactured primarily inflatable products and the North Adams Plant manufactured such things as gas masks and chemical warfare hoods X-TYAL was owned by its President, WILLIAM KICARA, Wappingers Falls, New York. Its General Manager was CHARLES SHEBANIE. Investigation conducted to date has identified a number of questionable and irregular transactions, summarized as follows:

This document contains neither recommendations nor conclusions of the FBI. It is the property of the FBI and is loaned to your agency; it and its contents are not to be distributed outside your agency.

ENCLOSURE
206-2551-4

A page from materials received from the federal government under the Freedom of Information Act (FOIA), pursued by X-Tyal worker supporters (Nine Against Government Scams, NAGS). Representative Silvio Conte helped pursue the case for the NAGS, and it is most likely his name that is blacked out.

RENT GOUGING BY TOLOCO INDUSTRIES

X-Tyal's plant in North Adams, Massachusetts, was rented from Toloco Industries, Limited (Toloco), which is solely owned by MARION ALEXOVITZ, the wife of WILLIAM KICARA. X-Tyal shared this space with Dutchess Industries, Poughkeepsie, New York, which is owned by JOHN KICARA, the brother of WILLIAM KICARA. X-Tyal was a subcontractor of Dutchess Industries. Toloco's rental charges appeared to be unreasonably high because it was alleged that they far exceeded the normal square footage rate for the North Adams area. In the twenty-eight month period, between October 1, 1982, and January 31, 1985, the following rental payments were made to Toloco, Industries:

Dutchess Industries	$396,076.00
X-Tyal	364,000.00
Total	$760,076.00

Toloco was reportedly purchased by ALEXOVITZ in 1980 for $76,000.00. Since X-Tyal's business was substantially all government, all the rental costs were charged to defense contracts.

In a related development, Dutchess Industries had a government contract which was terminated for the convenience of the government. Dutchess Industries claimed rent in the amount of $396,676.00 in its termination settlement proposal. The government (DCAS) referred to the less than "arm's length" relationship between Dutchess Industries and Toloco Industries and stated that, "Charges in the nature of rent between organizations under common control are allowable to the extent that such charges do not exceed the normal cost of ownership. The rental charge of $396,676.00 was reduced to $2,111.00, the applicable depreciation costs for the period." It is noted that there was an even closer relationship between Toloco and X-Tyal than there was between Dutchess Industries and Toloco.

PRE-BANKRUPTCY TRANSFER OF FUNDS FROM X-TYAL TO TOLOCO INDUSTRIES

In October 1984, X-Tyal transferred $100,000.00 to Toloco, which was then carried on X-Tyal's books as prepaid rent. On May 10, 1985, just before the filing of the bankruptcy petition, a credit of $106,438.00 was made against the prepaid rent account. It was suspected that this $106,438.00 credit was made to cancel the $100,000.00 payment to Toloco which the Trustee in Bankruptcy would otherwise have attempted to collect. KICARA, through the Trustee, produced records to support his claim that the $100,000.00 to Toloco was in payment for zippers and door frame assemblies, and that the $106,438.00 credit was made when the items were actually received. Although this explanation is questionable and the records offered in support are irregular, the receipt of the goods from Toloco is supported

b7D
FBI

Another page from the FOIA detailing what the government called "rent gouging."

b7c FBI

X-TYAL INTERNATIONAL CORPORATION,
HUDSON, NEW YORK;
FRAUD AGAINST THE GOVERNMENT -
DEPARTMENT OF DEFENSE;
THEFT OF GOVERNMENT SERVICES

THEFT OF GREIGE GOODS

LEONARD T. TOZER, JR., an Industrial Specialist from DCAS, went to the X-Tyal location in North Adams to determine the extent of damage following a fire at that location. While there, TOZER determined that there should have been 2,285,616 yards of greige (cloth) goods to complete two contracts for biological hoods. The greige goods had been completely paid for in two progress payments and were, therefore, the property of the government. TOZER calculated the number of hoods shipped, hoods in process, hoods ready for shipment, number of yards in storage at North Adams and number of yards at subcontractors for coating. He was able to account for only 1,872,052 yards in this manner, for an apparent shortage of 413,564 yards. Since the greige goods were worth about $2.00 per yard, the apparent shortage was valued at an amount in excess of $800,000.00. TOZER advised he did not have access to inventory records and did not interview any X-Tyal personnel since the plant was by then closed. He stated that none of the greige goods had been destroyed by fire.

Eastern Canvas Products, Haverhill, Massachusetts, received a letter from KICARA dated April 30, 1986, offering to sell and sending photographs and samples of a large quantity of rubber coated material and partially completed gas mask hoods.

DOUBLE BILLING ON PROGRESS PAYMENTS

TOZER further advised that while randomly verifying a progress payment on February 5, 1985, he discovered a "double billing" situation, wherein two invoices for materials totaling $227,692.00 were used to support requests for two separate progress payments. X-Tyal stated this was done in error. TOZER advised that as soon as the double billing was discovered, WILLIAM KICARA should have immediately written a check payable to the United States Government in the amount of $227,692.50. However, the DCAS Administrative Contracting Officer, JOHN SULLIVAN, Hartford, Connecticut, said that the overpayment would wash out in a future progress payment request. According to TOZER, it is not legal for an overpayment to be handled in this manner.

JOHN SUTO, hired by WILLIAM KICARA to be trained as the Comptroller for X-Tyal, advised that in approximately January or February 1985, KICARA instructed him and JOHN KICARA, WILLIAM

5

206-2551-6

"Theft" and "Double Billing" detailed in another page from the FBI report.

NOTES

1 *Berkshire Eagle*, August 3, 1985, 7.

2 Ibid., October 11, 1985.

3 *Transcript*, March 29, 1980.

4 Ibid., April 2, 1980, and February 25, 1981.

5 Ibid., September 23, 1982.

6 Ibid., May 15, 1984.

7 For an overview of the history of U.S. sweatshops and their return, particularly in New York and Los Angeles, see Robert J.S. Ross, *Slaves to Fashion: Poverty and Abuse in the New Sweatshops* (Ann Arbor: University of Michigan Press, 2009). The first paragraph of this section relies on the history that Ross presents. For a focus on New York, see Daniel Soyer, "Garment Sweatshops, Then and Now," *New Labor Forum*, No. 4 (Spring–Summer, 1999), 35–46; for a focus on Philadelphia, see Elizabeth McLean Petras, *Social Justice*, Vol. 19, No. 1 (47), (Spring, 1992), 76–114.

8 Ross, 98–100 for data on decline of apparel workers' pay.

9 As late as the 2010 Census, whites made up 93 percent of the population of North Adams, and 97.4 percent of the population was born in the United States. In Adams, the white percentage was 96.7 percent with the same percentage native born. www.usacityfacts.com/ma/berkshire/north-adams/ and www.usacityfacts.com/ma/berkshire/adams/.

10 Interview with author.

11 Ibid., July 26, 1984.

12 Ibid., March 16, 1985.

13 *Transcript*, May 31, 1985.

14 *Berkshire Eagle*, June 4, 1985.

15 Ibid., June 7, 1985.

16 Ibid., June 11, 1985.

17 Ibid., July 1, 1985.

18 *Transcript*, July 2, 1985. See Ch. 22 for discussion of the Sprague and Carol Cable actions.

19 *Springfield Morning Union*, July 15, 1985.

20 Ibid., July 24, 1985.

21 *Berkshire Eagle*, July 22, 1985.

22 *Transcript*, July 30, 1985.

23 *Berkshire Eagle*, July 27, 1985.

24 *Transcript*, July 30, 1985.

25 The above market value rent that went to the Kicara family was an added cost to the military and the tax-paying public.

26 *Berkshire Eagle*, August 1, 1985.

27 Ibid., August 1, 1985.

28 Ibid., August 1, 1985.

29 *Transcript*, July 31, 1985.

30 *Berkshire Eagle*, August 1, 1985.

31 Interview with author.

32 *Springfield Morning Union*, August 1, 1985.

33 *Berkshire Eagle*, August 3, 1985.

34 Williamstown *Advocate*, September 11, 1985.

35 *Transcript*, February 24, 1986.

36 *Berkshire Eagle*, August 3, 1985.

37 *Transcript*, August 22, 1985.

38 Ibid., December 31, 1985 and March 25, 1986.

39 Ibid., August 6, 1985.

40 Ibid., September 30, 1985.

41 Ibid., November 7, 1985; May 5, 1986; and August 24, 1988.

CHAPTER TWENTY-ONE

NORM ESTES: LABOR LEADER WITH LONG TIES TO THE AREA

PROBABLY ONE of the most well-liked union leaders in the North Berkshires, Norm Estes, has family ties in the region that go back four generations. Of French-Canadian descent, he grew up poor, was separated from his family, and for a while lived at the "city farm" or poorhouse. He went to work at age 16 at Wall-Streeter Shoes. There he stained and burnished heels, working at piece rate. Norm remembers it as a "terrible job . . . . The inside of my hand was so tough I could put a cigarette out with it." Recalling the early 1950s in North Adams, Norm spoke of plenty of industrial work, including textiles, a situation where you could easily quit a job one day and start a new one the next. But in 1951, he chose to leave his job and the area as well, at least for a while.

As his brother had done earlier, Norm joined the Navy and spent nearly four years at sea. Prior to enlisting, his farthest travels from North Adams had been to Brattleboro, Vermont, and to Utica, New York. The Navy trained him as a radioman and, on the whole, Norm had positive memories of his time in service. He pointed out, however, that the officers inhabited "another world," but that the enlisted men worked together, cooperating in helping each other out. While on leave, he visited North Adams, and in 1955, at the end of his tour of duty, he returned home for good. He took a manual job ("bull work," he called it) at a local rag company for four years, painted for a year, and in 1961 started work at Cornish Wire, the predecessor of Carol Cable, in Williamstown.

Cornish had a union, making it Norm's first experience with organized labor. After Sprague, Cornish's 600 employees made it one of the biggest plants in the area. The pay exceeded what Sprague paid, and Norm was lucky to have had a connection (the father of a friend), which he needed to get the job. The International Union of Electrical workers (IUE) had already been at the plant for five years. Prior to that time, Norm "never gave unions a thought." He had to join; he went to union meetings and generally thought that unions helped people who got into "trouble."

In 1972 he began his union activism when he decided to run for steward, an election he won. As for his motivation, he explained:

> I wanted to represent the people . . . . [W]hen you have problems . . . when you see something that's wrong you want to do something about it. Sometimes things happen, you go in and straighten them out, as opposed to standing around, not saying anything. So that's what got me first started.

In 1975, he won a seat on the negotiating committee, at a time when the company's future looked bleak. The workforce had declined to 400, then to 200. He won several elections for chief steward, and in 1984, his co-workers voted him in as union president, and re-elected him two years later.

In reflecting back on fifteen years of union work, he said he felt he "did a good job . . . arguing for the people . . . . I know how they feel . . . . I fought, did everything I could do to save peoples' jobs." Norm discussed a couple of examples in detail, stressing the importance of good preparation and knowledge of the situation and the law in preparing for grievance hearings. He also pointed out the value of good communication between the local union and the international one. The international, after all, had the expertise to help train stewards and officers about contract negotiations and, for example, incentive rates, an added wrinkle offered by management. Throughout, Norm came back to what was "fair."

In the mid-1980s, Norm became a founding member of the Northern Berkshire Labor Coalition. While he knew other members, several of whom led area IUE locals, the coalition also included faculty members from Williams College and North Adams State College. At one of the first meetings, Norm remarked that he hadn't considered academics as allies in the labor movement, but always stayed open to that possibility.[1]

Norm also served as one of the labor representatives on the Governor's Task Force on the economic development of the region. He felt the group did a good job, that "it worked out pretty good," though he saw "a lot of politics under the surface." He reminded others on the somewhat unwieldy task force not to "forget the people . . . . Labor should be involved . . . . Without labor, you might as well forget everything else."

He knew that management prepared well for grievances and negotiations and that the union needed to do the same. The union also needed to be wary of management tactics. Norm recounted an incident when management offered Norm a job for his son, at a time of ongoing contract talks. Recognizing it as some sort of bribe, Norm turned them down. "They figure they're going to buy me, but they never did . . . . I have no shame for what I did."

Norm Estes, on the right, supporting X-Tyal employees. On left, Jean Braman, and Valerie Rodriguez to Norm's right (Wilber collection).

NOTES

1 Biography based on an interview with Norm Estes by the author, 1986. I was pleased to have Norm's daughter, Dawn, in one of my classes later on. We remained friends, and my wife and I attended her wedding after she graduated.

CHAPTER TWENTY-TWO

SPRAGUE SHUTS THE DOOR

I say the enemy is attitude . . . . I'm talking about the attitude of a very small group of people within our employment, within the communities in Northern Berkshire. It doesn't take much to spoil the barrel.

—Sprague Vice President John Murphy, 1984.

I think Ronald Reagan cares more about this area than [John Murphy and John Sprague].

—Ray Bass Jr., President, International Union of Electrical Workers (IUE) #200, 1984.

Remember the golden rule. Whoever has the gold makes the rules.

—Favorite saying of Carl Lindner, Chairman, Penn Central Corporation, parent company of Sprague Electric.

SPRAGUE, PENN CENTRAL, AND 1984

AS THE X-Tyal and textile era were coming to an end in the mid-1980s, a similar fate was about to befall Sprague Electric. About a decade earlier (as mentioned in Chapter Eighteen), the company was sold. General Cable, later renamed GK Technologies, purchased a still-profitable Sprague in 1976. Then in 1981, Penn Central Corporation bought GK. As 1984 began, employment levels totaled about 1,600, a figure which included production, clerical, research, and management personnel. Sprague's corporate headquarters remained in the city, as did its research and development center. Yet all of that would soon change, and, in fact, within two years, Sprague Electric Company's history in North Adams would be over.

On January 24th, Sprague management called a news conference at its Marshall Street offices. While Dr. John Sprague, son of the company's founder, appeared to be the major spokesman, at least one Penn Central official had a seat at the table. Penn Central's presence, with all its symbolic meaning, played an important role in trying to assess blame for the upcoming layoffs, as local residents often switched from seeing Sprague as the decision maker to viewing the outsiders, the distant Penn Central Corporation, as the puppet master. It was John Sprague who delivered the news that the company had decided to move its corporate headquarters from North Adams to somewhere in the Boston vicinity. The company's headquarters, where all the top managers worked, had been in North Adams since the company located there in 1930. Now, over fifty years later, with a proud history of leading its international rivals in capacitor production, why make such a move?

In explaining the headquarters move at the press conference, John Sprague did not mention Penn Central at all. Instead he cited the company's desire to be closer to high-tech business and research, and with greater access to Boston's international airport. In addition, he pointed out that headquarters would be in closer proximity to Sprague's other New England plants, in Worcester, Massachusetts; Nashua and Concord, New Hampshire; and Sanford, Maine. It would mean being farther from North Adams, of course, and also from the Barre, Vermont, facility. The latter plant wasn't mentioned, probably because the company had already decided on its shutdown. John Sprague assured those at the press conference that North Adams would remain the home of its research and development unit and its production facilities along with its workforce.

Sprague said the move would only mean the loss of ten or eleven positions. That didn't seem like much to most North Berkshire residents. After all, less than two years earlier, the company had transferred its ceramics division out of North Adams with a cost of seventy jobs. That led to local protest, outrage, and a lot of handwringing by elected officials—but the transfer took place. So while Sprague employees had reason to be fearful of company moves, ordinarily a loss of fewer than a dozen jobs would not have been seen in very dramatic terms.

But this time, the announcement brought with it a great deal of fear and anxiety. North Adams residents knew that factories had been leaving the Northeast and Midwest in huge numbers, and they could foresee similar devastation in the North Berkshires, which was already suffering from high unemployment.[1] That fear resonated despite the fact that John Sprague assured the city's residents that the move, which would occur in about six months, would involve just himself and two others, with seven or eight top officers to be transferred within the next two years.

Sprague added that the move would expedite the company's goal of increasing sales to $1 billion by 1987. To reach that figure, John Sprague would have only a few years to more than double the company's 1983 sales figures of $428 million. Exactly how the company would reach this objective remained unclear for now, but evidence suggests that Penn Central had set that goal, somewhat arbitrarily.

Penn Central's desire to rapidly boost sales had to have been connected to the $2 billion in tax credits the corporation had accumulated during its earlier rise from bankruptcy. The Penn Central Transportation Company, a 1968 merger of two giant railroads, the Pennsylvania and the New York Central, ran into trouble and declared bankruptcy in June 1970, which was, at that time, the biggest corporate failure in U.S. history.[2] When the company emerged from bankruptcy in 1978, it received a huge tax credit and had become a conglomerate, basically a holding company for a variety of firms in diverse fields. The conglomerate form, a popular business model in the 1980s, had local resonance as Warren Buffet's Berkshire Hathaway investment arm had earlier included Berkshire Fine Spinning Company with numerous textile mills in North Berkshire. Also,

General Electric, a company that had dominated Pittsfield for many years producing electrical products, had expanded its reach into financial services and the media with its purchase of NBC. The gains that Penn Central could realize from the huge tax credit it received could be utilized only when it produced sales and income that could be taxed, so just holding onto assets, or helping Sprague grow by plowing money into its operations, wouldn't improve the bottom line that big sales would. For Penn Central, Sprague Electric had become a cash cow to be milked, to make the most of its resources and then sell it to the highest bidder.

Carl Lindner, already one of the country's richest men, a member of the *Forbes 400,* had built a fortune in the financial services industry from his Cincinnati-based firm, American Financial Corporation. Lindner, with holdings of almost one-third of Penn Central's stock, became chairman of the board in 1983. As the company's most powerful individual, while he didn't attend the 1984 meeting in North Adams, his business philosophy could possibly have influenced the Penn Central representatives there. According to *Business Week,* "asset redeployment" stood out as Lindner's main focus. For the employees at Sprague Electric in North Adams, that presented a scary prospect.[3]

Dr. Sprague offered the opinion that the news of the headquarters move would be a "psychological" blow to the city. That proved to be an understatement. It brought big, front-page news, the talk of the town, and with it feelings of gloom and depression. However, in their public pronouncements, North Adams's mayor and the leaders of the two biggest unions at Sprague showed some optimism. Mayor John Barrett III's comment noted approval of the company's reasoning: "I look at the positive aspect and think it will do a lot of good . . . . It's a good business decision that will benefit North Adams." Ray Bass, President of the International Union of Electrical Workers (IUE) 200, sounded more guarded in his optimism: "Whatever benefits the company attracts should benefit the people of North Adams . . . . But you never know what changes bring about." And Jack Boulger, president of the International Federation of Professional and Technical Engineers (IFPTE) Local 101 (formerly American Federation of Technical Engineers), weighed the issues and remained positive: "Psychologically, it's kind of a disaster . . . . We're losing a kind of security blanket. But there are a lot of positive signs and there's no reason to fear what's happening." Perhaps that note of hopeful optimism in the statements of all three leaders reflected their belief in the veracity of another statement that John Sprague offered at the press conference in which he said: "I would see North Adams employment remaining stable at present levels for the next several years."[4]

THE BACKLASH GROWS

By the next day, however, John Sprague had already qualified his prediction. "As long as we remain competitive, we'll be here," he said, "[b]ut that's true of any of our plants."[5] The sense of unease remained in North Adams, but no further announcements of layoffs or transfers followed. But for those who read an interview with John Sprague in the *Berkshire Eagle* a couple of months later on March 17, any feelings of anxiety probably intensified. Sprague noted that the "high profit contributors" to the company's bottom line could be found not in North Adams, but in Worcester, where Sprague personally headed the semi-conductors operations. Then, in words that few local residents would ever forget, he added, "This is a pretty depressing place . . . ."[6]

That description angered the mayor, but it took another announcement, that one on March 26, to cause tempers to flare, when Sprague management informed union leadership and the workers at Brown Street (the smaller of the two city operations) that the plant had become a money loser as had the filter division at the larger Marshall Street site. The company called for a turnaround within "the next quarter," a deadline that would impact the 125 employees who worked at Brown Street manufacturing motor-run capacitors and the 200 at Marshall Street who produced electronic noise filters. In response, trying to be good team players, the union agreed to work rule changes to increase productivity and hopefully avoid closings.[7]

However, the stakes had shifted from simply a headquarters move to the possibility of shuttering two production lines. The mayor reacted by calling John Sprague a liar: "I felt I was misled and lied to by Dr. Sprague, who indicated to me at the time of the move that things would be stable at Sprague."[8]

But by the following month, the mayor had halted his criticism amid weekly breakfast meetings (termed the "Croissant Club") with Sprague Vice President John W. Murphy, the executive selected to head the North Adams operations. After three such meetings, a quieter mayor sounded upbeat: "These meetings can only lead to positive things. [They] have been good, frank, honest and open discussions. We're moving toward our goal of a good economic environment for the city."[9]

Now in his twelfth year at the company, John Murphy came to North Adams after a stint at Sprague's Barre, Vermont, plant. A veteran corporate executive, he had diverse experience, having previously worked at American Cyanamid, a major chemical company based in Wayne, New Jersey; at Becton Dickinson, a leading producer of medical devices, headquartered in Franklin Lakes, New Jersey; and at GTE Sylvania, in New York, whose focus on electronic components familiarized him with the lines at Sprague.

The breakfast meetings couldn't, however, stop the upcoming layoffs or the hostility directed at Sprague. On September 19, the mayor went on local cable television, Northern Berkshire Community Television, in effect pre-empting Sprague management, to complain of future job cuts that he knew were coming. The mayor announced that he didn't foresee Sprague being in North Adams in 1990; instead, he feared the loss of "several hundred jobs . . . in the near future." He called for employees and local businesses to band together to keep Sprague there.[10] And, in fact, the next day the company did announce the upcoming elimination of 50–75 jobs at Brown Street and in filters. (The more sizable job losses that Barrett had predicted would be announced at a later date.)

Outright anger characterized the feelings of the rank and file as well as its union leadership. Workers complained of the company's lack of honesty—of praising their increased productivity while planning to move the product line anyway. Incensed union leaders called out the company for making the job loss announcement while they attended an international union convention in Pittsburgh. IUE 200 President Ray Bass minced no words: "They claim productivity is the problem . . . . We reject it, that's absurdity, if people in the filter division are not productive then no one in the U.S. is productive." Furious at the company's failure to discuss its plans with the union, Bass continued: "After 50 years in North Adams, we deserve a little conversation."[11]

While not going as far as the mayor in directly calling Sprague management liars, an editorial in the September 20 *Transcript* left little to the imagination. It read that the area needed "a certain amount of 'up-front' talk—it used to be called honesty—from major employers about their intentions . . . . That's the real mark of reliability." Most local residents who read the editorial no doubt recognized the "mark of reliability" phrase as Sprague Electric's slogan.

Events moved quickly. On October 3, Sprague Vice President John Murphy took a cue from the mayor by using the same local cable television for the next announcement. Apparently Dr. John Sprague didn't want to deliver any more bad news, so Murphy became the fall guy. In a way it seemed to be a good choice by Sprague. Murphy appeared to be the model of the hard-headed businessman. He illustrated his speech with charts that seemed to make the case that the company's decision to eliminate 600 jobs within a year and a half passed the rationality test. But when Murphy wavered from the rational model, he became a public relation man's nightmare.

Out of the blue, he quoted Shakespeare, without making too much sense and certainly without softening the blow. Instead he incurred the wrath of North Adams residents by blaming part of the problem on local community and worker attitudes:

> I say the enemy is attitude . . . . I'm talking about the attitude of a very small group of people within our employment, within the communities in Northern Berkshire. It doesn't take much to spoil the barrel. And if we have a relatively small percentage of our employees and residents here in Northern Berkshire that really do think negatively, they have a serious impact and serious effect on the remainder that *want* to think positively.[12]

For a workforce that had recently changed its work rules, had increased its productivity, had been employed at Sprague for years, had parents and grandparents who had done likewise, and who, in 1984, averaged only $7.15 an hour in wages, to hear that they had a "bad attitude" proved to be too much. A thirty-seven-year veteran at the company, 55-year-old Michael Morin, knew "[y]ou can't stop a company from moving if they want to. What people resent is that they worked hard to get them where they are today."[13] From that point on, John Murphy undoubtedly lost any legitimacy with Sprague workers, and a stronger defense of local attitudes and pride emerged.

For example, Ray Bass responded to Murphy's claim that the workers had an "attitude problem," with: "It's bullshit. And you can print that if you want. It's total bullshit." When asked if he thought Sprague and Murphy cared about the city, Bass responded, "I think Ronald Reagan cares more about this area than those people."[14]

A third generation resident, Ray Bass Jr., and his family forebears had lived on the same street for a century. Ray's father, Ray Sr., had founded the machinists' local at Sprague and had served as its president for fifteen years. Ray's mother and an uncle actively participated in Sprague unions and another uncle played a key role in the union at a local textile machine repair shop. Growing up, Ray knew that "to work in a place and not join the union would have been incomprehensible. [To be in the union] was like breathing."

He began work at Sprague in 1974 and within a year won election to steward. Reelected twice, he then won the presidency. During his eight years as IUE #200 president, he had a reputation of always being well prepared in grievances and contract negotiations.[15] It took a lot of work, but as he exclaimed, "Good God, there are twenty-four hours in a day, not eight." Now, with the company cutting jobs and preparing to close up shop, he fought back and tried to protect the production workers. He reached out to the community, supported research to uncover all the skills his membership had, pushed for new job training, served on the Governor's Task Force, and tried to bring new industry into town.[16]

Like Bass, Mayor Barrett had no hesitancy in attacking Sprague. In an interview with the weekly Williamstown *Advocate,* he continued his blunt criticism of Sprague, stating his belief that the company simply wanted to leave North Adams: "I don't think they like the area." Barrett went on to recount the early days of the company's life in the city:

> This has gotta be ripping Robert Sprague Sr. apart. It's got to be ripping him apart. Because he remembers those early days, back in 1929 when he came to North Adams and the business people of this area raised over $200,000 during a Depression and brought him here to this city. He was extended credit by every businessperson around. The workers went several weeks without paychecks. Some of them had to be paid in stock that was worthless at that time to keep that company going. And Mr. Sprague told the workers at that time, 'You're working for nothing now, but it's going to benefit your grandchildren.' The question is now, whose grandchildren? His, or the people's?

Barrett continued, criticizing the company for keeping out competing firms back in the 1940s and 1950s, companies like Dragon Cement, General Electric, and Westinghouse. "Sprague went around and bought up just about every piece of decent industrial property in the city of North Adams. And they basically made North Adams a one-industry town, [and] they kept it a one-industry town."[17]

While evidence suggesting that General Electric and Westinghouse had taken an interest in building plants in North Adams remains hard to find, a huge controversy over Dragon Cement establishing a limestone quarry and cement plant in North Adams had erupted in 1955 (see Chapter Fourteen). Initially, Dragon's proposal had received strong approval, as local residents wanted new industry, and one that paid higher wages than the current norm. But Sprague had immediately come out against it, and a huge battle erupted with countless letters to the editor, editorials, meetings, and presentations of the different sides, amidst a powerful public relations campaign presented by Sprague that argued that the cement dust would harm capacitor production.[18] Finally, when Sprague said it would eliminate 2,000 jobs in North Adams if Dragon received permission to build the plant, the city capitulated.[19]

Mayor Barrett's comments on Sprague and Dragon Cement came nearly three decades after Sprague emerged victorious. As to whether to blame Sprague or Penn Central (Sprague's parent company) for the decisions hurting North Adams in 1984, the mayor was emphatic:

> John Sprague is calling all the shots. And anybody who thinks differently is wrong . . . . John Sprague is president of that company. Penn Central has set goals and objectives as any intelligent company should do. And they have asked that those goals be met. And it is up to those people who are running those companies to meet those objectives and goals. To be very honest with you, I think that if Penn Central really knew what is going on here, they would put a stop to it. I really do.

Much later, in a book he authored about the company, *Sprague Electric: An Electronic Giant's Rise, Fall, and Life after Death,* John Sprague offered another explanation for the headquarters move. He claimed that Penn Central had dictated the corporate headquarter move out of North Adams, where, in the spring of 1983, a Penn Central corporate jet filled with board members and management had landed at the North Adams's Harriman-and-West Airport at the base of Mount Williams, an airport without a tower, with a relatively short runway and in a valley subject to windy conditions. Sprague imagined the anxiety of the passengers as they looked down at the landing area that looked "like a postage stamp." After their visit, a first time for many, "the visitors rushed back to the airport, happy to be gone and hoping that the Penn Central jet had enough power to take off and clear the surrounding hills." As John Sprague recounted it in his book:

> The feedback from Penn Central CEO Martinelli was swift and unequivocal. He made it clear that he was never going to fly into that airport again, that North Adams was no place for Penn Central's highest technology investment and that he wanted headquarters moved to somewhere appropriate, such as the Route 128 area of Boston.[20]

Early in 1985, John Sprague announced a change in John Murphy's status in the company: by March 1, Murphy would be leaving his position as head of North Adams operations in order to lead the company's "decentralization plan." The company also increased its estimate of job loss from 600 to 700, amounting to a 50 percent cutback in the voluminous Marshall Street plant. IFPTE union head Jack Boulger saw the shift in Murphy's status as one in which he would be "presiding over his own demise. I don't think there's going to be a need for a head of local operations," he added, "because there won't be any local operations." As for the ultimate "decider" in the job cuts in North Adams, Penn Central's spokesperson Kathleen M. Kucera "did acknowledge that 'clearly, any major decisions are talked about here before they take place.'"[21]

In any case, the layoffs continued, and in 1986 workers removed the iconic SPRAGUE sign atop one of the Marshall Street buildings. It was over. Production on Marshall Street had ended. For the first time since the erection of the buildings by Arnold Print Works in the nineteenth century, nothing would be manufactured within those walls. For all intents and purposes, Sprague had closed its doors in the city of North Adams.

The company still had a small plant on Brown Street that it wanted to sell. A team of workers and a separate group of managers put together proposals, and in July 1985 the Sprague Electric Board of Directors said "Yes" to the managers. Called CAPTECH, the new company initially refused to recognize the Sprague unions, but after being picketed by IUE #200, CAPTECH seemed to change its tune. However, the new company added contractual clauses that would eliminate the union and, after facing community pressure, CAPTECH decided to withdraw its purchase offer.[22]

Reluctantly, Sprague tried to continue production and opened bargaining with the 130 production workers. But when offered a concessionary contract, a split in the workforce developed. At first, union workers rejected the contract, which reduced wages by 14 percent, cut paid holidays, and made changes in work rules. But fearing a plant closure and the loss of precious jobs, pressure built for a second vote. That time the vote favored approval. It didn't end there, however, as dissident employees went to court in Springfield in an unsuccessful attempt to get one more vote.[23] In effect, the dissidents faced an alliance of management and the union, both wanting to keep the affirmative vote. U.S. District Judge Frank H. Freedman rejected the third vote proposal but, for the record, stated: "It was the first time in his career that he had 'seen counsel for the union and counsel for management sitting on the same side of the courtroom.'"[24]

As it turned out, the Brown Street facility remained open, but the company soon sold it to a Connecticut firm. The new owners renamed it Commonwealth Sprague. They recognized that the Sprague name still meant quality in the capacitor industry, even though the family and its legacy had departed.[25]

WILDCAT STRIKE IN WILLIAMSTOWN

In Williamstown, one manufacturing plant held on, though barely. In October 1983, General Cable Company announced it would close by year's end if it couldn't find a buyer. The cable company, like Sprague, was a subsidiary of Penn Central. Carol Cable, General Cable's chief competitor and number one producer of wire and cable products in the United States, turned out to be a prospective buyer. Williamstown Town Manager Howard Redfern had been involved in the negotiations between both companies, but he remained suspicious of Carol's intentions and had "extreme concern" that the new company might be buying the plant simply to close it down and reduce competition in the cable business.[26]

Carol Cable, however, managed to convince Williamstown to seek $1.3 million in state and federal funds to purchase the local factory. Holding all the cards, they pressured the union (IUE #299) to accept a giveback contract including pay cuts averaging 20 percent and the loss of family health insurance coverage. Outraged by the financial losses, the union turned it down, 67 to 50, in a March vote. However, fearful of losing their jobs, some of the workers petitioned for another vote. The second vote occurred six days later, and that time the contract found acceptance by 77 to 55. Newly elected union president Norm Estes probably expressed the mood of most of the employees: "[It is] a lousy contract. [But] [i]t's either this or we're out of a job . . . . There's nothing else. There's no hope. It's all we've got."[27]

Carol Cable won a favorable contract, but it didn't come with a happy workforce. After less than a year of working under the agreement, with numerous grievances and dissatisfactions with company policy, the Carol workers, now more unified than ever, went out on a wildcat strike in late April 1985. The spark that ignited the strike came from the company's bumping of a first shift union member to the third shift to make room for a foreman that management wanted back on the production line. But, according to union vice president Robert M. Sweet, the management ploy proved to be "the straw that broke the camel's back" as the workers had begrudgingly agreed to a takeback contract, and also found that their new incentive clauses brought them less pay than the company had indicated.[28]

There hadn't been a local strike for quite a while. In fact, nationwide, the 1980s proved to be a difficult one for the labor movement, with more plant closings, concessionary bargaining, and a weakened AFL-CIO. For many workers, the memory of President Ronald Reagan firing and replacing the 12,000 unionized air traffic controllers in 1981 proved dispiriting and gave management everywhere license to be tough with their employees.[29]

At Carol Cable, however, discontent bubbled up through the rank and file, and they acted without official union support. As a wildcat strike, the workers received no help from the international union, but the strikers remained united. Despite receiving two letters from the company that threatened termination and loss of medical benefits, only a handful of the 140 union members returned to work. According to some Carol employees, the company's personnel manager called the local unemployment office to tell them that the strikers would be ineligible for benefits. As the strikers told it, he was met with a "you run your business and we'll run ours" response.

Just over a week into the strike, the Northern Berkshire Labor Coalition (NBLC) organized a community support rally for the strikers. Members of the coalition had also been phoning residents of Williamstown to ask their town manager to bring Carol management to the negotiating table. They also tried to build local pressure against the town's releasing any further government loans to Carol until a settlement had been reached.

At the rally on April 30, close to 200 people attended: strikers, union and non-union area supporters, and students and faculty from nearby Williams College. IUE's Ray Bass, from Sprague, told the crowd, "We're the people who built this country and we're the ones who will keep it alive." Norm Estes, president of IUE #299 at Carol Cable, spoke as well, despite the prohibition of the official union supporting a wildcat strike. "I want you to continue what you are doing," he said, "[because] with people supporting us like this we can't lose." The crowd sang "Solidarity Forever," and the rally ended with a long, singing picket line that extended from the company parking lot to the main entrance, and moved slowly to serenade management personnel as they attempted to drive out of the lot.[30]

The scope of support for the Carol strikers widened the next day, May Day, when twenty union representatives from six other Carol plants in eastern Massachusetts, Rhode Island, and New Hampshire traveled to Williamstown to demonstrate their solidarity. The unions represented by the twenty fellow travelers included the International Brotherhood of Electrical Workers, the United Electrical workers, the IUE, and the United Steel Workers.

Soon the company agreed to negotiate, undoubtedly moved by the display of community support and worker solidarity. On May 8, the rank and file unanimously accepted the settlement in which the company agreed to return the "bumped" union member to his job on the first shift. The workers had won on principle though the settlement came with nine days of suspensions to seven union leaders in the walkout. However, in a powerful display of unity, "union members . . . agreed to finance the suspended employees 100 percent of their wages while they are out of work." As the strikers returned to work, union President Estes raised the American flag in front of the company's entrance, flanked by union members who, once again, were singing "Solidarity Forever."[31]

NEW JOBS: THE ROLE OF THE STATE AND THE STRUGGLES OF THE RANK & FILE

After Sprague had announced its massive layoffs in early October 1984 without giving the state any advance notice, a determined Governor Michael Dukakis commented: "It's a disappointment and a serious blow to our efforts to rebuild the economy in North Berkshire . . . . As a result we must redouble our efforts."[32] Later that month, speaking at North Adams State College (NASC) for the inauguration of the college's new president, Catherine Tisinger, Dukakis announced a state commitment to back the region's economic development. The consensus-seeking governor called it "The Governor's Task Force on Economic Development in North Berkshire," and said it was to be co-chaired by local Democratic Party activist and lawyer John DeRosa and NASC President Catherine Tisinger.

The task force, composed of more than sixty people from government, academia, law, business, and labor, began meeting in January 1985, continued meeting while the Carol Cable wildcat strike unfolded, and completed its report in March 1986. They met in seven different committees, and other than recommending immediate actions to deal with the depressed economy—supporting a worker assistance center, analyzing the skills of the local workforce and their needs, and bringing in more healthcare services—the suggestions focused on marketing the area as a region (North Berkshire) for both business and tourism.

The state's $8.5 million plan to develop a year-round resort and recreational center at Greylock Glen, in Adams, at the foot of Mount Greylock, became one of the centers of discussion. However, the Glen never came close to fruition, as it provoked a good deal of criticism for its aim to bring development to a pristine park area and the state's tallest site. Another recommendation that received significant press and also proved contentious would have provided for a new road, a "bypass" that would better connect North Adams to the Massachusetts Turnpike at Lee, 35 miles to the south. This highway also never made it off the planning documents.

Around the same time, the Sprague production workers' union took out a local newspaper ad that included a group photo with a caption that proclaimed it was an available workforce. However, no employers responded. The state supported training programs for unemployed workers, but skills weren't the problem; it was the lack of jobs. The state even tried to rescue the former Arnold Print Works from a second bankruptcy, but it didn't work.

In fact, as noted in Chapter Three, North Adams has a history of worker-owned enterprises that dates back to 1870, when out-of-work shoe craftsmen, members of the Knights of St. Crispin, opened their own factory. And over a hundred years later, out-of-work employees in North Adams looked to worker ownership, to co-ops, as a dignified way out of the economic crisis. A column in the February 24, 1984, *Transcript* had proposed employee-ownership plans as one local avenue to investigate. Also, the Northern Berkshire Labor Coalition had talked about such possibilities at its meetings in the summer of 1984, with broad-ranging discussions including examples of actual and proposed worker-owned facilities (e.g., two of the former A&P stores in Philadelphia and the Bridgeport Brass Company in Seymour, Connecticut). Coalition meetings had also introduced two new, innovative, Massachusetts state plans: the Cooperative Regional Industrial Laboratory and the Industrial Service Program. Both plans had been designed to provide funds for feasibility studies, and the latter program included a trust mechanism for funds to support the buyout itself. Shortly after, three groups of workers came up with plans to buy and own their own businesses—a supermarket, a paper mill, and, as mentioned earlier, a capacitor factory.

In the fall of 1984, a county grocery chain, Adams Supermarket, had announced its closure and the sale of five of its stores, including the ones in Adams and North Adams, to a larger regional chain, Big Y. While Big Y interviewed and hired many of the former Adams workers, the company brought back relatively few of the Adams meat department employees and, according to some accounts, gave them interviews that were "just a formality." It seemed obvious to many that anti-union animus must have been the cause of Big Y's behavior, as the meat department employees had been the only unionized sector of the Adams workforce. Gerald Burdick, who managed the meat department in Adams, stated that he received a "No" from Big Y, as did eight of the nine employees who worked with him. According to Peter Solari, who worked with Burdick in Adams, "People were hired off the street before we were considered."[33]

In response, the former meat department workers picketed the North Adams Big Y when it reopened, and they called for a consumer boycott. They received support from local workers and from the Northern Berkshire Labor Coalition. The coalition helped organize a Saturday picket of the store, came up with a boycott leaflet, and sent a letter of support to the local press. After meeting with the meat cutters' organizer, Gerald Burdick, the coalition planned a December 8 community meeting and invited a former UE union president and co-chair of the Unemployed Council from Greenfield to the speakers' rostrum.

After much discussion, the former Adams workers decided to explore the possibility of opening their own supermarket. In conjunction with the Industrial Cooperative Association (ICA), a worker-oriented consulting firm from Somerville, Massachusetts, the Northern Berkshire Labor Coalition, a state-sponsored agency, the Cooperative Regional Industrial Laboratory (CRIL), and faculty from the state college, the former Adams workers came up with a detailed business plan to buy a vacant supermarket and start their own worker-owned market.

Precedent for such a venture came from Philadelphia where, rather than being laid off, employees of the A&P stores bought them out and established their own supermarkets known as O&Os (Owner Operated Markets). At a Northern Berkshire CRIL meeting, Ronald Sage, a CRIL member who had also been active in an attempted employee buyout of Deerfield Specialty Papers Inc. in nearby Monroe, stated:

> "We're sick and tired of big businesses dictating our work, our vacations and our pay. And, then if a conglomerate decides to walk, there's nothing we can do about it."[34]

After a good deal of planning, fortified by $700,000 in financing, the Heritage Supermarket opened in 1988. The management team included seventeen owner-investors, each of whom put $10,000 of their own money in the project, with the rest coming from loans from local banks, the Community Development Corporation, and the Bank of New England West, guaranteed by the Federal Small Business Administration. Not a purely worker-owned supermarket, the owners needed to hire 40 other employees to keep the operation going. According to one co-owner, Kathleen T. Hoczela, "the emotional inequality between workers and management is minimized."

Hoczela, a meat-wrapper, characterized the supermarket relationships in the following way: "It's more like a family. Problems can arise, but there's no one trying to be lord and master looking over your shoulder, or the fear of being on the outside looking in."[35]

Heritage built up a customer base of over 6,000 customers a week. Unfortunately, facing a significant amount of local competition from two non-union chains, the market lasted less than three years.[36]

On January 3, 1985, another group of workers announced an employee-ownership proposal. Union members at Deerfield Specialty Papers Inc., including CRIL member Ronald Sage, publicized the formation of a nine-member board of directors to "oversee the workers' attempt to purchase the plant." After months of plant-closing rumors, the company announced that it would halt operation on January 4.

The plant, organized by the United Paperworkers International Union, had at one time employed 149, but that number had dropped to 68 when a final December layoff had occurred. Union President William Mazanec "blamed Deerfield's closing on 'mismanagement' and said the company was overloaded with people upstairs." Numerous state and federal officials and agencies had been contacted for a feasibility study and low-interest loans. Clearly, the workers had done their homework. About 65 former employees placed $500 each in an escrow account totaling over $30,000 to indicate the seriousness of their intentions.[37]

While the Deerfield process moved along, in March the press reported that a group of Sprague workers had begun consideration of a similar buyout plan of the company's Brown Street plant along with its two capacitor lines manufactured there. About 150 employees worked there, and with the support of two of their unions, the International Union of Electrical Workers (IUE) and the International Federation of Professional and Technical Engineers (IFPTE), they proceeded to elect an eleven-member steering committee to investigate the potential of a buyout. Ray Bass, the IUE local president, appeared cautiously optimistic about the proposal's success. "This is not a pipe dream," he said, "this is a reality."[38]

As with the Deerfield workforce, the ICA had been hired by the state to conduct a feasibility study of the Brown Street plant. Work proceeded on the study, and one proposal had the workers join several interested managers on a dual project, but in the end, the company rejected the workers' offer. Also at Deerfield, the company sold the specialized paper mill before the employees could receive a full hearing.[39]

While local interest had been focused on these efforts at worker ownership and the recommendations of the Governor's Task Force, news about a huge museum taking over the former Sprague buildings hit the media, and attention quickly turned to that possibility. The task force work took a distant backseat, along with the ideas and energy of its diverse local members. Instead, the residents of North Berkshire had to deal with a new big idea, one that emanated from the outside, from an elite institution. Thoughts of worker ownership, let alone of salvaging industrial jobs, soon found little resonance.

Sprague lunch hour, September 21, 1984, during a year of anxiety and recriminations, with a corporate office move and talk of layoffs (*Transcript*).

The Berkshire Eagle

CITY & TOWN

B

Tuesday, September 15, 1987

Page B1

Susan Plageman

LANDMARK Sprague Electric sign is dismantled on roof of Marshall Street plant by Dustin Wilk, left, and Kenneth Tetreault of the R.I. Baker Co. of Clarksburg. Removal signaled end of an era.

Removal of giant Sprague letters a sign of the times for N. Adams

By Alison Gendar

NORTH ADAMS — Letter by letter workmen took down the Sprague Electric sign from the top of Building 12 yesterday.

"Somehow this makes everything final," said Donald G. Roy of 176 North Summer St., Adams, as he was watched the sign come down during his lunch break.

"This is really it," he said.

Roy was one of the few who turned out to watch as two men from R.I. Baker Co. of Clarksburg lifted each letter and gently slid it down the roof of the building that used to house the tantalum division.

The 4½-foot black letters that used to mark Sprague Electric Co.'s international headquarters will be scraped and their stainless steel metal castings will be sold to a sign manufacturer.

"Those letters have been up there since at least 1960 and that might as well be forever," Roy said.

But by 3 p.m. the sign that had once been synonymous with the city of North Adams was gone and with it the final vestige of North Adams as a one-company town.

"Who's sentimental about that?" asked Lawrence W. LaBombard as he came off his shift. He has worked in the tantalum division for 38 years and is one of the 60 or so Sprague employees who still report to work at the Marshall Street plant. The rest have moved to Sprague's new quarters in the Robert Hardman Industrial Park. Removing the sign is just part of Sprague's abandonment of the building.

"So what's there to be sentimental about?" LaBombard commented.

Getting rid of the sign has been one of the most visible changes to the old mill buildings since the idea of turning them into the world's largest museum of contemporary art first surfaced.

Williams College and the city have proposed the $72 million project. The plans require $35 million in state funds, and last week Gov. Michael S. Dukakis pledged his support of the project.

Williams College is now negotiating with Penn Central, Sprague's parent company, for a deed to the Marshall Street complex.

But as one Sprague employee put it yesterday: "Seeing the signs come down was the first time all the talk about museum stuff seemed real."

"Seeing the signs come down was the first time all the talk about museum stuff seemed real."

Susan Plageman

LUNCH BREAK may have left a bitter taste in Sprague Electric workers' mouths yesterday. They knew bad news was on the way, and it came in the form of more layoffs.

Laid-off Sprague workers ponder uncertain future

By Dianne Cutillo

NORTH ADAMS — For many Sprague Electric Co. employees, yesterday's news about which jobs the company will cut, though bad news, came as a relief.

look here first for a new job but will move if forced to. For Koczela and other middle-aged workers laid off by Sprague, the prospect of moving means not only uprooting their families, but assuming a new, larger

and her husband, who also works at Sprague, did not know what they would do if both were laid off. Because the couple own a home and have young children, they did not want to leave the area. She received

Workers leave amidst more layoffs (*Berkshire Eagle*).

The Transcript

"We hold the western gateway"

Serving Northern Berkshire and Southwestern Vermont

142ND YEAR — No. 24 THURSDAY, OCTOBER 4, 1984 20 PAGES — 30 CENTS

G. Greenberg T. Chalmers B. Claremont V. Moran D. Rougeau J. Robinson D. Dean R. Janigo V. Vareschi T. Beckwith L. Townes V. Gay

Sprague worker reaction: 'They had to' vs. 'We got shaft'

By J. CHRISTOPHER WHITCOMB
Transcript correspondent

NORTH ADAMS — Reaction among employees of Sprague Electric Co. to the firm's announcement Wednesday morning that 600, or 39 percent, of the 1,550 jobs at the city's largest employer would be eliminated range from shock and anger to relief that about 1,000 jobs will remain.

Sprague senior vice president John W. Murphy made the announcement to union leaders and the press Wednesday and cited a 10-point plan to explain the electronics firm's decision. He said local employment now accounts for 12 percent of Sprague's 12,000 worldwide total, while less than two decades ago, when more than 4,000 workers had jobs here, the percentage was 65 percent.

Mr. Murphy cited "a bias toward older markets and older technology" as part of the reason for the removing the jobs here. Foreign competition, energy costs and negative attitudes here also account for problems, he said.

Sprague management, employees, and state and local officials must work together, Mr. Murphy said, toward a more positive attitude which will give the company strength and help it become more stable in the future.

To the 600 employees and their families who will be affected by the layoffs, a positive attitude might be difficult to maintain.

John A. Robinson of Williamstown, a Sprague Electric employee who believes he will not be affected by the layoffs, expressed his opinions on the matter in a letter to The Transcript.

"Losing 600 jobs over 18 months is scary, but the 900 or so who'll remain must take a deep breath, tuck in our shirt tails and carry on as usual," Mr. Robinson said. "But in order to do so there must be changes: changes in relations, attitudes and rules between production and management."

Can attitudes bred from years of labor and commitment be changed overnight?

Several Sprague employees, leaving the plant Wednesday afternoon, spoke about their feelings concerning the impending layoffs. Perhaps attitudes speak for themselves.

Victor Vareschi said, "This plant has excellent workers. If the company brings the work here, we can do it and do an excellent job. Jobs could be made here, but the company is transfering them to other plants for some reason."

"This makes for a for a very dismal picture in North Adams. I've worked for Sprague for over 36 years and I just found out I have until the end of November before I get laid off. It just isn't right," said Victor Gay.

Victor Moran was terse: "We're losing our jobs. What more needs to be said?"

Tammy Beckwith added, "What I have to say about the situation can't be printed."

See Reaction, p.12

Six hundred more jobs to go!

Fran Alibozek, left, and Francis Schonfelder, managers of Heritage Supermarket in North Adams, Mass. They are among the 17 people who used their personal savings to buy the store.

Where the Workers Are the Owners

By JOHN TOWNES
Special to The New York Times

NORTH ADAMS, Mass. — The man behind the meat counter at the Herit-

Local workers make it happen: worker-owned supermarket (John Townes, *New York Times*, June 12, 1988).

Outside unionists support Carol Cable "wildcat" strike on May Day (*Berkshire Eagle,* May 1, 1985).

Mark Mitchell

RAISING THE FLAG at Carol Cable is Norman J. Estes, president of the union that voted to return to work. Members are singing "Solidarity Forever."

"Solidarity Forever" as union president raises the flag celebrating Carol Cable strike settlement (*Berkshire Eagle,* May 9, 1985).

NOTES

1 Holly Taylor, *Berkshire Eagle,* October 8, 1983.

2 John C. Spychalski, "Rail Transport: Retreat and Resurgence," *The Annals of the American Academy of Political and Social Science*, Vol. 553 (Sept. 1997), 42–54, 47. To finalize the merger, the new company also had to include the bankrupt New York, New Haven and Hartford Railroad.

3 *Business Week*, June 6, 1983.

4 *Transcript*, January 25 and January 26, 1984.

5 Ibid., January 26, 1984.

6 The full statement regarding North Adams went like this: "This is a pretty depressing place and part of it is self-defeating . . . . It's not growing, that's the problem. Worcester, Boston—that's alive." Asked whether "he had to be pragmatic rather than sentimental toward the plants" in North Adams, Sprague responded, "I guess I have to . . . . My job is to maximize the profits of the Sprague Electric Co. I have to match what I feel about the community with what I have to do to make the company successful" (Gustav Niebuhr, "Sprague plans cause North Adams dilemma," *Berkshire Eagle*, March 17, 1984).

7 *Berkshire Eagle,* March 26, 1984.

8 Ibid., March 27, 1984.

9 Ibid., April 19, 1984, 1, 12.

10 *Springfield Union*, September 20, 1984.

11 *Transcript*, September 21, 1984.

12 Williamstown *Advocate*, October 10, 1984, 1.

13 Ibid.

14 Steve Leon, "Breaking Faith: The Sprague Story," *The Berkshire Sampler,* December 9, 1984.

15 Evelyn Jones, IUE #200 vice president while Ray served as president, remembers Ray's preparation and tenacity. In negotiations with the company, she knew the union had done its homework. "If you sneezed ten years ago Ray's got it down. And you won't get away with that again, saying you didn't sneeze, because he's got it right there. And before we went into negotiations we had meetings. And we had all of our stuff all prepared. And he would say, 'now, what if,' you know, 'what if.' And then we'd go and decipher that. And then he'd say, 'then what if this?' And so we had about five or six different ways we could go when we went in there." University of Lowell, Center for Lowell History, "Shifting Gears" Oral History Project, interviewed by Annette Gamache, May 18, 1988.

16 See interview by Robert Gabrielsky, January 31, 1989, "Shifting Gears" Oral History Project and interview with author, 1986 (transcript in author's possession). In one community meeting, led by Ray Bass, a local

priest made reference to a document on the economy recently written by American Catholic leaders. Based on their authority, he stated that it is "immoral" for a company to leave an area simply to increase its profits.

17 Williamstown *Advocate,* October 17, 1984, 1, 10, 28.

18 In an interview in 1998, former Mayor Joseph R. Bianco remembered how Sprague stopped Dragon: "They spent a lot of money to beat them . . . . They did everything in the book. They went all over taking pictures of cars covered with cement dust in Maine, where there was a factory." Joe Manning, *Disappearing Into North Adams* (Florence, MA: Flatiron Press, 2001), 118.

19 The Planning Board "said it was not yet convinced that cement-making would be detrimental to Sprague's operations, but that it could not reach an objective conclusion 'where 2,000 workers may be adversely affected.'" In a weekly review article entitled "Sprague Cracks the Whip" in the *Berkshire Eagle,* the unnamed journalist's concluding sentence proved prescient, stating that "the ill feelings stirred up by the knock-down fight would plague Sprague's community relations for a long time to come" (November 19, 1955, 15).

20 John L. Sprague, *Sprague Electric: An Electronic Giant's Rise, Fall, and Life after Death.* (North Charleston, S.C.: CreateSpace Independent Publishing Platform, 2015), 119, 120. Just five years later, John's younger brother, Robert Jr., died while trying to land the company plane at the same airport.

21 Chris Whitcomb, *Transcript,* May 7, 1985, 1.; Julie Sell, *Berkshire Eagle,* March 14, 1985, 16, and March 30, 1985, 1.

22 Mark White, "Brown Street Revisited: Rank and file dissent, management harassment and an uncertain future persists," *Labor Connection,* August, 1986, 4.

23 Susan C. Phillips, "Anger, burnout, pride feed Sprague's Brown St. rebellion," *Berkshire Eagle,* May 27, 1986.

24 White, 4. One Brown Street employee, Daniel Perreault, who had served on the negotiating committee and opposed concessions, had this to say about workers who supported the givebacks: "They understand there are cuts in vacation and holidays. But they can't understand why people are against (the contract) when it means the plant might close. 'Half a loaf is better than none,' they say. I've heard that so often I could scream." One very veteran employee, Vera Lombardi, in her forty-fourth year at Brown Street, saw the present struggle in the context of the ten-week 1970 strike: "We were fighting for better wages, for vacations. You have to work for these things . . . . The younger people don't realize . . . [Sprague] never gave us anything we didn't fight for" (Phillips).

25 Commonwealth Sprague subsequently moved to Curran Highway and was sold to Eaton Corporation in 2003. Vishay Intertechnology bought the Wet & Foil operation in 1991 from what Penn Central called Sprague Technologies, Incorporated (The STI Group), but left North Adams in

1995. Japan's Sanken Electric purchased the controversial Sprague Semiconductor facility in Worcester in 1989. That company remains profitably in business under the name Allegro Microsystems (Glenn Drohan, *Berkshire Eagle,* September 17, 1991, and John Sprague email, September, 2017).

As part of a transaction in 1992, American Financial Corporation increased its ownership in Sprague Technologies from what had been 32.5 percent to 80 percent. That led John Sprague to write, somewhat ruefully, "[I]n the eleven short years since the 1981 acquisition of Sprague Electric by the Penn Central Corporation, the once dominant force in electronic components will become an insurance company.

"That's right—*an insurance company!*" John Sprague, *Revitalizing U.S. Electronics: Lessons from Japan* (Boston: Butterworth-Heinemann, 1993), 249, emphasis in original.

26 *Berkshire Eagle*, December 8, 1983.

27 Ibid., March 26, 1984.

28 *Transcript*, April 23, 1985.

29 See Steve Early, "Strike Lessons from the Last Twenty-Five Years: Walking Out and Winning, *Against the Current*, Sept.–Oct, 2006, accessed January 15, 2017, http://wewww.solidarity-us.org/node/113 and Steve Early, *Embedded with Organized Labor: Journalistic Reflections on the Class War at Home* (New York: Monthly Review Press, 2009), 162–163, for some labor gains during the 1980s. On the whole, labor's retreat during the Reagan years, after the PATCO debacle, is stunning, as documented in Timothy J. Minchin, *Labor Under Fire: A History of the AFL-CIO since 1979* (Chapel Hill, NC: University of North Carolina Press, 2017). For the most part, labor gave up its most important weapon, the right to strike. In 1982, the Bureau of Labor Statistics reported on only 96 strikes of more than 1,000 people, and by 1988, just 40. Compare this with some 200 to 400 such strikes each year from 1945 to 1979 (70). Union organizing fell precipitously during the Reagan years as well, with over 8,000 elections for union representation in 1980 to just 4,152 in 1988 (141). Not surprisingly, from 1979 to 1989, the percentage of workers in unions (or union density) declined from 24.8 percent of the workforce to 16.8 percent (127).

30 *Berkshire Eagle*, May 1, 1985, and *Transcript*, May 1, 1985.

31 *Transcript*, May 8, 1985, and *Berkshire Eagle*, May 9, 1985.

32 Ibid., October 4, 1984.

33 James Niedbalski, "Ex-Adams workers to picket new store," *Transcript,* November 14, 1984, 1.

34 Kathleen Brunet, "Ex-Adams workers plan own supermarket," *Transcript,* September 13, 1985, 1.

35 John Townes, "Where the Workers Are the Owners," *New York Times*, June 12, 1988.

36 John Sullivan, "Store manager: 1-day sell-out no surprise," *Transcript,* August 9, 1990, 1.

37 *Transcript,* January 4, 1985, and *Berkshire Eagle,* February 5, 1985.

38 Julie Sell, "Sprague employees eyeing purchase," *Transcript,* March 2, 1985, 1.

39 Christopher Whitcomb, "Buyout plan KO'd?" *Transcript,* April 29, 1985.

CHAPTER TWENTY-THREE

BUILDING STRONG UNIONS AT NORTH ADAMS REGIONAL HOSPITAL

WHILE MANUFACTURING DECLINED nationally and with it the industrial unions that represented its production and office workers, the demand for health care services increased both nationally and locally. The community hospital, North Adams Regional Hospital (NARH), served for many years as a source for good jobs in North Berkshire. With the loss of Sprague, it became one of the area's major employers, along with Williams College and Massachusetts College of Liberal Arts (MCLA). Like the two colleges, the hospital had been in service for many years, starting operation in 1885. A fatal train accident in 1882 in the Hoosac Tunnel spurred the local population to establish a hospital, and three years later, after community organizing and fund-raising, it opened.[1]

Unlike industrial workers who won the right to collectively bargain in the 1930s, hospital employees had not been included in the original National Labor Relations Act, and were further hindered from organizing by the anti-labor Taft-Hartley Act of 1947. Pressure for health care workers to gain bargaining rights grew, and they won those rights with 1974 federal legislation.[2] Within two years, registered nurses at NARH had organized a chapter of the Massachusetts Nurses Association (MNA). Four years after that, in 1980, the hospital's technical and service staff had formed a chapter of the Service Employees International Union (SEIU).

One would have to credit the social movements of the 1960s for improving the organizing atmosphere and, for the nurses, the growing power of feminism. As one historian of nursing history wrote, "By 1970, women were working longer, interrupting their work less frequently and spending the majority of their child-rearing years in the workplace . . . and working because economically they needed to do so. Therefore [nurses] joined other women in asserting their right to receive adequate remuneration for their efforts and organized to make their claims known." Early on, nurses fought for safe staffing levels, and, in one study, 60 percent of nurses who engaged in strikes in Connecticut and Rhode Island reported that their actions led to increased staffing. Not surprisingly, staffing would be a critical issue for NARH nurses.[3]

Mary McConnell and Ruth O'Hearn served as co-chairs of the NARH MNA chapter for many years.[4] Mary grew up in North Adams, the third generation of a family with roots in northern Italy, French Canada, and Sweden. Her grandfather worked as a baker at DiLego's Diner, and both her parents, like so many of their generation in North Berkshire, found employment at Sprague Electric in the 1940s and 1950s.[5]

After high school and marriage, Mary worked as a service representative for the phone company in Hartford, and years later she remembered not understanding why her fellow employees went on strike. They did, after all, make "very good money." Not until she became an RN at NARH, working on a daily basis, did she realize the importance of the union, particularly in trying to improve staffing.

Ruth grew up in a strong union environment in Connecticut. Her father was a Teamster, and her mother, who worked at Hartford Hospital, helped organize the aides there. After high school and marriage, Ruth settled down in Readsboro, Vermont. She began her nursing career as an LPN, working in a long-term facility in North Adams. She knew she "always wanted to help people," and was grateful that she had grown up with two important role models. Deciding to pursue her RN degree, she earned it at Greenfield Community College in 1995 and began working at NARH in 1999.

Mary had chaired the local union chapter since 1994, and Ruth joined her five years later, soon after she started work at the hospital. According to Ruth, the key issue was "staffing, staffing, staffing"; the union focus was on safety for patients and for nurses as well. The workforce had seemed like a "very tight-knit community," and supportive of the union. Out of a total of 110 RNs at the hospital's closing, only a couple had paid an agency fee, rather than joining the union.

On the SEIU side, Jackie Rhinemiller, an LPN, served as chief steward from the early 1980s until 1986. She first worked at NARH from 1970 until 1975 when she left to raise a family. She returned in 1979 and noticed a significant change in atmosphere and work. "[T]here already had been two different administrators, and the director of nursing was still there, but she was leaving. And there was a lot of . . . unhappiness. You know, people were getting disciplined for being out sick; people . . . weren't getting raises . . . . [T]he postings for jobs went by whoever they wanted to give it to."

The hospital brought in more administrators from outside the area, and what Jackie had remembered about a family type atmosphere from her first stint at the hospital had dissipated. Not surprisingly, 1979 was the year that the SEIU unionization drive started. At that time, Jackie didn't know much about unions. She couldn't recall the word "union" even being mentioned in her home "or out on the street." She had grown up in a working-class family of French-Canadian background, the fourth generation of her family to live in North Berkshire. Her father had a variety of jobs that included farming, delivering milk, and working at a supermarket, and at Arnold Print Works in Adams. For the most part, Jackie's mother was a full-time homemaker, but she also worked in a doctor's office. One of four siblings, Jackie remembered, "We all slept in one room in two different beds."

Mike O'Brien, who would become SEIU chapter chair or president, arrived at the hospital in 1977. While he didn't have the experience that Jackie had of an earlier stint at the hospital, during his first years he did recognize that a shift was taking place. NARH's long-time administrator, George Lerrigo, had hired Mike. At the time, many considered the hospital a close, well-knit place, with a small town, "family" atmosphere reminiscent of Sprague Electric before the late 1960s. Lerrigo played the role of "the good father," comparable to R.C. Sprague. Lerrigo was personable and seemed to know everyone's name, something that R.C. Sprague had tried to accomplish. The hospital emphasized the importance of extra-curricular activities, hosting Christmas parties and summer picnics, in a familial Sprague-like manner.

But families can often be run on a top-down, authoritarian style—e.g., "we've always done it this way"—and Mike soon realized that he and others in the respiratory therapy department had few well-defined rights. The changes that Jackie had mentioned had become obvious: the hospital seemed to be becoming a colder place, more "business oriented, not patient-care oriented." Workers also felt underpaid; they wanted more security, and knew that "the hospital wasn't going to protect" them. One frustrated nursing assistant reached out to the SEIU for organizing help. SEIU, out of Boston, sent a representative who made house visits. He talked to members of the technical staff (respiratory, x-ray, LPNs), service staff (housekeeping, dietary, orderly), maintenance, security, and business (pharmacy, medical records) staffs about the value of having a union. The hospital responded to the threat of organizing with small raises, though without changes in the work rules.

It took Mike a while to get close to the union idea, but "by 1979 [he] could see where there were areas where a union would be a good idea." He started going to the union house meetings, and got involved in organizing. By 1980, a solid nucleus of technical and service staff supported the union, and, after an election, a chapter of SEIU 285 was formed. At that time, only the technical and service staff joined, with the others lacking the votes to become members. Perhaps because of his college degree and the trust they saw in him, Mike's fellow workers asked him to serve as chapter chair. He agreed. Being chair meant acting as liaison between the chapter and headquarters in Boston, as well as serving as leader/president of the chapter. So Mike began a thirty-three-year career as chair, which lasted until his retirement from the hospital in 2013. He may hold the regional record for longevity in leading a local union.

During his decades of service, Mike developed a reputation for knowing the contract and being willing to talk to management to defend it, though in a respectful way. In his own words, he said of his colleagues:

> [They] weren't that involved or interested in becoming union activists. That's very plain to see in between contract periods . . . . Membership's not interested or involved until new contract time . . . . One thing I've learned is if you want to get something accomplished, you have to do a lot of groundwork. At least getting the members in the mindset of possibly going out on strike, you have to start and educate them and keep them informed all along. You can't go up to them one day and say, "This is what we have. This is what they want to take from us or do to us. Do you want to strike?" It'll leave them cold. You have to bring them along and keep them informed.

At roughly the same time that Mike began his involvement with the union, so did Jackie. It took her a while. When the union organizer invited her to a house meeting, the first couple of times she said, "No," but the third time was a "charm," and she said "O.K." This was the same time that the hospital administration was sending notices to employee homes, going over all the reasons that a union wasn't needed, and promising raises, benefits, and a "big open door policy." They also approached employees at work with their anti-union arguments.

Pro-union employees did talk to others on the job, but had to do it out of earshot of administrators. The RNs, already unionized, seemed to be supportive, but stayed uninvolved, content with their own status. SEIU, meanwhile, hoped to organize not only the LPNs but also the full technical, clerical, maintenance, and service personnel. Differences emerged over which departments would be covered, and, although SEIU won an election within the year, the local didn't encompass some of the less "professional" employees.

With unionization, Jackie remembered enjoying more rights on the job. With the union in place, if there was a problem, administration had to respond to grievances. In 1982, one of the LPN stewards had to take a military leave, and Jackie agreed to replace him, to serve as steward. She later recalled:

> Going in to administration, I was pretty much afraid. I didn't know what to say or how to say it . . . . They were still my bosses and I couldn't distinguish myself any differently—being an employee and a steward. But then we had some training instructions that were real helpful and we had our first assertiveness training class. This was the first class they had for stewards at Berkshire Community College and that's where I went . . . a six week program.

Jackie remembered how the training helped her:

> I knew my rights. I knew what I could and couldn't do as a steward. I just started questioning a lot. And people would come and ask [about] problems or whatever. That's when I really became a little more active . . . . I felt people's rights were being violated. And I studied the contract more and I felt more comfortable after a couple of months."

Respected by her fellow employees for her union work, Jackie won election twice more, and then became chief steward.

It was a big job. When she had returned to the hospital in 1979 she'd worked part-time, twenty-four hours a week, but in 1982, as chief steward, she estimated she spent as much time on those responsibilities as on her actual nursing work. "I worked out my schedules and I wanted to do it and I really liked it," she said. "I just wanted to become more active . . . . I just felt . . . there were some issues that needed to be heard. And the people [said], 'We'll back you up, Jackie, if you . . . could be the spokesperson . . . .' Most people . . . didn't really understand what a union was . . . and what their rights were. And I enjoyed doing all that."

Fortunately, Jackie's husband, Dave, supported her union work and helped a lot with the care of their four children. Jackie had many meetings and often had to go out of town. "If it wasn't for [my husband], there's no way that I could have done all that I've done," she said. But it was the early 1980s, and a high-ranking woman union officer seemed to be a rarity for many. Jackie remembered walking into grievance meetings where the male administrators would focus on her male colleague to talk about sports, not "the issues," leaving her feeling invisible. When she went down to the Central Labor Council in Pittsfield, she would be the only woman, and they would ask her to "pour the coffee and pass the sandwiches," to which she responded:

> No, that's not my job, and if you want a maid, go . . . out and get a maid. I'm part of the group. I mean if you guys want a cup of coffee, you can walk up there and get it. They say, "Well, why are you here if you're not divorced or . . . ." It's like they didn't see many women in labor being involved in those types of positions . . . . You know they would support GE and everybody would go down, picket with those people, put statements in the paper and when it came to our organization [need for picketing help at Hillcrest Hospital or NARH], it was like they're not there—and I hounded them on the phone.

> I said, "Look, you know we're represented by you and . . . be here! I embarrassed them until they came."

When Jackie went out to different workplaces to get support for union issues—for example, for strike votes—she found that some of the male union leaders she had to communicate with still felt uncomfortable dealing with a woman. She did, however, find support and "generosity" also from other unions.

At NARH, Mike O'Brien remembered the 1983 negotiations as having been the toughest, a time when the chapter came closest to striking. With talks at a standstill, at the eleventh hour, the hospital took out an ad in the *Transcript,* advertising openings for all union jobs. Mike said:

> At the time I thought it would scare our people and they'd back down, but . . . it infuriated them that management could do such a tactic, plus we got a lot of support from the community. When the community saw what kind of wages we were getting paid, they were shocked they were so low. As it turned out, it really backfired on management. It pushed us over the edge in support. But we needed other conditions. The members wouldn't walk out over wages.

They also wanted assurances that once they came to work, they would put in a day's work, and not be told to leave if the census seemed too low. Just as staffing had always been a key issue for the RNs, Mike and SEIU shared worries about workers being overloaded.

Probably the longest-serving chief steward, Julie Blanchard took the reins of the post after Jackie left the hospital, and Julie held that position from 1988 to 2006. On her mother's side, Julie had Irish roots and, on her father's, French-Canadian. The fourth generation of her family in the area, she lived in Clarksburg. The work experiences of the generations before her were reminiscent of the working-class occupations of so many in the North Adams area: chambermaid, security guard, bartender, and machine shop operator. And they worked at a variety of familiar places like Arnold Print Works, Sprague, Excelsior/Crane, Bounty Fair, and Green Mountain Racetrack.

When Julie became active in the union at the hospital, she remembered that her grandfather, a union bartender, told her of how proud he was of the path she was taking. Julie graduated in 1977 from McCann Technical School and did a post-grad year at Drury High School to become a medical assistant. She soon started a thirty-five-year career at NARH: twenty-one years at rehabilitation services, and fourteen as a phlebotomist. She had started working as a temporary employee, not a union member, but soon realized that if she had a problem on the job, she would need help, group support.

When she became a permanent employee and a member of SEIU, she decided to get involved in the union, and her section elected her steward in 1983. She recalled receiving "wonderful training" both in North Adams and in Boston, learning about grievance work and building her confidence. She knew the contract well and won lots of grievances. The years of experience that Julie and other union activists had gave them an edge when dealing with new administrators. They knew "past practice" well, better than the managers, who never seemed to stay too long. Julie continued to learn, going to arbitration hearings in Springfield and Boston, and attending state conventions.

A second major shift in management behavior occurred in 1999 and continued on into the next century, as the hospital embarked on an expansion program, stepping away from the small, community full-service hospital that had served the region for over a century. In 1999, NARH purchased two properties in Williamstown: Sweetbrook, a long-term nursing and rehabilitation center, and Sweetwood, a retirement community. Called the "Sweets" by the employees, the deals turned out sour, leading to huge debts and the ultimate bankruptcy of the hospital. Not content to simply borrow and spend millions on the "Sweets," NARH also added a parking garage and renovated the main building. Making the main campus more attractive seemed a priority of management, under the theory, "if we build it, they will come."

For the campus expansion, the hospital initiated a community drive to garner contributions from the area residents. Many NARH employees pledged money for the effort, with management taking their contributions out of their paychecks. Years later, with the end of NARH, a plaque by the elevator in the front lobby lists the names of the employees who made contributions. As Ruth O'Hearn put it, "We believed in the North Adams hospital and the need for the community to have it." While both unions worked diligently to represent their co-workers, to provide them with a living wage, good working conditions, and safety for themselves and their patients, they lacked the power to stop management's empire-building, and could not stop its abrupt closing in 2014.

Billboards and lawn signs help connect RNs to the community (Seider photo).

NOTES

1 Paul Donovan, *North Adams Regional Hospital: A Historical Perspective, Part I: 1882–1910* (author's email address: emsportmed2015@gmail.com).

2 See Eleanor G. Feldbaum, "Collective Bargaining in the Health Sector: A Focus on Nurses," *Journal of Health and Human Resources Administration,* Vol. 4, No. 2 (Fall, 1981), 148–166, and "Our History, District 1199C," 1199cnuhhce.org/C1_OurHistory.html.

3 Feldbaum, 150, 152.

4 The following information from MNA and SEIU leadership comes from phone interviews with the author in September 2017, and earlier personal interviews with two SEIU leaders, Mike O'Brien and Jackie Rhinemiller, in the mid-1980s.

5 See interview with Paul F. DiLego about the diner in Joe Manning, *Steeples: Sketches of North Adams* (Florence, MA: Flatiron Press, 1997), 132–138, and more on the diner in Joe Manning, *Disappearing Into North Adams* (Florence, MA: Flatiron Press, 2001), 53, 54, and 323.

CHAPTER TWENTY-FOUR:

THE REGION GAINS A MUSEUM AND LOSES A HOSPITAL

"Historically, museums follow affluence, they don't usually create it."

—James Welu, Director of the Worcester Art Museum[1]

"MASS MoCA is like, well, like the savior of the community."

—Bob Canedy, Security Guard, MASS MoCA[2]

"They're not going to close a hospital. They just can't."

—Robin Simonetti, short stay unit nurse, one of 530 employees who lost their jobs

"[I]f the government can bail out the banks because they're too big to fail, we have to let our government officials know that hospitals are too big to fail."

—Dick Dassatti, North County Cares Coalition activist

ECONOMIC SETBACKS

BY THE MID-1980s, with the loss of manufacturing jobs, North Berkshire residents found themselves confronting the same set of problems that other historic industrial communities faced. Besides the layoffs at Sprague Electric, over 500 additional production jobs had gone by the wayside in 1984. The situation appeared so grim that Holly Taylor, a veteran local reporter, wrote: "The outlook is the worst since Berkshire Hathaway . . . pulled out in 1957, leaving . . . a jobless rate of 22 percent . . . ."[3] From 1984 to 1990, fourteen manufacturing plants in North Berkshire had closed, leaving 5,000 workers without employment. Besides the Sprague closing, the shutdown of Adams Print Works (formerly Arnold Print Works) hit the area hard. The company could not be saved, even with an eighteen-month reorganization and a $3.3 million loan transfusion from private and public sources.[4]

A workers' assistance center study concluded that over three-quarters of those who had lost their jobs wanted to stay in North Berkshire, but where would the new jobs come from? One possible solution came in 1986, when local activists and academics joined together and founded the Northern Berkshire Health and Human Services Coalition. The coalition had the single objective of trying to deal with the critical economic and social problems facing the region.[5]

In their 1982 path-breaking book, *The Deindustrialization of America,* economists Barry Bluestone and Bennett Harrison gave a name to the phenomenon that had hit the gritty Berkshires and much of the rest of Rust Belt America. The authors defined deindustrialization as the "widespread, systematic disinvestment in the nation's basic productive capacity . . . ." They wrote that "disinvestment" occurred, despite the fact that the corporations closing the factories—whether it be Penn Central, in control of Sprague in North Adams; GE in Pittsfield; Nabisco in Chicago; or RCA in Monticello, Indiana—remain flush with cash, and more than profitable. Rather, they decided to invest in other manufacturing locations, inside or outside of the United States, or in other sectors of the economy, including finance. The reasons were to achieve higher profits, but the results were "shuttered factories, displaced workers, and a newly emerging group of ghost towns."[6] Factory closings ordered by conglomerates, such as Penn Central, appeared to be even more devastating than those coming from independent, smaller companies.

In just four years, from 1981 to 1985, an estimated 11.5 million workers became unemployed due to deindustrialization, roughly 12 percent of the national labor force.[7] In the middle of the Rust Belt, Milwaukee's manufacturing job loss of 56,000 from 1979 to 1983 surpassed the city's job loss during the Great Depression.[8] And while the national media focused on the Midwest in stories on deindustrialization, the phenomenon also impacted New York State and New England, and even industrial communities in the South and California.[9]

The new jobs created after deindustrialization generally paid less, offered few if any benefits, and lacked security. Only half of the new jobs from 1979 to 1986 provided middle-income wages, compared to nearly 90 percent of new jobs from 1963 to 1973.[10] The state of Massachusetts added nearly 500,000 service-sector jobs in the 1980s and 1990s, but most of those that paid well could be found in the greater Boston area.[11] In North Berkshire, the only employment growth in the early 1980s emanated from the low-paying service sector. The best service-sector jobs—at Williams College, North Adams State College (soon to be renamed Massachusetts College of Liberal Arts), and North Adams Regional Hospital—stood in high demand, and could only employ a minority of the population. With the layoffs at Sprague accelerating in 1984, Williams College received 600 requests for non-teaching, service employment during the first week of September alone.[12] Absent other opportunities, many workers turned to X-Tyal, despite the fact that it provided a low-paying, unstable, and unsafe work environment.[13]

In 1986, North Adams had the highest unemployment rate in the state, ranging anywhere from 25 to 30 percent. In other social measures—teen pregnancy, child sex and physical abuse, and the high school dropout rate—the city fared quite poorly.[14] Clearly, new job opportunities and economic gains were needed, but none appeared on the horizon.

To make matters worse, the kinds of social programs to aid the unemployed and poor that had been developed during the New Deal and the 1960s War on Poverty were being dismantled.

Attacks on unions—the key institution that protected the rights and wages of workers—accelerated, particularly in 1981, after President Ronald Reagan fired the striking unionized air traffic controllers who were members of the Professional Air Traffic Controllers (PATCO). Reagan's action "made union-busting just another management program to reduce labor costs."[15]

MASS MoCA COMES TO TOWN

In 1982, North Adams Regional Hospital celebrated its centennial. Besides fully serving the region's medical needs, the hospital also stood as a major job provider. At the same time, the blue-collar job outlook looked grim, with the decline of Sprague and other smaller industrial plants. When Sprague closed in 1985, North Adams was faced with acres of empty productive space and no manufacturing suitors willing to step in.

While some still hoped for good-paying industrial jobs, tourism had moved to the top spot in local economic development plans. In February 1986, a big tourist idea arrived from outside the city. Thomas Krens, the director of the Williams College Museum of Art in the neighboring town of Williamstown, called on John Barrett, the blue-collar mayor of North Adams. Krens had connections with the world-renowned Guggenheim Museum in New York and represented an elite college located in Williamstown. The men seemed to be unlikely allies, but before long they reached an agreement to transform the Sprague buildings on Marshall Street into what would become the world's largest museum of contemporary art. More importantly for the region, the museum would be an engine of economic development.

Krens represented a new type of museum director, one who merged a background in art history with one in business, a director-entrepreneur as interested in expanding and building new museums as in bringing in popular exhibitions of art. He may have seen the vacant buildings in North Adams as a depository for the art that New York's Guggenheim didn't have room for, but in any case, his proposal called for a brand new museum of contemporary art. An up-and-comer in the museum world, Krens was a big guy, and a strong exponent for his point of view. He wanted the Sprague properties for the museum and had no problem providing the economic data that would impress the political elite in North Adams and the state for the project's economic development possibilities.

With his young assistant and Williams College graduate, Joseph Thompson, Krens wrote a two-volume business plan, which argued that the museum would be an economic benefit to North Adams and the North Berkshire region. (The fact that both authors had strong reasons for wanting the museum to become a reality, and that they hoped to receive state funds for it, would seem to question their neutrality or even objectivity in researching and writing the crucial report, yet no media outlet or government official raised that issue.) Relying on previous studies of culture-based development and economic models, they estimated that the museum would generate over 600 full-time equivalent jobs. They also anticipated numerous tenants in offices constructed within the museum complex, as well as a small hotel and restaurant on site. In addition, Krens and Thompon assumed that the Greylock Glen development project in neighboring Adams that was primed to include numerous "second homes" would bring an additional audience to the museum complex. (That version of Greylock Glen never got off the ground.)

Moving from the economic benefits of the museum, Krens and Thompson heralded its image-enhancing function for North Adams, a city not only devastated by unemployment, but one whose residents reportedly felt defeated.[16] Quoting from the Governor's Task Force, they noted their objective: "To promote the Northern Berkshire Region both to its residents and to others in order to build a positive self-image and to attract visitors and business." They further wrote that the Massachusetts Museum of Contemporary Art (or MASS MoCA as it came to be called), "[would] become . . . an unmistakable gesture of community achievement, and [that] community achievement is a vital factor in providing regional and personal esteem."[17]

Krens and Thompson then quoted from a 1983 report on Philadelphia, written by Michael Rubin and Theodore Hershberg:

> Perhaps the most important measure of a city's attractiveness is the quality of life it affords its residents. The term "quality of life" implies a comprehensive assessment of the accessibility and value of a wide variety of human services and facilities. *It is replacing "standard of living" as an index of general welfare.* (Italics added.)

For area residents whose standard of living had been in decline from massive deindustrialization and whose economic future appeared bleak, Krens and Thompson's seeming acceptance of a different meaning of "quality of life," should, at a minimum, have raised eyebrows. However, one should remember that the business plan had been written not for laid-off factory workers but for business and political elites. Interestingly, one of the museum's biggest backers whose disapproval would have doomed the museum's chances, Mayor John Barrett, also saw the psychological advantages of the museum yet downplayed its job-creating function:

> [Tom] Krens was saying it would create 600 jobs, I didn't see it that way. [T]his was an image game. If you ever go back and read about Ronald Reagan . . . . I didn't agree with anything he said but you know what, I adopted his philosophy: make people feel good even if isn't good. And if we could create that excitement in the community, people who had been downtrodden for years—you know, little or no hope— . . . they would start to believe in the community and people would come here . . . . That's what it was all about with me from day one: how can I use this to better the community? It went far beyond my wildest expectations.[18]

Without a well-publicized alternative proposal for the huge Sprague property, and with residents hungry for jobs, most residents of North Adams appeared supportive of the museum. Governor Michael Dukakis, who often vacationed in the Berkshires, liked the idea, and in 1988, the Legislature approved a bill granting $35 million for the development of the museum. That grant proved to be decisive for the museum's success. As Director Joe Thompson remembered it years later, "Absent that, there would have been no MASS MoCA."[19]

Not everyone expressed enthusiasm about the overall plan. What impact would it have on the poor? Some raised concerns about escalating rents in the working class neighborhood that bordered the prospective museum. Would the service-sector jobs that would be created as a result of the museum—part of the 600-job promise from Krens and Thompson—pay anything close to a living wage? Further, local artists worried that they might be shut out of the museum and access to the tens of thousands of tourists that MoCA officials anticipated. Still, 10,000 local residents signed a petition calling for the museum to be built.[20]

Anthropologist Cathy Stanton interviewed local residents, and many saw no other alternative for an economic revival than the museum. At best, it presented a mixed picture. After all, for former textile and Sprague workers who had produced cloth and electronic parts for most of their lives, they would "hav[e] . . . to come to terms with the fact that in the absence of other good options, they now find themselves becoming [a] service econom[y] . . . for wealthier regions and populations."[21] I heard that same concern voiced by some of the two-dozen North Berkshire workers that I interviewed during the same time period:

> So what am I going to do when I'm 45? Am I going to wash dishes or am I going to clean up rooms at the Glen? . . . I don't want to do that . . . . I don't just want to survive . . . I want to be able to improve my life . . . . I do not want to be a guard at an art museum . . . . North Adams

> is a grubby, beautiful . . . town . . . . I think it's marvelous.

Concern over low-wage service-sector jobs led one respondent to worry about the need to work two jobs and its consequences: "Working 'sunrise to sundown just to make ends meet' is no way to 'enjoy the Berkshires.'"[22]

Soon after he proposed MASS MoCA, Thomas Krens left the project to run the Guggenheim Museum, and Joe Thompson became the prospective museum's coordinator. At the same time, the state economy, the so-called "Massachusetts Miracle," went into decline, and a prime museum backer, Governor Michael Dukakis, lost his bid for the presidency. Unfortunately for the project, Dukakis's successor, Republican Governor William Weld, voiced skepticism about the museum's financing.

James Welu, director of the Worcester Art Museum and supporter of MoCA, shared his worries. "A major concern is whether a constituency could be developed to support such a large undertaking into the future," Welu said. And then, getting to the crux of the matter, he added, "Historically, museums follow affluence, they don't usually create it."[23]

Governor Weld told the museum planners to return $688,000 in planning and design funds that Dukakis had delivered in his last week in office. Weld also challenged the museum's supporters to raise more private funds to supplement the state monies. When museum supporters met the fund-raising challenge, Weld came back on board to back the museum.[24]

THE STRUGGLE FOR HOUSING SHELTER

Just as deindustrialization—as a word—had only recently entered the American vocabulary, "homelessness" (hardly mentioned in the late 1970s) had now become part of the American lexicon and, for millions of Americans, a reality in their lives. Demand for low-cost housing had risen as more and more Americans saw their paychecks diminish, but, at the same time, the availability of such housing had contracted. After 1970, from an estimated surplus of about 2.4 million low-income units, a dramatic shift in the national housing market meant a deficit of 3.7 million low-income units in 1985. The federal government had virtually disappeared from the market. In 1978, the Housing and Urban Development budget for subsidized housing stood at $32.2 billion, and ten years later the Reagan administration had slashed it to $9.2 billion. In addition, the government reduced incentives for private developers to build low-income housing and deregulated the savings and loan industry, which led to high interest rates for mortgages. And for those not able to buy, rents kept going up. The result: from 1.2 million to 2 million Americans were homeless by the late 1980s. Not willing to take any responsibility for the crisis, in 1984 President Reagan remarked: "People who are sleeping on the grates . . . the homeless . . . are homeless, you might say, by choice."[25]

The housing reality in North Berkshire reflected the problems nationwide. Already one third of households in North Adams faced monthly rents deemed "unaffordable." And now the publicity given to the coming of MASS MoCA and the Greylock Glen project in Adams heightened fears that gentrification would make its way to the area and raise rents for low-income tenants even more. After all, Thomas Krens himself had speculated that, in the future, River Street would be like Fifth Avenue, New York. Local realtors welcomed that future. For Mike Deep, it meant "We're catching up with the rest of the world . . . . North Adams has a new image, and the city feels better about itself." However, those households who could not catch up and needed subsidies to obtain rental units from the North Adams Housing Authority faced a lengthy waiting list.[26]

The cry for affordable housing grew, and by 1987 the local press, including the *Transcript*, the *Berkshire Eagle*, and the *Advocate*, reported extensively on the crisis. A new citizens group, the North Adams Tenants Organization (NATO), began organizing, and raised the issue of rent control as a way to stabilize the increased cost of housing. Michael Wilber, former union president at X-Tyal, served as chair of NATO and was one of sixteen candidates running for City Council—only two of whom supported rent control. Opponents saw it as "a bureaucratic intrusion in the free market" and instead called for more housing to be built. Ironically, at roughly the same time, the City Council, responding to pressure from neighbors who didn't want a thirty-six-unit housing development in their "backyard," voted against it.

Michael Wilber lost his Council race, but NATO continued to function, and the rent control issue gathered more support. Tenants packed City Council meetings and "almost uniformly spoke of sudden rent increases with no improvements to the property, while landlords . . . warned that rent control was discriminatory regulation of business, would discourage further investment and job creation in the city, and could lead to abandoned buildings and other problems." Wilber called for a sizeable committee, including local residents, to study the issue, but Council instead appointed a Rent Control Subcommittee composed of only three, all from the Council. In an editorial entitled "What's 'fair' in rent wars?" the *Transcript* reviewed the pro and con arguments, and stated the following:

> Rents are leaping, in some areas, more than 100 percent . . . . And the elderly, which make up more than 65 percent of the city's population, and who live on fixed incomes, just can't pay those prices . . . . Residents have pressured the City Council to take some action on rising rents in North County. That pressure is bolstered by Help Line's recent announcement that its calls about placement for homeless people has increased mightily . . . . There's no way to please everybody completely . . . . But it is the renters, especially, who look to the council for the definition of "fair."[27]

The subcommittee said "No" to rent control, but the NATO campaign continued, and they invited Council members and the press to inspect the conditions of rental units in the city. In two press reports on the inspection, readers learned of apartments with leaky pipes, a room without glass windows, unsteady fire escape stairs, poor wiring, cockroaches, and the lack of a second escape door. Wilber "hoped the tour would encourage councilors to push for stricter enforcement of city building codes." He went on to say that complaints to City Hall don't get filed. In response, Mayor John Barrett, who refused an invitation to go on the tour, stated that no complaints on the apartment in question had been filed. Then he added: "I'm tired of these people. They [NATO] haven't lifted one finger to help . . . out the city. They just set their own agenda for their own political reasons."[28]

Editorially, the *Transcript* viewed the role of NATO much differently than did the mayor: "NATO has done its part in bringing the issue of substandard rentals to public attention, by its very existence, by its tours, and by making City Council take notice." The newspaper exhorted property owners to respond.[29]

Just prior to the tour, a front-page article in the *Advocate* illustrated the responses of landlords to claims of substandard conditions in their rental units. Charles P. Norcross, co-owner of thirteen buildings with rental units, "blamed careless tenants for costing landlords thousands of dollars in otherwise unnecessary repairs." From Berkshire Valley Management partner Steven C. Morrison's view, "70 percent of all violations are caused by tenants and 30 percent from daily usage." Morrison went on to say that "landlords can limit tenant-caused damage" by "a more thorough screening of prospective renters." He spoke of a new North Adams landlord association that "will begin sharing information about good and bad tenants . . . . " Of that proposal, tenants rights' advocate Enid Shields responded, "This tenant blacklisting could only have a further chilling effect on renters who complained, formally or informally, of any substandard housing conditions."[30]

The reality of an increasing homeless population led the region's leading non-profit, the Northern Berkshire Health and Human Services Coalition, to set up a task force to bring in shelter services for those in need. To support the effort, Alan Bashevkin, the coalition's coordinator, along with two students from the University of Massachusetts Medical School, wrote a 1988 policy paper, backed up with their research findings, entitled "The Need for Comprehensive Shelter Services in the Northern Berkshire Area."[31]

Among their findings:

- Emergency Help Line calls that related to homelessness increased by 27 percent from 1985–87.
- Actual cases of homelessness were on the rise, with 44 percent of the cases involving families.
- The length of homelessness averaged 18.3 weeks.
- The vast majority of homeless people were in fact local.
- 50 percent of the households interviewed had at least one member who had been a steady full-time employee, but had lost his or her job through cutbacks or plant closings, or in some cases, they were single mothers who had to quit work to care for their children.
- A shortage of housing subsidies kept some from attaining rentals.

Finally, the task force recognized that, while numerous agencies provided helpful services, those services needed to be centralized.[32]

Two years later, with the help of the Northern Berkshire Community Development Corporation that was supported by state and local funds, the Family Life Support Center (FLSC) opened in Adams. The facility, a large house in Adams just across the town line to North Adams, provided housing for both individuals and families and programs to prevent homelessness. The FLSC was also called the Louison House, in honor of the decades of service that Terry Louison provided North Berkshire through her advocacy for the poor that went back to the 1960s when she first served as director of the local Community Action Agency.

NATIONAL NEO-LIBERAL POLICIES CONTINUE

The cutbacks continued under Democratic administrations as well as Republican ones, and were highlighted by policies promulgated by President Bill Clinton. Clinton pushed hard to "end welfare as we know it," joining Republicans in changing a program that had originally been fashioned to help mothers and their dependent children into a workfare program, which often took moms away from their children during the day. He also signed legislation increasing the length of prison terms for non-violent offenders, thus accelerating the growth of the prison population, a trend that hit African Americans particularly hard. He also turned against his labor union base by getting the North American Free Trade Agreement (NAFTA) passed, an act which only increased the loss of middle class jobs in the Midwest and Northeast.

The kinds of policies that Reagan, Clinton, and successive presidents—including Bush, Obama, and Trump—championed have come to be labeled "neoliberal." They include promoting the private market; cutting back on consumer safety, environmental, and financial regulation; reducing aid to the poor and working classes; cutting taxes on corporations and the rich, and privatizing public resources.[33] All the while, the military budget saw increases and American wars continued and accelerated. At the same time, the Democratic Party moved further and further to the right, depending on and supporting Wall Street banks, ignoring and even growing hostile to its previous connection with labor unions.[34]

MASS MoCA OPENS

By the late 1980s and early 1990s, the Massachusetts Museum of Contemporary Art grew closer and closer to reality.

The road ahead proved not to be without controversy as disputes over poorly designed retraining programs and the paucity of local construction workers hired for the renovation work broke out.[35] In 1995, below a huge banner headline, **"MoCA HAPPENS!"**, the *Transcript* covered an official ceremony at the courtyard of the former Sprague complex before 300 people. Lt. Governor Paul Cellucci signed a document certifying that the museum had satisfied all needed requirements and would be funded by the state. Under a subhead, "Cheers, tears of joy in city," *Transcript* reporter Rosemary Jette waxed poetic about the future awaiting North Adams: "Jubilation, pride and a sense of excitement not seen in the city for years mixed with the brilliant sunshine and clear blue sky, which were the perfect backdrop to what each official spokesperson at the event described as a cornerstone on the economic growth expected to follow the creation of the cultural factory of the 21st century."[36]

Four years later, on Memorial Day 1999, the museum opened to great acclaim amidst a crowd of 10,000. Thirteen years had passed since Thomas Krens first broached the idea to Mayor Barrett. Ironically, for a city that had put almost all of its eggs in the Sprague basket, only to be devastated when that company left, it seemed to be betting its whole purse on MoCA and what had come to be called the "creative economy." But could that new economy, powered by art and cultural innovation, be the answer? Would the shift from manufacturing work to service jobs—in hotels and inns, in gift shops, restaurants, and other retail outlets—provide local residents with a living wage and dignified work? Would those things be enough?[37]

In each of its first two years, MoCA attracted about 100,000 visitors.[38] In addition to the art, the museum offered films, concerts, and dance recitals. Over time, in the North Adams downtown, away from the museum, a mixture of the "old" and the "new" coexisted, with change being the constant. Long staples of the community, Molly's Bakery and Mr. Cobbler, closed, but so did a relative newcomer, Staples, the city's only big-box office supply store.

A year after MoCA opened, while vacancies still existed on Main Street, John Kifner of the *New York Times* wrote: "[m]ore than two-thirds of the town's shops are occupied." Kifner's upbeat article mentioned a "downtown-slick restaurant, 55 Main,"[39] a pricey business that clearly aimed at attracting tourists. Less than two years later, 55 Main had closed, and in 2001, Mayor Barrett faced a popular, youthful challenger in his reelection battle. Barrett's opponent, Paul Babeu, stood in front of the shuttered restaurant and blamed MoCA for inserting restaurants on its own site, thus taking business away from the city's downtown:

> When you allow restaurants and shops and all kinds of public businesses in MASS MoCA, how are we ever going to get these people to come to our downtown? . . . He [55 Main owner Ray Arsenault] is saying his business was dramatically impacted because of restaurants being allowed into MASS MoCA and an influx of multiple restaurants in the city.

Babeu went on to say that, if he had the power of the mayoralty and of the MoCA Commission head, "I would have never allowed that to take place . . . . We have created a city unto itself in MASS MoCA."[40]

Several other startups also failed after 55 Main, but later The Hub seemed successful. Less focused on the tourist trade, and with historical photos of North Adams on its walls, this restaurant seemed closer to the tradition of the previous longtime tenant, the Capitol Restaurant, a destination that always had been jammed with lunchtime patrons during the Sprague years.

Five years after MoCA's opening, a study by the museum claimed that the storefront occupancy rate had hit 75 percent, and that annual visitors to the museum had reached 120,000. But as of 2018, the Mohawk Theater remains, still waiting to be refurbished and reopened. Diagonally across the street, also in 2018, the Berkshire Food Project, housed in the

Congregational Church, stands as a reminder of the other North Adams, part of the "parallel universe" that the church's pastor, Reverend Jill Graham, often spoke of.[41]

Unlike Paul Babeu, Mayor John Barrett didn't chastise MoCA for bringing retail outlets that competed with Main Street onto its campus. Instead, the mayor blamed downtown property owners for failing to invest in their own locations. He claimed that, because they had not believed in MoCA, "They weren't ready for it. They didn't fix up their properties . . . . They had no faith." Barrett went on to state that all of the Main Street property owners resided in Williamstown, with one owner controlling "ninety-percent" of Main Street's north side. Barrett saw the property owners as being from outside of the North Adams community, and therefore uninterested in improving the city itself.[42]

THE PORCHES INN AND RENTAL HOUSING

One area that MoCA, the mayor, and a wealthy benefactor of MoCA wanted "cleaned up" was a block of River Street directly across from the museum. Old Victorian houses, many in need of repair, had apartments that offered low rent to poor and working-class families; not far from these homes stood a bar, a liquor store, the Harvest Soup Kitchen, and the Salvation Army. In the fall of 1999, Williams College alumnus John S. Wadsworth Jr. complained to Joe Thompson about the River Street view. According to Thompson:

> We were standing in the Mezzanine of Building 5 overlooking the Rauschenberg [painting], and you could look out those windows to the south and see our courtyard, and look to the north and see River Street . . . . He said something like "Oh, it's a shame. North Adams is looking so good, and yet when you look out these windows there's a mess out there." And I said something

> like "Well, someone like you could affect a transformation overnight if you wanted to."[43]

Wadsworth, then chairman of Morgan Stanley Asia Ltd., took on the challenge. He met with Nancy Fitzpatrick, whose family owned the iconic Red Lion Inn in Stockbridge as well as the retail business Country Curtains. She agreed to manage an inn that could replace the old housing; he agreed to contribute $5 million to the project. Less than two years later, The Porches Inn at MASS MoCA opened. Housed in six renovated row houses on River Street, it had fifty-two rooms, each with a television, high-speed internet access, a mini-bar, and antique furniture. The inn also sported a backyard lap pool and Jacuzzi area, several meeting rooms, and fourteen suites. When Porches opened in 2001, its prices ranged from $150 per night for a guest room to $430 a night for a two-bedroom suite.[44]

Just as MoCA replaced the Sprague manufacturing complex across the street, Porches stood as the successor to worker housing in those six buildings, undoubtedly occupied at some point by Sprague employees. Given the prices of the rooms at Porches, no former Sprague worker could have afforded to stay for a night. Ironically, according to a featured travel story in the *Boston Globe,* the more affluent guests who stay at the inn can enjoy morning breakfast, "delivered in bed, carried in 'galvanized metal lunch boxes workers used to carry . . . adorned with a small vase of flowers on the side.'"[45]

While it appeared that most neighborhood residents approved of the Porches project,[46] it was not without controversy. One lengthy article in an online newspaper by Marjorie Ransom and G.M. Heller detailed heavy pressure from the mayor's office to landlords to sell the buildings at low prices and to give the twenty-three tenants just thirty days to vacate their apartments. According to one resident, the new owners didn't offer her any help in getting a new rental. "Asked how she feels about having to move so quickly, she said, 'I've spent years buying paint and wallpaper to fix-up my place. I don't know where I'm going to go.'"[47]

At the time of the sale, Tina (Bushika) Holland, a single mom of two, had lived at 241 River Street for a few years, and "[d]espite the deterioration of the area, she enjoyed the comforts of a large apartment and some friendly neighbors." While there could be trouble in the neighborhood, for those living there "everybody looked out for everybody." Working for the landlord, Tina was in charge of "all the kids they hired" to make repairs. "The outsides looked like crap, but the insides were okay. Granted, [there was] wear and tear on the floor and paint chips and stuff. But most people kept [their apartments] up. They had carpets. Some of the apartments weren't too cool, but a lot of 'em were in good shape."

Ms. Holland heard rumors that the house would be sold, but her landlord assured her that it wouldn't happen. Two days later, she read in the paper that the house, indeed, had been sold. "It ended up the landlord locked me out. He allowed me just enough time to grab enough stuff to get me by for a few days." She didn't have time to empty her coolers and freezer, and by the time she found someone who would let her in, she "had to throw out everything . . . . Then I found this place on Union Street. I went from six really good-size rooms and an attic to four small rooms and no storage . . . . If I could, I'd go back to River Street in a heartbeat."[48]

Amidst the general rosy outlook on the neighborhood renaissance, neither the *Transcript* nor the *Berkshire Eagle* reported on the hardships faced by the evicted tenants.[49] In an interview before all the rehabilitation had been completed, Nancy Fitzpatrick, the Porches manager, stood in a messed-up apartment with broken fixtures on the floor and commented on the previous tenant:

> I think this does show something real about this community and the difficulty that some people in it are having with change. You know there's a certain amount of hostility in the way this was left by the people who left here . . . . And the so-called gentrification issues. You know, we're not going to avoid them. That's for sure."[50]

Extensive study of MoCA over its first seven years—and its varied effects on North Adams and North Berkshire—pointed out some improvements in housing stock, better self-images of the city, and greater integration of civic and community organizations in the area.[51] However, economically, by 2006, MoCA's contribution to both direct and indirect job creation totaled only 230, including some 77 museum employees, a far cry from the 600 full-time jobs that Thomas Krens and Joe Thompson had promised at the onset. Even eleven years later, in 2017, job creation had only reached 385, according to economist Stephen Sheppard, a bit under two-thirds of the founders' original goal.[52]

Despite the fact that the museum had not become the "engine of economic development" that it had promised, an introductory film on the museum's website begins with a smiling employee stating that MoCA was the "savior" of North Adams:

> When MASS MoCA came here, of course, it provided jobs. And it provided some place for the people to go, because until they came here, [between] the time that manufacturing ended and the time MASS MoCA began, there was really nothing—there was nothing. MASS MoCA is like, well, like the savior of the community.[53]

Historically, family incomes in North Adams lagged behind state and national averages. Toward the end of the Sprague years, in 1979, North Adams median family incomes had topped out at just 76 percent of the state median. Ten years later, after the Sprague closing and accelerating deindustrialization, that figure stood at 60 percent. In 1999, when MoCA opened, the percentage stood even lower, 54 percent. Ten years into MoCA, and admittedly with the economic crisis of 2007–8 in play, the percentage hadn't wavered (55 percent). Turning to the comparative unemployment rate between North Adams and the State of Massachusetts (a measure which historically saw the city's rate as higher than the state's), in 1999, the local rate was 19 percent higher than the state, a figure that had increased to 23 percent in 2009, ten years after MoCA's opening. By 2014, the difference had reached 32 percent.[54]

In a 2011 interview with the author, museum director Joseph Thompson made the point that North Adams had become more diverse since MoCA's opening, and that, while the downtown lacked the vibrancy of the 1960s and mid-1970s, more was happening there now than any time since Sprague had left, despite an occupancy rate of just 60–70 percent. When Thompson and Krens had written their business plan for the museum, they'd assumed that only about 5 percent of the visitors would be local (no more than 40 miles away), but that figure turned out to be 20 to 25 percent, reflecting more day trips and fewer tourists who needed to stay overnight, thus hindering the region's economy.

While he saw the museum doing "pretty well," not only artistically but also financially, Thompson told the author that MoCA's socio-economic impact had been "very slow." Some of that he blamed on the "market [being] remarkably slow to respond," due in part to the small number of local landlords on Main Street who did not rise to the occasion. (In that sense, he stood in agreement with former Mayor Barrett who had blamed the downtown landlords for their failure to invest in the new North Adams.)

Looking at the big picture, Thompson argued that it would take thirty or forty years to move from the industrial death of the city to a viable post-industrial mode. Thus, one couldn't effectively judge the museum and its economic development success until at least 2025.[55] In 2015, in another interview, Thompson remarked that the museum had just marked its fifteenth year of what he termed a thirty-year project—so now one would conceivably need to wait until 2030 to evaluate its economic effectiveness.[56]

MoCA EXPANDS WHILE THE HOSPITAL CLOSES

In March 2014, two dramatically different events illustrated the diverse directions that the museum and the city had taken. On March 5, the state House of Representatives passed a bill granting $25.4 million to MoCA to improve its facilities, including the addition of 120,000 square feet of gallery space. The addition meant the museum could double its space to 260,000 square feet, which would move it beyond its nearest competitor, in Beacon, New York, DIA:Beacon, and enable it to close in on the total space of the Los Angeles County Museum of Art. The Senate approved the bill as well, and, that August, Governor Deval Patrick signed the legislation, making the grant official.[57] Twenty days after the House announced that multi-million-dollar gift to MoCA, the North Adams Regional Hospital (NARH)—the city's largest employer—announced that it would close in just three days.[58]

On a national basis, a hospital closing doesn't often merit big news. After all, about one-third of hospital emergency rooms in the country had been closed over the previous twenty years, and, within the twelve months prior, eighteen hospitals had been shuttered. The closings tended to be in rural, poorer areas where hospitals relied on relatively low Medicare and Medicaid reimbursement rates. In Massachusetts itself, during the fifty-year period from the mid-1960s until 2014, the number of hospitals declined from about 140 to around 70.[59] Even so, the circumstances that surrounded the closing of NARH made it extremely unusual. First, despite a law requiring a 90-day notice of closure, the CEO of NARH, Timothy Jones, gave its employees and patients just three days.[60] Second, while the NARH Board claimed that its bankruptcy emanated from hospital operating losses, the reality indicated that its parent company had incurred huge losses due to trying to run a retirement community and an assisted living facility in neighboring Williamstown.

With the North Adams official unemployment rate already at 8.7 percent, the hospital's closing meant that 530 more employees would be out of work, and a local economist estimated that an additional 194 jobs would be lost in related businesses. In financial terms, the area's economy would suffer a hit of some $96 million.[61] That would make the closing the most devastating blow to the local region since the end of Sprague and the subsequent loss of 581 jobs in 1985. Former Mayor John Barrett III, who had been in office in 1984 when Sprague announced it would move its headquarters out of North Adams, called the hospital's precipitous closing worse, since, unlike the Sprague case, the three-day notice allowed no time to plan a response. Barrett warned, "It could be catastrophic; that's why the governor has to come in immediately."[62]

But the loss of hospital services, including the emergency room, a facility which had seen 20,000 visits the previous year, proved even more threatening to the local community. The nearest hospital, Berkshire Medical Center in Pittsfield, lay 20 miles to the south over crowded hilly roads, which were dangerous in the winter, and the distance proved even greater for residents in southern Vermont and in the mountainous area around Florida, Massachusetts, who used NARH.

On Tuesday, March 25, 2014, NARH CEO Timothy Jones announced that the hospital would close on Friday, March 28.[63] While local residents knew that the hospital faced financial obstacles and had recently closed its psychiatric wing, Jones's devastating message sent the region into shock, especially with only days to prepare a response. Robin Simonetti, a short-stay unit nurse, remembers receiving a call from her daughter who worked in medical records and said, "I heard we're closing." Robin replied, "No. I bet it's an announcement that we're either merging or being bought. They're not going to close a hospital. They just can't."[64]

At the hospital itself, Cindy Bird, SEIU chapter secretary and a twenty-six-year veteran at NARH, described a chaotic scene:

> There was an email saying [there would be a] mandatory meeting in cafeteria . . . . Everybody was screaming and saying what's going on . . . . We made our way down to the cafeteria, it was too crowded. It was shoulder-to-shoulder—people were crying, people in the hallway couldn't hear anything and were asking, people in the room were shushing us.

Then CEO Jones made the announcement.

Two days later, on the final morning of work at the hospital, Bird described an angry Jones, upset that "the unions weren't going quietly."

> We said, "Why didn't you tell us sooner?" He became very defensive and started screaming at us, so bad that in the adjacent cafeteria there was an employee assistance person . . . . She was going to call the police, she thought it was a maintenance person upset and devastated about losing their job.

In an interview over a year later, Jones denied acting angrily and described his efforts to keep the hospital open. He claimed that as late as two days before the announcement, he tried to get a deal with NARH's bondholders. "We thought we were going to get that done, and it just didn't play out that way, unfortunately."[65]

Mike Wilber, former union president at X-Tyal, immediately called for an occupation of the hospital to keep it from closing. "The only way we can fight this outrage is to show up," Wilber stated. He went on to say, "If you want [to] do anything, you have to fight. If you don't get hundreds of people, it means they really don't care . . . . If people want it to be open, they've got to be willing to fight to keep it open." Mayor Richard Alcombright phoned the governor, who "pledge[d] to do whatever he can to try to bring a positive outcome to this." Keeping hope alive, the mayor continued, "Until I hear that nothing can be done . . . it's not closed." [66]

The day after the announcement, two public health scholars from Boston University (B.U.) released a three-page document arguing that Governor Deval Patrick had the power to declare a public health emergency and keep the hospital open. Alan Sager and Deborah Socolar, co-directors of B.U.'s Health Reform Program, cited the justifications and precedent for such an action and included the long distances and travel times that North Berkshire residents would have to endure to reach another hospital. Furthermore, they made the point that, since residents in the service area were older and poorer than the state average, they more likely needed hospital care but were less likely to be able to travel longer distances to access medical attention. Finally, the state had a Distressed Hospitals Trust Fund that could be used to keep the hospital going. Toward the end of their document, they stated: "Now is the time for action, not words." But the governor chose not to act.[67]

For City Councilor Jennifer Breen, the news "feels like a death or worse." Brian O'Grady, the director of Williamstown's Council of Aging, added some specifics to the consequences of the closing:

> It's a total disaster. It's not just affecting seniors. It's affecting the 530 people who lost their jobs. What happens to them? . . . Every week we bring whole bunches of people up there for blood tests, the Wound Clinic, the eye doctor, whatever.

Without a hospital, let alone an emergency room, the local ambulance service faced a huge time burden. John Meany Jr., North Adams Ambulance Service general manager, noted that with NARH, turnaround time for local trips amounted to just fifteen to twenty minutes, but with the closure, the time increased to one-and-half to two hours to get to the hospital in Pittsfield or Bennington, Vermont.[68]

A day after the Tuesday closing announcement, more than 1,000 residents had signed an anti-closing petition and a Facebook anti-closure group had amassed 4,513 likes.

On Wednesday evening, after a community meeting, sixty protestors showed up at the hospital's lobby to demonstrate their anger. Two NARH employee unions—1199 Service Employees International Union (SEIU) and the Massachusetts Nurses Association (MNA)—as well as the April 4th Coalition—a community-union group that rallied locally in support of collective bargaining in Wisconsin in 2011—issued a call for an occupation of the hospital on the day of its closing.[69]

On that afternoon, a crowd of former employees and supporters congregated at the hospital and refused to leave. Sensing they would need help, the North Adams Police Department put out a call for mutual aid from around the county. When the help arrived, the protestors left the hospital to meet at the American Legion to plan a strategy.[70]

Regional government and state officials voiced their concerns over the closing, but, in the final analysis, they did nothing to stop it. No legislator or government official offered an explanation as to the ease by which the same state could find over $25 million to finance the museum's expansion, but at the same time could not figure out a way to save the region's most vital institution. The failure of a Democratic governor, a heavily Democratic legislature, and a fully Democratic Berkshire delegation to keep the hospital going, while at the same time finding millions for MoCA to expand, symbolized the shift in Democratic Party policies over the previous thirty-five years. Neo-liberalism had hit home.

Starting with deregulation under President Jimmy Carter and continuing the right-leaning direction of President Ronald Reagan during President Clinton's two terms, the party had become Republican-lite. With President Obama taking office amidst a financial crisis, the big banks that had precipitated the crisis received billions to stay afloat while homeowners who could not pay their mortgages received foreclosure notices. Both political parties paid homage to big business and Wall Street. Giving $25 million for MoCA to expand could only be seen as an example of conservative "supply side economics"—give money to big institutions in the hope that it would trickle down to ordinary citizens and to Main Street.

Hospital employees and local residents who protested NARH's closing saw Berkshire Health Systems (BHS), parent of the sizable Berkshire Medical Center (BMC) in Pittsfield, buy the bankrupt hospital for the bargain price of $4 million at the end of summer 2014. BHS restarted the emergency room and instituted several outpatient units, but—despite the needs reflected in a state mandated study and an analysis by the Massachusetts Nurses Association[71]—refused to make the North Adams unit (now Berkshire North) a full-service hospital. Residents continued to demand a full-service hospital, like BHS offered in its South Berkshire facility, Fairview in Great Barrington, which provided services for a smaller, but more affluent, population, with fewer annual births than the North Berkshire population.

As for the more than 500 hospital employees who lost their jobs when the hospital closed, about half have been hired by BHS for work either in their North Berkshire campus or at the Pittsfield hospital. However, the typical hire became part of the country's growing contingent labor force, working on a per diem basis, with no benefits and putting in fewer hours than she or he would like.[72]

Without a full-service hospital, North Berkshire residents had to travel more and more to BMC in Pittsfield, putting a greater strain on that hospital's resources. In particular, nurses there complained about understaffing and increased levels of stress in handling a greater population. According to the nurses' union, while patient volume increased 20 percent after the NARH closure, the staffing level had not gone up. (BMC's chief operating officer countered that the increase had only been 10 percent.) Not finding an adequate response from the hospital management, the BMC nurses voted to picket over the staffing levels.[73]

At the picket line, on a snowy Berkshire day eight months after NARH's shutdown, with motorists beeping support for the nurses, Shannon Weloure, RN, described a situation in which "[a]ll of our units are horribly understaffed." Prior to the North Adams closing, patient support was already "at a dangerous level . . . . It's getting unsafer by the day." A fellow nurse, Judy Sharpe, spoke of overcrowded conditions leading to patients being placed in hallways. "The hospital," she exclaimed, "has welcomed these patients [from North County], but they haven't provided us with the staffing resources to deal with them."[74]

In North County, activists continued to pressure government officials and senior officials at BMC to make North Adams's hospital full-service. Calling themselves the North County Cares Coalition (NCCC), they met on a weekly basis, lobbied their elected representatives, participated on a local cable television show and, on a cold, snowy March day—the one-year anniversary of the hospital's closing—they picketed in front of BMC.[75] They also drove down from North Adams City Hall in a caravan of cars, illustrating the time it took to travel to BMC for health-related problems.

Dick Dassatti, one of NCCC's co-directors, spoke to the protestors and the crowd in front of Berkshire Medical Center. He placed the demands for a full-service hospital in the context of the North Berkshire struggles:

> This is not about the closing of a factory or a business. It's not the loss of our local newspaper. It's not the loss of local ownership of our radio station. It's not that the state closed our employment office in North Berkshire, closed our welfare office in North Berkshire. We draw the line here. When we lose our full service hospital, you've hit the tipping point . . . . [W]e cannot accept our elected officials' lack of leadership and commitment to serve our community. . . [I]f the government can bail out the banks because they're too big to fail, we have to let our government officials know that hospitals are too big to fail.[76]

But government officials refused to intervene. State Senator Adam Hinds, who was elected in 2016 to represent North Adams and all of the Berkshires, illustrated that conservative approach when he explained why he supported state investments in MoCA even while the hospital serving North Berkshire lacked a full-service component. Neither when he briefly led the Northern Berkshire Community Coalition nor when he campaigned and began to serve in the Senate did he advocate for a full-service hospital. He did agree that maintaining medical services in North Adams is "a very real concern . . . . But [w]hen it comes to making the decision of what the state is going to invest in, we are going to invest in what seems to be demonstrating the most promise." And, for Hinds, the promise seemed to be with MoCA and its supportive cultural attractions: "They have created the buzz—you see that in other new projects and new investments coming in from outside Massachusetts. Every project has a critical juncture and MASS MoCA has reached that juncture."[77]

Outside North Adams City Hall, April 4th Coalition rallies to support collective bargaining for Wisconsin workers. Shaun Sutliff, former president of IUE local 231 at Chadbourne International in Williamstown, holds "I Pay More Taxes Than GE" and, to his right, stands Gary Ghidotti, National Association of Letter Carriers, President, Branch 286 (Gillian Jones photo, the *North Adams Transcript*, New England Newspapers, Inc., April 5, 2011).

North Adams firefighters hold signs and listen to speakers at April 4th Coalition rally. (Gillian Jones photo, the *North Adams Transcript,* New England Newspapers, Inc. April 5, 2011).

Part of the crowd at the April 4th Coalition rally (Seider photo).

Words to Remember: Back of Shaun Sutliff's shirt at April 4th Coalition rally (Seider photo).

Protesters walk through North Adams heading to City Hall for the April 4th Coalition March/Rally for Jobs, 2012 (Zeke Meginsky photo).

As the hospital closes on Friday, March 28, 2014, Karen Malloy, dietary worker and member of 1199 Service Employees International Union (SEIU), gets a hug of support from Mike O'Brien, retired chapter chair of the union (Jack Guerino, *iBerkshires*).

As the hospital closes, the man and the sign say it all! (Jack Guerino, *iBerkshires*)

More protesters at the hospital's last day (Jack Guerino, *iBerkshires*).

Veronica Turner, Executive Vice President of 1199SEIU state-wide, part of a union contingent from Boston, to offer support to hospital employees (Jack Guerino, *iBerkshires*).

Overflow crowd meets at the American Legion to plan strategy after hospital closes, April 1 (Stephanie Zollshan, *Berkshire Eagle*).

Mike O'Brien, former chapter chair 1199SEIU, and his daughter, Cindy Bird, chapter secretary, next to him at a community vigil, 1st Congregational Church, North Adams, March 30 (Gillian Jones, *Berkshire Eagle*).

About ninety hospital workers and supporters head to Boston on two buses with 12,000 signatures on petitions calling on Governor Deval Patrick and other state leaders to reopen the full-service hospital. On the left is Mike O'Brien, retired 1199SEIU chapter chair and on the right is Martin Pearson, hospital X-Ray technician (April 5, Gillian Jones, *Berkshire Eagle*).

At the first anniversary of the hospital's closing, March 28, 2015, a caravan of protestors travels from North Adams to Pittsfield to demand a full-service hospital. Here the protestors gather at North Adams City Hall prior to the drive to Berkshire Medical Center in Pittsfield.

At the protest in Pittsfield, North County Cares Coalition co-chair Dick Dassatti speaks out. To his left, co-chair Jim Lipa holds an "I CARE" message. Towards the conclusion of his speech, Dassatti stated: "[I]f the government can bail out the banks because they're too big to fail, we have to let our government officials know that hospitals are too big to fail" (Peter Dassatti, *Shutting NARH*).

NOTES

1 Grace Glueck, "A new museum's bright future becomes dim," *New York Times*, April 11, 1990, C11.

2 MASS MoCA accessed at massmoca.org.

3 *Berkshire Eagle*, Oct. 8, 1983.

4 While Adams Print Works ended in bankruptcy, Waverly Fabrics, its largest customer and operator of an Adams warehouse, continued to operate. Represented by Local 523 of the United Textile Workers of America, its employees sewed fabrics and warehoused the materials. In 1984, Ilene Dodge became the first female president of the local. Despite problems along the way, Waverly managed to maintain a presence in Adams, at least through 1990. In 1986, employees engaged in a short wildcat strike due to anger over reassignments and fears of seniority losses. "Workers' resentment reached the boiling point after a fabric cutter with 12 years' experience was transferred to a lower paying job . . . ." Union president Ilene Dodge maintained that employees feared becoming "another X-Tyal." In October 1989, Waverly's owner, F. Schumacher & Co., announced that it would open a new factory in Chester, South Carolina, which would produce the same kinds of goods that Waverly manufactured. About half of Waverly's 425 workers would lose their jobs, though the company planned on maintaining a regional office in Adams. Ilene Dodge, then a shop steward for the union, called the news "a big shock" to the workforce. With those plans, it would mean the end of textile production in North Berkshire, a history that went back to 1812. *Berkshire Eagle,* November 19, 1984; *Transcript,* September 9, 1986; and *Transcript,* October 11, 1989.

5 The coalition later changed its name to the Northern Berkshire Community Coalition and focused on neighborhood organizing, teen issues, transportation, homelessness, and food sustainability. An Amherst community organizer, Tom Wolff, had started a similar coalition in the Athol/Orange area and helped to replicate the model in North Berkshire in 1986 ("Celebrating Twenty Years," Northern Berkshire Community Coalition, 2006, brochure).

6 Barry Bluestone and Bennett Harrison, *The Deindustrialization of America: Plant Closings, Community Abandonment, and the Dismantling of Basic Industry* (New York: Basic Books, 1982), 6. For GE and Pittsfield, see June C. Nash, *From Tank Town to High Tech: the Clash of Community and Industrial Cycles* (Albany: State University of New York Press, 1989) and Max H. Kirsch, *In the Wake of the Giant: Multinational Restructuring in a New England Community* (Albany: State University of New York Press, 1998); for Chicago and Nabisco, see Marc Doussard, Jamie Peck, and Nik Theodore, "After Deindustrialization: Uneven Growth and Economic Inequality in 'Postindustrial' Chicago," *Economic Geography*, Vol. 85, No. 2 (April 2009), 183–207; and for Monticello, Indiana, see Earl Wysong, Robert Perrucci, and David Wright, *The New Class Society: Goodbye American Dream?* 4th ed. (Lanham, Maryland: Rowman & Littlefield,

2014,). The term "deindustrialization" had been publicly used decades earlier in the context of the "Allies' policy toward Germany just after World War II: an active process of victors stripping a vanquished nation of its industrial power." Jefferson Cowie and Joseph Heathcott note that, "to many workers who walked out of the factory gates for the last time in the sunset of America's golden age of industry, it must have felt exactly like an occupying force had destroyed their way of life." They then quote Joe Trotter Sr., who had worked in Youngstown, Ohio's steel industry for thirty-seven years, as he walked through the remains of the Ohio Works that U.S. Steel chose to dynamite rather than rehabilitate: "What Hitler couldn't do, they did it for him." Jefferson Cowie and Joseph Heathcott, "The meanings of deindustrialization," in J. Cowie & J. Heathcott (eds.), *Beyond the ruins: The meanings of deindustrialization* (Ithaca, NY: ILR Press), 1–15, Notes 306–307, accessed at http://digitalcommons.ilr.cornell.edu/cb/33, 1.

7 David Brady and Michael Wallace, "Deindustrialization and Poverty: Manufacturing Decline and AFDC Recipiency in Lake County, Indiana 1964–93," *Sociological Forum*, Vol. 16, No. 2 (June 2001), 321–358, 323, referring to a U.S. Senate, 1987, study.

8 Matthew Desmond, *Evicted: Poverty and Profit in the American City* (New York: Crown Publishers, 2016), 24.

9 James Feyrer, Bruce Sacerdote et al., "Did the Rust Belt Become Shiny? A Study of Cities and Counties That Lost Steel and Auto Jobs in the 1980s [with Comments]," Brookings-Wharton Papers on Urban Affairs (2007), 41–102, 45. Also, see Robert Forrant, *Metal Fatigue: American Bosch and* the *Demise of Metalworking in the Connecticut River Valley* (Amityville, NY: Baywood Publishing Co., 2009) for a study of the greater Springfield, Massachusetts, area.

10 Kathryn Marie Dudley, *The End of the Line: Lost Jobs, New Lives in Postindustrial America* (Chicago: University of Chicago Press, 1994), 33.

11 Forrant, 170.

12 *Berkshire Eagle*, Oct. 9, 1984.

13 Despite the great need for work, dissatisfaction at X-Tyal grew so great that the yearly turnover rate reached a high of 25 to 30 percent. Compare this to the Sprague turnover rate of about 3 percent in 1982 and 1983. "The Work Force," I.U.E. Local 200, Nov. 27, 1984.

14 *Boston Globe*, March 2, 1992, in Kay Oehler, Stephen C. Sheppard, et al., "Shifting Sands in Changing Communities: the Neighborhoods of North Adams, Massachusetts" (Williamstown, MA: Center for Creative Community Development, 2006). Also see, Alan Bashevkin, "Social Costs of Economic Decline: Northern Berkshire Region 1980–1990," Northern Berkshire Health and Human Services Coalition, January 23, 1991.

15 Nelson Lichenstein, *The State of the Union: A Century of American Labor* (Princeton: Princeton University Press, 2002), 235.

16 See the documentary film *Downside Up* by Nancy Kelly.

17 Pushing the "prestige" value of the museum might remind some cynics

of the buttons that blue-collar Harvard workers wore during a contract campaign with the administration, "You Can't Eat Prestige."

18 Interview by Alison Pincus on October 10, 2011, in *"The Mark of Reliability": From Sprague Electric to MASS MoCA in North Adams, MA* (Williamstown, MA: Williams College, 2012), 97.

19 Interview with author, 2011.

20 *Transcript,* October 19, 1988, 1; *Berkshire Eagle,* March 8, 1989, B6; *Transcript,* April 6, 1989, 1; and ibid., April 15, 1988, October 14, 1988, 1, December 9, 1988.

21 Cathy Stanton, "Ron Kuivila's 'Visitations': Social history as art at MASS MoCA," unpublished paper for FAH 160/Museum History and Theory, Tufts University, December 21, 1999, 7, and interviews by author.,

22 Maynard Seider, "Is this what we want?" *Berkshire Eagle,* February 17, 1989, A9.

23 Grace Glueck, "A New Museum's Bright Future Grows Dim," *New York Times,* April 11, 1990.

24 Grace Glueck, "Massachusetts Says New Art Museum Must Help Pay Costs," *New York Times,* December 4, 1991; Joseph Thompson, "Director's Statement," *Mass MoCA: From Mill to Museum,* ed. Jennifer Trainer (North Adams: MASS MoCA Publications, 2000). For a description and analysis of where the project stood in 1995, including the lack of local input, see Sharon Zukin, *The Cultures of Cities* (Cambridge, MA: Blackwell Publishers, 1995), Ch. 3, "A Museum in the Berkshires," with Philip Kasinitz.

25 Daniel Weinberger, "The Causes of Homelessness in America," *Democracy Now,* June 11, 2004; Peter Dreier, "Reagan's Real Legacy," *Nation,* February 4, 2011.

26 Much of the material and references in this paragraph and the six succeeding ones come from a paper by Enid Shields, *How the Other Half Lived in the Late 1980s: The North Adams Tenants Organization and the Struggle for Decent, Affordable Housing in a Former Massachusetts Mill Town.* North Adams, MA: Massachusetts College of Liberal Arts, 2010.

27 *Transcript,* February 22, 1988; earlier quote in paragraph from Shields, 26.

28 Linda Burchard, "Housing tour dramatizes low-income tenants' plight," *Berkshire Eagle,* August 14, 1988; and Paul Moriarty, "Councilors 'awakened' to housing stock conditions in city," *Transcript,* August 15, 1988. Quotations are from the *Transcript.*

29 *Transcript,* September 9, 1988 and in Shields.

30 Eileen Gloster and Bill Densmore, "Landlords react to code cleanup: 'Tenants' fault," *Advocate,* July 20, 1988; Shields, 30.

31 Bashevkin's co-authors for the August 1988 paper were Kelton Burbank and Andrew Schamess from the UMass Medical School.

32 More in-depth findings and discussion can be found in the document by Alan Bashevkin, Kelton Burbank and Andrew Shamess, "The Need

for Comprehensive Shelter Services in the Northern Berkshires Area," Northern Berkshire Health and Human Services Coalition, August, 1988.

33 A case could be made that neo-liberal policies began with President Jimmy Carter, who introduced the deregulation policies, specifically of trucking, airlines, and finance. Judith Stein, *Pivotal Decade: How the United States Traded Factories for Finance in the Seventies* (New Haven: Yale University Press, 2010), 243–4.

34 For a description of that shift, covering the years from Bill Clinton's presidency to and including Barack Obama's two terms in office, see Thomas Frank, *Listen Liberal: Or, What Ever Happened to the Party of the People?* (New York: Henry Holt & Co., 2016).

35 *Transcript*, November 8, 9, and 19.

36 April 21, 1995.

37 In an interview that same year, MoCA curator Laura Heon matter-of-factly emphasized the economic development goal of the museum: "To fulfill that mission we need to bring in lots of rich New Yorkers. We're very upfront about that." Cathy Stanton, "Outside the Frame: Assessing Partnerships between Arts and Historical Organizations," *The Public Historian*, 27, 1 (Winter 2005), 19–37, 29.

38 Interview of Joe Thompson by Jennifer J. Card, *From Industrial to Postindustrial: The Rebirth of North Adams Massachusetts* (Amherst, MA: Hampshire College, 2002), November 7, 2001, 69.

39 John Kifner, "Museum Brings Town Back to Life," *New York Times*, May 30, 2000, A14.

40 Karen Gardner, "Babeu: MASS MoCA limits downtown opportunities," *Transcript*, November 3, 2001, A 1, 8.

41 *New York Times*, May 28, 2004, B 31, and Graham interview in *Farewell to Factory Towns?*

42 Card, 73–4, and very much the same perspective in *Downside Up*.

43 Mark Randall, *Transcript*, May 20, 2000.

44 Williamstown *Advocate*, March 6, 2002, in Card, 79. When discussing with my class the nightly costs for staying at Porches, one local student responded in disbelief, "Why would anyone spend $300 a night to sleep on River Street!"

45 *Boston Globe*, October 14, 2001, in Card, 79. Anthropologist Cathy Stanton uses a concept advanced by Barbara Kirshenblatt-Gimblett ("the reciprocity of disappearance and exhibition") in describing Porches, referring to the "recontextualizing of materials while helping to consign them to the past by, for example, depicting as a 'homage to mill workers' families' an inn that no working-class person could afford to stay in" (Cathy Stanton, 31). Paradoxically, with the virtual end of the industrial working class, the Porches Inn "honors" them with "galvanized metal lunch boxes," in the same way that tourist shops along Route 2 (the Mohawk Trail) sport huge wooden Indians and sell so-called Indian memorabilia, after the

decimation of local Native Americans. In a speech that museum director Joe Thompson delivered to Williams College Reunion 2011 ("Hardware to Software, Material to Immaterial: 150 Years of Manufacturing and Art in North Adams"), he seemed to blame the Sprague workforce for its own demise. There had been an exhibit at MoCA, "The Workers," which included a walled exhibit of the first union contract signed after the 1970 strike. Thompson referred to it as "misguided" and stated that the "rigid nature of the language in this union contract agreement with Sprague in some ways was the beginning of the end of Sprague Electric as we know it today." He went on to say, "The kind of thinking that was implicit in that document . . . is a cautionary tale . . . . The lesson is you nurture creativity or you risk becoming a museum."

46 Card, 80.

47 Marjorie Ransom and G.M. Heller, "Details emerge about sleazy deals: Fitzpatrick's Porches Inn Displaces 23 North Adams Families," *Berkshire Record*, May 24, 2000, accessed at http://berkshirerecord.com/porches.html.

48 Not all tenants had such a favorable impression of their years at the River Street apartments. Joe Manning's interviews of them, including Ms. Holland, can be found online at the following Joe Manning websites that cover the history of the apartments as well as the transition to Porches:

https://morningsonmaplestreet.com/2001/07/25/porches-inn-brings-new-era-to-river-street-chapter-one/

https://morningsonmaplestreet.com/2001/07/26/porches-inn-brings-new-era-to-river-street-chapter-two/

https://morningsonmaplestreet.com/2001/07/27/porches-inn-brings-new-era-to-river-street-chapter-three/

Mr. Manning was hired by MASS MoCA to write about the residents who lived in the houses that would become "Porches." See the piece he wrote for Nicholas Whitman, *Porches: Art and Renewal on River Street* (North Adams: MASS MoCA, 2002). The entire text can be found in the three chapters cited above.

49 Ransom and Heller.

50 *Downside Up*.

51 Stephen C. Sheppard et al., *Culture and Revitalization: The Economic Effects of MASS MoCA on its Community,* C3DK Report NA3.2006; and Kay Oehler et al., *Network Analysis and the Social Impact of Cultural Arts Organizations*, C3D Report NA4.2007.

52 Linda Enerson, "The Promise of MASS MoCA," *CommonWealth Magazine,* 22, 3 (Summer 2017), 44–45.

53 Bob Canedy, Security, on MASS MoCA website, accessed at massmoca.org.

54 Adam Forrester, class paper, North Adams, MA: Massachusetts College of Liberal Arts, 2010.

55 Interview by the author, November 29, 2011.

56 Steve Barnes, *Times-Union*, January 18, 2015.

57 Adams Shanks, *Berkshire Eagle*, March 6, 2014; Judith H. Dobrzynaki, *New York Times*, August 20, 2014.

58 Forty-one years earlier, another local hospital closed. W.B. Plunkett Memorial Hospital in Adams, smaller than NARH, was closed in 1973 after sixty years of operation (*Berkshire Eagle,* November 1, 1982).

59 Alan Sager statement in Grant Walker, "LGH-Tufts union maintains local control, boosts power to face industry challenges," *Lowell Sun*, April 20, 2014.

60 The three-day notice apparently became the new low bar for hospital administrators to announce closings. Later that year, the Quincy Medical Center announced on November 5 that it would close by the end of the year, a violation of a sixty-day major layoff notice and a ninety-day health care closing notice. On November 6, an executive at Steward Health Care, the parent of Quincy Medical Center, reportedly told the Quincy employees that they were receiving "much better" treatment than those accorded the NARH employees, who only received three days notice. Sandy Eaton, "The Demise of Acute Health Care in Quincy, Massachusetts: Implications for Surviving Community Hospitals," *Open Media Boston*, January 6, 2015.

61 Stephen Sheppard, *The Economic Impact of Closure of the North Adams Regional Hospital*, March 30, 2014 (Williams College, Center for Creative Community Development).

62 Jim Therrien, *Berkshire Eagle,* March 26, 2014.

63 The hospital's trustees wrote a letter to the staff, not commenting on the three-day notice, but stating: "Everyone in the organization, along with our state and federal legislators, has been working to avoid this outcome. In the end, as revenues declined precipitously it was simply impossible to continue operations. We had hoped for purchase by another party, but [as] our financial position quickly weakened it became clear that we could not complete a sale." Tammy Daniels, *iBerkshires*, March 26, 2014 (from letter in possession of the *Berkshire Eagle*).

64 *Shutting NARH*, a documentary written and directed by Peter Dassatti, 2015.

65 Quotes from Bird and Jones from David Brooks, "Concord Hospital COO oversaw closure of Mass. Hospital in 2014," *Monitor*, November 8, 2015. The article began by reporting that Jones had been hired as Chief Operating Officer at Concord Hospital in New Hampshire, about a year and a half after NARH's closure. Jones describes himself as following the Toyota system of "lean management." It focuses on efficiencies of operation, but he hastened to add, "Efficiency is not about laying people off."

66 "Local Reactions Continue Over Hospital's Closing," Tammy Daniels, *iBerkshires*, March 26, 2014.

67 The document is headlined "GOV. PATRICK SHOULD DECLARE A PUBLIC HEALTH EMERGENCY TO PREVENT NORTH ADAMS

REGIONAL HOSPITAL FROM CLOSING," March 26, 2014. After serving two terms, Governor Patrick left office in 2015. His new full-time job—at Bain Capital—provided the perfect symbol of the Democratic Party's neo-liberal direction (Beth Healy, "Deval Patrick takes investing role at Bain Capital," *Boston Globe*, April 14, 2015). During the 2008 presidential campaign, the Democrats continuously hammered Republican candidate (and former governor of Massachusetts) Mitt Romney for his role in starting Bain Capital and its policy of firing workers in companies they took over. Governor Patrick was one Democrat who did not criticize Romney. Now Patrick, the former Democratic governor, often seen as a progressive, has morphed into Mitt Romney.

68 "Local Reactions Continue . . ." op cit.

69 Edward Damon, "Community expresses outrage, demonstrations planned through Friday," *Berkshire Eagle*, March 27, 2014.

70 Pittsfield Police Department Sergeant James Roccabruna letter, March 29, 2014, RE: NARH Protest Detail.

71 The state's Department of Public Health had hired Stroudwater Associates of Maine to evaluate NARH's service region for its health care needs and led to what came to be called the Stroudwater Report (Stroudwater Associates, Healthcare Market Assessment: Northern Berkshire County, Massachusetts, September 17, 2014). The Massachusetts Nurses Association study is entitled "Berkshire Medical Center North (BMCN): The Case for Restoring a Full Service Hospital for Northern Berkshire County."

72 Phone interview with Julie Blanchard, phlebotomist, resident of Clarksburg, who worked thirty-five years at NARH and ended up commuting for work to Pittsfield (May 1, 2017).

73 Ibid., "Berkshire Medical Center: Nurses to picket staffing levels; hospital disputes union's statistics," December 4, 2014.

74 *Shutting NARH.*

75 Scott Stafford, "Advocates say Northern Berkshire full service hospital sustainable, deserved," *Berkshire Eagle*, accessed at http://www.berkshireeagle.com/local/ci_27509421/northern-berkshire-group-report-shows-full-service-hospital.

76 *Shutting NARH.*

77 Enerson, 47.

CHAPTER TWENTY-FIVE

TERRY LOUISON: BIOGRAPHY OF A COMMUNITY ACTION PIONEER

A DEDICATED ADVOCATE for the poor, Terry Louison was born during the Great Depression in Pittsfield in 1930. As one of the founders of Louison House noted, Terry "provided inspiration. Here was a woman who devoted herself tirelessly to improving the lot of others. We knew statistics; she knew people. She knew their stories. She knew their despair and hopelessness."[1] A graduate of Pittsfield High School in 1948, Terry learned to utilize the "War on Poverty" programs in the 1960s when she directed the Adams Community Action Center and its successor, Northern Berkshire Community Action (NBCA). She began as a volunteer in Adams and ended up as executive director of NBCA for twenty-five years.

Terry appreciated the radical mandate for membership on the Community Action board of directors: one-third had to come from the people being served; one-third from the public sector; and one-third from the private sector. It would not be a top-down organization, run by people who thought they knew what was best for the poor, but a board that would have to listen to and learn from the poor themselves. Terry remembered always having a supportive board. They had VISTA volunteers who came in during the mid-1960s and did a needs-and-housing study, documenting the substandard housing in the area, with most homes having been built prior to 1930.

Helping to start vital programs including Legal Services, Head Start, Elder Services, Meals on Wheels, and a twenty-four-hour hot line for people in emergency need, Terry also proved to be a strong advocate for women's programs, including family planning. She knew the importance of working with young girls, helping them with their self-esteem, hoping to prevent them from an early pregnancy. "Terry knew that domestic violence was a great contributor to women's poverty," remembered Gail Bobin, who worked at the Elizabeth Freeman Center. "Her interest in family planning was connected to that, as was job training, childcare, and education for this cohort."[2]

When she was interviewed in 1996, just a few years after she retired, Terry talked about the importance of "listening to the poor . . . . We actually listened . . . . We got out in the community. We wanted people to feel comfortable . . . . It took a lot of years to build up credibility." Rather than running to Boston on a constant basis, she preferred to work locally, needing to gain "the trust of the people."[3]

North Berkshire, from her experience, had "always been a wonderful community" that responded to those in distress, in ways such as bringing in new and used clothes to help needy families. When something new arose, Terry would contact the *Transcript,* and her message would reach the local audience. Good, affordable housing, always a big issue in North Berkshire, became a priority for Community Action and Terry. She tried to institute a home ownership program for low-income people, which brought with it a federal subsidy to help pay the mortgage. Terry remembered having to teach the local banks about the program.

In addition, she fought Mayor Joseph Bianco to improve housing codes in the city. City Council passed higher code standards, but the mayor vetoed the bill. Terry viewed him as "a great friend of slumlords . . . a slumlord himself." (See Chapter Sixteen for Mayor Bianco's attack on Legal Services.) But the City Council overrode the mayor's veto, legitimizing the pressure to get housing up to standard.

From needs assessment studies that included asking low-income people about their problems and their issues, Community Action tackled the perennial transportation dilemma, helping people get to where they needed to be when they lacked cars and had to rely on costly and irregular bus service. Terry wanted and received statistics on homelessness, and she met with others to try to deal with it. But she realized that each person, each case, represented someone different and unique.

When questioned about a growing homeless population in 1987, she noted that the reasons for lacking shelter varied: some folks, "transients," were temporarily without housing; others, adolescents, had left their parents' homes for various reasons; and then there was "the growing problem of displaced people who are unable to keep up with the rising costs of rent or who lose their home in a fire or some other crisis." As for the adolescents, Terry attempted mediation to resolve the problems, but, if that didn't work, then separation became at least a temporary fix. She realized that the fastest-growing segment of the homeless comprised those who had been displaced, who had lost factory jobs and were left with employment at a minimum wage and no benefits. "Reduced wages, coupled with the rapidly rising cost of rents, and the lack of affordable housing, has serious implications for workers here." Terry added that larger families, those who "have lived here for a good many years paying fairly low rent," could end up in crisis with quickly rising rents in a tightening market. Also, of "special concern" were the elderly who were living on a fixed income. "When their rents suddenly increase 300 percent, there is no place for them to get the extra money."

Terry always did her best to maintain good relations with other local social service agencies so they could work together. In doing so, she modeled a practice that an important umbrella agency, the Northern Berkshire Health and Human Services Coalition—headed by Al Bashevkin for many years—would practice as well. As Bashevkin recalled, "When we started the . . . Coalition, Terry was out in front. When we started talking about homelessness, Terry was out in front."[4]

One of the principles Terry followed when something new was needed, like Legal Services, was to use local resources to get it started, and then work on gaining additional funds. Her theory was that, if a community could show a degree of self-sufficiency, it would be more successful that way. She hoped to get people in a place where they could help themselves, not to be in a state of dependency. Striking a prophetic tone, she believed that we "will never eliminate poverty," but could work with people to "make things better."

From the 1960s through the early 1990s, Terry had seen and responded to a lot: mill closings, the long strike at Sprague, and political attacks on the poor. She watched the community come together in times of need, whether it be through volunteers helping to distribute government food packages, poor people organizing themselves, or agencies working in tandem to alleviate problems and supporting new programs to aid the poor. No one could simply be labeled a poor person. Terry "knew the importance of breaking poverty down into individuals' stories," recalled Gail Bobin, whose local clients availed themselves of Community Action services. "One person may be 'temporarily' poor, i.e., just lost job, illness, etc. Others will be entrenched in poverty from birth to death. [Terry] knew and respected them all, did what she could to help, and got them to help each other."[5]

When interviewed in 1996, Terry grew very concerned about President Clinton's so-called welfare reform, as he followed through on his campaign promise "to end welfare as we know it." Congress passed the measure, and the president signed the "Personal Responsibility and Work Opportunity Reconciliation Act of 1996," an act that ended Aid to Families with Dependent Children, placed a five-year limit on receiving federal funds, forced mothers into the workplace after two years of receiving aid, and empowered the states by providing them with block grants.[6] In retirement, Terry speculated that if it was a bad reform, people needed to "get enough people to fight it, and maybe something good will come out of it."

Terry died in 2015 at the age of 84, and it should be remembered that, at the same time she "devoted herself tirelessly to improving the lot of others," she helped raise seven children of her own.

State Representative Gailanne Cariddi delivers a proclamation of appreciation from the state legislature thanking Terry Louison for her "endless devotion to the community" (*iBerkshires*, November 23, 2014).

NOTES

1 Mark Gold, http://www.iberkshires.com/community/printerFriendly.php ?ob_id=10702.

2 Email from Gail Bobin, September 13, 2017. Thinking back on the programs initially instituted to help poor women, Bobin remembers the negative consequences of President Clinton's so-called "welfare reform": "Women lost opportunities for all of the above under [Clinton's] Welfare Deform."

3 Interview by Gail Bobin, "Social History of North Adams" class, North Adams, MA: Massachusetts College of Liberal Arts, 1996.

4 Paul Hopkins, "Louison House 25th Anniversary Fetes Namesake," *iBerkshires*, November 23, 2014.

5 Email from Gail Bobin, includes material in the following paragraph.

6 At that time, I remember that on the same day two of my college students had to drop out of school mid-semester because Massachusetts did not count college hours as work hours. The new program, entitled Temporary Assistance to Needy Families (TANF), treats the poor in a more punitive fashion and remains in effect in 2018.

CHAPTER TWENTY-SIX

"THE NEXT NEW THING"

It wasn't a messianic vision in the beginning. I wasn't looking to do that. But then you look and start to add up the components.[1]

—Thomas Krens, on his creation of a cultural corridor between Williamstown and North Adams

If it's not a non-profit, it's not a museum.

—Michael Conforti, former director of the Clark Art Museum on Krens's proposed for-profit museum for North Adams

THOMAS KRENS'S POST-MoCA CAREER

IN 1986, not long after he made the case for MASS MoCA, Thomas Krens left the Berkshires to run the Guggenheim Museum in New York City. He first served as a consultant and, in 1988, he became the storied museum's director. In that post he quickly established himself as a controversial figure in the world of entrepreneurial art, with his corporate-sponsored exhibitions and expansion of Guggenheim museums around the world. In 2005, he left the director's position to run the Guggenheim Foundation as senior advisor for international affairs. His primary goal: to complete a huge museum designed by Frank Gehry in Abu Dhabi, United Arab Emirates.[2]

Not hesitant to use superlatives, Krens stated that the Abu Dhabi project "will be truly global . . . representing art from the Middle East, Russia, Eastern Europe, Asia, Africa, as well as Europe and America. It will change the model of the art museum." More than a third larger than his signature global museum in Bilbao, Spain, the Emirates museum would have "a staff of about a dozen people" just focused on getting it going.[3] Not only has the museum not been completed by its promised 2013 date, but "the site [was] nothing more than a scatter of concrete pilings." Financial issues, skepticism on the part of Gehry, Krens's disagreements with the Guggenheim board, and outrage over the "modern day slavery" treatment of Emirates' migrant workers have overshadowed the project. By 2010, Krens was out as its director.[4]

(While in 2018 the Guggenheim still anticipated that the museum would be built, Krens seemed unsure: "It may not be such a good idea these days to have an American museum, essentially with a Jewish name, in a country that wasn't recognized diplomatically by the Emiratis, meaning Israel, in such a prominent location at such a big scale." Previously, while Krens was director of the project, no record exists that he spoke out or showed concern that Israelis could not enter the Emirates. Nor was there any evidence of his having spoken out about the Emirates' anti-gay policies or treatment of migrant workers.[5])

A *New York Times* profile of Krens described him as "[a] towering 6 foot 5, with an MBA in management from Yale and a manner that is often taken for arrogance . . . . Mr. Krens . . . is best known for his ambitions for developing an international network extending from Las Vegas to Bilbao, Spain, and for the types of high-profile exhibitions he presented, including shows like 'The Art of the Motorcycle,' a personal passion, and ones that tackled entire countries like China and Brazil."[6] Krens had been credited with success in new ventures in New York, Venice, Berlin, Bilbao, and Las Vegas. But, though Krens thought big and charged full speed ahead, his resume also included numerous failures, projects in Taiwan, Brazil, Japan, Singapore, Russia, and Mexico that never got off the ground.[7]

THOMAS KRENS RETURNS TO NORTH ADAMS

In 2015, apparently without a major national or international project to work on, Thomas Krens returned to North Adams and proposed two new museums in addition to the renovation of an historic theater.[8] His return came close to thirty years after he'd conceived of MoCA and then quickly exited the area. On August 11, 2015, he announced plans to build a museum at the city's Harriman-West Airport. A special meeting of the city's Airport Commission heard Krens out, then quickly and unanimously agreed to begin lease negotiations with him.[9]

In typical grand style, he called the project the Global Contemporary Collection and Museum, with a price tag of between $10–15 million. Plans included the collection of 400 pieces of art in a building with 100,000 square feet for the gallery and 40,000 square feet for storage. Krens labeled it a for-profit museum, which would house "a world-class collection of contemporary art," but one that would not compete with the Clark Art Museum in Williamstown or MoCA. He said he'd been thinking about the project for around five years, and that he originally planned it for China. As for the very significant change in location, Krens, who has a home in Williamstown, would only say, "The idea of spending a little more time in the Berkshires was attractive to me."[10]

At his announcement, the now 68-year-old hinted that there would be more to come. "The region needs a couple of more cultural destinations and a marketing package to pull it all together," he said. As Alanna Martinez, of the New York *Observer,* reminded her readers, Krens "is a pioneer of cultural tourism, the idea that a magnet institution, like the Guggenheim Bilbao in Spain, can alter the economy and character of a region."[11]

Less than a month later, Krens literally roared into town on a motorcycle, accompanied by actors Laurence Fishburne,

Jeremy Irons, Lauren Hutton, and Harold Perrineau, all members of the so-called Guggenheim Motorcycle Club. On a journey to the Adirondacks for the purpose of memorializing a late club member, Dennis Hopper, Krens convinced his friends to stop in North Adams. There he met with Mayor Richard Alcombright and Building Inspector William Meranti, and the group toured the interior of the partially renovated Mohawk Theater. Without making any promises, Krens called a new Mohawk something that needed to happen, and made a vague nod to Heritage State Park as a necessary third attraction to balance out his airport museum proposal.[12] Then the group roared off.

About two months later, Krens returned to North Adams without his Hollywood entourage. He did, however, have two former Massachusetts governors by his side, a Democrat, Michael Dukakis, and a Republican, William Weld. Architect Richard Gluckman, with whom Krens had been working on the concept, was also there. At a press conference at the Heritage State Park, Krens told the crowd he would build the Extreme Model Railroad and Contemporary Architecture Museum (EMRCA) at the park. The museum, based on a similar facility in Germany, would use two miles of track for its trains in a building 670 feet long. It would also house models of famous buildings, like the Empire State Building, and would employ sixty staff.[13] In addition, plans also included a railcar restaurant, a distillery, and retail space for a MASS MoCA gift store in the newly configured park.

Along with the airport museum and the hoped-for Mohawk Theater renovation, the model railway would be the third attraction that would complete the "cultural corridor" from Williamstown to North Adams, thus giving tourists more reasons to visit the area, stay over for a night or two, and bolster its economic development. At that point, Krens admitted that MASS MoCA had not been the "silver bullet" that the city's economy had needed. Curiously, while hyping the three new projects, Krens confessed that only a quarter of the big projects he had worked on "have come to fruition."[14]

Krens, Gluckman, and the two former governors all spoke. Mayor Richard Alcombright explained that the five of them had been discussing development plans since early 2015. Yet none of the men offered new details about the renovation of the Mohawk, nor did anyone say where the $25–30 million needed for the museum and model railroad would come from.[15] Krens did suggest that the model railway project would bring in revenue and that "perhaps" the state could help. The for-profit museum would rely on private funding. When pushed on what a for-profit museum would look like, Krens admitted it might be much like a gallery with the paintings for sale.[16]

The following summer Krens once again visited North Adams where he made his presence known at the Northern Berkshire Economic Summit, hosted by the Massachusetts College of Liberal Arts. In addition to the three projects he had previously announced, his plans now included rehabbing the Norad mill, adding an antique clock museum and distillery inside the Heritage State Park, and "inviting developers to build a luxury art hotel downtown."

Krens's confidence in the viability of his vision stemmed from the prospective audience that could make it to North Adams, some thirty-six million people who lived just a "half-day's drive" away. "It's all about audience," Krens said. "'I know how to do these projects," he added, referring to his work on the ongoing, massive, Guggenheim Abu Dhabi project. The press report on the summit didn't mention any corrective to his boast even though the Abu Dhabi project had not yet been built, and Krens had been relieved of directing it years earlier.

Krens's vision for North Adams received a boost from Jay Ash, Massachusetts Secretary of Housing and Economic Development, who also spoke at the summit. Ash promised "to be supportive [with] resources to support good planning." He even specified a 25 percent boost in funding the MassWorks program, "which could well end up supporting any of the initiatives Krens described."[17]

Soon the Krens team realized that the Extreme Model Railroad museum needed more space than Heritage State

Park could provide. After two executive sessions with the North Adams Redevelopment Authority, Krens negotiated an agreement to purchase not only the Heritage site but also the Sons of Italy building next door. Seeking taxpayer money for the project, Krens and the city applied for a $5.4 million MassWorks grant to fund the demolishment of the Sons of Italy building and the rebuilding of an access bridge.[18] Several months later, the state denied the multi-million dollar grant, but that didn't stop Secretary Ash from being optimistic about the grant's future: "They were not selected for this round [but w]e continue to be very interested in the project, and I'll be coming back to talk to them about it."[19]

Former Governor Weld returned to North Adams for Krens's next press conference along with the star attraction, world-renowned architect, Frank Gehry, who would design the model railway museum. Krens confidently predicted that the funding for the museum would be raised by June 2018. In an earlier interview, Krens reflected on his cultural corridor creations and his role in all of it: "It wasn't a messianic vision in the beginning. I wasn't looking to do that. But then you look and start to add up the components."[20]

Economist Stephen Sheppard, more earthbound, also spoke at the press conference, giving some details of his economic impact study on the various Krens projects, which now had added a motorcycle museum and the possibility of an architectural museum. According to Sheppard, all twelve projects would cost about $300 million, with the funds coming from a variety of sources: "some private, some for-profit, some not-for-profit . . . [and] some state support money . . . ." Should they all be built, Sheppard concluded, "they will totally transform the North Adams-Williamstown area."

For the first time at the various press conferences that Krens held over the previous three years, a doctor spoke. Dr. Gray Ellrodt, Berkshire Medical Center's chief of medicine, stated that health systems have only a 20 percent impact on health, while "nearly 70 percent of outcomes and healthy living can be attributed to a community's economic and social health; poorer communities, like North Adams, have higher rates of smoking, obesity, and drug and alcohol abuse, for example." Ellrodt went on to say, "If we are going to effectively address the epidemic of diseases of despair for our community . . . we will need brave and bold economic development in this community."[21]

From press reports of the event, neither Ellrodt nor anyone else mentioned that Dr. Ellrodt had invested in Krens's company, the for-profit Global Cultural Asset Management and EMRCA Inc. Was Ellrodt speaking as a health care professional in downplaying investment in "health systems" or as an investor in Krens's project? Was there a possible conflict of interest?[22] The theory that economic development would be more likely to improve health outcomes in North Berkshire than further investments in "health systems" would likely also find support from Dr. Ellrodt's employer, Berkshire Medical Center. By then BMC had an additional rationale to maintain the status quo, to keep their North Berkshire campus as a less than full-service hospital.

NOTES

1 John Seven, "On Track: Master museum builder has big plans for North Adams," *Berkshire Magazine,* August 2016.

2 There is no shortage of written and online writings on Krens. Key background used here includes Vicky Ward, " A House Divided," *Vanity Fair,* January 1, 2007; Jerry Saltz, "How to Rebuild the Guggenheim," *New York Magazine,* September 25, 2007; Charles Giuliano, "Tom Krens Resigns from the Guggenheim," www.berkshirefinearts.com/02-28-2008_tom-krens-resigns-from-the-guggenehim.htm.; Carol Vogel, "Guggenheim's Provocative Director Steps Down," *New York Times,* February 28, 2008; Negar Azimi, "The Gulf Art War: New museums in the Emirates raise the issue of workers' rights," *New Yorker,* December 19 & 26, 2016; "On Tom Krens, the charismatic former Guggenheim director. Dangerous are those with nothing to lose," *Judith Benhamou-Huet Reports,* March 28, 2017; Martinez, "He's Back: Former Guggenheim Czar Tom Krens Plans For-Profit MegaMuseum in Berkshires," *Observer,* August 12, 2015; and Amah-Rose Abrams, "Ex-Guggenheim Director Thomas Krens Thinks Abu Dhabi Project Should Be Scaled Back," *Art World,* March 30, 2017.

3 Vogel.

4 Azimi and *Observer,* December 2013.

5 Alyssa Buffenstein, "The Guggenheim and Rockbund Museums Call Off Exhibition of Middle Eastern Art in Shanghai," *artnetNews,* March 22, 2017; Amah-Rose Abrams, "Manuel Rabate Named Director of Louvre Abu Dhabi," *artnetNews,* September 21, 2016; Saltz.

6 Vogel.

7 Saltz.

8 On noting that the North Adams project appears to be Krens's only one, Judith Benhamou-Huet warns us: "Dangerous are those with nothing to lose."

9 Still, "as a public entity, the commission must also issue a request for proposals in accordance with Massachusetts law" and gain approval by the Federal Aviation Administration (Adam Shanks, "Update: Mass MoCA visionary Thomas Krens envisions new, massive art gallery for North Adams," *Berkshire Eagle,* August 11, 2015).

10 Alex Greenberger, "Thomas Krens Is Planning Another Contemporary Art Museum for North Adams, Massachusetts," *ARTnews,* August 12, 2015.

11 Martinez.

12 Tammy Daniels, "Guggenheim Motorcycle Club Makes Mohawk Theater Pitstop," *iBerkshires,* September 8, 2015. In 1998, Krens brought "The Art of the Motorcycle" to the Guggenheim and initially accepted a free motorcycle from BMW, raising a conflict-of-interest issue. Guggenheim Board Chairman Peter Lewis objected to Krens's motorcycle club also serving "as a BMW promotion." With numerous objections to Krens's

style and performance, Lewis wanted the Board to fire Krens. The Board refused to listen to Lewis, despite his overall donations of $75 million to the museum, and Krens stayed on, while Lewis left (Ward).

13 On reading about the press conference, one commentor wrote, "Better than a model train museum would be a fast train connecting Cape/Boston/North Adams/NY City," www.berkshirefinearts.com/12-05-2015_tom-krens-outlines-plans-for-a-cultural-corrider. One indication of the scale of the project: the model Empire State Building would take up 288 square feet, and would have three, one-inch windows of all of its four sides (John Seven, *Berkshire Magazine,* August 2016).

14 Adam Shanks, "Mass MoCA visionary Krens announces plans to revitalize Heritage State Park," *Berkshire Eagle,* December 6, 2015.

15 Larry Murray, "Plans for a North-Adams-Williamstown Cultural Corridor advance,"https//berkshireonstage.com/2015/12/05/plans-for-a-north-adams-williamstown-cultural-corridor-advance/.

16 Charles Giuliano, "Tom Krens Develops Business as a Museum: A For-Profit Paradigm for North Adams," www.berkshirefinearts.com/12-08-2015_tom-krens-develops-business-as-a-museum. As for the for-profit museum, Michael Conforti, former director of the Clark Art Museum, bluntly stated: "If it's not a non-profit it's not a museum" (Giuliano, 12–05–2015).

17 Phil Demers, "Arts, vision, are keys to Northern Berkshire's economic strength," *Berkshire Eagle,* July 17, 2016. In response to the summit, I wrote a letter to the *Berkshire Eagle,* July 22, 2016, which included the following: "I wonder what Mr. Krens would discover if he took a week to walk the neighborhoods of North Adams and ask its residents about their economic development desires. He could walk along with Mr. Ash, who stated that he doesn't want to lead in North Berkshire, 'but I have to figure out how to follow' . . . . [T]hey could ask local residents: Would you rather have a full service hospital or a huge model railroad? Would you prefer another museum by the airport or a government program to put people to work repairing our bridges, weatherizing our homes and subsidizing good quality child-care?"

18 Adam Shanks, "As bigger museum plans emerge, option to buy Heritage State Park on table," *Berkshire Eagle,* April 19, 2017; Adam Shanks, "Famed architect Frank Gehry to design Extreme Model Railroad and Contemporary Architecture Museum," *Berkshire Eagle,* August 30, 2017.

19 *Berkshire Eagle,* November 16, 2017, 1.

20 John Seven.

21 Tammy Daniels, "World-Class Architect Climbs Aboard Model Railroad Museum," *iBerkshires,* September 1, 2017.

21 "Krens has managed to attract a number of local investors to his team, some of whom were also involved in bringing MASS MoCA to life . . . as well as new members like Dr. Gray Ellrodt" (John Seven).

CHAPTER TWENTY-SEVEN

BACK TO THE BEGINNING: THE HOOSIC RIVER REVIVAL

NORTH BERKSHIRE could not have developed as it has without the labor power of its diverse immigrant population. That energy, combined with the power of the Hoosic River, enabled the region to industrialize and become a manufacturing center for much of the nineteenth and twentieth centuries. The 70-mile-long river, which flows throughout the region's communities into southern Vermont and New York State, ultimately empties into the Hudson River. In Berkshire County it has provided its residents with recreation as well as a source of food, but it has also overflowed its banks from time to time. Starting as far back as 1785, floods ravaged the city in 1869, 1927, 1938, and 1948. Besides the destruction of homes, bridges, and factories, at least two lives have been lost.[1]

The havoc created by the floods led officials in Adams and North Adams to request help from the federal government. Beginning in 1950 and concluding in 1961, the Army Corps of Engineers created a flood control system that stopped the flooding but left both communities with concrete instead of grass, plants, and trees, by the river's banks. While the river still flows through its three-sided crumbling cement flood chute for some two and a half miles within North Adams, its previous roar has become a whisper, and, aesthetically and culturally, the region has lost a natural gift.

Now, with MASS MoCA the center of the new tourist economy, plans have been implemented to bring back the Hoosic River, to restore it to its more beautiful, natural state, while maintaining flood protection. As part of her work for Storey Publishing Company, North Adams resident Judy Grinnell visited San Antonio, Texas, and Providence, Rhode Island, in the 1990s. In both places, she marveled at the revival of the rivers and the rivers' influence in bringing downtown areas back to life. She came back to North Adams, looked at the two branches of the river that flowed right through the middle of the city, and asked herself: "Why shouldn't North Adams also have a vibrant downtown with a restored riverfront?" So, in 2008, she invited members of the community—activists, government officials, and river experts—to discuss the possible revitalization of the river. Thirty people showed up, and the non-profit Hoosic River Revival got to work trying to bring the river back to its pre-industrial beauty, perhaps even as clean as it once was, before it powered the mill's machines and received the effluent from those same factories—an effluent that, in the nineteenth century, W.B. Du Bois had written and spoken about concerning the county's southern river, the Housatonic.[2]

By 2018, while working in stages, Hoosic River Revival received over $800,000 in funding for the project from individuals, foundations, businesses, and the state of Massachusetts, which considered it a "Priority Project." Though it is a long-term endeavor (up to twenty years) with a $200 million price tag, the goal remains the same: to restore the river as much as possible to its natural flow; to enhance it as a home for fish and wildlife; and to maintain protection for the city with a twenty-first-century flood control system, its banks as an ecologically sustainable environment that can provide river access, pedestrian walking/biking paths, and opportunities for commercial development.

The Hoosic, like the Hudson that it flows into, and the Housatonic to its south, has been contaminated by Polychlorinated Biphenyls—PCBs—a chemical used by General Electric and Sprague Electric Company. Sprague dumped the chemical into the Hoosic River from the 1950s until the late 1970s when federal law prohibited its use. The chemical has been classified as a carcinogen by the International Agency for Research on Cancer. When the toxins accumulate in the fatty tissues of fish in contaminated waters, those fish become too dangerous to eat.[3]

After Sprague could no longer dump the PCBs into the river, they stored the hazardous wastes in barrels at their Brown Street site and in the old Fairground neighborhood of North Adams. The successor firm to Sprague, American Annuity Group of Cincinnati, took ownership of the needed cleanup. After the local residents united to protest the ongoing danger of living in chemically contaminated houses, American Annuity was forced to compensate them.

Hoosic River Floods in North Adams, 1927 (North Adams Public Library).

1936 Flood Damage all the way up to Brooklyn Street, North Adams (North Adams Public Library).

Constructing flood control chutes in the early 1950s.

View of Hoosic River and cement chutes near YMCA, Rt. 2, North Adams (Seider photo).

What a restored river could look like: the view from Denver (https://hoosicriverrevival.org/).

NOTES

1 Sandra Brookner, "The River Once Ran Wild," Social History of North Adams class paper, North Adams, MA: Massachusetts College of Liberal Arts, 2001.

2 In his autobiography, Berkshire County's most renowned citizen, W. E. B. Du Bois writes that he was "born by a golden river" in Great Barrington in 1868. Du Bois was describing the color of the Housatonic River, a color that he knew came from the mills and other sources of pollution by its banks. *The Autobiography of W.E.B. Du Bois: A Soliloquy on Viewing My Life from the Last Decade of Its First Century* (New York: International Publishers, 1968), 61. In 1930, already in his sixties, Du Bois returned to Great Barrington, where he delivered a speech to the alumni of Searles High School, the same school he had graduated from in 1884. The speech focused on the Housatonic River, a river whose unnatural gold, as he explained, came from the pollutants that poured into the water from the "[m]ills, homes, and farms . . . outhouses and dung heaps have lined its banks." He ended his speech by urging us to "rescue the Housatonic and clean it as we have never in all the years thought before of cleaning it, and seek to restore its ancient beauty; making it the center of a town, of a valley, and perhaps—who knows?—of a new measure of civilized life." "Reflections upon the Housatonic River," reprinted in the *Berkshire Edge,* April 3, 2016. Du Bois's hopes for the renewal of the Housatonic find resonance in the hopes of another great American, Pete Seeger, who helped spark a revival for the Hudson River in the 1960s. In 1966, Seeger "announced plans to 'build a boat to save the river.'" The *Clearwater* was built, and it became a lodestar of inspiration to clean the river of its chemicals, sewage, and other effluents (www.clearwater.org/about/the-clearwater-story/). As the Hoosic flows into the Hudson, the building of the *Clearwater* can be a powerful symbol for North Berkshire residents who work for a revived Hoosic.

3 Jay Kleberg, "The pollution of the Hoosic River and the continuing battle to clean it up," *The Williams Record,* January 16, 2008.

CHAPTER TWENTY-EIGHT

"LIFT ME UP TO THE LIGHT OF CHANGE"*

[T]he community has been amazingly supportive of [the] organization's mission . . . . People like to give back . . . . [T]his community in particular gives back.

—Kathy Keeser,
Executive Director, Louison House

"They have *a plan. We need our* own *plan."*
"Right, and we have to stick together just like we did in 1970."
"O.K. But aren't you worried about what they'll do?"
"No, not really. What matters most, after all, is what we do*."*

—Actors, playing workers displaced by the closing of Sprague, from "The Sprague Years," 1995.

* *From "I Am Willing" by Holly Near*

MoCA EXPANDS, DOWNTOWN DOESN'T

AS LOCAL ACTIVISTS persisted in their struggle to make the regional hospital a full-service facility, MASS MoCA continued to expand. Bolstered by a state grant of $25.4 million and an additional $40 million in private funds, the museum's huge new gallery, Building #6, opened on May 28, 2017, to sizeable crowds and critical acclaim. MoCA increased its staff and, with other tourist-oriented projects underway, museum director Joe Thompson was bullish on the future. He informed *CommonWealth Magazine*'s Linda Enerson: "[I]n the next few years, the museum will far exceed the initial projection of stimulating 600 jobs."[1]

At the same time, Williams College economist Stephen Sheppard told Enerson that MoCA job creation, both direct and indirect, stood at only 385. Despite the expansion and the increasing crowds, the city's downtown had not yet been rejuvenated, some eighteen years after MoCA opened:

> [O]n a Sunday afternoon in June . . . Main Street itself was nearly empty, in stark contrast to the museum, which bustled with visitors a few blocks away. A pizza place, a café, and a dollar store were open . . . . About half a dozen storefronts were vacant.[2]

THE OPIOID CRISIS HITS HOME

By the second decade of the twenty-first century, the national opioid epidemic had become front-page news. In particular, stories in the print and electronic media focused on increased rates of addiction in rural areas, in New England and the Midwest, and disproportionately among whites. *USA Today* reported that in 2015, whites accounted for around 90 percent of opioid and heroin overdoses in the country. That racial disparity undoubtedly added to the increased publicity of the problem and to governmental and non-profit agencies making great efforts to deal with it as a public health issue. In earlier times, when young African American men in urban communities became addicted, they were portrayed as the enemy in a war on drugs. Sociologist Michael Eric Dyson pointed out the differences: "White brothers and sisters have been medicalized in terms of their trauma and addiction. Black and brown people have been criminalized for their trauma and addiction."[3]

As the opioid epidemic swept through Massachusetts, it had a particularly devastating impact on the more rural areas like Berkshire County. Back in 2013, the Department of Public Health (DPH) reported that age-adjusted opioid death rates in Berkshire County exceeded those for the state as a whole. For that same year, Berkshire County topped all of the western Massachusetts counties for opioid-related, non-fatal overdose hospital and emergency room visits—with a rate even higher than that of urban Springfield, the largest city in the region.

Deaths from overdoses in Berkshire County continued to increase. In 2016, North Adams residents accounted for six of the thirty-five deaths in the county. The assistant chief at North Adams Ambulance, Amalio Jusino, told the *Berkshire Eagle:* "Responding to overdoses is 'pretty much a daily occurrence . . . .'" In fact, over a ten-year period, North Adams residents requesting treatment for opioid abuse skyrocketed, increasing by 376 percent.[4]

In one response to the crisis, Berkshire Medical Center (BMC) in Pittsfield announced plans to provide a 30-bed unit where patients could receive fourteen to thirty days of treatment to deal with their addictions. BMC's vice president for acute care, Brenda Cadorette, stated: "This service really fills the gap between detoxification and long-term recovery."[5] Missing from BMC's concern were their neighbors twenty miles to the north as Cadorette announced no plans to add such a facility to BMC's campus in North Adams—despite the likelihood that the North Berkshire treatment need exceeded that of Pittsfield and South County.

North Berkshire had the highest poverty and unemployment rates in the county, both factors associated with increased rates of addiction. A member of BMC's own psychiatry department in Pittsfield, Dr. Alex Sabo, highlighted the "stress of poverty" as a key factor in the causes of drug abuse in the county.[6] In 2017, for the third year in a row, the Voices for Recovery Rally, Walk, and Vigil in North Adams focused on the epidemic, connecting residents with the available support services in the area. The event attracted about 100 people who rallied and then marched through the city's streets calling attention to the issue.[7]

When neither the Northern Berkshire Community Coalition nor the mayor called on BMC to provide an inpatient addiction unit for North Berkshire, a citizens group stepped into the breach. On May 10, 2016, the North County Cares Coalition (NCCC) brought a resolution to North Adams City Council to call on BMC to open an inpatient addiction center at their North County campus. The Council agreed to have a committee study it, and on June 28 they heard arguments for the proposal.

In their resolution, NCCC pointed out that the Stroudwater Report, which had been commissioned by the Department of Public Health, concluded that North County needed ten to eleven inpatient beds for substance abuse cases. They explained that, in 2014, nearly 200 local residents had sought such treatment, a huge jump from 42 in 2005. The group added that "poverty, the lack of transportation, and high incidences of other health problems" in the region "exacerbated" the opioid epidemic. The resolution received strong support from community residents at the council meeting and, despite a written note against the resolution by the mayor, the council adopted the following by an 8 to 1 vote:

> [W]e call upon Berkshire Health Systems and state officials to respond to the urgent healthcare needs of North Adams and North County residents and open inpatient detox treatment and inpatient crisis stabilization at the North Adams campus, in conjunction with outpatient services, to meet the needs of people with opioid addiction and provide them with the best chance for a full recovery.[8]

Following on their success with the North Adams City Council, the NCCC found support as well from the select boards in neighboring Clarksburg and Adams, but not in Williamstown, where the governing officials cited the need for help, but refused to specify inpatient services.[9]

As of mid-2018, undeterred by the lack of response from Berkshire Health Systems, the coalition continued to advocate for a full-service hospital.

"Huddled together outside City Hall, a group of advocates for health care in the Northern Berkshires urged: Keep fighting."[10] At a candlelight vigil marking the third anniversary of NARH's sudden, shocking closing, about twenty-five people braved the cold rain to continue their support for a full-service hospital, one that included a maternity ward and inpatient addiction services. One of the coalition's members, Rachel Branch, called the "decimat[ion]" of the North Adams community hospital a "travesty of justice," and encouraged everyone to "remain steadfast and continue working to restore our full-service hospital with inpatient beds."[11]

By then, North Berkshire comprised the largest geographical region of the state lacking a full-service hospital—and a region with the hilliest terrain and toughest winters.

A LOCAL ECONOMIC AND SOCIAL SNAPSHOT

North Berkshire continued to lose population, down some 20 percent in 2017 since 1970 when nearly 47,000 residents had called it home. Berkshire County as a whole also declined in numbers over the same period, though at a lower rate, down 12 percent. Within North Berkshire, the biggest population losers were the historical mill towns, North Adams and Adams, the former declining 29 percent and the latter 28 percent.

As of 2017, the field of education employed the most people in North Berkshire—especially since the loss of North Adams Regional Hospital—with Williams College, the Massachusetts College of Liberal Arts, and the city, town, and regional school districts of the region leading the way. While industrial unions, like the International Union of Electrical workers at Sprague, became almost a thing of the past, and with the loss of union jobs at the former NARH, most organized workers in the area belonged to unions representing teachers or other public employees. For example, most of the 353 full-time employees of the North Adams school district belonged to six bargaining units, represented by the Massachusetts Teachers Association (MTA), American Federation of State, County and Municipal Employees (AFSCME), and the United Steelworkers (teacher assistants). For the 294 full-time employees at MCLA, the MTA and AFSCME headed the bargaining units. Williams College remains the biggest single employer in North Berkshire with 1,273 faculty and staff, all non-unionized. Just down the road in Williamstown, employees at Wild Oats Market have voted to join the United Food & Commercial Workers union, Local 1459, but as of 2017 had yet to achieve a contract. If they did, they would be represented by the same union to which Stop & Shop workers, across the town line in North Adams, belong.[12]

The economic and social problems that the region continues to face—low wage jobs, poverty, inadequate health care, poor transportation—more and more typify other regions of the United States, particularly in what might be termed the "Rust Belt." In 2017, the North Adams poverty rate passed 21 percent, and its unemployment rate (6.6 percent) placed it fifth among all the state's cities and towns. In that same year, its median household income ($37,654) made up just 56 percent of the state average, and the Adams median ($41,807) came in at 62 percent.[13] Yet, at a time with a heightened need for economic and social services, the state closed both the local employment and welfare offices.

The Berkshire Food Project (BFP), which provides free lunches and a pantry, found itself more and more in demand, serving 35,000 meals in 2017 from the social hall of the First Congregational Church, the same church that Social Gospel leader Washington Gladden led in the nineteenth century. Founded in 1986, the project "was supposed to be small and temporary," as volunteer and former board member Peter Buttenheim reflected on its history. It started serving forty to fifty people three times a week, but a little over twenty years later, some one hundred diners come five times a week. A stalwart of the project, Valerie Schwarz, served as kitchen manager and executive director for twenty-four years before her retirement. Emblematic of the intergenerational support for the BFP, Valerie had learned of its existence when her son Mathew, a Boy Scout, volunteered serving meals there. As Valerie remembered: "One day I came down with him, and I just loved it."[14]

Nearby on Eagle Street, the Friendship Center Food Pantry, hosted by the North Berkshire Interfaith Action Initiative also was in demand, necessitating a move in 2017 into bigger quarters, in order to provide food for about 2,000 families a year. Former MCLA sociologist Steve Green, one of the pantry's founders and a longtime North Adams volunteer, said he didn't "think we knew what to expect when we opened, how busy it would be, how great the need would be. The need is still there."[15]

Further north in North Adams, the Salvation Army (the North Adams Corps Community Center) and the Harvest Christian Ministries Soup Kitchen on River Street, both continue to offer food and meals to local residents. Symbolic of the economic divide facing local residents, the facilities stand just blocks away from the most exclusive address in the area, Porches Inn at 231 River Street.

Not surprisingly, homelessness remains a big problem. Louison House served over 3,500 individuals since it opened in 1990, but it faced an additional crisis on June 24, 2016, when a fire made it uninhabitable. The disaster hit just before Kathy Keeser, veteran community organizer, was about to take over as executive director of what had been officially called the Family Life Support Center. Finding a new home became the first priority and, with it, fund-raising. Success on both accounts, including an interest-free loan of $867,000 from the state, brought the agency a home on Church St. in North Adams, the Flood house, and the plans to rehab the fire-damaged home in Adams. In addition to the state loan, the agency was to receive $360,000 from insurance for the fire damage, and, importantly, raised close to $100,000 through its local campaign, "Rebuilding Hope."

THE NEW DIRECTOR'S CONCERNS

In a September 2017 interview, Kathy Keeser anticipated that with the completion of repairs, in addition to the twenty-two-bed shelter, new apartments will be added to both houses. Along with community apartments that the agency oversees, families in need will have access to fourteen supportive housing units/ apartments.

Though not a native of North Berkshire, Keeser has lived and worked in the region for over twenty years.[16] A native of Kentucky and Missouri, with an organizing and social work background, she arrived in late 1996 to work on Northern Berkshire Neighbors, a program of the Northern Berkshire Community Coalition (NBCC). While there, she teamed up with long-time local activist Sister Natalie Cain in the Neighbors programs and on other NBCC projects.

When she left NBCC in 2009, with an in-depth knowledge of local needs and resources, she began to work part-time at the Mohawk Forest Apartments as its residence service coordinator, writing grants and developing programs for their residents who live in 190 units. It became a full-time job in 2012, and Keeser held it until 2016 when the Louison House board asked her to lead the agency. She accepted the job knowing that "the community has been amazingly supportive of [the] organization's mission." As she put it, "People like to give back . . . . [T]his community in particular gives back."[17]

Keeser does worry about affordable housing in the region, a problem she sees getting worse as rental prices increase while wages stagnate; she sees "so many people struggling to make ends meet, some with substance abuse and mental health issues." Demand has overtaken supply for Section 8 assistance, and the federal government hasn't stepped up to make a difference. Right now, applicants seeking subsidized units in North Adams face a three-to-five-year wait time.[18]

For young people needing housing, the job market in North Berkshire continues to hold little promise. Beyond entry-level jobs paying minimum wage like Super Walmart, pickings remain slim. When individuals and families can't make the rent, some move in with others and "couch surf," but that leads to overcrowding and, often times, landlords halt the practice. Aleta Monecchi, a Louison board member, pointed out "the need for both buildings . . . . We see so many homeless people in this area and I don't think people around here believe or understand what's really going on."[19]

While more jobs will arrive if the Extreme Model Railway Museum and other promised museums come to the area, Keeser anticipates that most will pay minimum wage and offer no benefits. And rents might very well go up as more people move into the area.

The loss of the full-service hospital has also hurt the clients that Louison House tries to help. Getting down to BMC for treatment or to visit a family member or friend means a twenty-dollar round-trip bus fare and, if it's by ambulance, a significant co-pay. A Neighborhood for Health grant brought in a variety of useful, outpatient services, but, without being renewed, it operated for less than two years. With more and more doctors leaving the area, residents face additional health care worries.

ONGOING REGIONAL POLITICS

Politically the region remains a Democratic Party stronghold. In North Adams, about five times as many voters are registered Democrats than Republicans, which is higher than the state margin of three to one. In the 2016 presidential election, the Clinton percentage in North Adams (65.3 percent) ranked even higher than the state margin (60.8 percent). Massachusetts has historically had legislatures overwhelmingly controlled by Democrats, but often serving with "moderate" Republican governors.

The state's current Republican governor, Charlie Baker, defeated North Adams native and attorney general Martha Coakley in 2014. Baker had served in the administrations of previous Republican governors William Weld and Paul Cellucci, and, like them, holds liberal positions on social issues but leans conservative on fiscal policy. When out of government, he worked in both the corporate and nonprofit world of health care. Indicative of the political overlap between Massachusetts Democratic governors and their "moderate" Republican opponents, in 2006, Governor-elect Deval Patrick chose Charlie Baker to be on his transition team as a member of the Budget and Finance Committee.[20] Four years later, Baker, the Republican nominee for governor, challenged Governor Patrick in the election, an election that Patrick won.

In a career move that signaled the rightward shift of the Democratic Party, nationally and locally, after Governor Patrick left office he became a managing director at Bain Capital. In doing so, his new role joined him to his predecessor, former Republican Governor Mitt Romney, who himself helped start Bain Capital in 1984. Bain had become notorious for buying out companies, putting them in debt, laying off their workers and then walking away with huge profits. Locally, Bain had purchased KB Toys, headquartered in Pittsfield, in 2000. Bain then forced KB to borrow huge amounts of capital and had bankruptcy declared in 2004, resulting in the loss of 90 jobs in Pittsfield and 3,500 nationally.

During the 2012 presidential campaign, Democrats hammered presidential candidate Romney in his run against President Obama for his connection with Bain. Democratic National Committee Chairwoman Debbie Wasserman Schultz put it this way:

> Mitt Romney . . . is more of a job cremator than a job creator . . . . He dismantled companies. He cut jobs. He forced companies into bankruptcy and he outsourced jobs and sent jobs overseas.[21]

One Democrat who didn't join the attacks at the time and instead defended Bain was Deval Patrick, describing Bain as "a perfectly fine company."[22] And three years later, the former governor, who already had solid corporate credentials in his legal work for Texaco and Coca-Cola before assuming the top political spot in Massachusetts, joined the firm that Mitt Romney helped start.

A NATIONAL SNAPSHOT

While much has changed in the country and region since industrialization took off in the second half of the nineteenth century, the business cycles, including the recessions and depressions endemic to capitalism, have not. Historian Alexander Keyssar examined those cycles that impacted working people in the first part of the twentieth century (see Chapter Three). Using an example of a 70-year-old man in 1921, Keyssar wrote that that man would have experienced about a dozen "downturns" in the economy in the previous fifty years. For a similarly aged man or woman at the start of America's "Great Recession," which began in 2008, nine economic declines would have occurred in the previous fifty years, the period of transition from a manufacturing-based economy.[23] But, unlike previous recessions, the weak growth, the scarcity of good paying jobs, and the increase of suffering from that Great Recession continued for a much longer period of time.

The level of inequality in 2017 can be compared to that of the "Gilded Age," and the future, without industrial jobs and with the reality of climate change, may be worse than that faced by residents of the North Berkshire region at the end of the nineteenth century. One-tenth of the top 1 percent own as much wealth as the country's bottom 90 percent; 21 percent of U.S. children live in poverty, and that's according to the government's very conservative definition of poverty. Much of the population lives paycheck to paycheck; half are poor or close to poverty, and without assets.[24]

The United States spends more on its military than all the rest of the advanced economies combined and has 800 bases worldwide. The ongoing wars waged by the United States have become the new normal. The military has either invaded and/or bombed Iraq, Afghanistan, Pakistan, Somalia, Syria, Libya, and Yemen off and on since 2001. Since that year, the costs for military and homeland security total $4.79 trillion, and take in well over half of all federal discretionary spending. The National Priorities Project calculates that North Adams taxpayers have paid over $28 million in taxes toward the costs of all U.S. wars since 2001. At the same time, the North Adams city treasury remains starved for funds, leading to cuts, for example, of nine full-time teachers in its 2018 budget.[25]

While supporters of increased military spending often point to it as a job creator, numerous studies undermine that argument. For example, Heidi Garrett-Peltier concludes that for every $1 billion in federal spending on the military, a total of 11,200 jobs will be created, directly and indirectly. In comparison, for the same money spent on clean energy, job creation totals 16,800; for health care, 17,200; and for education, 26,700.[26] Given the dangers of human-induced climate change, and the concurrent need for good jobs, a growing call for another New Deal, a "Green" New Deal, has been developing. The goal would be an integrated struggle against environmental racism and militarism, and for new green jobs and a just transition for workers in fossil fuel industries.[27]

For much of the period that this book has covered, from the middle of the nineteenth century until the 1970s, virtually all U.S. workers had an employer, and many, if not most, had full-time, seemingly permanent work. Even though most had "employee at will" status and could be fired without cause, job security still appeared fairly certain. For employees under civil service contracts and those with union contracts, their job security seemed limitless.

But all that has changed. Over the past forty years or so, the percentage of workers in unions has fallen from 35 percent to 10.7 percent (even lower in the private sector)[28] for two reasons: industries where unions had been prevalent (blue-collar work in steel, rubber, electronics, auto, etc.) have disappeared or significantly declined, and also because federal and state governments as well as corporations have gone on the offensive against unions.

Witness the anti-union attacks in Wisconsin. In that state, despite massive protests in the state capitol, Governor Scott Walker survived a recall vote and passed legislation significantly restricting the collective bargaining rights of public-sector workers. The results: union membership has declined; take-home pay has fallen at the same time that pension and health-care costs have risen; and, in at least one county, public employees have lost the "just cause" provision of their contracts, leaving them no legal recourse if fired.[29]

Across the country, more and more workers have become contingent—contingent on an employer needing them, contracting with them at the employer's pleasure. Workers don't have permanent jobs. They work part-time and lack benefits, a perfect storm for anxiety and insecurity. One academic study found that all of the employment growth from 2005 to 2015, including the "recovery" years, came from the contingent, the gig, or "alternative work arrangement" economy. Further, during that same time period, the percentage of contingent workers holding more than one job increased from 7.3 percent to 32 percent.[30] The 530 medical employees who lost their jobs when NARH closed well exemplify this employment shift. Some have moved to hold similar jobs elsewhere—e.g., doctors and RNs—but most have stayed in the area working at the North Adams campus or in Pittsfield, part-time, without benefits, without a union, and with no control over their hours or schedule. For example, Julie Blanchard, a phlebotomist, worked thirty-five years at NARH, where she also served as a chief steward for the Service Employees International Union 285. When the hospital closed and she lost her full-time position, she had to travel to Pittsfield to BMC for work. Now, besides a much longer commute, she has fewer hours, gets paid on a per diem basis, and receives no benefits. She estimates that her co-workers' incomes have declined by 25 percent or more. Her own annual income has fallen by $10,000. [31]

These former NARH employees have become more and more the face of the "typical" American worker, whether laboring at McDonald's, as an adjunct at the University of Massachusetts, or as an LPN at Berkshire Medical Center. The power balance has shifted significantly to the employer, whether it is the government or a private employer, and any significant change for this pattern in the immediate future seems unlikely. It's a question of both structural change, with the end or diminution of factory/blue-collar work, and the loss of union or organized labor influence. The social contract that appeared to be in place at the end of World War II, in which corporations tolerated unions and both worked to maintain stability, has evaporated. For the workers of that generation who had achieved middle-class status, the appellation "happy worker," suggested by Wharton School Professor of Management Peter Cappelli, might seem to fit. Now, however, in the present era, Cappelli uses the term "frightened worker."[32]

SIMILARITIES AND DIFFERENCES

In the Introduction to this book, North Berkshire, particularly North Adams, is viewed in the context of industrializing communities in the country, even with its relatively small population and geographical isolation. As time went on, as North Berkshire underwent the same social forces as the rest of the nation—wars, business cycles, waves of unionization, globalization, deindustrialization, and a growing service economy—the responses of its working class in many cases mirrored that of the nation as a whole, and in other cases diverged from it.

But one way in which North Berkshire differs in a critical way from other Rust Belt communities, particularly those in the Midwest, is that the "Great Migrations"—the twentieth-century movements of southerners, both black and white, to northern cities in search of work and greater freedom—never arrived in North Berkshire. The region's isolation and relatively low wages offered too little of an inducement for internal migrants. Black and white Southerners had good reason to travel to Akron or Detroit to become part of a burgeoning auto industry, rather than make the trek to rural New England where low-paying textile jobs had already begun to decline. In fact, for Massachusetts as a whole, both the black and white "Great Migrations" hardly factored in at all, with just 2.7 percent of the state's population in 1970 having southern origins, a very low figure compared, for example, with Ohio's percentage of 12.8.[33]

The great migrations to North Berkshire occurred in the second half of the nineteenth century and the first two decades of the twentieth, not from within the United States, but from Canada and Europe. They changed the area ethnically and religiously from white English Protestant to predominantly white Catholic of Irish, French, Italian, and Polish extraction. And the heritage of that ethnic mix still characterizes North Berkshire, particularly Adams and North Adams, with fourth and fifth generations of that immigrant population remaining. In the North Adams census, leading ancestral backgrounds are French Canadian, followed by Irish and Italian. In Adams, not surprisingly, Polish ancestry stands on top, followed by French, Italian, and Irish. For the descendants of those early immigrants, their background has meaning, and helps to explain, for example, the historic vigil at St. Stanislaus Church in Adams. There some 200 people took part in a non-stop occupation for more than three years (2009–2012), finally convincing the authorities in the Vatican—bypassing the diocesan officials in Springfield—-to keep their church open.[34]

The population of both communities ranks older than the state average, as younger residents have been leaving, particularly with the decline of the industrial economy since the 1970s. The geographical isolation of the area, and its failure to attract new population, made it more self-reliant, a pattern that was explored earlier, during the Great Depression era.

WORKERS IN NEED OF A PLAN

In 1995, when MASS MoCA had already received an initial $35 million grant from the state, but four years before it opened, I headed a project presenting a local history play at MCLA. The play, "The Sprague Years," focused on labor-management relations at Sprague during its early years, the war years, the 1970 strike, and the company's closing. In the last scene of the play, a group of former Sprague employees, men and women, stand outside the main gate—which is by then locked and soon to be occupied by MoCA—and discuss the future, particularly what the next occupant of the facility will do.

> WOMAN: It makes you wish you knew what was going on in their heads, so you could figure out what to do yourself. (OTHERS NOD IN SAD AGREEMENT.)
>
> WALTER: It doesn't matter what they're talkin' about. They're gonna do what they're gonna do. (OTHERS REACT.) This gate was locked when R.C. got here, and look, it's locked right now.
>
> MABEL: (CATCHING ON.) The next company to unlock this gate is gonna want to take over, too, and we have to make sure that they don't.
>
> MACK: What will they want to do? We don't even know their plan.
>
> MABEL: And we probably never will. But that's just the point. They *have* a plan. We need our *own* plan.
>
> ALAN: That's right. It's *our* community.

MABEL: It's *our* jobs.

ALAN: It's *our* lives.

WALTER: Right, and we have to stick together—just like we did in 1970 [year of the 10-week strike].

MACK: O.K. (PAUSE) But aren't you worried about what they'll do?

ALAN: (nonchantly) No, not really. (PAUSES. LOOKS AT AUDIENCE, AND CLEARLY ENUNCIATES.) What matters most, after all, is what *we* do.

That sentiment, that it matters what *we* do, could stand as a credo for the residents of North Berkshire, for the working class of the area, whether anyone contemplates the historical past, or the present, or the future. The narrative began in the mid-nineteenth century with mill workers coming together to demand better wages and working conditions, and moved on to Crispin activists starting their own worker-owned shoe factory. Joining with the national Knights of Labor, a coalition of workers took off work to enjoy more leisure time, a Labor Day celebration, and, as the twentieth century emerged, skilled workers from a variety of crafts came together to form a central labor union. Immigrant textile workers, many without a craft, founded local unions on the basis of ethnicity and occupation, and they supported each other by uniting with mill workers across the region to improve their bargaining power. After World War II, they shifted from local independent unions to national ones, and in 1970, took on the biggest employer in the area with a ten-week strike.

As deindustrialization hit hard, they mobilized to try to form worker cooperatives and committed civil disobedience to stop "their" machines from being auctioned off. In the twenty-first century, workers formed community coalitions to save their jobs and support local strikers, and they rallied to support their co-workers in the Midwest when they were threatened with the loss of collective bargaining.[35] Finally, they protested the precipitous closing of their cherished local hospital, and, against great odds, continue the struggle to bring back the full-service facility that has been a mainstay in the community for over a hundred years.

They not only fought the owners of privately owned mills and factories, but also had to battle the state for support, whether it be for worker ownership or maintaining a full-service hospital. As Dick Dassatti said earlier about the state buyout of the Adams Print Works: "You have to talk to the people working there to find out what's wrong. Rather than people coming in and saving it, they should let people participate and point out where the problems were."[36]

If the people of North Berkshire did in fact participate not only in their workplace decisions, but also in the economic development priorities of their region, would they be saying "Yes" to a tourism-dominated future? Would a service-sector economy characterized by gift shops, distilleries, museums, restaurants, and gas stations be their first choice? Would they support a plan bringing in thousands and thousands of cars of day-trippers, coming and going, fouling the air and contributing to the climate crisis that is wreaking havoc on the planet?[37] Would they raise questions about the ability of elites—cultural, economic, and political—to create a huge model railroad museum in the city, but ignore the desperate need to bring back the passenger rail service their ancestors enjoyed up until the 1950s? With all the needs the communities of North Berkshire face—renewable energy, good, affordable housing, good-paying jobs, reliable mass transit, safe bridges, full-service health facilities, well-funded schooling—and given an option, what would the people choose?[38]

TOURISM AND THE ARTS, NATIONWIDE

In 1986, with the hope that tourism would revitalize the region's economy, plans for a huge museum of contemporary art to inhabit the twenty-six buildings on the 16 acres near North Adams's downtown went forward. More than three decades later, the bet on tourism doubled, perhaps tripled, with the prospect of additional museums, including the much ballyhooed "extreme" model railroad museum, to be built in the small city. During that same time period, numerous other cities across Rust Belt America have also shifted to tourism to help them survive a post-industrial future.

Most of the Rust Belt cities are much bigger than North Adams. For example, historian Aaron Cowan studied Cincinnati, St. Louis, Pittsburgh, and Baltimore, each of which has tried to rebuild their downtowns to attract visitors with money. Hotels, conventions centers, new stadiums, and attractive harbor areas replaced the factories and mills that helped power these cities in the past. While their post-industrial images may have been brightened in the popular press, and while tourists have indeed spent time and money in the renewed sections of town, most of the poor and working-class residents of these four cities have not seen their standard of living rise. In his Epilogue, Cowan writes of a "disconnect between the visitor-based economy and the needs of the local populace . . . ":

> The promises of tourist industry wealth spreading throughout the urban economy seem to ring hollow in the face of grim reality. Baltimore, Cincinnati, Pittsburgh, and St. Louis, despite extensive tourist development, continue well into the twenty-first century to be among the nation's poorest cities . . . . Pittsburgh—frequently cited as the model for

> post-industrial economic adaptation and for its livability—has the highest rate of black poverty of any major American city. A full two-thirds of Cincinnati city public school students drop out before graduation.[39]

Cowan does not dismiss the contribution that tourism might make in a city's development, but worries that "an overzealous dedication" to an economy that attracts temporary visitors takes precedent over "the needs of local residents."[40]

Daniel D'Oca, an urban designer and teacher at the Maryland Institute College of Art, looks specifically at the arts and economic development, and, like Cowan, focuses on Baltimore. In an interview, he stated that "[a]rtists can certainly bring value to a neighborhood and to a city [b]ut, obviously to address larger issues, there's a lot more that you need to do." When asked if he had a million dollars to donate, would he give any to the arts in Baltimore, D'Oca responded, "No . . . . There are worse problems in inner cities."[41]

In her review of the research on small and medium-sized cities that have turned to the arts for economic development, Myrna Breitbart finds results not very different from Cowan's.[42] In her own research on Holyoke, Massachusetts, and in the case studies she edits, she finds that local involvement in the arts through community-based organizations can bring about better outcomes for its working-class residents than top-down planning by local or out-of-town elites. How do we know if art-based economic development is working? Breitbart explained:

> In the end, success will be measured by more than the number of visitors who call in to a flagship museum or the number of new cafés that open to serve young entrepreneurs. It will be measured by the numbers of young people and displaced workers who are introduced to career trajectories and productive enterprises that take advantage of their potential and provide stable, high quality jobs.[43]

The leading advocate for art-led economic development early in the twenty-first century was Richard Florida. With his 2002 book, *The Rise of the Creative Class,* Florida, an academic economist, became a cultural phenomenon, jet-setting around the world, lecturing and consulting on the "creative class," a concept of his creation. Within three years, two more books followed: *The Flight of the Creative Class* and *Cities and the Creative Class.* To use the subtitle of his first *Creative* book, Florida argued that the creative class "is transforming work, leisure, community, & everyday life."[44]

While most economic development specialists focus on enticing industry and commerce to come into a city—often with tax breaks of one sort or another—Florida advocated building up the creative class whose efforts would enhance development. But what exactly is the creative class, and who falls into it? According to Florida, it encompasses some 30 percent of the labor force, workers who "share a common creative ethos that values creativity, individuality, difference, and merit." That includes not just artists, musicians, and writers, but also "people in science and engineering, architecture and design, education . . . business and finance, law, health care, and related fields."

On the lecture and consulting circuit, Florida played the role of an urban prophet, as one who advises city planners and government officials on what is to be done to move their cities forward. He used charts and anecdotes to argue for developing an environment that favors the migration of the creative class to America's cities, including an increase in local spending on amenities (e.g., museums, bike paths) to support their entry. Florida argued that, once sufficient numbers of the creative class settles down in any community, economic development will follow.

As time passed, Florida came to realize that cities that had captured significant numbers of the creative class also exhibited widening levels of inequality. Eleven years after his first "creative class" book, he wrote: "[T]alent clustering provides little in the way of trickle-down benefits."[45] Simply put, the 70 percent of the population that Florida had categorized into the working- and service- sector classes have not done well, but have fallen further and further behind with the loss of middle-class jobs and neo-liberal government policies.

Despite the failure of Florida's original "creative class" economic development thesis, cities, groups and organizations across the country, including Berkshire County, continue to use Florida's concepts and hope that his original thesis will bear fruit. Thomas Frank has been a leading critic of the national focus on art and artists as drivers of economic development. He compares Depression-era policy toward artists with our contemporary age:

> In the thirties, the federal government launched a number of programs directly subsidizing artists. Painters got jobs making murals for the walls of post offices and public buildings; theater troupes staged plays; writers collected folklore; photographers combed the South documenting the lives of sharecroppers. But no one expected those artists to pull us out of the Depression by some occult process of entrepreneurship-kindling. Instead, government supported them mainly because they were unemployed. In other words, government then did precisely the opposite of what government does today: in the thirties, we protected artists from the market while today we expose them to it, imagining them as the stokers on the hurtling job-creation locomotive.[46]

THE NEW MUSEUMS, TOURISM, AND THEIR ECONOMIC IMPACT ON THE REGION

The economic impact study of the Krens-related projects in the Heritage State Park and the Extreme Model Railway Museum next door relies on estimates of the number of visitors who will come and their spending habits. Economist Stephen Sheppard anticipates that, by 2020, the sectors that will gain the most revenue "are full-service restaurants, hotels and motels, museums and historical sites, distilleries, retail—including food and beverage stores—and real estate." Job growth, Sheppard estimates, will stabilize at 2,063. Given the vagaries of financing and construction, those expectations may be seen as optimistic at best.

If all goes as planned, Sheppard expects that the jobs that will result from the Krens-related development will pay an average of $16.00 an hour in 2020.[47] But what does it cost to live in Berkshire County? While the minimum wage refers to the legal wage that the employer must pay, the living wage refers to the wage that an individual must realistically earn to support her or his family—just the basic necessities, no luxuries. In all cases, the living wage is higher than the minimum wage.

A research group at Massachusetts Institute of Technology (MIT) has calculated the living wage for residents of Berkshire County: it varies by size and composition of family, taking into account local child care and housing costs, for example. Based on 2016 data, a single mom, working full-time with one child, would need an hourly living wage of $23.62. With more children, the needed living wage would rise, and, for adults without children, the wage would fall. Looking at the range of possibilities, one can see that already, four years *before* the 2020 Krens completion date, the anticipated average wage for that date will provide less than a living wage for Berkshire County residents.[48]

THE FUTURE?

As inequality increases, as more and more Americans have a hard time making it—at least half with no savings at all—one wonders how much worse it could get. There is resistance, locally and nationally, whether in the form of movements to protect the environment, Fight for Fifteen and a Union, Black Lives Matter, or immigrant rights.[49] But the individual struggles haven't yet coalesced into an unstoppable surge to change the rightward direction of the country. It's hard to predict when the next big "upsurge" will occur.[50] Who, after all, anticipated the great movements birthed in the early 1930s or at the beginning of the 1960s? As an undergraduate in 1963–1964, this author recalls reading sociologists like Daniel Bell and Seymour Martin Lipset, who wrote that we had reached homeostasis, harmony, in the United States, that our basic problems had been solved, and that there would be no more significant change in the future.[51] Almost as soon as we had read those words in our classes, we looked out the window and the Civil Rights Movement and Anti-War Movement had erupted.

It is important to remember our own history, just as we need to recall the examples of social change in the past. Change for the better often comes unexpectedly. As evidenced in this book, much of the written record and documentary evidence ignores the reality of the lives of marginalized groups, while focusing on and often glorifying those with wealth and power. In the nineteenth century, William C. Plunkett was lionized as a great industrialist, philanthropist, and man of moral character, while the historians and journalists of that time ignored his pro-slavery sentiments; in the current era, the local press portrays museum impresario Thomas Krens as the region's savior, recounting his successes and adventures with his Hollywood friends, while downplaying or ignoring many of his costly failures.

At the same time, little has been documented about "ordinary" people, their individual strivings and group efforts. Perhaps that explains our surprise when social change movements erupt: we have not seen them percolating from below. The daily press doesn't document unknown activists; YouTube videos do not include their informal meetings, or, if such videos exist, a would-be viewer must know where to find them. Some descendants of those industrial workers who did not appear in *Downside Up* may well be at the forefront of the progressive change that the North Berkshires need. The turnaround would be welcome, though difficult. And no one knows exactly what it will look like.

In Massachusetts, one candidate to spark that turnaround might well be the union of hospital nurses, the Massachusetts Nurses Association (MNA). An activist union, with an overwhelmingly female membership and a female leadership as well, the union has been a strong and persistent advocate for safe staffing levels and patient safety. At a time when the strike has virtually disappeared from the union playbook, three locals of the MNA went on strike in 2017 alone, over the staffing issue. In June of that year, 200 nurses struck the Baystate Franklin Medical Center in Greenfield, and the following month, 1,200 nurses went on strike at Tufts Medical Center in Boston. During the first week of October, 800 nurses at Berkshire Medical Center in Pittsfield and at its North County campus in North Adams went on strike: it was to be a one-day strike, but management locked them out for four more days, satisfying a contract they signed with "replacement" nurses.[52]

But the nurses knew what they were up against, and they stayed strong and enthusiastic during the whole week. The democratic ethos that pervades the union undoubtedly bolsters their strength. Unlike many other unions, any member can attend contract negotiations, not just a small committee, and information is readily shared. In a very unusual step, back in 2000, the MNA created a system by which union members could pay their dues directly to the union, rather than using a management payroll-deduction system, thus creating a stronger bond between union members. As Julie Pinkham, MNA director of labor relations described it, "The strength of the union is weakened when the relationship between you and your local unit resides in the technology of your employer."[53]

Prior to the strike and lockout, the nurses had numerous rallies, informational picket lines, petitions, and open meetings for the public. They and their supporters used social media and wrote letter after letter to the local press explaining the staffing issues. While the bulk of the picketing went on in Pittsfield at the main BMC site, some 100 nurses and their supporters picketed at the North County campus. Mary Bryant, a former nurse who worked at North Adams Regional Hospital for forty years before it closed in 2014, and now a BMC patient, picketed as well. Mary was joined by members of the North County Cares Coalition, including coalition co-chair, Dick Dassatti, who "described the nurses as 'speaking truth to power.'"[54]

Several political candidates joined the demonstration including Jason LaForest, a nurse in Williamstown and a candidate for City Council. LaForest, who went on to be elected to Council a month later, criticized the "people at the top" . . . [for] "trying to turn the country against nurses and other workers."

The nurses, the patients they served, and their supporters didn't get the improved staffing ratios they wanted. Not as of mid-2018. But they have kept hope alive, and continue the generational struggles that their North Berkshire forebears have waged over the past two centuries. Whether they know the words or not, they march in the spirit of Holly Near: "For to be hopeless would seem so strange, It dishonors those who go before us, So lift me up to the light of change."[55]

Sign at third-anniversary vigil for a full-service hospital, North Adams City Hall (Stephanie Zollshan, *Berkshire Eagle*, March 28, 2017).

Julie Blanchard holds a candle at the third-anniversary vigil (Stephanie Zollshan, *Berkshire Eagle,* March 28, 2017).

NOTES

1 Scott Stafford and Adam Shanks, "Building 6's big bang attracts thousands to Mass MoCA's new expanded footprint," *Berkshire Eagle,* May 28, 2017; Linda Enerson, "The Promise of MASS MoCA," *CommonWealth Magazine,* 22, 3, Summer, 2017, 44–45.

2 Enerson, 44 and 45–46.

3 Nationwide, over half a million Americans died from drug overdoses from 2000 to 2015, the results in part from vastly increased prescriptions for opioids (*Naked Capitalism,* March 29, 2017). "Inside a Killer Drug Epidemic: A Look at America's Opioid Crisis," *New York Times,* January 6, 2017; Kevin McKenzie, "Opioid crisis points to racial divide," *USA Today Network,* March 27, 2017.

4 Ralph Brill Associates, "Opinion: How Did Opioid Abuse Overtake the Berkshires? And What is Next?" *The Greylock Glass,* June 16, 2016; "Opioid Overdose in Western Massachusetts: Springfield and Western Counties compared to statewide data," *Baystate Health, Public Health Issue Brief,* October, 2015; Phil Demers, "New Berkshire Medical Center unit to provide longer-term treatment for opioid addictions," *Berkshire Eagle,* April 26, 2016; "A Closer Look," Berkshire Taconic Community Foundation, 2017; Derek Gentile, "Heroin, opioids now top alcohol as No. 1 substance treatment at Brien Center," *Berkshire Eagle,* June 27, 2014; and from resolution North County Cares Coalition submitted to North Adams City Council, May 10, 2016. Adam Shanks, "Vigil recalls those lost to addiction and hope for those recovering," *Berkshire Eagle,* September 24, 2017.

5 Phil Demers, *Berkshire Eagle,* April 26, 2016.

6 *Boston Globe,* March 28, 2016.

7 Adam Shanks, *Berkshire Eagle,* September 24, 2017.

8 Resolution submitted by North County Cares Coalition; Tammy Daniels, "North Adams Council Backs Resolution Calling for Detox Center," *iBerkshires,* June 29, 2016.

9 Stephen Dravis, "Williamstown Adopts Resolution on Opioid Addiction Services," *iBerkshires,* August 24, 2016.

10 Adam Shanks, "Vigil marks third anniversary of North Adams Regional Hospital closing," *Berkshire Eagle,* March 28, 2017, 1.

11 Ibid. I was invited to speak at the vigil and focused my remarks on criticizing my former employer, MCLA, for awarding the CEO of Berkshire Medical Center an honorary degree for public service at the upcoming college commencement. I argued that not until David Phelps makes the North Adams campus a full-service hospital will he have earned the degree.

12 Ellen Sutherland, assistant to the superintendent, North Adams school district email; "MCLA President's Report, 2016–2017," 70; Simone Anderson, Williams College human relations email, July 25, 2017. The North Berkshire unionization rates reflect the national trend of higher

union density among public sector workers as compared to those in the private sector. In 2016, the public-sector percentage stood at 34.4 percent and the private-sector just 6.4 percent, and the total unionization percentage at 10.7 percent ("Economic News Release; Union Members Summary, *Bureau of Labor Statistics,* January 26, 2017). http://hillcountryobserver.com/2017news/july2017wildoats.htm

13 For an example of the difficulties of surviving on a fast-food worker wage in North Adams, see Megan Woolhouse, "Between haves, have-nots, an ever greater gulf," *Boston Globe,* August 21, 2011; Enerson, *CommonWealth Magazine,* 44, 45–46; "2010–2014 American Community Study," *U.S. Census Bureau.*

14 Adam Shanks, "Over 24 Years with the Berkshire Food Project, Valerie Schwarz Retires," *Berkshire Eagle,* September 4, 2017.

15 *Berkshire Eagle,* May 11, 2015.

16 For a lengthy interview with Kathy Keeser, see Joe Manning, *Disappearing into North Adams* (Florence, MA: Flatiron Press, 2001), 181–184.

17 Tammy Daniels, *iBerkshires,* October 26, 2017.

18 Brad Gordon, Berkshire County Regional Housing Authority, at Northern Berkshire Community Coalition February 2017 Forum. For the county as a whole, Gordon estimates that 56 percent of renters are "rent burdened" and 29 percent "severely rent burdened."

19 Adam Shanks, "Louison House readies for an upgrade," *Berkshire Eagle,* September 22, 2017. In late October 2017, the number of people who had received service at the agency over the past year totaled more than 400, compared to 288 in 2016 (*iBerkshires,* October 26, 2017).

20 https://web.archive.org/web/20070110152159http://www.patrickmurraytransition.org/press/Transition_Groups112206.pdf (accessed 8/12/2017).

21 Beth Healy, "Deval Patrick takes investing role at Bain Capital," *Boston Globe,* April 4, 2015; Clarence Fanto, "Bain Capital's role in KB Toys' demise still a point of controversy," *Berkshire Eagle,* October 28, 2012; Alexander Bolton, "Bain gives more campaign money to Democrats than it does to Republicans," *The Hill,* January 19, 2012.

22 "Bain Capital gains former Massachusetts governor," *The Hill,* April 14, 2015.

23 National Bureau of Economic Research, www.nber.org/cycles.html (accessed July 15, 2017).

24 Paul Street, "Russia Trumps Ecocide at the Petroleum Broadcasting System," *Counterpunch,* July 14, 2017. Racial minorities face even greater difficulties.

25 David Vine, *Base Nation: How U.S. Military Bases Abroad Harm America and the World* (New York: Henry Holt & Co., 2015); Neta C. Crawford, "US Budgetary Costs of Wars through 2016: $4.79 Trillion and Counting: Summary of Costs of the U.S. Wars in Iraq, Syria, Afghanistan and Pakistan

and Homeland Security," *Watson Institute, Brown University,* September 2016; www.nationalpriorities.org/cost-or-war/ (accessed January 5, 2018); "North Adams Budget Goes to City Council," WAMC, June 12, 2017; Kevin Zeese and Margaret Flowers, *Counterpunch.org,* July 31, 2017. The National Priorities Project website also has a "Trade-Offs" section where you can see, for example, the number of teachers who could be hired; the number of clean energy jobs created; the number of Head Start slots for children that could be funded, etc., for the comparable tax dollars spent on war. See *Farewell to Factory Towns?* for trade-offs for North Adams as of 2012.

26 www.truth-out.org/news/item/27921-cost-of-war

27 See Jeremy Brecher (newlaborforum.cuny.edu/author/jeremy-brecher/); work being done at the Political Economy Research Institute at the University of Massachusetts, Amherst, by Robert Pollin and colleagues (https://www.peri.umass.edu); the Green New Deal proposed by the Green Party (https://www.jill2016.com/greennewdeal); and the work of the National Priorities Project (https://www.nationalpriorities.org), which documents the benefits for local and state budgets by cutting the military budget. Part 3 of *Farewell to Factory Towns?* uses National Priorities Project data to illustrate the specific educational, health, and environmental benefits that would come to the citizens of North Adams absent the costs of war; for the fight against environmental racism, see greenfaith.org/programs/environmentaljustice; and for a recent book that covers many of these themes, Naomi Klein, *This Changes Everything: Capitalism vs. the Climate* (New York: Simon & Schuster, 2014).

28 "Union Members Summary for 2016," *Portside,* January 28, 2017 (https://portside.org).

29 Steven Greenhouse, "Wisconsin's Legacy for Unions," *New York Times,* February 22, 2014.

30 Mike Whitney, "The 'Gig Economy'; Another Vicious Attack on Ordinary Working Slobs," *Counterpunch,* April 6, 2016.

31 Telephone interview.

32 Peter Cappelli, *The New Deal at Work: Managing the Market-Driven Workforce* (Boston: Harvard Business School Press, 1999).

33 James N. Gregory, *The Southern Diaspora: How the Great Migration of Black and White Southerners Transformed America* (Chapel Hill: The University of North Carolina Press, 2005).

34 As parishioner Robin J. Loughman put it, "We had a close knit parish with a lot of Polish traditions and we wanted to keep that going . . . . I think it helped keep pressure on the diocese to show our dedication . . . ." Lori Stabile, "After three-year vigil, St. Stanislaus Church in Adams reopening for services," *Springfield Republican,* February 18, 2012.

35 The April 4th Coalition organized in North Berkshire to support public workers under attack in Wisconsin. Along with protestors in over 1,200 communities across the Unite States, the coalition rallied with speeches

and music at City Hall in North Adams on April 4, 2011. Scenes from the rally can be seen in *Farewell to Factory Towns?* a documentary written and directed by the author, 2012.

36 *Farewell to Factory Towns?*

37 In his economic analysis of the new model train museum, Stephen Sheppard anticipates that the museum will attract between half a million and three quarters of a million visitors a year to North Adams. "The Economic Impacts of EMRCA: The Extreme Model Railroad and Contemporary Architecture Museum," Center for Creative Community Development, Williams College, 2017, 12. How many cars will that mean, in a region without passenger train service and infrequent bus service? How much carbon dioxide will those cars emit in a year? While the carbon emissions might be thought of as an "externality" in any economic analysis, the reality is that they add to the rapidly poisoning of our planet. So far, I haven't heard or read of any proponent of the museum showing any concern over that.

38 Three young local men have answered that question themselves by starting a production company manufacturing tiny houses in North Adams's Windsor Mill. The three, former Hoosac Valley High School classmates, employ more than forty workers, who build small—even tiny—affordable homes. They apparently had no problem in hiring employees with the skills to do the work, and they buy most of their supplies locally (Tammy Daniels, "North Adams Tiny House Builders See Growth in Affordable, Custom Housing," *iBerkshires,* September 19, 2017). A voluminous literature concludes that domestic, New Deal–type of federal spending is the fastest and greatest contributor to job growth. See, e.g., "Study says domestic, not military spending, fuels job growth," May 25, 2017, https://news.brown.edu/articles/2017/05/jobscow. Passenger service, which took residents to Boston or New York City, ended in 1958. In 1973, in remarks prepared for the North Adams commemoration of the centennial of the Hoosac Tunnel opening, U.S. Representative Silvio O. Conte said, "[T]he nation must 'restore a profitable rail system to the Northeast—the kind of viable network envisioned by the men who planned and constructed the Hoosac Tunnel.'" Conte had a strong family connection to the tunnel as his father had worked there, and, on his mother's side, her family provided lodging for tunnel laborers. ("Hoosac Tunnel opening marked in ceremonies, *Transcript,* Nov. 28, 1973, reprinted in "Centennial Edition, Oct. 27, 1995, 28.)

39 Aaron Cowan, *A Nice Place to Visit: Tourism and Urban Revitalization in the Postwar Rustbelt* (Philadelphia: Temple University Press, 2016), 157.

40 Ibid., 159.

41 Greg Harrison, "Can the arts save struggling cities?" November 4, 2011 (http://grist.org/cities/2011-11-03-can-the-arts-save-struggling-cities/).

42 Myrna Margulies Breitbart, *Creative Economies in Post-industrial Cities: Manufacturing a (Different) Scene* (Burlington, VT: Ashgate Publishing Company, 2013).

43 Ibid., 307. Breitbart critically asks, "Where are the visions for change in post-industrial communities derived, and how, if at all, are residents brought in the planning process?" (3). The plan for MoCA, of course, as well as the more recent proposals by Thomas Krens, originated from the outside without the involvement of North Berkshire's working class residents. Breitbart has examined MoCA and its consequences and notes "locally anticipated high paying jobs for residents and tourist spillover effects have yet to materialize" (7).

44 Richard Florida, *The Rise of the Creative Class* (Cambridge, MA: Basic Books, 2002); *The Flight of the Creative Class: The New Global Competition for Talent* (New York: HarperCollins, 2005); and *Cities and the Creative Class* (New York: Routledge, 2005).

45 Richard Florida, "More Losers Than Winners in America's New Economic Geography," *Atlantic,* January 20, 2013. The bulk of the subtitle of Florida's latest book (*The New Urban Crisis,* New York: Basic Books, 2017) bears witness to the author's recognition of what's happened to contemporary cities, despite the growth of the "creative class": *How Our Cities are increasing Inequality, Deepening Segregation, and Failing the Middle Class* . . . .

46 Thomas Frank, "Dead End on Shakin' Street, *The Baffler,* #20, 2012.

47 Sheppard, "The Economic Impacts of EMRCA . . . ." See, especially pages 12 and 19.

48 Amy K. Glasmeier and the Massachusetts Institute of Technology, "Living Wage Calculation for Berkshire County, Massachusetts," http://livingwage.mit.edu/counties/25003. Of course, legislating a living (not minimum) wage faces roadblocks (See David Kassel, "Living wage in Massachusetts suffers a setback," https://cofarblog.wordress.com/2017/07/31/living-wage-in-massachusettts-suffers-an-setback/). With the state minimum wage now at $11 an hour, progressives are mobilizing to put a referendum on the November 2018 ballot to increase that number by $1 a year until it reaches $15 an hour in 2021 (Dick Lindsay, "Berkshires-based Raise Up Mass backs $15 minimum wage, paid leave ballot effort," *Berkshire Eagle,* September 18, 2017).

49 For examples of such activism, see Karen Andrews, "Physician fleeing Pennsylvania gas wells fights Berkshire pipeline," *the Berkshire Edge,* August 3, 2014; Tammy Daniels, "North Adams Rallies Protest, Support Trump's Travel Ban," *iBerkshires,* February 4, 2017; Tony Dobrowolski, "Berkshire businesses oppose 'pipeline tax,'" *Berkshire Eagle,* March 21, 2017; and J.D. Allen, "A North Adams Mayoral Candidate without Mail Outs, Lawn Signs," WAMC.org, July 17, 2017.

50 Dan Clawson, *The New Upsurge: Labor and the New Social Movements* (Ithaca: Cornell University Press, 2003). Clawson argues that "A new upsurge . . . will fuse the unions of today with the issues and styles of the social movements of the 1960s, producing new forms and taking up new issues" (x).

51 Daniel Bell, *The End of Ideology: On the Exhaustion of Political Ideas in the Fifties* (Cambridge, MA: Harvard University Press, 1960; and Seymour Martin Lipset, *Political Man: The Social Bases of Politics* (Garden City, NY: Doubleday, 1960).

52 Larry Parnass, *Berkshire Eagle,* October 4, 2017.

53 Jane McAlevey, "The Massachusetts Nurses' Union is Reviving the Strike," *Nation,* July 19, 2017.

54 Adam Shanks, "100-plus locked-out BMC nurses rally in North Adams," *Berkshire Eagle*, October 5, 2017, 1.

55 www.hollynear.com/show_up.html (see "I Am Willing" under TRACK LISTING).

CHAPTER TWENTY-NINE

GENERATIONS PAST, PRESENT, AND FUTURE

AT THE BEGINNING of the twentieth century, immigrants from what is now northern Italy traveled to North Adams and to Readsboro, Vermont, to begin life in the "New World." They came from South Tyrol, which, prior to World War I, was part of the Austro-Hungarian Empire. Dick Dassatti is a fourth-generation descendant from that pioneer group, and, with children and grandchildren living in North Adams, the Dassattis can claim sixth-generation status.

In 2011, Dick helped organize the April 4th Coalition, which brought together local unionists and supporters to rally against Wisconsin Governor Scott Walker's attempt to dismantle public-sector collective bargaining. In 2014, when the North Adams Regional Hospital (NARH) closed with three days' notice, he joined the campaign to reopen it and helped found North County Cares Coalition, which continues to advocate for a full-service hospital in North Adams.

Dick's ancestors have a history of community and labor activism. His maternal great grandmother, Virginia Donati, worked as a midwife in her native Austria and immigrated to the United States with her husband, Enrico, around 1880. She received the required certification in New York to maintain her profession, which she continued to practice in North Adams. Her middle daughter, Annie Maroni, Dick's grandmother, was born in 1901 in the Flatiron building, just above the train tracks on West Main Street.

When Annie retired after a blue-collar career at Sprague Electric Company, she became a VISTA volunteer, served with the Northern Berkshire Community Action agency, and eventually received the Carol Hess award for her community service. While a member of VISTA, she tutored young people, and later, volunteering for the Commonwealth Service Corps, she assisted in a hot lunch program for the elderly. Her continued work with the elderly led to her appointment to the North Adams Council on Aging. The Carol Hess Memorial Committee voiced their pleasure in giving "public recognition to a woman who is widely known and loved for her deeds of service and warm concern for others."[1]

Annie's husband, Cherubino Maroni, worked for many years at the Mt. Hope Farm estate in Williamstown, where he headed the gardening crew. Concerned that all the employees lacked benefits, he tried to organize them to pressure management for additional help, including life insurance coverage. Dick remembers his grandfather telling him about management's response. Once they learned about the developing battle, a management spokesmen lectured the workers about asking for too much amidst the insecurity of their jobs. With the fear of unemployment in the air, the organizing drive dissipated. One of Annie and Cherubino's sons, Henry, kept the organizing spirit alive, however, in his role as president of the North Adams Police Association in 1965.

Dick's paternal grandfather, Emilio Dassatti, settled in Readsboro, where he worked in the wood pulp and wooden chair factories. He was one of 200 workers from South Tyrol who was recruited in just one year to work in the mills in Readsboro. In the 1920s, he left Vermont for North Adams, where he worked shoveling coal for the Boston-Maine Rail Road, earning enough to purchase two houses—for his own family and for rental income. In North Adams, he helped found the Tyrolean Mutual Aid Society, which provided social support as well as insurance and burial aid for fellow immigrants and their families.

Dick's father, Erminio, left school after eighth grade and worked in a tie factory and for the railroad before he got drafted in 1942. While serving in North Africa, he learned that he had a job waiting for him as a custodian at Drury High School back in North Adams. Happy about that future, Dick's father told his sergeant, who responded, "Get back down in the foxhole or you won't make it back to take the job." At Drury, he joined the union that represented both the custodians and the teachers. Later, in the 1960s, when a split developed, he started a separate custodians' union, and served as its president, representing custodians in all of the city's schools.

Both sides of Dick's family came from the same village in Tyrol, settled in the State Street neighborhood of North Adams, and involved themselves in the Tyrolian Society. Dick grew up in an extended family, with all relatives living in the two houses next to each other that his grandfather had purchased. Their lives revolved around work, family, community, and church.

Dick remembers the emphasis his immigrant community placed on education for his generation. Many of his friends and family went off to college and settled away from North Adams. Dick had no desire to leave the area. "To me it was great," he said. "We had Little League baseball, basketball, the YMCA downtown. There was a lot to do. It was quite a community." He grew up during the "Great Society" days in the 1960s and recalls summer playgrounds where college students, young men and women, were able to get government-funded jobs working at the recreation centers. Dick got some paid work in the "Youth Corps" at age 13, cutting grass and doing other outdoor work; he continued working summers at local parks through the age of 18. He remembers the Reagan years when those kinds of jobs ended, and views toward the federal government began to change. "For some reason there's people in the society who think giving people of low income a job when they're young . . . is a bad thing."

He started college at the University of Massachusetts, where he joined a student-organizing project, and back at home in the summer he worked at "Help Line," training volunteers to help people in need who called in their distress. As a high school student, he had been a "Help Line" volunteer. At UMass,

Dick took a variety of liberal arts courses and liked them. One day, after listening to three different lectures on the Marxist theory of alienation, he recognized his own alienation, and he decided he needed time off from school. He went home and took a job at Arnold Print Works (APW) in Adams.

Though the older workers teased him for being a college boy, he found community there, working with some of the same people who had earlier worked with his grandfather. For five years, he went back and forth to college and APW. He also got married, became the father of two children, and finished his college career at North Adams State College.

He learned a lot at APW, about craft and skill, about hierarchy, and about working together. When the company filed for bankruptcy, Dick saw opportunity:

> Here's a chance we could run this place. We could have a worker-owned mill here. I think we could do it. The state came in and bought it. All these guys came in to reorganize it. There was one guy, Teddy Kondell. I worked with him in the shipping department. He [had] worked with my grandfather. He was there for over twenty-five years . . . . All these politicians and everybody came in and they were going to save APW. They walked by Teddy and everybody else. They didn't know how to change the structure. You have to talk to the people who work there and find out what's wrong. Rather than people coming in to save it, they should have tried to let people participate and point out where the problems were.

Thinking back on that experience some twenty-five years later, Dick sees similar problems today. "Our whole society is top down. The social structure has to be reversed."

After APW, Dick had a variety of jobs including a stint at a factory chicken farm in Williamstown where he tried to organize a union, mostly for safety reasons. He and his family lived in Shelburne Falls for a couple of years but finally moved back to North Adams in 1984, living in the house of his birth, taking the apartment above his parents. He began a career, which he still follows, as a letter carrier for the Postal Service. An activist in his union, he served as steward and legislative liaison for more than a decade.

He got to know the community really well, and worried about the economic and social problems caused by the mid-1980s factory closings. He saw worker cooperatives and worker ownership as a way of dealing with runaway shops. As a member of the Northern Berkshire Labor Coalition, he worked with laid-off supermarket employees who eventually started Heritage Supermarket. When he heard about the development of small, craft cottage industries back in Tyrol, he began to inquire about the possibility of a similar constellation to fill the empty buildings that Sprague abandoned. He suggested it to a local group looking into the future of that site, but any other plans got preempted by the coming of MASS MoCA.

After he finished his formal college study, Dick read on his own, learning about Liberation Theology and the importance of focusing on the poor, of seeing their perspective and recognizing their spirituality. Active in his church, he enjoyed teaching eighth graders, discussing social issues. From the writings of Jane Jacobs, he grew to appreciate the value of looking at one's own community as an economic and social resource.

While Dick supported the entrance of MoCA into North Adams, he knew it wasn't the cure-all for the region's economic problems. It had, however, brought new blood into the community, including artists with innovative and creative ideas.

Still, poverty seemed intractable and good jobs, scarce. Dick knew that a good job was central to a full life. "If you're employed, you have a network . . . someone that you interact with on a regular basis, something that you can participate in . . . . For people not to have that network, you're outside of society."

With times hard in North Adams, in 1995 Governor William Weld threatened to make things even worse. Dick grew concerned when he learned that, in Weld's efforts to enact welfare "reform," he had sent letters to everyone on welfare stating that, unless the Legislature acted, all benefits would end in one month.

Along with other members of his church, Dick brought welfare recipients together to discuss Weld's letters and his policy goals. When they learned that the governor planned on visiting North Adams, they organized a protest. On the day Weld met with local officials, they stood in front of City Hall. "We were holding signs," Dick said. "I think Sister Natalie Cain was there. And I was selected to go in and talk to the governor's aide to tell him why we were out there."

Dick told the aide that the recipients were worried that, if they lost their checks, the Department of Social Services would come and take their kids. "They think you want to steal their children. I don't think that's what you want to do, but they don't understand that. Could you please come out and just talk to them about what you're trying to accomplish?"

The aide refused, and, when the governor exited City Hall, he "just whisked by us, [didn't] even acknowledge that we [were] there." Later, Weld appeared on the local radio station. When asked about the protest, he responded, "They're just a bunch of people who didn't want to work."

Dick has continued to support efforts to reduce poverty in his volunteer efforts for Habitat for Humanity and the Berkshire Food Project. As he phrased it: "Any economy that increases poverty is doomed for failure. We cannot continue like this. Our whole economy is based on a few people consuming a lot of items. We have to turn things around." In speaking specifically about North Adams, he said:

> Until those people that used to work in the mills have a place within our economy where they can be productive and contribute, we won't be successful as a community—I think that we will build an economy that includes them, but it's going to take another generation . . . [a] younger generation.

Dick's son, Peter, a member of that younger generation, heard about the sudden NARH closing in the spring of his junior year at Wheaton College. Coincidentally, the announcement came on the same day in 2014 that he had to decide on the topic for his senior thesis. Peter immediately knew that he had to publicize and protest the hospital's closing; he decided that a documentary would be his vehicle. He had minimal experience with film production, but spent the summer learning the craft and conducting interviews in North Adams. He completed the interviews during his winter break and finished the project in the spring of 2015. The film, *Shutting NARH*,[2] tells the story of the closing of the hospital through the use of powerful, emotional interviews with some of the 530 employees who lost their jobs. In addition, Peter's on-camera interviews with EMTs and local residents illustrate the ripple effects throughout the community of a lost hospital, business closings, and fears of dealing with unmet health and safety needs. Finally, the film highlights the protest that developed, and on the first anniversary of the hospital closing, it follows a cavalcade of residents driving to Berkshire Medical Center in Pittsfield in a March snowstorm to demand the return of a full-service hospital to North Berkshire.

Two years after his college graduation, Peter works for a health care company in Quincy, Massachusetts. He lives in Boston and is employed as a business analyst, after starting as a call center operator. Peter describes his job as helping people who face surgery or other medical procedures get second opinions on their medical condition. The people he talks to have very good insurance, which allows them to receive additional medical advice and support. Peter's hope is to stay in the field of health, but to work in a setting where he can help underinsured people get the same high-quality medical advice that his company now offers more affluent patients.

Peter credits the experiences he had growing up in North Adams as the biggest influences on his life. He sees his parents, grandparents, and even his junior hockey coach as central to his development. He learned the importance of family, of community, and of hard, persistent work. He did manual labor on a local farm and for a roofing company, where he learned to value the importance of quality work and the need to pay attention to detail.

When asked about the future of a real hospital in North Adams, he doesn't know how it will all turn out. He worries about it, is still upset over its "illegal" closing, and the "unfortunate" consequences for the North Berkshire region. He realizes that it's "business," not health care needs, that keeps the hospital from becoming "full-service." And he bemoans the fact that, in 2017, "the public college in North Adams" granted an honorary degree in public service to David Phelps, the CEO of Berkshire Medical Center, who continued to refuse to make the North Adams campus a full-service facility.

Like many others of his generation, Peter has college loans to pay off. If he had the financial security of a good job, he would move back to North Adams. As he puts it, he would "100 percent" like to live there. "It's home, it's a beautiful area, and the mountains can't be taken away."[3]

Dassatti extended family gathering, circa 1960, at Maurice "Buddy" Maroni's apartment porch, four or five houses from Dick Dassatti's family apartment. The man in the photo is Buddy Maroni, a city firefighter and Dick's uncle and godfather. The visible woman is Mary "Mammie" Cimmonetti, who lives upstairs from Buddy. All the children are either first or second cousins of Dick's. He, four or five at the time, is to the right, closest to the camera and looking sideways. To the far right is Dick's cousin Cary (Dassatti family collection).

Tyrolese Society family picnic, probably from the 1940s (Dassatti family collection).

NOTES

1 Interview with Dick Dassatti, February 6, 2018, and *Transcript* obituary, August 3, 1982. Much of the information on the Dassatti family comes from the interview with Dick, as well as an additional filmed interview for *Farewell to Factory Towns?*

2 https://www.youtube.com/watch?v=yRfBUIR5h0M

3 Information from Peter Dassatti from series of phone calls and emails, December 2017 to February 2018.

ACKNOWLEDGEMENTS

I owe a great deal of gratitude to the librarians, historians, and archivists who have provided me with the photos, manuscripts, documents, books, and news articles that have made this book possible. Many thanks to Gene Carlson, Justyna Carlson, Chuck Cahoon, and Paul W. Marino of the North Adams Historical Society; Eugene Michalenko of the Adams Historical Society; Sarah Currie, director of the Williamstown Historical Museum; Mike Miller, Williamstown History Email Group; Linda Kaufmann, Massachusetts College of Liberal Arts research librarian; Katie Nash, Williams College archivist; Kim DiLego and Robin Martin, North Adams Public Library research librarians; Janine Whitcomb, Special Collections Archives Manager, University of Massachusetts, Lowell; staff at Pittsfield's Berkshire Athaneum; Will Garrison and John Dickson, Berkshire County Historical Society; and to the archivists at the University of Massachusetts, Amherst; Khell Center for Labor Documentation and Archives, Cornell; Wisconsin Historical Society; and the University of Pittsburgh. And special thanks to Leon Beverly, who efficiently shepherded me through the Sprague Electric Company archives.

While the *Transcript* no longer exists, much of its photo file does, and its photographs, many taken by the legendary Randy Trabold, have helped to illustrate *The Gritty Berkshires*. The *Berkshire Eagle* Community News Coordinator and Librarian, Jeannie Maschino, has helped me discover and sort through numerous valuable photographs, and the *Eagle's* own photographers, Gillian Jones and Stephanie Zollshan, have graciously allowed me to use numerous contemporary photographs that they have taken. Finally, I owe a debt of thanks to the North Berkshires online newspaper, *iBerkshires*, and its editor, Tammy Daniels, for additional help with local news and photos.

At a time when the manuscript was long but rough, I was fortunate to meet a young historian/librarian, Seth Kershner, who works at Northwest Connecticut Community College in Ralph Nader's hometown, Winsted. Seth was as interested in working class history as was I and knew an awful lot about U.S. labor history. As he was also a published writer, I was wise enough to ask him to edit my chapters and he agreed. He worked quickly, and we went through it all, chapter by chapter, with stylistic and substantive suggestions. The latter led me to read more books on labor history, which enabled me to provide the context for much that I had written on labor struggles in North Berkshire. Many thanks, Seth.

The impetus for my writing on North Adams and North Berkshire history has been my teaching at what began as North Adams State College in 1978 and ended as Massachusetts College of Liberal Arts in 2010. Many of my students were first generation college students, working-class and from the area. I learned much from them informally, in classes, through their internships, and in joint community work. They cared about the community and its history, and we often worked together to learn and write about that vibrant history. I hope I taught them half as much as they taught me.

Outside of the classroom, the Northern Berkshire Labor Coalition served as a vehicle for learning about the region's problems and opportunities and a safe place for discussing new ideas, whether they were worker ownership or inter–union cooperation. The camaraderie and activism that the coalition fostered helped keep me focused on the day-to-day realities of life in the region during a tough time of deindustrialization. Many of the names of coalition members can be found in the pages of this book. Towards the end of my stay in North Adams, a long–time resident of the community named Dick Dassatti helped start the April 4th Coalition and, later, the North Community Cares Coalition, dedicated to supporting collective bargaining and a full–service regional hospital. From my first years in North Adams to the present, Dick has been a good friend and has helped me understand the history of the area, its needs and its strengths. His abiding optimism and community involvement have made him a model social activist that many have come to admire and appreciate, as have I.

Over the years of my writing, I have enjoyed and learned much from conversations with other friends and writers including Joe Manning, Irv Seidman, Ben Jacques, and Rabbi Shirley Idelson. They have helped to keep me going, as has the enthusiasm for the project that Linda Roghaar, publisher of White River Press, has expressed. My son Aaron has always offered optimism and support for the project and practical editing help as well. Appreciation to long–time friend Elliot Silberberg for his interest in the project and editing help as it developed. Joe Manning, Jon Weissman, and Sue Birns volunteered some critical proofreading along the way. I owe them all a good deal of thanks.

As an author who studies the history of work and the workplace, I have come to appreciate and gratefully acknowledge the commitment, art, and craft of the professionals who have helped bring this book to publication: copy editor Jean Stone, designer Douglas Lufkin (Lufkin Graphic Designs), indexer Rachel Nishan (Twin Oaks Indexing), proof reader, Kitty Burns Florey, and, once again, publisher Linda Roghaar, who has kept her sharp eye on the big picture as well as the small.

From the late 1970s to 2012, I lived in western Massachusetts, but moved to Philadelphia in 2012 to be closer to our first grandchildren. I have been fortunate to have a sizable and loving family, all within driving distance from Philly to New York, Connecticut, and Massachusetts. I thank them all: my son Aaron, my step children Abby and Ezra, and my sister Vera and everyone in their growing families for their smiles and hugs and warmth whenever I knocked on their doors. Throughout the years, now decades, of working on this book, Rabbi Sheila Peltz Weinberg has been a great support, a believer in the project, a fine editor and a wise and loving partner. The biggest thanks goes to her.

Towards the end of the project, I received the sad news that John (Jack) Boulger had died at the age of 83. At Sprague Electric, Jack helped to bring in a national union serving the office and technical employees, a unit that played a key role in the lengthy 1970 strike. Jack became a long–time president of the union local and proved always willing to share his memories with me and other researchers in labor history. We were in communication about my book towards the very end of his life. After he died on January 13, 2019, Jack's wife, Sylvia, mailed me some notes he had previously written for me about Sprague history. May he rest in peace.

BIBLIOGRAPHY

Abrams, Amah-Rose. "Manuel Rabate Named Director of Louvre Abu Dhabi." *ARTnews* (September 21, 2016).

A Closer Look. Berkshire Taconic Community Foundation, 2017.

Allen, J.D. "A North Adams Mayoral Candidate without Mail Outs, Lawn Signs." WAMC.org, July 17, 2017.

"American Community Study, 2010–2014." *U.S. Census Bureau.*

Andrews, Karen. "Physician fleeing Pennsylvania gas wells fights Berkshire pipeline." *The Berkshire Edge* (August 3, 2014).

Anonymous. "Memoirs of a Salaried Scab." 1970.

Architectural Heritage of North Adams, Massachusetts, The. Ithaca, NY: Herschensohn and Reed Associates, Historic Preservation Planners, 1980.

Baker, Elizabeth. "Blackinton: A Case Study of Industrialism, 1856–1876." *Historical Journal of Massachusetts* (January, 1981): 15–26.

Ballou, Lydia. "Great Events." *Hoosac Trails*. North Adams Historical Society (November, 2011).

Baptist, Edward E. *The Half Has Never Been Told: Slavery and the Making of American Capitalism*. New York: Basic Books, 2014.

Bashlevkin, Alan. *Social Costs of Economic Decline: Northern Berkshire 1980–1990*. Northern Berkshire Health and Human Services Coalition (January 23, 1991).

Bashevkin, Alan, Kelton Burbank, and Andrew Schamess. *The Need for Comprehensive Shelter Services in the Northern Berkshire Area*. Northern Berkshire Health and Human Services Coalition (August, 1988).

Baystate Health. "Opioid Overdose in Western Massachusetts: Springfield and Western Counties compared to statewide data." *Public Health Issue Brief* (October, 2015).

Bedford, Henry F. *Socialism and the Workers in Massachusetts, 1886–1912*. Amherst, MA: University of Massachusetts Press, 1966.

_________. editor. *Their Lives & Numbers: The Condition of Working People in Massachusetts, 1870–1910*. Ithaca, NY: Cornell University Press, 1995.

Bell, Daniel. *The End of Ideology: On the Exhaustion of Political Ideas in the Fifties*. Cambridge, MA: Harvard University Press, 1960.

Bennett, Richard V. "The Crispins, Calvin, and the Chinese." Middletown, CT: Wesleyan University master's thesis, 1986.

Berkshire Eagle. "Sprague Cracks the Whip" (November 19, 1955).

Berkshire Hills, The. "A Great Berkshire Industry," Vol. 3, no. 6 (February 1, 1903).

Bernstein, Irving. *A Caring Society: The New Deal, the Worker and the Great Depression.* Boston: Houghton Mifflin, 1985.

________. *The Lean Years: A History of the American Worker, 1920–1933.* Boston: Houghton Mifflin, 1960.

________. *The Turbulent Years: A History of the American Worker, 1920–1933.* Boston: Houghton Mifflin, 1969.

Birdsall, Richard D. *Berkshire County: A Cultural History.* New Haven: Yale University Press, 1959.

Blewett, Mary H., editor. *Surviving Hard Times: The Working People of Lowell.* Lowell, MA: Lowell Museum, 1982.

Bliss, Raymond C. "A Study of Union History at the Sprague Electric Company in North Adams, Mass. 1929–1970." Williamstown, MA: Williams College thesis, 1976.

Bluestone, Barry and Bennett Harrison. *The Deindustrialization of America: Plant Closings, Community Abandonment, and the Dismantling of Basic Industry.* New York: Basic Books, 1982.

Bobin, Gail. Email (September 13, 2017) re interview with Terry Louison.

___________. Interview of Terry Louison for "Social History of North Adams" class. Massachusetts College of Liberal Arts, 1996.

Bolton, Alexander. "Bain gives more campaign money to Democrats than it does to Republicans." *The Hill* (January 19, 2012).

Bossi, Arnold. "The Traditions and Spirit of the Arnold Print Works." *The Arnold Print.* Vol. II, no. 6 (North Adams, MA: 1919).

Boston Sunday Globe. "An Old-Time Democrat Dead." January 20, 1884.

Bowditch, Vincent Y. *Life and Correspondence of Henry Ingersoll Bowditch.* Vol. I. Boston: Houghton Mifflin Co., 1902.

Boyer, Paul. *Urban Masses and Moral Order in America, 1820–1920.* Cambridge, MA: Harvard University Press, 1978.

Boyer, Richard O. and Herbert M. Morais. *Labor's Untold Story.* New York: United Electrical, Radio and Machine Workers of America, UE, 1955.

Brady, David and Michael Wallace, "Deindustrialization and Poverty: Manufacturing Decline and AFDC Recipiency in Lake County, Indiana 1964–93." *Sociological Forum.* Vol. 16, no. 2 (June, 2001).

Brecher, Jeremy. *Banded Together: Economic Democratization in the Brass Valley.* Urbana, Illinois: University of Illinois Press, 2011.

__________. newlaborforum.cuny.edu/author/Jeremy-brecher/.

Breitbart, Myrna Margulies. *Creative Economies in Post-industrial Cities: Manufacturing a (Different) Scene.* Burlington, VT: Ashgate Publishing Company, 2013.

"Brief History of the Houghton Memorial Building, A, Now the Home of the North Adams Public Library." North Adams Public Library (n.d.).

Brody, David. *Workers in Industrial America.* New York: Oxford University Press, 1980.

Brookner, Sandra. "The River Once Ran Wild." North Adams: Massachusetts College of Liberal Arts student paper, 2001.

Brooks, Robert R.R. Interview with author, 1991

_______.editor. *Williamstown: The First Hundred Years, 1753–1953 and Twenty Years Later, 1953–1973.* 2nd ed. Williamstown: Williamstown Historical Commission, 1974.

Brooks, Thomas. *Toil and Trouble.* New York: Delacorte, 1971.

Brunet, Kathleen. "Ex-Adams workers plan own supermarket." *Transcript* (September 13, 1985), 1.

Bryson, Matthew S. "The North Adams Shoe Manufacturers: How They Created a Successful Industry Only to Abandon It." Williamstown, MA: Williams College thesis, 1999.

Buffenstein, Alyssa. "The Guggenheim and Rockbund Museums Call Off Exhibition of Middle Eastern Art in Shanghai." *artnetNews* (March 22, 2017).

Burchard, Linda. "Housing tour dramatizes low-income tenants' plight." *Berkshire Eagle* (August 14, 1988).

Burns, Stewart. "Capacitors and Community: Women Workers at Sprague Electric, 1930–1980." *The Public Historian.* Vol. 11, no. 4 (Fall 1989).

Cappelli, Peter. *The New Deal at Work: Managing the Market-Driven Workforce.* Boston: Harvard Business School Press, 1999.

Card, Jennifer J. "From Industrial to Postindustrial: The Rebirth of North Adams, Massachusetts." Amherst, MA: Hampshire College thesis, 2002.

Carlson, Gene and Tina Peters. "Thomas Gustus Mallory—Lydia Ballou's hero and mystery man . . ." North Adams Historical Society (n.d.).

Carney, William. *A Berkshire Sourcebook: the history, geography, and major landmarks of Berkshire, Massachusetts.* Pittsfield, MA: Junior League of Berkshire County, 1976.

Carter, Mark W. "Adams. Massachusetts, And the American Civil War." Williamstown, MA: Williams College thesis, 1976.

Cassagio, Danielle. "The Berkshire Street Railway." North Adams: Massachusetts College of Liberal Arts student paper, 2009.

"Celebrating Twenty Years." Northern Berkshire Community Coalition, 2006.

Child, Hamilton. *Gazetteer of Berkshire County, Massachusetts, 1725–1885.* Syracuse: Journal Office, 1885.

Chomsky, Aviva. *Linked Labor Histories: New England, Colombia, and the Making of a Global Working Class.* Durham, NC: Duke University Press, 2008.

Clark, Christopher. *The Roots of Rural Capitalism: Western Massachusetts, 1780–1860.* Ithaca, NY: Cornell University Press, 1990.

Clawson, Dan. *The New Upsurge: Labor and the New Social Movements.* Ithaca, NY: Cornell University Press, 2003.

Cloward, Richard and Frances Fox Piven. *Poor People's Movements: How they Succeed, How They Fail.* New York: Pantheon, 1977.

Cohen, Adam. *Nothing to Fear: FDR's Inner Circle and the Hundred Days That Created Modern America.* New York: Penguin Press, 2009.

Cole, Carin Lynn. *Between Two Worlds: The Business Career of Albert C. Houghton.* Williamstown, MA: Williams College thesis, 1991.

Coogan, Timothy. "The Forging of a New Mill Town: North and South Adams, Massachusetts, 1780–1860."New York: New York University dissertation, 1992.

Cooke, Rollin Hillyer, editor. *Historic Homes and Institutions and Genealogical and Personal Memoirs of Berkshire County, Massachusetts.* New York: The Lewis Publishing Co., 1906.

Cowan, Aaron. *A Nice Place to Visit: Tourism and Urban Revitalization in the Postwar Rustbelt.* Philadelphia: Temple University Press, 2016.

Cowie, Jefferson and Joseph Heathcott. "The meanings of deindustrialization," in J. Cowie & J. Heathcott, eds. *Beyond the ruins: the meanings of deindustrialization.* Ithaca, NY: ILR Press, http://digitalcommons.ilr.cornell.edu/cb/33,1.

Coyne, Terrence E. "The Hoosac Tunnel." Worcester, MA: Clark University dissertation, 1992.

_______. "The Hoosac Tunnel: Massachusetts' Western Gateway." *Historical Journal of Massachusetts.* Vol. 23:1 (Winter 1995).

Crawford, Neta C. "US Budgetary Costs of War through 2016: $4.79 Trillion and Counting: Summary of Costs of the U.S. Wars in Iraq, Syria, Afghanistan and Pakistan and Homeland Security." Watson Institute, Brown University (September, 2016).

Cuyler, Lewis. "Wall-Streeter Shoes: A lot of class." *Transcript* (November 29, 1973).

_________. "Wall-Streeter to close." *Transcript* (November 28, 1973).

Dalzell, Robert F. Jr. *Enterprising Elite: The Boston Associates and the World They Made.* New York: W.W. Norton, 1987.

Damon, Edward. "Community expresses outrage, demonstrations planned through Friday." *Berkshire Eagle* (March 27, 2014).

Daniel, Clete. *Culture of Misfortune: An Interpretive History of Textile Unionism in the United States.* Ithaca, NY: Cornell University Press, 2001.

Daniels, Tammy. "Guggenheim Motorcycle Club Makes Mohawk Theater Pitstop." *iBerkshires* (September 8, 2015).

_________. "Local Reactions Continue Over Hospital's Closing." *iBerkshires* (March 26, 2014).

_________. "North Adams Council Backs Resolution Calling for Detox Center." *iBerkshires* (June 29, 2016).

_________."North Adams Rallies Protest, Support Trump's Travel Ban." *iBerkshires* (February 4, 2017).

_________. "North Adams Tiny House Builders See Growth in Affordable, Custom Housing." *iBerkshires* (September 19, 2017).

_________. "World-Class Architect Climbs Aboard Model Railroad Museum." *iBerkshires* (September 1, 2017).

Dassatti, Peter. *Shutting NARH.* Documentary, written and directed (2014).

Dawley, Alan. *Class and Community: The Industrial Revolution in Lynn.* Cambridge, MA: Harvard University Press, 1976.

Day, Joseph. *Dew Upon the Mountains: A History of St. Francis of Assisi Parish, North Adams Massachusetts in the Berkshires.* North Adams, MA: St. Francis of Assisi Parish, 1989.

Demers, Phil. "Arts, vision are keys to Northern Berkshire's economic strength." *Berkshire Eagle* (July 17, 2016).

________. "New Berkshire Medical Center unit to provide longer-term treatment for opioid addictions." *Berkshire Eagle* (April 26, 2016).

Desmond, Matthew. *Evicted: Poverty and Profit in the American City.* New York: Crown Publishers, 2016.

Dobrowolski, Tony. "Berkshire businesses oppose 'pipeline tax.'" *Berkshire Eagle* (March 21, 2017).

Dodge, L. Mara. "Anna B. Sullivan, 1903–1983: The Formative Years of a Textile Union Organizer (Holyoke, Massachusetts)." *Historical Journal of Massachusetts.* Vol. 36, no. 2 (Summer 2008).

Donovan, Paul. *North Adams Regional Hospital: A Historical Perspective. Part 1: 1882–1910* (n.d.). Author's email address: emsportmed2015@gmail.com).

Doussard, Jamie Peck and Nik Theodore. "After Deindustrialization: Uneven Growth and Economic Inequality in 'Postindustrial' Chicago." *Economic Geography.* Vol. 85, no. 2 (April, 2009), 183–207.

Dravis, Stephen. "Williamstown Adopts Resolution on Opioid Addiction Services." *iBerkshires* (August 24, 2016).

Dreier, Peter. "Reagan's Real Legacy." *Nation* (February 4, 2011).

Drew, Bernard A. "Wall and Streeter, maker of shoes." *Berkshire Eagle* (July 5, 2014).

Du Bois, W.E.B. "Reflections upon the Housatonic River." Reprinted in the *Berkshire Edge* (April 3, 2016).

________. *The Autobiography of W.E.B. Du Bois: A Soliloquy on Viewing My Life From the Last Decade of Its First Century.* New York: International

Publishers, 1981.

Dudley, Kathryn Marie. *The End of the Line: Lost Jobs, New Lives in Postindustrial America.* Chicago: University of Chicago Press, 1994.

Early, Steve. *Embedded with Organized Labor: Journalistic Reflections on the Class War at Home.* New York: Monthly Review Press, 2009.

__________. "Strike Lessons from the Last Twenty-Five Years: Walking Out and Winning." *Against the Current* (Sept.–Oct., 2006).

Eaton, Sandy. "The Demise of Acute Health Care in Quincy, Massachusetts: Implications for Surviving Community Hospitals." *Open Media Boston* (January 6, 2015).

"Economic News Release; Union Members Summary." *Bureau of Labor Statistics* (January 26, 2017).

Editorial. "More misery for poor." *Transcript* (March 10, 1979), 4.

Eisenmenger, Robert W. *The Dynamics of Growth in New England's Economy, 1870–1964.* Middletown, CT: Wesleyan University Press, 1967.

Encarta World English Dictionary. New York: St. Martin's Press, 1999.

Enerson, Linda. "The Promise of MASS MoCA." *CommonWealth Magazine*, 22, 3 (Summer 2017).

Estall, R.C. *New England: A Study in Industrial Adjustment.* New York: Praeger, 1966.

Etman, Andy. "Sanford Blackinton, His Mill and a Wool Sorter Named John W. Jones." North Adams: Massachusetts College of Liberal Arts SOCI 500 paper, 2006.

Fanto, Clarence. "Bain Capital's role in KB Toys' demise still a point of controversy." *Berkshire Eagle* (October 28, 2012).

Federal Writers' Project of the Works Progress Administration for Massachusetts. *The Berkshire Hills.* New York: Funk & Wagnalls Company, 1939.

Feldbaum, Eleanor G. "Collective Bargaining in the Health Sector: A Focus on Nurses." *Journal of Health and Human Resources Administration*, 4, 2 (Fall, 1981), 148–166.

Feyrer, James, Bruce Sacerdote, et al. "Did the Rust Belt Become Shiny? A Study of Cities and Counties That Lost Steel and Auto Jobs in the 1980s [with Comments]." Brookings-Wharton Papers on Urban Affairs (2007), 41–102.

Field, David Dudley and Chester Dewey. *A History of the County of Berkshire, Massachusetts, in Two Parts: The First Being a General View of the County; the Second, an Account of the Several Towns.* Berkshire county: S.W. Bush, 1829.

Fink, Leon. *Workingmen's Democracy: The Knights of Labor and American Politics.* Urbana, IL: University of Illinois Press, 1983.

Flint, Anthony. "10 Years later, did the Big Dig deliver?" *Boston Globe Magazine* (December 29, 2015).

Florida, Richard. *Cities and the Creative Class.* New York: Routledge, 2005.

________. *Flight of the Creative Class, The: The New Global Competition for Talent.* New York: Harper Collins, 2005.

________."More Losers Than Winners in America's New Economic Geography." *Atlantic* (January 20, 2013).

________. *New Urban Crisis, The: How Our Cities are Increasing Inequality, Deepening Segregation, and Failing the Middle Class.* New York: Basic Books, 2017.

________. *Rise of the Creative Class, The.* New York: Basic Books, 2002.

Forrant, Robert. *Metal Fatigue: American Bosch and the Demise of Metalworking in the Connecticut River Valley.* Amityville, NY: Baywood Publishing Company, 2009.

Forrester, Adam. (North Adams: Massachusetts College of Liberal Arts student paper, 2010).

Frank, Thomas. "Dead End on Shakin' Street." *The Baffler*, #20 (2012).

Freeman, Joshua, Nelson Lichtenstein et al. *Who Built America? Working & The Nation's Economy, Politics, Culture & Society, Vol. Two: From The Gilded Age To The Present.* New York: Pantheon Books, 1992.

Friedlander, Peter. "The CIO after 50 Years." In Brody.

Gabrielsky, Robert Paul. "The Evolution of the Marshall Street Complex in North Adams." *Historical Journal of Massachusetts* (Winter, 1991).

Gardner, Karen. "Babeu: MASS MoCA limits downtown opportunities." *Transcript*, (November 3, 2001).

Garstka, John Edward. "A Producing and Performing Arts Complex: A Study in 19th Century Mill Recycling." Amherst, MA: University of Massachusetts master's thesis, 1974.

Gentile, Derek. "Heroin, opioids now top alcohol as No. 1 substance treatment at Brien Center." *Berkshire Eagle* (June 27, 2014).

Gerstle, Gary. *Working-Class Americanism: The Politics of Labor in a Textile City, 1914–1960.* Cambridge, MA: Cambridge University Press, 1989.

Giuliano, Charles. "Tom Krens Develops Business as a Museum: A For Profit Paradigm for North Adams." www.berkshirefinearts.com/12-08-2015_tom-krens-develops-business-as-a-museum.

Gladden, Washington. *From the Hub to the Hudson: with sketches of nature, history and industry in north-western Massachusetts.* Greenfield, MA: E.D. Merriam, 1870.

Glasmeier, Amy K. and the Massachusetts Institute of Technology. "Living Wage Calculation for Berkshire County, Massachusetts." http://livingwage.mit.edu/counties/25003.

Global Nonviolent Action Database. "Lawrence Mill Workers strike against wage cuts, 1919." nvdatabase.swarthmore.edu.

Gloster, Eileen and Bill Densmore. "Landlords react to code cleanup: 'Tenants' fault.'" *Advocate* (July 20, 1988).

Glueck, Grace. "A new museum's bright future becomes dim." *New York Times* (April 11, 1990).

__________." Massachusetts Says New Art Museum Must Help Pay Costs." *New York Times* (December 4, 1991).

Goldberg, Deborah A. "Louis Slobodkin's North Adams Reliefs." Williamstown, MA: Williams College student paper, 1987.

Golden Jubilee: St. Anthony's Church, North Adams, Massachusetts, 1958.

Goode, Kenneth. "Economic Change and Political Behavior: Berkshire County, Massachusetts, 1831–1860." Williamstown, MA: Williams College thesis, 1976.

Goodwyn, Lawrence. *Democratic Promise: The Populist Moment in America.* New York: Oxford University Press, 1976.

Gordon, Brad. Berkshire County Regional Housing Authority. Northern Berkshire Community Coalition Forum (February, 2017).

Grande, Joseph A. "Workers, academics join to discuss saving, attracting jobs." *Transcript* (October 29, 1984), 3.

Green, James. *Death in the Haymarket: A Story of Chicago, the First Labor Movement and the Bombing That Divided Gilded Age America.* New York: Pantheon, 2006.

_________. *The World of the Worker: Labor in Twentieth Century America.* New York: Hill and Wang, 1980.

Greenberger, Alex. "Thomas Krens is Planning Another Contemporary Art Museum for North Adams, Massachusetts." *ARTnews* (August 12, 2015).

Greenhouse, Steven. "Wisconsin's Legacy for Unions." *New York Times* (February 22, 2014).

"Green New Deal." Green Party. https://www.jill2016.com/greennewdeal.

Gregory, James. N. *The Southern Diaspora: How the Great Migration of Black and White Southerners Transformed America.* Chapel Hill, NC: The University of North Carolina Press, 2005.

Gyory, Andrew. *Closing the Gate: Race, Politics and the Chinese Exclusion Act* (Chapel Hill, NC: University of North Carolina Press, 1998).

Hardy, Christopher D. "The Reaction of Local Elites to Modernization: Berkshire County, Mass., 1800–1860." Williamstown, MA: Williams College thesis, 1976.

Harrison, Greg. "Can the arts save struggling cities?" November 4, 2011. http://grist.org/cities/2011-11-03-can-the-arts-save-struggling-cities/.

Hartford, William F. *The Working People of Holyoke: Class and Ethnicity in a Massachusetts Mill Town: 1850–1960.* New Brunswick, NJ: Rutgers University Press, 1990.

________. *Where is Our Responsibility? Unions and Economic Change in the New England Textile Industry, 1870–1960.* Amherst, MA: University of

Massachusetts Press, 1996.

Healy, Beth. "Deval Patrick takes investing role at Bain Capital." *Boston Globe* (April 14, 2015).

Hernandez, Timothy Z. *All They Will Call You.* Tucson, AZ: University of Arizona Press, 2017.

Hill, The. "Bain capital gains former Massachusetts governor" (April 14, 2015).

Hitchcock, John. "Pulitzer winner sounds warning on labor's future." *The Morning Union* (September 2, 1986).

Hopkins, Paul. "Louison House 25th Anniversary Fetes Namesake." *iBerkshires* (November 23, 2014).

Horwitt, Pink. *Jews in Berkshire County.* Williamstown, MA: DOR Company, 1972.

Hungerford, Edward Rev. "A Memorial discourse delivered at the funeral of gen. Wm. C. Plunkett in the First Congregational Church, Adams, Massachusetts, Tuesday, January 22, 1884 by Rev. Edward Hungerford with remarks by Rev. Mark Hopkins, D.D., ex-president of Williams College." Boston: Franklin Press; Rand, Avery & Co., 1884.

Johnston, Katie. "Tourism booms but locals struggle: Behind the two worlds of the Berkshires." *Boston Globe* (September 15, 2017).

Jones, Steven E. *Against Technology: From the Luddites to Neo-Luddism.* New York: Rutledge, 2006.

Kaplan, Carolyn. *Congregation Beth Israel Centennial.* North Adams: Congregation Beth Israel, 1995.

Kassel, David. "Living wage in Massachusetts suffers a setback." https://cofarblog.wordpress.com/2017/07.

Katznelson, Ira. *Fear Itself: The New Deal and the Origins of Our Time.* New York: W.W. Norton, 2013.

Kelly, Nancy. *Downside Up.* Documentary, written and directed (2002).

Keyssar, Alexander. *Out of Work: The first century of unemployment in Massachusetts.* Cambridge, England: Cambridge University Press, 1986.

Kifner, John. "Museum Brings Town Back to Life." *New York Times* (May 30, 2000), A14.

Kirkland, Edward. *Men, Cities and Transportation.* Vol. II. Cambridge, MA: Harvard University Press, 1969.

Kirsh, Max H. *In the Wake of the Giant: Multinational Restructuring and Uneven Development in a New England Community.* Albany, NY: State University of New York Press, 1998.

Kleberg, Jay. "The pollution of the Hoosic river and the continuing battle to clean it up." *The Williams Record* (January 16, 2008).

Klein, Naomi. *This Changes Everything: Capitalism vs. the Climate.* New York: Simon & Schuster, 2014.

Koch, William Jr., editor. *The Diary of Elsie Kleiner Koch: 1932.* JeanShadrack Publishing, 2008.

Lee, Anthony. *A Shoemaker's Story: Being Chiefly about French Canadian Immigrants, Enterprising Photographers, Rascal Yankees, and Chinese Cobblers in a Nineteenth-Century Town.* Princeton, NJ: Princeton University Press, 2008.

Lee, Philip A. *Sesquicentennial Edition, Transcript* (November 19, 1993).

Leikin, Steve. *The Practical Utopians: American Workers and the Cooperative Movement in the Gilded Age.* Detroit: Wayne State University Press, 2005.

Leon, Steve. "Breaking Faith: The Sprague Story." *The Berkshire Sampler* (December 9, 1984).

Levine, Bruce, Steve Brier et al. *Who Built America: Working People and the Nation's Economy, Politics, Culture and Society, Vol. One: From Conquest & Colonization Through Reconstruction & The Great Uprising of 1877.* New York: Pantheon Books, 1989, 1992.

Levinson, David, editor. *African American Heritage in the Upper Housatonic Valley.* Great Barrington, MA: Berkshire Publishing Group, 2006.

Lewis, David Levering. *W.E.B. Du Bois, Biography of a Race, 1868–1919.* New York: Henry Holt, 1993.

Lichtenstein, Nelson, *The State of the Union: A Century of American Labor.* Princeton, NJ: Princeton University Press, 2002.

Lindsay, Dick. "Berkshire-based Raise Up Mass backs $15 minimum wage, paid leave ballot effort." *Berkshire Eagle* (September 18, 2017).

Lipset, Seymour Martin. *Political Man: The Social Bases of Politics.* Garden City, NY: Doubleday, 1960.

Lockwood, John H. *Western Massachusetts: A History, 1636–1925.* Vol. 2. New York: Lewis Historical Publishing Company, 1926.

Loewen, James W. *Lies My Teacher Told Me: Everything Your American History Textbook Got Wrong.* Revised and updated. New York: Simon & Schuster, 2007.

Lynd, Robert S. and Helen Merrell Lynd. *Middletown in Transition: A Study in Cultural Conflicts.* New York: Harcourt, Brace &World, 1937.

Maloy, Kailey. "Occupations of African-Americans in North Adams, 1850–1930." North Adams: Massachusetts College of Liberal Arts student paper, 2010.

Manning, Joe. *Disappearing Into North Adams.* Florence, MA: Flatiron Press, 2001.

________. "Porches Inn brings new era to River Street," in Nicholas Whitman, *Porches: Art and Renewal on River Street.* North Adams: MASS MoCA, 2002. https://morningsonmaplestreet.com/2001/07/25/porches-inn-brings-new-era-to-river-street-chapter-one/ and https://morningsonmaplestreet.com/2001/07/26/porches-inn-brings-new-era-to-river-street-chapter-two/ and https://morningsonmaplestreet.com/2001/07/27/porches-inn-brings-new-era-to-river-street-chapter-three/

________. *Steeples: Sketches of North Adams.* Florence, MA: Flatiron Press, 3rd ed., 2001.

Marx, Karl. *The Eighteenth Brumaire of Louis Bonaparte.* New York: International Publishers, 1852.

Massachusetts Nurses Association, Nykole Roche. *Berkshire Medical Center North (BMCN): The Case for Restoring a Full Service Hospital for Northern Berkshire County.* (n.d.)

Matles, James J. and James Higgins. *Them and Us: Struggles of a Rank-and-File Union.* Englewood Cliffs, NJ: Prentice-Hall, 1974.

McAlevey, Jane. "The Massachusetts Nurses Union is Reviving the Strike." *Nation* (July 19, 2017).

McGaw, Judith A. *Most Wonderful Machine: Mechanization and Social Change in Berkshire Paper Making, 1801–1885.* Princeton, NJ: Princeton University Press, 1987.

McKenzie, Kevin. "Opioid crisis points to racial divide." *USA Today Network* (March 27, 2017).

Melder, Keith E. "The Polish Immigration in Adams, Massachusetts: A Case Study of the American Melting Pot." Williamstown, MA: Williams College thesis, 1954.

Metzgar, Jack. *Striking Steel: Solidarity Remembered.* Philadelphia, PA: Temple University Press, 2000.

Metzger, Andy. "'We're broke,' North Adams mayor says." *Boston Globe* (June 27, 2014).

Michalenko, Eugene F. *In This Valley: A Concise History of Adams, Massachusetts.* Adams, MA: Adams Specialty and Printing Company, 2002.

Middleton, William D. and William Middleton III. *Frank Julian Sprague: Electrical Inventor & Engineer.* Bloomington, IN: Indiana University Press, 2009.

Miles, Lionel G. "The Red Man Dispossessed: The Williams Family and the Alienation of Indian Land in Stockbridge, Massachusetts, 1736–1818," in Alden T. Vaughan, editor, *New England Encounters: Indians and Euroamericans, ca. 1600–1850.* Boston: Northeastern University Press, 1999.

Millet, Anne L. "They're Big Boys Now." *Berkshire Eagle* (March 21, 1970), 13.

Mills of North Adams, The. 1986 documentary by middle school students; at Visitors' Center, Western Gateway Heritage State Park, North Adams.

Minchin, Timothy J. *Labor Under Fire: A History of the AFL-CIO since 1979.* Chapel Hill, NC: University of North Carolina Press, 2017.

Mixon, Scott. "The Crisis of 1873: Perspectives from Multiple Asset Classes." *Journal of Economic History.* Vol. 78, no. 3. (September, 2008).

Moriarty, Paul. "Councilors 'awakened' to housing stock conditions in city." *Transcript.* (August 15, 1988).

Morris, A. H. "Interesting Facts in the Early History of North Adams." The *Adams Transcript* (1859–1860).

Munley, Michael W. "Unemployed shoe company workers face a bleak Christmas." *Transcript* (December 20, 1975).

Murray, Larry. "Plans for a North-Adams-Williamstown Cultural Corridor Advance." https//berkshireonstage.com/2015/12/05/plans-for-a-north-adams-williamstown-cultural-corridor-advance/.

Nash, June. *From Tank Town to High Tech.* Albany, NY: State University of New York Press, 1989.

National Priorities Project. "Cost of War." (https:///www.nationalpriorities.org).

Near, Holly. "I Am Willing." www.hollynear.com/show_up.html.

Nelson, Peter Martin. "Legal Services: Emerging Institution or Crack in the Dike?" Williamstown, MA: Williams College student paper, 1976.

New York Times. "Inside a Killer Drug Epidemic: A Look at America's Opioid Crisis" (January 6, 2017).

Niebuhr, Gustav. "Sprague plans cause North Adams dilemma." *Berkshire Eagle* (March 17, 1984).

Niedbalski, James. "Ex-Adams workers to picket new store." *Transcript* (November 14, 1984), 1.

Nierenberg, Jay Louis. "North Adams: A New England Mill Town: A Political, Economic, and Psychological Study." Williamstown, MA: Williams College thesis, 1942.

O'Connor, Thomas H. *Lords of the Loom: Cotton Whigs and the Coming of the Civil War.* New York: Scribner's, 1968.

Oehler, Kay, Stephen C. Sheppard, et al. *Network Analysis and the Social Impact of Cultural Arts Organizations.* Williamstown, MA: Center for Creative Community Development, 2007.

_________. *Shifting Sands in Changing Communities: The Neighborhoods of North Adams, Massachusetts.* Williamstown, MA: Center for Creative Community Development, 2006.

"Our History, District 1199C." 1199cnuhhce.org/C1_OurHistory.html.

Owens, Carole. "The Good Millionaire," *Berkshire Eagle* (October 4, 2016).

Parise, Anthony F. "North Adams and the Hoosac Tunnel." Williamstown, MA: Williams College thesis, 1971.

Petras, Elizabeth McLean. *Social Justice*, 19/1. Vol. 47 (Spring, 1992).

Phillips, Susan C. "Anger, burnout, pride feed Sprague's Brown St. rebellion." *Berkshire Eagle* (May 27, 1986).

________. "Museum would generate jobs, dollars, report says." *Berkshire Eagle* (June 2, 1987).

Pidgeon, Daniel. *Old World Questions and New World Answers.* London, 1884.

Piendak, George A. "The Independent Condenser Workers Union, Local #2: A Study of Local Unionism." Williamstown, MA: Williams College thesis, 1965.

Pierson, William H. "Industrial Architecture in the Berkshires." New Haven, CT: Yale University dissertation, 1949.

Pincus, Alison. "The Mark of Reliability: From Sprague Electric to MASS MoCA in North Adams, MA." Williamstown, MA: Williams College thesis, 2012.

Pollin, Robert et al. Political Economy Research Institute. University of Massachusetts, Amherst. https://www.peri.umass.edu.

Portside. "Union Members Summary for 2016." January 28, 2017. https://portside.org.

Powell, Daniel Edmund. "Another Williamstown: The Cotton Textile Industry in a New England Community 1826–1929." Williamstown, MA: Williams College thesis, 1979.

Pugliese, Phil. "Black Heritage: Traditions and Culture Enrich Area." *Transcript,* (March 11, 1989).

__________. "Irish Fled Famine in Old Country for New World and Hope." *Transcript,* (March 17, 1987).

__________. "Local Jews recall rich history." *Transcript* (August 15, 1987).

Rhodes, Richard. "The General and World War III." *New Yorker* (June 19, 1995).

Roberts, Janet E. "A History of the French Canadians in North Adams." Williamstown, MA: Williams College thesis, 1975.

Prude, Jonathan. *The Coming of Industrial Order: Town and Factory Life in Rural Massachusetts, 1810–1860.* Cambridge, England: Cambridge University Press, 1983.

Ralph Brill Associates. "Opinion: How Did Opioid Abuse Overtake the Berkshires? And What is Next?" *The Greylock Glass* (June 16, 2016).

Ransom, Marjorie and G.M. Heller. "Details emerge about sleazy deals: Fitzpatrick's *Porches Inn* Displaces 23 North Adams Families." *BerkshireRecordDotcom.* http://berkshirerecord.com/porches.html.

Richard, Mark Paul. *Not a Catholic Nation: The Ku Klux Klan Confronts New England in the 1920s.* Amherst, MA: University of Massachusetts Press, 2015.

Richmond, Clinton Q. "Adams and North Adams." *New England Magazine,* 21 (1899–1900).

Richmond, Clinton Q. III. *An Annotated Bibliography of North Adams, Berkshire County, Massachusetts.* Brookline, MA: Muddy River Press, 1999.

Roberts, Janet Ellen. "A History of the French Canadians in North Adams." Williamstown, MA: Williams College thesis, 1975.

Roccabruna, James. Pittsfield Police Department Sergeant, letter re NARH Protest Detail (March 29, 2014).

Romer, Robert H. "Higher Education and Slavery in Western Massachusetts." *The Journal of Blacks in Higher Education.* No. 46. (Winter, 2004–5).

______. *Slavery in the Connecticut Valley of Massachusetts.* Florence, MA: Levellers Press, 2009.

Rondeau, Mark. *A People of Faith, Hope and Love: The First 100 Years of St. Anthony of Padua Parish, 1903–2003.* North Adams: The St. Anthony 100th Anniversary Committee, 2003.

Ross, Robert J.S. *Slaves to Fashion: Poverty and Abuse in the New Sweatshops.* Ann Arbor, MI: University of Michigan Press, 2009.

Rowe, H.G. and C. T. Fairfield, editors. *Index to North Adams and Vicinity Illustrated, 1898.* Pittsfield, MA: Berkshire Family History Association, 1995.

Rubin, Lillian. *Worlds of Pain: Life in the Working Class Family.* New York: Basic Books, 1976.

Rudolph, Frederick. "Chinamen in Yankeedom: Anti-Unionism in Massachusetts in 1870." *American Historical Review,* 53 (October, 1947).

______. Editor. *Perspectives: A Williams Anthology.* Williamstown: Williams College, 1983.

Ruger, Theodore W. "Changing Times: A Study of Industrial Transformation and Working-Class Culture in Nineteenth-Century Williamstown." Williamstown, MA: Williams College thesis, 1990.

Sager, Alan and Deborah Socolar. "Gov. Patrick Should Declare a Public Health Emergency to Prevent North Adams Regional Hospital from Closing." Document, March 26, 2014.

Schatz, Ronald. *The Electrical Workers: A History of Labor at General Electric and Westinghouse, 1923–1960.* Urbana, IL: Illinois University Press, 1983.

Schexnayder, Cliff. *Builders of the Hoosac Tunnel: Baldwin, Crocker, Haupt, Doane, Shanley.* Portsmouth, NH: Peter E. Randall, 2015.

Schroeder, Alice. *The Snowball: Warren Buffett and the Business of Life.* New York: Bantam Books, 2008.

Scribner's Magazine. Vol. 1, no. 10

Seeger, Pete. Clearwater, 1966. www.clearwater.org/about/the-clearwater-story/.

Seider, Maynard. *A Year in the Life of a Factory.* Chicago: Charles H. Kerr, 1993; Singlejack Books, San Pedro, CA, 1984.

_________. "Contested Beliefs and Rebellion in a New England Mill Town: Sprague Electric Workers in North Adams." *The Mind's Eye* (1997).

_________. *Farewell to Factory Towns?* Documentary, written and directed,

2012.

_________. "Is this what we want?" *Berkshire Eagle* (February 17, 1989),.

_________. "The CIO in Rural Massachusetts: Sprague Electric and North Adams, 1937–1944." *Historical Journal of Massachusetts.* Vol. 22, no.1 (Winter 1994).

_________. "The Sprague Electric Strike Adams, 1970." *Historical Journal of Massachusetts.* Vol. 42, no. 1 (Winter, 2014).

Seif, Michael (Storch Associates and Michael Seif). *Historical Documentation*

Report for Western Gateway Heritage Park. Commonwealth of Massachusetts: Department of Environmental Management, 1981.

Sell, Julie. "Sprague employees eyeing purchase." *Transcript* (March 2, 1985).

Seven, John. "On Track: Master museum builder has big plans for North Adams." *Berkshire Magazine* (August, 2016).

Shanks, Adam. "As bigger museum plans emerge, option to buy Heritage State Park on table." *Berkshire Eagle* (April 19, 2017).

__________. "Famed architect Frank Gehry to design Extreme Model Railroad and Contemporary Architecture Museum." *Berkshire Eagle* (August 30, 2017).

__________. "Louison House readies for an upgrade." *Berkshire Eagle* (September 22, 2017).

__________. "Mass MoCA visionary Krens announces plans to revitalize Heritage State Park." *Berkshire Eagle* (December 6, 2015).

__________. "Over 24 Years with the Berkshire Food Project, Valerie Schwarz Retires." *Berkshire Eagle* (September 4, 2017).

__________. "Update: Mass MoCA visionary Thomas Krens envisions new, massive art gallery for North Adams." *Berkshire Eagle* (August 11, 2015).

__________. "Vigil marks third anniversary of North Adams Regional Hospital closing." *Berkshire Eagle* (March 28, 2017).

__________. "Vigil recalls those lost to addiction and hope for those recovering." *Berkshire Eagle* (September 24, 2017).

__________. "100-plus locked-out BMC nurses rally in North Adams." *Berkshire Eagle* (October 5, 2017).

Shears, Bethany. "Berkshire County: Then and Now." North Adams: Massachusetts College of Liberal Arts student paper.

Shepard, Karen. *The Celestials.* Portland, OR: Tin House books, 2013.

Sheppard, Stephen C. *The Economic Impact of Closure of North Adams Regional Hospital.* Williamstown: Center for Creative Community Development (March 30, 2014).

__________. *The Economic Impacts of EMRCA: The Extreme Model Railroad and Contemporary Architecture Museum.* Center for Creative Community Development, 2017.

Sheppard, Stephen C., Kay Oehler, et al. *Culture and Revitalization: The Economic Effects of MASS MoCA on its Community.* Williamstown, MA: Center for Creative Community Development, 2006.

Shields, Enid. "How the Other Half Lived in the Late 1980s: the North Adams Tenants Organization and the Struggle for Decent, Affordable Housing in a Former Massachusetts Mill Town." North Adams: Massachusetts College of Liberal Arts student paper, 2010.

Shutting NARH. Documentary written and directed by Peter Dassatti, 2015. https://www.youtube.com/watch?v=yRfBUIR5h0M.

Smith, J.E.A., editor. *History of Berkshire County, Massachusetts, with Biographical Sketches of its Prominent Men, 1885.* Two volumes. New York: J.B. Beers Co., 1885.

Smith, Jenn. "Groups redouble efforts to reduce food insecurity in Berkshires." *Berkshire Eagle* (April 11, 2016).

Soyer, Daniel. "Garment Sweatshops, Then and Now." *New Labor Forum*, No. 4 (Spring-Summer, 1999), 35–46.

Spear, W.F. *History of North Adams, Mass., 1749–1885.* North Adams: Hoosac Valley News Printing House, 1885.

Sprague, John L. *Revitalizing U.S. Electronics: Lessons From Japan.* Boston: Butterworth-Heinemann, 1993.

__________. *Sprague Electric: An Electronic Giant's Rise, Fall, and Life after Death.* North Charleston, South Carolina: CreateSpace Independent Publishing Platform, 2015.

Sprague, John L. Sprague and Joseph J. Cunningham. "A Frank Sprague Triumph: the Electrification of Grand Central Terminal." http://magazine.ieee-pes.org/januaryfebruary-2013/history-6/.

"Sprague's Union Eyes." UE local newsletter (December 15, 1938).

Springfield Republican. "Picketers Charge Official of Mill Endangered Lives" (September 7, 1934), 1, 4.

Springfield Republican. "Textile Strikers to Invade Pittsfield Tuesday in Effort to Force Local Mills to Close: Flying Squadrons from Adams Will attempt to Make 1000 workers in Four Local Mills Join Walkout" (September 10, 1934), 1.

Spychalski, John C. "Rail Transport: Retreat and Resurgence." *The Annals of the American Academy of Political and Social Science*, Vol. 553 (September, 1997).

Stabile, Lori. "After three-year vigil, St. Stanislaus Church in Adams reopening for services." *Springfield Republican* (February 18, 2012).

Stafford, Scott. "North County Cares Coalition: Report shows full-service hospital needed, viable." *Berkshire Eagle* (February 12, 2015), 1.

Stafford, Scott and Adam Shanks. "Building 6's big bang attracts thousands to Mass MoCA's new expanded footprint." *Berkshire Eagle* (May 28, 2017).

Stanton, Cathy. "Ron Kuivila's 'Visitations': Social history as art at MASS MoCA." Unpublished paper for FAH 160/Museum History and Theory, Tufts University (December 21, 1999).

Starratt, Ruth. "Urban renewal in North Adams: a case study in community decision-making." University of Massachusetts master's thesis, Department of Sociology and Anthropology, 1968.

Stedman, M.S. "The C.I.O. Comes to North Adams," *Sketch,* Williams College (November, 1938), 18.

Stein, Judith. *Pivotal Decade: How the United States Traded Factories for Finance in the Seventies.* New Haven, CT: Yale University Press, 2010.

Stevens, Lauren R. "Groups Have Lived in Harmony." *Berkshires Week* (September 11, 1987).

________. "Sprague Electric, and the man who started it all." *The Advocate* (March 30, 1988).

________. "The Joys of Hiking in a Berkshire Autumn." *Berkshire Eagle* (October 2, 2016).

Street, Paul. "Russia Trumps Ecocide at the Petroleum Broadcasting System." *Counterpunch* (July 14, 2017).

Stroudwater Associates. *Healthcare Market Assessment: Northern Berkshire County, Massachusetts* (September 17, 2014).

"Study says domestic, not military spending, fuels job growth." May 25, 2017. https://news.brown.edu/articles/2017/05/jobscow.

Sullivan, John. "Store manager: 1-day sell-out no surprise." *Transcript* (August 9, 1990), 1.

Task Force Report, The: The Governor's Task Force on Economic Development for Northern Berkshire. Assisted by Landscape Architecture and Regional Planning, University of Massachusetts Amherst in Conjunction with LANDUSE INC. Hadley, MA, 1986.

Tavelli, Dick and John Hauck. "The Italians in North Adams: A History of Their Cultural and Political Contributions." Williamstown, MA: Williams College paper, 1972).

Taylor, Courtney. "The Windsor Mill Project." North Adams: Massachusetts College of Liberal Arts student paper, 2010.

Taylor, Holly. "N. Berkshire workers form labor coalition." *Berkshire Eagle* (October 29, 1984), 18.

Therrien, James P. "New union shop steward 'caused quite an uproar.'" *Transcript* (December 5, 1979).

Thompson, E. P. *The Making of the English Working Class.* London: Victor Gollancz, 1963.

Thompson, Joseph. "Director's Statement," Jennifer Trainer, ed. *MASS MoCA: From Mill to Museum.* North Adams: MASS MoCA Publications, 2000.

__________. "Hardware to Software, Material to Immaterial: 150 Years of Manufacturing and Art in North Adams." Speech delivered at Williams College Reunion, 2011.

Thores, Nick. Interviewed January, 1984, Winter Study "Oral History Project." North Adams: Massachusetts College of Liberal Arts.

Townes, John. "Where the Workers Are the Owners." *New York Times* (June 12, 1988).

Transcript. "Florsheim workers assured on U.S. funds," (November 15, 1976).

________. "Hoosac Tunnel opening marked in ceremonies." Centennial Edition (October 27, 1995).

________. "Little If Any Progress in Ideals in Modern Times Says Rabbi Silver." (December 22, 1925).

________. "Local Woolen Mills Announce Pay Raises for 900 Workers." (March 26, 1937),

________. "North Adams and Vicinity Illustrated." 1897.

________. "Notable Progress Seen in Adams During Year." (January 1, 1937).

________. "Rabbi Wise Wants U.S. in World Court; Holds Mussolini is Most Dangerous." (November 17, 1925).

________. "Welfare group quizzes King." (June 15, 1979).

Twain, Mark and Charles Dudley Warner. *The Gilded Age: A Novel of Today.* New York: New American Library, 1969, 1874.

Uberti, David. "The labor beat is dead; long live the labor beat." *Columbia Journalism Review* (March 12, 2015).

Veblen, Thorstein. *The Theory of the Leisure Class.* New York: Oxford, 2007, 1899.

Vine, David. *Base Nation: How U.S. Military bases Abroad Harm America and the World.* New York: Henry Holt & Co., 2015.

Von Frank, Albert J. *The Trials of Anthony Burns: Freedom and Slavery in Emerson's Boston.* Cambridge, MA: Harvard University Press, 1998.

Walker, Grant. "LGH-Tufts union maintains local control, boosts power to face industry challenges." *Lowell Sun* (April 20, 2014).

"Wall-Streeter Shoe Company." Document, North Adams Historical Society. (n.d.)

WAMC. "North Adams Budget Goes to City Council." June 12, 2017.

"W.C. Plunkett & Sons: 1814–1914, One Hundred Years of Business." Berkshire Cotton Manufacturing Company Inc. 1899, 1914.

Weinberger, Daniel. "The Causes of Homelessness in America." *Democracy Now* (June 11, 2004).

Werth, Barry, "The Father, the Sons, and the Town." *New England Monthly* (June, 1985).

Whitcomb, Christopher. "Buyout plan KO'd?" *Transcript* (April 29, 1985).

White, Mark. "Brown Street revisited: Rank and file dissent, management harassment and an uncertain future persists." *Labor Connection* (August, 1986).

Whitney, Mike. "The 'Gig Economy'; Another Vicious Attack on Ordinary Working Slobs." *Counterpunch* (April 6, 2016).

Wilder, Craig Steven. *Ebony & Ivy: Race, Slavery, and the Troubled History of America's Universities.* New York: Bloomsbury Press, 2013.

Wilk, John Addison. "A History of Adams, Massachusetts." Ottawa, Canada: University of Ottawa dissertation, 1945.

Willison, George P. *The History of Pittsfield, Massachusetts, 1916–1955.* Pittsfield: City of Pittsfield, 1957.

Woolhouse, Megan. "Between haves, have-nots, an ever greater gulf." *Boston Globe* (August 21, 2011).

"Work Force, The." I.U.E. Local 200, November 27, 1984.

Wysong, Earl, Robert Perrucci, and David Wright. *The New Class Society: Goodbye American Dream?* 4th ed. Lanham, MD: Rowman & Littlefield, 2014.

Zieger, Robert H. "Toward the History of the CIO: A Bibliographical Report." *Labor History,* XXVIII (Fall, 1985).

Zinn, Howard. *A People's History of the United States, 1492–Present.* Revised and updated. New York: HarperCollins, 1995.

INTERVIEWS

University of Massachusetts, Lowell, Center for Lowell History Oral History Collection: Shifting Gears Project, North Adams Interviews conducted in 1988 and 1989.

Bass, Raymond F., interviewed by Robert Gabrielsky.

Bernardi, Ruth A., interviewed by Selma Sabin.

Boulger, John A., interviewed by Robert Gabrielsky.

Griswold, Phyllis, interviewed by James Ivancic.

Harris, Florence, interviewed by Gailanne Cariddi.

Hartranft, Esther G., interviewed by Nancy Hart.

Jones, Evelyn L., interviewed by Annette Gamache.

O'Neill, Catherine, interviewed by Alexandra Glover.

Uberti, Vera, interviewed by Melissa Cahoon.

Wood, Walter D., interviewed by Bruce W. Saunders Jr.

Wood, Walter, interviewed by Robert Gabrielsky.

Zawislak, Stella, interviewed by Janet Keep.

INTERVIEWS BY AUTHOR (FROM 1984–2016)

Auge, Bernie

Bass, Raymond F.

Bateman, George

Blanchard, Julie

Boulger, John

Braman, Jean

Chenail, Norman

Cyr, Leo

Dassatti, Peter

Dassatti, Richard

Estes, Norm

Gould, Emma

Harley, Hugh

O'Brien, Louise (joint interview with Chet Gallup)

O'Brien, Michael

Ouellette, Reney (joint interview with Karen Rose)

Rhinemiller, Jackie

Rodriguez, Valerie

Russell, Kenny

Stackpole, William

Steinberg, Rhoda

Thompson, Joseph

Wilber, Michael

ARCHIVAL COLLECTIONS

Independent Condenser Workers Union Local 2 (ICW #2, Sprague)—University of Massachusetts, Amherst.

International Ladies Garment Workers Union (ILGWU)—Kheel Center for Labor Documentation and Archives, Cornell University.

Sprague Electric Company archives (no longer available).

Textile Workers Union of America (TWUA)—Wisconsin Historical Society, Madison.

United Electrical, Radio and Machine Workers of America (UE)—University of Pittsburgh.

NEWSPAPERS (INCLUDING ONLINE)

Advocate (Williamstown, MA)

Berkshire Eagle

BerkshireRecord.com

Berkshire Sampler, The

Boston Globe

Boston Globe Magazine

Boston Sunday Globe

iBerkshires

Greylock Glass, The

Labor Connection

Morning Union, The

New York Times

Springfield Republican

Times-Union (Albany)

Transcript

USA Today Network

Williams Record, The

INDEX

A

B

C

D

E

F

G

H

I

J

K

L

M

N

O

P

R

S

T

U

V

W

X

Z